RABBINIC INTERPRETATION OF
SCRIPTURE IN THE MISHNAH

Rabbinic Interpretation of Scripture in the Mishnah

ALEXANDER SAMELY

OXFORD

UNIVERSITY PRESS

Great Clarendon Street, Oxford, OX2 6DP

Oxford University Press is a department of the University of Oxford.
It furthers the University's objective of excellence in research, scholarship,
and education by publishing worldwide in

Oxford New York

Athens Auckland Bangkok Bogotá Buenos Aires Cape Town
Chennai Dar es Salaam Delhi Florence Hong Kong Istanbul Karachi
Kolkata Kuala Lumpur Madrid Melbourne Mexico City Mumbai Nairobi
Paris São Paulo Shanghai Singapore Taipei Tokyo Toronto Warsaw

with associated companies in Berlin Ibadan

Oxford is a registered trade mark of Oxford University Press
in the UK and certain other countries

Published in the United States
by Oxford University Press Inc., New York

© Alexander Samely 2002

The moral rights of the author have been asserted

Database right Oxford University Press (maker)

First published 2002

British Library Cataloguing in Publication Data

Data available

Library of Congress Cataloging in Publication Data

Data applied for

ISBN 0–19–827031–3

1 3 5 7 9 10 8 6 4 2

Typeset in Palatino by
Regent Typesetting, London
Printed in Great Britain
on acid-free paper by
Biddles Ltd, Guildford and King's Lynn

Preface

The present study is a synthesis of research begun in the summer of 1992. I am grateful to the British Academy for its support of the database project from which the book draws its material (1994/5); and to the Humanities Research Board of the British Academy and my Department for enabling me, in 1998/9, to take the research leave necessary to complete the book.

I am grateful to a fraternity of colleagues in my Department and beyond who keep alive a subversive sense of scholarly integrity in an environment largely defined by other priorities. I owe a significant debt in particular to Philip Alexander and to the late Norman Calder for many a conversation on reading, law, and the rabbis through the years. Julian Abel has read an earlier draft of this book and saved me from a number of embarrassing errors. Bernard Jackson's penetrating criticism and structural suggestions have considerably improved the book. Their help is much appreciated.

A further, stranger, debt needs to be acknowledged. It concerns the wondrous ability of music to cut new paths for thought, exemplified in Berg's Violin Concerto and the Piano Trio and Violin Sonatas of Ravel.

Manchester
Spring 2000

For
Batsheva and Maurice

Contents

List of Tables

Abbreviations and Special Signs

ABBREVIATIONS FOR WORKS AND TERMS

General Abbreviations

b	In front of abbreviated tractate name: tractate in the Babylonian Talmud
Bacher	W. Bacher, *Die exegetische Terminologie der jüdischen Traditionsliteratur I, Die bibelexegetische Terminologie der Tannaiten* (Leipzig: Hinrichs'sche Buchhandlung, 1899)
BDB	Francis Brown, S. K. Driver, and C. A . Briggs, *Hebrew-English Lexicon of the Old Testament* (Oxford: Clarendon Press, 1906; repr. 1951)
BerR	*Midrash Bereshit Rabba*, ed. J. Theodor and Ch. Albeck, 3 vols., 2nd edn. (Jerusalem: Wahrmann, 1965)
CD	Damascus Document
Clines	D. J. A. Clines, *The Dictionary of Classical Hebrew*, vols. I–IV (Sheffield: Sheffield Academic Press, 1993–8)
D	Dictum (see Glossary and Index)
E	With biblical references, English translation verse numbering (except in JPS, which follows the Hebrew)
Heb.	In Hebrew
Jastrow	M. Jastrow, *A Dictionary of the Targumim, the Talmud Babli and Yerushalmi, and the Midrashic Literature*, 2 vols. ([Philadelphia, 1903], numerous reprints)
JPS	Jewish Publication Society translation of the Hebrew Bible = *Tanakh: A New Translation of the Holy Scriptures According to the Traditional Hebrew Text* (Philadelphia/New York/Jerusalem: Jewish Publication Society, 1985)
L	Lemma (see Glossary and Index)
m	In front of abbreviated tractate name: Mishnah tractate
ShirR	Shir Rabba, part of Midrash Rabba on the Song of Songs
t	In front of abbreviated tractate name: tractate in the Tosefta
y	In front of abbreviated tractate name: tractate in the Palestinian Talmud (Yerushalmi)

Tractate Names

Arak	tractate Arakhin	Naz	tractate Nazir
Avot	tractate Avot	Ned	tractate Nedarim
AZ	tractate Avodah Zarah	Neg	tractate Nega'im
BB	tractate Bava Batra	Nid	tractate Niddah
Bek	tractate Bekhorot	Parah	tractate Parah
Ber	tractate Berakhot	Peah	tractate Peah
Bik	tractate Bikkurim	Pes	tractate Pesahim
BM	tractate Bava Metsi'a	Qid	tractate Qiddushin
BQ	tractate Bava Qamma	Qin	tractate Qinnim
Dem	tractate Demai	RH	tractate Rosh
Eduy	tractate Eduyyot		Hashanah
Erub	tractate Eruvin	San	tractate Sanhedrin
Git	tractate Gittin	Shab	tractate Shabbat
Hag	tractate Hagigah	Shebi	tractate Shevi'it
Hal	tractate Hallah	Shebu	tractate Shevu'ot
Hor	tractate Horayyot	Sheq	tractate Sheqalim
Hul	tractate Hullin	Sot	tractate Sotah
Kel	tractate Kelim	Sukkah	tractate Sukkah
Ker	tractate Keritot	Taan	tractate Ta'anit
Ket	tractate Ketubbot	Tam	tractate Tamid
Kilaim	tractate Kilaim	Tem	tractate Temurah
Maas	tractate Ma'aserot	Ter	tractate Terumot
Mak	tractate Makkot	TY	tractate Tevul Yom
Makh	tractate Makhshirin	Uqtsin	tractate Uqtsin
Meg	tractate Megillah	Yad	tractate Yadayyim
Men	tractate Menahot	Yeb	tractate Yevamot
Mid	tractate Middot	Yoma	tractate Yoma
Miqw	tractate Miqwa'ot	YT	tractate Yom Tov
MQ	tractate Mo'ed Qatan	Zab	tractate Zavim
MS	tractate Ma'aser Sheni	Zeb	tractate Zevahim

SPECIAL SIGNS

* used before a resource name or resource code: only one example of this resource is found in the Mishnah

* used between a resource name and a digit: representing another digit which may differ for different resources

[] square brackets used with the resource code or resource name: the resource does not appear in the Mishnah

[] square brackets used for references to chapter 6 of the Mishnah-tractate Avot: evidence of this tractate is not used for the hermeneutic profile of the Mishnah

[] square brackets in translated texts: parts of a biblical quotation supplied by the translator

() round brackets mark Mishnaic words that are not represented in all text witnesses

SIGNS MARKING FORMAL FEATURES IN HERMENEUTIC PROFILES

For fuller explanation see final section of Appendix I.

π   Expressive use of Scriptural wording
§   Reiteration and explication of a biblical term from a Mishnaic list
Δ   A situation or Dictum or practice marked as lying in the past
Σ   Lemmatic chain
Ω   Position at the end of a tractate
◊   Position in the final *mishnah* of a chapter inside a tractate, or in the penultimate *mishnah* of a tractate
¶   Part of a dispute structure
•   Ascribed to a named rabbi
®   Double representation of the Mishnaic position in a midrashic unit
≈   Same resource as in a neighbouring unit
¬   Presented so as to be refuted; or implicit rejection of a resource due to use of another resource
‡   Continuation format of presentation of paraphrase of Lemma
i   Lemma provides the protasis of a Mishnaic protasis–apodosis unit

1

Hermeneutic Orientation and Introduction

THE HERMENEUTIC SITUATION

The Hebrew Bible is fundamental to the historical context from which all post-biblical Jewish groups emerge. Understanding the way these groups read their Bible means understanding how they saw their own origins. Origins are the main, and elusive, prize in historical research. Although no direct path leads from the rabbinic reading of Scripture to Scripture as the origin of rabbinic Judaism,[1] this is the larger historical agenda to which this study wishes to make a contribution.

I offer a systematic description of the explicit hermeneutics of early rabbinic Judaism as reflected in its foundation document, the Mishnah. While my account deliberately concentrates on one work of rabbinic literature, its sights are set on core aspects of the hermeneutic enterprise as it appears in rabbinic literature as a whole. In the Mishnah explicit interpretation occupies only little room. But outside it and after it biblical interpretation becomes the dominant expression of rabbinic Judaism. The categories and tools of description here introduced were created with a view to expansion and adaptation for other rabbinic documents. Even as arising from the limited Mishnaic hermeneutic material, these categories cut broad swathes through the complexity of midrashic and Talmudic hermeneutics.

My description has the following characteristics. It breaks down unified but internally complex hermeneutic operations into individual components. It provides explicit definitions for these individual components as hermeneutic procedures. It furnishes a catalogue of definitions based on the *totality* of the evidence of the rabbinic work under discussion,that is, it does not pre-select the evidence in some other manner. And the definition for each individual procedure reflects other hermeneutic phenomena arising from the same corpus; the terms of descriptions are mutually

[1] More on this in Ch. 3 below.

compatible or complementary. I aim to provide a *comprehensive* catalogue of hermeneutic components, that is, a full hermeneutic profile of the Mishnah. My language of description is independent of specifically rabbinic terminology. This prepares the ground for fairly direct comparison with non-rabbinic hermeneutic traditions; it also lays one of the foundations for a diachronic study of rabbinic hermeneutic terminology. Wherever possible the definitions of hermeneutic components draw on the rich and diversified conceptual apparatus supplied by academic discourses on linguistics, reading, and philosophy of language. As far as the scholarly context is concerned, my aim is to make rabbinic hermeneutics accessible to these discourses as well as to historians of culture through use of the lingua franca of modern linguistics.[2] (The terminologies both of that lingua franca and of rabbinic studies are explained in the Glossary.)

What do my raw data look like? I concentrate on passages in the Mishnah where Scripture is alluded to or explicitly quoted. In such passages we find largely unexplained, or even undeclared, hermeneutic dependencies between Mishnaic norms or statements on the one hand and Scripture's words on the other. Since there is no fully explicit or consistent account of these dependencies in the Mishnah, my explication of them is a matter of reconstruction and of categorization. My descriptions of hermeneutic components thus constitute an interpretation of rabbinic interpretation.

Yet the word 'interpretation' does not convey the full flavour of the decisions which we are obliged to impose on the material. As historians, we preserve an attitude of detachment regarding any direct expression of opinion or alleged fact in our sources. But units of interpretation are not direct expressions of opinion or fact: they establish hermeneutic links. For direct claims we preserve a professional neutrality, a dis-interest. Between the Athenians and the Spartans the ancient historian need not, and perhaps must not, take sides. And the historian qua historian is not concerned with whether the Jerusalem priesthood or the Qumran covenanters had the *correct* festival calendar.[3] But such neutrality is not even theoretically possible in the case of interpreting the rabbinic interpretation of Scripture. For historical scholarship is, among other things, *a method of reading*. Modern historical scholarship has its 'own' opinion on the meaning of any historical text, and in the case of Scripture this is a fully articulated, long-standing, and fairly unified opinion.[4] It is the basic claim of the

---

[2] I am aware that my descriptions are nevertheless very heavily contextualized by the rabbinic evidence in ways that I could not eliminate; so that the linguistic lingua franca in this book is bound to be *distorted* in specific ways.

[3] Here and in what follows the modern historical-scholarly approach is to some extent defined in tacit contrast to other modern approaches to historical sources, such as deconstruction. It is precisely the commitments of the former, but not of the latter, which produce the tension which is here explored.

[4] Cf. Porton's statement that 'the distinction between "hidden" and "plain" is often a result of our present view of Scripture' ('Defining Midrash', 59).

contemporary offshoots of the historical-critical approach to make available the 'historical' meaning of man-made documents. This meaning is thought of as the meaning a document had in its original context. Even where that meaning remains conjectural, the method narrows down the options by weeding out the inappropriate, unhistorical interpretations. And among these are any that bring to the text dogmas from a time later than that of the composition, for example, the idea of one, unified will which controls simultaneously all the document's parts down to the last detail.[5] But this is only the most fundamental of the 'unhistorical' preconceptions brought to the biblical text. There are others, equally unacceptable to the historical approach. In the matter of reading method, most modern scholarship is committed, not neutral. So, when confronted with an approach to the same text which produces interpretations which are very often historically inappropriate, modern historical scholarship cannot even classify them without noting that they are precisely that—inappropriate, unhistorical, anachronistic.[6] The modern historical approach as such, not some personal and illegitimate lack of objectivity, *judges* rabbinic interpretation. The contemporary understanding of the biblical text is enshrined in the vast majority of secondary literature, in translations, academic Bible commentaries, and dictionaries. It is also instilled in scholars as part of a historical training in the various subjects of Jewish studies at university. It is thus unavoidably the foil setting off the rabbinic reading of Scripture, but not merely a foil. The modern historical understanding of the Bible is a *rival* to rabbinic reading.[7] Scholars with a historical agenda do not criticize or correct rabbinic interpretation; but they do correct their students if they come up with rabbinic-style explanations for any historical text.

Where this hermeneutic situation is not taken into account, some fundamental misunderstandings can result—misunderstandings, that is, in terms of historical appropriateness. Lack of hermeneutic awareness can

---

[5] This is what the word 'canon' entails, if used to refer to a traditional idea of the Hebrew Bible. For the modern scholarly reading, on the other hand, any book of the Bible is potentially a book of parts, even if the confidence of marking out the exact boundaries of sources or traditions has diminished in recent decades.

[6] Judah Goldin is both outspoken and accurate when saying: 'We describe such interpretations as anachronistic and homiletical, which they plainly are, and forthwith dismiss them from serious consideration because they are not literal exegesis. They are certainly not to be treated as literal exegesis . . .'. But Goldin goes on to explain how precise the midrashic engagement with the biblical text actually is, calling it 'disclosing commentary' (*The Song at the Sea*, 22 f.).

[7] It is no accident that some scholars who have ceased to subscribe to the claims of historical-critical scholarship are presenting the rabbinic approach as an alternative to it, effectively as a forerunner of post-modern methods of reading. See nn. 102 f. below. Gadamer links the origins of modern hermeneutics to Luther's criticism of Roman Catholicism: 'Modern hermeneutics, as a protestant discipline of the art of interpreting scripture, is clearly related in a polemical way to the dogmatic tradition of the catholic church. It has itself a dogmatic denominational significance', *Truth and Method*, 296 (*Wahrheit und Methode*, 314 f. [315]). Similar is the claim that modern biblical criticism is based on a critique of revealed religion and not its result, for which see Strauss, *Spinoza's Critique of Religion* (and cf. Gadamer, *Truth and Method*, 159 f.; *Wahrheit und Methode*, 184 f. [169]).

lead to the denial that rabbinic reading is genuine interpretation, basically because its results are too far-fetched in comparison with those of modern scholarship.[8] Alternatively, it can lead to an apologetic reclassification of rabbinic hermeneutics as 'literal interpretation', 'plain meaning', or 'philology'.[9] Reflection on the rivalry between *our* reading of Scripture and that of the rabbis should make any such moves suspect. Using these terms for rabbinic hermeneutics is like saying that J. S. Bach almost achieved, or regrettably failed to achieve, the orchestral colours of Romantic music.[10] It is more complimentary, but not in principle different, to claim that rabbinic 'philology' was 'creative', in the famous and influential formulation of I. Heinemann.[11] Let us not forget that such creativity is drummed out of our students in the course of their historical *training*. The answer is to admit that rabbinic hermeneutics is not a derivative form of our hermeneutics— neither 'philology' nor 'historiography'.[12] The first step towards an ade- quate historical understanding of rabbinic interpretation is to offer some resistance to describing it as a variation of what we ourselves do when doing historical scholarship.[13] I take it, by the way, that we cannot simply 'outgrow' the historical agenda itself; and practitioners of deconstruction

[8] For individual rabbinic interpretations this is a very common judgement (see the first section of Ch. 3 below). A more general judgemental attitude towards rabbinic hermeneutics is found in Maass, 'Von den Ursprüngen der rabbinischen Schriftauslegung'.

[9] An anachronistic use of the word *peshat* often compounds this confusion. Rosenblatt's *The Interpretation of the Bible in the Mishnah* is an exponent of this trend. After an admirable summary of how and why rabbinic reading of the Bible is different from that of modern scholarship, Rosenblatt continues: 'With these reservations the exegetes of the Mishnah may be said to have engaged in what would today be called literal exegesis. That they were interested in discovering the פשט or simple meaning of the text is evident not only from certain verbal remarks, but also from their practice in the Mishnah . . .' (p. 4 f.). In this respect, as in others, Rosenblatt's work is less rigorous than the earlier book by Aicher, *Das Alte Testament in der Mischna*. Both these works have recently been sub- stantially supplemented by a further study of Mishnaic exegesis, Pettit's *Shene'emar* (I am grateful to Prof. Moshe Bernstein of Yeshiva University, New York, for drawing my attention to this work). *Peshat* has frequently functioned as a modern term for all that is philologically respectable in rabbinic hermeneutics. On its meaning, see esp. Loewe, 'The "Plain" Meaning of Scripture in Early Jewish Exegesis', 140–85; Halivni, *Peshat and Derash*. This apologetic tendency survives the change of scholarly paradigm from history to post-modernism, as the example of Handelman shows (*The Slayers of Moses*, 76).

[10] I am not denying that these ahistorical comparisons have their uses; they can be extremely illuminating. However, if their proponents consider themselves to be historians, they should retain an awareness of their ahistorical character.

[11] *Darkhey Ha-Aggadah* (Heb.). This is updating with a vengance. For the cultural framework in which Heinemann created his picture of rabbinic hermeneutics, see Boyarin, *Intertextuality*, ch. 1.

[12] Nor, I might add, 'etymology'. On the latter point, see Ch. 14 below. As far as 'creative' philo- logy and historiography are concerned, see Heinemann, *Darkhey Ha-Aggadah*, 4 ff., and the titles of the first two main sections in his book.

[13] I am presupposing in the above my *experience* with the historical and critical reading. If users of this book have had a different experience with it, they will perhaps see no need to explicate the differences (or these particular differences) as part of a description of rabbinic reading. But that could not be remedied by quoting a book on the nature of modern historical approaches to texts. I am not talking about the theoretical justification or articulation of this approach, but about a socially mediated practice of reading which is learned in its application to a scholarly subject. Barton, *Reading the Old Testament*, offers an overview of methods in biblical studies, including a concise account of ' "traditional" biblical criticism' (155 f.) which, to my mind, provides the context in which much scholarly literature on *rabbinics* was and still is produced.

are mistaken if they suppose it *frees* them from that agenda. Historical appropriateness is surely as much part of the conceptual presuppositions and historical nexus of post-modernist thinking as structuralism is part of post-structuralism.

Instinctive assimilation of rabbinic hermeneutics to the modern historical project may reflect a conviction that the historical reading is basically a universal mode of reading, for example, when it separates the meaning of a document on the one hand from its truth and relevance on the other.[14] But such a separation is far from universal, and may indeed be very rare, historically speaking. Brief reflection will show that there are many contexts in which reading (and communication in general) is done quite differently. Here are some hypothetical situations in which historians and philologists might read a text with an eye to immediate relevance; these furnish some parallels to the basic attitude assumed by the rabbinic reader vis-à-vis Scripture.

(1) A person who is not used to assembling three-dimensional objects has bought a bookshelf for self-assembly. He now sits on the floor, with two-dozen wooden parts and an assortment of screws around him, looking at a page printed with instructions, numbers, and drawings. (His lips form silent words and his hands are sweaty.) In his mind, every word and every number carries heavy emphasis so that no information is lost. Every sign is vital, the smallest difference between otherwise similar signs or drawings translates into a decisive difference for the manner in which the parts are put together. Every line of text counts, because there is no repetition. Reading is slowed down to a syllabic stammer as if the text were in a foreign language, and from time to time certain wooden parts are held together to try out a meaning hypothesis—if the pieces do not fit, the text is scrutinized again until a mistake in the interpretation is identified and corrected. Progress of assembly depends wholly on the correct decoding of the document.

(2) As before, but the manufacturer has by mistake enclosed the instructions for a *different* model of bookshelf. The process of interpretation begins as in (1) above. The bookshelf is not very obviously different from the model presupposed in the text. The user never questions that the instructions are correct, because he is certain of the manufacturer's skill and reliability. He therefore perseveres in his reading of the text. He even starts to modify the physical dimensions of the shelves and parts in order to make them conform to the text; he selects alternative screws from his toolbox instead of the ones enclosed, succeeding eventually in putting together something like a bookshelf of the model for which the instructions were

---

[14] This certainly shows how successful historical training can be; however, it betrays a lack of historical perspective for the phenomenon of historical scholarship itself. The separation of meaning from truth is performed explicitly, for the purposes of reading the Bible, by Spinoza in his *Tractatus Theologico-Politicus*.

intended. Alternatively, he guesses the method of assembly from reading the instructions, extracting its principles and applying them by analogy without following the detail of the text step by step. In either case, he takes the successful assembly as confirmation of the text's accuracy.

(3) An historian has found in an obscure library evidence that a certain medieval event known to scholars took place in a certain (hitherto unknown) manner. Perusing an older collection of articles on the topic, she finds one by an eminent historian who speculates about that event in terms which approximate what she knows, on the basis of her newly found evidence, to be the truth. In publishing her findings she quotes the older article in a footnote, presenting it as a working hypothesis which she can now confirm with evidence. She does so without investigating ambiguities and vagueness in the earlier author's account (as she would with a primary source), and without stressing certain discrepancies between her own and the other scholar's description of events. She interprets the other's paper, in the light of her evidence of what happened, as confirmed.

(4) A Latinist, seeing himself as keeping an open mind on the merits of astrology, comes across his horoscope for the week. He interprets the text, which consists of general formulations, with an eye to the concrete circumstances of his situation, identifying without hesitation the specific events and persons to which the words must refer. The upbeat final sentence he takes as encouragement to go ahead with a funding application he has been doubtful about.

All of these imaginary contemporary settings illustrate types of interpretation which construe meaning under the expectation of the text's immediate relevance in the situation. They take a strong orientation in the nature of the subject-matter—as known to and of concern to the reader.[15] This orientation is a guiding principle for the construction of meaning. In fact, the expectation of relevance may even, in suitable circumstances, be decisive for the determination of the very subject-matter or the referent of a text (as in (2), where bookshelf and text are not meant for each other). The historical context, by contrast, plays no role in determining the text's meaning, not even where the reader concerned has trained historical habits—as in (3) and (4). The point of the text is sought in its (partly technical) *information contents*.

From such examples of reading we can perhaps replenish our historical imagination as to how varied the construction of meaning can be. Apparently alien manners of reading, usually put down to the distorting influence of a tradition or ideology, can be found in everyday circumstances of the here and now. In fact, the direct alignment of a text's meaning

---

[15] The same thing is being done at this point in the present book, namely, taking certain everyday aspects of *our own* experience with the phenomenon 'reading' as a preliminary orientation in the subject-matter. The main difference is that the subject-matter is reading itself, i.e. the orientation is of a reflective nature.

with the situation of reading predominates in many walks of life. I am leaving open the question whether as historians and philologists we are so very far away from such hermeneutic strategies even when concerned with our primary sources.[16] Current scholarly trends in the reconstruction of rabbinic hermeneutics, for example, can quite easily be read as part of a larger *contemporary* dispute on the force of the irrational in human affairs, or the perceived failure of the European Enlightenment. Our very own historically unique context and the things that make *us* tick may well shape the parameters in which our reading of the rabbis proceeds.[17]

The historical mode of reading is, then, by no means the only one known even to historians and scholars. An approach to Scripture which is prima facie very different from it cannot be simply treated as a variant, let alone a deficient variant, of the historical mode of reading Scripture. Nevertheless, the historical perspective on Scripture provides the inevitable horizon of any historical appreciation of rabbinic hermeneutics. For a start, the limits of our description of rabbinic hermeneutics are defined by what is con-spicuous or characteristic about it. And that is, to some extent at least, what is different from *our* reading of Scripture. Furthermore, in order to express what any specific rabbinic interpretation does with a biblical passage we have to imply our own understanding of that passage, sometimes shared with the rabbinic one, more often quite different. 'Our' way of reading this passage from Jeremiah:

> Blessed is he who trusts in the Lord,
> Whose trust is the Lord alone[18]

may admit a great variety of notions. Among them will probably be an appreciation of the fact that it forms part of a longer passage couched in general terms, praising trust in God and condemning ill-gotten gain or reliance on human devices. But biblical scholarship does not connect these biblical words to the case of a person who, while poor enough to be entitled to the corn left standing after harvest (*Peah*), does not wish to take it. There is no mention of the *Peah* in this Jeremiah passage or anywhere near it. Neither does the historical approach provide for the following under-standing of the verse: Blessed is the (needy) person trusting in God (as opposed to *Peah*), *for* God will provide his security [trust].[19] But this is how the Mishnah understands the verse, in mPeah 8:9 I (4).[20] The verse is on the one hand linked to the case of a needy person who refrains from taking

---

[16] The main attack on such hermeneutic naivety is the work of Gadamer and Derrida. See below.

[17] More on this below.

[18] Jer. 17:7, in the JPS version (ברוך הגבר אשר יבטח בה׳ והיה ה׳ מבטחו); RSV renders, 'Blessed is the man who trusts in the Lord, whose trust is the Lord.'

[19] Cf. the paraphrase in the commentary *Peney Mosheh* (Mosheh ben Shim'on Margoliot) on yPeah 8:8 end (ed. Zhitomir).

[20] This unit, while succeeded by textually suspect material, is well represented in the MSS and the text used by Maimonides for his *Commentary* (trans. Qafih, *Zera'im*, 78). Cf. Bauer, *Pea*, 71; Albeck, *Untersuchungen über die Redaktion der Mischna*, 140 f.

Peah. On the other hand, its second half is read as containing God's *response* to such behaviour.[21] Such are the hermeneutic decisions that need explaining—interpretations which we do not already understand on the basis of our understanding of Scripture. They will inevitably provide the focus for describing the hermeneutic mechanisms in rabbinic texts. And the sum total of all instances of conspicuousness in individual interpretations will shape quite fundamentally our overall appreciation of rabbinic hermeneutics, even if our description eventually achieves a more comprehensive treatment of all aspects.[22]

So we select, in the first instance, aspects of rabbinic hermeneutics which *require* description because they are not shared by us. But this is only one manifestation of the impact of our contemporary reading of Scripture. Others are linked to the question of the division of Scripture into smaller segments. Here we find very roughly two trends in recent biblical scholarship, insofar as it keeps an interest in the Bible's historical context. The one gives priority to the shape in which the larger biblical units are now found, and construes the book's coherence accordingly.[23] The other is inclined to accept as decisive or final any evidence of incoherence suggesting that pre-existing units were put together in the formation of the biblical text. But both agree that the text is ultimately put together by man, and that the idea of *one simultaneous* will controlling all its parts is unhistoric and cannot be allowed to dictate the outcome of the interpretation. On the other hand, they also agree that, where there are no traces of text growth, any shorter biblical passage has to be understood first and foremost in the light of its immediately surrounding text. This priority of the co-text for determining the local meaning of clauses, words, metaphors, and so on is a fundamental corollary to the idea of the 'original' meaning. In these two points the modern historical approach is united *against* rabbinic hermeneutics. On the one hand, the latter accepts the idea of unified overall control mostly to such a degree that no textual evidence can withstand it. Inconsistency is merely apparent,[24] repetition means that the two redundant expressions are not about the same topic.[25] Neither inconsistency nor repetition is a sign

[21] The response is to reward the behaviour by complementing it symmetrically: he did not take *Peah* when he needed it, therefore he will become wealthy enough to support others in (*Peah-*) need. This is likely to presuppose the rabbinic principle, 'measure for measure' (on which cf. Ch. 5 below).
[22] It would be more accurate to say that an initially 'naive' astonishment at certain rabbinic interpretation results gives way to a discipline that looks for the astonishing element in all rabbinic interpretation results.
[23] For an important example, see Sternberg, *The Poetics of Biblical Narrative*. I am assuming that only some of the most recent approaches to the biblical text as a whole, or as a 'canon' (see Barton, *Reading the Old Testament*, 77 ff.), will go as far as simply neutralizing all the results of the historical-critical dissection of the biblical text, and accept *all* phenomena of repetition, discontinuity, or internal contradiction in Scripture as meaningful. Here it seems necessary to make a distinction between the theory that scholars profess and how they actually read biblical texts (cf. Barton, *Reading the Old Testament*, 84 ff.). See n. 13 above, and also my attempt to review Boyarin's *Intertexuality* ('Justifying Midrash', 30 f.).   [24] See Ch. 10 below.
[25] See Ch. 13 below.

of historical growth, that is, the meaningless, accidental, or involuntary result of insufficient control of meaning. Modern scholarship's word for this attitude is 'harmonization', which means the inappropriate manufacture of coherence. And on the other hand, rabbinic hermeneutics divides the text into (topical) segments whose meaning is quite often determined in *isolation* from the surrounding biblical text.[26] These phenomena are conspicuous—to us; we take them as characteristic of rabbinic hermeneutics, because they are so different from our reading of Scripture.

When describing rabbinic interpretation of a biblical passage there is thus a confrontation between the average current scholarly view of its meaning and the rabbinic view. And the operative word is 'current'. This confrontation causes our description of rabbinic hermeneutics to carry the index 'twentieth century'. It carries the mark of a specific juncture in the history of human discourse. The idea of historical scholarship as presupposed in biblical studies is itself such a sign of the times. As for Scripture in particular, the modern scholarly reading is a tradition in whose genesis Christian, rabbinic,[27] and secular-historical elements are inextricably mixed.

Since we can neither avoid nor ignore the impact of our own reading of Scripture on our reading of the rabbinic reading of Scripture, we need to bring it into the open; to make it as *explicit* a part of our description as we can. Perhaps the most important difference that needs to be articulated is the above-mentioned role accorded to the surrounding biblical text when determining the significance of a segment of Scripture. This aspect is also present in my earlier summary of the interpretation of Jer. 17:7. The modern historical approach will attempt to determine more specifically the meaning of a sentence whose wording is vague by looking at its links to the surrounding sentences. And, if there is nothing more specific to be found there, then the presumption is that nothing more specific is intended; a presumption clearly not shared by the Mishnaic interpreter of Jer. 17:7. This is a typical difference and lends itself to being spelled out when rabbinic hermeneutic resources are defined.[28] Concrete details of the scholarly understanding of the biblical text are often also presupposed in our description of a rabbinic interpretation, most importantly with regard to biblical lexicography. We cannot explain the meaning choices made for words by the Mishnah without reference to what biblical scholarship, distilled in the biblical dictionaries,[29] considers to be the semantics of the word in question.

[26] See Chs. 2 and 14.
[27] Mostly as filtered through Christian exegesis.
[28] See Ch. 2 below.
[29] The current investigation is being undertaken by someone who is not a biblical scholar, and who depends very much on the broad reference tools of biblical scholarship. Consequently, some aspects of the historical understanding of the Bible used here as a foil for rabbinic hermeneutics are bound to be behind the times, or incomplete. There may be a paradoxical advantage to that, in that I am forced to present an *average* and approximate position in the modern historical understanding

In some respects the difference between the rabbinic approach to Scripture and that of modern scholarship will be underplayed in this study. For example, the English translations of biblical verses incorporated into my citations from the Mishnah are really an attempt to prepare the reader for the hermeneutic operation, not an attempt to present the sense of the biblical sentence.[30] The English version is designed where possible to represent all Hebrew words by an English word, to preserve their sequence, and to produce calques of the asyndetic or paratactic linkages typical of Hebrew phrases.[31] Rabbinic hermeneutics, applied to such fragmentary and obscure fragments of English, will often look *more natural* than in its application to the Hebrew. The best antidote, apart from consulting the Hebrew directly, is to use one of the thoroughly modern English versions, such as the new Jewish Publication Society translation, which have no qualms about relinquishing the original structures to say directly what they perceive as the Hebrew's sense. The difference is also underplayed throughout most of this book by its frequent acceptance of the biblical wording's boundary as chosen by the Mishnah. I shall not place back into its biblical setting every single quotation consisting only of one sentence (although I shall do it with some). Often the clarification of individual words is negotiated wholly on the level of the sentence, when biblical scholarship looks to larger units. Also, there is no attempt to compare the results of textual criticism, where it separates neighbouring text parts, with rabbinic reading. In all these ways my presentation, by not confirming the difference anew for each instance of interpretation, tends to reduce the appearance of difference between the two hermeneutic approaches.

DESCRIBING RESOURCES OF INTERPRETATION

How do I intend to capture the concrete regularities of Mishnaic Bible interpretation? By empirical investigation, classification, and description of all occurrences of Scripture in the text of the Mishnah. This includes all passages in which the meaning of Scriptural words is explicitly addressed; it also includes many instances of the use of Scriptural wording for the Mishnah's own formulations.[32] The totality of the evidence is contained not

---

of the Bible which gives sharper relief to the contrast with rabbinic hermeneutics. I would, however, gladly forgo that advantage in exchange for an expert's knowledge in biblical studies.

[30] This issue, not unimportant for the hermeneutic situation, is explained very clearly in the introduction to Lauterbach's Mekhilta edition (vol. I, pp. lxi f.). It also concerns the extent of the quotation: I shall supply in square brackets all unquoted parts of a verse (or neighbouring verses) which are either necessary to establish the sense of the biblical sentence, or are presupposed in the working of the interpretation. On the question of how we know which biblical parts are required, see n. 82 below.

[31] It is no accident that this sentence reads like an instruction for producing the base text of a Targum; see my 'Scripture's Segments and Topicality', 101 ff.

[32] But with regard to this phenomenon, explained as expressive use in Ch. 4, the study is not based on a survey of *all* cases.

in this study but in my *Database of Midrashic Units in the Mishnah*. My descriptions are the result of an internal comparison and contrast of passages, as well as of the employment of the descriptive categories of contemporary linguistics, philosophy of language, and hermeneutics. They are the result of a sustained process of interpretation and abstraction. As such they are deliberately grounded, as the previous section has shown they must be *nolens volens*, in my own explanatory needs. They speak the language of the modern scholarly reader, not the language of the rabbis or the language of Scripture. In describing interpretations as they are actually found in a rabbinic text, the explicit hermeneutics of the rabbis are not of decisive help (see below); nevertheless, I shall from time to time point to relevant rabbinic terms or rules.

This project of description started out as an attempt at defining each hermeneutic operation as a whole. This is the standard modern as well as traditional approach for most individual units of rabbinic interpretation. However, it became evident that this merely means that the most conspicuous feature of the operation lends its name (if it has one) to the complex whole, and other features are not named, let alone explicated. Most Mishnaic units of interpretation turn out to be unsuitable for description by one undifferentiated hermeneutic technique. In particular, if we seek underlying similarities between different interpretations, the description needs to unpack the hermeneutic package. The descriptive categories here used capture *components* within complex hermeneutic operations. These components recur in other passages in combination with other components. Thus, when speaking above about the use of Jer. 17:7 in mPeah 8:9 I (4) I *separated* two questions. The first is: 'How can we understand the thematic link to the case of a needy person not taking *Peah*?' The second is: 'How can the second half of the verse be taken as specifying a change of fortune for the person trusting in God when it merely seems to repeat the meaning of the first half?' Answers to both questions are given through the formulation of hermeneutic procedures, but two *different* procedures. It is the *combination* of these two hermeneutic components into a unified hermeneutic operation which accounts for the interpretation of Jer. 17:7 as a whole.

From here on I shall call such hermeneutic components *resources*, resources of interpretation, or hermeneutic resources, using this term in preference to the words 'methods' and 'techniques', let alone 'rules'. All of these latter terms are employed in modern discussions of rabbinic hermeneutics; however, they have very strong overtones of *instrumentality*, and such an instrumental character is unlikely for rabbinic hermeneutic procedures, as will be seen below. The word 'resource', on the other hand, points more in the direction of something that is available, but in a 'raw' or undefined form; or something that can come in many forms. A resource is more like an energy than like a tool. At the point of its use a resource is hard to objectify or to make the focus of attention. One can draw on a resource *one did not know one had*. In precisely this sense rabbinic hermeneutic components are 'resources'. It is an added bonus that the semantic make-up of the word (when taken as a verb, which is not how I am going to use it) suggests the idea of connecting something to a *source*, and of connecting it for a second time, or to a different source than before.[33]

Exactly why is it unhelpful to think of the rabbinic reading habits as methods, in the sense of individual and well-defined tools spread out in readiness for a job? Historically speaking, rabbinic hermeneutic procedures are unlikely to have been reified in explicit formulation. The image of the toolbox is a tempting one to use, in particular once the tools are spread out for inspection, as in this book. But historically speaking, the image is almost certainly misleading, and the so-called hermeneutic rules of rabbinic literature indirectly confirm this by their incompleteness, scarceness, and lack of real explanatory intent.[34] The nature of reading itself mitigates against any purely instrumental or mechanical application of hermeneutic rules to textual phenomena. For example, the rules of textual criticism are the most mechanical or 'scientific' section of the modern scholarly methodology, which takes pride in the explicitness and even-handed application of methods. But even these rules do not allow for purely mechanical application, and are usually accompanied by emphatic caveats against such automatic or unthinking use.[35] Nevertheless, the word 'method' here has a place, in that there is indeed some obligation to treat all similar linguistic or textual phenomena by the same method or set of methods—in fact, methodically. No distinction is admitted which rests on the nature or the origin of the document; no text can *a priori* be exempted from the treatment. There is an inherent claim to universality in these methods, and their legitimacy depends on it. Rabbinic resources of interpretation are very different in this respect. The result of an interpretation, if it is an un-rabbinic proposition, cannot be made acceptable merely by showing that a legitimate procedure has been applied correctly to an eligible piece of Scripture. Rabbinic positions are justified in a variety of ways, and the 'correctness' of an abstract method of interpretation is only one of them.[36] Rabbinic resources of interpretation are always specific, applied to a concrete biblical text with concrete results. There is also no sign of a rabbinic commitment to a finite *set* of methods. And rabbinic resources of interpretation have no inbuilt universality, that is, they involve no

[33] In other words, a verbal meaning 'to re-source something'. I shall argue in Ch. 3 that the literary units which contain interpretations of Scripture cannot be taken as spontaneous or immediate reflexion of an exegetical idea in its original historical occurrence. The mediation implied in 're-source' is thus welcome.

[34] More on the rabbinic hermeneutic 'rules' below.

[35] See e.g. Aland and Aland, *Der Text des Neuen Testaments*, 282 ('Zwölf Grundregeln').

[36] See in particular the restrictions for application of the *a fortiori* and the analogy, briefly treated in Chs. 7 and 8 below.

commitment to treat all similar cases in a similar manner. Under the conditions of reading envisaged here there is a choice of resources for the rabbinic reader; but that choice is not between abstract stratagems of reading, but rather is constrained or triggered by the text's subject-matter and the reader's concern. This also provides a model for the proliferation of resources in the emergence of rabbinic hermeneutics: a spread from one or several *topics* with which they are successfully connected to other topics; also from one Lemma, whose treatment in a given biblical location is remembered, to the same Lemma elsewhere in Scripture. In other words, we should envisage dissemination of hermeneutic resources by analogy from one concrete application to another, not on the basis of abstract formulations.[37]

In my attempt to forge suitable concepts for the components of complex (and mostly unexplained) hermeneutic operations, the whole breadth of the modern understanding of language is, in principle, relevant. Helpful in particular are the insights gained from the study of conversation, or face-to-face communication.[38] But the totality of resources found in the Mishnah (as presented in Appendix I) shows that a wide variety of categories in modern linguistics is useful in explaining how the rabbis construed Scripture's explicit or implied messages. An important exception to this is the absence of procedures which highlight specifically artistic or poetic qualities.[39]

In addition to a technical vocabulary derived from modern linguistics and philosophy of language (explained in the Glossary), there are more general and diffuse conceptual links to contemporary discourse in this book, which are no less influential on the interpretative decisions I have taken. Language, meaning, and reading have been among the dominant topics in the discourse of (Western) modernity for more than a century. Major groupings of contemporary discourse, often perceived as mutually exclusive, may well be perceived in the future as sharing a common concern: Heidegger-inspired hermeneutics,[40] Wittgenstein-inspired ordinary language philosophy,[41] linguistic pragmatics and discourse analysis,[42] structuralism,[43] and Derrida-inspired deconstruction[44] all emphasize the

[37] For the term 'Lemma', see Glossary. We would expect, if this is true, the formation of *clusters* of interpretations in which there is a similarity of resources, and a similarity of biblical Lemma, but a different biblical location and / or a different rabbinic topic. The Mishnah seems to offer one example of just such a cluster, or rather a pair: mShebi 10:8 I–II (2), passage **[132]** below. The phrase linking them is כיוצא בו.

[38] See also my 'Scripture's Implicature'.

[39] See on this further in Ch. 2 (text after n. 93) and Ch. 13 (text following n. 76).

[40] See Gadamer's *Truth and Method*.

[41] Apart from Wittgenstein's *Philosophical Investigations*, see in particular Austin, *How To Do Things with Words*; Grice, *Studies in the Way of Words*; Black, *Models and Metaphors*.

[42] Of central importance are Sacks, *Lectures on Conversation*, and Grice, *Studies in the Way of Words*. Summaries are found in Levinson, *Pragmatics*, and Yule and Brown, *Discourse Analysis*.

[43] e.g. Jakobson's work, and the influence of Saussure in Lyons.

[44] Many of the publications on rabbinic exegesis over the last decade and a half are in the deconstructionist vein. A better starting-point is Derrida himself (in particular his *Of Grammatology*).

ties that bind the linguistic expression to social practice and 'real life'.[45] The *theoria* they provide is itself best learned in the application, not through verbal explanation. They all seem to provide categories designed to do justice to the richness of cultural practices and habits of thought embedded in language. The influence of these approaches is felt at various points in this study, and underpins it with an understanding of reading as a phenomenon of communication, language-in-use, and time. Gadamer's insistence that reading is rooted in an orientation in the truth of a matter (*Sache*) brought a decisive reorientation in my studies, and has helped me to jettison some unhelpful preconceptions.[46] These philosophical positions, too, tie this study to a specific context, a time and a place.

There is thus no neutral or automatic mechanism which would generate the descriptions of resources presented here. They remain *interpretations* of the rabbinic material, couched in terms that are relevant to us (me), now. Other, more fruitful categories may well be found and replace the ones offered here. At some later stage it should also be possible to articulate the relationship between the concepts used here and the metalinguistic terminology of the rabbis.[47] It can already be seen that, in many cases, there will be no one-to-one correspondence between rabbinic term or rule on the one hand and resource on the other. But our first task must be to establish at least *one* internally coherent interpretation of rabbinic interpretation which explains it for us, and whose terms are systematically related to each other.

The terms in which the resources are defined in this study are drawn from modern linguistics in the widest sense; so are the headings under which the individual resources are gathered in groups. They are listed in Table 1.1, together with the chapters in which they are discussed; also listed is the technical name given to each family of resources. This name is terminological in that its natural meaning fits some of the individual resources better than others. Their family relationships cannot be summed up in *one* term; nevertheless, the family name's meaning will perhaps help in recalling a resource's definition. For database purposes it is simpler if each resource family occupies only one letter of the alphabet; accordingly, sometimes the name chosen was not the most obvious one, but rather one which started with an as-yet unused letter of the alphabet. In a number of cases this has led to somewhat forced or metaphorical names (e.g. Habit, Keying, Map).

Within the resource families, individual resources are distinguished by

---

[45] Biblical and related studies have felt the impact of this sort of approach for more than a century; a case in point is the notion of *Sitz im Leben*. The latter provides a model for a context which determines the meaning of signs in written texts, i.e. transmitted without that context. Recently, biblical (legal) texts have been examined also from the perspective of speech acts; see Bernard Jackson, *Studies in the Semiotics of Biblical Law*, in particular sec. 2.3.1. I am indebted to Professor Jackson for allowing me to use the typescript of his book.

[46] See his *Truth and Method*, 337 ff. (*Wahrheit und Methode*, 380 f. [357 f.]).

[47] But we will still not be able to say *in their words* how their interpretation works, unless we have first filled their words with our sense.

TABLE 1.1 *Resource families*

Hermeneutic or linguistic category	Family name	Chapter
1. Word constitution and semantics		
Choices for word constitution and word meaning	WORD	14
Semantic and paradigmatic opposition	OPPOSITION	11, 12
Taxonomic relationships between lexemes	EXTENSION	9
Semiotic options beneath the level of the complete word	ICON, GRAPHEME	14
Logical constants and conjunctions	LOGIC	9
2. Syntax, text structures		
Neutralizing or utilizing the biblical co-text	COTEXT	2, 14
Syntactic relationships within the sentence or between clauses	SYNTAX	13
Redundancy of similarity, repetition, and synonymy	REDUNDANCY	13
Inconsistency, inner-biblical contrasts and differences	DIFFERENCE	10
Position in the text	MAP	13
3. Subject-matter		
Imposing the perspectives of topical orientation	TOPIC	3, 4
4. Analogical procedures		
Analogy, *a fortiori* argument	ANALOGY	7, 8
Analogy between two occurrences of the same lexeme	KEYING	8
5. Narrative		
Biblical events as exemplifying a norm	NORM	6
6. Pragmatics		
Canonical traits, existential presuppositions	HABIT	10
Fixed wording (biblical or non-biblical) used as utterance about biblical events	USE	5
Verses performed; used as utterances about events	PERFORMANCE	4, 5

a number added to the family name (without space). This produces individual resource names such as Norm5, Opposition2, Topic8, or Word6. Sometimes a second digit is used, as in Analogy4.1, marking it as a subtype, in this case of Analogy4.[48] A complete list of resources, together with

[48] Analogy4.1 will be found by the search program of my *Database of Midrashic Units in the Mishnah* when Analogy4 is the search term.

their definitions and in their systematic order, is found in Appendix I. The sequence in which resources are discussed in the body of the book is guided by considerations of frequency and functional similarity in the Mishnah, and also by presentational convenience.

A complete hermeneutic operation usually requires several resources to be completely analysed. The resource names, in alphabetical and numerical sequence, make up a resource *profile* for the whole operation. The profile is thus a coded, shorthand description of all hermeneutic features of a given unit of interpretation. Thus the interpretation of Jer. 17:7 at mPeah 8:9 I (4) discussed above has the profile: 'Ωπ Opposition1Redundancy6.1Syntax5.2 Topic0Topic2Word1' (abbreviated as O1R6.1S5.2T0T2W1). In this code, Opposition1 points to a contrast between *Peah* and God; Syntax5.2 means that a paratactic biblical construction is read as implying a causal relation; Redundancy6.1 means that the double occurrence of 'trust' in the verse is given separate significance, so there is no repetition; Word2 means that a different semantic nuance ('security') is given to the word otherwise meaning 'trust'; Topic0 points to an unexpressed auxiliary assumption,[49] and Topic2 signals that the biblical Lemma is tied into a hypothetical case set up by the Mishnah (namely, that of someone entitled to *Peah* but not wishing to take it). The hermeneutic profile provides a summary of a complex and highly specific interpretation, but in terms that are general and allow precise comparison with other interpretations. The first two symbols in the above profile, the Greek letters *omega* and *pi*, belong to a different dimension of the description, namely literary format (see next section). In the *Database of Midrashic Units in the Mishnah*, whose creation accompanied my work on this book, all passages carry such a profile.[50] An extract of this *Database*, listing all Mishnaic units of interpretation together with their profile, is found as Appendix II at the end of this book. Similarly, each Mishnaic passage translated in this book has a footnote which presents its hermeneutic profile. In the *Database* the profile code can be used to search for hermeneutic similarity in independence of all other formal or material factors, including Mishnaic locality, biblical Lemma, subject-matter, rabbinic terminology, rabbi's name, and so on.

My discussion of the individual resources, of which there are more than one hundred, presents usually at least one Mishnaic example in translation. These Mishnaic texts are numbered sequentially in square brackets for ease of reference. Altogether there are 142 of them, and several are quoted more than once. An example is selected for the clarity with which it illustrates the resource under discussion at that point in the book (its other resources are sometimes briefly addressed as well). Resource definitions

---

[49] In this case, that there is a correspondence between the action and the reward, a מדה כנגד מדה.
[50] The *Database of Midrashic Units in the Mishnah* offers, among other things, a hermeneutic commentary on every Mishnaic passage of interpretation, of which there are more than 600. The support of the British Academy for the database project (during 1994/5) is gratefully acknowledged.

often resemble each other in format, in particular within the same resource family. But they do vary nevertheless in the manner in which they pinpoint the hermeneutic movement. They are general in their formulation, but aim to be as concrete and robust as possible. Some of them can be used like a 'recipe' for the fresh production of midrashic units of interpretation, others depend to a greater degree on the contextual information supplied in the discussion. In the body of the book the resource definitions are marked out in bold type. Resource *family* names are always printed in small capitals. The overview of all resources in Appendix I also indicates where in the book a resource is introduced and defined. Mishnaic passages are quoted in the usual way according to tractate, chapter, and *mishnah* numbering. However, where there is more than one unit of interpretation in a single *mishnah*, these are distinguished by sequential numbering in Roman numerals, and the total number of units in that *mishnah* is given in brackets in Arabic numerals. Thus, in the reference mPeah 8:9 I (4) the last two figures mean: in the *mishnah* 9 there are altogether 4 units of interpretation, of which the one mentioned is the first. This internal numbering also extends to alternative interpretations presented in a dispute format.

THE MISHNAIC SETTING OF THE HERMENEUTIC DATA

What sort of hermeneutic picture does the Mishnah offer us? The Mishnah is probably the first literary manifestation of rabbinic Judaism, emerging in a Palestine ravaged by two military confrontations with the Roman empire, in 66–70 and 132–5 CE. It is the first thematically organized and unified statement of rabbinic Judaism, its final redaction is usually dated to the first half of the third century CE. Most of its discourse is dedicated to the casuistic treatment of religious obligation and permission, that is, *halakhah*. The document is regarded as consisting of small, semi-independent items of text or information taken from an earlier rabbinic tradition and arranged in a thematic sequence. Many of these units are presented in the name of a rabbi, but even the anonymous ones are considered to be quotations.[51] In the Mishnah itself the treatment of halakhah largely proceeds in a case-by-case fashion, with hypothetical legal cases forming the smallest thematic units.[52] Cases are supplemented by lists, highly formalized disputes, reason clauses, and Scriptural quotations. There is also material incorporating meta-halakhic principles and comparisons, and occasionally short narrative units. The discourse proceeds largely through primary or secondary thematic centres, grouped in sixty-three tractates; there is hardly any

---

[51] Goldberg, 'Der verschriftete Sprechakt als rabbinische Literatur', quotes the earlier literature for this concept (i.e. *Traditionsliteratur*); see also Goldberg, 'Zitat und Citem'.

[52] See my 'From Case to Case' and below Ch. 4 (text to nn. 74 f.).

nesting or hierarchy of topics; instead, they are juxtaposed by large-scale parataxis. Scriptural wording finds its place in this structure only occasionally. There are approximately 600 individual interpretation units found in the Mishnah, if the counting is restricted to the explicit treatment of Scriptural formulations.[53] If all instances of *allusion* to biblical wording are included, the number is much higher than that.[54]

The Mishnah is a relatively stable textual entity compared to other works of rabbinic literature. It is also quite homogeneous in a literary sense; relatively few and quite rigid literary formats account for much of its text.[55] Many of the units from which the Mishnah is composed, including its units of interpretation, also appear in other works of rabbinic literature, in different literary settings. There is only one rabbinic document whose overall format and thematic orientation resembles that of the Mishnah: the Tosefta. It is usually dated later, and its precise relationship to the Mishnah seems to vary from tractate to tractate. There are other texts which consist wholly of units of interpretation, arranged in the order of the biblical texts they explain. The earliest of these are mainly concerned with legal parts of biblical text, such as Sifra (on Leviticus), Sifre (on Numbers and Deuteronomy), and Mekhilta (on Exodus). Sifra in particular has frequent overlap of units with the Mishnah, and the historical relationship between these so-called 'halakhic Midrashim' and the Mishnah is an open question.[56] The most common historical model for the explanation of the recurrence of the same units in several rabbinic works at once is a mixture of oral and written transmission, or (for some works) oral transmission alone. None of these questions can be decided without careful considera-tion of the literary setting of these recurrent units in the different works, and research into the forms and compositional conventions of rabbinic literature has increased both in sophistication and in quantity in recent decades.[57]

The Mishnah became accepted as the central articulation of rabbinic Judaism in later times. Its text is quoted paragraph by paragraph in the two Talmuds.[58] It constitutes there the object of explicit commentary; it also

---

[53] Pettit, *Shene'emar*, pegs the number at 511 exactly.

[54] I shall define the idea of 'allusion' which is relevant here in Ch. 4 below (sign π).

[55] The work of Jacob Neusner on the Mishnah has brought to the fore this fact, and demonstrated very clearly that it is vital to a proper understanding of the nature of the text. See esp. his *History of the Mishnaic Purities*, part 21; furthermore his *The Memorized Torah*, and his *Judaism: The Evidence of the Mishnah*, 243–8.

[56] See Reichman, *Mishna und Sifra*, who attempts to reopen the case for the priority of a Sifra-like text. For a clear statement of the contrary position, see Neusner, *History of the Mishnaic Law of Purities*, part 7: *Sifra*; also his *Uniting the Dual Torah*, and his *Judaism*, 217–19. Cf. also Norman Solomon's review of Neusner's work in *Scottish Journal of Theology*.

[57] The question of whether the Mishnah was first 'taught' in isolation from the Scriptural text or linked to it is not directly relevant to our topic; it concerns the prehistory of the text (but cf. Ch. 3 below). Cf. Albeck, *Einführung*, 58 f. See also Fishbane, *Biblical Interpretation*, 274 ff.; Halivni, *Peshat and Derash*; Lauterbach, 'Midrash and Mishnah'.

[58] See Albeck, *Einführung*, 183, for the way the Talmuds present the Mishnaic text.

serves as a springboard of much ramified discourse on matters of obligation and permission, as well as an almost encyclopaedic range of further
topics. These discourses also present units of Scriptural interpretation in
support of Mishnaic statements without Scriptural links. Most rabbinic
works after the Mishnah consist to a considerable extent, if not in their
entirety, of units of biblical interpretation.

The fact that in the Mishnah the explication of Scripture is embedded in a
thematically arranged discourse (not in a discourse whose topic is the text
of Scripture) is of profound importance in reconstructing the hermeneutic
choices. It imparts a thematic orientation on nearly all Scripture use,[59] and
this directly accounts for a number of features often considered typical of
rabbinic hermeneutics in general. In *positioning* a biblical quotation within
the Mishnaic discourse, the author-editors of the Mishnah have to decide
on the topic to which it is relevant—which is often, as we shall see, the
fundamental hermeneutic decision to take. This is not the case in the
halakhic Midrashim mentioned above. The position of a unit of interpretation in those works has no direct prognostic value for the topic which the
interpretation will ascribe to a verse, for it is determined by the biblical
order of verses. Nevertheless, many units of interpretation in works of
Midrash also have a Scripture-independent thematic orientation (which
can change totally from one unit to the next). It is too early to say how inti-
mate is the connection between the topical orientation of interpretation on
the one hand, and the topical arrangement of the units on the other.[60]

As I said above, the boundaries of the work 'Mishnah' are better
defined than those of any other work from the rabbinic period. Yet they
were still fluid to some extent between the final redaction (third century CE)
and the Middle Ages. This is relevant to units of interpretation because
many of them appear at the end of tractates, that is, at points especially
vulnerable to secondary text growth.[61] In fact, the very structure of amplification which *any* explicit Scriptural quotation creates in the Mishnaic text
can mask later additions.[62] Other units of interpretation are considered
suspect by some scholars because they appear where there are 'seams' in
the text, and also occur elsewhere in rabbinic literature. The appearance
of units of interpretation, in particular if they are non-halakhic in theme,

---

[59] See in particular Chs. 3 and 4.

[60] The question of how such a thematic orientation influences the nature of the Targums is raised
in my 'Scripture's Segments and Topicality'. On the appearance of a 'running commentary' format
in the Mishnah, see n. 74 below.

[61] Cf. Noy, 'The Aggadic Endings in the Tractates of the Mishnah'; Epstein, *Mavo*, 974–9; Albeck,
Untersuchungen über die Redaktion der Mishnah, 134 f.; id., *Einführung*, 182 ff.; Kuyt and Uchelen (eds.),
History and Form. There are also some beginnings of tractates which are textually suspect, including
one passage cited by me (the passage number is given in square brackets): mBQ 1:1 **[25]**; also the
chapter beginning mSan 10:1 I (2) **[82]**. Two other tractate beginnings are also quoted in this study:
mHag 1:1 **[139]** and mZeb 1:1 **[65]**.

[62] See on this Epstein, *Mavo*, 684 ff.; the Scriptural quotation produces redundancy on the
Mishnaic text surface, on which cf. my 'Delaying the Progress from Case to Case'.

coincides with such Mishnaic seams quite often, making them suspect.[63] But it is possible that they were placed there as a literary signal of transition or closure (parallel, for instance, to the division of tractates into chapters).[64] It is quite obvious that in today's Mishnah many end-of-tractate units have that *literary* function. The question is, are they *all* secondary, that is, was that literary function itself superimposed on an otherwise finished Mishnaic text without such signals?[65] In order to facilitate a text-critical perspective on Mishnaic hermeneutics without prejudging this issue, I have marked *all* units of interpretation which come either in the last *mishnah* of whole tractates or in the final *mishnah* of chapters within tractates.[66] The hermeneutic profile for these passages will be prefixed by the *omega* sign Ω (end of tractate) and by the diamond sign $\Diamond$,[67] respectively. The latter sign marks both the final *mishnah* of a chapter and the *penultimate mishnah* in a tractate. There are about forty Ω-units[68] and approximately fifty units of the $\Diamond$-type. It is important to remember, however, that the signs Ω and $\Diamond$ give *synchronic* information, namely, about the *mishnah*'s proximity to boundaries within the Mishnaic text.[69] Where a Mishnaic resource is established (as Mishnaic, in any case) only by one single example, its resource name is marked by an asterisk; where that single example also happens to be a Ω-unit or a $\Diamond$-unit, that resource is furthermore marked by the sign $\Diamond$ or Ω (this occurs only once).[70] The tractate Avot is included in the analysis;[71] however, its contribution to the material of this book is minimal.[72]

[63] A perusal of Albeck, *Untersuchungen über die Redaktion der Mischna*, 135 ff., illustrates very clearly the extent to which considerations of cohesion and thematic unity play a role in Mishnaic textual criticism. But the *standards* of cohesion are taken for granted in this historical criticism just as much as in the hermeneutics of harmonization (on which see Ch. 10 below).

[64] Which Albeck points out as known to the Talmuds (*Einführung*, 187 f.); Stemberger, *Introduction*, 121.

[65] If not, one needs to distinguish between two types of units fulfilling the same literary function, namely closure.

[66] Albeck, *Einführung*, 182 ff., treats chapter endings and tractate endings as equally vulnerable to accretion.

[67] The following $\Diamond$-units are used as illustrations in the body of this study: mSheb 10:8 I (2) **[132]**; mYoma 3:11 **[40]**; mBQ 4:9 II (3) **[87]**; mBQ 5:7 **[76]**; mBM 9:13 I (4) **[113]**; mBM 9:13 II (4) **[78]** **[110b]**; mMak 3:15 I (4) **[137]**.

[68] They are the following passages (often multiple interpretation units); those used as illustrations in this study have next to them their sequential number(s) in square brackets: mBer 9:5 I–IX (9) **[15]** **[82a]** **[114a]**; mPeah 8:9 I–IV (4), see above; mYoma 8:9 I–III (3) **[4]**; mTaan 4:8 I/II (3) **[96]**; mTaan 4:8 III (3) **[51]**; mMQ 3:9 I–II (2); mNaz 9:5 I–II (2) **[93]**; mSot 9:9 I–II (2); mSot 9:11; mSot 9:12; mSot 9:15 I–II (2); mGit 9:10 I–III (3); mQid 4:14 I–IV (4); mMak 3:16 **[133]**; mEduy 8:7; mMen 13:11; mHul 12:5; mKer 6:9 I–IV (4) **[131]**; mTam 7:4; mQin 3:6 I–II (2); mYad 4:8 I–II (2); mUqtsin 3:12 I–II (2).

[69] But even of that, they are only an approximate measure, since there are variations in the numbering of *mishnayyot* in the textual witnesses.

[70] Resource Use2, which is accordingly marked *Use2$_\Omega$ (see Ch. 5).

[71] It is excluded from the project of Pettit in *Shene'emar* (21 f.); cf. Neusner, *Torah . . . Part Three: Doctrine*, 31 f. Avot is indeed absent from the Yerushalmi and has no equivalent in the Tosefta. But see Albeck, *Einführung*, 187 f. for evidence that the Bavli knows of a tractate Avot as part of the Mishnah; see also Stemberger, *Introduction*, 119; Epstein, *Introduction to Tannaitic Literature*, 232 f.

[72] Two passages from Avot are used as (additional) illustrations for a resource: mAvot 3:2 I (3) **[36]** and mAvot 4:1 III (4) **[120]**. It is clear from this that all resources occurring in Avot 1-5 also occur elsewhere in the Mishnah. The evidence of the very late sixth chapter of Avot (*Qinyan Torah*), although

In a considerable number of cases the question of the Mishnaic textual shape can be tested against the manuscript evidence, although complete manuscripts of the Mishnah are, on the whole, scarce. Where available, I have checked critical editions for all the passages quoted in this book (not merely end-units). Where I could not do this, or where I had doubts, I have checked the facsimile of manuscript Kaufmann.[73] My translations either represent Kaufmann's text or provide the readings of that manuscript in brackets or footnotes.

On the whole, textual variants are unlikely to make a difference to the constitution of resource descriptions. Any resource which we have defined in this study whose presence in the Mishnah is weak or doubtful is likely to account for numerous rabbinic interpretations outside the Mishnah. On the other hand, for establishing a resource as belonging to specifically *Mishnaic* hermeneutics, one secure occurrence is enough. In other words, text-critical arguments may well affect the allocation of a given resource to Mishnaic hermeneutics (and thus the comparative and diachronic agendas which we also wish to further), but not its presence in rabbinic hermeneutics as such.

In this context it is important to note that the Scriptural organization of a topic, with a few rather well-defined exceptions,[74] does not provide the order in which the Mishnah deals with the same (halakhic) topic.[75] Another important feature of the hermeneutics of the Mishnah is its *silence* about Scripture, sustained over large stretches of text. This silence is compatible with divergent attitudes. At one extreme, Mishnaic norms and statements which are presented without any link to Scripture may nevertheless at first have been accepted into rabbinic thought by way of their link to a specific biblical passage.[76] At the other extreme, a *contradiction* between Scripture and the Mishnah may be treated with silent indifference. Since Scriptural information is otherwise frequently presupposed in and often

included in my *Database of Midrashic Units in the Mishnah*, is excluded from establishing the existence of a Mishnaic resource, and from the statistics. Cf. Herford, *The Ethics of the Talmud*, 13; Epstein, *Mavo*, 978; Albeck, *Einführung*, 182; Stemberger, *Introduction*, 115; Marti and Beer, *Abot*, 158 f.; Strack, *Die Sprüche der Väter*, 8. I use one Avot 6 passage, mAvot 6:3 I (3) **[52]**, as an outlook on hermeneutic developments *outside* the Mishnah in Ch. 5.

[73] Kaufmann is called 'the most important' of all Mishnaic manuscripts by Abraham Goldberg (*The Mishnah Treatise Ohalot*, 10 and see 39; cf. also Stemberger, *Introduction*, 141). It also provides the base text for most (but not the early) critical editions published as part of the project of the 'Gießener Mischna' (see Bibliography, sec. A). The facsimile of Kaufmann was produced by Beer. On the manuscript situation and critical editions, see Stemberger, *Introduction*, 139–44; see also Bar Asher, 'The Study of Mishnaic Hebrew Grammar'.

[74] See the Σ-format discussed in Ch. 12 (a list of passages in n. 47 there). Pettit is ambiguous in his explanation of how he handles these in his analysis (*Shene'emar*, 18 and n. 29), and I am not sure if they are included in his total of 511 Mishnaic units of interpretation. Cf. Albeck, *Einführung*, 133 and 453 f.

[75] 'The very redactional structure of Scripture, found so serviceable by the writer of the Temple scroll, is of no interest whatever to the organizers of the Mishnah and its tractates, except in a few cases (Yoma, Pesahim)', Neusner, *Judaism*, 217.

[76] There is, of course, the question of how we could ever gain certain knowledge of such instances (on this, see below). However, they are extremely likely to exist, given the other features of Mishnaic employment of Scripture. See the opening section of Ch. 3 below.

fundamental to the Mishnaic discourse,[77] certain explanations are excluded: namely, that Scripture was basically not relevant to the Mishnaic discourse or that Scripture has no chronological priority over the Mishnah.[78]

In identifying passages of interpretation in the Mishnah I have limited myself to the evidence of the Mishnah itself. I have thus excluded biblical proof-texts for Mishnaic positions supplied in later rabbinic works. The provision of links to Scripture is one of the major self-appointed tasks of rabbinic Mishnah-commentary. These are not included in the primary evidence here, regardless of how plausible they may appear; for I am engaged in constructing a *benchmark* of plausibility in the first place. Sticking to interpretations about which the Mishnah is not silent means that these results can be used for comparative purposes, both between different parts of the Mishnah and between it and other rabbinic documents. Something similar holds for rabbinic opinions presented as part of a dispute. Frequently the first position in a Mishnaic dispute is not linked to a Scriptural support, while the second, rival position is (for the opposite constellation, see mBik 1:2 I (2) **[34]**). The imbalance in the provision of proof-texts is important, in particular where the first position is also given anonymously, which in the style of the Mishnah suggests that it is more widely accepted.[79] But while this raises interesting questions, there is no getting over the fact that the first position does *not* quote Scripture. We have thus no direct evidence for any hermeneutic resource,[80] and rabbinic parallels in other works cannot serve as substitute.[81] It has to be admitted,

[77] See Neusner, *Judaism*, 167–229 and 329–51; also the sections 'From Mishnah to Scripture' (dealing with the order of Purities) in his *From Mishnah to Scripture*. The biblical verses corresponding in topic to the themes of a Mishnaic tractate are identified in some of the modern editions, e.g. Albeck's *Shishah Sidrey Mishnah*, and also in Steinsaltz's edition of the Babylonian Talmud.

[78] Neusner says: 'The Mishnah in no way is so remote from Scripture as its formal omission of citations of verses of Scripture suggests' (*Judaism*, 222). However, Neusner's oft-repeated notion that Scripture provides the Mishnah with *facts* (e.g. 'Scripture provides indisputable facts', *Judaism*, 223) manages, by its very inappropriateness, to block out all issues of *reading*. Neusner's work on the Mishnah could perhaps be characterized as a heroic and very instructive attempt to understand the relationship between Scripture and Mishnah *without* considering it as hermeneutic. The general outlines of a hermeneutic relationship are given: 'But the framers of the Mishnah had their own world with which to deal . . . They were bound, therefore, to come to Scripture with a set of questions generated other than in Scripture. They brought their own ideas about what was going to be important in Scripture.' Neusner adds, 'This is perfectly natural', and I agree (see the opening pages of this chapter). But if so, the task of describing what is distinctive about rabbinic hermeneutics only begins here. Cf. Pettit, *Shene'emar*, 103, n. 130; Porton, 'Defining Midrash', 65 f.

[79] See on this n. 57 in Ch. 5 below. In thematically organized units, the named unit tends to be an alternative opinion. Otherwise, naming occurring outside dispute formats tends to indicate that a statement has no fixed place in the order of themes (see e.g. mAZ 3:6 II (2) = mShab 9:1 **[69]**), and/or that its subject-matter is not halakhic (e.g. in Avot).

[80] Rosenblatt, *Interpretation*, 60 ff., tends to supply the 'other' party's interpretation from outside the Mishnah. In many cases he accepts the idea that *the same verse* is used by both participants in the dispute, which often means that the two hermeneutic links are of very unequal transparency (see e.g. *Interpretation*, 74, n. 79). Pettit is rightly critical of this procedure, *Shene'emar*, 28 f. Where two disputing voices use the same verse as argument that fact tends to be given prominence, as in mTer 6:6 and mShab 8:7.

[81] Bringing all material together which can be gathered on the basis of an attribution to an 'early' rabbi or group results in confusion, as is illustrated by Brewer's *Techniques and Assumptions in Jewish*

however, that in the course of construing the link between the biblical text
and the Mishnah one is often involved in deciding on the *scope* of hermeneutic link-up, and sometimes this means finding the hermeneutic effect of
biblical wording at more than one point in the surrounding Mishnaic co-
text.[82] None of the resources identified in this study depends on a passage
subject to this sort of ambiguity. I am, however, crossing the line into *tacit*
interpretation in any case, since I include biblical allusions (see Chapter 4)
as well as explicit quotations in the scope of this investigation.

At this juncture it may be useful to spell out how I have selected illustrative passages. All the normal difficulties in interpreting the Mishnah are
heightened when it comes to units of interpretation. The Mishnah as a book
is implicit and terse to an extraordinary degree; and we have no better
access to its historical context than the text itself. Thus, there is plenty of
room for scholarly disagreement on the interpretation of individual
Mishnaic interpretations. As I have just mentioned, for many Mishnaic
passages of interpretation there are available hermeneutic analyses from
other (usually later) rabbinic literature; these often tie the Mishnaic interpretation into a new and complex network of concerns as well as an agenda
of harmonization. Sometimes the later rabbinic interpreters of the Mishnah
find great complexity where our resource analysis finds relative simplicity.
To identify clear or neat examples for individual resources was easy in
most, but not all, cases. Some passages were excluded from use as illustrations because their hermeneutic mechanism is tied up with complex
halakhic issues which require lengthy explanations or are unclear to me;
others, because one has a choice between two or three resources in constructing the link. In the case of a few resources, the sample passages are an
island set in a sea of ambiguity or incomprehension on my part. In such
cases my discussion will make it clear that evidence for the resource (from
inside the Mishnah, at least) is particularly scarce or ambiguous. A general
perusal of units of interpretation in the Mishnah armed with our manual of
resources is made possible by the list of passages attached to each resource
in the Overview of Resources (Appendix I), and the Index of Mishnaic
Units of Interpretation (Appendix II) gives the full (if still preliminary)
picture. Far from everything is clear, however, as the presence of question-
marks amply demonstrates; and in some cases my resource definitions
merely articulate clearly alternatives between which it is impossible to
decide. A comprehensive discussion of all Mishnaic passages, pointing to
obscurities or ambiguities for individual texts, is contained in my *Database
of Midrashic Units in the Mishnah*.

Exegesis Before 70 CE. He accepts the reliability of attributions, and ignores co-textual functions, to
such a degree that the distinction between different rabbinic documents and genres becomes irrelevant.

    [82] More on the construction of the limits of the biblical segment is found in Ch. 2 below (text start-
ing at n. 109) and Ch. 14 (text following n. 26). Cf. also the format *reprise*, explained in the final section
of Ch. 12.

Interpretations which appear in Mishnaic disputes are included in this book as evidence for resources. They are marked in the passage's hermeneutic profile by the paragraph sign, ¶. Their deliberate inclusion in the Mishnah, the general frequency of literary dispute forms, the strength of common ground in most disputes, the ascription of alternatives to persons classified as 'rabbi', as well as the almost universal refusal of the Mishnah's controlling voice to take sides explicitly—all of these things indicate that the minority opinion in a dispute is usually thought to share a *basic* acceptability with the prevailing rabbinic opinions.[83] If the position itself is seen *in principle* as admissible in the polyphony of rabbinic voices, then there is no reason to exclude from this its biblical support, for we are looking for *principles* of reading. The same goes for positions whose manner of presentation indicates that they are only suggested in order to be rejected.[84] While their application *at this point in Scripture* may be considered dubious by the rabbinic majority tradition, they mark one hermeneutic *option*.[85] However, the relationship of Mishnaic dispute structures to other literary formats, including those of quoting Scripture, deserves an investigation in its own right.[86] Some further consideration will be given to this matter in Chapter 12.

I make no distinction in this book between types of evidence on the basis of contents. Rabbinic literature is often seen to have two general 'modes' of exegesis: one concerned with legal topics (halakhah) and another concerned with narrative and theological themes (aggadah).[87] The best way to test this is not by introducing the distinction into material which makes no claim or appeal to it, but by treating all units of interpretation in the same way to see if, in order to achieve *hermeneutic* precision, some such distinction needs to be introduced. That this indeed happens, and how it is tied in with the manner in which the resources work, can be seen in Chapter 6

---

[83] mEduy 1:4–6 gives specific reasons for the transmission of disputes in rabbinic tradition. These cannot count (and are not offered) as full explanation for what constitutes in effect a fundamental feature of the Mishnah's discourse. The giving of reasons and the admission of alternative positions must be seen as belonging together. On the Mishnah as a text of 'persuasion', see von Uchelen, *Chagiga*, 62 f.

[84] This discourse structure, too, has a symbol in the hermeneutic profile for our translated passages: the negation sign, ¬. See Ch. 7 below.

[85] See text belonging to n. 86 in Ch. 9 below. Perhaps the strongest rejection of any individual interpretation to be found in the Mishnah is the treatment of a non-literal Aramaic version of Lev. 18:21 in mMeg 4:9 (the interpretation is marked as coming from outside the rabbinic discourse itself). Even in this case, the hermeneutic options exercised through the Aramaic paraphrase are acceptable elsewhere in the Mishnah (see e.g. resource Cotext5 in Ch. 2). There is one resource, the *a fortiori* analogy, which seems to be found more often in refuted positions than in accepted ones (see Ch. 7).

[86] Some aspects of the question are treated in Pettit, *Shene'emar*, albeit not with specific reference to a literary structure conveying disputes. See also my 'Delaying the Progress from Case to Case'.

[87] The main locus of this distinction seem to be certain rabbinic restrictions imposed on the application of individual hermeneutic 'rules'. See esp. Guttmann, 'Foundations of Rabbinic Judaism', who deals with one of the prime passages in this regard, bPes 66a / yPes 6:1 (33a), cf. also Chajes, *The Student's Guide*, 9 (bKet 38b and bYeb 24a). See also Bloch, 'Midrash', 33 f.; id., 'Methodological Note', 53 ff. See also below.

below.[88] As a pair of *opposed* concepts, 'aggadic' and 'halakhic' are nearly useless for modern descriptive purposes.[89] The Mishnah often contains material which, while intimately linked to the halakhic discourse, is not in itself halakhic in the sense of being normative.[90]

I have just reviewed some of the Mishnaic literary structures into which Scriptural wording is integrated (e.g. tractate-end Ω, chapter-end ◊, dispute ¶). There are also certain textual features inside the units of interpretation which carry useful information. Most of these are explicitly introduced or defined in other parts of this book. All of these formal features are represented by specific signs (of which Ω is an example) in the hermeneutic profile of each translated passage. They are listed all together at the end of Appendix I, and are also explained in the List of Abbreviations and Special Signs at the beginning of this book.

The question, however, of what function biblical quotations and allusions fulfil in the overall literary structure or discourse of the Mishnah requires a separate investigation, and is not pursued here in its own right.[91] For the present purposes, the Mishnah is primarily evidence for the pool of rabbinic hermeneutic resources available at the time of its production, and we take account of their literary setting merely in order to secure maximum information on how they work.

---

[88] Which distinguishes resources Norm1–5 from Norm8 along such lines. Another example are the resources Analogy4 and Analogy5. Fraenkel speaks of 'methods of midrash halakhah' as being used for 'midrash aggada' (*Darkhey*, ii. 488). Does this not imply that the methods themselves are neutral with regard to the distinction? The same is implied in rabbinic injunctions to use certain 'rules' (see preceding note) only for aggadic interpretation. Fraenkel's account points to the following differences between aggadic and halakhic interpretation: the subject-matter of the biblical verse (487); the purpose of the midrashic unit (491: '*Midrash halakhah* wants to create a bridge between the *halakhah* and the verse'); and, directly linked to this, the fact that *midrash halakhah* aims at unequivocal meaning, when *midrash aggadah* does not (491 f.).

[89] Using the term 'aggadic' as a category of description for the analysis of inner-biblical interpretation (as in Fishbane's *Biblical Interpretation*) seems to have the worst of both worlds; no conceptual clarification is achieved, while a blatant anachronism is committed.

[90] Johann Maier, in his *Geschichte der jüdischen Religion*, sometimes uses the word 'Motivschicht' to characterize the 'aggadic' (19 ff., and also p. 95; see also s.v. 'Motivierung' in the index to the first edition of the book). This ties the function of the aggadic discourse firmly to the life of halakhah. Loewe puts a different accent on the matter when he defines aggadah as 'concerned with the inculcation of God-awareness into mental attitudes; and although it may condition the approach to law and institutional practice, it is self-substantive' ('Jewish Exegesis', 346). Important is also the discussion of the two terms with regard to textuality provided by Faur, *Golden Doves With Silver Dots*, 84 ff. Cf. further the distinction of a 'normative' (halakhic?) from a 'formative' (aggadic?) social body of knowledge constituting cultural identity in Assmann, *Das kulturelle Gedächtnis*, 141 f. Within biblical studies, the strict separation of 'law' from other types of value judgements in a variety of social and 'narrative' settings has become increasingly questioned; see Jackson, 'Law, Wisdom and Narrative', and the literature quoted there.

[91] Again, Pettit's *Shene'emar* is relevant, but does not address what one might call the 'distributive' angle of the question.

THE RABBINIC HERMENEUTIC RULES AND TRENDS
IN THE STUDY OF RABBINIC HERMENEUTICS

What I said above about evidence that is only found outside the Mishnah also goes, *mutatis mutandis*, for the three main lists of hermeneutic 'rules' found in rabbinic literature. No resource definition offered in this study is based on any of the seven, thirteen, or thirty-two *middot* ascribed to Hillel, Ishmael, and Eliezer ben Yose respectively.[92] Not only is their *historical* relationship to the units of interpretation found in the Mishnah unclear; these lists also belong to a different aspect of the question, namely, the rabbinic 'theory' of hermeneutics. The present study, however, is interested almost exclusively in explaining what we can *see* the (Mishnaic) rabbis do with the Bible. Any help which their own explanations can give us in understanding that manifest *practice* of reading is gratefully received. But it would be bizarre to take on trust the nature of rabbinic hermeneutics as summarized in three obviously incomplete and conceptually opaque lists, while the vast primary evidence of how the rabbis employed Scripture is available to us.[93] Consequently, the scope of the current study is in no way limited by and is only incidentally concerned with, the hermeneutic 'rules' of the rabbis. I am also not restricted to hermeneutic methods for which the rabbis had names.[94] I shall from time to time speculate on the relationship between a resource and a rabbinic hermeneutic term; but since rabbinic terms are not *defined* in rabbinic literature, no direct comparison of *definitions* can take place.

The three rabbinic lists of rules have in fact been allowed to dominate and circumscribe many modern accounts of rabbinic hermeneutics (in particular the briefer ones).[95] Quite a few of the modern summaries are therefore not conceptual expositions but collections of unexplained hermeneutic *curiosa*. But there are also modern treatments which go far beyond the confines of these *middot*. The two main comprehensive accounts of rabbinic hermeneutics, by I. Heinemann and Y. Fraenkel,[96] are on the one hand much more ambitious than the present study, in that they each cover

[92] They are found in the following locations: Tosefta San 7:11 (Hillel's Seven), the opening section of Sifra (Ishmael's Thirteen), and the *Mishnah of Rabbi Eliezer or the Midrash of Thirty-Two Hermeneutic Rules* (ed. Enelow). The traditional text of the latter is found in the opening pages of the Wilna edition of BerR. For a modern attempt to catalogue Mishnaic interpretation according to these named techniques, see Albeck, *Einführung*, 83 ff.; also Brewer, *Techniques and Assumptions*, 14–23.

[93] See the clarification provided by Alexander, 'The Rabbinic Hermeneutical Rules and the Problem of the Definition of Midrash', 114 f.; id., 'Jewish Interpretation', 308b. Cf. also Fraenkel, *Darkhey*, ii. 501–3.

[94] This is clearly articulated by Alexander ('The Rabbinic Hermeneutical Rules', 114 f.), who also speaks of the 'lack of intrinsic meaning' of these names (113).

[95] Ideological reasons why the lists, and in particular the one ascribed to Ishmael, should have been given preferential treatment in some earlier scholarship are identified by Elman, 'Towards a History of *Ribbuy* in the Babylonian Talmud', 87.

[96] Isaak Heinemann, *Darkhey Ha-Aggadah*, and Y. Fraenkel, *Darkhey Ha-Aggadah weha-Midrash* (quoted as Fraenkel, *Darkhey*).

large sections of rabbinic literature; but on the other hand, they are much less ambitious in that they do not attempt to build up from scratch the conceptual foundations of description.[97] They also deliberately restrict themselves to what they perceive as 'aggadic' exegesis. As for less comprehensive scholarly treatments, several important trends can be discerned. Of some importance has been the direct comparison of rabbinic hermeneutics, mostly only in its terminology, with terms from the legal and literary discourse in the Graeco-Roman world.[98] Another branch of research investigates rabbinic tendencies to bring to the surface suppressed mythological elements in Scripture.[99] Extremely influential in recent times has been the attempt to understand rabbinic hermeneutics as a continuation of much earlier hermeneutic tendencies, visible already in the Hebrew Bible itself.[100] In this respect, as in others, scholarly work on the Qumran documents has revived interest in and provided new material for comparative and developmental perspectives.[101] In many historically oriented studies of rabbinic hermeneutics the historian's own position as reader of Scripture used not to be considered problematical. This has changed dramatically in more recent scholarship, which derives its methods from deconstruction and similar theories of language and literature.[102] Sometimes this scholar-

[97] They do introduce important terminology from outside rabbinic literature, but these imports are not conceptually co-ordinated and do not provide a unified language of description. Also, rabbinic terminology seems to be used where available, apparently in the belief that this amounts to understanding the evidence on its own terms (see Fraenkel, *Darkhey*, i. 67 f.). On Heinemann, see nn. 11–12 above.

[98] See esp. Liebermann, *Hellenism*, 57 ff.; Daube, 'Alexandrian Methods of Interpretation and the Rabbis'; id., 'Rabbinic Methods of Interpretation and Hellenistic Rhetoric'; see recently Alexander, 'Quid Athenis et Hierosolymis?'

[99] e.g. Boyarin, *Intertextuality*, ch. 6; Fishbane, *The Garments of Torah*; id., ' "The Holy One Sits and Roars" '; Goldberg, 'Kain: Sohn des Menschen oder Sohn der Schlange?'; Handelman, *The Slayers of Moses*; Niehoff, 'The Return of Myth in Genesis Rabbah on the Akedah', offers much on the recent relevant literature, also quoting the psychoanalytical background. Cf. also Faur, *Golden Doves With Silver Dots*, pp. xxvi f.

[100] See esp. Geiger, *Urschrift*; Seeligmann, 'Voraussetzungen der Midraschexegese'; Maass, 'Von den Ursprüngen der rabbinischen Schriftauslegung', esp. 143 ff.; Clines, 'Nehemiah 10 as an Example of Early Jewish Biblical Exegesis'; Fishbane, *Biblical Interpretation*. A revisionist twist is given to this position by David Weiss Halivni in his *Peshat and Derash*, ch. 5. See further Weingreen, *From Bible to Mishna*; Alter, *Putting Together Biblical Narrative*.

[101] Rabbinic hermeneutics was/is used by many scholars as a point of reference when explaining Qumranic exegesis. See e.g. Fishbane, 'Use, Authority and Interpretation of Mikra'; Brooke, *Exegesis at Qumran* (who is careful to draw some necessary distinctions); Schiffmann, *Halakhah at Qumran*. Among the first to do this was Brownlee, 'Biblical Interpretation Among the Sectaries of the Dead Sea Scrolls' (see the criticism by Elliger, *Studien zum Habakuk-Kommentar*, 158 ff.). For a recent summary, see Fraade, ' "Comparative Midrash" Revisited: The Case of the Dead Sea Scrolls and Rabbinic Midrash'. More literature is given in Ch. 5 below.

[102] Hartman and Budick (eds.), *Midrash and Literature*; Handelman, *The Slayers of Moses* (who believes the biblical view to be 'a kind of "deconstruction" of the classical idea [of philosophy]', 28); Boyarin, *Intertextuality*; Faur, *Golden Doves With Silver Dots*, e.g. p. xviii; Faur offers an account (pp. xxvi–xxix) of how Judaism escaped logocentrism: 'Rabbinic tradition is the only intellectual and cultural movement to have continued developing since antiquity without a primaeval rupture—an inaugural split—resulting in an endless series of hierarchical oppositions' (p. xxvi). This account is in itself mythical, and its suggestion that our reading (even in a Jewish tradition) could be untouched by the 'hierarchical oppositions' is surely naive from a deconstructionist point of view.

ship is marked by apologetic or indeed triumphalist overtones, for its practitioners tend to consider rabbinic hermeneutics as an alternative to discredited 'logocentric' modes of reading which are seen to have dominated Western culture. At times they join hands with a much older speculative-scholarly tradition of contrasting underlying Greek and Jewish 'modes' of thinking.[103] Another scholarly interest recently revived is the concern with parallels between rabbinic hermeneutics and ancient dream interpretation, which is now sometimes combined with a Freudian critique of 'logocentrism'.[104]

The descriptive language of the present book is in principle compatible with most of these approaches, even those which deny the possibility of disinterested historical reconstruction. The reason for this is that its method is synchronic, although it anticipates diachronic uses of synchronic results. I shall not attempt to conform to a widespread practice of identifying specific but *tacit* religious, emotional, political, or ideological concerns in the rabbis' interpretation to Scripture.[105] But the system of componential resources which I introduce provides a framework for describing *how* any reader concerns could have been made to engage *hermeneutically* with the biblical text.

The literature on rabbinic hermeneutics has increased dramatically in recent decades. Moreover, the present topic has strong links to biblical studies and to research into the cultures of the Middle East in antiquity; to general linguistics and literary studies; to legal history and legal interpretation; not to mention rabbinic literature and history. The range of potentially relevant publications is therefore vast, and only a small part of it is familiar to me, and is explicitly referred to in this book. Within these limits, I have not encountered a model or predecessor for the main thrust of this study.

A MANUAL AND A POINT OF COMPARISON

This book aims to provide a comprehensive and conceptually unified description of rabbinic hermeneutics, as represented in a redactionally limited but seminal corpus of interpretations. The description is meant to be comprehensive for the Mishnah, and thus be used as a catalogue of hermeneutic procedures for that work. As such a complete catalogue, it provides that *configuration* of rabbinic hermeneutic resources which is represented in the Mishnah. Other documents of rabbinic literature may

[103] This continuity is perhaps most obvious in Handelman's *The Slayers of Moses*, but it is present in other authors using this approach.

[104] Examples of the interest in dream interpretation (whether or not from the psychoanalytical angle) include Liebermann, *Hellenism*, 70–8; Alexander, 'Bavli Berakhot 55a–57b'; Niehoff, 'A Dream Which Is Not Interpreted'; Faur, *Golden Doves With Silver Dots*; Handelman, *The Slayers of Moses*; see also the literature quoted in the final section of Ch. 5 below.

[105] See, as one example, Fraenkel, *Darkhey*, i. ch. 4 (pp. 67–85); also 210 ff.

well have other configurations of resources: there will be additional resources yet to be described, some that are known from the Mishnah will be absent, and others will exist in variations still undefined. The nomenclature of the resources caters for these changes: some resource families are only small, in anticipation of further members; many numbers and several letters of the alphabet are as yet unused, and gaps are placed between some resources names in the same family (more on this is found in the introduction to Appendix I). Yet there is the hope (a hope supported by considerable anecdotal evidence) that large numbers of interpretation units outside the Mishnah can be accounted for by the resource definitions here offered for the Mishnah, or by fairly straightforward variants of them. So the same configuration of resources which is a (provisional) *end* as far as the Mishnah is concerned is a *beginning* with respect to other works of rabbinic literature.

As a fixed entity, the Mishnaic configuration of resources also offers a starting-point for comparative and diachronic tasks, both within and outside the confines of rabbinic Judaism. Among the many possibilities of direct comparison within rabbinic literature (once the hermeneutic configurations of some other works have been provided) is the parameter of *complexity* of hermeneutic operations. My description provides a *measure* for such complexity: the number of resources making up a complete hermeneutic operation. As a quick perusal of the passages quoted in this study will show, this complexity tends to be high. We very rarely find a one-resource operation. This could be typical for the Mishnah in comparison with later rabbinic works; if so, the decrease in complexity might point to a growing hermeneutic self-awareness, or a programmatic attitude.[106]

Our overall picture of rabbinic hermeneutics in the Mishnah will be presented in the following topics. Fundamental is the licence to cut Scripture into segments and separate them from their biblical co-text (Chapter 2); this frees up fuller meaning possibilities for the segments, which are narrowed down in a new direction by the thematic agenda (perspective) of the Mishnah, manifest in the *new* co-text now surrounding the biblical segments (Chapters 3, 4). The hermeneutic interaction with the biblical text, given its argument function in the Mishnaic discourse, need not be read as historical reports on the origin of certain rabbinic ideas (Chapter 3). The words of Scripture can be adopted to express directly Mishnaic ideas (use); or they can be quoted with their message reduplicated by the Mishnaic voice (the midrashic unit). It may be possible to discern distinct hermeneutic attitudes as giving rise to these two different hermeneutic formats (Chapter 4). Where whole Mishnaic utterances are performed using the words of Scripture, their often striking interpretation is implicit in the manner they engage with a unique set of circumstances

---

[106] See Ch. 4 below on the notion of a programmatic hermeneutic attitude in rabbinic Judaism.

(Chapter 5). In reduplicated (midrashic) format, biblical words can be used to support the exemplary character of biblical behaviour (Chapter 6), or to provide the basis for analogical extensions of norms and categories (Chapters 7, 8). The semantics of biblical words also serve as the basis for further resources of category extension, in which Mishnaic paradigms (lists of halakhic subjects) play a role. Certain biblical connectors and particles can be treated as if they carried logical force (Chapter 9). The meaning of a biblical segment can be determined in the light of its difference, contrast, or potential conflict with another segment, and its existential presuppositions may be spelled out (Chapter 10). Mishnaic paradigms are again brought to bear in the interpretation of a given biblical word choice as *excluding* something (Chapter 11). The format of reduplication (the midrashic unit) as found in the Mishnah involves a commitment which is not restricted to the validity of the interpretation (the hermeneutic operation), but embraces simultaneously the validity of biblical Lemma and rabbinic Dictum (components of the midrashic unit, Chapter 12). Apparently redundant items of the biblical wording can be made to complement each other by distribution to semantically or numerically matching paradigms of the Mishnaic discourse. In the interpretation of syntactic links between clauses, there is a tendency to transform purely temporal links into those of causal or final dependency (Chapter 13). In the treatment of biblical word meaning, the combined effect of separation from original co-text and imposition of a Mishnaic thematic perspective allows the Mishnah to shift to other semantic nuances of the same word, to homonymic meaning, or to switch between literal and metaphorical meaning (Chapter 14). I shall end by reflecting on the nature of the project to which this book aims to contribute, and the type of further research which it may help to stimulate into rabbinic Judaism and beyond (Chapter 15). Appendix I offers a list of resource definitions in systematic order (i.e. gives that configuration of rabbinic hermeneutics which is proper to the Mishnah), together with the page on which they are discussed in this book, the number of occurrences in the Mishnah, and a list of those Mishnaic passages (complete if the total is up to twenty occurrences). Appendix II offers an index of Mishnaic units of interpretation together with their resource profiles. At its end is also found a sample entry from the *Database of Midrashic Units in the Mishnah*.

2

Creating Scriptural Segments

Mishnaic interpretations do not target *the whole* of Scripture, or any one of its larger parts, but rather segments approximately of sentence length. The hermeneutic licence to cut the text into small units which can be interpreted *as if they stood alone* creates a wide hermeneutic choice. Its fundamental effect is that the segment, taken in isolation, is *less* determined in topic, reference, or meaning than as part of a Scriptural environment (co-text). The Mishnah, in surrounding the segment with different co-text, can thus appoint a fresh topic, reference, or meaning for the biblical words.

How do we find out what Scripture means to the rabbinic readers whose discourse is presented in the Mishnah? By far the most important evidence are the new words which surround Scripture as it appears in the Mishnah. These words show what Scripture was taken to mean by *constraining* it to mean that.

Modern views on how meaning is conveyed in linguistic signs allocate a crucial role to the concrete setting of language-in-use, the context or situation of speaking.[1] And a special dimension of this overall context is the way words interact *with each other* in an extended utterance or text. This linguistic environment, the *co-text*,[2] is taken to make a contribution to establishing the meaning of a given word or clause. For the individual word or even clause is usually open to several different meanings. It is the co-text which shows which of these meanings is actually conveyed. Compare, for example, the meaning of 'to compose' in 'I composed a letter' with 'I composed a string quartet'. In this chapter one fundamental mechanism of rabbinic hermeneutics will be shown as consisting in *cutting a Scriptural*

---

[1] Cf. e.g. Lyons, *Introduction to Theoretical Linguistics*, 97; Stevenson, 'Contextualism'.

[2] For concise definitions of the concepts of co-text, context, as well as context-sensitive words, see e.g. Pope, *The English Studies Book*, 364 f. See further, Brown and Yule, *Discourse Analysis*, 46 ff.; Halliday and Hasan, *Cohesion in English*; Levinson, *Pragmatics*; Frawley, *Linguistic Semantics*, 36 ff.; Lyons, *Introduction to Theoretical Linguistics*, 413. Of great interest and clarity is also Johnson-Laird's account on how the meaning of a word is determined by its linguistic environment (for which he uses the word 'context', not 'co-text'): *Mental Models*, 233–42. More on his account below.

segment off from its co-text, and thus opening up some of the ambiguities which the linguistic signs harbour when taken in isolation. But the first thing we encounter when reading the Mishnah is not Scripture in isolation. It is Scripture embedded in the Mishnaic text. In other words, we encounter Scripture with its ambiguities of meaning *removed (or reduced) by new, different co-text*. Insofar as these ambiguities of Scriptural meaning are created in the first place through the process of cutting biblical text off from its own co-text, the meaning as determined by the Mishnaic co-text is *different* from the meaning as determined by the biblical co-text. In exploring this hermeneutic difference, the two aspects will be separated for analytical purposes: the Mishnaic treatment of biblical co-text will be looked at in this chapter, while the effect of the new, Mishnaic co-text will be addressed in Chapters 3 and 4.

The Mishnah, a written document for us, incorporates another document written earlier, Scripture.[3] Not only is the Scriptural text surrounded by new, Mishnaic, text; we also find that the Scriptural text is not *whole*; only small cuttings from it are used at any one point in the Mishnah.[4] Compared with the size of the Hebrew Bible or even its most important part in rabbinic times, the Pentateuch, the biblical passages used are tiny,[5] usually no more than a sentence at any time. The Mishnah thus incorporates far-reaching decisions about the boundaries of meaningful units in Scripture. The delimited units of Scripture are treated as capable of making sense as quotation or allusion, or of having some function in the new text which alludes to or quotes them. In separating parts of Scripture from their original co-text and placing them into a new co-text, the Mishnah creates textual *segments*. This hermeneutic movement alone virtually guarantees that the meaning of the segments does not remain constant compared to the original setting. The new Mishnaic co-text is often radically different from that of Scripture, and it always has its own thematic orientation. This is true whether the meaning of the biblical words become the explicit topic of the Mishnah or not;[6] for even where the new co-text is an *explication* of the biblical message, that explication does not consist of a recapitulation of the *biblical* co-text.

We have access to the Hebrew Bible as used by the Mishnah;[7] therefore

---

[3] Our evidence is therefore quite different, methodologically speaking, from evidence for inner-biblical interpretation. For a clear account of the differences and parallels, see Fishbane, *Biblical Interpretation*, 6–13; also 283 ff. The diachronic perspective earlier–later is embedded in the very act of quoting.

[4] In rabbinic documents of the type Midrash, the arrangement of the document depends to some extent on the segmentation of Scripture and thus becomes itself problematical. See Kern, 'Die Verwendung von Schriftversen in rabbinischen Texten', 136 f.

[5] For the evidence of biblical manuscripts from antiquity, see Tov, 'Sense Divisions in the Qumran Texts, the Masoretic Text, and Ancient Translations of the Bible'.

[6] For the distinction implied here, see Ch. 4 below.

[7] Assuming that the consonantal text of the Masoretic tradition is, at least in the vast majority of cases, the text used by the Mishnaic interpreters.

we can describe the shift of meaning between old and new co-text. But for us, the Mishnaic co-text of Scriptural segments is the *only* guide to discovering what meaning the Mishnah takes the Scriptural segment to have in its original co-text. For the two components—selecting a segment from a textual continuum, and embedding it in a new textual continuum—are only separate in our analysis. They are facets of the same complex move of interpretation. It must be assumed that the Mishnaic reader of Scripture selects segments (that is, defines boundaries) that make a certain sense to him,[8] and that he embeds them in a discourse in such a way that they help to express or support this sense. In concrete terms, the Mishnaic reader of Scripture recognizes in some Scriptural passage a treatment of a subject-matter of importance to him, and his own treatment of that subject-matter is the place into which the segment thus recognized is moved.

NEUTRALIZING THE CO-TEXT RELEASES THE MAXIMUM RANGE OF MEANING

Creating textual segments must always involve, in varying degrees, the isolation of a word, phrase, or clause from its surrounding Scriptural text. Units of Scripture are treated as independent to some extent, otherwise the option of using only part of Scripture would simply not be available. The licence to divide the text and select one of its parts on the one hand, and the licence to neutralize the co-text on the other, thus belong together. But the choice is not between Scripture taken as a whole versus Scripture divided into (any) units. The size and nature of the units is also critical. The Mishnah does not take the boundaries of larger literary units or some other intermediary division in the Bible as defining its segments. The segment is in general not determined in terms of literary units, such as the biblical book, the thematic legal unit, the episode, the narrative cycle, the song, and so on.[9] Instead, it usually has the size of a sentence or part of sentence. Quite

---

[8] I shall use the masculine pronoun when speaking about rabbinic interpreters, instead of using both masculine and feminine. Speaking of women *as if* they had been equal contributors to the rabbinic enterprise is historically misleading and helps in no way to combat an injustice that is troubling us today.

[9] This means that certain types of interpretation are quite rare in rabbinic literature. I am thinking here in particular of attempts to identify the general thrust, or the 'spirit' of the Bible as a whole. One of the rare exceptions is the idea ascribed to Hillel that the meaning of 'Torah' can be reduced to one principle (cf. bShab 31a and the comments by Urbach, *The Sages*, 955 f., n. 93). Here the word 'Torah' serves as the name of a text, as well as the name of its main message (something similar is true of the word 'Gospel'). Once such a main message is articulated, it can serve as a *guide* for reading the whole, and this could be implied in calling the whole of Torah the 'explanation' (פירושה) of the principle. But our study provides no direct evidence for such an approach. Identifications of the gist of Scripture are, however, central to some other hermeneutic traditions. To pick just two representatives. A recent papal encyclical ('Evangelium Vitae') treats the Scriptural link of its main concept merely in a footnote, saying: 'The expression "Gospel of life" is not found as such in Sacred Scripture. But it does correspond to an essential dimension of the biblical message' (*Evangelium Vitae*, 4). And H. W. Wolff writes, in an academic context: 'a section of text can be understood aright only in its

often the surrounding Scriptural text is taken into account. But even where this happens, typically only one specific strand of the multitude of intertextual relationships is selected. It is almost never the whole complex network of original co-textual relationships which is utilized (let alone explicated) in the Mishnah. The Mishnaic segmentation of Scripture tends to go hand in hand with an added emphasis or shift of emphasis which, as such, could not be accommodated by the *totality* of the surrounding Scriptural sentences. Only if taken in some measure of isolation do the words of the biblical segment offer the meaning chosen by the rabbinic interpreter, that is, only then do they provide that one meaning option among a wider range of latent meanings. The new selection of meaning can take place only after the ties to the biblical co-text have been weakened. This weakening is what is presupposed by the new textual environment in the Mishnah. The Mishnaic environment takes the biblical words into a new thematic framework or places them into a new perspective. While the light which the biblical co-text sheds on the Lemma's meaning is dimmed, a new light source is provided.[10] This is the nature of what is often labelled the 'atomistic' approach of rabbinic midrash.

At times the topic identified for a Scriptural segment by the Mishnah has no presence in the surrounding biblical text at all. In such cases the interpretation can only work if a high degree of isolation from the biblical co-text is imposed on the segment. Such cases constitute the most 'atomistic' end of the spectrum. It is clear that the neutralization of biblical co-text needs to be identified and explicated as one contributing component to many hermeneutic operations. In some cases other hermeneutic resources cannot be formulated without explicit reference to the weakening of co-textual links.[11] However, the mechanism can be present to a higher or lesser degree in a hermeneutic operation. It is in any case important to note that, even where there are no visible effects of neutralization of co-text, segmentation is still presupposed.[12] A 'mild' version of neutralization of co-text which pervades Mishnaic interpretation in general, and which may be assumed to be a silent partner in almost all hermeneutic operations, can be articulated:

context. This rule has not been adequately observed if only the immediate literary connections have been investigated. We cannot avoid the question of the *total* meaning of the Old Testament' ('The Hermeneutics of the Old Testament', 165; emphasis mine). Cf. Grech, 'The Regula Fidei as a Hermeneutical Principle in Patristic Exegesis'.

[10] The manner in which a given unit of text 'has' a topic has been of intense interest to linguistics in recent decades. See e.g. Brown and Yule, *Discourse Analysis*, ch. 3; Coulthard, *Introduction to Discourse Analysis*, 79 ff. On the effect of co-text in particular, see Beaugrande and Dressler, *Introduction to Text Linguistics*, chs. 4 (Cohesion) and 5 (Coherence); van Dijk, *Text and Context*, ch. 4 (Coherence), 98 ff. A very clear example of the manner in which the new co-text determines afresh the meaning of a quotation is discussed by Gabrion, 'L'Interpretation de l'écriture à Qumran', 787 f.

[11] Cf. the WORD and KEYING resources (Chs. 14 and 8, respectively). See below.

[12] Such cases need in fact to be understood as instances of the Mishnaic perspective coinciding with the perspective provided in biblical co-text. See below, and next chapter.

Neutralization of the ability of Scriptural co-text to narrow down the semantic range, topic or referent of the Lemma, thus allowing fresh thematic selections or semantic[13] and syntactic options.

No attempt shall be made in each case to identify exactly which aspect of linguistic meaning is the starting-point of the operation. Thus, all the parameters which determine meaning shall be treated together, unless the nature of the evidence allows distinctions. Current linguistic terminology speaks of 'sense' as well as 'reference'; of 'intension' as well as 'extension'; or again of *signifiant* and *signifié*; also of the 'topic' of a sentence, and so on.[14] The identification of the subject-matter about which Scripture speaks is absolutely central to the hermeneutic movements in the Mishnah. Quite often it makes sense to think of this identification as relating to the *referent* of a linguistic entity, that is, the extra-linguistic object;[15] but often it may be more appropriate to say that there is an identification of the concept signified, the *signifié*. However, most of the time it is not clear from the way the interpretation is presented which of these meaning decisions (in the wider sense of the word) came 'first', and which came 'later'. In other words, we do not know from which end to unpack the whole package of meaning with which we are presented, and we need in any case to capture the *togetherness* of all these elements in rabbinic hermeneutics.[16] Or, perhaps rabbinic hermeneutics is typically concerned with the *meaning of words* as such *only* in connection with their *use*, namely in Scripture.[17] Furthermore, there is no consensus in current linguistic theory as to the application of these terminological distinctions—they tend to operate in different fields of the study of language, and each is limited or even controversial in some respect. One account, by Johnson-Laird, of the manner in which the co-text narrows down meaning is extremely attractive for the purposes of this study. This is his crucial thesis for how the meaning of a complete utterance is constituted:

the *reference* of some expressions . . . [plays] a role in determining the *senses* of other expressions.[18]

This brief statement can help in explaining the *ripple effect* produced by the recognition (or appropriation) of what it is that Scripture is speaking about

---

[13] Such as the 'literal' option, or the option to choose a certain subsection of the semantic range of a word (see the WORD resources, Ch. 14). On the idea of 'literal' meaning as meaning isolated from use, see Frawley, *Linguistic Semantics*, 2.

[14] For all the terms mentioned here, see e.g. Crystal, *Dictionary of Linguistics and Phonetics*, 190 f., and 279; cf. also Lyons, *Semantics*, i. 95 ff.

[15] Strikingly so in the case of the referent of deictic terms, see Ch. 5.

[16] This is what is often referred to as the *application* of Scripture in rabbinic exegesis. The present study could be understood in large parts as an articulation of what 'application' is and how it engages linguistic meaning. See also below in Ch. 5 (section 'Quoted Use of Scripture and Mishnaic Use of Scripture').

[17] For such a distinction between meaning and use, see Searle, *Speech Acts*, 146 ff. See also n. 72 in Ch. 4 below.

[18] *Mental Models*, 241.

in a given expression. Once that topic, or referent, is identified by the Mishnaic reader, the rest of the phrase, or sentence (at times even a whole section), is reinterpreted so as to fit the identification of referent/topic. And where that process of reinterpretation meets its limits, becomes impossible on linguistic grounds, that is where the boundaries are of the segment created by the identification. From that point onwards, or in that semantic dimension, the original co-text's contribution is ignored by the reader: co-text is neutralized. This mechanism provides one possibility for a linguistic transcription of a hermeneutic attitude discussed in the next chapter (topical alignment), as well as for the notion of 'perspective' presented there and in Chapter 4.

However, this does not solve the problem of description in our case. For it is not known, from the literary unit presenting the interpretation, whether the identification of the referent of a biblical expression came first, before there was the semantic adjustment of meaning (Johnson-Laird's 'sense') in the rest of the sentence—and 'to come first' does not have a straightforward chronological meaning here. It may have been the other way round, or something else altogether might have taken place.[19] So, an attempt to distinguish for each resource between the different contextual, co-textual, and semantic aspects of the notion of 'meaning' would lead in the first instance to a confusing increase in the number of resources: many would have to be formulated in, say, three different versions (one each for 'semantic nuance', 'topic', and 'referent', to start with). More seriously, resources defined in this way would force upon us choices of description for which there is often no data from the literary evidence. Some of the distinctions mentioned above, therefore, will be used occasionally, where the evidence allows that a resource be defined in a specialized manner. Otherwise, however, we shall speak of how the Mishnah construes Scripture's 'meaning' and list in our resource definitions elements such as topic, semantic range, referent together.[20]

To return to the COTEXT resources. The option to read the Scriptural segment in independence of its Scriptural co-text is always available, and follows almost automatically from the fact that the segments are routinely as short as a sentence or shorter. Some co-textual relationships can be maintained, others not; the severity of the isolation varies. Selecting a Scriptural segment goes hand in hand with the reader bringing his own topical focus to the text, and that opens up the possibility of neutralizing the biblical co-text whatever the size of the segment. But the high frequency of Mishnaic

---

[19] See the opening section of Ch. 3.

[20] Imposing a radical and automatic separation of 'sense' and 'reference' or 'meaning' and 'relevance' might well make it impossible to understand linguistic meaning in general; but it would certainly make it impossible to understand the type of reading of which rabbinic interpretation is one historical example. On this issue in the context of biblical studies, see Barton, *Reading the Old Testament*, 175 ff., and cf. Searle's position quoted in n. 17 above; Hesse, 'Texts Without Types and Lumps Without Laws'.

interpretations which presuppose such neutralizing may well be linked to the fact that the size of a typical segment is smaller than even the smallest literary units of biblical literature.[21] In other words, the predominant segment size is a direct manifestation of the interpretative approach: one that reads a segment to some extent *against* the grain of the surrounding text, suspends the *textuality* beyond the sentence. But the most obvious manifestation is the dissolution of grammatical relationships, that is, a suspension of links *within* the sentence or clause. The suspension of grammatical relationships within complex expressions or short phrases will be taken as a special case (labelled Cotext2).[22] More frequently, the relationship of a phrase to the clause in which it occurs is suspended, that is, becomes impossible to construe in the light of the new meaning; and even more frequently, the grammatical cohesion within the complete clause or sentence requires to be (and is capable of being) adjusted to accommodate the new meaning, but the link from there to the immediately surrounding text cannot be re-created and thus retained. These latter two forms of suspending the co-textual relationships will be treated together as forming the resource Cotext1:

Cotext1: Neutralizing the semantic effect of the biblical co-text at the sentence, clause, or phrase boundary, leading to a readjustment or, if necessary, dissolution of grammatical dependencies.

The co-text's effect is, as we said, to narrow down the range of meaning available for the Lemma: it is that effect which is being cancelled by Cotext1. The semantic options are opened up to their full range, approximating the *plurality* of meanings given in the entry for a single word in a dictionary.[23] At some virtual moment in the hermeneutic process the word, expression, clause, or sentence has all its potential meaning nuances available to it, has maximal ambiguity—before, that is, it is narrowed down again, to some other meaning which meets the concerns of the Mishnaic reader. But imposing reader perspective and suspending co-textual relationships within Scripture are not two movements; they are one. And we only *know* that the co-textual relationships have been cut, suppressed, or adjusted because the biblical meaning as determined in the Mishnah cannot be put back into Scripture, or only up to a point. Cotext1 separates out, for our analytical purposes, one component of an integral hermeneutic whole.

An illustration will serve to clarify this. The following interpretation identifies the topic to which a measurement mentioned in the text belongs, after it is liberated from the constraints of its co-text.

---

[21] A very important exception to this are the short texts containing maxims or proverbs belonging to the biblical wisdom genre. See below and Ch. 5.

[22] See the second section of Ch. 13.

[23] I shall make concrete use of the notion of the dictionary entry when discussing the Mishnaic treatment of words and word-forms in Ch. 14.

[1] = [93a] mSot 5:3 I (2)[24]   Num. 35:5 and 4

That same day R. Aqiva expounded, 'And you shall measure outside the city for the eastern side two thousand cubits . . .' and another[25] verse says, '. . . from the wall of the city and outward a thousand cubits round about'. It is not possible to say 'a thousand cubits', for it is already said, 'two thousand'; and it is not possible to say 'two thousand', since it is already said, 'a thousand'. (How so?)[26] A thousand [constitutes] the outskirts and two thousand the Sabbath limit.[27]

Here we have a fairly complex midrashic operation. It presents verses 5 and 4 of Num. 35 as contradictory (1,000 cubits is not 2,000 cubits). It proceeds to solve the contradiction by saying that these two verses speak about two *different* subjects. One of these subjects is available from the biblical segment itself: the boundaries of the outskirts of the Levitical city; the other is supplied by the rabbinic discourse: the limit of the distance permissible to walk outside a city on a Sabbath. Thus, the measure of 2,000 cubits is *appropriated* by Aqiva for the rabbinic topic of the Sabbath limit; of that topic there is no trace in the verses or their biblical co-text. It can in fact not even be accommodated by the biblical sentence without loss of internal coherence, because the sentence has 'outskirts' as its subject.[28] In other words, the measurement of 2,000 cubits has to be taken *out* of the grammatical and textual relationships in which it is found in Num. 35:4 f., so that it becomes *free* to be available for the new topic (Sabbath limits). However, this is not a total separation from the biblical theme. One co-textual link does not need to be suspended: the fact that the distance is measured *outside the city*; that is a link which the new theme of Sabbath limit can accommodate and therefore must appropriate.

Here is an example for Cotext1 as the neutralization of the syntactic bond between two clauses:

[24] Hermeneutic profile: • ¶C1≈D2T1T3. Such a profile, giving a summary of all resources used in a Mishnaic interpretation, will from now on be given for each passage translated in this book.
[25] The reading of most text witnesses, including Kaufmann. The first print of the Bavli has אחר instead of אחד, as well as providing the phrase הא כיצד given in brackets further down.
[26] MS Kaufmann and other important witnesses have, instead of this question, the following: 'And why is it said "a thousand cubits" and why is it said "two thousand cubits"?' This seems to conflate two slightly different formats in setting up the hermeneutic problem (see Bietenhard, *Sota*, 96 and 190). However, the differences do not affect the main terminological characteristics, nor the hermeneutic operation. See note to passage **[93a]** in Ch. 10 below.
[27] On the problems raised by the biblical text, see Milgrom, 'The Levitic Town: An Exercise in Realistic Planning'. I have used this example before in 'Scripture's Segments and Topicality', 94. Cf. also Albeck, *Einführung*, 83.
[28] bErub 51a offers a hermeneutic argument for the link of Num. 35:5 to the topic of the Sabbath limit. It is of great complexity. There is a widespread assumption in modern scholarship that Num. 35:4 f. provided the measure for post-biblical definitions of a Sabbath limit (1,000 or 2,000 cubits), in conjunction with Exod. 16:29. The earlier literature is summarized in Schiffman, *Halakhah at Qumran*, 91–8, who also presumes such a derivation of the rule from the text of Scripture. On such assumptions in general, see Ch. 3 below. The relevant passage in the Damascus Document (CD 10:21) betrays no link to a Scriptural passage. Cf. also Albeck, *Shishah Sidrey Mishnah, Seder Nashim*, 245 (s.v. שבת תחום), who stresses the link to the city, which is of course part of the biblical topic. Interesting examples of radical re-topicalization are discussed in Halivni, *Peshat and Derash*, 56 f., 62 f.; in particular, one of them, bErub 23b (pp. 6 f.) involves a very similar hermeneutic move to our case **[1]**.

[2] mGit 9:10 III (3)[29]   Deut. 24:1

And R. Aqiva says: [He may divorce his wife] even if he finds another one more pleasant than her, as it is said, 'And if she does not find favour in his eyes'.[30]

Aqiva, in spelling out the range of valid reasons for divorce, treats the first part of the sentence as if it were not qualified at all by the subsequent part introducing a reason, beginning with 'because' (כי). Accordingly, the field of reasons becomes very wide indeed. But only *if* the effect of the second half of the verse is suspended can the clause mean that the husband has the right to divorce whatever the reason—merely as long as 'she finds no favour in his eyes'.[31]

NEUTRALIZING THE CO-TEXT IN OTHER RESOURCE FAMILIES

As we said before, the licence to neutralize the co-text is only the starkest manifestation of the general effects of segmentation and the tendency to explore meaning by lifting a Scriptural sign at least partly out of its original environment. This tendency is built into a number of resource families. Resources in group WORD, mostly concerning semantic choices for lexemes, are defined by favouring word meaning not privileged on the level of the biblical co-text. The resources of the REDUNDANCY family treat the biblical Lemma as repeating information from the co-text—as long as a meaning for that Lemma is chosen whose links to the co-text are intact. Since the co-text is excluded *ex hypothesi* from repeating the Lemma, this provides a warrant to choose a meaning for the Lemma which is to some extent alien to the co-text, for example, as concerning a fresh topic. Something similar is true of resources of the DIFFERENCE family, concerning apparent inconsistency in Scripture. Our passage [1], mSot 5:3 I (2), shows how the observation of inconsistency can be used to eliminate co-textual constraints on meaning. In cases where there is no quotation, but Scriptural wording is adopted for the Mishnah's own formulations (see sign π in Chapter 4 below), the relationship between the chosen segment and its original co-text is not addressed. However, such adoption of Scriptural wording often proceeds without regard to co-textual links; and where it employs biblical wording to explain narrative (the PERFORMANCE and USE resources), it typically uses segments which have undemanding links in their biblical settings, such as

---

[29] Ω•¶C1 O8W1W6.2 or S6/W1.2(*ki*).

[30] The biblical verse continues: 'because he has found something indecent . . .'.

[31] Cf. Rosenblatt, *Interpretation*, 79, n. 256; bGit 90a explains Aqiva's argument differently, namely, as rooted in the semantics of כ. According to this the conjunction is taken to mean 'or when'. This is an issue of more general import: where the rabbis determine the relationship of two clauses, do they always also reflect an interpretation of the lexical meaning of the conjunction? See passage **[130b]** in Ch. 13 below.

proverbs or poetry.[32] Resources belonging to the family KEYING provide for the co-text to be superseded in favour of a (suitably selected) co-text of the same lexeme in a *different* place in Scripture. All of these suspend or limit to some extent the biblical co-text's ability to narrow down the meaning range of biblical expressions. The result is that they are wide open to receive a different type of narrowing down, namely, through the reader's concerns. The main resources and formats which are predicated on a neutralization of the co-textual relationships are:

- adopting a Scriptural text into the Mishnah's thematic perspective (treated in Chapters 3 and 4);
- using Scripture's words as Mishnah's utterance (Chapters 4 and 5);
- exchanging Scriptural co-texts of two occurrences of the same lexeme (Chapter 8);
- allocating a fresh topic or referent to inconsistent expressions (Chapter 10);
- allocating a fresh topic or referent to redundant expressions (Chapter 13); and
- exploring semantic options for lexemes in isolation from their co-text (Chapter 14).

Insofar as the neutralization of co-text is an element inherent in or combined with the resource groups identified above, we shall be concerned with it in a number of other chapters in this book. And, since it forms a routine part of Mishnaic interpretation, we shall encounter it in many illustrative passages even in chapters which deal with the other resource families.

Rabbinic literature (though not the Mishnah itself) knows a term which seems to capture the effect of neutralizing the co-text's contribution to the Lemma's meaning: מופנה (*mufneh*). It is usually translated as 'rendered free'.[33] It is employed to qualify the second in the thirteen hermeneutic principles ascribed to R. Ishmael. Its exact import with respect to that rule was the object of a dispute between two 'schools' of exegesis, linked to the names of R. Aqiva and to R. Ishmael.[34] This could be quite an important detail. If the ascription of styles of interpretation to the two rabbis is correct, then rabbinic hermeneutics as we now know it is dominated by Aqiva's

---

[32] In other words, it makes use of biblical segments which already have a high degree of ambiguity or generality.

[33] In mYeb. 3:5 it denotes 'unmarried', a suggestive use in our present context. Bacher translates it as 'frei, ledig', and explains it as: being 'open' to interpretation (i. 149). Mielziner paraphrases the term as: ' "empty", that is, seemingly *superfluous*, or pleonastic, and not already engaged for another deduction of the traditional interpretation, to enable it to be used for an analogy of Gezera Shava' (*Introduction*, 150; emphasis original). Hirschfeld renders it as pleonasm in his *Halachische Exegese*, 462–7. Jastrow (1188a) renders: 'free for interpretation, unnecessary for the plain sense or context' (!). Liebermann, *Hellenism in Jewish Palestine*, 61, translates it as 'vacant'. BDB, 815a, s.v. פנה, offer no meaning obviously relevant to this technical usage.

[34] See e.g. Alexander, 'Midrash', 453.

approach. It would make very good sense if the decisive battle was fought over the contribution of the *co-text* to meaning.[35] However, the problem of co-text, as captured in the term *mufneh*, seems to have been highlighted by the rabbis only with regard to a few of the 'rules' of hermeneutics. The evidence from the Mishnah, on the other hand, indicates that the suspension of co-textual links is of principal importance across the configuration of resources.[36]

STRESSING OR PRESUPPOSING THE DEPENDENCY OF MEANING ON THE CO-TEXT

In Mishnaic interpretations, the Scriptural co-text is robbed of its influence on the meaning of the Lemma often and with determination. However, this needs to be placed into perspective by showing that there are other interpretations which make very specific use of the co-text or presuppose knowledge of it. Such use of co-textual relationships we shall label Cotext5.

Cotext5: Explication of the meaning of an expression in the light of the biblical co-text, where the latter is linked by cohesive signals or narrative connectedness beyond the clause.[37]

The existence and frequency of the Cotext5 resource provides a perspective in three important respects:

(1) It shows that the 'atomistic' Cotext1 approach, while prominent, is very far from being universal in Mishnaic hermeneutics. (It also demonstrates indirectly that the neutralizing resource Cotext1 is not the result of negligence or misunderstanding, which would be intrinsically unlikely in any case.)

(2) Since neutralization is a resource available in the Mishnaic hermeneutic configuration, interpretations which make use of or rely on co-textual relationships are not the *default* option. This means the co-text is *allowed* to narrow down the meaning—presumably because its perspective approximates that of the Mishnah.

(3) Neutralizing co-textual links and fostering them very often work hand in hand; some links between a segment and its co-text may be ignored while others are promoted. Both Cotext1 and Cotext5 are thus expressions of the same underlying licence to emphasize, utilize, or neutralize co-

---

[35] Cf. e.g. Bacher, i. 15 and the literature quoted there.

[36] Cf. the frequency with which the phrase 'elsewhere' or 'its neighbour' occurs in the *Mishnat R. Eliezer* (ed. Enelow). On the link between analogy and redundancy, see Ch. 8 (resource Keying2) and esp. Ch. 13 (resource Syntax2).

[37] I here give preference to the notion of the clause over that of the sentence. I do so with a case like mNed 3:11 I (10) in mind. Jer. 9:26, a long and complex sentence, is there interpreted by connecting its opening to its closing.

textual relationships. There is no hermeneutic obligation, as there is for the modern historical or philological approach,[38] to give pride of place to a text's linguistic surroundings when determining meaning.

Let us first look at an example of the Mishnah's use of a *narrative* nexus.

[3] = [57a] = [130a] mShab 9:3 II (3) = mShab 19:3[39]   Gen. 34:25

Whence [do we know] that one bathes a child[40] [even] on the third day [after circumcision] that falls on the Sabbath? For it is said, 'And it came to pass on the third day when they were in pain . . .'.

There is narrative link here. Verse 25 continues from the unquoted verse 24, which reports that the inhabitants of Shechem submitted to circumcision. The link between that event and pain on the third day is generalized (resource Norm8). But before the causality between circumcision and pain can be established, it needs to be assumed that the subject of verse 25 ('they') is identical with that of the immediately preceding verse (i.e. that it is the people of Shechem who are in pain). This is simply taken for granted, and with it the textual coherence of these two sentences.

[4] mYoma 8:9 II–III (3)[41]   Jer. 17:13 (or 14:8)

R. Aqiva said: Blessed are you, O Israel! Before whom are you made clean and who makes you clean? Your father in heaven, as it is said, 'And I will sprinkle clean water upon you and you shall be clean; [from all your uncleanness and from all your idols I shall cleanse you]' (Ezek. 36:25). And it says: 'O hope [*miqweh*] of Israel, Lord'—as the *miqweh* [immersion pool] cleanses the unclean so does the Holy One, Blessed be He, cleanse Israel.[42]

We are concerned only with the second biblical quotation. The word *miqweh* allows two meanings: hope, and gathering of water (which, in rabbinic contexts, is a ritual bath). Here the second meaning is chosen in a syntactic slot where it is odd (namely, addressing God as 'ritual bath of Israel', as effecting cleansing), so maybe co-textual dependency is meant to be suspended. But on the other hand, the theme of water, and indeed of God as compared to water, is present in the co-text: this very verse concludes with God being called 'fountain of living water', while in Jer. 14:8 the same vocative stands in the wider context of the idea of a drought. So the meaning 'gathering of water' chosen for *miqweh* strengthens, as well as weakens, some links to the biblical co-text.[43]

---

[38]   See the first sections of Ch. 1 above and of Ch. 14 below.

[39]   C5N8S5.2T2T3.1.

[40]   The popular prints have here 'the circumcision', i.e. the wound of circumcision. (Nowack's apparatus in *Schabbat*, 143, gives no clear idea of the variants.)

[41]   ΩA5E9C1C5T3W1.

[42]   The function (and MS presence) of this midrashic unit at the end of the tractate is discussed in Goldin, 'Reflections on a Mishnah', 141–9; Albeck, *Einführung*, 182; Epstein, *Mavo*, 1306. MSS Kaufmann and Cambridge have this unit, while MS Munich and some prints do not (Meinhold, *Joma*, 80).

[43]   The Targum translates the opening *miqweh* of Jer. 17:13 as 'hope', and so do modern translations.

[5] mBQ 5:5 I (2)[44]   Exod. 21:33

The person who digs a 'pit' in a private domain and opens it up to the public domain, or [digs it] in the public domain but opens it to a private domain, or [digs it] in a private domain and opens it to another private domain, is liable. If he digs a 'pit' in the public domain and an ox or ass falls into it (and dies), he is liable. Whether he digs a pit, a trench or cavern, ditches or channels, he is liable. If so, why is it said 'pit'? Just as a pit which is deep enough to cause death is ten handbreadths deep, so any [cavity] deep enough to cause death [must be] ten handbreadths deep.[45]

We are concentrating here on the answer to the metalinguistic question, 'Then why is it said "pit"?' (אם כן למה נאמר בור?). The answer gives a class-defining criterion: ability to cause death (further defined in terms of a minimum depth, Topic8). Restricting the theme to *death* caused by a pit allows the unquoted verse 34 to be taken into account, which contains the phrase 'and the dead beast shall be his'. This phrase presupposes that the fall into (or sojourn in) the pit spoken about in verse 33 has caused death; and this co-textual relationship is read, understood, and developed by our Mishnaic norm. A similar, if perhaps less remarkable case, of pre-supposed information is the creation of a link between a speech report on the one hand, and the direct speech introduced by it on the other. For instance, in mQid 1:7 III (3) the commandment given in Lev. 21:1 is taken to exclude women presumably because the 'priests, the sons of Aaron' are the addressees mentioned at the beginning of that verse. Here is another Cotext5 case:

[6] = [52a] mSan 2:3 II (2)[46]   2 Sam. 3:31

If a relative of his [the king] dies, he may not go out of the door of his palace. R. Yehudah says: If he wants to leave after the bier he may leave. For thus we have found it with David, who went out after the bier of Abner, as it is said, 'And king David walked after the bier'. They said to him: The thing happened only to appease (the people).[47]

The argument against interpreting David's behaviour as providing an example of a norm (a resource of the NORM family) rests on the links of the quoted sentence with the whole of the narrative unit in which it is found, that is, the lengths to which David went to dissociate himself from Abner's murder.[48] The logic of the argument is: the event does not have exemplary character because the reasons for its occurrence are unique or exceptional, in other words, rooted in the circumstances *reported in the surrounding text*.

---

[44] πA1C5E1.1E1.2T8.
[45] The meaning of the last sentence is clarified by the next sentence: the person is not liable for an animal which dies upon falling into a pit less than ten handbreadths deep. This is how the hermeneutic question is formulated in MS Munich (see n. 47): 'If so, what does Scripture teach in saying (מה תלמוד לומר), "pit"?' Cf. Windfuhr, *Baba qamma*, 90.
[46] ¶C5¬N1T2.
[47] 'The people' is found in MS Munich and the printed editions. Cf. Krauß, *Sanhedrin-Makkot*, 386.
[48] Verse 37 reads: 'So all the people and all Israel understood that day that it had not been the king's will to slay Abner the son of Ner' (cf. the opening section of Ch. 6 below).

It may be noted in this context that there are a number of metalinguistic maxims in rabbinic literature which seem to stress the role of some kind of co-text. Among them is, very likely, the maxim, 'A verse can never take leave of its *Peshat*';[49] also, 'The Torah speaks the language of man',[50] and quite explicitly, no. 7 of the hermeneutic rules ascribed to Hillel (reappearing as the first part of the twelfth rule in the list of R. Ishmael).[51] However, the meaning of the latter is perhaps more closely linked to Cotext5.2, to be defined presently. In which case the operative rabbinic term, *inyan*, signifies not so much 'thematic context' as the very different notion of 'textual proximity'.[52]

Among the Cotext5 cases in the Mishnah, one group stands out. It defines the linking effect created by a *discourse deixis* (such as the English 'below'). We shall define this as a sub-category of Cotext5, adding a differentiating second digit to the code:

Cotext5.2: Explication of the meaning of an expression in the light of a co-text whose limit depends on (or calls for an adjustment in) the scope of a demonstrative pronoun understood as a discourse deixis.

This resource is as much about the semantics of biblical deixis as it is about the co-textual relationships. And yet it would be fruitless to attempt to define it in terms of the meaning of words such as 'this', or 'that' (i.e. as a WORD resource). For it is clear that it is not the semantic possibilities of the biblical demonstratives (few in number) that trigger the interpretation. Rather, it is the textual proximity and its opportunities for Mishnaic relevance first, and the deictic opportunities in the textual neighbourhood second.[53] Our definition of Cotext5.2 is couched in general terms ('whose limit depends on'), for the reason that the scope of the discourse deixis can de-emphasize certain co-textual relationships at the same time as emphasizing others.

---

[49] This sentence (אין מקרא יוצא מידי פשוטו) is found in bYeb 11b, bShab 63a, and bYeb 24a. Halivni comments on these passages (*Peshat and Derash*, 54 ff.), stressing the co-text as defining criterion: 'That *peshat* here meant context is indisputable' (56, and see 55).

[50] Found e.g. in Sifre Num. ad 15:31 (ed. Horowitz, 121): דברה תורה כלשון בני אדם; cf. Samely, 'Scripture's Implicature'.

[51] Rule 20 in *Mishnat Rabbi Eliezer* is different (cf. Bacher, i. 134). The wording of the Hillelite rule is: דבר הלמד מעניינו (cf. Bacher, i. 142, n. 1). Cf. also Stemberger, *Introduction*, 27; Mielziner, *Introduction*, 176 f.; Braude and Kapstein (trans.), *Pesikta de-Rab Kahana*, pp. xl–xli.

[52] Stemberger, *Introduction*, 27. See further below. Cf. Bacher, i. 140; Braude and Kapstein (trans.), *Pesikta de-Rab Kahana*, p. xli; Fraenkel, *Darkhey*, i. 196; also Samely, 'Between Scripture and Its Rewording', 47 (on the flow of the text for the *Kelal u-frat*), and Jackson, 'On the Nature of Analogical Argument in Early Jewish Law' (see further Ch. 8 below).

[53] This is different from interpreting the biblical deixis as pointing to something outside the text, e.g. something present in the situation of reported speech. The latter too is an important resource of rabbinic hermeneutics. See Goldberg, 'Rede und Offenbarung in der Schriftauslegung Rabbi Aqibas'; Roitman, 'Sacred Language and Open Text'; Boyarin, *Intertextuality*, 120 f.; Fraenkel, *Darkhey*, i. 102–5. There is no example for this in the Mishnah, but see the Performance8 and Use8 resources discussed in Ch. 5 below. In some Mishnaic passages a biblical demonstrative is being deprived of its discourse function (mSheb 10:8 I (2) **[132]**; cf. also **[116]** mYeb 12:3 I (2) and **[127]** mSot 7:4 II (2)).

We have defined Cotext5 as dealing with segments whose linguistic make-up shows that they are linked to the co-text. We now come to cases where the Mishnah construes co-textual links in the absence of explicit or implicit cohesive signals. Here is the resource:

Cotext6: Explication of the meaning of a biblical expression in the light of a contiguous co-text not connected by grammatical links, lexical iteration, or other cohesive signals.

An example is:

[7] mSan 4:1[54]   Lev. 24:22 (Deut. 13:15)

Non-capital and capital cases are alike in [forensic] 'examination and inquiry' (cf. Deut. 13:15), for it is said, 'One law you shall have [the foreigner shall be as the native, for I am the Lord your God].'

Two elements in the Dictum[55] seem not to be supported by the verse's wording: the idea that it is capital and property cases which are 'one law' (no such dichotomy is mentioned), and that they are 'one law' in respect of the procedures for judicial probing (as opposed to, say, measures of punishment). The former perspective, however, almost certainly draws tacitly on the segment's relationship to the preceding verse.[56] That verse reads: 'He who strikes dead a beast shall make payment for it; and he who strikes dead a man shall be put to death.' These two cases of killing can obviously be distinguished along the lines of the categories employed in the Mishnah: destruction of possessions versus destruction of humans. In fact it is conceivable, but not likely, that verse 21 with verse 22a were read as a textual unit: '. . . shall be put to death—[but] one law you shall have [for both].' In that case, this interpretation would be an illustration of the next resource to be defined below, Cotext7.[57] But the Mishnah gives no hint of such a redefinition of grammatical units; and this would not solve the problem of the *torso* of verse 22, given in brackets in our translation above. Rather, the interpretation is likely to be based on a deliberate 'switching on' of verse 21 as a co-text which sets the theme of the quoted segment (at the same time 'switching off' verse 22b). It is thus a case of Cotext6. It is also a very clear illustration of how neutralization of and emphasis on co-text can coexist with each other. In this case the two are separated along the lines of 'preceding co-text' (emphasized) and 'subsequent co-text' (neutralized). And yet, since there is left in verse 22 a piece of text which cannot be

---

[54] πA2A3(one law)C1C6E1.2T1T3.

[55] We call the rabbinic formulation 'Dictum', and the biblical passage linked to it 'Lemma' (the terminology is explicated in Ch. 12). The latter term only applies if there is a *duplication* of the biblical message, on which criterion see Ch. 4 below.

[56] Cf. Albeck, *Einführung*, 90. For the imposition of a different thematic perspective (TOPIC) on the 'one law' expression, which could not so draw on the co-text, see bBQ 84a (cf. Jackson, *Studies in the Semiotics of Biblical Law*, sec. 10.4).

[57] Cotext6 requires the absence of grammatical links; Cotext7 is neutral with regard to such links; they can thus appear together.

properly connected (the foreigner shall be as the native, for I am the Lord your God),[58] the licence to *suspend* co-textual relationships is clearly fundamental even in this Cotext6 interpretation.

The hermeneutic terminology of the rabbis includes the term *semukhin* (סמוכין),[59] seemingly applied in particular to cases where the biblical text offers some explicit transition between distinct but contiguous narrative episodes. In such cases the last verse of the preceding episode (or its whole narrative import) is taken to shed light on the first sentence of the subsequent episode. For this resource there is no example in the Mishnah.[60] However, the word is also used for the linking of contiguous segments outside narrative structures. Rabbinic usage of this term seems not to distinguish two different groups of cases: readings which retain the same thematic focus from one Scriptural segment to the next (our resources Cotext5 and Cotext6), on the one hand; and readings where co-textual relevance is taken to create room for an analogy (i.e. a combination of resources Cotext5 and Analogy2).[61] *Semukhin* also labels interpretations in which not merely proximity (as in Cotext5 and Cotext6), but also *sequence* is important. In addition, the term may name hermeneutic operations which create grammatical links across verse boundaries. This type of *semukhin* is our next topic, and we shall name it Cotext7.[62] For, occasionally, decisions about the scope of syntactic relationships[63] can lead to the co-option of text which lies outside the Masoretic verse boundaries. Here is the general structure of this resource:

Cotext7: Explication of the meaning of an expression in the light of an extension of the grammatical period to co-text beyond the Masoretic verse boundary.[64]

The clearest example in the Mishnah is the following (the backslash is used to mark the verse division):

---

[58] It can of course be also connected to 'One law you shall have', but surely not *at the same time* as '. . . shall be put to death'.
[59] See Bacher, i. 132 f.; ii. 142 f.; Mielziner, *Introduction*, 177 f. (regarding the legal 'juxtaposition', which is quite different from the narrative mechanism explained here, but similar to resource Analogy2.1, Ch. 8 below); Goldberg, 'Die "Semikha" ', 6–11.
[60] Cf. on this I. Heinemann, *Darkhey Ha-Aggadah*, 140 ff.; Fraenkel, *Darkhey*, i. 183 ff. A very clear example is the transition from Gen. 21 to 22 as interpreted in BerR 55:4 (שם היו דברים הרהורי, ed. Theodor-Albeck, ii. 587); also that between Gen. 14 and 15 (BerR 44:4–5, ed. Theodor-Albeck, i. 427 f.). Both are linked to the biblical phrase, 'And it was after these things . . .'. On this phenomenon in the Targums, cf. Samely, *Interpretation of Speech*, 62, 76 f.
[61] See Goldberg, 'Die "Semikha" ', 8 f., and Stemberger, *Introduction*, 20, for the distinction of the two types of hermeneutic operation.
[62] Examples in Mielziner, *Introduction*, 178 f.
[63] For resources of this type, see the SYNTAX family in Ch. 13.
[64] Cf. L. Blau, 'Massoretic Studies III', 140, who distinguishes the case where the verse boundary is in doubt from the case where the interpretation does not mean to question the boundary. Cotext7 simply records the fact that a Masoretic verse boundary is not accepted as limiting the co-text. Bacher quotes further examples (i. 132 f.).

[8] mMak 3:10[65]   Deut. 25:2–3

How many lashes do they inflict on a man? Forty minus one, for it is said, 'by number\forty'—a number near to forty.

The two verses involved here read:

Then if the wicked person deserves to be beaten, the judge shall cause him to lie down and be beaten before him according to his wickedness by number.\Forty [lashes] one may scourge him (with)—no more; lest, if one should go on to beat him with more stripes than these, your brother be degraded in your sight.

The Mishnah reads this period as follows: 'Then if the wicked person deserves to be beaten, the judge shall cause him to lie down and be beaten before him. According to his wickedness—by the number forty—one may beat him; no more.' The effect of reading the preposition *bet* as 'around' (resource Word1.2),[66] while at the same time taking into account the 'no more' of verse 3, is this: 'about forty'; means not forty exactly; and it cannot be *more* than forty, so not forty-one; thus thirty-nine.

The list of hermeneutic *middot* ascribed to R. Eliezer contains a rule (no. 11) which seems to cover such a phenomenon. The option to connect text which is separated by the Masoretic division is identified under the name מסדור שנחלק.[67] The biblical passages quoted there are 2 Chron. 30:18–19 and Job 17:4–5. But even between these two passages, quoted in the same breath, there are significant differences.[68] It is not clear if מסדור שנחלק presupposes that the two verses need be construed so as to leave no grammatical torso. In the interpretation I have given to case **[8]**, this happens to be the case. In other words, the Mishnaic reader, at the same time as construing text across verse boundaries, makes use of a syntactic ambiguity of the consonantal text (Syntax3, see Chapter 13 below).

There is another structure for allocating special significance to the co-text. Where the segment forms (part of) direct speech, typically *conversational* coherence may be emphasized.[69] This is of particular interest to the Mishnah where the speech needs to be uttered in performing a legal act (Performance4, Chapter 5 below).

---

[65] ®¶C5C7S3W1.2(*bet*) or G2W3(*bet*).

[66] Instead of taking it in the sense of 'according to'. Cf. BDB, 89a, where *bet* is taken to denote 'proximity'; BDB, 90b defines the *bet* in this verse as: 'of a standard of measurement or computation with, by'. See resource Word1.2 (Ch. 14).

[67] *Mishnat Rabbi Eliezer*, ed. Enelow, 22 f.

[68] The *mem* in the formula is conntected to the heading of the list, 'By 32 Middot is the Torah expounded'. It is actually the examples that make clear that the topic here is segmentation beyond verse boundary. The formula used in the examples is: סדור היה ראוי להיות אלא שנחלק. Cf. Alexander, 'The Rabbinic Hermeneutical Rules and the Problem of the Definition of Midrash'; Stemberger, *Introduction*, 25 f. Of relevance is also the rabbinic term *hekhrea*', הכרע כתובה, on which see Bacher, i. 87; Fishbane 'Use, Authority and Interpretation of Mikra at Qumran', 368; Albeck, *Einführung*, 85; Breuer, 'Biblical Verses of Undecided Syntactical Adhesion'; cf. also Blau, 'Massoretic Studies III', 139, n. 2.

[69] On conversational phenomena such as turn-taking and 'adjacency pairs', see Sacks, *Lectures on Conversation*, ii. 521 ff.; Levinson, *Pragmatics*, 296 ff., 303 ff.; Brown and Yule, *Discourse Analysis*, 230 f.

Cotext9: Explication of the meaning of a biblical expression in the light of its response function in a sequence of reported utterances by different speakers.

Several of the Mishnaic Cotext9 cases are concerned with the Lemma 'Amen, Amen', taken from the ordeal imposed on the wife suspected of adultery (*Sotah*) in Num. 5:22. Here is the first of these interpretations:

[9] = **[124]** mSot 2:5 I (5)[70]   Num. 5:22; 5:21

Why[71] does she say, 'Amen, Amen'? Amen to the 'curse' (הָאָלָה), Amen to the 'oath' (הַשְּׁבוּעָה).

The explanation suggests that two words are separately affirmed by the repetition of the 'Amen' in the speech of the woman suspected of adultery. These two words, curse and oath, come from verse 21 where they form part of the speech of the priest: 'may the Lord make you a curse and an oath among your people.' The same words appear once more, and linked to each other as genitive compound, in the speech report belonging to this priestly utterance: 'And the priest shall make the woman swear the swearing of the curse, and say to the woman' (verse 21). The interpretation in **[9]** removes the impression that the repetition of Amen in the woman's answer is meaningless or merely emphatic. The double 'Amen' is shown to have two different reference points (Redundancy8.1) in the preceding text.[72] But the two words to which the two 'Amen's respond are in themselves redundant: they belong to the same lexical field, are employed in the same syntactic function, and occur twice each in the same verse. That redundancy too is accounted for (Redundancy4.1); all four terms (Amen, Amen, curse, oath) are justified as having distinct significance. And this is achieved, at a stroke, by construing the woman's utterance emphatically as a *response* to something said before. In other words, it emphasizes the *co-text* as structuring a *conversation*. The same *mishnah* offers three further suggestions of how to explain the redundancy of 'Amen, Amen'; all of them create links to the preceding priestly utterance.

SCRIPTURAL *PAROLE* AS MISHNAIC *LANGUE*; TECHNICAL LANGUAGE; PROVERBS

We shall now briefly consider parallels for the way in which biblical segments, in their Mishnaic treatment, convey meaning. We shall mention three: the proverb, the *langue*, and the technical language.

Considered on their own, certain types of biblical segments can be quite

---

[70] Σ?¶C9P4R4.1(oath/curse)R8.1(amen).
[71] The reading למה, found in most texts. MS Munich and the first print of the Babylonian Talmud (Venice 1522) have על מה instead (see list III at the end of Ch. 12 below). Cf. Bietenhard, *Sota*, 188.
[72] REDUNDANCY resources are discussed in Ch. 13.

ambiguous as to *what they are about*. Partial or total de-cotextualizing can thus render a segment 'atopical'.[73] The degree to which the topic of a Scriptural segment becomes indeterminate by separating it from its co-text is variable. Our passage [1] mSot 5:3 I (2) above illustrates one end of the scale. The measurement '2,000 cubits' is treated as readily available for any suitable topic that might be linked to it from the Mishnaic perspective (see next chapter); and what is suitable is decided at least in many cases on the basis of the available range of subjects, not on the basis of the relations of the Lemma to the co-text and the topics found there.[74]

This is especially pronounced if the Lemma appears in a sentence which is vague, highly general, or metaphorically employed.[75] Such sentences, if removed from their original textual or situational setting, can appear as admitting a bewildering number of possible thematic foci. The latter is typical of the sentences or phrases used as proverbs.[76] The segmentation of Scripture into sentence-sized bits whose links to the co-text are suspended or weakened can be seen as a 'proverbialization' of Scripture. Midrashic interpretation treats Scripture as 'proverbial' in that it turns it into a conglomerate of atopical sentences in search of a topic. But some procedures in the Mishnaic application of Scripture can be characterized as treating Scriptural verses (of *any* genre) as proverbial in a much more specific manner also.[77] Thus, we shall encounter cases where a Scriptural segment is used as whole utterance in a proverb-like way, and cases where Scriptural proverbs are used to characterize a situation in a manner in which we would expect proverbs to work in oral use.[78] We shall also investigate the use of sentences from Scripture in the explanation of Scriptural narrative, another functional parallel to proverbs in oral use.[79] In our present context it is important to stress that rendering atopical a Scriptural sentence is a direct consequence of (and often wholly dependent on) neutralizing its links to the biblical co-text. The potential for different types of 'proverbialization' is thus always there, given the standard small-scale segmentation of Scripture.

We can approach this phenomenon also from the angle of the language system (and proverbs too are amenable to such an analysis). Linguistics after Saussure distinguishes the concrete instances of speech produced in a speech situation, called *parole*, from the language system, called *langue*. The latter provides the elements and principles whose selection and

---

[73] This is how Harvey Sacks characterizes the proverb, in his *Lectures on Conversation* (i. 109). See further Chs. 4–5 below.

[74] I shall come back to this in Ch. 4 (the hermeneutic attitude of 'topical alignment').

[75] Being metaphorical is not a property of words in isolation. For the metaphorical character of proverbs, see Hasan-Rokem, *Proverbs in Israeli Folk Narratives*, 15.

[76] Sacks, *Lectures on Conversation*, i. 109–12; Hasan-Rokem, *Proverbs in Israeli Folk Narratives*.

[77] More on this in the last section of Ch. 5.

[78] See Chs. 4 and 5 below.

[79] Cf. Hasan-Rokem, *Proverbs*, sec. 2.2 ('Proverb as a Key for Complexity of Plot'); Sacks, *Lectures on Conversation*, ii. 421 ff. This is our topic in Ch. 5.

combination creates the individual instance of speech (i.e. a *parole*). One can describe aspects of the Mishnaic treatment of Scripture by saying that individual biblical *paroles* can be turned into systematic elements of Mishnah's *langue*.[80] For example, what in Scripture is a unique combination of words, can become a fixed, standing phrase of the Mishnah with a stable and specific meaning (see next chapter).

And there is a third way in which we can approach the phenomenon called 'proverbialization' above. It is one of the hallmarks of a technical language that its terms are less dependent in their meaning on the context than the terms of everyday speech.[81] Is this linked to the way the Mishnah reads Scripture? Is the tendency to neutralize biblical co-text evidence of a Mishnaic propensity to find in Scripture *technical* terminology? There are a number of observations which seem to support this. There is the fact that the Mishnah's reformulation of the Scriptural meaning is often technical: quite a few of the terms offered as Mishnaic counterparts to biblical words have a standardized and precise sense in the Mishnaic discourse.[82] However, this merely shows that the Mishnah assumes that its own technical terminology can be linked to Scriptural wording, not necessarily that it treats Scriptural language as technical. For that to be the case, we would expect that the same lexeme is in fact understood in the *same* manner at all or at least most of its occurrences in Scripture; but that does not seem to happen, at least in the Mishnah. Nevertheless, the possibility of a 'technical' treatment of Scripture needs to be kept in mind,[83] and there is one Mishnaic resource group (LOGIC) which fits the bill: the interpretation of negation and certain conjunctions as having a precise, quasi-logical, import.[84] Also, the functionality of modern specialist languages is linked to an economy of information: as much information as possible is packed into as few words as possible.[85] And this is also an important feature of Mishnaic hermeneutics: the assumption that the density of information in Scripture is very high, and the corollary that biblical expression is *economical*.

---

[80] Cf. Saussure, *Course*, secs. 2 and 3; Lyons, *Introduction to Theoretical Linguistics*, 51 f. With regard to the proverb, the terminology is explained thus by Hasan-Rokem (p. 16): 'Each use of a proverb . . . is conceived of as a specific realization of the text, according to the Saussurian distinction between *Parole* (use) and *Langue* (text) . . .'; cf. Jakobson and Bogatyrev, 'Die Folkore als eine besondere Form des Schaffens'. See also our discussion of passages **[25]** and **[26]** in Ch. 4. The importance of this observation for midrashic literature is explored in Boyarin, *Intertextuality*, 29. See also Fishbane, 'Midrash and the Meaning of Scripture', 552 f.: 'the *parole* of Scripture becomes the *langue* of each and every midrashic *parole*.'

[81] This is one distinguishing characteristic of technical lexemes according to Fluck, *Fachsprachen*, 47 ('präziser und kontextautonomer'). Cf. also Richards, *Philosophy of Rhetoric*, 48. According to Jackson, *Semiotics and Legal Theory*, 41, 'monosemicity' is a feature of technical (including legal) language.   [82] See the next chapter (Topic3).

[83] There is, for example, the apparently hyperbolic formula '[the word] X means nothing but Y', which is at times linked to resource Keying2/*gezerah shawah* (Ch. 8 below). See Bacher, i. 4; Reiss, 'Wortsubstitution als Mittel der Deutung'; Fraenkel, *Darkhey*, i. 105 ff. Related is also the introduction: 'In each place where it says X, the meaning is . . .' (Bacher, i. 116, 4 f.).

[84] This is typical for technical languages according to Fluck, *Fachsprachen*, 48 f. Cf. the concluding section of Ch. 9 below.   [85] Fluck, *Fachsprachen*, 56.

TOPICAL DIVERSITY AND SEGMENT SIZE

What does it mean to say that the Mishnah expects Scripture to have a high information density? On the level of hermeneutic presentation in the Mishnah, this question is linked to the quantity of discrete topics which the Mishnaic discourse traverses.[86] The link to Scripture presented for at least some of these discrete topics implies that they are based on the resolve to seek guidance for a life of Torah. In the rabbinic context, the life of Torah consisted of sanctifying (in a non-cultic or para-cultic manner) the ordinary. This was to be achieved through fulfilling God's commandments on a daily basis, in the context of everyday life, all the year round. Torah was considered the source from which the information required for a life of Torah must come.[87] And Torah is two things: it is on the one hand the written document whose material presence is addressed in its very physicality by the rabbis.[88] And on the other hand, it is the halakhic competence, traditional knowledge, and experience transmitted in the *doing* of the life of Torah, that is, embedded in a social practice.[89] This is at least one aspect of the so-called 'Oral Torah'. As far as we can see, the legal positions of the 'Oral Torah' were the first to be articulated in separation from that context of practice, providing the material adopted in the document Mishnah. There may have been a growing tendency in post-Mishnaic Judaism to furnish links to Scriptural wording for statements and norms that started life as verbal articulations of a competence embedded in a non-verbal practice. Be that as it may, Torah as the written document was likely to have been important from the start as a source of information on the commandments of God and the life of Torah; it may also have provided a verbal guide for *formulating* competence derived, not from written Torah, but from a non-verbal practice of the life of Torah.[90] Once the idea that specific segments of text conveyed specific points of information was entrenched,[91] there could have been an accelerating movement of increasing the number of focused segments and paring down their size (i.e. differentiating them against each other). There could have developed, up to a point, a correlation between the quantity of discrete topics on which concrete information

---

[86] See esp. resource Topic2 (Ch. 4 below).

[87] Cf. the maxim 'turn it [Torah] and turn it again, for all is in it', ascribed to Ben Bag-Bag in mAvot 5:22.

[88] See Goldberg, 'The Rabbinic View of Scripture'; Green, 'Writing with Scripture'.

[89] Cf. Goodman, 'A Note on Josephus, the Pharisees and Ancestral Tradition', for a timely reminder that 'oral' can mean *not fixed verbally* as well as *not written down*. This distinction is the key to a proper understanding of the notion of 'Oral Torah'. Important rabbinic passages are analysed in Schäfer, *Studien zur Geschichte und Theologie*, 153–97. Kadushin correctly stresses the *lack of verbal definition* of central 'organismic' concepts of rabbinic Judaism (in *Organic Thinking* and *The Rabbinic Mind*). Cf. also Segal's notion that 'law' was at first tied to specific decisions in concrete circumstances for the early rabbis ('Jewish Law during the Tannaitic Period', 107 f.).

[90] Cf. also the first section of Ch. 3 below.

[91] Perhaps through something like the attitude of 'topical alignment' discussed in Ch. 4 below.

was sought, and the size of the segments of Scripture in which an answer was located. Information density means economy of words, and this economy implies that each new semantic, grammatical, or literary entity carries a new focus, a new topic or sub-topic, in any case something *new* when compared to the co-text. That is how the economy of technical language works, mainly embedded in its lexemes.[92] But there is another type of information density which uses many more linguistic structures in addition to the lexemes for conveying extra information: the economy of poetry.[93] For example, where the sound patterns crafted from the selection and combination of words make a contribution to their message,[94] one is in the presence of high information density. Structures contributing to the message in poetic language might embrace the level of syntax as much as that of vocabulary, as well as sound quality, rhyme, rhythm/metre, and others. Rabbinic interpretation has the option to look for Scriptural meaning on such levels too, as the Mishnaic resources of the ICON and GRAPHEME family show.[95] But when making use of structures other than the sentence and its words,[96] rabbinic exegesis is not compelled to *integrate* the evidence of all levels for the same segment, as is modern poetic analysis. Instead, some of the co-textual links at least are routinely neutralized. Yet, some typically 'poetic' structures of language are in fact scrutinized for their message. This means that we have a third analogy of the type of text Scripture is when the links between its parts are cut: the poetic, in addition to the proverbial and technical.[97]

The identification of structures in Scripture that can store information, beyond what the Scriptural words say when taken as an uninterrupted flow, increases information potential. The need for this arises from the *difference* in the amount of detail required by the rabbinic reader on the one hand, and that offered by the words-in-co-text of Scripture on the other.[98] Any expectation of finding significance of this kind is not fixed in the text; it becomes fixed between the text and reader. Therefore the *resolve* to find

---

[92] Fluck, *Fachsprachen*, 48. See on the question of the *number* of segments also the second section of Ch. 13 below (text following n. 76).

[93] For literature, see n. 78 in Ch. 13.

[94] For a famous modern example see ' "Le chats" de Charles Baudelaire', by Jakobson and Lévi-Strauss. Cf. also Jakobson, 'Linguistics and Poetics'.

[95] These resources are listed in Ch. 14 below.

[96] Braude and Kapstein (trans.), *Pesikta de-Rab Kahana*, p. xliii, put it like this: 'The fourth category of norms takes every word, every phrase—in fact, every syllable and letter—of Scripture as a *self-contained* unit of divine radiance, shedding the light of its meaning around it and illuminating the sense of the verse or passage in which it occurs' (emphasis mine). Contrast with this Jakobson's maxim, 'No linguistic property of the verse design should be disregarded' ('Linguistics and Poetics', 365).

[97] In the case of the 'poetic' treatment, the rabbinic search for meaning remains oriented towards the type of information that can be *separated* from the text and turned into a contribution to the details of the life of Torah. It is compatible with denying Scripture any genuine poetic function (in the modern sense of the word). We shall return to the topic in Ch. 13.

[98] The level of detail is addressed by resources Topic2 and Topic5 defined in Ch. 5. My paper 'From Case to Case' addresses halakhic detail as a discourse phenomenon.

detailed information, once it has been established, cannot be undone by the text itself.[99] A text as long, internally diverse, and complex as the Hebrew Bible is very amenable to such a treatment. Its high degree of literary discreteness, its frequent repetitions, inconsistencies, and gaps, are taken by historical scholarship as traces of growth, accretion, and redaction.[100] But in rabbinic hermeneutics these simply join hands with a much more radical refraction of the text through its rabbinic division into segments.[101] It is therefore perhaps the expectation of high information density which informs the preference of rabbinic hermeneutics for the neutralization of co-text, and thus also for the division of Scripture into many small segments. To put it very crudely: 100 sentences, taken as redundantly complementing each other in the manner of ordinary textual coherence, speak perhaps only about ten or twenty different topics or sub-topics. But the same sentences, cut into many discrete units on various levels, may be able to speak about 500 different topics or sub-topics—if the separate perspectives are there to separate these topics. The unity of theme for any stretch of text disappears with the disappearance of the co-textual relationships; as I said, isolated segments are much more open with regard to their thematic and meaning possibilities than segments which are textually integrated. Rabbinic hermeneutics is free to locate meaning on levels both below that of the complete clause, or even complete word, and on the level above. And the licence to suspend co-textual influence means that there is no obligation to tie together the results from different levels for the same segment. In a large text like the Hebrew Bible this approach produces such a large quantity of potential points of information that the text, far from having too few topics to yield the amount of detail necessary for a fully determined life of Torah, becomes *inexhaustible*. Ultimately, this phenomenon is rooted in the fact that for the rabbinic reader the semiotic level on which meaning or information is encoded in Scripture is not determined in advance of the reading process (as, also, it is not for modern poetic texts).

While smaller units are often found, the segment-size of sentence seems privileged. There are good reasons for such a perception (whether on the part of the rabbis, or from the point of view of this study). The sentence is a plateau of independence for meaning and information; isolated words do not yet have a message.[102] Although the synthesis of message and meaning does not stop at the sentence (its meaning is further determined by the text

---

[99] Grice has shown that even in ordinary conversation the assumption of co-operation is so strong that certain distortions will rather be construed as indirect messages than as nonsense ('Logic and Conversation', 49 f.). For rabbinic hermeneutics, the co-operation of the divine partner is never in doubt (see my 'Scripture's Implicature', 194 ff.)—its theological name is revelation.

[100] For a different way to read them, see e.g. Sternberg, *The Poetics of Biblical Narrative*.

[101] Notwithstanding the fact that the rabbis treat contradictory biblical passages as ultimately consistent. See the DIFFERENCE resources in Ch. 10.

[102] For the linguistic view, see Bloomfield, *Language*, 170. I explore the link between sentence and segment in 'Scripture's Segments and Topicality', 107 ff.

in which it appears), the sentence is the only privileged intermediary point for arresting the process of synthesis between the isolated sound or letter on the one hand, and the full text within the setting of texts that make up a culture on the other. The sentence approximates in many cases the stable unit of information which we isolate as the Mishnaic Dictum (and which *balances* the biblical segment; see below). And it is also reflected in the general and rabbinic use of sentences as proverbs, and as self-contained declarations or proclamations with legal effect (see the resources discussed in Chapter 5). Both of these specifically hermeneutic uses of the sentence (as independent *utterances*) could have had an influence on shaping the hermeneutic habits of segmentation, in addition to the general mechanisms discussed here.

SEGMENT SELECTION, SEGMENT BOUNDARIES

In selecting one location in the Scriptural text from thousands of locations of similar size, and in determining the boundaries of that location, the rabbinic reader directs a focus on the text. This focus presupposes a guiding interest or concern. The selection and the concern belong together, even though we are separating them for analytical purposes. The same is true of the midrashic collections which present units of interpretation in the sequence of their Lemmas in Scripture (i.e. works of Midrash). They too select a Lemma, and therefore a topic, from the flow of the text. The midrashic units densely populate certain given areas of Scripture (e.g. Gen. 1),[103] while covering others only barely. Nevertheless, the impression is received that there is a running commentary and that the coverage is somehow total. But such exhaustive coverage is not possible, unless it is determined in advance which features or semiotic levels of a text can convey meaning. Do the words carry meaning? Does the choice of words matter, and their metaphorical or literal use? Do whole sentences carry meaning? How about the paragraphs in which they appear or the stories which they tell? Is there separate meaning conveyed by formal features of the writing: the way in which a narrative is told, the format of a poem or song, the repetition of linguistic structures at certain intervals, the metre or length of sentences, parallelism, and so on? Preliminary answers to these questions are given—for the modern reader—by information on genre, time and place of composition, intended audience, and author, to name but a few aspects. For the rabbinic reader the author of Scripture is divine, and that does indeed provide rabbinic hermeneutics with a dominant genre expectation for Scripture: a book of commandments, Law. And yet this identification of authorship does not narrow down the options for

---

[103] Alexander, 'Pre-emptive Exegesis', argues that the density of interpretations at the beginning of Genesis in BerR is meant to crowd out heterodox interpretations of the same text.

encoding meaning. On the contrary, it ultimately destroys all possibility of limiting the structures of meaning. Rabbinic interpretation does neglect some of the avenues of meaning named above, but it knows of others. There is, for example, the orthography of Scripture: is a word written *plene* or *defective*? Does it form an acrostic, unfolding into a whole phrase or sentence? Do the letters indicate meaning through their numerical value? Which language is it?[104] The list could be continued. If we take into view the maximal catalogue of questions which we know to be in principle admissible in rabbinic hermeneutics,[105] it becomes clear that no part of Scripture, and maybe no single verse in Scripture,[106] is ever treated exhaustively by the rabbis in the sense that it is discussed *from all these angles in turn*. This means that the midrashic compilations we possess do not come close to being total in their coverage of the meaning possibilities of their base text, according to rabbinic expectations. Whether they were meant to attempt total coverage, or to create its impression, is a different question.[107]

If the features of the text which can carry meaning are not determined in advance for the Mishnaic reader, then neither is the size and boundary of the Scriptural segments. The segmentation itself, or the focusing it expresses, must be guided by an interest, or the relevance of the text to the reader's concerns. This is why these reader concerns are inseparable even from the constitution of the hermeneutic question, let alone from its answer. However, they become *visible* to us only in the answer, in the Dictum or rabbinic proposition. Although we do not know how important the Dictum was in the 'real world', outside the rabbinic discourse, we know this: the concerns expressed in the Dicta were important enough to the rabbis to recognize and record recognition of their presence in Scripture. One way to express this very important if somewhat formal historical certainty is to say that these topics mattered in the universe of discourse[108] of the Mishnah. The manner in which that universe of discourse imposes a perspective on the Scriptural signs is the topic of the next three chapters.

There is one more question on segmentation that needs to be explored in a preparatory manner.[109] How do we know what the segment's boundaries actually are? The first answer is: by the extent of the wording quoted or used. But that is not enough; it is quite common to find that the quotation

---

[104] A biblical sign may occasionally be interpreted as the use of a Greek word, for example. Cf. Fraenkel, *Darkhey*, i. 115–18; Liebermann, *Hellenism in Jewish Palestine*, 51; Braude and Kapstein (trans.), *Pesikta de-Rab Kahana*, pp. xliv–xlv; Rosenblatt, *Interpretation*, 33. See also Ch. 14 below (resource Icon6).
[105] Even the shorter catalogue of Mishnaic resources is sufficient here.
[106] Not even Gen. 1:1 is likely to be an exception. See also n. 103 above.
[107] See the section on programmatic exposition in Ch. 4 below.
[108] For the use of this term in linguistics, see Lyons, *Introduction to Theoretical Linguistics*, 419; Lyons, *Semantics*, i. 157 f., 166; van Dijk, *Text and Context*, 26; Allwood *et al.* (*Logic in Linguistics*, 5) define it as: 'everything that is talked about in a certain text or a certain conversation'; see also ibid. 62: 'everything that we speak about in a certain context'.
[109] For the following, cf. my 'Scripture's Segments and Topicality', 97 f.

ends after the first half of the verse, while the Lemma is in the second.[110] Abbreviation signs such as וגו׳ (=וגומר) or וכו׳ (=וכוליה, both 'etc.') are commonplace in rabbinic texts. More importantly, the biblical quotations in rabbinic literature are particularly vulnerable to scribal intervention or transmission errors. Their textual shape (harmonizations in the light of the accepted biblical text), as well as their extent, is liable to be 'corrected' in the manuscripts; by the time we see a manuscript or a printed edition, the length of a given quotation may well have been abbreviated and expanded several times.[111] This is, of course, possible because the source of the quotation is known and the quotations themselves may be very familiar to copyists. But it does also mean that if there was ever an attempt to use the quotation as a *precise* indication of where the segment begins and ends, we cannot assume that it has reached us intact. There may even have been systematic revisions of quotations in some works of rabbinic literature. This, then, is not how we know the extent of the segment. The real answer is that we *construct* the segment when understanding which biblical Lemma the interpretation engages. At that point, when seeing which Lemma is being focused on, and how it is understood, we try to project that meaning back into the biblical co-text. If the new meaning can be built into the whole of the biblical sentence, that is, if the co-textual relationships can be adjusted to accommodate the meaning determined for the Lemma, then that will be the segment. If they only work in part of the sentence, and we have to abandon the rest, the segment will only extend that far. But since we cannot simply assume that the quotation actually *contains* the Lemma, how do we find out in the first place if it is there, or in the unquoted part of the verse? The answer is that we read the biblical text *in the light of the rabbinic formulation* which accompanies it. We look for a convergence of sense between the quotation and the Mishnaic statement or norm. If that convergence of sense can only be achieved by the unquoted part of a verse, or improved by it, then we know that the unquoted part of the verse defines the segment or forms part of it. The hermeneutic operation, and the boundaries of the segments, are constituted together. Unless we understand how a word or words from the biblical verse can have the meaning the *Mishnaic* formulation conveys, we do not know where the segment starts and ends. The segment is thus a construction of ourselves as readers of the rabbinic unit of interpretation.[112] In most cases, the quotation given will at least identify the verse (although there are some cases of ambiguity, as in **[4]** above). In most other cases, the quotation will furthermore be quite precise in giving the most important part of the verse, and often in instances of radical neutralization of co-text the quotation will contain the isolated

[110] Examples for this and similar cases are listed in Albeck, *Einführung*, 85 f.

[111] For the Mishnaic passages translated in this book I have often quoted a larger part of Scripture than all or most MSS. These parts are enclosed in square brackets.

[112] I shall explain this further in Ch. 14 below, with regard to resource Word2.

words and no more. Maybe this is so because the author of the original interpretation limited the quotation in that way, and it was preserved in the transmission. Just as likely, however, is that the precision is due to the competence of later copyists and editors in picking out the two or three operative words from a larger verse. Either way, they help us, up to a point, to construe our own convergence of sense between biblical and Mishnaic formulation.

Even in cases where the understanding achieved for the interpretation reveals that the segment is briefer or longer than indicated by the extent of the quotation, the *scale* of size does not usually change. The Scriptural segments required or allowed by the Mishnaic interpretation are rarely longer than a sentence, and are often shorter.[113] This also means that there is a quantitative *balance* between the Mishnaic formulation and the biblical segment. The Mishnaic statement (or Dictum, as it is called here) and the biblical segment (whose focused element is the Lemma) are of roughly matching size. If anything, the biblical quotation is shorter; for often the information contained in a *phrase* is reformulated in a whole Mishnaic sentence. What we do not find is a Mishnaic statement or norm consisting of one sentence, accompanied by a Scriptural quotation of twenty pages, or even half a page. And the reverse is also true: there seems to be no example of larger literary units of Mishnaic text linked hermeneutically to one biblical sentence (or even two). This is so despite the fact that, with regard to explicit thematic framework, the latter often represents the actual scale of relationships. The Mishnah will frequently deal with 'the same' subject-matter that occupies a handful of sentences in Scripture in as many pages. We also do not find a string of biblical sentences which, *as a unit*, is hermeneutically linked to a string of Mishnaic sentences, also taken as a unit.

This quantitative balance of Dictum and Lemma is actually a very conspicuous phenomenon, and points us in an unexpected direction. The individual Dictum is, on its own, as vague or ambiguous as the individual Scriptural segment. It receives its meaning from the whole configuration of Dicta, both in the surrounding Mishnaic text and further afield. It forms a consistent whole with other Dicta, and is parallel or analogical or even superordinate or subordinate to other Dicta. Could it be that, by way of this network of interrelated rabbinic propositions, Scripture also becomes a network of interrelated propositions? Does the atomistic hermeneutic linkage on the level of the individual sentence create a new coherence for Scripture, Scripture as a configuration of values and norms, not Scripture as a text? If so, the new coherence is as implicit for Scripture as it is for Mishnah. For the

---

[113] The occasional quotation of a *chain* of connected verses is a different phenomenon altogether. It will be explained in Ch. 12, and is represented by the *sigma* sign (Σ) in the hermeneutic profiles of our passages. If, however, occasionally some totally different segment size were intended by a unit of interpretation, would we necessarily notice? Are some of the interpretations we find difficult to understand of that type?

Mishnah does not articulate its underlying principles, it does not explain the manner in which all the different parts, whether thematically defined or in some other way, make a whole. In other words, the Mishnah's coherence as a configuration is left to interpretation; the readers and users of the Mishnah create that coherence, for example, by comparing and contrasting parts of the Mishnah which are not textual neighbours, and are not linked in any other manner in the Mishnah. And, insofar as the interpreters of the Mishnah believe that Scripture's coherence as a configuration of values and norms is congruent, or isomorphic, with that of the Mishnah, they will construe the Mishnah's coherence and Scripture's coherence together. That is to some extent what happens in post-Mishnaic rabbinic literature, I believe. In other words, the question of the wholeness of Scripture returns; the hermeneutics of neutralizing the co-text may have been embedded in a hermeneutics of undeclared relationships to the whole. A construction job quite different from the one performed in this study would be necessary to show that this could be the case, although it would have to take account of the relationships on the level of individual Dicta and Lemmata as explicated here. Such a job could probably also not restrict itself to the evidence available from the Mishnah, although it is difficult to see where exactly a new limit could be created among the works of rabbinic literature. The main problem, however, is to know where the historically plausible stops and harmonization in the service of tradition starts. Given sufficient interpretative ingenuity and no upper limit for the complexity of the explanations, it may well be possible to construct a coherent totality as rabbinic configuration which implies Scripture as a coherent configuration. But would that prove that rabbinic hermeneutics incorporates a constantly present picture of the conceptual integrity of Scripture while dissolving its textual integrity? Would that prove that there is a centre, or an organic network of shifting and flexible ties, which informs, directs, and limits the neutralization of co-text?[114] And is that a plausible picture of the gradual and collective emergence of an internally diversified and complex hermeneutic practice?

Be that as it may for the whole of the Mishnah and the whole of Scripture, there could well be certain parts of the hermeneutic discourse which provide a new implicit (thematic) integrity for Scripture far transcending the one-sentence segment. If so, this lies beyond the horizon of the present investigation.[115]

---

[114] As an assumption or theological claim, this position is expressed with superb conciseness by Emmanuel Levinas when he speaks of Midrash as 'in fact restoring the spirit of the whole to a purely "local" meaning, deepening and reinforcing it' (*Beyond the Verse*, 154). See n. 9 above for some other theoretical statements which privilege the whole, or the 'spirit', before the part.

[115] It is also likely that, for this question, the difference in types of biblical topic is important (narrative coherence versus juxtaposition of casuistic laws).

3

Quotes and Causes. The Imposition of a Perspective on Scripture

In presenting Scriptural wording as part of its normative discourse, the Mishnah does not usually make historical statements. Rather, it is concerned with the validity of a normative position. Ascribing to the rabbis the claim that a Scriptural proof text was the *origin* of a rabbinic position goes beyond the evidence afforded by the hermeneutic link. The fundamental hermeneutic move is an appropriation of Scriptural segments for the Mishnaic topical agenda. That appropriation can take the form of integrating Scriptural segments into a new textual environment which has a circumscribed, usually narrower, thematic (halakhic) identity. The biblical words take on a fresh topic, reference, syntactic function, or level of generality because of the perspective imposed on them by the new, Mishnaic, co-text in which they occur. This is particularly clear in, but not restricted to, cases where their meaning is reformulated with the help of specific Mishnaic terminology, or where the relationship of two Scriptural segments is organized around a Mishnaic pair of concepts.

The Mishnah, as was seen in the preceding chapter, imposes a segmentation on Scripture. At the same time, and as part of the same hermeneutic movement, it imposes a perspective. We know of this perspective because the text with which the Mishnah surrounds the Scriptural segment is always (by definition) different from, and often bears no resemblance to, the co-text of that segment in Scripture. This and the next chapter aim to provide a classification of the different ways in which the Mishnaic perspective manages the meaning of the words adopted from Scripture. We shall take these manifestations of perspective to be hermeneutic resources belonging to the TOPIC family. The following resources need to be distinguished in the first instance: the general thematic orientation of the discussion into which the Scriptural wording is placed, Topic1; the use of specifically rabbinic or Mishnaic expressions as companion terms in the explication of Scripture, Topic3; the tacit presupposition of a Mishnaic position known from elsewhere, Topic0; and the use of *pairs* of Mishnaic concepts for explaining the relationship of two Scriptural passages, Topic4. Before we start, however, we need to undermine a perspective often automatically supplied for rabbinic interpretation by the modern reader. There is a tendency in historical scholarship to interpret the quotation of a biblical segment, presented as the reason or warrant for a rabbinic statement, as a tacit claim that that segment was the historical 'cause' of that statement, or that the interpretation of that biblical quotation called forth the rabbinic position. To this tendency we must now turn.

EXEGESIS IS NOT GENESIS

The question of hermeneutics in the Mishnah is inextricably linked to the question of format and literary structure. Here a distinction must be assumed between the setting of the literary production of the Mishnah as an early expression of a basically mature rabbinic world, and the emergence or genesis of that rabbinic world. The origins of rabbinic Judaism are not directly available to our inspection in the Mishnah. This applies to passages which make reference to Scripture as much as to passages which do not. Units of interpretation cannot without further ado be translated into statements of the form: 'This biblical verse is the remembered historical origin of that norm/idea of rabbinic Judaism.' What happens if such translations become routine is that each unit of interpretation is viewed as a reliable or unreliable report on historical origins.[1] And the decision whether it is the one or the other can be reached by the modern historian—in the absence of other evidence, that is, in most cases—only by a judgement on the cogency of the individual rabbinic interpretation. Judging the cogency of interpretation, however, often involves an unacknowledged and thus uncontrolled projection of the scholars' modern standards of reading. The alternative, namely, an explicit standard of reading built up by systematic investigation of rabbinic interpretation, is not yet

---

[1] Here is a particularly succinct formulation of the two alternatives: 'Gelegentlich rufen solche Stellen den Eindruck hervor, daß versucht wurde, eine von allen oder von der Mehrheit anerkannte Halacha *nachträglich* mittels eines solchen Hinweises biblisch zu begründen . . . Es gibt jedoch auch Mischnastellen, in denen es anders zugeht und in denen die *Entwicklung* einer Halacha *aus* einem Bibelwort nachweisbar ist' (emphasis mine); taken from Boertien, 'Einige Bemerkungen zu Bibelzitaten in der Mischna', 73. Such statements are almost ubiquitous in the modern literature, underlying, for example, also the distinction between 'exegesis' and 'eisegesis' sometimes made (e.g. Alexander, 'Midrash', 457). See also Albeck, *Einführung*, 59 and 62 ff., 87–91. Albeck assumes that, where one finds what we here call the Mishnah's imposition of a perspective, the halakhic result was decided beforehand; but that is unwarranted. See further n. 33 below. Cf. also Fishbane, *Biblical Interpretation*, 274 f.; also Urbach, *The Halakhah*, 101–8 on Scriptural exposition as a source of law.

available.[2] We simply do not know what, for the rabbis, was the difference between a weak and a convincing interpretation. But it should make us suspicious that, according to our standard of historically contextualized meaning, *most* interpretations preserved in rabbinic literature are not cogent. And the equation of exegesis with genesis has other flaws. It assumes that a questionable interpretation cannot have been historically effective, or that a good one cannot have remained ineffectual—obviously unwarranted assumptions. Both the projection of modern ideas of interpretative cogency, and the assumption that cogency equals impact, have distorting effects in the historical construction.[3] And there are no clues available from the individual passage of interpretation. Attempting to guess from the format or appearance of an exegetical argument alone if a rabbinic idea was *originally* prompted by the Scriptural passage is quite hopeless, and that is why it usually involves scholars in uncontrollable judgements of cogency.[4] At the heart of the identification of interpretation with original influence, however, seems to be a misunderstanding of the nature of the rabbinic hermeneutic discourse. Units of Scripture, such as those found in the Mishnah, always present something like *warrants*, but by no means necessarily *origins* for the rabbinic Dicta connected with them. Even superficially, this is clear from the frequent appearance of Scriptural warrants on both sides of a Mishnaic dispute with mutually exclusive Dicta.[5] The historical origins of the rabbinic Dictum may or may not be linked to the verse as interpreted; but the reason we find it in the Mishnaic discourse is its *argument function*. Can we get to the historical influence behind the argument function? Sustained interpretation of Scripture is a defining moment of the historical construct 'rabbinic Judaism' for us. The one thing we know about it is that it was a culture committed to reading and construing as relevant the same text again and again—like some other post-

[2] It exists, of course, in the intuitive competence of many scholars in the field. The current study is meant to make a start at transforming such intuition into an explicit standard (with proper flexibility and distinction between documents and historical phases of rabbinic Judaism).

[3] Sanders, in his work on 'common Judaism' (*Judaism: Practice and Belief 63BCE–66CE*), proposes not to project the Mishnah or its exegetical material back into the pre-Mishnaic centuries, but he shares one of the assumptions of scholars for whom exegesis is a claim to historical origin. He subscribes to the belief that our idea of what Scripture says would have coincided readily with that of ancient interpreters, in particular the 'common' ones. As a consequence, he occasionally describes their religious practice, in fairly general terms at least, by the simple expedient of quoting a Scriptural (!) text (see e.g. 137, 152, 154).

[4] Scholars sometimes offer corroborating external evidence when doing this, but very often they do not. Even where such non-hermeneutic evidence is adduced, decisive weight tends to be given to the historian's ad hoc judgement on the cogency of the interpretation. Cf. the examples quoted in my 'Scripture's Segments and Topicality', 120f.

[5] See Pettit, *Shene'emar*, 88–146; cf. also my 'Delaying the Progress from Case to Case'. Albeck (*Einführung*, 58–67) makes much of the fact that certain Mishnaic disputes seem to stake a halakhic decision on a Scriptural interpretation. But the question is: who decides on the alternatives between which Scripture is taken to arbitrate? As a rule, Scripture is as heavily perspectivized in these disputes as in other Mishnaic interpretations. The parties tend to agree on the (often very specific) rabbinic articulation of the problem, even when it is not thematic in Scripture. See below and the next chapter.

biblical groups, only more so. In such a historical setting there is never a *tabula rasa* 'before' the text, and never a stable *status quo* 'after' the text, as if the text had suddenly become irrelevant. This goes both for the individual and the collective.[6] To sketch only one possible scenario, likely to be particularly relevant to the case of the norms of rabbinic Judaism: the discourse on Scriptural *warrants* and their explicitness may develop and increase long after the discourse on the substance of the norms has reached its peak. This is one model to explain the explosion of dedicated hermeneutics in the rabbinic literature *after* the Mishnah.

To show just how complex the historical reality might be which hides behind the rabbinic link of one of its norms or ideas with a Scriptural passage, it may be useful to produce a list of the possibilities. We shall use the phrase 'historically appropriate' in the following as shorthand for 'plausible co-textually integrated sense of Scripture for a historically trained modern scholarly reader', in a word, *our* plain sense of Scripture. Here are the various possibilities, spelled out for the formulation of a rabbinic notion which actually *depends* on Scripture in some way. We shall call the rabbinic notion the Dictum (D); the Scriptural passage to which it is linked, the Lemma (L).[7] We shall highlight the successive differences with the help of italics and bold print.

1. D came into being as repetition or reaffirmation of an idea contained in the historically *appropriate* meaning of L.
2. D came into being as repetition or reaffirmation of an idea contained in a historically *inappropriate* meaning of L.
3. D came into being as repetition or reaffirmation of an idea contained in a historically appropriate meaning of L *but is now linked to a historically inappropriate meaning of L* (or *vice versa*).
4. **Shifts from one L to another.** D came into being as a repetition or reaffirmation of an idea contained in a historically appropriate meaning of L1 *but is now linked to the historically appropriate meaning of L2*.
5. D came into being as a repetition or reaffirmation of an idea contained in a historically appropriate meaning of L1 *but is now linked to a historically inappropriate meaning of L2*.
6. D came into being as a repetition or reaffirmation of an idea contained in a historically *inappropriate* meaning of L1 *but is now linked to a historically inappropriate meaning of L2*.[8]

---

[6] Rereading the same book over generations can never be a repetition of an earlier reading event, and even one and the same person cannot reread the same book in exact repetition of an earlier reading. Important texts are in fact expected to *change* the reader (this historicity of reading becomes thematic in Gadamer's *Truth and Method*).

[7] I am simplifying matters in considering merely the case which requires only one Scriptural passage; some reading strategies involve of course two or more biblical segments.

[8] For this case, and perhaps also cases 4 and 5, there may be examples from the *literary* relationship between Mishnah and Sifra. Ronen Reichman, in a recent study, identifies potentially literary changes which resulted in a modification of the hermeneutic operation (i.e. an accidental change in

7. **Re-creation of interpretation.** D came into being as a repetition or reaffirmation of the idea contained in a historically appropriate meaning of L, *but this was forgotten; later, the coincidence of D and L was rediscovered and the two were exegetically linked.*

8. **No single L.** D came into being in dependence on a larger meaning structure in Scripture, but is now being linked to the historically appropriate/inappropriate meaning of the smaller segment containing L.

There is also, very importantly, the following possibility:

9. **Exegetical silence.** D came into being as repetition or reaffirmation of an idea contained in a historically appropriate or inappropriate meaning of L, *but is not linked to any L in the Mishnah.*[9]

This is only one group, and the simplest; it deals with verbalized rabbinic notions. Perhaps more relevant for real developments is a second group: D came into being as Scripture-*independent* formulation of a *practice* which originally started in direct response to an idea contained in L. In other words, we would have a rabbinic formulation which articulates a rabbinic *practice*; and that practice (but not its formulation) is linked in its origins somehow to the wording of L. All the above possibilities apply in this case also: that response shaping a practice could have been selecting a historically appropriate meaning of L, or an inappropriate one;[10] the independent formulation arising from that practice might now be tied hermeneutically to a different L altogether (whether appropriately or not). Again, we could have the case of the re-creation or rediscovery of a link, the absence of a link to a *single* Lemma, and the absence of any link in the Mishnah when historically speaking there was one. And although we are grossly simplifying matters already, we still have not exhausted even the main possibilities. For a link between D and L could be presented in the Mishnah while the rabbinic notion or rabbinic practice does not derive from Scripture at all. And here too we could find links to historically inappropriate meanings of L as much as to appropriate ones; the shift between Lemmata and the loss of a link and its rediscovery. We also have a new possibility: the rabbinic notion or practice could have an unbroken link to *pre*-Scriptural times, and its expression in D is historically speaking *parallel* to its expression in L.[11]

hermeneutics) approximately of the type formulated as number 6 (e.g. mHor 3:3). Literary dependency of two rabbinic documents is of course not the same as the historical dependency envisaged above.

[9] A further set of possibilities is captured by substituting 'idea presupposed' or 'idea implied' for 'idea contained' in the preceding cases and the following ones.

[10] Sometimes we find alternative ways to connect the same Dictum to the same Lemma in so-called parallels between distinct rabbinic documents (cf. Ch. 4, text to n. 43).

[11] See the very interesting example in Seeligmann, 'Voraussetzungen der Midraschexegese', 166 f. (on mPeah 5:6 and Prov. 22:28). On a larger scale, this idea was recently proposed by D. W. Halivni. In his view some of the rabbinic interpretations which neutralize the biblical co-text preserve the original biblical meaning, while the biblical text, through the 'sin of Israel', was allowed to

Under such circumstances too we could have the absence of any link, that is, a 'silence' which in this case has the *correct* historical implication, despite the availability (and post-Mishnaic use) of a suitable Lemma in Scripture. Among the cases articulating a practice, one further possibility is of special interest. The practice is not originally linked to the quoted Lemma (or any Scriptural Lemma), but its rabbinic *formulation* is contaminated by Scriptural categories or wording. For example, a practice surviving from a historical context in which Scripture was not all-dominating becomes *articulated* for the first time in a Scripture-quoting climate, and then linked hermeneutically to the L which influenced its formulation.

This is a pedantic list, even a tedious one; and it is far from exhaustive. But its possibilities must surely be intuitively available to scholars who wish to reconstruct biblical interpretation as historical influence. The list prepares a number of observations. First and foremost, it brings to the surface the fundamental ambiguity of the explicit or deliberate use of Scripture with regard to the question of historical origin. All these possibilities are in principle compatible with a Mishnaic Dictum being supported by the wording of a Scriptural quote. The ambiguity is no accident but, as we said before, due to the functionality of quotations in the Mishnaic discourse. The most common formula for the introduction of quotations is the expression 'for it is said' (שנאמר).[12] The anchor of this 'for' is in the present tense of the Mishnaic discourse, and it is in the present that Scripture speaks to the rabbinic reader.[13] 'For it is said' means: if you understand the Lemma properly, you have to accept the Dictum as valid. Without such a meaning, the 'for' has no function. It invites the reader to read the Lemma in the light of the Dictum, to allow the sense of Dictum and Lemma to converge. The alternative is to say that, despite the formula's surface meaning, the Dictum is *historically* connected to the Lemma. That would include the possibility that the link is *merely* historical, that is, that it carries no current conviction for the participants in the Mishnaic discourse. Most individual interpretation units in the Mishnah give no hint that an interpretation is reported for its historical interest rather than its contemporary relevance. But some seem to imply that the interpretation belongs to a time (or a group) different from the contemporaneous fellowship of rabbis included in the timeless present tense of Mishnaic discourse.[14] Even in such cases, we have nothing like a report on historical origins, as the following example shows.

be corrupted. This explanation depends on an acceptance of the divine origin of Torah and the reliability of rabbinic tradition (*Peshat and Derash*, 132 ff. and 153). This view too destroys the *hermeneutic dependency* of the rabbinic Dictum on the biblical Lemma; the midrashic interpretation has the status of a textual 'emendation' (p. 133), or substitutes for a textual emendation (p. 146 f.). And, in the very act of removing a critical historical stance, Halivni takes the aims of text-critical scholarship and rabbinic hermeneutics to coincide (see also n. 89 in Ch. 11 below).

[12] This term and other formulas are investigated in Ch. 12 below.

[13] See Goldberg, 'The Rabbinic View of Scripture', and cf. n. 30 below.

[14] See also Section 2 in Ch. 5, on the *delta* format (Δ).

[10] mPes 5:5[15]   Exod. 12:6

The passover offering was slaughtered [by the people] in three groups, for it is said, 'and the whole assembly of the congregation of Israel[16] shall slaughter it'— 'assembly' (קהל) and 'congregation' (עדה) and 'Israel'.

This passage is followed by a detailed account on how the three successive groups[17] actually went about killing the animals in the temple and interacting with the priests. The verse or its co-text mentions neither the temple (the setting is the Egyptian passover narrative) nor do they articulate explicitly any problem of sequence,[18] but the Mishnah does. The Mishnah links the verse to a Dictum on a temple practice, and the Dictum and the Lemma together function as the introduction to a report on this matter stretching over several *mishnayyot*. Let us assume[19] that the Mishnah means to ascribe the essential point of the interpretation to the temple authorities of pre-Mishnaic times, namely, something like this: the words 'assembly of the congregation of Israel' mean 'three groups'.[20] How are we to understand such a claim: did the priestly authorities organize the slaughter of the passover offering in three groups because they read the verse in the manner suggested? Or did they slaughter it in three groups because there was not enough room in the temple area to do it any other way—only afterwards looking for a passage in Scripture which could be understood to address the difficulty? Or did they encounter the problem, looked for a Scriptural verse addressing the difficulty, found this verse, and concluded from this verse that *three* groups was the answer? It is very plain that the interpretation unit itself does not answer such questions—even *if* we are ready to accept that it relates to the time of the origin of the problem and solution. In other words, the problems we have of deducing historical origins from hermeneutic links simply spring up again in the more distant past. The historical link becomes even more tenuous when we consider that there might never have been a practice corresponding to this Dictum. E. P. Sanders, in a detailed calculation, comes to the tentative conclusion that three groups would not have been sufficiently many for busy Second Temple times.[21] What, then, about the Scriptural proof? If the report is unhistorical, the Scriptural wording is the *only* reason given for deciding that there should have been (from the Mishnaic perspective) three groups. Was this meant to be the theoretical solution of a practical problem the rabbis remembered but with whose actual solution during the Second

---

[15] ΔC2C5R9T1T5.

[16] כל קהל עדת ישראל.

[17] Thereafter referred to as 'first group', 'second group', 'third group'—not *qahal, edah,* and *Israel*.

[18] The interpretation dissolves a syntactically integrated (i.e. simultaneous) structure into steps in a sequence; the resource here involved is Cotext2 (Ch. 13).

[19] Taking 'for it is said:' as meaning 'for they said, for it is said:'; which is by no means a necessary interpretation.

[20] On the distributive aspect of this operation, see Redundancy9 in Ch. 13 below.

[21] *Judaism: Practice and Belief 63BCE–66CE*, 136 f.

Temple they were unhappy? Or was the interpretation remembered by the rabbis as having been accepted by the temple authorities, who found themselves regrettably unable to implement it? There are plenty of possibilities here, and absolutely no help from the interpretation unit, which gives us nothing more than the *hermeneutic* link between the Dictum and the Lemma.[22] The interpretation unit gives a warrant for a rabbinic position, that is, the Scriptural wording is presented for what it may prove in the discourse of the Mishnah. Being grounded in the discourse on timelessly valid law and the arguments of the present, the answer to the question 'What warrant in Scripture?' effectively *masks* for us the answer to the question 'What historical origin in Scripture?'

Let us generalize the point. The environment in which the link to Scripture is now found is that of a discourse *different* from Scripture's own, one whose structures are no longer explicable with reference to any one passage of Scripture, including the specific passage of Scripture that is being quoted. The format in which these links are created in the Mishnaic text is clearly already conventional—it is a *format*, not the spontaneous expression of an exegetical idea, or a recollection of such a spontaneous event (see further in the next chapter).[23] We are not invited to be present at the birth of a rabbinic idea; we are not given that idea untouched by the ideas of the generations which accepted, transmitted, and used it. As for recollecting an earlier interpretation: recalling the first interpretation of a passage is quite different from recalling an event. The text itself remains present, but our interpretation of it never stands sufficiently still for its various phases and versions to be separately available to recall. And even if a fixed, articulated record was created at the very first time of reading (an extremely unlikely event both for an individual and a collective!)—what is the point of reporting it if its *current* validity as interpretation is not endorsed by the generation transmitting it? Is there anything less relevant than an interpretation that has been discarded? Will it not be replaced or improved upon, rather than repeated in its original form? Or will the original form, if preserved, not be reinterpreted in the light of the current context and requirements of persuasive discourse? Any interpretation which makes a contribution to an ongoing, current discourse (such as that

[22] Let us assume for a moment that 'genuine' interpretations point to historical influence. Since the interpretation in [10] is certainly far-fetched by the standards of historical reading, we shall not be surprised to discover that there never was such a practice. But then we are left with a report on a custom that never existed derived from an unconvincing reading of Scripture—and thus an apparently pointless Mishnaic text. Alternatively, the temple authorities accepted an unconvincing interpretation which imposed an obligation on them which they were unable to meet—again, why accept it in the first place? Thus, we are referred back to the *function* in the contemporary discourse of the Mishnah.

[23] It is also clear, from the homogeneity of the Mishnah's discourse style if nothing else, that earlier traditions were not in all cases presented by repeating an earlier fixed wording. This assessment, established very convincingly by Neusner, is confirmed broadly by units of interpretation. The 'present tense' of the discourse of the Mishnah does not seem to be interrupted much by the introduction of arguments from the past which had ceased to make sense to its participants.

of the Mishnah in its own time) will give primarily the contemporary view of the meaning of Scripture. If recollection occurs, it is incidental to the function of the interpretation unit in its current discourse setting. So, while one cannot exclude the possibility of finding actual or intended cases of remembered earlier interpretation, powerful reasons mitigate against the transmission of obsolete earlier interpretations for purely historical reasons,[24] and against the transmission of currently accepted earlier interpretations in their exact earlier formulation (if there was one). Any dogmatic and universal assumption along the lines of 'Since D is the valid interpretation of L, D must be as old as L' must of course be discounted, whether it was intended by the Mishnaic redactors or not.

Moreover, the large influence that Scripture can be assumed to have had in one way or another on the genesis of the Mishnaic world is not available to us in interpretation units any more directly than in other parts of the Mishnah.[25] We are inherently no closer to the historical process of influence in these passages than we are when reading a Mishnaic passage without any allusion to Scripture. The presence or absence of Scriptural wording is, among other things, a choice of *presentation* of discourse. The overall scarcity in the Mishnah of explicit Scriptural references could not otherwise be explained, unless one wants to argue that only those Mishnaic passages which employ Scriptural wording are in their substance influenced by Scripture. It is not the function of Scriptural interpretation in the Mishnah to preserve the points of original and formative contact, nor the nature of that contact. Taken in a general manner, this is not so unusual. Among the abstract parallels that may further an understanding of this phenomenon is the distinction, in the theory of sciences, between the 'context of discovery' and the 'context of justification',[26] also found in jurisprudence.[27] Another structural similarity inviting comparison is E. P. Sanders' classification of criteria of membership in the early Christian church according to 'getting in' and 'staying in'.[28]

---

[24] There are many other potential reasons for presenting earlier positions with which one disagrees; polemics is one of them. Any pair of mutually exclusive interpretations belong in this group, as well as reports on priestly interpretations 'to their own advantage', as found in mSheq 1:4.

[25] It is therefore quite consistent to try to *improve* both on the quality and on the quantity of rabbinic links to Scripture when investigating the historical influence of Scripture on the formation of rabbinic ideas, as does e.g. Maccoby, 'Corpse and Leper'.

[26] See e.g. Patzig, *Tatsachen, Normen, Sätze*, 94.

[27] See e.g. Jackson, *Making Sense in Jurisprudence*, ch. 9, dealing with the distinction between legal decision and legal justification.

[28] Cf. his *Paul, the Law, and the Jewish People* (e.g. pp. ix, 114, 143). On the (socio-) linguistic construction of 'membership', see esp. Sacks, *Lectures on Conversation*. In the context of Paul's theology Sanders also speaks of 'the solution as preceding the problem' (*Paul and Palestinian Judaism*, e.g. 442 ff.), also a suggestive formulation from the angle of hermeneutics.

IMPOSING ON SCRIPTURE A PERSPECTIVE, SURROUNDING IT WITH NEW CO-TEXT

It follows in a sense from the methodical framework favoured in this study that the text which *surrounds* Scriptural wording in the Mishnah is the Mishnah's in a privileged sense, not Scripture's. This is true in particular where Scriptural words are directly embedded in the Mishnaic expression. But it also holds where the Mishnah provides a dedicated reformulation of a Scriptural quotation.[29] The Mishnah's words make sense in the first instance to the participants of the discourse represented in the Mishnah; their meaning and connotation is rooted in the Mishnaic world; their consequences, practical or conceptual, are consequences in the world of the Mishnah. In other words, the process of *updating* Scripture's meaning is assumed here to be pervasive and taking priority—at least methodologically speaking.[30] Even where the Mishnah uses words that Scripture also uses, it does not simply *repeat* Scripture's meaning, because it cannot repeat Scripture's utterance. The utterance in this sense is defined as context-sensitive in its meaning, and the utterance collection 'Mishnah' belongs in a different context from the utterance collection 'Scripture'. The Scriptural words, repeated in the Mishnah's voice, have their Mishnaic connotations and consequences, not their Scriptural ones. The meaning of all the words the Mishnah employs (including the technical ones; see below) is defined by the conceptual configuration of rabbinic Judaism (available to us only through the textual configurations of the Mishnah and other rabbinic works), not by the conceptual configuration 'Hebrew Bible', or 'Pentateuch'. It is not that Scripture had no influence on the Mishnaic configuration or its terms; but the Mishnaic configuration retains priority for finding out what the Mishnah means when it tells us, in its own terms, what Scripture means.[31]

---

[29] The distinction ('expressive use'/π *versus* 'midrashic unit') is explained in detail in the next chapter.

[30] For the emphasis on updating in rabbinic reading, see Bloch, 'Midrash' (esp. 32 f.); Goldin, *The Song at the Sea*, 13 ff. ('The Past made Present and Immediate') and *passim*; see also the summary in Porton, 'Defining Midrash', 59 f. Cf. n. 13 above. I see some problems in making 'updating' a criterion for defining 'midrash'. Updating is probably the rule, not the exception, in reading (see Ch. 1 above), so it is not distinctive enough. Also, 'updating' is a circular concept as long as we have no external evidence for reader concerns. The greater the extent to which 'updated relevance' becomes a methodological assumption on our side (because almost all reading, and midrashic reading in particular, is like that), the more circular it becomes to say of any one concrete theme: since the rabbis found this particular meaning in Scripture, this theme or issue must have mattered to them; therefore, this tells us something about the rabbinic world. It does tell us something, but maybe more about the rabbinic universe of discourse than about the rabbinic social, economic, or political 'realities'. The relationship between extra-linguistic realities and interpretations may well be different from one passage to the next.

[31] The approach here taken leads to ultimate results very similar to those formulated by Neusner in his general summary of the relationship of Scripture and Mishnah: 'once people had chosen a subject, they knew full well how to develop their ideas about that subject by examining and reflecting upon relevant verses of Scripture. But what dicated the choice of subject awaiting amplification

The words with which the Mishnah explains or surrounds the words of Scripture are thus our main evidence for determining what meaning the Mishnah finds in a biblical passage. The Mishnah gives the Scriptural text a thematic perspective, effectively replacing the original co-text in Scripture with a new, Mishnaic one. Why need we say that this new co-text also amounts to a new perspective? Because of the contrast of thematic arrangements and agendas, taken together with the division of Scripture into segments. This combination ultimately guarantees that a fresh perspective is imposed. How does this imposition of a fresh perspective become visible to us *in concreto*—apart from being the consequence of certain abstract and axiomatic features of our approach? It becomes visible *to us* mostly by its distance from the historically appropriate context and perspective of the Scriptural passage. Mishnaic perspective is most conspicuous when it presupposes that the biblical co-text is neutralized (Cotext1; see preceding chapter), that is, when it radically alters the topic or referent of a Scriptural word from what its textual setting suggests to us. Thus our sample passage [1] seems to us to import the topic of the Sabbath limits. A very similar redefinition of the Scriptural topic in terms of the halakhah of the Shabbat can be found in mShab 9:6, where the prohibition against retaining banned objects from the apostate city (Deut. 13:18) is transposed into a prohibition to carry any quantity of idols on the Sabbath. But such are merely the conspicuous cases. There are many instances where the Mishnah remains within the general topic of a Scriptural passage, and yet imposes a very specific perspective. In such cases, the clearest way for us to characterize the perspective is to say that Mishnah reads the Scriptural passage as an answer to a question which does not lie on the same level of generality, but is more specific or (less commonly) more general. The level of generality chosen by the Mishnah is different from the level favoured by the biblical co-text, but regular grammatical relationships are not suspended by the Mishnaic choice. And there are other cases still where the Mishnah seems to move wholly with the flow of the larger Scriptural environment. This we can now interpret as another type of imposed perspective, namely, as the Mishnaic affirmation and adoption of a perspective that happens to be the same as that of the Scriptural co-text (at least the immediate co-text). The perspectives embodied in the Scriptural co-text provide some of the options available to the rabbinic reader for choosing a perspective and thus narrowing down the meaning of the Lemma. We can say that the co-text is the text's self-selected thematic or narrative perspective for a given Scriptural segment. The perspective imposed by the Mishnah's reader-concerns on the one hand, and the Lemma's own co-text on the other, are functionally equivalent in narrowing down the meaning range (or referents) of terms appearing in the segment. Where Mishnaic perspective

and expansion was hardly a necessary or ineluctable demand of Scripture' (*Judaism. The Evidence of the Mishnah*, 168; see also 170).

and original co-textual perspective coincide, we do not notice any perspectivization at all. And yet, such an imposition of a perspective is present: it consists in the Mishnah's decision to *allow* the biblical co-text to narrow down the meaning. In rare cases this, to us, is indistinguishable—in particular in aggadic exegesis—from reading Scripture in a historical, or philological perspective. I am not aware of an instance of such apparent philology in the Mishnah, but it is certainly not wholly absent from the classical midrashic corpus (which in any case comprises divergent styles of interpretation).

MANIFESTATIONS OF PERSPECTIVIZATION

We shall now discuss various manifestations of the imposition of a perspective. We start with cases where Mishnaic words surrounding the biblical words indicate that the topic as a whole or its level of generality is imposed on the Lemma against a measure of resistance or indifference in its co-text (Topic1). We shall then look at cases where the Mishnaic words accompanying Scripture are terminological or technical in some sense, thus marking their meaning as the Mishnah's own in an overt manner (Topic3, Topic3.1).[32] We shall conclude with an examination of Mishnaic concept *pairs* in their role of explaining and relating to each other two separate Scriptural Lemmas. Further phenomena of perspectivization are discussed in the next chapter.

Topic1: Providing a perspective which re-topicalizes, or limits the meaning choices for, a biblical expression or clause. In providing a thematic orientation, or in integrating the biblical expression/clause into a specific place in the Mishnaic discourse, the Mishnah takes over the role of the original biblical co-text.

As will be clear by now, I view as methodologically naive attempts to separate, say, 'pure' exegesis from 'applied' exegesis for single rabbinic passages on the basis of ad hoc criteria. My concept of 'perspective', as embodied in the TOPIC resources, is of course relevant to such a distinction. Yet, it is conceived along different lines, in two fundamental respects. (a) It assumes that most if not all interpretations contain a TOPIC element (therefore, that it cannot be used as a criterion for grouping interpretations), and that this is acceptable *in principle* in rabbinic hermeneutics. (b) It rejects the assumption implicit in at least some of the secondary literature that we can

---

[32] Fraenkel devotes ch. 4 of his *Darkhey* to the interface between the 'world view' of the rabbis and their reading of Scripture (i. 67 ff.). For a nuanced account of our problem in terms of Gadamer's 'fusion of horizons', see now Reichman's 'Zur Analyse des Applikationsmoments im talmudischen Diskurs'. (Reichman is concerned with the way the Gemara reads the Mishnah, on which see n. 84 in the next chapter.)

distinguish instances of 'pure' exegesis (also called 'genuine' exegesis) merely by their results or the format in which they are presented.[33] We can see resource Topic1 at work in a number of sample passages already quoted, among them case **[10]**. In passage **[10]** the Mishnah treats the biblical verse as if it was meant to answer the following question: did all the people present in the temple area slaughter the passover lamb at one and the same time? No expression of this topic can be found in the quotation or its biblical co-text.

Mishnaic interpretation determines both semantic and pragmatic meaning through the imposition of a thematic perspective. For this, the following two passages are a useful illustration. They interpret the same Lemma (*davar*) in the same semantic sense ('word'), which is not the sense privileged by the co-text ('matter'). And yet the *perspectives* are different.

[11] mMak 2:5 II (2)[34]   Deut 19:4

And they give him [the manslayer] two disciples of the sages, so that if he [the avenger] attempts to slay him on the way, they may talk to him [the avenger]. R. Meir says: He [the manslayer] also may speak for himself, for it is said, 'This is the matter/word (דבר) of the manslayer'.

[12] mMak 2:8 = mShebi 10:8 II (2)[35]   Deut 19:4

Similarly, the manslayer who is exiled to his city of refuge: If the men of the city wish to honour him, he needs to say to them: I am a manslayer. If they then say to him: Nevertheless [we wish to honour you],[36] he may accept it from them, as it says, 'And this is the matter/word of the manslayer'.

The clause 'This is the word of the manslayer' has—in the biblical co-text—the function to introduce the *topic* of the manslayer (after the topic of the cities of refuge). דבר ('thing', 'matter', 'word') here has the sense of 'subject-matter'; RSV translates 'provision', JPS 'case'. But in both passages, the Mishnah takes דבר in another sense, which is also linked to this word, namely that of (spoken) 'word'.[37] If דבר is something like 'word', then the

---

[33] Cf. my 'Scripture's Segments and Topicality', 120 ff., n. 68. For the various positions synthesized above see Vermes, 'Bible and Midrash'; Alexander, 'Midrash', 457 ('eisegesis'); Halivni, *Peshat and Derash* ('reading in'). L. Schiffman discerns 'contrived' derivations of rabbinic halakhah from the biblical text (*Halakhah at Qumran*, 17), placing them into contrast with genuine derivation. For him exegesis could have 'conditioned the law of the sect' (*Halakhah*, 9). But the claim that Qumran law 'represents a certain understanding of Scripture' (represents it presumably to *us*) is very different from seeing a certain understanding of Scripture as 'conditioning', creating, or causing Qumran law. Confusing the two produces a false dichotomy between 'actual origins of law' and 'later attempts to give support to already existing practices' (p. 17). Ch. 3 of *Halakhah at Qumran* repeatedly transposes exegetical links into—backdated—historical origins. Similar to the word *peshat*, the availability of a rabbinic term *asmakhta* ('biblical support') has helped to cement a flawed conceptual foundation in modern scholarship, which simply takes it to indicate an exhaustive division of rabbinic hermeneutics into contrived and natural.   [34] •¶C5.2S4T2T3W1.

[35] C5.2T1T2W1.

[36] Krauß, *Sanhedrin-Makkot* (pp. 351, 348) points to the possibility of a high priest being the manslayer (making it plausible that the city would honour him); cf. mMak 2:7.

[37] This choice between semantic alternatives (Word1) is explained in Ch. 14, in connection with mShebi 10:8 I (2) **[132]**.

whole phrase comes to refer to an act of speaking on the part of the manslayer. So far, the hermeneutic choices in [11] and [12] are very similar. But the actual utterance envisaged under 'word', and the situation in which it arises, is totally different in the two cases.[38] In [11] mMak 2:5, the manslayer is speaking to his pursuer, presumably in order to warn him of the consequences of killing him (cf. tMak 3:5, ed. Zuckermandel, 440; bMak 10b). It is possible that the speech here envisaged, even in Meir's opinion, is a technical 'warning' to the person about to commit a crime, halakhically necessary for later conviction;[39] the presence of two skilled witnesses points in that direction.[40] In any case, the Scriptural 'speaking' becomes embedded in a specific theme of interest to the Mishnah at this point, but not to Scripture. The same goes for [12] mMak 2:8 (which actually belongs in the co-text of mSheb 10:8).[41] But here the manslayer's speaking is an *obligation* on his part and consists of full disclosure to the inhabitants of the city of his status as manslayer. Thus the actual interpretation of דבר in the sense 'word', chosen, as we said, despite the fact that the sense 'subject-matter' is privileged by the biblical co-text, is common to both of these passages, and so is the overall halakhic theme 'norms linked to the manslayer'. But the speech act taken to be conveyed by Scripture's employment of דבר is wholly distinct: different words, uttered in different situations, with different effect. The topical *relevance* of this דבר to the Mishnah diverges between the two interpretations. As a consequence, the biblical דבר occupies two different locations in the Mishnaic grid of halakhic themes mapped out by the larger theme 'manslayer'. This illustrates very clearly the power of perspective for determining the impact and meaning, including pragmatic meaning, of a Scriptural quotation. It also shows that determining the thematic contribution to the Mishnaic discourse is foundational for the whole hermeneutic operation, although it is of course circumscribed by what the biblical words can actually convey. Everything else, such as semantic adjustments, the extent and degree of neutralization of co-text, and so on, follows from this fundamental orientation in the subject-matter. There seems to be at least one metalinguistic maxim referred to in rabbinic literature (outside the Mishnah) which captures important elements of the imposition of perspective, or the power to re-topicalize. It reads: 'If it has no bearing on its own subject, apply it elsewhere.'[42]

---

[38] If the interpretation suggested by Goldschmidt of a passage in bMak 10b is correct, this fact becomes thematic in the Gemara. See Goldschmidt, *Der Babylonische Talmud*, ix. 184, n. 118.

[39] Whether the avenger who kills a manslayer on his way to the city of refuge is guilty of death is a question raised in bMak 10b.

[40] However, Meir's opinion is usually understood to say that, since the manslayer's speech is mentioned in Scripture, no Sages are to accompany him. In that case, the speech is of the nature of persuasion.

[41] Cf. Krauß, *Sanhedrin-Makkot*, 350.

[42] Halivni's translation (*Peshat and Derash*, 61). The maxim is found repeatedly in Sifra and other midrashic works. As found in an example in Mekhilta Ishmael Pisha 18 (ed. Lauterbach, i. 162), the form of words is: . . . 2 תנהו ענין (לנופף) ו ענין אינו אם.

Often the new Mishnaic perspective is manifest in the use of a technical rabbinic term in connection with the biblical quotation. In the following interpretation, the biblical topic is taken to be the third section of the *Shema'* (called 'Going forth from Egypt'), a concept of rabbinic, not Scriptural, discourse:

[13] mBer 1:5 I (2)[43]   Deut. 16:3

'Going forth from Egypt'[44] is mentioned [lit. remembered] [also] at night. R. Eleazar ben Azariah said: Behold, I am now like one who is seventy years old and I have not succeeded [in demonstrating] why 'Going forth from Egypt' should be recited at night until Ben Zoma expounded it: For it is said, 'That you may remember the day of your going forth from the land of Egypt all the days of your life.' 'the days of your life'—the days; 'all the days of your life'—[including] the nights.

The biblical verse and co-text know nothing of the third part of the *Shema'*, or of the fringes (the topic of that part of the *Shema'*). Instead, the clause is found in the context of Passover and is surrounded by references to the seven days of unleavened bread.[45] In determining the actual topic of the clause, the rabbinic reader introduces a non-biblical concept, the (third part of the) *Shema'*, which is of systematic importance in the Mishnaic discourse at this point, dealing with obligations related to the *Shema'*.[46]

The word *Shema'* forms part of the vocabulary of the Mishnaic discourse which is established as having a standard, in parts even narrowly technical, meaning. Items from that vocabulary are recognized mostly by their recurrence in technical usage; sometimes they are even subject to a definition elsewhere in the discourse of the Mishnah.[47] The meaning of items from that vocabulary is determined by their routine use in non-exegetical contexts, or their repeated use in exegetical contexts in the Mishnah. This is particularly clear in cases where they embody concepts that are non-Scriptural as here (although the *word* may well also occur in Scripture). Here is an attempt at pinning down the effect of such vocabulary[48] when used as the new co-text for Scriptural segments:

---

[43] ®•¶C1D2≈L1T1T3×2 T9W1×2.

[44] i.e. the third section of the *Shema'*, Num. 15:37–41.

[45] The tension or redundancy between these seven *days* and 'all the *days* of your life' may have been taken to 'free' the latter expression for a topic (recitation of the *Shema'*) which is foreign to the Scriptural passage. See Ch. 2 (text following note 33).

[46] Use is furthermore made of a *double entendre* for the word 'remember', meaning on the one hand 'recall' (in the biblical passage) and on the other (in later Hebrew and in the Dictum) 'reciting' (combining Word1-Topic3, see first section of Ch. 14). There is even an overlap between the phrase 'Going forth from Egypt' as the name of a part of the *Shema'*, and its appearance—albeit linked to 'day'—in the Lemma.

[47] On definitions for items of Mishnaic vocabulary which are also Scriptural, see Ch. 4 below (resource Topic8).

[48] M. Kadushin has emphasized the terminological status and significance of a number of key terms in rabbinic literature, in particular insofar as they give expression to 'values' (see his *Organic Thinking* and *The Rabbinic Mind*).

Topic3: Explication of a Scriptural expression by way of a Mishnaic companion term whose meaning is specific, standardized, or defined by its recurrent use or interdependence with other terms in the Mishnaic discourse.

Typical for the effect of a transposition of what Scripture says in a more defined Mishnaic terminology is the following passage. In it, biblical expressions ('good–bad') are furnished with Topic3 companion terms by the Mishnah; thus, the message is reduplicated and, in the process, re-created.

[14] mTem 1:2 I (2)[49]   Lev. 27:10

They may substitute cattle for small cattle, and small cattle for cattle, sheep for goats and goats for sheep, males for females and females for males, unblemished [animals] for blemished ones and blemished ones for unblemished ones, for it is said, 'He shall not alter it nor change it, a good for a bad [or a bad for a good]'. Which is 'a good for a bad'? Blemished ones whose consecration preceded their blemish.

Two terms with a general or vague meaning ('good'/'bad') are transposed into precise technical language, 'blemished'(בעל מום)/'unblemished'(תם), anchored in the Mishnaic discourse on cultic suitability of animals. The cotext of Scripture is clearly respected, and the thematic framework has not changed.[50] The subtle difference between speaking of 'good' animals as opposed to 'unblemished' ones marks the boundary between the discourse of Scripture and the discourse of the Mishnah. In the discourse of the Mishnah there is a strong interest in further differentiating the goodness and badness of things into the more detailed category of halakhic goodness or badness in which they might belong, and that halakhic category also standardizes the meaning of the terms. And what Scripture says is made to fit these categories or shown to fit them. It is not simply that ambiguity has been removed and that the Mishnaic terms are narrower in their meaning than the Scriptural ones; the 'good–bad' difference has been projected onto a whole plane of interrelated terms and halakhic concepts, implying part of the Mishnaic discourse on cultic suitability and beyond.

The expression 'evil/good inclination' in the following midrashic unit provides another example of a Topic3 companion term:

[15] = [82a] = [114a] mBer 9:5 I (9)[51]   Deut. 6:5

Man is obliged to perform blessings over evil just as he performs blessings over good, as it is said, 'And you shall love the Lord your God with all your heart and with all your soul and with all your might'. 'With all you heart'—with your two inclinations, with the good inclination and with the evil inclination; 'and with all

---

[49] L3R4.4?T3(blemished, etc.).

[50] While the Mishnah also manages to allocate a function to the constellation 'good for bad'. The resource involved (Topic2), is explained in the next chapter.

[51] ΩL1O6T3(two inclinations).

your soul'—even if he takes away your soul; 'and with all your might'—with all your wealth.

Concentrating on the interpretation of 'all your heart', we can see that the rabbinic concept pair 'evil inclination–good inclination'[52] is used to put into perspective the idea of a 'whole' heart, that is, to articulate the parts which make up a heart whose wholeness is stressed (Logic1).[53] This stands in the context of discussing the obligation to pronounce blessings over things evil as well as good. The idea of the two inclinations is current in rabbinic discourse, not in Scripture, and there is no trace of it in the biblical co-text.

[16] mArak 9:3 II (2)[54]   Lev. 25:30

The person selling a house from the houses of a walled city, behold this one may redeem it at once, or may redeem it throughout all the twelve months. Behold, this is like a kind of usury, but it is not [really] usury. If the seller dies, his son may redeem it. If the buyer dies, he may redeem it from the hand of his son. And he only counts the year from the time when he sold it to him, as it is said, 'Until the completion for him of a full (תמימה) year'. And when it says 'full' [year], this is to include an intercalated month.

The concept of the extra month in the year is a standard element of the Mishnaic discourse on the calendar; it is here used as a Topic3 companion term to the biblical 'full year', endowing that term with a technical meaning whose thematic orientation is not available from the quotation or its biblical co-text.

Where the Mishnaic term is a word different from the biblical Lemma, as in cases **[14]** to **[16]**, there is no problem about locating the hermeneutic mechanism. But in some cases the Lemma and the Mishnaic companion term are identical. In such interpretations we find an equivocation of two different concepts represented by the same word, and despite the apparent identity of terms, the imposition of a perspective is as resolute as when the Mishnaic term is conspicuously different from the biblical one. Consider the meaning of 'Torah' in this passage:

[17] mQid 4:14 IV (4)[55]   Gen. 26:5

And thus you find with our father Abraham, that he fulfilled the (whole) Torah before it was given, as it is said, 'Because Abraham listened to my voice and kept my charge: my commandments, my statutes, and my *torot*'.

The emphatic expression 'whole Torah' (את כל התורה כלה)[56] in the Dictum

---

[52] On the concept of the יצר (inclination), see Schechter, *Aspects of Rabbinic Theology*, ch. 15 (pp. 242–63); for the idea of a *plurality* of hearts, see 257. Urbach attempts to harmonize the scattered testimonies to this concept in the framework of a rabbinic anthropology in *The Sages*, 471–83 ('coined by the Sages', 471); cf. Maier, *Geschichte der jüdischen Religion*, 152 f.

[53] More on this treatment of כל is found in Ch. 9 below.

[54] O8(full)T3.

[55] Ω(•)(O1.4)R4.4T0T1T3(Torah)W1(*torah*).

[56] The text of MS Kaufmann, however, only has 'fulfilled the Torah', as indicated by the round brackets. It also has 'came into the world', instead of 'was given'.

almost certainly means the Sinaitic revelation of the commandments in their—rabbinically—complete form, that is, supplemented by the oral tradition. In the opening section of this *mishnah* (not translated here) the term Torah is used for what is to be taught to the next generation in preference to all crafts.[57] In a parallel text in the Tosefta (tQid 5:21) the expression 'Torah' is first used in the Dictum and afterwards paraphrased as 'the words of Torah and the words of scribes'. This concept of Torah has its specific use and definition in the Mishnaic (and wider rabbinic) world, not in Scripture's universe of discourse.[58] In other words, the biblical 'Torah' is given a very specific transposition and perspective by identification with the Mishnaic 'Torah'. Since the same term is used, the role of the biblical co-text may seem less important (and the identification of senses may even look historically appropriate); but it is still that co-text, and the larger historical context, not the word itself, which fully determines the specific meaning in a given utterance.[59] In fact, the Mishnah treats meaning nuances which belong to different 'stages' of Hebrew (or its context of use) as simultaneously available for interpretation. This means that the rabbinic idea of 'Torah' is treated as one of the semantic nuances presently contained in the biblical word 'Torah', to be accessed by the reader where appropriate.[60] As a hermeneutic procedure, this is in principle no different from selecting one meaning from the full semantic range of a biblical word (the range being defined roughly as a modern dictionary of biblical Hebrew would define it).[61]

Another very important function of Mishnaic terminology is to express a contrast between what Scripture says and what Scripture might have said but did not, and therefore excludes. Where this happens, the Mishnaic contrast terms identify the precise place of the biblical phrase in the network of *Mishnaic* topics. I shall address the pertinent resources of OPPOSITION in Chapter 11.[62] Here is just one example, which shows how the Topic3 terms establish the halakhic paradigm[63] which ties Scripture's words into the Mishnaic discourse.

---

[57] 'R. Nehorai says: I would set aside all the crafts in the world and teach my son only Torah . . . when a man falls into sickness or old age, or troubles and cannot engage in his work, behold, he dies of hunger. But with the Torah it is not so; for it guards him from all evil while he is young, and in old age it grants him a future and a hope.' This is followed by Scriptural quotations leading up to passage [17], which concludes the whole tractate (and is missing in some texts of the Mishnah, e.g. in Maimonides' text, but not in Kaufmann).

[58] Cf. Neusner, *Torah. From Scroll to Symbol in Formative Judaism*, esp. 31 ff. Cf. also Schäfer, *Studien zur Geschichte und Theologie*, 153–97.

[59] Such a treatment of the term 'Torah' is also found in mQin 3:6 II (2), ad Job 12:12.

[60] This is not a question of anachronism. Rather, all of Scripture's *contemporary* meaning possibilities are taken to be intended by the divine author for each successive period of reading. The results are not trivial equations of meaning, i.e. not a philological *faux pas*.

[61] For this resource (Word1), see Ch. 14 (and cf. n. 21 there).

[62] The OPPOSITION resources do not need to involve specifically Mishnaic terminology; thus, in passage [13] 'night' is taken to be excluded by 'day'.

[63] Cf. my 'Stressing Scripture's Words', 199–201. This idea I now define, in its hermeneutic function, as a special type of perspectivization. More on paradigms in Ch. 11.

[18] = [118] mBQ 4:3 II (4)[64]   Exod. 21:35

The ox of an Israelite which gores that of the sanctuary, or that of the sanctuary which gores the ox of an Israelite[65]—[the owner] is not liable, for it is said, 'the ox of his neighbour'—and not the ox of the sanctuary (של הקדש).

The category 'of the sanctuary' is anchored in the Mishnaic discourse on the special status of temple property. To say that the use of the word 'neighbour' *excludes* this category is to place the Scriptural phrase into the same context or perspective (the next sentence of the Mishnah establishes another contrast, with the term 'non-Jew'). Even while the Mishnaic category is declared to be not covered by the Scriptural text, that text is placed on the same level of specificity as the Mishnaic term. Scripture is taken to include or to exclude, but not to be indifferent to or incompatible with this Mishnaic topic. Its meaning is identified as one item from a list, a paradigm, thereby excluding the other or others;[66] but the paradigm is provided by Mishnaic concerns, and is not visible in the Scriptural quotation or its textual setting. Even while saying what Scripture does *not* say, the interpretation establishes the topical framework or perspective in which Scripture is made to provide its information.[67]

Very similar to the terminology presupposing specifically Mishnaic concerns or concepts are explicit maxims, which can be used to manage the transition from the words of Scripture to the words of the Mishnah.

Topic3.1: Explication of a Scriptural expression by way of an express rabbinic maxim whose validity is treated as unproblematic.[68]

An example is afforded by the Mishnaic discussion of the number of judges required to perform the rite of breaking the heifer's neck:

[19] = [121a] mSot 9:1 II (2)[69]   Deut. 21:1

(The [ritual concerning the] heifer whose neck is broken [is performed] in the holy tongue, as it is said, 'If a slain person is found in the ground . . . and your elders and judges shall come forth [and measure towards the cities which surround the slain person] . . .') Three [judges] from the great *Bet Din* (court) which was in Jerusalem used to come forth. R. Yehudah says: Five, for it is said,[70] 'your elders'—two; 'and your judges'—[another] two; and no *Bet Din* is even-numbered, [so] they add to them one more.

---

[64] ®O1T2T3.

[65] Some texts have here the word 'commoner' (הדיוט) instead of 'Israelite', making explicit a precise legal implication for the word 'Israelite'; see n. 160 in Ch. 13.

[66] Neusner's work on the Mishnaic lists is summarized in 'The Mishnah's Generative Mode of Thought: *Listenwissenschaft* and Analogical-Contrastive Reasoning'. He is correct in speaking of list items as pointing 'in one direction and not in another' (p. 317).

[67] A similar effect can be achieved by spelling out what is *included* by a biblical term; see Ch. 9 below.

[68] Again, such maxims are not necessarily technical in character; thus mSan 10:3 IX (10) **[70]** relies on the statement that a day, once passed, does not return.

[69] •¶ΔO1.4O7R4.2T0T1T3.1.

[70] MS Munich does not have 'for it is said'.

We restrict ourselves here to R. Yehudah's position and Lemma. The principle that the court must have an uneven number of members is added to the discussion as an accepted proposition, not to be proved from the Scriptural text or from anywhere else. Nevertheless, its validity is assumed for the interpretation of the biblical verse *itself* (otherwise R. Yehudah would be saying that in biblical times the court consisted of four members). In other words, the rabbinic principle performs an auxiliary hermeneutic function.

We also find cases where a specific auxiliary assumption is necessary to come to the suggested interpretation, and is in principle available from other parts of the Mishnah or rabbinic literature, but is not spelled out in the unit of interpretation. In these cases, it makes nevertheless sense to construe the interpretation unit as partly dependent on such an assumption. We shall assign the label Topic0 to such a *tacit* auxiliary assumption.[71]

Topic0: Tacit use of a specific assumption rooted in the Mishnaic discourse for the explication of a Scriptural expression.

Let us examine an example for Topic0.

[20] mBQ 9:11 (and see 9:12)[72]   Num. 5:8

The person who steals from a proselyte and swears to him [falsely], and he [the proselyte] dies—behold that one pays the value and the added fifth to the priests, and a guilt offering to the altar, as it is said, 'And if the man has no kinsman to whom restitution can be made, the amount repaid shall go to the Lord for the priest—in addition to the ram of expiation with which expiation is made on his behalf'.[73]

The application of the biblical verse to the proselyte in this interpretation must remain wholly mysterious unless linked to the accepted assumption that the proselyte has, legally speaking, no family even if members of his non-Jewish family are alive. That legal construction, therefore, enters as an indispensable component into the hermeneutic operation.

Finally, certain pairs of concepts (or concepts implying duality) otherwise also embedded into the discourse of the Mishnah[74] are sometimes used to explain the mutual relationship of two elements in Scripture, thus creating a perspective for determining the meaning of the operative biblical terms.

Topic4: Explication of two (or more) biblical expressions or clauses by way of functional concepts with a binary (or tripartite, etc.) structure whose

---

[71] The use of zero indicates the *absence* of a factor otherwise defining the resource family. Since the TOPIC family is characterized by imposing an explicit perspective on a Scriptural segment (there must be some Mishnaic *text*), the *tacit* assumption deserves to be marked off as different in principle. Cf. the introduction to App. I below.

[72] E1.0T0T2.

[73] JPS translation.

[74] Fraenkel, *Darkhey*, i. 67 ff., addresses the role of oppositions in the world view and hermeneutics of the rabbis; halakhic categories are also treated by him, 77 f.

meaning is defined by their recurrent use or interdependence with other terms in the Mishnaic discourse.[75]

We have already come across a binary Mishnaic concept in this chapter: the notion of the *two* inclinations in passage **[15]**. However, in that interpretation the binary concept does not fulfil a binary hermeneutic function; it does not treat two Lemmas but one (and is thus labelled Topic3, not Topic4).[76] In the following passage, by contrast, the binary concept does in fact link two Lemmas.

[21] mSan 10:3 VI (10)[77]   Num. 14:37

The scouts have no share in the world to come, as it is said, 'those men that spread calumnies about the land died', 'of plague before the Lord'; 'died'—in this world; 'of plague'—for the world to come.

The concept pair 'this world—the world to come' is found in the Mishnaic discourse in many places, in particular in hermeneutic contexts,[78] and in particular in this chapter of tractate Sanhedrin, the so-called *Pereq heleq*. It is used here in **[21]** to allocate separate meaning (two types of death, so to speak) to two semantically (and syntactically) related terms.[79] The Scriptural co-text offers no perspective on the question of afterlife, while the Mishnah is concerned with such questions at this point of its discourse.[80] This particular binary pair and variations of it (such as 'this world—days of the Messiah')[81] are by far the most common in the Mishnah. But there are other concepts which serve the same Topic4 purpose, for instance, the dichotomy between loving and fearing God in mSot 5:5 I (2).

Terms can also serve to relate *narrative* Scriptural elements. In that case, I take the functionality to be of a different order, involving unique events, causality, and motivation. In such operations, the Topic4 terms combine with resources of the USE family concerning narrative plotting.[82] The next example is going to be of this type. It also happens to involve not a pair of concepts, but an integral rabbinic proposition or maxim. Where whole rabbinic propositions have the distributive functionality typical of Topic4 (for terms), we shall use the label Topic4.1 (in exact analogy to the difference between Topic3 and Topic3.1).

---

[75] This resource now clarifies and replaces my notion 'material terms of exegesis', employed in 'Scripture's Implicature', 202.

[76] But elsewhere the same concept is in fact used for Topic4 (see e.g. Fraenkel, *Darkhey*, i. 72).

[77] R9T3T4.

[78] As, for instance, in mAvot 4:1 III (4) **[120]**, 5:19. Cf. Schäfer, *Studien zur Geschichte und Theologie*, 244–91.

[79] The resource involved is Redundancy9 (see Ch. 13). This particular unit is found in MS Munich, the *editio princeps* of the Mishnah and popular prints, but not in other MSS, nor in Maimonides's text (trans. Qafih, *Neziqin*, 145); Krauß (*Sanhedrin-Makkot*, 276, 398) thinks the original setting, as a *Baraita*, is bSan 109a.

[80] Cf. tPes 8:12.

[81] Used in the continuation of passage **[13]**, mBer 1:5 II (2).

[82] See further in Ch. 5.

Topic4.1: Explication of two (or more) biblical expressions or clauses by way of a functional proposition which articulates a binary (or tripartite, etc.) structure and whose validity is treated as unproblematic.

Here is my example for Topic4.1. The binary proposition which fulfils hermeneutic function here is also known under the standard phrase מדה כנגד מדה, i.e. 'measure for measure':

[22] mSot 1:8 I (4)[83]   Judg. 16:21

[*mishnah* 7: With whatever measure a man measures they measure him in turn: Sotah case . . .] Samson went after [the desire of] his eyes, therefore the Philistines put out his eyes, as it is said, 'And the Philistines seized him and gouged out his eyes'.[84]

The two narrative elements in Scripture, Samson's desire for Delilah and his blinding by the Philistines, are related to each other (and thus given a perspective determining their significance) with the help of the rabbinic idea of 'measure for measure'. That maxim envisages poetic justice; divine punishment is expected to fit the crime in some semiotic manner. This principle is first applied (in mSot 1:7), not to a narrative case, but to the *Sotah* procedure itself. It is thus used to explain a judicial punishment. The special narrative quality of the biblical material here in *mishnah* 8, by contrast, engages with the principle in a different manner: poetic justice now structures a story and the events within it (resource Use6; see Chapter 5). The Mishnaic expression 'went after his eyes' (הלך אחר עיניו), a metaphor for Samson's sexual desire, frames the correspondence in identical terms (by expressing 'seeing' in terms of 'eyes').[85] It may be meant to invoke biblical language for the hankering 'after' other gods.

It may be noted in passing that the distinction between 'stringent' (חמר) and 'lenient' (קל) norms or their application, that is, another binary concept, is important for a common type of Mishnaic analogy, the *a fortiori* argument (see Chapter 7).

We have pointed repeatedly to the hermeneutic importance of different levels of generality between the Mishnah and Scripture. We shall deal with this very effective way to impose a perspective in the next chapter. First, however, two main formats for the adoption of Scriptural wording into the Mishnaic text need to be considered.

---

[83] (≈N8)T3.1≈T4.1≈U6 .

[84] The concluding phrase ('as it is said' plus quotation) is missing from the MSS Kaufmann, Munich, Parma de Rossi 138, Cambridge; it is present in the *editio princeps* of the Mishnah Naples 1492. Cf. Bietenhard, *Sota*, 186.

[85] Samson's first involvement with a Philistine woman starts with an act of 'seeing' (Judg. 14:1). That same biblical narrative also stresses other aspects of the balance (or imbalance) of retributive acts, see Jackson, *Semiotics of Biblical Law*, sec. 10.2.

4

Scripture's Words, Mishnah's Speech

The Mishnah often uses Scripture's words to express *itself*, that is, without providing a separate reformulation of Scripture. In such cases the meaning of Scriptural words does not become thematic, only the topic addressed by employing them. In other cases Scriptural words and Mishnaic reformulation are both found: this is the midrashic unit. The existence of these two hermeneutic *formats* points to the possibility of two hermeneutic *attitudes*. The first of these would appropriate Scriptural wording for a concern contemporaneous with the reader, and do so on the basis of a conviction that Scripture qua Torah is directly relevant to the 'life of Torah' (the attitude of topical alignment). The second attitude would make Scripture as such the object of attention, and pursue a programme of sustained interpretation across a variety of thematic concerns (the attitude of programmatic exposition). The integration of Scriptural words into Mishnaic speech appropriates them for the reader's concern, and can lead to a blurring of the boundaries between author and reader, as when the biblical term's meaning is 'defined' by the rabbinic voice. Of particular importance for the appropriation of Scripture is the integration of Scriptural segments into the Mishnaic formulation of hypothetical halakhic cases.

EXPRESSIVE USE OF SCRIPTURE

So far, we have encountered Scripture as a separate text embedded explicitly into the text of the Mishnah. All the passages examined hitherto have the *midrashic format*. This is a literary unit which contains an explicit quotation from Scripture, followed or preceded (or both)[1] by a rabbinic

---

[1] This format, *reprise*, is discussed at the end of Ch. 12.

formulation whose meaning is presented as congruent with that of Scripture. This structure, with its internal doubling of the biblical message, is explicitly hermeneutic.[2] There is, however, also a more incidental or integral use of Scriptural wording in the Mishnah. In it, the relationships of figure and ground are reversed; the Scriptural wording does not become a topic in its own right, but serves to express a Mishnaic idea; and often there are no obvious markers of the presence of a quotation. Distinguishing it from the reduplication of the midrashic format, I shall call this format the 'expressive use' of Scripture (or simply 'use'). In the profiles of Mishnaic passages it is represented by the *pi* sign, π (see below). Somewhat related distinctions have been made,[3] more recently in particular for Qumran writings, and terms such as 'allusion'[4] or 'reuse'[5] have been employed. A careful examination of expressive use in the Mishnah is not only important because it is one of two surface formats in which hermeneutic work can be located in the Mishnaic text. It is important also because expressive use is a formal manifestation of a process of appropriation and integration of Scriptural material. In the absence of a duplication of the message, the very words of Scripture become those of the Mishnah, because there is no alternative formulation.[6] It may seem that expressive use is a peripheral phenomenon, a limiting case of the format of explicit interpretation found in the midrashic reduplication. But I am proposing to give equal heuristic weight to the inverse perspective, namely, that the format of reduplication is a limiting case of expressive use, that is, biblical allusion.[7] Furthermore, the existence of a format of expressive use points to the possibility of two distinct hermeneutic attitudes in the history of rabbinic hermeneutics. Before unfolding this idea, we need to understand the difference of formats more clearly.

---

[2] I shall address the format and pragmatics of the midrashic unit in Ch. 12.

[3] Cf. Pettit, *Shene'emar*, 17–19, distinguishes 'explicit citations' of Scripture with and without citation formula. It is not clear from his explanation, however, how the latter are 'explicit', or how they differ from 'allusions' which he wishes to exclude from his investigation. He also excludes Mishnaic terminology adapted from Scripture (p. 19), which is an unwarranted restriction of hermeneutic evidence. See further below on 'expressive use', and resource Topic8.

[4] Expressive use of Scriptural wording is found often in Dead Sea Scroll texts. See e.g. Campbell, *Use of Scripture in the Damascus Document*, who distinguishes 'allusions' from 'citations' or 'virtual citations' (pp. 9, 25, 29, 31, 55 ff.) but finds the difference 'largely relative and essentially formal' (p. 29), or 'blurred' (p. 31). Cf. also Fishbane, 'Use, Authority and Interpretation of Mikra at Qumran', 347 ff.; id., Fishbane, *Biblical Interpretation*, 9 ff. Gabrion ('L'Interprétation de l'écriture à Qumran') speaks of 'citations explicites' in contrast to 'allusions bibliques' (pp. 787 ff.). The decisive difference in his view is the use of citation formulas (p. 787, n. 48). Gordis, 'Quotations as a Literary Usage in Biblical, Oriental and Rabbinic Literature', speaks of 'unexpressed quotation' (p. 179), in particular in dialogue (also pp. 166, 173, 179). See also Epstein, *Mavo*, 1129 ff.

[5] Cf. Fishbane, 'Use, Authority and Interpretation of Mikra'; id., *Biblical Interpretation*.

[6] I examine the redundancy of reduplicated biblical messages in 'Delaying the Progress from Case to Case'.

[7] There is a paradoxical third 'format' for biblical interpretation which will eventually need to be taken into account. It is the use of Scripture for Mishnaic positions which have no wording link to Scripture at all (called 'exegetical silence' at the beginning of Ch. 3 above). As yet, I cannot see how this task of conjecture can be satisfactorily tackled.

Let us first look at the midrashic format. The biblical segment stands in a special relationship to the Mishnaic text which surrounds it: it is distinguished as *not* directly expressing the thoughts of the voice which does the quoting. It points to an earlier time in which the text quoted was formulated, for uptake in the present time. And the validity of the quoted words is not, as such, the responsibility of the quoting voice.[8] This is why a quotation can be used as *argument* in a discourse: its status is different from the voice quoting it. This displacement of commitment and authority is anchored in the fact that the quotation is accompanied by a second statement or norm. This second statement is made directly by the same voice which quotes, and there is an implicit or explicit claim that the sense of these two textual units converges or is partially identical, that is, that the statement is a restatement. Thus an explicit hermeneutic utterance is created, the midrashic utterance. The duplication of the message shows that the two statements do not belong to the same level—they cannot be read as continuous, nor as a mere repetition.[9] The quoted wording has to be understood as being spoken *about*. It is this metalinguistic constitution which characterizes the midrashic unit. It has the underlying form: 'Scriptural sign X means Y.' Whatever else is expressed with the help of a midrashic unit, a rephrasing of the meaning or message of a Scriptural segment is always also provided, the validity of a certain interpretation is claimed. Insofar as the direct relationship between the biblical words and the extra-linguistic reality to which they refer is suspended in this format, the biblical words are quoted as linguistic signs (as we say, in quotation marks). In the context of linguistic philosophy a distinction is made which is of some relevance here, namely that between *use* and *mention*. In the sentence

There is a major difference between women and men.

the word 'women' is *used*. In the sentence

There is a difference of two letters between 'women' and 'men'.

it is *mentioned*. The reference in the second sentence is to the *word* 'women', the reference in the first is to half of humankind. This technical distinction between 'use' and 'mention' is not without its inherent conceptual complexities[10] and we do not need to adopt it for the description here. But when

---

[8] I shall place these formal features into a wider context in Ch. 12.

[9] Cf. on this Samely, *The Interpretation of Speech in the Pentateuch Targums*, 163.

[10] See Quine, *Methods of Logic*, 37–8, 208 f.; see also Garver, 'Varieties of Use and Mention'. Searle, *Speech Acts*, 73–6, stresses that the expression which is 'mentioned' does not conventionally *refer* to the things normally taken to be referred to by that expression. On the 'reflexive' aspect of 'mention', see Lyons, *Semantics*, i. 5 f.; further Levinson, *Pragmatics*, 86 and 247 ('mention' is metalinguistic, while 'use' is performative). The notion of 'mention' should not be construed as implying that what is inside quotations marks makes no contribution to the meaning of the larger syntagma in which it occurs. See further on this problem Wierzbicka, 'The Semantics of Direct and Indirect Discourse', 267–307; Geach, *Mental Acts* (ch. 18: 'Psychological Uses of *oratio recta*'), 80 ff.; and Davidson,

Scripture is quoted something similar happens: biblical *words* become a focus (as well as what they are about). In the format of reduplication the message of the Mishnah can and must be construed, in the first instance, through its 'own' words; the contribution of Scripture is, to start with, like a black box—unknown. Scripture's contribution can be bypassed in constructing the gist of the Mishnah. In a similar way, the reference of 'women' can be bypassed in our example above when ascertaining if the difference to 'men' is indeed two letters. In expressive use, on the other hand, biblical wording is applied *directly* to a Mishnaic subject-matter. Scripture is not topic, and *no potential for difference* between two formulations is acknowledged; there is only one formulation. The biblical words cannot be bracketed: interpreting their meaning is a precondition for construing the Mishnaic message. In other words, the Mishnaic co-text and thematic progress totally dictate the terms for that biblical meaning, totally construe it in a Mishnaic perspective.

Here is an example of the expressive use of a biblical phrase:

(A) If you are still childless, you should *be fruitful and multiply*.

The same biblical words are 'mentioned' (that is, have their direct situational interaction suspended) in the following format, which I take as constitutive for the midrashic unit:

(B) If you are still childless, you should have children,
for it is said, 'be fruitful and multiply'.

In (B) the precept concerning children occurs twice: once in the voice of the person speaking ('you should . . .'), and once in the voice of Scripture as quoted by that voice. If the Scriptural wording were to be removed, the obligation would still remain expressed, but not so in (A). There would be no message left (and no grammatical sentence). Let us consider a real case:

[23] mSot 4:3 II (2)[11]   Gen. 1:28

Sterile women, aged women, and women who are not fit for children do not drink [the bitter waters], and do not receive their Ketubah. R. Eliezer says: He [the husband] has the right to take another wife and *to be fruitful and multiply* from her.

Scriptural wording is obviously employed here for direct expression. R. Eliezer does not 'mention' the words of Scripture, he uses them. He speaks about the activities that Scripture speaks about, *using* Scriptural words.[12] Here is a definition of this format for the appearance of Scriptural text in the Mishnah, for which I shall employ the *pi* sign:

'Quotation', in *Inquiries into Truth and Interpretation*, 79–92. In mRH 2:9, in a narrative rabbinic setting, the words 'master' and 'disciple' are first 'used' then 'mentioned'.

[11] •π.

[12] They appear in modified form: instead of the imperative ('be fruitful and multiply!'), the infinitive is used. See the definition of expressive use below (π).

π: Use of a biblical word, phrase, or clause, in its original or a modified form, in the expression of a Mishnaic proposition or norm without a separate, non-biblical, restatement of the meaning.

In other words, this format offers no reduplication of the message, thereby collapsing any distinction between the biblical message and the Mishnaic one. In using the Greek π for representing this format in the hermeneutic profile of Mishnaic passages, I allude to the initial letter of the PERFOR-MANCE resources (see below and next chapter).

Less obvious than in [23] is the expressive use of Scriptural wording in the following text:

[24] = [37a] mPes 7:1 I–II (2)[13]   Exod. 12:8

How do they 'roast' the Passover offering? One thrusts[14] a skewer of pomegranate-wood through it from its mouth to its anus, and places its legs and entrails inside it—these are the words of R. Yose Ha-Gelili. R. Aqiva says: That would be in the category of cooking; but rather, one hangs them outside it. [mishnah 2] The Passover-offering is roasted neither on a [metal] spit nor on a grill . . .

The word 'roast' is not marked out by any irregularity or conspicuous structure in the text. We could perhaps not be sure of a deliberate link to the Scriptural phrase 'roasted by fire' (צלי־אש) in Exod. 12:8, were it not for the contrast term *cooking* (בשׁל) in Aqiva's objection. This shows that 'roast' is emphasized and that the Mishnaic question deliberately uses for its own utterance the same word that Scripture uses.[15]

This passage illustrates two things. First, that it can be difficult to recognize Scriptural allusions in large rabbinic texts such as the Mishnah, in particular if they consist of the use of only one word which is not technical or conspicuous in its rabbinic setting.[16] The second point is that not every use of biblical phraseology needs to reflect deliberate appropriation of Scriptural text of the type investigated here. Although likely to be rare in a technical discourse like that of the Mishnah, there is in principle the possibility of stylistic or rhetorical (associative) use of biblical phrases. Not that these do not imply hermeneutic activity, albeit of a different kind. Post-biblical Judaism knows of texts which are a veritable pastiche of biblical phrases, of which some Qumran documents provide good examples. How we should interpret the hermeneutic activity behind such extensive use of Scriptural wording depends on other features of the documents in question, and external information available for them.[17]

[13] •¶π≈T5T8.

[14] So MS Kaufmann; other MSS and prints have plural verb forms throughout; cf. Beer, *Pesachim*, 207.

[15] Cf. the Opposition2 resource at Mekhilta ad Exod. 12:8 Pisha 6 (ed. Lauterbach, i. 46; see also 47).

[16] A fair number of expressive use passages are included in my *Database of Midrashic Units in the Mishnah* (see App. II below). However, the *Database* is far from comprehensive in this regard. See also Albeck, *Einführung*, 190–2, for whom such passages are relevant to the question of whether Mishnaic Hebrew was part of an independent living language (p. 193).

[17] Cf. Campbell, *Use of Scripture*, 29, 31; Lim, *Holy Scripture*; further also Maier, *Temple Scroll: An*

TOPICAL ALIGNMENT AND PROGRAMMATIC
EXPOSITION AS HERMENEUTIC ATTITUDES

We have distinguished two formats of Scripture use in the Mishnah, expressive use (π) on the one hand, and reduplication on the other. As we said, the latter is typical for the format of the midrashic unit, which says *again* what is taken to be the message of the Scriptural wording also presented. This formal distinction will now be used as starting-point for some historical speculations on hermeneutic modes or *attitudes* in rabbinic Judaism.[18] It should be stressed from the outset that literary formats are not spontaneously connected to specific hermeneutic attitudes; as formats, they are in fact interchangeable to a large extent, and there is no doubt that interpretations did 'cross over' from one format to another. It is also not suggested that only one of the following two attitudes can stand behind any rabbinic passage of interpretation—there are others. It is therefore necessary to keep separate the evidence of literary structures from the historical constructs here referred to as hermeneutic attitudes, if the case for the constructs' existence should be found convincing at all.

The two hermeneutic attitudes that I wish to distinguish are assumed to have left their traces in particular in those parts of rabbinic literature containing discourse. However, there are other contexts of Scripture use, and thus hermeneutic attitudes, of which one can catch a glimpse in that literature.[19] It seems to me that the reading involved in the scribal copying of Scripture must constitute one of these.[20] The discourse on the shape of the Scriptural text, its exact transmission, division, and vocalization, which led to the Masorah must surely constitute another.[21] Then there is the *performance* or use of Scriptural passages as utterance in the context of prayer.[22] There is furthermore the use of a Scriptural quotation as direct utterance in a speech situation; we shall treat literary accounts of such speech events in

Introduction, Translation and Commentary, esp. 3 ff., 8 ff., and notes (quoting more literature). On anthologies, see next chapter, text to n. 113.

[18] For the following, cf. my 'Scripture's Segments and Topicality'; the attitude here referred to by the name 'topical alignment' is called 'topical appropriation' in that article.

[19] Perhaps the idea of hermeneutic attitudes is similar to the categories of exegesis distinguished (not clearly defined) by Michael Fishbane in *Biblical Interpretation*: scribal corrections and revisions, legal exegesis, aggadic exegesis, and mantological exegesis. The question to what extent rabbinic hermeneutics continues, supplements, and discontinues types of inner-biblical hermeneutics remains open; some parallels will be drawn in the next chapter, as occasionally elsewhere in this study. Fraade attempts to give the rabbinic commentary format *as such* a performative function or hermeneutic context (namely, 'study'), see *From Tradition to Commentary*, 18 f.

[20] See mMeg 3:3, which presupposes that copying can also be reading.

[21] This may be a natural home for rabbinic interpretations which have a 'philological' or 'historical' tendency; but such interpretations could also have had a home in the attitude of programmatic exposition.

[22] e.g. the biblical quotations in the *Qedushah* of the Eighteen Benedictions; the *Shema'*; the Ten Commandments as preserved in the Nash Papyrus. On Mishnaic USE and PERFORMANCE resources, see the next chapter.

the next chapter (Performance2/8). Moreover, there is the delivery of the Scriptural text as synagogue reading, requiring its own set of decisions on interpretation (such as the division of segments,[23] the division of *parashiyyot*, the placement of stress, or the manner of delivery). Another hermeneutic mode is that of translation which was, in complex ways, connected with the production of Targums.[24] It is to such a list that the following two would be added: the generalized search for meaning in Scripture as an object of study on the one hand; and the incorporation of Scriptural topics into thematically oriented discourses of the rabbis on the other. It is this pair of attitudes which I wish to discuss further with special reference to the two formats of reduplication and expressive use distinguished above. I shall refer to the two attitudes as *programmatic exposition* and *topical alignment*, respectively. I have already emphasized that they are offered here as historical constructs. They are not directly available to us in the individual interpretation units of rabbinic literature (which do not verbalize hermeneutic attitudes), but require interpretative construction which involves our own experience as readers. Unless they help us understand known features of the rabbinic evidence or discover new ones, they have no *raison d'être* (although I admit it is much easier to add an unnecessary concept to the scholarly discourse than to get rid of one).

Topical Alignment

This is the unmediated and implicit alignment of a Scriptural subject-matter with a reader's topic or concern. Scripture is simultaneously recognized as dealing with that topic, and as dealing with it in a manner directly relevant, informative, corroborative, or valid to the reader. The Scriptural segment's boundary, its relevance to the reader's concern, its accuracy in the eyes of the reader (or its validity in the case of a norm) are all established in the same breath as determining *what* the segment's subject-matter is. Put differently, the topic on which Scripture speaks is established in direct dependency[25] on whether what Scripture says is true and relevant, while the assumption that Scripture is being true and relevant on *some* topic is axiomatic.[26]

Do we know about topical alignment from our own experience of

---

[23] On this, see my 'Scripture's Segments and Topicality', 109–13.

[24] See ibid.

[25] The methodological framework adopted in this study suggests that some measure of dependency is quite normal in reading. The expectation that the text says something true is unimportant for determining what it means only in certain varieties of the historical-critical approach, and even there it is not absent. See Grice, 'Logic and Conversation', and Gadamer, *Truth and Method*, 158 ff. (= *Wahrheit und Methode*, 183 ff. [168 ff.]).

[26] Truth and relevance are two main expectations guiding the interpretation of utterances in face-to-face conversation. They can be used routinely to convey information by *implication*. Cf. the seminal work by H. P. Grice, *Studies in the Way of Word*; see also Levinson, *Pragmatics*, and Yule and Brown, *Discourse Analysis*. Grice's ideas are strikingly relevant to the phenomenon of midrashic interpretation, as I tried to show in 'Scripture's Implicature'.

reading? I think so. The key to understanding the phenomenon in rabbinic times probably lies in a rabbinic expectation of *shared expertise* in the field of halakhah. In this model of the author–reader relationship, the rabbinic reader and the divine author are both legal experts. As we hinted in the first chapter, the way academics tend to read each other's work (not their primary sources) provides a parallel. We seem to be constantly appropriating, and at times misappropriating, each other's concepts. I can certainly find many footnotes in my own publications which rope in a colleague's position as supporting my own, based on nothing more than a single, quite superficial point of contact. And that point of contact consists of a *term or phrase* which makes striking sense—in my *own* current project (i.e. perspective). And, of course, sometimes simply rereading the colleague's passage shows that a quite different point was intended. But it is clear that, in certain limited contexts, we read another person's words *on the strong assumption that they are relevant and correct.*[27] In other words, we determine the topic (and thus aspects of the meaning) of a text in the light of what we *know to be true*. And something similar might well characterize the atmosphere in which the rabbis read Scripture. We might say: A word (דבר) to the wise (חכם) is enough.[28] Where a common set of experiences or shared special competence is assumed, reading becomes even more like jumping to conclusions then it is usually, and successfully so. The participants of the discourse we find in the Mishnah may well have looked upon themselves as experts whose familiarity with the manifestations of halakhah (in particular if acquired through the experience of a social practice) put them in direct touch with the *subject-matter* of the norms of the Pentateuch. And they may have thought, in suitable humility, to understand the divine draftsman as well as two persons understand each other who share a craft. Such an assumption of common expertise would allow them—from time to time or in specific stages in the development of rabbinic hermeneutics—to feed the Scriptural wording directly into their *own* conception of its perceived topic: without separating Lemma from Dictum, author from reader, sign from subject-matter, and without investigating the internal textual relationships. The Scriptural words are brought in line and appropriated by—*aligned with*—the reader's topical interest.[29]

[27] But the opposite can happen: putting as much distance as possible between one's own work and that of colleagues also seems to be effected by such immediate imposition of a new perspective.

[28] We might continue, in the spirit of rabbinic hermeneutics: . . . and if it is more than one word where one word suffices, the surplus is free (*mufneh*) for a new topic (see Ch. 13 below). The Latin form often quoted for this saying, *verbum sapienti sat est*, apparently goes back to a passage (using *dictum*, not *verbum*) in *The Persian* of Plautus (cf. Partington (ed.), *The Oxford Dictionary of Quotations*, 517/4).

[29] Another relevant experience many users of this book will recognize is the following. After finishing writing, but before publishing, an academic finds a relevant article she/he had no knowledge of which treats the same topic from a different angle. Reading what she/he has written in the light of the other author's words, certain adjustments and reinterpretations of the academic's *own words* take place. It turns out that it is sufficient to add the new reference to existing footnotes without further changes. In that case, one is able to reinterpret one's own words with regard to the new

And that interest is not, as such, constrained by the unity of the biblical topic, nor bound to treat the same word as having the same or even a compatible meaning in different places in Scripture.[30] Topical alignment, in our own experience as readers of secondary literature in particular, may be most often connected with the *initial* stages of a meaning hypothesis. However, it would be wrong to conclude from this that its results could not have been sufficiently stable or not convincing for long enough to produce a lasting effect on the formation of some rabbinic ideas.[31] It is also unwarranted to think that, since its results can be understood as incomplete initial stages of a fully fledged exegetical argument, topical alignment constituted a simple, primitive, naive, or generally 'early' stage of rabbinic reading. We cannot form an opinion on how simple or complex an instance of topical alignment is without explicating its features, and such explication destroys its very nature (instead of, perhaps, merely distorting that nature in some ways, as in the case of programmatic exposition). On the contrary: it is likely that the implicit interpretation will always call for a more complicated explanation than an interpretation which has at least some measure of explicitness to start with. There is thus no reason to assume that topical alignment was an 'earlier' or simpler phase of rabbinic hermeneutics. As for the segment of Scripture picked out by topical alignment, it is bound to be small or very small—a phrase, a complex expression, or even a single word. The segment is unlikely to contain complex syntactical dependencies which require disentangling.[32]

The conceptual features of this hermeneutic attitude find their counterpart in the textual structures of the expressive use of Scriptural words (π)— the attitude is defined so as to fit the evidence of the passages of expressive use. Nevertheless, no specific unit of expressive use can be tied historically to the attitude of topical alignment merely on the basis of its format. For the link between attitude and format cannot be other than deliberate or conventional. Literary formats do not give *spontaneous* expression to anything, let alone events of interpretation. Interpretations that may originally have

line of thought in such a way that they coexist, or *align*, with the points made by the other author. But in this rereading they receive a new boundary or take on new resonances; the contour of their meaning becomes more clearly defined, without any change in the text itself. This is what happens to the biblical text in the rabbinic reading: new resonance without change of a single letter.

[30] There is no discernible attempt in the Mishnah to co-ordinate the treatment of the same biblical expression appearing in different verses. The Mishnah shows no concern for some ultimate semantic unity of an expression across its different themes (and this fragmentation of meaning is not tied to the plurality of *biblical* co-texts, or *biblical* themes). The diverse treatment of biblical *davar* affords an example (mGit 9:10 I–II (3); mShebi 10:8 I–II (2) (= mMak 2:8 **[12]**), and mMak 2:5 II (2) **[11]**; mHor 1:3; and mZeb 8:10 II (3)).

[31] There is also another mode of interpretation which might have been combined with topical alignment. This places *isolated* words or phrases without any recognizable 'home' in Scripture into the context of an ongoing thematic discussion, exploring their linguistic meaning in isolation from any context of use. See below, n. 70.

[32] More on the link between segment size and attitude, including the attitude of translational rendering, is found in my 'Scripture's Segments and Topicality'.

been conceived in the attitude of topical alignment could now be found, created anew, in the format of the midrashic unit.

Programmatic Exposition

This places the Scriptural text at a distance as a separate object. What the reader knows about a topic is usually still brought to the text as an imposition of perspective—but the fusion of Scripture's concern with the reader's concern is accepted as potentially *problematic*. 'Problematic' does not mean that the reader is necessarily in doubt about that fusion, or Scripture's truth and validity; or that the force with which a perspective is imposed is any weaker than for topical alignment. Rather, the fusion of the reader concern and the meaning of Scripture becomes (up to a point)[33] a matter for explication and demonstration, and Scripture can be used as a warrant or argument for the validity of a rabbinic position. In addition to Scripture's perceived topic Scripture itself becomes topical; its meaning is problematic in that sense, and *in principle*. The topicality of Scripture is joined at all points by the topicality of its topics.[34] This also means that Scripture is problematic *everywhere*, independently of the theme to which the text is taken to make a contribution.[35] The programmatic search for meaning is not, as such, topically selective. Its tendency is all-inclusive, insofar as Scripture has meaning in all its parts and that meaning is in principle problematic. Programmatic exposition thus stands between the hermeneutic attitude of topical alignment on the one hand, for which topical selectivity is constitutive, and attitudes such as translational rendering on the other, which aim for total inclusiveness and cannot give expression to an independent topical agenda.[36]

Although programmatic exposition may increase, through the accumulation of individual segments of Scripture receiving an interpretation, it cannot exhaust the meaning possibilities of the text since no textual element and no semiotic level is *a priori* excluded as potential carrier of meaning.[37] In addition, there is no pressure through genre constraints (as in the case of translation) to restrict the quantity of interpretations per biblical Lemma to one. To create even the *appearance* of total coverage for a given stretch of Scriptural text is an expression of the attitude of programmatic exposition,

---

[33] And not without contribution from the reader of the interpretation, who constructs the convergence of sense between the Dictum and Lemma. See Ch. 2 (text starting at n. 109) and Ch. 14 (text following n. 26).

[34] 'Scripture's Segments and Topicality', 97.

[35] At this point it would become possible for Scripture to be approached in its 'historical' meaning, by holding urgent reader concern in abeyance and suspending the imposition of TOPIC perspective. This was clearly not the route taken by rabbinic hermeneutics as a whole, but each unit of interpretation has to be taken on its merits. I am not aware of an example for 'historical' reading in the Mishnah.

[36] Cf. my 'Scripture's Segments and Topicality', 103.

[37] See Ch. 2 on the resulting inexhaustibility of the meanings of Scripture; and Ch. 14 for some of the semiotic dimensions in which Scripture is read by the rabbis (GRAPHEME, ICON resources).

and this appearance is achieved in the midrashic works of the so-called 'exegetical' genre,[38] that is, works which order midrashic units according to the sequence of the biblical verses.

The search for meaning conceives of the voice and position of Scripture as *separate* from the voices and positions of its readers—Scripture is expositional, receives exposition. Separating the rabbinic position from that of Scripture, even if only to demonstrate their identity, also creates the option to explicate or name the mechanism of demonstration, that is, the resource of interpretation. The literary format to which the features of the attitude of programmatic exposition are meant to correspond is of course the midrashic unit. The midrashic unit separates Scripture (as quotation) from the Dictum (as expressive statement by the rabbinic voice); it reduplicates the message of the former by the latter or claims meaning convergence for the two; it has room for an explication of the mechanism of interpretation; and it speaks about the topic of the Dictum as well as speaking about the linguistic signs of Scripture, having topical as well as a metalinguistic orientation.[39] Again, the match between attitude and format is circular. And yet, as we said above, there is no necessary link between attitude and format for any specific passage of interpretation. It is more than a theoretical possibility that some interpretation results which came about and were originally accepted as part of the programmatic exposition of Scripture were later couched in terms of expressive use, and that this is now the only format in which they survive.

Table 4.1 gives a summary of the features of the two attitudes.[40]

The results of interpretations in the attitude of topical alignment are most conspicuous to us when the subject-matter identified as Scriptural is wholly absent from the wording and co-text of the Lemma (Cotext1). In such cases, the reader's interest catches the eye. But topical alignment does not carefully neutralize the co-text's contribution (as can happen in programmatic exposition). Rather, it has no opinion on it, in a manner of speaking. Topical alignment is as compatible with full co-textual appropriateness as it is with inappropriateness. Its unquestioned certainty about the truth on the subject-matter that *could* be the topic of the Scriptural segment translates hermeneutically into an unquestioned certainty that it is indeed its topic—and the internal textual relationships of Scripture are simply of no concern.

We may find the trace of a topical alignment interpretation in mSot 5:3 I (2), quoted as passage [1] in Chapter 2 above. In that midrashic unit the expression '2,000 cubits' is taken to refer to the Sabbath limit despite the fact that it appears in a paragraph concerned with other matters. This

---

[38] On the terminology, see e.g. Alexander, 'Midrash'; Stemberger, *Introduction*, 240.
[39] More on the formal features and nature of the midrashic unit is found in Ch. 12.
[40] A similar table, but including the attitude of translational rendering, may be found in my 'Scripture's Segments and Topicality', 97.

TABLE 4.1 *Summary of hermeneutic attitudes*

Characteristic	Attitude	
	Topical alignment	Programmatic exposition
Scripture as separate object	no	yes
Scripture's meaning universally problematic	no	yes
Technique of interpretation potentially explicit	no	yes
Topical orientation	yes	yes[a]
Metalinguistic orientation	no	yes
Topical selection only	yes	no
Maximal segment size smaller than a sentence	yes	no
Co-text taken note of (neutralized or admitted)	no	yes
Midrashic unit as possible format (reduplication)	yes	yes
Expressive use as possible format	yes	yes
Targumic unit as possible format[b]	yes	yes

Notes: [a] One must allow for the possibility of interpretations which are in fact the expression of a topical orientation, but are 'historical'; so the 'yes' in this row is a qualified one only. See also n. 35 above.

[b] See my 'Scripture's Segments and Topicality'. Targum stands here merely as an example of other manifestations and formats of rabbinic hermeneutics in which the results of interpretations in the two hermeneutic attitudes could be presented. A further, quite hypothetical, example is the intonation or even the gestures of the person reading the Torah in the synagogue. The hermeneutic effects of a tradition of cantillation also belong here.

interpretation of Num. 35:5 could have started life as a topical alignment. Finding a number in the text which was firmly established as the Sabbath limit could have been what determined for the rabbinic reader the topic of the text (not the other way round).[41] If so, this happened without reifying Scripture as an object of examination, without explicating the assumptions of reading, without investigating the relationship of '2,000 cubits' to the text that surrounds it. If we continue with our hypothetical reconstruction, all of this, in particular the latter, took place at a later stage when the original interpretation was transposed from the attitude of topical alignment to fit the format of the midrashic unit. In that transposition the observation of an internal inconsistency in the biblical paragraph was added. It is this preliminary observation of inconsistency which now creates the hermeneutic space for the introduction of an otherwise alien topic.[42] But this trans-

[41] Cf. n. 28 of Ch. 2 above.
[42] See Ch. 10 on the DIFFERENCE family of resources, dealing with inconsistency.

position to the midrashic format also re-created the original interpretation in a new attitude (namely, that of programmatic exposition); it did not preserve the implicitness constitutive for topical alignment. The fact that a switch between formats affects the nature of the hermeneutic operation has a bearing on the problem of *parallels* for the same interpretation in rabbinic literature. From a merely synchronic point of view it is clear that the hermeneutic link between a Dictum and a Lemma is not totally determined by the nature of these two textual elements. Given the variety and richness of the pool of resources, alternative hermeneutic ways can lead from one to the other. In the Mishnah the hermeneutic operation is sometimes subject to a challenge even when the fact that a specific Dictum is linked to a specific Lemma is conceded.[43] Although the input of the reader of rabbinic interpretation is indispensable in identifying the resources, the way in which the interpretation is *presented* often decides between equally viable alternative routes (see Chapter 12 below). Therefore, *parallel* units of interpretation in two rabbinic documents need to be scrutinized for clues to see if the operation linking Lemma and Dictum is really the same in both cases.

While topical alignment is most visible to us when it results in the neutralization of co-text, it is reasonable to assume that many and perhaps most interpretations in the attitude of topical alignment were compatible with the contribution from the co-text even without being concerned with it. The cases of expressive use quoted above as **[23]** and **[24]** are examples (if we assume for a moment that they preserve the implicitness of an original topical alignment interpretation). On the other hand, topical alignment's disregard for the internal textual relationships of Scripture is likely also to have generated readings which could be justified in *explication* only by a neutralization of the co-text.[44] In other words, interpretations on the basis of topical alignment may have helped establish or confirm the hermeneutics of small segments and neutralization of co-text, that is, what is called the *atomistic* character of rabbinic hermeneutics.

The dominant format for the appearance of Scripture in rabbinic discourse as we know it is the midrashic unit, and that form's explicitness makes it very suitable for presenting interpretation results conceived in the attitude of programmatic exposition. But it is likely that at least some of the interpretations preserved as midrashic units started life as topical alignment or as one of the other attitudes mentioned at the beginning of this section, most of which are less explicit. And explicitness is not something

---

[43] An examples of this is found in mSot 5:1 II–III (3).

[44] Once an implicit link between rabbinic topic and Scriptural word was required to be explicated, re-creation of the interpretation would become necessary. But there is no reason to assume that the midrashic re-creation of the interpretation would select the same passage in Scripture as Lemma for the rabbinic position that was originally appropriated by topical alignment—unless the link was already a fixed part of the tradition, for example by expressive use in the Mishnah. I have allowed for a switch between Lemmata in my list of possibilities at the beginning of Ch. 3 above.

that is added on to an otherwise finished interpretation; it interacts with its substance, as we have seen.

SOME VARIETIES AND FUNCTIONS OF EXPRESSIVE USE OF SCRIPTURAL WORDING

A fruitful way to look at the embedded, expressive, use of Scriptural wording in the Mishnah is to think of it as the transformation of a Scriptural phrase or clause employed in ordinary parlance into a standard phrase or technical term of Mishnaic discourse.[45] This is part of a more general phenomenon I mentioned before: a Scriptural *parole* becomes a systemic part of the *langue* of the Mishnaic interlocutors, and appears as such in many instances of Mishnaic *parole*.[46] Here is an example of Scriptural terms being implicitly but centrally embedded in the discourse of the Mishnah:

[25] mBQ 1:1[47]   Exod. 21:28–22:5

The four main branches of damages are 'the ox' and 'the pit' and the crop-destroyer (המבעה) and 'the fire' (ההבער). The distinctiveness of the ox is not like the distinctiveness of the crop-destroyer and the distinctiveness of the crop-destroyer is not like the distinctiveness of the ox; and neither this nor that, in whom there is the breath of life, is like the distinctiveness of the fire (אש) in which there is not the breath of life, and neither this nor that, whose manner is to move and cause damage, is like the distinctiveness of the pit, whose manner is not to move and cause damage.[48]

The terms naming the branches of tort are taken from a cluster of verses between Exod. 21:28 and 22:5 (Hebrew numbering), with the exception of the word 'crop-destroyer', which is not found there.[49] These terms are not marked as quotations from Scripture and are perfectly ordinary words of Mishnaic discourse; it is therefore theoretically open to doubt that they are biblical allusions. Yet their appearance in the Mishnah is parallel to the appearance of three of them in the same Scriptural co-text and in the biblical sequence, making it rather certain that they are used expres-

---

[45] Cf. Albeck, *Einführung*, 190 f. Albeck distinguishes Mishnaic technical terms of biblical origin ('auf Grund der Thora-Sprache geschaffen') from 'admixtures' of biblical wording, but he does not explain the criteria for this (cf. p. 190 with 191).

[46] See Ch. 2 (text to n. 80) on these Saussurian terms. Crystal summarizes the distinction thus: *parole* is the individual utterance or instance of language use, *langue* is the 'collective language system of a speech community' (*Dictionary*, 221).

[47] πC5D6E1.3×3 [E7?]T1T3 (crop-destroyer, damage, branches)T8×3.

[48] There are some striking links between the language of this passage and the formulation of rules nos. 3 and 4 in the Thirteen Middot of R. Ishmael (see Ch. 1 above). I shall touch upon the latter when defining the EXTENSION resources in Ch. 9. Cf. also Fraenkel, *Darkhey*, ii. 587, n. 55.

[49] This is where the terms appear: the ox is mentioned in an active role in 21:28, 29, 32, 35, 36; the pit in 21:33, 34; the *mab'eh* does not appear, instead 22:4 uses the words *yab'er* and *be'iroh*; both terms for fire appear in 22:5. MS Munich does not have the sentence which puts the crop-destroyer into contrast with the ox, cf. Windfuhr, *Baba qamma*, 87. For an analysis of the reasoning in this passage, see Jackson, 'On the Nature of Analogical Argument in Early Jewish Law', 164 ff., who also cites relevant literature.

sively.[50] But the function of the three biblical terms has changed. In Scripture the word 'ox' refers to an ox which is somehow generalized, but in any case an ox; in the Mishnah 'the ox' is the name of legal category, and functions like an adjectival qualification of the word 'damage'. It thus provides a new item in Mishnaic *langue*, namely 'the goring ox-type damage', as used in the Mishnaic *parole* that constitutes our passage mBQ 1:1. Here is a similar case:

[26] mHul 12:1[51]   Deut. 22:6; 22:7

[The law to] 'let [the dam] go [from] the nest' is binding both in the land [of Israel] and outside the land.

The Mishnaic opening phrase, שלוח הקן, is adapted from a Scriptural sentence; but it is clear from the abundance of square brackets in this translation that the relationship is not straightforward. The Mishnaic term is wholly of the language of the rabbis while its elements are Scriptural.[52] It combines two terms coming from verses Deut. 22:6 and 22:7. The second half of the Mishnaic term, 'nest', picks up a noun from verse 6 (which is the protasis of the biblical norm): 'If you chance upon the nest of a bird . . .' (. . . כי יקרא קן־צפור), while its first component is a nominalization of the verb commencing the biblical apodosis in verse 7: '. . . you shall surely let go . . .' (שלח תשלח). The result is an evocative and concise transformation of the Scriptural text of a norm (a biblical *parole*) into a name for that norm, resulting in an expression which has no transparent independent meaning at all—it is not the *nest* that is to be let go.[53] This is a clear indication that it is a standard phrase, a terminological part of the Mishnaic language (as *langue*).

The names of norms formed by expressive use of biblical wording are available for syntactical constructions as nouns, for example 'it and its young' with the preposition *bet* ('through', 'by') in the following case:[54]

[50] As for the fourth word, the Mishnaic term המבעה (crop-destroyer), it is a paraphrase of the contents of verse 22:4 in one of two rival rabbinic interpretations we know about. In other words, it too occupies its position according to the arrangement of the biblical text. It is possible that the Mishnah deliberately *avoided* expressive use of the biblical terminology of that verse because of its known problem of ambiguity. The issue is bound up with the question of the antiquity of Targumic texts. On this aspect, see Kahle, *The Cairo Geniza*, 205–7 and J. Heinemann, 'Early Halakah in the Palestinian Targumim'. On the question of how old this *mishnah* might be, and what its precise relationship is to the biblical verse, see Jackson, 'The Fence-Breaker and the *actio de pastu pecoris* in Early Jewish Law'; id., 'Maimonides' Definitions of *Tam* and *Mu'ad*', 169 f.   [51] ת.

[52] The processes of linguistic adaption from the language of Scripture to that of the rabbis are complex and interesting. Two examples are analysed in Boertien, 'Einige Bemerkungen zu Bibelzitaten in der Mischna', 74–6; cf. Saénz-Badillos, *A History of the Hebrew Language*, 174 ff.

[53] In its lack of semantic transparency, the expression is exactly like an *opaque compound* in ordinary language (cf. Bauer, *English Word-Formation*, 19 f.). Although קן can be used in rabbinic Hebrew to refer to the bird, not only the nest, it is doubtful that the Mishnaic expression could be translated as 'the letting go of the bird' with reference to the dam. Cf. Jastrow, 1387b ('the duty of letting the mother bird go when a nest is taken out'); the Mishnaic word *qinnim* refers to the sacrifical pair of birds (e.g. mQin 2:1); cf. Albeck, *Einführung*, 353; Danby, *The Mishnah*, 599. The expression contained in our passage Albeck paraphrases as 'die Vertreibung des Muttervogels vor dem Ausnehmen eines Vogelnestes' (p. 360). Cf. Holtzmann, *Qinnim*, 10 f., 17.

[54] Similar in some respects is the expression משום, 'because of' (Jastrow, 1536a). It can be used to

[27] mHul 4:5[55]   Lev. 22:28

If a man slaughtered a beast and found in it . . . a living nine month's birth it needs to be slaughtered and he [thereby] becomes culpable by [virtue of the law of] 'it and its young'—these are the words of R. Meir.

The biblical wording in cases like these has no direct probative function; it is not given as an warrant for the applicability (or inapplicability) of the norm to the legal case which is the Mishnah's topic. Neither the words which make up the name of the norm, nor any other part of the verse from which they are taken, need to provide such an argument—their actual meaning plays only a minimal role. This is obvious when the norm's name is found in a statement of the form, '[Norm] π applies inside the land and outside the land', as in passage **[26]**; and the phrase 'it and its young' is used as the subject of a sentence in a similar statement in mHul 5:1.

Terms created by expressive use of Scriptural wording are treated in every respect as the Mishnah's own language. Thus their Scriptural meaning can be quite irrelevant for their terminological function in the Mishnah's discourse. This can be seen where a Scriptural term which has been adopted into Mishnah's own language is treated as *problematic* in meaning. In such cases, a clarification is mostly not given by going back to Scripture (but see case **[30]** below). Instead, a *definition* of the term *in its Mishnaic use* is given.

[28] mYeb 8:2 I (3)[56]   Deut. 23:2 (E 1)

Who is 'he who is wounded by crushing'? He whose testicles are wounded and even if it is only one of them. 'And he who has his privy member cut off'? He whose member is cut. But if there remains of the crown as much as the thread of a hair, he is fit.

The answer to the second definition question makes no attempt to link the defining moment (measure of remaining crown) back to the Scriptural expression or its co-text. Similarly for the next passage:

[29] mBek 7:3[57]   Lev. 21:18

A person 'mutilated' (החרום) is disqualified [from priestly service]. Who is 'mutilated'? He who can paint both his eyes together.

The Mishnaic term is defined, and *thereby* also the legal meaning of the biblical term. But the Mishnah is not interpreter of a biblical term at this

---

introduce a Scriptural quotation with or without a verb of speaking (compare mBik 1:2 I (2) with mMak 1:3). Related is the phrase יש בו משום, found e.g. in mBM 9:12 I (3); cf. also the use of מפני for a quotation (mHallah 4:10 = mBik 1:3). In mMen 10:4 I (2) Scriptural wording is introduced with the word *mitswah* in the phrase כדי לקיים בו מצוה. In the case of prohibitions, the construction '*bal* plus verb' is used, as in mQid 1:7 II (3). See further in Ch. 12 below (n. 103).

point, but user of a Mishnaic one, and as such its voice can pronounce a definition. Here is an attempt to articulate the various possibilities of adapting and defining:

Topic8: Explication of a biblical term (or an adaptation of it), when in expressive use (π), by the provision of a legal or otherwise globalized definition. The definition is presented with a view to the term's Mishnaic function and without explicit or discernible recourse to its Scriptural one.

Topic8 is the most extreme form of imposing a perspective on a Scriptural word. It could be said that the biblical term is not so much perspectivized as re-created; and if an elucidation of the meaning of the term as *Scriptural* is intended, that is often not obvious. It thus also neutralizes, although by default, the Scriptural co-text. If there is more than one suitable biblical occurrence (see case **[31]** below), it is sometimes not even clear where the biblical term was taken from. The biblical term is used expressively, its meaning is treated as if it was wholly Mishnaic, and there is no 'Lemma' in a fixed biblical location.

In the following passage use is made of the Scriptural meaning of a term; and, as in the preceding texts, its meaning is thereafter put into question. In this case, however, the meaning is clarified by going back to the biblical passage from which the expression was adopted in the first place.[58] And yet it is the previous use in a Mishnaic list which is being clarified; Scripture thus provides evidence in a curious reversal of hermeneutic polarities:

[30] mMiqw 9:1–2[59]   Ps. 40:3 (E 2)

[*mishnah* 1] These interpose in the case of a person [between the water and the body]: ... [*mishnah* 2] ... 'miry clay', potter's clay, and road-lime. What is miry clay (טיט היון)? This is the clay of pits, as it is said, 'And he lifted me out of the watery pit, out of the miry clay'.

The expression 'miry clay' is used in the biblical verse to refer to the place also described as 'pit' in the parallel phrase. Accepting that they refer to the same location (Syntax3), and generalizing the relationship, the one is taken to illuminate the meaning of the other: 'miry clay' is the clay one finds in pits. However, this leads to an explanation of what the *Mishnah*, which used the term before, means by 'miry clay'.

Although this is not a case of Topic8, it shares with some of the passages quoted above the feature of an איזה question (what is?). The איזה question usually recalls a term that is used in a preceding Mishnaic passage, often an item in a list. In a considerable number of cases the Mishnaic term thus put into question is a biblical expression in expressive Mishnaic use, that is, not reduplicated. The relevant word remains thus embedded in the Mishnah's voice, and the question of meaning is not raised for the *Scriptural* use; the

---

[58] The expression יון occurs only in two biblical passages, and is only in Ps. 40:2 combined with טיט.
[59] §πC1(¬R1.1)S2T3.

term does not become a biblical Lemma. Here is a description of the format recalling a previously used biblical term for the purpose of defining it in some manner:

§:   Reiteration and explication of a biblical term used expressively in an earlier (Mishnaic) list.[60]

In most cases the definition does not involve a reconnection of the term with a biblical occurrence. But as our case [30] shows, even when a biblical setting is considered, Scripture's meaning does not necessarily become the focus of a hermeneutic gesture. Scripture's use is merely evidence towards determining the meaning of the word in the Mishnah's use.

The iteration of the list item can be separated by some distance from the list in which it originally figured, or it can be very close, as in the following case:

[31] mPeah 4:10[61]   Lev. 19:9; 23:22

[*mishnah* 9] The 'gleanings', the 'forgotten' [sheaf],[62] and *Peah* of a non-Jew are liable to tithes . . . [*mishnah* 10] What are 'gleanings' (לקט איזהו)? Whatever drops down at the moment of reaping.

The term לקט occurs only twice in the Hebrew Bible;[63] and the Mishnaic use and definition of the term, having no apparent exegetical orientation, yields no evidence as to which of these two passages is seen as the biblical location. This is not surprising, as it is the normative *topic* of the Mishnah which is the focus of the Mishnaic passage, not the Scriptural Lemma.[64]

Just as there are Mishnaic names for norms formed from the linguistic material of Scripture, so there are names for Scriptural texts formed from words occurring in them. In such usage it is again not the meaning of a Scriptural passage that is referred to, but primarily the passage as textual object. Often, the name given to an entity of text is its *beginning* or opening verse, as in the following passage:

[32] mTam 5: 1[65]   Deut. 11:13[–21]; Num. 15:37[–41]

The officer said to them: Pronounce one benediction! They pronounced a benediction and recited the 'Ten Commandments' (עשרת הדברים), *Shema'*, 'And it shall come to pass if you shall hearken' (והיה אם שמוע), 'And [the Lord] spoke [unto Moses]' (ויאמר) . . .

---

[60] Cf. my 'Scripture's Implicature' (pp. 168 f., n. 4). We are now able to describe a case such as the 'sorcerer' in mSan 7:11 quite precisely, namely as combination of π, §, and Topic8. There are at least 25 cases of the combination π-§ in the Mishnah, quite a few of them quoted in this study: mMQ 3:9 I (2) [99], mHag 1:5 [35] [99a], mYeb 8:2 I (3) [28], mKet 3:5 II (2) [93], mSan 8:1 [102], mBek 7:3 [29], mArak 3:5 II (2) [59], mTem 6:3 I (3) [140], mMiqw 9:2 [30].

[61] §πT8.

[62] Cf. Deut. 24:19.

[63] And once at Qumran (4QD⁼ 6.3₅), see Clines, iv. 576a.

[64] In all its features, this passage may be considered as compatible with the attitude of topical alignment discussed above, so it could preserve an interpretation of that type.

[65] ΔT9.

'And it shall come to pass if you shall hearken' is the title or name given to a definite piece of Scriptural text, namely the passage that starts with these words (the same goes for the name *Shema*'). The conventional nature of the naming is more obvious in the biblical section mentioned subsequently, under the name 'And he spoke'. On the basis of its wording alone it is impossible to determine which specific piece of text is intended; one needs to know the name's conventional meaning. The opening words of the verse have thus terminological status, which is also clear from the fact that they mark the beginning of a passage, but not its end. In using biblical wording in this way the Mishnah imposes a perspective, so they belong to the TOPIC family.

Topic9: Use of a Scriptural expression or clause as the name of a definite textual entity from Scripture beginning with that expression or clause, or containing it.

As passage **[32]** shows, there are also other names for a biblical text segment which are not formed from its opening words (or indeed any of its words), such as 'Ten Commandments' (of biblical origin: Exod. 34:28; cf. e.g. mSot 7:8 II (3)). There is also a format which combines the names of biblical protagonists with the word מעשה (perhaps best translated as 'incident') into a complex expression. Such expressions (e.g. 'incident of Tammar'), when used in Scriptural exegesis, constitute the resource Topic3, not Topic9.[66] In other places the word *parashah* ('pericope') is used for similar combinations (e.g. פרשת שקלים in mMeg 3:4). Both of these types need in turn to be distinguished from Mishnaic expressions which are used to refer to biblical objects but not to text parts. Examples include 'Generation of the Flood', 'Generation of the Dispersion', or 'Men of Sodom' (all from mSan 10:3). Although these partly employ words used in Scripture to tell the story,[67] they do not function as textual allusions (i.e. π), nor as names for textual entities. They are in fact the rabbinic names of *events* or clusters of events in the history of the people of Torah which is presupposed as known. They work like the expressions 'the survivors of the Titanic', 'the beneficiaries of the New Deal', or 'the students of Tiananmen Square' in current English.[68] The rabbinic names refer to the events as directly *known*; and it is incidental for this usage that Scripture is the source of that knowledge. In that they do not refer to texts, they are a direct 'historic' equivalent of aggadic terms such as 'Aqedah' (the 'binding' of

---

[66] A number of them are found together in mMeg 4:10, a list which includes the items: מעשה ראובן מעשה עגל... מעשה תמר... מעשה דוד ואמנון... See further, Bacher, i. 112 f.

[67] Not, however, in the case of the דור הפלגה; cf. also BDB, s.v. מבול, (550), observing that the word 'the flood' is used almost like a proper name in Scripture itself.

[68] Cf. Coseriu's notion of 'universeller historischer Kontext' (*Textlinguistik*, 98 f.). Coseriu distinguishes from this 'okkasioneller Rede-Kontext', 'kultureller Außer-Rede-Kontext' and 'Redeuniversum'. In the rabbinic discourse, the contents and words of Scripture form an essential part of the last two categories as well.

Isaac), or halakhic ones such as 'Sotah' (the wife suspected of adultery). But while names for text parts consisting of biblical wording also belong in that category, they need to be kept apart, since they retain the *potential* to be looked at for the meaning of the words quoted to make up the name. They have an ambiguous status as Mishnaic term on the one hand and as quotation of Scripture inviting exegesis on the other.[69]

How can one distinguish cases of expressive use (i.e. π) from Mishnaic terms that merely happen to have a Scriptural origin (or are identical with a Scriptural word)? Apart from their actual function in the Mishnaic co-text, an important general criterion seems to be whether the Scriptural expression can be anchored to a specific biblical passage and co-text, that is, whether it can be understood as *lemmatic*, not lexemic. *Hapax legomena*, with their guaranteed unique location in Scripture, or one-word expressions whose conventional meaning identifies a unique location (Topic9) have such a lemmatic status by default. Otherwise, that status depends to some extent on the number of biblical words appearing on the surface of the Mishnah—the more words the better the likelihood of a specific location. The isolated word is only *lemmatic* if it is treated as having a Scriptural sense-in-use, as opposed to a general dictionary item. The latter, that is, the word as 'lexeme', can also become the target of attention among the rabbis.[70] In that case its occurrence somewhere in Scripture is taken for granted, but its analysis resembles an abstract reflection of a native speaker on a word from her/his language. Biblical expressions in the Mishnah should thus perhaps only be classified as expressive use (π) if they retain their potential to be treated as biblical Lemmas; that potential depends on *one* location of Scripture being identifiable as their textual home. The clearest case, on the other hand, of non-allusive use of a Mishnaic word which is also biblical, is its employment as paraphrase of a quoted biblical term in a midrashic unit (Topic3). Even if the Mishnaic term and the biblical one happen to be identical,[71] the functional difference ensures that the former belongs unambiguously and wholly to the language of the Mishnah. It cannot function at the same time as a reduplication of the Scriptural term and as an allusion to it.

---

[69] The last unit of mTam 7:4 is an example for a quotation which, while being used to identify a Scriptural text, is turned into the object of exegesis on the basis of the wording quoted. This is somewhat similar to resource Word9 (Ch. 14).

[70] The only Mishnaic case of such a 'lexemic' treatment of which I am aware is mSheq 3:3, where the literal meaning of 'Terumah' is presupposed. An instance outside the Mishnah is, for example, the treatment of *devir* and *'aron* in BerR 55:7 (ed. Theodor-Albeck, ii. 591). Resources such as Word6.1 and Cotext3/4 seem to be favourites for the treatment of words without a Scriptural 'home', and also GRAPHEME and ICON resources. For all of these, see Ch. 14 below. A literal, decontextualized treatment of meaning is said to belong to 'semantics' by Frawley (*Linguistic Semantics*, 2). Perhaps it would make sense to distinguish a 'semantic' from a 'textual' mode of rabbinic interpretation; see also n. 31 above.

[71] As in [17] above, where the term *Torah* is used to represent the message of a biblical occurrence of *Torah*; and cf. [33] below.

SCRIPTURE AS MISHNAH'S APODOSIS

An important recurrent format for the presentation of halakhic information in the Mishnah is the case schema. It links two elements: a hypothetical situation or circumstance on the one hand, and an obligation or evaluation arising out of that situation/circumstance on the other hand. The link between these two components is often created in a conditional sentence or a syntagma fulfilling a conditional function.[72] The conditional clause (or 'if' part) is referred to as *protasis*, the main clause (the 'then' part) as *apodosis*,[73] and I shall use the terms 'case schema' and 'protasis–apodosis unit' interchangeably. Individual case schemata, or sets of mutually related case schemata, can provide a very effective perspective for any biblical segment integrated with them, be it in expressive use or as midrashic quotation. Two effects of this are of special hermeneutic interest: the effect of reading a biblical clause as conditional when the co-text does not mark it as conditional,[74] and the effect of reading it on a different level of generality from that suggested in its co-text. We shall distinguish three resources in particular:

- reading an unconditional Scriptural syntagma as apodosis of a Mishnaic protasis–apodosis unit (Topic2);
- reading a biblical norm as apodosis of only one protasis–apodosis unit in a Mishnaic set of such units, when its meaning in co-text could equally apply to the others (Topic2.1);
- reading the protasis of a biblical protasis–apodosis unit as generating a specific set of mutually differentiated Mishnaic protases (Topic2.2).

We shall also explore more general ways in which the specificity of the Mishnaic discourse may put into perspective a Scriptural segment (Topic5).

The most direct manner of involving Scripture in a Mishnaic protasis–apodosis unit is to identify a Scriptural segment as yielding or supporting the apodosis. This usually makes a Scriptural segment conditional where its original co-text does not.[75] It also often gives emphasis to some element of the segment unstressed in the biblical co-text;[76] or results in a topic defini-

---

[72] See Azar, 'The Conditional Clause in Mishnaic Hebrew', esp. 67 f. (conditions expressed in non-conditional clause forms).

[73] For the terminology, which was applied to casuistic biblical law before it was applied to rabbinic literature, see e.g. Patrick, *Old Testament Law*, 19 f.; Neusner, for example, in *The Memorized Torah*. See n. 82 in Ch. 9.

[74] This is not to say that the biblical norm (to take an example) must have been meant in an 'absolute' manner, merely because it is not made to depend on conditions through its co-text. There may well have been contextual constraints, or 'regular' circumstances, to which the application of the norm was meant to be tied in biblical times. See on this Jackson, 'The Original Oral Law'.

[75] Using the terminology introduced by A. Alt into the study of biblical law (see above n. 73), one could say that an apodictic biblical norm is placed into a casuistic structure.

[76] See on this Ch. 11 (Opposition6).

tion that is much more specific in the Mishnaic setting than in the biblical one.

[33] mSan 2:1[77]   Lev. 21:12

If a member of his family dies, he [the high priest] does not go out after the bier, but when they are out of view, he is seen, and when they are seen, he is out of view. And [in this manner] he goes out with them up to the gate of the city—these are the words of R. Meir. R. Yehudah says: He does not go out from the sanctuary, as it is said, 'From the sanctuary he shall not go out [and he shall not profane the sanctuary of his God . . .]'.

R. Yehudah's complete case schema runs as follows: If a member of the high priest's family dies (= protasis), he may not go from the sanctuary (to follow the bier = apodosis). It is *as apodosis* that the latter part of the case schema is supported by the verse Lev. 21:12. That sentence is taken to belong thematically to verse 11 (Cotext6), which reads: 'And upon any dead body he may not come; for his father and his mother he shall not make himself unclean.' The leaving of the sanctuary (verse 12) is thus linked to the danger of attracting corpse impurity (verse 11). There are many concrete circumstances which could be envisaged for this link; for example, the high priest could unintentionally come near graves while taking a stroll, and so on. All such circumstances would cater for the link of verses 11 and 12. But the Mishnah has no interest in casual strolls or unspecified activities involving fuzzy risks of corpse contamination. Instead, it envisages a very specific circumstance qua protasis: a (close) relative of the high priest dies, the bier with the body is being carried to the graveyard—how is he to act? The answer is (in R. Yehudah's opinion) *literally* supplied by Scripture: *Under such circumstances*, 'he shall not go out from the sanctuary'. Scripture, in form of a paraphrase by R. Yehudah which changes not a single word,[78] becomes the apodosis of a non-biblical protasis. For there is no trace of such a protasis–apodosis unit in Scripture itself, despite the fact that corpse impurity through mother and father is mentioned in verse 11. The biblical co-text allows for other relationships between verses 11 and 12, for there is no explicit signal of conditional dependency between them. And even those interpretations which are compatible with the Mishnaic employment of the verse, such as, 'The high priest is not under any circumstance to leave the sanctuary in order to avoid attracting corpse uncleanness', are much more general than the meaning now accorded to the verse by the protasis, 'If a relative of his dies and they bring out the bier . . .'. Thus we find, despite the reappearance of so many biblical features in the Mishnah, Mishnaic specificity *added* to information supplied by Scripture. And as the passage shows, this effect is achieved by merely positioning the Scriptural segment

---

[77] Yehudah •¶C1C6L3T2T7.

[78] Only tense and word order are changed, not the choice of words. Scripture says: ומן־המקדש לא יצא, while R. Yehudah (by way of the Mishnah) says: אינו יוצא מן המקדש. The resulting repetition (see also Ch. 6 below) is stylistically conspicuous (on this, see my 'Delaying the Progress from Case to Case').

at a specific (apodosis-) point of a discourse moving in protasis–apodosis units. As was said, R. Yehudah's own expression of the apodosis repeats the biblical text in every word.[79] Thus, the new co-textual position and function, not a rephrasing of the original idea, achieves the hermeneutic result. The effect of that new function on a biblical clause could be summarized by saying: The biblical segment is prefixed by the phrase, 'Under such circumstances . . .'.

The integration of biblical quotations in protasis–apodosis units provides one of the most effective Mishnaic mechanisms for reading a Scriptural segment as more specific than suggested by its co-text. More common than a case like [33], in which rabbinic and biblical wording are almost identical, is the case where additional resources are involved in adapting the meaning of the biblical quotation to its new function. Here too, other meaning possibilities are silenced, where necessary through Cotext1, in favour of Scripture's contribution to a specifically defined question.[80]

[34] mBik 1:1–2 I (2)[81]   Exod. 23:19a; cf. 34:25

[*mishnah* 1] There are some who bring the first fruits and recite [the declaration], some who bring but do not recite, and there are some who do not bring. These are those that do not bring [the first-fruits]: The one who plants within what is his, but bends it [to continue growing] into what belongs to someone else or into what belongs to the public; the one who bends it [to continue growing] from what belongs to someone else or from what belongs to the public into what is his. The one who plants within what is his and bends it [to continue growing] into what is his, but someone else's path or a public path is in the middle, behold this one does not bring [the first fruits]. R. Yehudah says: Such a one does bring. [2] For what reason may he not bring? Because (מִשּׁוּם) of what is said, 'The first fruits of your ground [you shall bring to the house of the Lord your God]'—[you may not bring them] unless all of the growth is from your ground.

There is no trace in the verse or its surroundings[82] of a differentiation of circumstances for the obligation to bring first fruits. The preceding verse deals with temple sacrifices, the second half of this verse with the prohibition to cook a kid in its mother's milk. The biblical imperative itself is expressed without qualification or distinction of circumstances, indeed without condition. The Mishnah places the biblical phrase 'your ground' into a network of highly specific circumstances, for which the biblical 'your' can be taken to be relevant (if emphasized) in excluding other personal

---

[79] In so doing, R. Yehudah also commits himself to the validity of these words; the hermeneutic utterance makes Scripture, in the meaning fixed by the discourse, part of the commitment of the Mishnah and its voices. See on this Ch. 12.

[80] It is worth recalling here the modern practice of lawyers, in adversarial litigation, to curtail hostile witnesses' answers and to insist that they fit the format of the question precisely. See Goodrich, *Languages of the Law*, who labels such courtroom exchanges 'the language of annexation and reformulation' (pp. 193 ff., with transcripts from trials).

[81] O0O1O1.3T2.

[82] Verse 16 mentions *bikkurim* but in a different context; none of the other biblical occurrences offer information on the ownership of 'ground'.

pronouns.[83] Put into this Mishnaic context, the Scriptural wording produces a decision (an apodosis): no first fruits may be brought, because it has to be the bringer's ground. The Mishnah goes on to list various types of control over property and its growth other than that of the full owner, thus presenting a further list of conditions. All of these are also taken to be excluded by the biblical '*your* ground'. In these hermeneutic operations the Mishnaic co-text provides highly differentiated protases which the quoted Scriptural text is taken to engage with. In this way norms or biblical expressions within norms are determined in their significance on a level of detail much greater than that suggested in the thematic context and co-text of Scripture.

Topic2: Determination of the meaning and subject-matter of a biblical expression or clause through its linkage to a Mishnaic apodosis. The apodosis can be one of several rival apodoses, and is part of a Mishnaic protasis–apodosis unit (or of a series of such units). The conditional alternatives belonging to this Mishnaic apodosis subdivide a larger halakhic theme not so subdivided in the Scriptural co-text; where the biblical text is not part of a conditional structure, this resource also conditionalizes the biblical segment.[84]

In other words: (1) Scripture is linked to the apodosis of a Mishnaic protasis–apodosis unit;[85] (2) the Mishnaic protasis–apodosis unit is part of a division of the larger halakhic theme; (3) no such division and/or no protasis–apodosis unit is expressed in the verse taken as Scripture's treatment of the same theme, or in its co-text.

The Mishnaic case schemata which impose a perspective on segments of Scripture can often be seen to form a set, or a paradigm.[86] These sets are mostly created by varying one element of the protasis ('if'-clause), that is, one situational circumstance, at a time.[87] Of particular interest is the integration of a Scriptural segment into such sets where the wording, taken in its biblical co-text, is so general as to fit *all* of the cases, but is allocated to only one of them in the Mishnah. This brings about a dramatic reduction in generality. Instead of functioning like a heading for the whole set, the segment's relevance (and meaning) is limited to only one of the members of the set. Here is an example:[88]

---

[83] '*Your* ground'—as opposed to the ground of others. On the use of contrasts as hermeneutic resource (Opposition0/Opposition1), see Ch. 11.

[84] The provision of a context of conditions, distinctions, and qualifications of which there is no sign in the lemmatic text is an important strategy in the Gemara's reading of the Mishnah.

[85] For the link of biblical wording to the protasis of a Mishnaic protasis–apodosis unit, see format 'i' treated at the beginning of the next chapter.

[86] The notion of the protasis–apodosis unit as a functional unit in the Mishnaic discourse is inherently linked to the idea of a sequencing of such units, forming paradigms of protases. I shall make repeated use of the notion of paradigm (in particular in Ch. 11, but also in Chs. 6, 9, and 13).

[87] I have attempted to describe this in 'From Case to Case'.

[88] Cf. Fraenkel, *Darkhey*, i. 79, who says this midrashic unit resembles aggadic midrash.

[35] = [98a] mHag 1:5[89]   Deut. 16:17

He who has many eaters and few possessions brings many peace offerings and few whole offerings;[90] [he who has] many possessions and few eaters brings many whole offerings and few peace offerings; [he who has] few of these as well as those, about him they said [עַל זֶה אָמְרוּ], in *mishnah* 1:2]: a *meah* of silver, and: two pieces of silver; [he who has] many of these as well as those, about him it is said (עַל זֶה נֶאֱמַר): 'Each man [shall give] according to the gift in his possession, according to the blessing of the Lord your God which he has given you.'

The biblical norm quoted here seems to give a comprehensive rule for the value of the (pilgrimage) offerings, namely, by leaving the actual worth flexible to fit varying circumstances. The Mishnah instead allocates and restricts the position of biblical flexibility to only one of the four hypothetical possibilities it distinguishes. These possible situations are mutually differentiated protases within the *same* thematic framework as the biblical norm. The four situational circumstances, or the paradigm of case schemata, are created by way of permutation from the elements 'quantity of possessions' and 'quantity of eaters'. It is likely that these two elements, from which the four cases are 'computed', are even hermeneutically linked to two parallel expressions in the quoted verse: 'gift' is interpreted as possessions, while 'blessing' is taken to refer to family (children).[91] Sets of four protasis–apodosis units, generated from the permutation of two elements in two modifications, are repeatedly found in the Mishnah.[92] In cases where a biblical verse is attached to them, it is mostly restricted in its generality by being allocated to only one member of the set or paradigm. Here is a definition of the resource embodied in [35]:

Topic2.1: Determination of the meaning and subject-matter of a biblical clause or sentence (conditional or not) by linking it to the apodosis of one of a set of Mishnaic protases. This set of protases can be generated from the permutation or stressing of linguistic items in the biblical segment, thereby subdividing the larger halakhic theme not so subdivided in the biblical segment or its co-text.

The phrase 'linking it' is chosen to cover both the format of explicit re-

---

[89] πC5P3R4.1T2.1.

[90] From the latter type of offering, the person bringing the sacrifice does not benefit, but from the former he does. By changing the mix in favour of the latter, the apodoses accommodate poverty. Fraenkel, *Darkhey*, i. 79 f., even sees a link between the two types of offerings and the parts of the biblical verse, in which case the 'according to' would point to parity (of whole offerings and peace offerings) and 'blessing' would refer to both the blessing of children and the possessions. Cf. bHag 8a on Deut. 16:10. MS Kaufmann reverses the order in which the 'possessions' and 'eaters' are mentioned the next clause (the sense is the same).

[91] See mMS 5:13, where the phrase 'bless your people Israel' (Deut. 27:15) is extended and explained by the Mishnaic '—with sons and with daughters'. Cf. Fraenkel, *Darkhey*, i. 80.

[92] See e.g. Lightstone, *The Rhetoric of the Babylonian Talmud*, 181: 'Mishnah will, in addition, permutate lists of circumstances in order to produce a series of cases, each requiring classification under one rule or another.' Cf. the treatment of Deut. 23:19 in mTem 6:3 II (3). There are also *iterative* mechanisms in the provision of protases, such as in mBQ 9:7 (added fifth of the added fifth, etc.).

duplication and that of expressive use. The formula used in **[35]** to introduce the biblical quotation is, as often in such cases, על זה נאמר.[93] This phrase
is remarkable in that it uses biblical words to express what the Mishnah has
to say while *marking* them as biblical.[94] There is thus no room for a reduplication of the biblical message in the Mishnah's 'own' words. We shall look
at such cases, where the Mishnah quotes and yet uses for its own expression
a Scriptural segment, in the next chapter. But the present case in which
the Scriptural segment is used to express specifically an apodosis, can be
treated here. The following definition is meant to include any hypothetical
'if–then' structure, whether halakhic as in **[35]** or non-halakhic as in **[36]**.

Performance3: Use of a Scriptural expression or clause as rabbinic utterance directly expressing (π) the apodosis of a Mishnaic protasis–apodosis
unit.

Here is another example of Performance3:

[36] mAvot 3:2 I (3)[95]   Ps. 1:1

R. Hananiah ben Teradion says: Two who sit and words of Torah are not [spoken]
between them, behold this (הרי זה) is the 'seat of scorners', for it is said, '[Happy the
man who does not walk in the counsel of the wicked and does not stand on the way
of the sinners] and in the seat of scorners does not sit [(2) but finds delight in the
Torah of the Lord and meditates on his Torah day and night]'.

The situation (protasis) that two sit together without exchanging words of
Torah, receives the evaluation (apodosis) 'seat of scorners' (in which one
ought not to sit). Other hermeneutic resources are also at work: the biblical
metaphor of sitting/seat (coming after walk and stand) is applied to a
concrete situation of sitting in conversation (Word6.2). And the topic from
verse 2—Torah—is made immediately relevant to verse 1 by reading it as
a contrast. Thus, the meaning of 'scorn' is not determined through its
semantic features in isolation, but through its specific textual contrast to
'Torah' (Difference5). But the Mishnah does not express anew what sort of
thing it is when two sit and do not exchange words of Torah—it uses the
words of Scripture to do so. In other words, the characterization or judgement of the hypothetical situation (in this case non-halakhic) is expressed
only in the words from Scripture, 'seat of scorners'. These words are
marked out as quotation; that marking is already achieved by the demonstrative, 'this is'. At the same time they are directly used to characterize a

---

[93] For the use of על, see Bacher, i. 174 f. (s.v. קרא); 5 f. (s.v. אמר); cf. also 155 (s.v. פרש). Van Uchelen,
'The Formula על זה נאמר in the Mishnah', touches upon matters of interpretation in his functional
analysis, but only incidentally. Thus, he does not link the formula to others which are functionally
very similar, such as ועליו הכתוב אומר in mPes 8:9 I (4). See also van Uchelen's *Chagigah*. The formula על
זה נאמר is used in mBQ 3:9 II (4) in the same manner as in **[35]**. On other formulas of this type, see the
closing section of Ch. 12.

[94] It may be noted that our passage **[35]** contains a similar phrase, על זה אמרו, introducing a
quotation not from Scripture but from the Mishnah itself ('about him they said: a *meah* of silver . . .').

[95] •πC5D5P3T2T3W6.1(sit).

repeatable, hypothetical situation in a format which can be understood as a protasis–apodosis unit, that is, a conditional structure. These are the features pinpointed by the Performance3 resource (which will be complemented by similar resources in the next chapter).

The formula employed in [35], על זה נאמר, is also used to introduce a biblical quotation *added* to a Mishnaic formulation of the apodosis.[96] Yet, even with such reduplication of the Scriptural wording the intensity and directness of perspectivization resembles that of expressive use. It may be an exaggeration, but a useful one, to say: the control over meaning exerted by the mere positioning of a Scriptural segment into a Mishnaic protasis–apodosis structure is not far removed from the control of authorship itself. For then the biblical wording is like semantic *raw material* for the expression of Mishnaic ideas. In a manner of speaking (literally, a manner of *speaking*), the Mishnah becomes Scripture's author.[97]

We turn now to a case where the biblical norm itself has conditional structure. Here too, a Mishnaic case schema can be used to impose a highly defined perspective on the Scriptural wording. All main elements of the wording of the biblical protasis are given specific circumstantial meaning.[98] But their apodosis is taken to be determined by the actual biblical apodosis.

[37] mBM 8:1 I–II (2)[99]   Exod. 22:14 and 13 (E 15 and 14)

He who 'borrows' [lit: asks, i.e. asks for loan of] a cow and 'borrows' its owner['s services] 'with it'; or if he [hired the cow and] hired its owner 'with it'; or if he 'borrowed' the owners[100] or hired them and afterwards 'borrowed' the cow—'and it died', he is not liable, as it is said, 'If its owner is with it, he does not pay [if it was hired it came for its hire]' (verse 14). But if he 'borrowed' the cow and afterwards 'borrowed' the owners, or hired them—'and it died', he is liable, as it is said: 'Its owner not being with it, he shall surely pay' (verse 13).

The unfolding of the various protases corresponds to the lexical items in the biblical verse partly indicated by the quotation marks in the translation. The two biblical terms 'hire' and 'ask' (in the sense of 'borrow') are taken up in the Mishnaic reformulations, as are the two subjects—the animal and its owner. The Mishnah also uses the Scriptural expression 'with it' (עמו, in the Mishnah עמה) and interprets it as meaning two things: that the owner's *services* also are part of the agreement,[101] and that the borrowing or hire of

---

[96] Examples of this are mPeah 7:3 II (2), cf. 5:6; mSukkah 2:6; mHag 1:6; mSan 3:7.

[97] As I said before, Scripture's wording can be seen to become *langue*, rather than *parole* in Mishnah's hands. As for the paradoxical notion of Mishnah becoming the *author* of Scripture while using Scripture's own words, the story 'Pierre Menard, Author of the *Quixote*' by Jorge Luis Borges is of some help in thinking this through (*Labyrinths*, 62–71). The phenomenon will concern us further in the next chapter.

[98] The mechanism of emphasizing parts of the biblical wording unstressed in their biblical setting is explained in Chs. 11 and 12 below; the operative resource in this passage is Opposition6.

[99] πE1.0O6T2.2T3.

[100] The plural could be used for the singular here, as is sometimes the case with biblical בעל in the sense of owner (but with suffixes); so Windfuhr (*Baba meṣia*, 89), with reference to Gesenius–Kautzsch, *Hebrew Grammar*, sec. 124 i.   [101] His physical presence is not decisive.

Table 4.2 *Protases and apodoses in passage [37]*

If the animal died:	'to hire'	'to borrow'
Animal first	(1) liable	(4) liable
Owner first	(2) not liable	(5) not liable
Owner together 'with' animal	(3) not liable	(6) not liable

the animal either precedes that of its owner(s) or is simultaneous with it. Thus a paradigm of possibilities is generated by the two types of legal agreement, the two objects of the agreement, and their sequences. To these possibilities, the apodoses of verses 13 and 14 are allocated accordingly. Table 4.2 shows how this is done, with apodoses numbered. To each of the six cases in Table 4.2, one of the two biblical apodoses is linked: two of them are tied to the apodosis of verse 13, 'he shall surely pay' (rephrased with the Mishnaic 'liable', חייב), and four of them are allocated to the apodosis of verse 14, 'he shall not pay' ('not liable', פטור in the Mishnah). Here is a general description of this resource:

Topic2.2: Differentiation of elements in the biblical wording of a conditional syntagma into a Mishnaic set of separate protases leading to the same Mishnaic apodosis, the latter being a repetition or rephrasing of the biblical main clause.

This operation is found twice in **[37]**: once with verse 14 (the owner is with it), and a second time (without its owner) with verse 13.

Even without imposing or refining conditional structures, the Mishnah can embed general biblical formulations into very specific accounts.[102] I give such hermeneutic embedding the resource name Topic5 and define it in the following way:

Topic5: Determination of the meaning of a biblical expression or clause by embedding it into a Mishnaic account of the same topic whose greater internal diversification is not linked to any differentiation of signs in Scripture.[103]

We have already encountered an instructive example of this in passage **[24]** above. Here it is again:

[37a] = [24] mPes 7:1 I (2)[104]   Exod. 12:8

How do they 'roast' the Passover offering? One thrusts a skewer of pomegranate-wood through it from its mouth to its anus, and places its legs and entrails inside it—these are the words of R. Yose Ha-Gelili.

---

[102] In some cases (as often in tractate Yoma), a sequence of actions is treated in chronological but interdependent fashion (fulfilment of one triggers obligation of the next). Passage **[38]** below is embedded in such a larger structure, the ritual of the *Sotah*.

[103] In mSot 7:5 the Topic5 operation is also marked as coming from a pre-Mishnaic past (Δ). See Neusner, *A History of the Mishaic Law of Women*, pt. IV, pp. 65 f.   [104] • ¶π≈T5T8.

While the basic topic of this unit is found in Scripture, the detail is not, nor is any attempt made here to derive it from the biblical text. There are many other ways to roast a lamb; there are other types of skewer one could use (one is explicitly excluded in *mishnah* 2); there must be other ways to apply the skewer to the animal; there are, according to R. Aqiva's objection (not here repeated, see [24]), other and better ways to deal with legs and entrails. All of these variants would still satisfy the wording of the basic biblical norm and the term 'roast'.[105] Thus, the biblical text is embedded into an account of a practice (or ideal practice) in which its terms convey concrete detail, and in so doing receive very specific meaning. In sum, the Mishnaic details impose a perspective on the meaning of the biblical word 'roast' (Topic5), thereby answering a Mishnaic question about the *definition* of the term's meaning (Topic8) in the expressive *use* of the Mishnah (π).

A similar effect can be achieved without explicit definitional goal. The next example is in some respects similar to mPes 5:5 ff., whose opening section was quoted above as case [10]. There as here, the detail-rich practice is presented as coming from pre-Mishnaic times (see next chapter on the *delta*-format Δ).

[38] mSot 2:2[106]   Num. 5:17

He [the priest] entered the sanctuary and turned to the right and there was a place, one cubit by one cubit, and a marble flagstone on which was fixed a ring. Having raised it, he took dust from beneath it and put in [the bowl] enough to be visible on the water, as it is said, 'And of the dust that is on the floor of the tabernacle the priest shall take and put it into the water'.

Through its placement at the end, the biblical sentence is made to sound like a *summary* of the wealth of detail preceding it. But the Scriptural co-text contains none of the details, and the Mishnah makes no attempt to link them to the biblical quotation or its environment.[107] Speaking formally, there is no correspondence in number between the divisions imposed on Scripture and the items of information presented in the Mishnah. Each of the operative words in the quotation is placed in perspective by being embedded into a whole sentence, giving concrete detail: the words 'floor', 'tabernacle', and 'take' assume thus a very specific, and indeed graphic, meaning. But there is no attempt to point to individual signs in Scripture which correspond to the information 'flagstone', 'ring', 'marble', 'turned right', 'one cubit', and so on. The new description *as a whole* is spread out over the biblical description *as a whole*. We are stressing the last point in order to place it in contrast with another Mishnaic resource which provides for a numerical matching of individual items (Redundancy9; see Chapter 13).

---

[105] Cf. n. 3 in Ch. 3 above.

[106] ΔT3T5T7.

[107] Which is not to say that such a derivation using perhaps a different Scriptural passage might not be found elsewhere in rabbinic literature; it is also not to say that, if no derivation is found, this means that Scripture played no part in the details of this account (see n. 7 above and n. 114 in Ch. 2).

5

Using Scripture as Hermeneutic Utterance

Expressive use of biblical wording is compatible with signalling the biblical origin of the wording while employing it. Such signals are common where the Mishnah applies Scriptural sentences to unique occurrences or persons to evaluate them or to endow them with special meaning (in a manner similar to the application of proverbs). The basic mechanism in all varieties of such expressive use is the identification of unique events or individuals as *referents* of a general biblical wording, often presented by deictic terms. The hermeneutic effect consists in the fresh, largely unpredictable interaction between the new situation—told or selected by the Mishnah—and the fixed biblical words, selected and uttered by the Mishnah *about* the situation. The Scriptural verse is uttered anew, and in the process is confirmed or 'fulfilled'. The same basic hermeneutic mechanism explains the application of a general biblical sentence to a unique *biblical* occurrence. A special variation of the latter resource (not found in the Mishnah, but otherwise common) is that the evaluating verse is quoted alongside a separate quotation of a biblical verse actually reporting the unique occurrence. The second quotation then invites meta-linguistic scrutiny of the biblical wording; a scrutiny which is additional to the indirect determination of meaning resulting from the basic movement of *application*.

DECLARED AND UNDECLARED USE OF SCRIPTURAL WORDING

So far we have seen the Mishnah use Scriptural words when speaking about general topics, or normative situations (π). I shall presently turn to the use of biblical words for speaking about *unique* (as opposed to general) events or persons. But first I shall continue my examination of the expressive use of biblical words for general and normative topics with the following question. Does it matter if the biblical text is marked as biblical or not? In passage [35], presented earlier to illustrate expressive use, Scriptural wording is both marked by a quotation formula and used as Mishnaic utterance. Let us examine another passage which declares its wording as biblical:

[39] mBQ 9:7[1]   Lev. 5:21 f. (E 6:2 f.)

So, too, with a 'deposit', for it is said,[2] '. . . in [a matter of] deposit or of security or through robbery, or if he has oppressed his neighbour (22) or has found lost property and dealt falsely in it and sworn to a lie . . .'—such a one must pay (זה הרי משלם) the value and the [added] fifth and [offer] a guilt-offering.

Despite the occurrence of an explicit quotation formula ('for it is said'), the biblical clause is *used* for the Mishnaic expression of the protasis. What is decisive is that there is no Mishnaic reformulation of the biblical message: eliminating the words of Leviticus from the Mishnaic passage would amount to destroying the Mishnaic protasis–apodosis unit. For in this passage it is a protasis (not the apodosis, as in [35]) which is expressed by way of a biblical segment:[3] the deixis 'such a one' refers to the behaviour described in the biblical quotation. In other words, the biblical wording appearing in the protasis or the apodosis of Mishnaic case schema (and in other general topics) can be recognized as expressive use by the absence of reduplication alone. It is not necessary that biblical words are *tacitly* used in order to be *used*. Where the biblical wording is explicitly quoted but is necessary to express a Mishnaic point, we shall speak of *declared* expressive use of Scriptural wording. But the hallmark of expressive use whether declared or not, is the absence of a reduplication of the biblical message in extra words. It is important to have this established, for in the resources to which we now turn biblical words are often marked as biblical, and yet they carry the self-expression of the rabbinic voice.

---

[1] ®πᵢT2T8. The sign 'ᵢ' symbolizes the link of Scriptural wording to the protasis of a Mishnaic protasis–apodosis unit (without prejudging if Scripture is used expressively or reduplicated). See, however, n. 3 below.

[2] Not all witnesses have the reduplication of 'deposit' in [39] together with the phrase 'for it is said', i.e. the formal feature which we are here investigating. See Epstein, *Mavo*, 1132.

[3] There is a noteworthy difference between links of biblical wording to the protasis and to the apodosis. An unconditional Scriptural segment supporting a Mishnaic apodosis is often reduplicated, i.e. presented in midrashic format. But for a segment linked to a Mishnaic protasis, expressive use (π) seems to be preferred. The only Mishnaic case of a protasis in the midrashic format is mTaan 3:3. (and cf. mQid 3:4 I (2)). The passage also has an unusual syntactic structure and employs the rare Aramaic expression דכתיב (see Ch. 12 below). Epstein (*Mavo*, 685) collects the arguments for the secondary status of the biblical quotation in mTaan. 3:3.

USING A SCRIPTURAL QUOTATION
AS SITUATED UTTERANCE

Rabbinic use of Scripture is essentially 'application'—that has often been said, and the resources to which we are turning now are perhaps the most obvious manifestation of this. But what does 'application' mean? I shall try here, as throughout this study, to draw out single strands, that is, explain 'application' in terms which are more specific and make fewer assumptions than that word. The notion of expressive use is going to be central. My claim is going to be that there are Mishnaic resources which consist in the *expressive use* of general biblical wording for *unique* events, facts, or persons.[4] The stress is on 'expressive use' on the one hand—as opposed to the reduplication of Scripture's message, as we just explained. And on the other hand, on the singularity of the items about which the rabbinic voice speaks—as opposed to general topics. The hermeneutic effect of such application of biblical words *on those words themselves* can be very striking, and yet remains largely implicit. I shall distinguish the following main types:

- a biblical clause or sentence is said about a singular or unique non-biblical occurrence or person (Performance2);
- biblical words are used to perform, by uttering them, a uniquely situated legal act (Performance4);
- general biblical wording is said about a singular biblical occurrence or person (Use1–4);
- general rabbinic wording (maxims, parables) is said about a singular biblical occurrence or person (Use5/6).

All of these are different from expressive use occurring in Mishnaic protasis–apodosis units, in that a general biblical formulation is applied either to a unique occurrence, or in a unique, unrepeatable situation. In other words, the biblical signs are presented so as to interact directly with unique circumstances. There are important parallels between this hermeneutic movement and the employment of proverbs,[5] in particular where the Scriptural segment used constitutes a whole sentence.[6] In that case, a non-biblical voice may use a biblical clause or sentence as a complete, self-contained utterance in a new situation of speaking. Our next passage shows how this works. In it the anonymous voice of the Mishnah has recourse to a ready-made Scriptural sentence in giving a moral judgement on a specific set of (non-biblical) events:

---

[4] This means: the events, facts, or persons are unique in place and time. It does not necessarily mean that this event/fact/person *exhausts*, in the Mishnaic view, what is referable to by the biblical wording (another similarity to the use of proverbs). See below.

[5] See Ch. 2 (text following n. 75), and the closing section of this chapter.

[6] Cf. the observation of Hasan-Rokem, *Proverbs*, that the proverb, in contrast to the quotation, needs formally speaking to be a complete sentence (p. 54).

[40] mYoma 3:11[7]   Prov. 10:7 (a + b)

Nicanor . . . and he was remembered for praise. [*mishnah* 11] But these [were remembered] for disgrace: They of the House of Garmu were unwilling to teach how to prepare the bread of presence. They of the House of Abtinas were unwilling to teach how to prepare the incense. Hygros ben Levi had special knowledge in singing but was unwilling to teach it. Ben Kamtsar was unwilling to teach the art of writing. Of the first it is said, 'The memory of the righteous is for a blessing', and of these [others] it is said, 'But the name of the wicked shall rot'.

The two halves of the verse Prov. 10:7 are applied to two groups of priests whose behaviour is described in the preceding Mishnaic sentences. The biblical quotation directly expresses a value judgement about historically unique individuals. What, seen in its biblical co-text, is a general maxim (the words 'righteous' and 'wicked' have no specific referent there) characterizes specific deeds and persons in the Mishnah. As in our text **[35]**, the introduction of the biblical quotation involves the preposition *al* ('upon', 'about') together with a demonstrative pronoun or anaphoric expression.[8] In our present context this is readily understood as a Mishnaic format for picking out *from the Mishnaic report* a referent and thereby something like a topic for the Scriptural quotation, constituting a manner of perspectivization. Of these specific persons or their specific behaviour there is, of course, no trace in the biblical co-text.

Performance2: Use of Scriptural wording as utterance to characterize or judge a singular non-biblical event or person, or unique non-biblical set of circumstances.

This contrasts with the Performance3 resource in that the former applies Scripture to hypothetical and repeatable events, for example, events viewed from a normative perspective; while Performance2 concerns happenings in their singular unrepeatability. Performance2 subsumes an individual instance under a general linguistic expression from Scripture, that is, takes a decision on the range of applicability of a Scriptural segment. Such 'judgements' are extremely important for the process of hermeneutics as well as for the process of applying law.[9] It seems to me that Performance2 is one of the main resources found in the Qumran *Pesher*, in that it ties the *singular* events of the sect's history and present to biblical sentences taken to be *about* them.[10] Here are two further examples:[11]

[7] ◊ΔπC1?D5P2.

[8] The terminology used here is: על הראשונים נאמר . . . ועל אלו נאמר. On the use of demonstrative pronouns, see below; also list VI.2 in the final section of Ch. 12, and the middle section of Ch. 13.

[9] See n. 122 below.

[10] I have not found this feature identified as central to the hermeneutics of *pesher*, but that may be due to my limited knowledge of the secondary literature. See the works quoted below and, for a brief account, Fraade, *From Tradition to Commentary*, 3–6. Cf. also below on the *Petihah*.

[11] See Fraenkel, *Darkhey*, ii. 496. The narratives analysed in Fraenkel's 'Bible Verses Quoted in Tales of the Sages', are examples for the PERFORMANCE family of resources, but Fraenkel barely touches on their *hermeneutic* function (cf. also his 'Paronomasia in Aggadic Narratives'). Slomovic

[41] mYad 4:3 III (3)[12]　Ps. 25:14

And when R. Yose the son of the Damascene came to R. Eliezer in Lydda, he said to him: What new thing did you have in the house of study today? He said to him: They voted and decided that Ammon and Moab must give tithe of the poor in the seventh year. R. Eliezer wept and said: 'The secret (סוד) of the Lord is with them that fear him, (and his covenant he will let them know)'.[13] Go and tell them: Be not anxious concerning your vote, for I have received from Rabban Yohanan ben Zakkai, who heard it from his teacher, and his teacher from his teacher, a halakhah [given] to Moses from Sinai, that Ammon and Moab give tithe of the poor in the seventh year.

The biblical expression 'those that fear him' is applied by Eliezer to his rabbinic colleagues who reached the right decision in the absence of crucial evidence. An immediate consequence of this is the necessity to interpret the biblical סוד in the sense of 'secret, counsel', rather than 'intimacy' or 'friendship'.[14]

[42] mSot 9:9 II (2)[15]　Micah 7:1

When Yose ben Yo'ezer (man) of Zeredah and Yose ben Yohanan (man) of Jerusalem died, the 'grape-clusters' ceased, as it is said, 'There is no grape-cluster (*eshkol*) to eat, [no] first-ripe fig which my soul desires'.

The application of the Micah verse to the situation after the death of the two masters hinges on the meaning of 'grape-clusters', or *eshkol*. There has been some discussion on this point, but it would seem that what is presupposed here is an epithet 'man who contains it all', *ish she-ha-kol bo* (note that the Mishnah goes out of its way to call them *ish*, man).[16] Whatever the linguistic mechanism allowing the two men to be referred to by use of the word *eshkol*, the movement of application itself is not in doubt. The verse proclaiming the absence of grape-clusters is used to characterize the situation after the death of the two Yoses, and is in turn placed in a perspective by such use. Thus, for example, the *absence* of the grape-clusters must be understood as a *cessation*. This is the effect which we pointed out earlier: 'the *reference* of some expressions . . . [plays] a role in determining the *senses* of other expressions.'[17] Exactly parallel is the above-mentioned necessity to interpret *sod* as 'secret' rather than 'intimacy' in **[41]**.

pays careful attention to the interaction of story and quotation in 'Patterns of Midrashic Impact', which is especially relevant to Performance2 and Performance8 (see his n. 34 on p. 70).

[12]　Δ≈πP2W1.

[13]　The text given in brackets is absent from a Genizah fragment of this part of the Mishnah (Taylor-Schechter, E1/151), see Lisowsky, *Jadajim*, 90.

[14]　The latter is the translation given in RSV. The two meanings are connected, see BDB, s.v. סוד (p. 691b).

[15]　C5C3I3≈P2W1W3.

[16]　Cf. bSot 47b; see further Geiger, accepting *ish she-ha-kol bo*, as a translation of 'katholikos', *Urschrift*, 116 f.; Loewe, 'Rabbi Joshua ben Haniniah: Ll.D. or D. Litt.?' (p. 139), thinks *eshkol* derives from 'schola'—school; this too would involve the application of a general term to a unique individual. The unit is considered as secondary by Epstein, *Mavo*, 684 f.

[17]　In the words of Johnson-Laird, *Mental Models*, 241 (quoted in Ch. 2, n. 18).

There is an apocalyptic mood in the *mishnayyot* preceding our passage [42]; later in the text a transition to openly eschatological material is made. Among the eschatological units is found the following, again using a Micah text (this time undeclared):

[43] mSot 9:15 III (3)[18]   Micah 7:6

Youngsters shall shame elders, and elders shall stand before minors, 'the son dishonours the father, the daughter rises up against her mother, the daughter-in-law against her mother-in-law, the enemies of a man are the members of his own house'. The face of the generation is like the face of the dog, the son is not put to shame by the father—and on whom can we lean? On our Father who is in heaven.

The Micah verse is used expressively to characterize events at the time of the 'footprints of the Messiah'.[19] Thus biblical words constitute part of a Mishnaic utterance on the shape of things before the arrival of the Messiah, thereby making that topic the topic of the biblical verse. Eschatological situations, of course, frequently provide occasion for expressive use of Scriptural utterances in post-biblical and pre-rabbinic Jewish literature (or for reports on such use), in particular in the Dead Sea Scrolls and the New Testament. Both of these literatures preserve traces of intense hermeneutic activity, and it is as important for our understanding of their interpretative stances as it is for rabbinic hermeneutics to explore, in its own terms, the mechanism by which Scripture as a new utterance interacts with the (non-Scriptural) situation in which it is uttered. For this mechanism of 'interpreting' Scripture by allocating it to a unique situation, or indeed by uttering it again *inside* a situation to which it applies, is quite different from making the text the topic of an utterance. (Some of the distinctions made earlier between topical alignment and programmatic exposition are relevant here.) We shall address this difference in more detail later, and also speak of the 'fulfilment' of biblical prophecy in terms of the use of a biblical segment, a re-utterance.[20]

Most robust and striking is the interaction between the situation to which the utterance is applied and its (Scriptural) wording when it contains a context-sensitive expression, such as a demonstrative. The referents of deictic terms change with circumstances and speaker (e.g. 'I', 'you', 'this', 'here', 'now').[21] Strong context-sensitivity of any biblical expression will be marked as Performance8, in addition to other markers such as Performance2.

[18] Ω(•)πC5P2.
[19] This expression (in Aramaic) appears earlier in this final section of the tractate Sotah. The same Micah verse is also an unmarked part of an utterance ascribed to Jesus at Matt. 10:35 f. On this part of the tractate, see Goldin, *Studies*, 360; MS Parma (de Rossi 138) and the *editio princeps* do not have the text of which [43] forms part; see Epstein, *Mavo*, 976 f.; Bietenhard, *Sota*, 196 f.
[20] Bietenhard, in trying to explain the function of the verse in our earlier case [42], has recourse to the language of prophetic fulfilment: 'Mi 7, 1, das sich mit dem Tode eben der beiden Rabbinen erfüllt hat' (*Sota*, 157, n. 8).
[21] See the account in Lyons, *Introduction to Theoretical Linguistics*, 413.

Performance8: Use of context-sensitive or deictic Scriptural wording as rabbinic utterance.

The role of demonstrative pronouns and deictic terms in biblical texts is of some importance in general for rabbinic exegesis.[22] In the PERFORMANCE resource (and USE; see below), the exploration of these terms consists of allowing them to interact with the new situation of use (rather than reformulating them). As in our next example: a ready-made biblical 'you' (which has no specific referent) fastens onto a unique person, Honi the Circle-Drawer, because Shim'on ben Shetah addresses him with biblical words:

[44] mTaan 3:8[23]   Prov. 23:25

Because of any trouble that might come upon the general public they sound [the shofar], except too much rain. An incident when they said to Honi the Circle-Drawer . . . [narrative of Honi calling upon God several times to get just the right amount of rain]. Shim'on ben Shetah sent to him, said to him: You ought to be placed under the ban.[24] But what shall I do to you? For you are petulant before God (and He does you your will); as a son (כבן) who is petulant against his father and he does him his will. And about you (עליך) Scripture says, 'Your father will be glad, as well as your mother; and she that bore you will rejoice'.

It is not easy to determine the exact significance of the application to Honi of the biblical verse.[25] What is clear is that a biblical sentence with indeterminate referent is being applied as utterance to a single individual (the 'you' = Honi). There are several reasons for our difficulty in pinning down the significance of Shim'on's utterance, among them Shim'on's patently ambiguous attitude towards Honi. But they all converge in the utterance's implicit *format*, namely, the use of the biblical phrase *without* repetition of the message in the speaker's or the Mishnah's own words.[26]

---

[22] See on this n. 53 in Ch. 2 above.

[23] ΔC1P2P8T3.1(*mashal*).

[24] This is the first sentence of Shim'on in the MSS; the *editio princeps* of the Bavli (Venice 1520 ff.) and popular Mishnah prints read: 'Had you not been Honi, I had decreed the ban over you!' Cf. Correns, *Taanijot*, 91, 136. They also have the clause translated in round brackets, while it is absent from the manuscripts.

[25] See Green, 'Palestinian Holy Men', 626 ff., and esp. 636–9 on the possible growth of the text. Green takes the biblical quotation to show 'that Honi has in some sense *fulfilled* a teaching of Scripture' (p. 639, emphasis mine). Brewer calls this interpretation *'Peshat'* (Brewer, *Techniques and Assumptions*, 25); Pettit (*Shene'mar*, 209 f.) says that with a 'change in context, however, the verse is otherwise read literally'. Both of these explanations are wholly inadequate. Vermes (*Jesus the Jew*, 264, n. 86) suggests that only two words ('Your father will be glad') of the Hebrew verse are applied to Honi (the reference to Prov. 23:23 should read Prov. 23:25). He speaks of the application of the verse as 'quasi-biblical prophecy' (with reference to yTaan 67a). The expression 'mother's joy' can be employed as an honorific, cf. mAvot 2:8. See also next note.

[26] Although Shim'on's parable (indulgence of a petulant son) prepares the applicability of the word 'father' in the quotation, the main message of the biblical verse (joy) is not phrased independently. In the biblical co-text the reason for that joy is the wisdom of the son (verse 24). It is quite likely that the 'mother' of the verse is taken as metaphor for the congregation of Israel (see below, [51]); otherwise, this term would have to be left out of the hermeneutic operation despite the parallelism between father and mother (making it a Cotext1 operation).

Insofar as Performance2 produces an identification of a biblical term's *referent*, its effect is to determine what the biblical sentence is *about*. This is a central concern of Mishnaic hermeneutics, as we have already seen. But here it is used to explain the significance of an event or a component in a narrative, as in cases **[40]** to **[42]** and **[44]**. This is how proverbs are employed in many cultures. Proverbs are applied quotations of a fixed formulation; their wording remains the same; only the situations to which it is applied change. Proverbs are often used, in oral exchanges both of ordinary discourse and in a folk-tale setting, to bring to the surface the evaluation, plot-line, or meaning of a narrative.[27] Hasan-Rokem speaks of the proverb as a key for the complexity of the plot. In oral Jewish settings proverbs can be used to highlight the plot-line of biblical narratives.[28] They can be used to string together individual narrative units[29] (as does the principle 'measure for measure' in the first chapter of mSotah, from which our cases **[22]** and **[49]** come). They are also sometimes conceptualized in the Saussurian categories of *langue* and *parole*,[30] and we have seen earlier that one may view the language system (*langue*) of rabbinic literature as containing elements of biblical *parole*.

Considered for their linguistic message, in separation from any one 'application', proverbs can appear *atopical*.[31] They are considered to be 'correct about *something*'.[32] Three of the verses used in these examples could in fact be proverbs of a sort, and two of them come from the biblical book called משלי ('proverbs' or 'parables'). However, it is not any intrinsic quality of the biblical verses, but the function to which they are put which is the main reason for their similarity with proverbs in general.[33] The whole of Scripture is potentially available for Performance2 and the related resources, not merely its 'proverbial' parts. Any general or metaphorical biblical sentence is particularly amenable to these procedures. But these two characteristics of a sentence depend to some extent on its integration into or isolation from the co-text. Neutralizing the co-text (Cotext1) can have the effect of *creating* sentences which have a general import or metaphorical potential,[34] readying them (among other things) for application to unique events. In other words, Cotext1 can prepare the ground for the 'proverbial' use of a verse. Presumably, there is no feature of a biblical

---

[27] See Hasan-Rokem, *Proverbs*, 12: 'summing up the narrative plot' or 'generalizing an individual experience'; also 73.

[28] Hasan-Rokem, *Proverbs*, 68 (the proverb as elaborating a biblical plot-kernel). It is of course possible that this habit is a distant echo of the hermeneutic habits of rabbinic literature, i.e. a case of life imitating art. She discusses plot complexity on pp. 77 ff.

[29] Ibid. 93.

[30] See n. 35 below.

[31] See Sacks, *Lectures on Conversation*, i. 109; cf. Ch. 2 above (n. 73).

[32] Sacks, *Lectures on Conversation*, i. 105 (emphasis added).

[33] Quite apart from the fact that it may be difficult to give a cross-cultural definition of a proverb relating to the wording alone, and in abstraction from the way speakers employ it.

[34] This is what we have called 'proverbialization' in the general sense in Ch. 2 (text to n. 73).

verse that would make it impossible *a priori* to use it in this way; not even the appearance of a proper name can prevent it (see 'Solomon' in [51] below). In the performance of a rabbinic utterance consisting of biblical words, we encounter again the potential for Scripture's *parole* (here, the individual Scriptural sentence) to become available as a structure of Mishnah's *langue*.[35]

In the Mishnah we find two further quasi-proverbial uses of Scriptural segments. The first is the utterance of a verse in the performance of a pre-scribed verbal act with fixed halakhic effect (in contrast to being uttered spontaneously). The second is the application of a verse to singular *biblical* (as opposed to rabbinic) occurrences and specific persons.

USING A SCRIPTURAL QUOTATION AS A PRESCRIBED UTTERANCE

Some Mishnaic norms require the use of biblical verses in the performance of certain obligations. Questions of how to perform certain acts of reading, quotation, avowal, or declaration are treated as halakhic in the same manner in which other acts of obligation or permission are discussed in the Mishnah. The difference is that where these prescribed speech acts involve biblical wording, the wording can potentially interact directly with the situation of performance. This interaction is repeatedly explored by the Mishnah. The following passage contains a report on King Agrippa, on the occasion when he fulfilled the obligation, incumbent on a Jewish king, of reading out part of the Pentateuch in public. In the performance of reading the king utters a line of text which points up a gap between norm and fulfilment in the very *situation of reading*:

[45] mSot 7:8 II (3)[36]   Deut. 17:15

. . . King Agrippa received it [the scroll] standing and read it standing, and for this the Sages praised him. And when he reached, 'You may not put a foreigner over you who is not your brother', his eyes flowed with tears. But they called to him: Do not fear, oh Agrippa, our brother are you, our brother are you, our brother are you!

In this narrative the weeping of the king, of Idumean extraction, constitutes a *comment* on the text's application to one of the features of the situation of reading. Agrippa is the person having been 'put over' the persons he reads to; they are the 'you' addressed in the text; and Agrippa, by also being the 'foreigner' of the text, embodies a breach of the norm he is reading out. This passage gives a report on one prescription requiring the performance of a Scriptural text—in this case, an act of reading involving an extended piece

---

[35] For the application of this pair of concepts to folklore and proverbs, see Jakobson and Bogatyrev, 'Die Folklore als eine besondere Form des Schaffens', 146 f., and Hasan-Rokem, *Proverbs*, 56.

[36] πP2(P4)P8T9.

of biblical text. More common than a narrative report is the direct treatment of the obligation as Mishnaic precept, as in [47] below. And in most cases, the utterance is not read out, but is uttered as the person's proclamation. Here is a definition of this resource:

Performance4: Use of Scriptural wording as utterance necessary in the performance of an obligation prescribed or reported in the Mishnah.

The interaction between the situation of utterance and the wording is again particularly striking when context-sensitive terms appear in the biblical segment.

[46] mBik 3:2[37]   Jer. 31:5b (E 6)

How do they take up the first fruits [to Jerusalem]? All cities belonging to the *Ma'amad* gather in the [main] city of the *Ma'amad*. And they stay overnight in the open space of the city and they used not to go into the houses. Early in the morning, the officer used to say: 'Arise you and let us go up to Zion, to the Lord our God.'

In the Mishnaic account, the first-person plural markers in the utterance apply to a group of pilgrims during Second Temple times.[38] The biblical co-text is actually eschatological, and the speakers are otherwise unspecified 'watchmen' (verse 5a), but in verse 4 appears a word connoting the enjoyment of first fruits,[39] so that this theme is actually present (Cotext5). However, in the situation reported by the Mishnah the 'you' refers to the pilgrims of the *Ma'amad*, not any watchmen.

The Mishnah is alert to the effect of context-sensitive biblical words in the performance of normative speech acts also when they are an obstacle to realizing the norm, as in the following ruling:

[47] mBik 1:4 I (2)[40]   Deut. 26:3

These bring [first fruits], but do not recite [the declaration].[41] The proselyte brings but does not recite, for he cannot say, 'which the Lord[42] swore to our fathers to give to us'. And if his mother was an Israelite, he brings and recites. And when he prays on his own, he says: God of the fathers of Israel; and when he is in the synagogue, he says: God of your fathers. And if his mother was an Israelite, he says: God of our fathers.

---

[37] ΔC5P4P8T3T5.

[38] The *Ma'amad* is a regional group of non-priests attached to one of the 24 priestly watches and accompanying 'their' group of priests when it is their turn to officiate in the Temple. See Liver and Sperber, 'Mishmarot'. The Yerushalmi (yBik 3:3, 7b) specifies further biblical passages to be performed as utterances by the pilgrims on their way, producing further reinterpretations of context-sensitive biblical expressions.

[39] Cf. Deut. 20:6; BDB, s.v. חלל III (p. 320b).

[40] H6O1.4P4P8T3.

[41] The text whose performance should accompany the bringing of first fruits is Deut. 26:5 ff. Scripture prescribes also Deut. 26:3. See also mBik 1:5 and mMS 5:14.

[42] So MSS Kaufmann, Cambridge, and a Hamburg MS (Stadtbibliothek, Codex 18); other recensions (transmitted together with the Babylonian Gemara) use the verb 'to swear' in the second person; see Albrecht, *Bikkurim*, 57.

The biblical phrase 'our fathers', if spoken by a proselyte, does not apply, insofar as the proselyte has no Israelite ancestry and the word 'our' must include the speaker. Another way of putting this is to say that the expression has an existential presupposition which is not fulfilled in the case of a proselyte (Habit6).[43] Thus, if the proselyte were to utter this phrase he would proclaim what is not, literally speaking, true.[44] The Mishnah is literal-minded enough to disallow such a proclamation. The subsequent treatment of the different prayer situations in which the proselyte is to use different versions of the biblical formula 'God of our fathers' (e.g. in Deut. 26:7) reads like an exposition of the different degrees of context-sensitivity of the pronouns of the first, second, and third person.[45]

QUOTED USE OF SCRIPTURE AND MISHNAIC USE OF SCRIPTURE

It is important to distinguish the narrative structures in which the utterance of the biblical sentence is reported from the narrative event which they are used to explain: Shim'on's quotation explains the Honi 'miracle', Eliezer's quotation explains the decision of the Sages in his absence. It is those comments on events which is the narrative level we are currently addressing, not the story in which the comment is reported (see below).

In investigating the perspective of an utterance, and the manner in which original biblical wording might interact with a new situation or a new context, we have made a tacit distinction in the earlier parts of this chapter which it is now time to explicate. In one type of Mishnaic passage Scripture is embedded and used by the main textual voice of the Mishnah (including at least all anonymous *mishnayyot*). Many cases of expressive use therefore belong to the level of the Mishnah's own voice, and sometimes that use is declared unambiguously, as in passages **[35]** and **[39]**. This means that the new context in which the words are spoken is that of the Mishnah as Mishnah, although we may actually not know very much about that context. It partakes of the generality, commitment, and original relevance of the Mishnah as a whole. There are, however, also passages containing expressive use of Scripture in which the Mishnah reports on a specific person speaking biblical words. Since in such cases the Mishnah quotes someone else's quotation of Scripture, all the effects of contextualizing the biblical text belong to the situation *depicted* in the Mishnah, not the situation

---

[43] More on the hermeneutic investigation of presuppositions of this type in Ch. 10.

[44] On the issue of presuppositions of utterances and how they affect the truth of propositions, see the opening section of Ch. 10.

[45] On the halakhic issue and its echoes in later rabbinic literature (including further examples of deictic terms in prescribed speech causing difficulty for converts), see Cohen, 'Can Converts to Judaism Say "God of our fathers"?', and his *The Beginnings of Jewishness*, ch. 10 (pp. 308 ff.). Cf. mKet 4:3 **[91]** (the expression 'door of her *father's* house' of Deut. 22:21 cannot be applied to a proselyte woman).

of the Mishnah. Examples include narrated cases such as **[41]**, **[44]**, and **[45]** where the Bible is used *inside* Mishnaic stories.[46] The Mishnah's claim is quite clear in these passages: Eliezer, Shim'on ben Shetah, and King Agrippa contextualized Scripture on one unique occasion, situated in the past from the point of view of the reporting voice.[47]

It thus seems necessary to distinguish between cases where the Mishnah ascribes to some earlier occasion the fresh utterance of Scripture, and others where the Mishnah performs that fresh utterance itself. It seems possible to distinguish a rough diachronic series of contexts for biblical words, thus: our context for biblical words, the Mishnah's context for them, the Mishnah's named voices' context for them, the original context of composition. However, the Mishnah is in fact often ambiguous about (or better, uninterested in) the point in time when a biblical wording came to be used as utterance. We have met this lack of interest in historical differentiation before, when analysing the ambiguities of a passages such as **[10]** mPes 5:5, apparently claiming that there was a Temple practice to deal with the passover sacrifices in three groups.[48] We find a similar ambiguity for the application of Scripture, as in passage **[40]**. Did someone stand up after the death of Hygros ben Levi and say: 'The name of the wicked shall rot'? Or did someone say it to his face? Was the verse applied to these priests (together as a group?) after one generation, or two? Or only when the *report* on their behaviour was compiled, that is, *for the first time* for the purposes of the Mishnaic text or its source? Consider these questions for the following case:

[48] = **[54a]** mSot 7:6 = mTam 7:2[49]   Lev. 9:22

The priestly blessing—how? In the country they say it as three blessings, and in the sanctuary as one blessing; in the sanctuary they say the Name as it is written, and in the country by circumlocution; in the country they raise their hands to the height of their shoulders, and in the sanctuary over their heads, except for the high priest who does not place his hands higher than the forehead-plate. R. Yehudah says: The high priest too places his hands above the forehead-plate, as it is said, 'And Aaron raised his hands towards [onto?] the people and blessed them'.[50]

---

[46] Pettit (*Sheme'emar*, 204) excludes such cases from the analysis, attempting a total separation of hermeneutic operations for which the Mishnah bears responsibility from those on which it merely reports. But these two types cannot be separated on the basis of the criterion 'reported speech' alone, as Pettit does. That would also exclude many disputes with a hermeneutic dimension, since one of the parties is usually a named rabbi whose position is cited by the stratum of commitment of 'the Mishnah', and therefore *earlier*.

[47] Fraenkel offers reflections on the narrative dynamics of such structures in 'Bible Verses Quoted in Tales of the Sages'.

[48] See on this the opening section of Ch. 3.

[49] ∆¶C5N1.1(T0)T3T5; and if the biblical wording is meant to support R. Yehudah's Dictum: §•¶∆W1.2?.

[50] The final unit containing R. Yehudah's opinion (but not the Scriptural verse) is missing from MS Munich, but a scribal error (*homoioteleuton*) is likely. See also Brody, *Der Misnah-Traktat Tamid*, 144.

As the sentences follow each other, the Scriptural quotation seems to relate to R. Yehudah's opinion. However, it is clear from the continuation of the verse Lev. 9:22 that Aaron is elevated above the people; the verb 'descend' (ירד) is used to describe his movement after the blessing.[51] I thus find more likely that the verse is meant to support the anonymous Dictum preceding, that is, the halakhic position *opposed* by Yehudah.[52] For the present purposes it is irrelevant which of the two Dicta is taken to be supported by the verse. Both make a claim about priestly practice during Second Temple times. But which claim exactly? That the high priests understood Lev. 9:22 as implying '(not) higher than the forehead-plate', and therefore acted accordingly? Or that the high priests acted like this, but did not know why, and that rabbinic reading can now prove their practice to be correct? Or that the high priests acted in such a way in imitation of Aaron through the generations, and that the Scriptural report can serve as a source of information on this? Or, more generally, that the high priests *must have acted thus*, because that is what Scripture shows should be done? Apparently it is not what the high priests *should* have done that is in dispute here, but what they did—so where exactly does the verse come into it? Is it not simply the case that the *historical* question holds no interest for Mishnah? That there *is* no clear separation between what should have happened and what did happen? The *literary* link between a Dictum or practice on the one hand and its Scriptural support on the other is as contingent and formulaic as all literary structures: deliberate, not necessary. It is therefore unwarranted to read every occurrence of the formula שנאמר as the claim that the Scriptural proof (use) comes from the same time as (or has historically 'caused') the Dictum it supports. However, to exclude that possibility would be just as dogmatic.

Among the passages which seem to admit a time difference between the speaking of the Mishnah and the quotation or use of the Scriptural verse, we have two types: first, those which specify a definite situation or practice of the past, marked as such in a narrative manner (as in the case of Honi in **[44]** or the officer of the *Ma'amad* in **[46]**).[53] Second, the case when Scripture is mentioned as warrant for an earlier or obsolete norm (or practice, and so on), but it is not clear if only the norm, or also its link to Scripture, is meant to belong to that earlier time. The *quantity* of the time difference (that is, the point of *origin* for the interpretation) is almost never thematized. In the hermeneutic profile of Mishnaic passages the *delta* sign, the symbol for

---

[51] It is possible that the biblical *el* (usually, 'towards') is understood as having the meaning of *al* ('over', 'onto'); see Clines, i. 263b ff. and cf. the appearance of *al* in Ben Sira 50:20, preceded by the act of 'coming down'. But in view of the fact that in Leviticus Aaron descends *after* the blessing, this cannot be the solution for our passage. As for resource Cotext1, it is not, to my knowledge, used to neutralize links to words which show the *opposite* of what is assumed in the Dictum (as here, Yehudah's Dictum).

[52] Cf. Brody, *Der Misnah-Traktat Tamid*, 144.

[53] There are some very clear passages ascribing an explicit interpretation to a pre-Mishnaic time and an extra-rabbinic tradition, notably mSheq 1:4, mSheq 6:6 I (2).

small difference in mathematics and physics,[54] marks both types of passages:

Δ: A situation, Dictum, or practice to which biblical wording applies is marked as lying in the past or as obsolete, or the application of biblical wording itself is presented as an act of the past.

Such a time difference should also be the norm in any report on the position of a named Tanna (Mishnaic rabbi), for that Tanna must have spoken before the time of the voice reporting his opinion. And the Mishnaic employment of the past tense of 'to say' seems to confirm this. However, 'said' seems to alternate freely with the present tense 'says'. The frequent occurrence of speech reports of the form 'Rabbi X *says:*' in the Mishnah seems, in fact, to deny that the time difference matters: the discourse of the Mishnah is time-less in its constitutive elements, and that includes 'earlier' positions.[55] And quoted sayings of named Tannaim are mostly not treated in a narrative format, unless one wishes to interpret the formula 'Rabbi X said' as narra-tive while interpreting the formula 'Rabbi X says' as something else. Rather, Tannaitic quotations are presented as contributions to a discourse with roots in the past but conducted in the present. They are projections onto the plane of the Mishnaic discourse, which deals with questions of current or future obligation. There is a general gesture of ratifying in the present tense (a selection of) what a *tradition* 'says', and the use of Scriptural wording discussed in this and the preceding chapter could be considered merely a special case of that ratification. Even in the anonymous *mishnah*, it is not necessarily the redactor of the Mishnah who speaks, but an unmarked quotation from tradition.[56] A new utterance is created by repeat-ing the wording of an earlier one. It is this continuity of a commitment to a wording which, while not leaving its meaning unchanged, is tradition—frozen into a text (see below). The later attachment of a Scriptural support to a position which is accepted as valid or which has the potential of being valid is always possible. On the other hand, positions from the past which are somehow marked as non-rabbinic, for example, designated priestly traditions, are treated by the Mishnah with a distance compatible with a claim that their employment of Scripture also comes from that earlier time. Distinctions are in fact blurred between the categories 'past' and 'extra-rabbinic' or 'non-rabbinic'.[57] Under these circumstances, the allocation of the *delta* sign Δ even in the catch-all formulation given above is far

[54] 'The increment Δ*x*, "delta *x*", suggests a small amount added to, or subtracted from, a given value of a variable *x* . . .' (Gullberg, *Mathematics*, 104). Here, '*x*' is the time of the discourse of the Mishnah.
[55] This is a feature of discourse in general (whether on norms or facts, see Patzig, *Tatsachen, Normen, Sätze*, 19 f.). See also Ch. 6 below (paragraph after n. 66).
[56] See on this Ch. 1 (n. 51).
[57] The difference of named versus anonymous Dictum has an equally *functional* meaning in the Mishnah. The named Dictum is marked for *disagreement*, and usually as *minority* opinion; so the anonymous Dictum is more authoritative. See further n. 79 in Ch. 1 above.

from straightforward. I have tended to mark passages with *delta*, when in doubt.

APPLYING A RABBINIC MAXIM OR PARABLE
TO BIBLICAL EVENTS

Turning now to a new group of resources, we are concerned with the rabbinic imposition of a theme or a meaning on biblical, as opposed to non-biblical, events. Again, we are concentrating here on the case of a fixed wording being spoken about unique occurrences or persons, or spoken in unique situations.[58] In contrast to Performance3, these are singular and unrepeatable; and in contrast to Performance2, they are biblical. Among the fixed verbal formulations which can be applied to biblical individuals are biblical quotations (in parallel to Performance2 and Perfomance3), or non-biblical quotations (see above, on the similarity of using Scripture and using proverbs). I shall name the family of resources which evaluate biblical events (as opposed to non-biblical ones) USE. I shall distinguish three main constellations: a non-biblical statement is used to characterize biblical events summed up in non-biblical language (Use5/6); a biblical quotation is used to characterize biblical events summed up in non-biblical language (Use1, Use2); and a biblical quotation is used to characterize biblical events whose narration is also represented as biblical quotation ([Use3], [Use4]). The latter case is here included for systematic purposes only; it is not found in the Mishnah,[59] but is very important in other documents of rabbinic literature.

Let us start with a biblical event being evaluated by a non-biblical formulation, a rabbinic maxim or principle. The first chapter of Sotah contains the rabbinic maxim, 'With whatever measure a man measures they measure him in turn'.[60] I shall refer to this as the poetic justice principle, for short. Having been spelled out in *mishnah* 7, this principle is tacitly applied to Samson (see passage **[22]** above) and Absalom in mSot 1:8. This is followed by further applications of the maxim to biblical stories. Here is the relevant evaluation and explanation of Absalom's fate:

---

[58] The next chapter deals with biblical events interpreted as exemplary, which constitutes another way of endowing them with theme or meaning.

[59] Its absence from the Mishnaic corpus is marked by its enclosure in square brackets.

[60] במדה שאדם מודד בה מודדין לו, mSot 1:7. Cf. Towner, *The Rabbinic 'Enumeration of Scriptural Examples'*, 84. Cf. the saying attributed to Ben He-He in mAvot 5:23: 'According to the suffering (or: trouble) is the reward.' The biblical narrative offers many 'pairs' of events which can be linked by the poetic justice schema. See Daube, *Studies in Biblical Law*, 191 ff., 253 f. Cf. Alter, *Putting Together Biblical Narrative*. A systematization of poetic justice material can be found in Urbach, *The Sages*, 371 ff. See also Fraenkel, *Darkhey*, i. 438 (on the format of the saying); Goldin, *The Song at the Sea*, 23 f. (and index s.v. 'measure for measure'); Kadushin, *Organic Thinking*, 10, 112. See above for some parallels to the use of proverbs.

[49] mSot 1:8 II (4)[61]   2 Sam. 14:25 f., 18:9

... Absalom took pride[62] in his hair, therefore he was hanged by his hair.

Absalom's taking pride in his hair is alluded to in the biblical narrative; 2 Sam. 14:25 f. contains an account of his annual haircut. His head becoming entangled in an oak is reported in 2 Sam. 18:9. The link between these two happenings, on the other hand, is a Mishnaic interpretation of their meaning. The meaning attaches to the events directly: poetic justice explains why it *happened* that way. The *words* in which Scripture tells the story are neither quoted nor alluded to; the word 'hair' does not even occur in the account of Absalom's death (although the word 'hang' does, in 2 Sam. 18:10). Knowledge of the story is presupposed, but not knowledge of the very words in which Scripture tells it. The maxim 'measure for measure' explains the correspondence between the pride of Absalom and his punishment; ultimately it points to the motivation of God as indirect protagonist. The story from the Bible is not, in principle, treated differently from an extra-biblical story (such as priests not sharing their knowledge in [40]). The main difference (apart from the rabbinic provenance of the maxim) is that here events are presupposed as known and unproblematic;[63] they surface as Mishnaic topic in form of a summary, retelling, or naming. We have encountered the latter phenomenon before, in the Mishnaic Topic3 terms 'Generation of the Flood' and 'Men of Sodom'.

The rabbinic poetic justice principle imposes a binary structure on the events, and involves the reader in *selecting* a pair of suitable events from the flow of the narrative. As a maxim imposing a perspective on two biblical segments, 'measure for measure' belongs to the inventory of Topic4.1 principles or assumptions (see above, case [22]). It also occurs with non-narrative material (serving to explain the punishment of the adulterous wife in mSot 1:7). And it can be used to predict the divine punishment of certain sins (e.g. mPeah 8:9), that is, it generates a conditional prognostic structure.[64] In its narrative application to biblical events as in [49], the poetic justice principle illustrates the following resource:

Use6: Use of a rabbinic maxim to articulate the underlying structure, meaning, or evaluation of a biblical event or chain of events or the character of a biblical person.

---

[61] ≈C5(≈N8)T4.1≈U6 .

[62] The reading נתגאה, found in MS Munich and the *editio princeps* of the Talmud Bavli (Venice 1522); other important witnesses have נתגרה instead, which means 'to be vain'. Cf. Bietenhard, *Sota*, 186; Jastrow, 887a.

[63] The reverse of this structure is found in an example in mAvot 5:17: a general rabbinic maxim is applied first to an event of rabbinic history and then to an event of biblical history (constituting a Use6 interpretation). Both events are presupposed as known and referred to by the names of their protagonists (Hillel/Shammai, Moses/Korah).

[64] It is possible that Prov. 11:27, quoted in mPeah 8:9, is meant to give a biblical equivalent for the rabbinic poetic justice principle.

This includes maxims which are used to speak about two events in their mutual relationship (as in [49]) as well as single events (cf. the difference between Topic4.1 and Topic3.1). For the Topic4.1–Use6 operation as found in [49] there seems to be a rabbinic hermeneutic rule in the *Mishnat R. Eliezer.* Using a word also appearing in the poetic justice principle (כנגד), rule number 27 is called *mi-neged* ('[interpretation derived] from a correspondence'), and provides for a similar structuring of biblical events. However, it may be restricted to finding a *numeric* repetition in the biblical text.[65] The paragraphs surrounding passage [49] in the Mishnah contain a number of such numerical correspondences (on the event level) under the same general poetic justice principle.[66] In any case, *middah* 27 in Eliezer's list seems to allude to a special type of Top4.1–Use6 operation, and its example is concerned with the specific correspondence between transgression and retribution. This correspondence is of course thematized in the Hebrew Bible itself as a major rule by which historical events are interpreted and predicted, and can serve to pick out many explicit structures in the biblical narrative.[67] The poetic justice principle is also found combined with another hermeneutic resource: the interpretation of biblical metaphors as concrete. In mSot 1:8 IV (4) the fact that Absalom 'stole hearts' (figurative hearts, that is),[68] is linked to the fact that he died having his heart (the concrete heart) pierced. This kind of link can provide a very striking *semantic* basis for the correspondence which the poetic justice principle requires.[69]

There is another important variant of the Use6 resource: the use of a rabbinic parable or *mashal* for the elucidation of a biblical narrative structure. The text quoted above as [44] contains a rudimentary parable: Honi is like a son whose petulance does not induce his father to refuse his request.[70] The rabbinic parable plays an important part in aggadic midrashic literature.[71] The word *mashal* is used in rabbinic parlance both for proverbs (as in the Bible), and for parables. The exegetical *meshalim*, insofar as they are so

---

[65] Cf. Stemberger, *Introduction*, 28; Bacher, i. 125; see also Fishbane (*Biblical Interpretation*, 450) regarding the correspondence of numbers in dreams and their interpretations ('numerological' technique). This is different, however, because the correspondence does not hold between two events (inside the narrative), but between the narrative and its 'meaning'. See also below.

[66] Towner, *The Rabbinic 'Enumeration'*, 82 f., investigates the parallels in Mekhilta de-Rabbi Ishmael.

[67] Cf. e.g. Clines, *Theme of the Pentateuch*, 61 ff. Clines assimilates or subordinates (pp. 64, 78 f.) the idea of transgression and retribution (what one might call a symmetry) to the idea of promise (a dynamic asymmetry). The two 'themes' are obliquely related to each other, and the reading of the rabbis seems, on balance, to stress the former rather than the latter.

[68] Cf. 2 Sam. 15:6.

[69] See the interpretation of biblical text as metaphorical treated in Ch. 14 below.

[70] The (minimal) narrative structure of the *mashal* needs to be carefully separated from the idea of metaphor: God is of course metaphorically addressed as father in rabbinic language, or as king, or as artisan (*yotser*). But functionally, these metaphors are not constitutive for parables in which he is compared parabolically to fathers, kings, or artisans. Within the *mashal* (as in [44] above), the father has to be a real father, otherwise there is no narrative counterpart for God.

[71] Cf. recently Stern, *Parables in Midrash*; more analytical rigour in the treatment of the hermeneutic function is found in Goldberg, 'Das schriftauslegende Gleichnis im Midrasch'. See also Boyarin, *Intertextuality*, ch. 8. There is a noteworthy parable in a halakhic context in mSuk 2:9.

announced,[72] are parables. They are a special type of a rabbinic utterance, namely a *narrative* imposing a perspective on the biblical narrative (that is, unique persons or events). This special hermeneutic interaction between two narratives requires its own resource in the USE family.

Use5: Use of a rabbinic parable to articulate the underlying structure, meaning, or evaluation of a biblical event or chain of events or the character of a biblical person.

The relational structure provided by the *mashal* for biblical events has the essence of narrative, the 'before–after' structure; often, however, it will account more narrowly for the *motivational* link between the before and the after. This is very important in cases where God's behaviour is explained by the *mashal* (for example, in the rabbinic parables of king, householder, father). Transferring a model of motivation from the *mashal* to the biblical narrative is therefore a major mechanism in explaining the *causality* of biblical events (cf. also Norm8 in the next chapter).

UTTERING BIBLICAL VERSES ABOUT BIBLICAL EVENTS

What happens if the object of elucidation is a biblical event, and the judgement applied to it is a biblical formulation itself? The hermeneutic structure underlying Use5/6 and Performance2 also holds here: a fixed verbal formulation which does not, as such, speak about any unique event, is applied to such an event. The only difference is that the event is biblical (as it is not in Performance2) and the fixed formulation is also biblical (as it is not in Use5/6). The main point is: the biblical verse can only highlight and explain singular events or specific persons if the exegete *utters* that verse *anew*—namely, *about* an event or person. This 'about-ness' turns the quoting into an *uttering*—it can only be performed by expressive use. It is an exact parallel to the manner in which a verse is uttered anew when being applied to the non-biblical persons Honi or Hygros ben Levi. Instead of employing a verse to talk about Honi, our next passage employs it to talk about the men of Sodom:

[50] mSan 10:3 IV (10)[73]   Ps. 1:5

. . . But they [i.e. the Men of Sodom, will] stand in judgement.[74] R. Nehemiah says: These as well as the others [i.e. the Generation of the Flood] do not stand in judgement, for it is said, 'Therefore the wicked shall not rise in judgement nor the sinners in the congregation of the righteous'. 'Therefore the wicked shall not rise in

---

[72] Among the more common introductory formulas for rabbinic parables are למה הדבר דומה? ‏ל־ /משל ל־ /ל־ .

[73] • ¶πC1≈R2.1T1T3U1.

[74] That is, even though they do not have a share in the world to come.

judgement'—this (זה) is the Generation of the Flood; 'nor the sinners in the congregation of the righteous'—these (אלו) are the Men of Sodom.[75]

The biblical events are presupposed as known and referred to by their Mishnaic names (Topic3); these names do not only stand for the persons, but for what these persons did and what happened to them. The verse Ps. 1:5 is quoted and used to articulate the wickedness of the two biblical groups,[76] by stating that they will not (even) rise to be judged at the end of time.[77] The 'about-ness' I mentioned above is performed by the demonstrative pronouns 'this' and 'these'.[78] These deictic terms *point* the biblical quotation to the events: they assume the rabbinic interpreter (not Scripture) as the speaking voice. In the process the Mishnah determines what the quoted verse is *about*—not by speaking about its wording, but by *using* it to speak. The identification locates the two protagonists 'generation of the flood' and 'men of Sodom' *in* the wording of the verse, or, put differently, the verse as utterance 'contains' these groups, has them *in view*.[79] The verse has these events in view *because* the reader does.[80] The use of deictic terms, representing the gesture of pointing, is very common in rabbinic hermeneutics; it also appears at Qumran and earlier both in the Hebrew Bible (in the context of dream interpretation) and in its wider ancient Near Eastern environment.[81] As always, the application of a fixed wording to a unique occurrence has consequences for the meaning of its words. In our case, the expression 'to rise in judgement' (משפט) must be taken to mean 'to be judged' when its biblical co-text suggests rather 'to be acquitted'. This is the sort of adjustment typically generated by fixing the referent for one of the terms in a sentence.[82] Here is the hermeneutic move in a nutshell; the term 'tenor verse' will be explained presently.

Use1: Use of a biblical sentence making no specific reference to a singular event or specific person as utterance about a specific biblical event, chain of

---

[75] This is the version of the popular prints; the *editio princeps* and MSS have the biblical verse only once, interrupting it with the explanatory clauses plus demonstrative pronouns. See Krauß, *Sanhedrin-Makkot*, 274, 398.

[76] The redundancy inherent in the parallelism of the tenor verse is neutralized by allocating two different referents to the terms 'wicked' and 'sinners', i.e. Redundancy2.1.

[77] On the issue, see Abrahams, 'The Second Death', *Studies in Pharisaism and the Gospels*, ii. 41–9.

[78] The protagonists which the words 'wicked' and 'sinners' are taken to refer to are presented by the demonstrative pronouns זה and אלו. The grammatical number of the pronouns is governed by the grammatical number of the object identified (singular in the case of the generation, plural in the case of the men).

[79] Arnold Goldberg has explained this hermeneutic mechanism using Bühler's notion of 'deixis ad phantasma' ('Versuch', 23 f.); cf. Bühler's concepts 'Zeigfeld' and 'Symbolfeld', *Sprachtheorie* (ch. 2 'Das Zeigfeld der Sprache und die Zeigwörter', 97–148). Cf. also Bregman, 'Seeing with the Sages: Midrash as Visualization in the Legends of the *Aqedah*'. Goldberg also understood the direction of the pointing to be both *to* the events and *into* the text ('Versuch', 45 f.).

[80] Personal pronouns such as הוא are used in demonstrative function e.g. in CD, see Fishbane, 'Use, Authority and Interpretation of Mikra', 374.

[81] Cf. Fishbane, *Biblical Interpretation*, 446–57, who also addresses the segmentization achieved by these formulas.

[82] See my discussion of [42] above and text with n. 18 in Ch. 2 above.

events, or person. The sentence (the tenor verse) is thus used to endow biblical happenings or characters with articulated structure, meaning, or evaluation.

The basic hermeneutic movement is this: a biblical event or person is being elucidated or evaluated by the reader's application to it of a biblical sentence coming from outside the biblical account of the event. This targets the underlying structure, meaning, or evaluation of a unique occurrence: that is what the biblical sentence articulates. Put differently, the *tenor* of the story in which the event is embedded is identified by the verse. I shall therefore call the verse which is used to evaluate the biblical event the *tenor verse*. And in order to engage with a singular biblical event (not figuring as such in the tenor verse) the reader of the tenor verse has to become its *speaker*. The tenor verse is quoted from Scripture, but is also *used* to express the Mishnah's message.

What about the verse which reports the biblical events? In our above passage the biblical occurrences are referred to by a Mishnaic shorthand; they are summarized, their detail is presupposed, and their account in Scripture treated as unproblematic. But the verse actually reporting the biblical event may also be quoted, alongside the tenor verse. This sets up a more complex hermeneutic structure: we find *two* biblical quotations apparently directly *interacting with each other*. This resource does not occur in the Mishnah; however, because of its systematic relationship to Use1 I shall define it here.

[Use3]: Use of a biblical sentence containing no specific reference to a singular event or specific person as utterance about a specific event, chain of events, or person referred to in a second biblical sentence, also quoted. The unspecific sentence (the tenor verse) is thus used to endow biblical happenings or characters with articulated structure, meaning, or evaluation. At the same time its linguistic relationship to the verse directly referring to these happenings or characters (the event verse) is also highlighted.

This resource plays a crucial role in the hermeneutics of rabbinic literature redacted after the Mishnah. It frequently underlies the so-called *Petihah* found at the opening of midrashic homilies.[83] Its underlying mechanism is the same as that of Use1: the uttering of a general wording about a singular occurrence or specific person. But it offers, *in addition*, room for resources which exploit the linguistic interaction between the wording of the event

[83] In the scholarly terminology of the *Petihah*, our tenor verse corresponds to the so-called '*Petihah*-verse', while the event verse is the '*Inyan*-verse' or '*Seder*-verse'. The hermeneutic movement found in the *Petihah* is often called *Petirah*, after the opening formula: 'Rabbi X *patar*' (on which see below). For the *Petihah* and its terminology, see Goldberg, 'Versuch'; Lenhard, *Die Rabbinische Homilie*, 33 ff. Fraenkel clearly articulates the dynamics of a general wording and individual referent when explaining the *Petirah* (*Darkhey*, i. 180). See also below, on Qumranic *Pesher*.

verse and the tenor verse. In other words, almost all other resources can be integrated into the movement of *application*, once the wording of the tenor verse becomes *also* the focus of metalinguistic attention through the juxtaposition of the event verse. This makes Use3 and its variations one of the most fertile as well as characteristic mechanisms of rabbinic hermeneutics. Here is an illustration. Bereshit Rabba offers a passage in which the general sentence 'The Lord tests (יבחן) the righteous one . . .' (Ps. 11:5) is brought together with the concrete event report, 'And it was after these things that God tried (נסה) Abraham . . .' (Gen. 22:1).[84] In this operation Gen. 22:1 is the event verse, Ps. 11:5 the tenor verse. The basic movement consists of uttering Ps. 11:5 about the *events* related in Gen. 22. This provides a specific and individual referent for the expression 'righteous one' in Ps. 11:5, namely, Abraham (the person, not the word 'Abraham'). But in addition to this, and at the same time, the linguistic overlap between the tenor verse and the event verse is highlighted. Thus, the synonyms for 'to test' (נסה/בחן) appearing in the two biblical locations become a focus, and the hermeneutic operation provides for a convergence of sense between them.[85] (None of this, by the way, implies that Abraham is taken to be the only possible referent of 'righteous one'.)

The juxtaposition of two verses may suggest that the tenor verse speaks about the event *verse*. But this is not so. The tenor verse speaks about the events about which the event verse speaks. This is clear from a comparison with the earlier examples quoted in this chapter. We see the same structure throughout: a biblical verse (or a rabbinic maxim), is spoken about a unique situation, or spoken into the unique situation (as in case **[44]**). But in all cases we only have access to the interaction of quoted wording and events through the verbal Mishnaic account of the events. In other words, the unique occurrence or situation is *re-presented* in verbal form. Verbal representation of the event is an integral part of these operations. So, providing a verbal representation for the singular event is not what the quotation of an event verse from Scripture in Use3 adds to the mix. What is different in Use3 is that this verbal representation is itself a quotation from Scripture, an event *verse*. And, as such, it can become the target of metalinguistic scrutiny (which would not usually happen to a rabbinic formulation), in addition to providing a report of the event at which the tenor verse is aimed.

Another important member of the USE family employs the tenor verse to articulate the narrative *interrelationship* of two distinct biblical events.[86] We shall refer to it as Use2; and since in the Mishnah it is found in only one

[84] Thus found in BerR 55:2 (ed. Theodor-Albeck, ii. 585 f.).

[85] The choice 'to test' as meaning of בחן is not necessary (JPS translate 'to seek out'), but itself favoured by its application to Abraham's trial. The movement of application induces maximal semantic convergence between the tenor verse and the event verse.

[86] This is analogous to the distinguishing factor between resources Topic3 and Topic4.

passage and at the end of a tractate, its definition is marked by an asterisk as well as the *omega* sign:

*Use2$_\Omega$: Use of a biblical sentence containing no specific reference to a singular event or specific person as utterance about two or more specific biblical events or persons. The sentence (the tenor verse) is thus used to articulate the structure, meaning, or evaluation of these biblical happenings or characters in their relation to each other.

Rabbinic interpretation takes the Song of Songs as speaking about the historical relationship between God and Israel.[87] Such an assumption is consistent with using verses from Canticles as tenor verses for biblical events. The following passage contains the only Mishnaic example for Use2:[88]

[51] mTaan 4:8 III (3)[89]   Cant. 3:11 [Exod. 19 ff., 1 Kgs. 8:2]

R. Shim'on ben Gamliel said: Israel had no (holi)days equal to the fifteenth of Av and Yom Kippur, for on them the daughters[90] of Jerusalem used to go out in white garments . . . And likewise it says, 'Go, O daughters of Zion, and look upon King Solomon [in his crown, with which his mother crowned him] on the day of his wedding'—that is the giving of Torah; 'and on the day of the joy of his heart'—that is the building of the sanctuary.[91] May it be built speedily in our days!

Two events are highlighted from the continuous chain of events that make up the biblical story of Israel: the giving of Torah and the building of the Temple. These are individually linked to two separate elements in the wording of the tenor verse: 'day of his wedding' and 'day of the joy of his heart'. And, since they are both being projected onto a common syntagmatic plane, they receive significance from each other as well. In the process, the apparent redundancy of the parallelism in the tenor verse is eliminated, for now it speaks about two separate referents . I shall deal with the distributive mechanism which achieves this (REDUNDANCY) in Chapter

[87] The literature on this topic is rather large. Examples include Heinemann, 'Allegoristik des Mittelalters'; Boyarin, *Intertextuality*, ch. 7; and Grözinger, *Ich bin der Herr*, 220, who identifies three main narrative (Pentateuchal) themes linked to the Song of Songs: the exodus from Egypt, the giving of Torah, and the sojourn of the *Shekhinah* in the tabernacle.
[88] Sifra ad Lev. 9:24 identifies all the other components of the Canticles verse in *Petirah*-fashion (see above n. 83), but in the context of the tabernacle. Cf. Bacher, *Die Prooemien der alten jüdischen Homilie*, 16. The unit is classed as secondary by Epstein, *Mavo*, 686 f., 975. See also Pettit, *Shene'emar*, 205 ff. However, it is apparently found in all the witnesses, see Correns, *Taanijot*, 137.
[89] ΩΔπC5R5.1U2W7.
[90] Some MSS, including Kaufmann, have here 'sons' or 'children', while Parma (de Rossi 138) and Munich as well as most prints have 'daughters'. Cf. Correns, *Taanijot*, 126 (n. 111), 137. The structure of the whole unit is very complex. What the maidens say actually includes, in some versions of the Mishnaic text at least, Prov. 30:30. Then verse 31 is quoted (see notes on passage [97] below), followed by the quotation formula translated above, 'And likewise it says'. Cf. Pettit, *Shene'emar*, 205–7, 210 f. On the 15th Av, see Schürer (ed. Vermes, *et al.*), *History of the Jewish People*, ii. 273.
[91] So Kaufmann and others. Other MSS, including Cambridge, Munich, and a Genizah fragment (Cambridge, Westminster College Talmudica II/117b and II/44b), have here the full quotation first; cf. Correns, *Taanijot*, 137.

13; but it may be noted in passing that the parallelism of the tenor verse in passage **[50]** above receives a similar differentiation ('wicked'–'sinners').

Here in **[51]** the two topics qua events constitute distinct temporal *stages* in the story of God's relationship with Israel, namely, God's revelation to Israel and God's taking permanent residence in the midst of Israel. The story of Israel is thus accentuated, or articulated by the binary structure of the tenor verse. The biblical events engage with the metaphorical potential of all the expressions in the tenor verse; the king is in fact tacitly identified with God, the mother with Israel.[92] The identification is also determined by the occasion of the maidens' utterance, which the verse is taken to point to: the fifteenth of Av and Yom Kippur. According to rabbinic tradition, the second tables of the law were given to Moses on Yom Kippur, and the First Temple was dedicated on that day.[93] Thus, the wedding and the joy fall on the same day in the liturgical year, the 'Day' (!) of Atonement. And, because of the way in which the interpretation puts things together, in the year in which Solomon finished the Temple (1 Kgs. 8:2) the Day of Atonement was also the day of dedication, and the maidens were summoned to admire the Temple by the words, 'Go and look upon . . . king Solomon on the day of his joy [= dedication]' (see below on Use8). Within this complex network of relationships the tenor verse is used to explicate the hidden rhythm of the events between Israel and God, providing a spotlight on two interrelated landmark events.

The Use2 resource, too, exists in a version which takes into account the biblical wording of the narrative which reports the events, and thus provides for an interaction on the level of linguistic signs between two or three biblical verses,[94] in addition to the applied use of an unspecific tenor verse for specific biblical events. In analogy to the pair Use1 and Use3, this variant shall be labelled Use4. I shall provide a definition here because of its systematic relationship to the other use resources as well as its importance outside the Mishnah. Inside the Mishnah, however, no example is found, so the code is again enclosed in square brackets.

[Use4]: Use of a biblical sentence containing no specific reference to a singular event or specific person as utterance about two or more biblical events or persons referred to in a second (or third, etc.) biblical sentence, also quoted. The unspecific sentence (the tenor verse) is thus used to articulate the structure, meaning, or evaluation of these biblical happenings or

---

[92] The whole of the Cant. 3:11 co-text is applied to the Sinai/Sanctuary situation; for the preceding verses, see ShirR 3:7, whose *Petirah*-function is discussed in Goldberg, 'Versuch', 13 ff. (and see n. 83 above). In ShirR 3:7 'King Solomon' is interpreted as מלך שהשלום לו, 'the king to whom belongs peace', i.e. God (resource Word9). Cf. also Braude and Kapstein (trans.), *Pesikta de-Rab Kahana*, pp. xxxiii ff.

[93] More material is found in ShirR ad loc. (Wilna edn., 22a), as follows: wedding = Sinai revelation, and joy = words of Torah; also, wedding = tabernacle, and joy = Jerusalem sanctuary. Targum Cant. 3:11 links the gathering of the people with the feast of dedication for Solomon's temple.

[94] Each event may have its own event verse, so that three passages are quoted: a tenor verse, event verse 1, and event verse 2.

characters in their relation to each other. At the same time its linguistic relationship to the verse(s) directly referring to these happenings or characters (the event verse/s) is also highlighted.

I have now reviewed a whole collection of resources which use biblical or non-biblical fixed wording to pronounce an evaluation of singular biblical or non-biblical events or persons, with or without interaction of more than one Scriptural quotation, and with or without a 'grouping' of more than one event/person. The components that need to be conceptually distinguished for the complex resources Use3/4 have thus been shown to be able to function on their own or in combination with other components.[95] The received text of the Mishnah contains one example of a resource which adds a further twist to the complexity of Use3/4; yet it looks to be a simple device. The example is not part of the original body of the Mishnaic text; it is found in a secondary addition to the tractate Avot. I am using it here merely as an outlook on hermeneutic phenomena found outside the Mishnah. It will not be taken into account for the overall hermeneutic contour of the Mishnah.[96]

[52] [mAvot 6:3 I (3)][97]   Ps. 55:14 (E 13)

He that learns from his fellow a single chapter or a single Halakhah or a single verse or a single expression or even a single letter, must pay him honour, for thus we find it with David, king of Israel, who learned only two things from Ahitophel, but called[98] him his teacher (רבי), his companion, and his familiar friend; for it is said, 'But it was you, a man my equal, my companion and my familiar friend'.

Let us first deal with the hermeneutic components which are not the theme here, but which need to be understood. The behaviour of David in praising Ahitophel is taken as exemplary, as embodying a Mishnaic norm (see Norm1 in the next chapter). Further, the notion that Ahitophel twice gave advice is narrative information simply presupposed here (Topic3.1), not problematized. If we now turn to the component of applied use, we find a tenor verse from Ps. 55. It is used to highlight a situation involving Ahitophel and David: the event of David honouring Ahitophel after having learned from him (again, the Mishnah is reporting events whose status is treated as unproblematic). By naming the two protagonists, and by the overall meaning of the tenor verse, the event of 'honouring' is placed in a very precise narrative setting: the story of how Ahitophel sided with Absalom against David, although these events are not mentioned but presupposed. Presumably, the moment after David learns of Ahitophel's betrayal is intended (2 Sam. 15:31). What is new here is that, because of

[95] Which does not mean that the more complex resources must be chronologically later. See on this Chs. 1, 3, and 4.
[96] On this part of Avot (Qinyan Torah), see Epstein, Mavo, 978; Albeck, Einführung, 182; Stemberger, Introduction, 115, 229 f.; see further n. 72 of Ch. 1 above.
[97] A5C5N5T2T3.1U2U8W1.
[98] Some texts have here 'made', cf. Marti and Beer, Abot, 166, 197.

the deictic 'my' and 'you', the utterance is meant to apply directly *in* the situation: Ahitophel is the 'you' of the verse, just as Honi is the 'you' of Prov. 23:25 in passage [44].[99] But while Shim'on ben Shetah in [44] utters Scripture in a situation of which he is part, here the rabbinic interpreter utters Scripture *on behalf* of a protagonist in the Scriptural situation of which that protagonist (but not the rabbinic interpreter) is a part. In other words, the exegete in [52] places a tenor verse in the mouth of a protagonist in order to be able to speak directly into a biblical narrative situation as if that situation was *present* (in the way in which Honi was present when Shim'on applied the verse to him).[100] This is what David could indeed have said or thought, as imaginary (!) conversation, as reflection on the fact that his trusted adviser, his 'teacher', is siding with Absalom. The non-specific image of betrayal in the Psalm verse thus receives a concrete reference, and suddenly a whole string of verses from its co-text can be given a concrete reading:[101] 'It is not an enemy who taunts me—then I could bear it; it is not an adversary who deals insolently with me—then I could hide from him. But it is you, my equal, my companion, my familiar friend. We used to hold sweet converse together; within God's house we would walk in fellowship.'[102] The tenor verse becomes an evaluation of the meaning *of* the situation *in* the situation, a reflection on events *as they unfold*. It is contextualized.[103] In our case the exegete is very likely to have drawn confirmation for the pairing of tenor verse and event from the fact that the assumed human speaker of the psalm is David himself (identified in the psalm superscription, more on which below). But such identity of the personas of narrative protagonist (in the biblical event) and prophetic author (of the tenor verse) is not necessary for the hermeneutic operation.[104]

Here is the USE resource illustrated by passage [52]:

[99] For an example of a similar application of Ps. 110:4, which identifies Abraham as the Psalm's 'you', see BerR 55:5 (ed. Theodor-Albeck, ii. 589). The identity of the speaker just as that of the addressee is wholly dependent on the choice of situation made by the exegete (apart from linguistic mechanisms between the various wordings). David is the presumed author-speaker of Psalms; but as the BerR example just mentioned shows, this does not limit the application to events from the David narratives. See also Fishbane, *Biblical Interpretation*, 404.

[100] Scripture as 'speaker' is addressed below; cf. also Goldberg, 'Versuch', 8.

[101] The inclusion of the co-text of the tenor verse in *Petihot* is addressed by Goldberg, 'Versuch', 15. Narrative structures, insofar as they are created by the rabbis themselves, may reflect not just one but a cluster of biblical verses drawn from the same co-text. See on this Slomovic, 'Patterns of Midrashic Impact on the Rabbinic Midrashic Tale' (n. 75, p. 80 is concerned with the rabbinic link of Ps. 55 to Ahitophel and David).

[102] RSV, slightly adapted. If 'God's house' is taken to mean temple, then the last verse cannot be included in the projection into the narrative setting.

[103] The contextualization of texts *as a hermeneutic construct* (as opposed to the direct involvement in a situation of utterance) is very common. One example is the historical-critical approach which attempts to reconstruct the situation in which a text might have had sense—its 'original' meaning or its *Sitz im Leben*. Other examples are the allocation of individual letters of Paul to specific points in the story of his life, or the traditional Muslim allocation of situations in the life of Muhammad to individual suras of the Qur'an.

[104] The other hermeneutic components involved in this interpretation will be encountered in Chs. 6 (biblical example) and 7 (*a fortiori* inference).

[Use8]: Use of a biblical sentence containing context-sensitive or deictic terms but no specific reference to a singular event or specific person (tenor verse) as utterance placed into the mouth of a biblical protagonist articulating the underlying structure, meaning, or evaluation of a biblical event in which he/she is involved.

THE CO-TEXTUAL INTERACTION OF THE TENOR VERSE AND EVENT VERSE (PETIHAH 1)

The most complex use of a tenor verse is its *juxtaposition* to an event verse, in addition to its *application* to the occurrence which the event verse reports. For this constellation, absent from the Mishnah, we have used the label Use3 above. It requires some further comment, not only because of its importance in midrashic literature outside the Mishnah, but also because it puts into sharper relief the other USE and PERFORMANCE resources.

When the event verse interacts, on a linguistic level, with the tenor verse, their relationship is governed by the dynamics of *co-text*. Under the assumption that they speak about the same events (that is, have the same topic), they coalesce *as if* in each other's proximity. Rabbinic hermeneutics is often said to increase the textuality or coherence of Scripture, and more recently this has been referred to as Scripture's *intertextuality* for the rabbinic reader.[105] But how exactly does this work? As shown above for Use3, a referent is determined for the general tenor verse in the light of the singular referent of the event verse. This is analogous to the following mechanism: a general sentence *immediately following* a concrete sentence in a coherent text receives a narrowed-down meaning from the latter's referent. In each of the following examples the referent of the more general term (given in italics) is reduced to one specific and identifiable item on the basis of the co-textual relationship:[106]

'Ro's daughter is ill again. *The child* is hardly ever well.'[107]
'Napoleon arrived at the palace. *The conqueror of Austria* was in high spirits.'[108]
'Now, Fairview had had its golden age. Mass production had seen to that. *The little town's* methods of production could not compete with the modern factories that had sprung up overnight in the neighbouring districts.'[109]

---

[105] Boyarin, *Intertextuality*, e.g. 80 (a 'self-glossing text'). Although that claim grows out of an (approximately) deconstructionist practice of literary criticism, it must be different from deconstruction's general claim of the pervasiveness of intertextuality, otherwise it could not characterize rabbinic Judaism in particular. See also Fraade, *From Tradition to Commentary*, 7 f.

[106] The terms are said to be co-referential, the relationship is substitutional. In addition to the references given in the subsequent three notes, see Vater, *Einführung in die Textlinguistik*, 31–49, 133–54.

[107] An example for 'co-reference relation' in Brown and Yule, *Discourse Analysis*, 193.

[108] Used as an example for the progression from more specific to less specific pro-forms in a text in de Beaugrande and Dressler, *Introduction to Text Linguistics*, 64.

[109] Quoted in van Dijk, *Text and Context*, 132 (section 'topics of discourse'); the quotation is from J. H. Chase, *Just the Way It Is* (London: Panther Books, 1975).

There is a plurality of items in the world referred to by each of the expressions 'child', 'conqueror of Austria', or 'little town' (cf. Gen. 19:22) taken in isolation. But in the above textual units, the co-textual dependency has the effect of picking out just one singular referent for each of these terms: Ro's daughter, Napoleon, Fairview. The dependency is marked by the definite article. The mere fact that these proper names (or, in the case of Ro's daughter, a singular expression) immediately precede the much more general expressions used in the subsequent sentences determines the referent of the latter. This is analogous to the relationship of the individual event reported in the event verse and the general term of the tenor verse taken to refer to it. And while the tenor verse is never found in the biblical text immediately succeeding the event verse, the hermeneutics of Use3 can be imitated by rearranging two suitably selected biblical verses. It is possible to imitate the effect of the sequence 'Ro's daughter is ill again. The child is hardly ever well.' with a pair of verses encountered above, putting the general verse second and the specific one first.[110]

(A) And it was after these things that God tried Abraham and said to him: 'Abraham', and he said: 'Here I am.' The Lord tests the righteous one.[111]

How can the expression 'the righteous one' in this sequence of sentences *not* be read as a regular cohesive substitution for the proper name Abraham? But of course the two verses are not found in this sequence in Scripture, and rabbinic hermeneutics does not pretend that they are. One format in which the transfer of reference is presented very clearly is the following, quoted from a work of Midrash:

(B) Another interpretation. 'The Lord tests the righteous one'—this is (זה) Abraham, '[And it was after these things that] God tried Abraham'.[112]

We have addressed above the use of the demonstrative pronoun זו (appearing in [50] and [51]) as characteristic for Use1/2 and the *Petihah*. It may be a useful heuristic procedure to transform passages of the form (B) into the format (A); that could help in clarifying further the Use3/4 mechanisms, and perhaps in making relevant distinctions regarding the relationships found in *Petihot*. It may be noted in passing here that this sort of interaction through proximity does not seem typical of surviving examples of biblical

[110] A sequence actually found in many *Petihot*. The combination of quotations comes from BerR 55:2–3 (ed. Theodor-Albeck, ii. 585 f.). The sequence of the two types of verses (tenor and event) in *Petihot* is influenced by a number of factors. Usually, where we have the above sequence, the two verses are in fact separated by an introductory formula for the tenor verse (e.g. רבי פלוני פתח; הדא הוא דכתיב; זה שאמר הכתוב; כתיב, etc.). Cf. Lenhard, *Die Rabbinische Homilie*, 33 f.; on the aspect of juxtaposition see also ibid. 31.

[111] Gen. 22:1 and Ps. 11:5, the latter divided and shortened according to the requirements of the Use3 resource. The complete verse reads: 'The Lord tests the righteous and the wicked and the lover of violence his soul hates.'

[112] So found in BerR 55:3 (Wilna edn., 111b; ed. Theodor-Albeck, ii. 586).

anthologies or florilegia,[113] hermeneutic genres which were clearly of some importance in pre-rabbinic times.

INTERPRETING AND BEING INTERPRETED: THE TENOR VERSE (PETIHAH 2)

To recapitulate the formal and hermeneutic distinctions made for the expressive use of Scriptural wording in the Mishnah: where we find a (usually) undeclared use of Scriptural wording and the absence of reduplication in a Mishnaic treatment of norms or general topics, we have expressive use π, or performative use Performance3. Where we find a (usually) declared use of Scriptural wording and the absence of reduplication in a Mishnaic treatment of unique occurrences or individuals, we have expressive use of Performance2, or Use1–Use4 types.

This is what the Scriptural words are being used for: to formulate general Mishnaic statements (π, Performance3); to perform a Mishnaic obligation involving an utterance (Performance4, Performance8); to speak about singular past or future—non-biblical—events (Performance2, Performance8); to speak about biblical events in Mishnaic perspective which elsewhere in Scripture are explicitly reported (Use1, Use2, Use8); or finally, to speak about biblical events whose biblical report is also quoted (Use3, Use4). All these have in common the characteristic that Scripture is not interpreted as spoken about, but interpreted as used. How the Mishnah understands the verse so used is not explained so much as made manifest; and made manifest in what the Mishnah speaks *about* with the help of the verse. In particular with regard to the tenor verse, whose subject-matter is identified as being the stuff of the biblical narrative itself, we must ask the question: what exactly happens to the verse when it is uttered about biblical events? If we supplement the Mishnaic evidence with USE examples found in other rabbinic sources, the following points emerge.

1. The tenor verse is in some way *confirmed* in its validity, because its truth is 'fulfilled' by the individual case to which it points. Relevance and truth of a specific biblical segment are thereby demonstrated. This sets up some structural parallels to the way in which proverbs and prophecies are confirmed when they can be meaningfully applied.

2. The meaning of words of the tenor verse is adjusted to produce maximal convergence with the singular person or event. (This convergence is part of the work done by the reader of the rabbinic interpretation; it is not

---

[113] At least not on the level of segments of sentence-length. For the co-textual interaction of the larger segments, a systematic review of the evidence along the lines suggested here might be worthwhile. On florilegia at Qumran, see Brooke, *Exegesis at Qumran*; Lim, *Holy Scripture in the Qumran Commentaries and Pauline Letters*, 149–58. An important extant example is the Nash Papyrus, see Würthwein, *The Text of the Old Testament*, 34, 144 f.; Sanders, *Judaism*, 196; Tov, 'Harmonisations in Biblical Manuscripts', 18 f.

explained in the Mishnaic text.) Tenor verses tend to be comparatively general in their meaning, or often have weak or ambiguous links to their biblical co-text—as is typical for poetry and proverbs in Scripture. Tenor verses tend not to contain singular expressions[114] or proper names; or if they do, these are first reinterpreted by other resources.[115] Weak co-textual relationships are sometimes tacitly further weakened through the neutralization of co-text (Cotext1). The meaning range for the tenor verse is thus wide, or, put differently, open to narrowing down in a number of directions. This narrowing down takes place when the tenor verse is uttered about a singular event. The event (represented by its verbal description or summary) becomes a *perspective* for the tenor verse. In particular, the identification of a specific *referent* brings with it semantic (or syntactic) adjustments.[116] The resulting shifts or selections for, say, word meaning can often (not always) be pinpointed; thus, 'rise in judgement' must be understood as 'rise for judgement', not 'be acquitted' in [50]. As for the referring expressions of the tenor verse, they are affected by receiving their concrete referent. The meaning of the general term is to some extent 'determined' by the selection of the singular item which is taken to be picked out by it: that the men of Sodom are taken to be referred to by the word 'sinners' does fix the word's meaning in a certain dimension, and (more obviously, perhaps) the same is the case for the word 'wicked' in passage [40]. But this sort of determination does not need to translate into specific semantic differences. The 'usual' range of meanings carried by the words is enough to establish the relationship of reference. The expressions 'wicked/righteous' in [40], 'those that fear him' in [41], 'fathers' and 'sons' in [43] (but the fathers and sons in *that* generation), 'you' in [44], 'you' and 'foreigner' in [45], 'our fathers' in [47], 'sinners/wicked' in [50], and 'you' and 'my' in [52] all have their ordinary lexical meaning. This is clearest for the demonstratives and deictic terms: they can only be applied *because* they retain their normal deictic function. The identity of the referent of the deictic term 'you' in any given situation does not become part of the semantic meaning of the word.[117] The same holds true for the other words. Thus, there is no suggestion that the interpretation in [50] commits the exegete to saying that the word 'wicked' can everywhere only refer to the Generation of the Flood, and the word 'sinners' only to the Men of Sodom. Where there is a change of meaning against what is suggested by the co-text, as in the case of *eshkol* in [42], or the metaphorical understanding of 'father' in [44] and 'king', 'mother', 'wedding', and 'crown' in [51], this is accounted for by

---

[114] These (also called singular referring expressions) fit only one unique entity, such as 'the first president of the USA', or 'the last person to modify the text of the Mishnah'. See Evans, *Varieties of Reference*, 1 f. Code-names are a case in point: thus, 'teacher of righteousness' in Qumranic literature is used as a singular expression.

[115] As is probably the case for the name 'Solomon' in [51]. See above, n. 92.

[116] See on this my discussion in Ch. 2 (at n. 18).

[117] For the distinctions here necessary see Frawley, *Linguistic Semantics*, 23.

additional resources also found on their own (that is, separate from USE resources).

3. A perspective is imposed on the tenor verse by its engaging a unique item as referent. This means that the effect of the hermeneutic operation cannot be fully translated into or exhausted by a metalinguistic reformulation. Something is being done to the tenor verse which no amount of talking *about it* can do—only talking *with it* can do it. And there is in fact no *explanation* of the meaning of the tenor verse. The tenor verse is only explained *insofar* as *it* explains the events.[118] There is something bottomless and uncontrollable about the interplay between unique items and the utterance of the tenor verse. That interplay can be explored along all the words of the tenor verse, and into the co-text of the tenor verse (which is what *I* did in explaining [52], see above). This particular way to determine the meaning of a linguistic structure, this 'message' of Scripture in the tenor verse, could not be comprehensively reformulated: it is inherent in the *use* of words as utterance. This means, formally speaking, that 'uttering about' is a very different mechanism from the midrashic unit, whose essence is re-formulation.[119] PERFORMANCE and USE resources do not provide for an *objectification* of the tenor verse (and are in this related to the hermeneutic attitude of topical alignment discussed in Chapter 3).

4. Applying the tenor verse involves the faculty of judging that an individual thing, person, or happening is an *instance* of a general rule or term, a faculty basic to all language use. Applying conceptual or linguistic structures (of necessity *general*) to a specific item is a routine requirement of linguistic and social interaction. Its importance has been articulated in particular in the philosophical[120] and legal[121] contexts, but also with regard to hermeneutics.[122] The basic structure of the movement is: the interpretation of the individual as instance of the general does not merely limit explication (see point 3); it also limits justification (which would involve an

---

[118] Cf. Goldberg, 'Versuch', 13.

[119] The USE resources can only superficially be accommodated by the notion of a midrashic 'sentence' as developed by Goldberg. He was aware of there being a problem, saying that the *Petirah* has the 'Form des auslegenden, erklärenden Midrasch, aber eine andere Funktion' ('Versuch', 27; also 33).

[120] Cf. the Greek notion of *phronesis*, or the German *Urteilskraft* (judgement). See Aristotle, *Eth. Nic.*, vi. 7 f., esp. 1141a14 (similar at 1141a25). For the Platonic articulation of this question, see Wieland, *Platon und die Formen des Wissens*, 28 ff., 162 ff. (regarding the notion ἀκρίβεια in *Euthyphro*). Goodman, 'A Note on Josephus, the Pharisees and Ancestral Tradition', draws attention to the importance in antiquity of learning through imitation rather than through verbal instruction. Cf. the section 'Topical Diversity and Segment Size' in Ch. 2 above. See further Kant, *Critique of Judgement*: 'Judgement in general is the faculty of thinking the particular as contained under the universal' (p. 15; German, p. xxvi). Kant also points out that there can be no *rule* regulating the correct application of any rule without infinite regress (see ibid., p. 5; German, p. vii).

[121] See e.g. Aristotle, *Eth. Nic.*, v. 14 (1137a30–b1138a3); Hart, *The Concept of Law*, 121–5; Gadamer, *Truth and Method*, 281 ff. (*Wahrheit und Methode*, 320 ff. [299 ff.]); Derrida, 'Deconstruction and the Possibility of Justice'.

[122] See esp. Gadamer, *Truth and Method*, 29 ff., 278 ff. (*Wahrheit und Methode*, 36 ff. [27 ff.], 317 ff. [295 ff.]).

infinite regress insofar as rule-conformity is concerned). This has consequences for the idea of authority of interpretation (see next point).

5. The reader, as speaker of the tenor verse, is like any user of language in that he assumes the faculty of judgement (see preceding point). In doing this with Scriptural words, he claims truth and validity *not unlike* Scripture itself. If the divine author produced sentences which are true about some things, the rabbinic reader has the competence to *identify* those things, and utter the biblical words as his own. This makes it impossible, for the USE resources, to separate the divine or inspired text on the one hand from the human reader as merely receiving instruction on the other.[123] This comes as no surprise; the rabbinic authority assumed in dividing Scripture into segments is of the same order.[124] Turning it into a *theologoumenon*, we might say that the application of Scriptural sentences (more than their midrashic exposition) has an aspect of revelation or inspiration.[125] In this respect, the PERFORMANCE and USE resources are significantly different from resources which tie the biblical quotation to its reduplication in the midrashic unit: in the Mishnah at least, the latter form part of a fabric of reasons in a discourse of persuasion (see in particular Chapters 6, 7, and 12 below).

SCRIPTURE SPEAKS

In resources Use1–4, Scripture provides the words which the Mishnah speaks (tenor verse) about biblical persons or events. In Use8 this 'speaking about' furthermore appears to be performed by a biblical protagonist for whom the event or person is present. In [52] none other than David himself *utters* the tenor verse; he is the special case of a prophet or author of revelatory texts who is *also* a protagonist in a biblical story (Solomon is another). Rabbinic literature knows of other speakers who can suddenly appear on the stage of events, and can pronounce on them by quoting a tenor verse. They are in particular the *Bat Qol*,[126] the Holy Spirit,[127] God, and (pre-prophetic) prophets (such as Abraham or Joseph). The first three are latent

---

[123] Cf. Brooke, *Exegesis at Qumran*, in disagreement with Patte, *Jewish Hermeneutics*.

[124] See Ch. 2. Contrast with this a hermeneutic position which gives priority to the whole, e.g. the position of Wolff cited in n. 9 of Ch. 2 above.

[125] Against Goldberg, 'Versuch', 11 who contrasts 'Wissen aus der Offenbarung' to 'Wissen aus der Schriftforschung' with regard to the rabbinic *Petirah*. The differences between rabbinic Use1/2 and Qumran *Pesher* (often Performance2) are not to be sought along the lines of the more or less 'authoritative' (Goldberg, ibid.), or 'dogmatic' (Fishbane, 'Use, Authority and Interpretation of Mikra', 373 f.). Fishbane stresses *pesher* identifications which are not backed up by verbal links. But the hermeneutic structure explained above (and see the end of n. 120 above) directly accounts for the absence of proof-texts, so no special 'dogmatic' attitude is necessary.

[126] Fishbane's suggestion (*Biblical Interpretation*, 456, n. 39) that the *Bat Qol* in rabbinic literature is parallel to the phenomenon of regarding 'chance remarks or sounds as an omen', i.e. kledonomancy, is misleading.

[127] Cf. Goldberg, 'Versuch'. In mSot 9:6 IV (5) [125] (Ch. 13 below), the Holy Spirit is identified as uttering a segment of Scripture which is redundant. For a similar case in Targum Neofiti, see Samely, *Interpretation*, 127 f.

participants in any biblical (or indeed rabbinic) event; they can appear as (speaking) *deus ex machina* in any situation. And there is one further speaker who regularly represents the rabbinic reader in applying the tenor verse to a biblical event: Scripture itself. Rabbinic hermeneutics construes Scripture as uttering its tenor verses about its events. This may have reinforced (or been reinforced by) the widespread terminological personification of Scripture.[128] This personification of Scripture as speaker is formulaic in the rabbinic terminology of citation, for example 'Scripture says'/אומר הכתוב[129] and 'Scripture speaks'/דבר הכתוב.[130] One might say that this is the final, crowning achievement of the imposition of segmentation and perspective: that the biblical text curves in upon itself, that it is made to speak about itself and to itself—and that the reader as speaker of the biblical words *vanishes*. The rabbinic voice uses the tenor verse as utterance applied to a specific person or occurrence—that is the nature of the hermeneutic operation. But that same rabbinic voice is made to disappear from the surface of the text containing the interpretation, leaving Scripture to talk, as it were, *on its own*. Modern parlance provides phrases which obscure the role of the reader in a similar manner (which may have affected the scholarly discussion of rabbinic hermeneutics). For us too, Scripture *'says'* (as does indeed any text).[131] Yet it is a metaphor—perhaps *the* metaphor of hermeneutics. A text only 'says', in the sense of making an utterance into the situation of the reader, when it is read. No situation can interact with the text without a reader using the text; it is the reader who *speaks* the text.

Tenor verses may have had an effect on the rabbinic perception of biblical narrative, that is, on how biblical events were seen and in how much detail they were seen. Biblical events are presented as forming many different narrative structures and sub-plots, while also being the elements of the one overall story which the words of Scripture tell.[132] The light in which they are presented by tenor verses produces something of a distorting mirror: accents may be set which are not determined by the narrative structures themselves. There is only one hermeneutic treatment of events (qua events) which is of comparable importance in rabbinic literature (and of greater

---

[128] The formula found frequently in (anonymous) *Petihot* is זהו שאמר הכתוב, or הדא הוא דכתיב in Aramaic; cf. Bacher, *Die Prooemien*, 17 f., 29 ff.; Bacher, i. 180 f.

[129] Cases in the Mishnah include text **[44]** above, and also mPeah 8:9 I (4) (a normative case), mQid 1:10 (normative), mArak 8:7, and mYad 4:4 I (4). It can also mean, depending on the co-text, 'the verse says'.

[130] Used e.g. in mBQ 5:7. More on the Mishnaic vocabulary of quoting Scripture in Ch. 12 below.

[131] Cf. the perceptive account in Warfield, *The Inspiration and Authority of the Bible* (p. 148, apropos the New Testament): 'Scripture is thought of as the living voice of God speaking in all its parts directly to the reader.' Warfield goes on to stress the use of the *present tense* of the verb 'to say' in citation formulas. Cf. Bloch, 'Midrash', 33: Scripture 'always involves a living Word addressed personally to the people of God and to each of its members'. But, in the words of H. L. A. Hart, 'the rule itself [cannot] step forward to claim its own instances' (*The Concept of Law*, 123).

[132] The free matching of tenor verses and biblical events would have been constrained by a number of contextual factors. Prominent among them must have been the conventional articulation of the Pentateuch into weekly portions for the lectionary cycle (the *Seder*; see above, n. 83), possibly privileging the opening verses of *Sedarim* (see Mann, *The Bible as Read*).

importance in the Mishnah) than the evaluation by the tenor verse: the subsumption of a narrative instance of behaviour under a fixed normative schema. We shall discuss this resource, the interpretation of biblical events as *exemplary*, in the next chapter. But one idea unites these two hermeneutic treatments of biblical events for the rabbis: biblical events are expressive of God's will and motives. This is true whether biblical heroes conform to a divine norm of behaviour or whether they are subject to the causality of divine justice.[133]

FIXED LINGUISTIC FORM MEETS UNIQUE ITEM: PSALM SUPERSCRIPTION, PROPHECY, PROVERB

It remains now to point, very briefly, to hermeneutic phenomena which have certain similarities with the USE and PERFORMANCE resources, and could be historically connected to them. They are: psalm superscriptions; the interpretation of prophetic utterances as fulfilled; proverb application; and, to some extent, dream interpretation. The first three share with the resources discussed above this basic characteristic: the (declared or undeclared) expressive *use* of a ready-made formulation to articulate features of a unique situation different from the situation to which the formulation first applied; or the (declared or undeclared) expressive *use* of a ready-made general formulation to articulate features of a unique situation.

Psalm Superscriptions

Since the biblical text is marked by a considerable amount of internal cross-referencing or recapitulation of earlier events, the use of tenor verses could be said to have a distant biblical ancestor. Psalm texts are often linked with narrative material, through their superscriptions.[134] These would certainly have imposed a perspective on the psalms for the rabbinic reader, and the growth of the USE family of resources in rabbinic exegesis might be fuelled by a generalization to the whole of Scripture of the phenomenon of one biblical text appearing to *recapitulate* obliquely events from earlier biblical accounts.[135] The hermeneutic movement is defined by the difference in generality between the narrative account proper and the non-individual terms of oblique recapitulations, or of texts that were never intended as recapitulations. In this context we must mention one specific instance of

---

[133] See on this my account of the *mashal* (Use5) above.

[134] Recent developments are summarized by Fishbane, *Biblical Interpretation*, 403 ff. His use of the rabbinic term *semukhin* to describe this inner-biblical phenomenon confuses the issue. See above Ch. 3 (Cotext5); cf. Slomovic, 'Toward an Understanding of the Formation of the Historical Titles in the Book of Psalms', 352–3.

[135] See on this theme Jackson, *Studies in the Semiotics of Biblical Law*, Chs. 8 and 9.

inner-biblical exegesis which prefigures the USE resource in all basic respects. Psalm 68 seems to allude to Israel's desert wanderings (verse 7). Verse 8 reads: 'The earth quaked, the heavens poured down rain, at the presence of God—this is Sinai—at the presence of God, the God of Israel.' Michael Fishbane shows that the phrase 'this is Sinai' (זה סיני) is an explanatory gloss, saying in effect 'this [earthquake caused by Elohim] refers to [the theophany of] Sinai'.[136] Thus, an early interpreter of this psalm read the non-specific description as referring to a unique happening reported earlier in the Bible, and identified that earlier event in exactly the same manner as is employed by the Mishnah in [50]: by the *name* of an event ('Sinai'—as explicated in Fishbane's rephrasing above, the equivalent of a *biblical* Topic3 term) combined with a demonstrative pronoun.

Fulfilment of Prophecy

I have said above that the ability to apply the general verse to the individual item confirms the validity of the proposition or norm contained in that verse. This is actually an oversimplification: it is not easy to say exactly what receives confirmation in the verse 'But it was you, a man my equal, my companion and my familiar friend' in [52]. And yet, even if we retreat to the formulation that the application merely shows the *applicability* of the tenor verse, this still says something about its relevance and 'truth' as a Scriptural segment. There is a class of biblical segments which were frequently applied to explain the meaning of events in post-biblical Judaism: biblical prophecies. The events to which they were applied were non-biblical and in a complex sense contemporary: part of the prophecy applied to events in the recent or immediate past, so that other parts (those predicting judgement or salvation) could be applied to the imminent future. In such cases, the biblical predictions were said to be 'fulfilled' (biblical מלא, functionally related the rabbinic קים).[137] We can understand the fulfilment of prophetic utterances as confirmation of their applicability in a certain interpretation (the perspective imposed by the application itself). The imposition of perspective is achieved on the basis of *using* them to point to, and thus evaluate the meaning of, unique events or circumstances: *speaking about* unique occurrences *in terms of* the prophetic verses. Often the identification is mediated by schemata with hermeneutic functions, such as the 'birth pangs'[138] of the Messiah (or his 'footprints', see [43]), as well as a framework of successive stages found in apocalyptic literature from Daniel onwards,

---

[136] *Biblical Interpretation*, 55.

[137] The former is used in the Hebrew Bible a few times to refer to the fulfillment of words or promises (BDB, 570b). Bacher has no examples of such a use in rabbinic terminology (Bacher, ii. 111 f.). Rabbinic Hebrew sometimes uses קים for 'fulfil', as e.g. in mBQ 3:9 III–IV (4) and mSheq 6:6 II (2). Cf. Bacher, i. 170 f., but see Metzger, 'The Formulas Introducing Quotations of Scripture in the NT and the Mishnah'.

[138] Cf. Matth. 24:8 (ἀρχὴ ὠδίνων).

with Qumran[139] and the New Testament[140] as prime examples. They are the *signs*, the *semeia*, of recognition ('signs of the times'), and the recognition means: the events to which the descriptions found in the Bible belong have been *found*, are present or in the immediate past (in the past from the perspective of the pronouncement of the exegete, in any case). Although rabbinic hermeneutics seems to play down the contemporary relevance of prophetic utterances, centuries of intense eschatological reading of Scripture in pre-rabbinic Judaism may well have left their mark on rabbinic procedures even when devoted to other topics. The claim that a given verse from Scripture understood to be prophetic is *fulfilled*, therefore, is similar to the basic structure of Perfomance2 and Use1/2 in that it fits the utterance to a situation for which it is (or, is also) meant. And also similar in that, while explaining the event in terms of the verse used to speak about them, the speaker commits himself to the meaning and validity (fulfilled status) of the utterance.[141]

Proverb Application[142]

The linguistic phenomenon of proverbs is of fundamental interest to us in two respects. Just as the tenor verse in Use1–4, the proverb is a fixed linguistic entity not containing names or singular expressions which is applied to characterize a singular situation. And, just as the tenor verse, the proverb can be used in folklore and everyday conversation to summarize or evaluate *narrative*.[143] Among the similarities two are of special interest: proverbs can be used to bring to the surface the evaluation, plot-line, or meaning of a narrative;[144] and they offer the opportunity to string together individual narrative units.[145] For the latter the Mishnah also offers a literary example in the first chapter from Sotah (from which our cases **[22]** and **[49]** come). Here we need to address the observation that some tenor verses are in fact biblical proverbs. That is not surprising. The co-textual links within proverbial biblical texts (just as in prophetic and psalmodic poetry) can be very weak, thus making them similar to proverbs which are transmitted without a fixed co-text altogether—'atopical', in Sacks' word. Yet, the fact

---

[139] For a brief treatment of Qumran, cf. Fishbane, 'Authority, Use and Interpration of Mikra'; see also Brooke, *Exegesis at Qumran*; Slomovic, 'Towards an Understanding of the Exegesis of the Dead Sea Scrolls', 7 f.

[140] See, e.g. the instructive overview by Marshall, 'An assessment of Recent Developments'; Ellis, 'Biblical Interpretation in the New Testament Church', 704; Rothfuchs, *Die Erfüllungszitate*, 92; Dodd, *According to the Scriptures*, 12 f., 131.

[141] The aspect of commitment, which is automatic when Scriptural wording is used as utterance, is also important for the midrashic unit. See Ch. 12 below.

[142] See the discussion following case **[44]**. Cf. also Jackson, 'Law, Wisdom and Narrative'.

[143] The notion of proverb was used for *listings* of Scriptural 'examples' by Towner, *The Rabbinic 'Enumeration of Scriptural Examples'*, 59 ff. He deals only to a limited extent with the hermeneutic function of the numerical patterns involved (pp. 128 ff.).

[144] See Hasan-Rokem, *Proverbs*, 12: 'summing up the narrative plot' or 'generalizing an individual experience'; also 73.

[145] Ibid. 93.

that Scripture actually contains proverbs, and that they are also used as tenor verses, is not the reason for the hermeneutic similarities with proverb application.[146] Decisive is the similarity of the act of uttering a fixed and non-specific formulation about a unique occurrence or person. But the existence of a rabbinic-biblical proverb tradition as such could still be an important general cultural background factor.[147]

Dream Interpretation, Qumranic Pesher, and Rabbinic Petirah

Some modern interpreters of rabbinic hermeneutics have suggested that rabbinic interpretation is linked to practices of dream interpretation shared among many cultures of the ancient Mediterranean.[148] Apart from an overlap in specific hermeneutic methods, it is two formal features of rabbinic interpretation which are thought to support such a connection. There is first the occurrence of the verb *patar* in many rabbinic *Petihot* on the one hand, and in the explanation of dreams (biblical *patar*, only in Gen. 40 and 41) and the Qumran *Pesher* on the other (see below). There is, furthermore, the employment of demonstrative pronouns (e.g. 'this' /זה) in the segmentation of dreams as well as in the rabbinic segmentation of Scripture.[149] I shall deal with some pertinent aspects of the use of demonstratives in Chapter 13 (resource Redundancy9). Here I only need to say that the use of demonstrative pronouns in the presentation of the interpretation (a formal observation) must be kept separate from the question of whether a fixed formulation is applied to a singular referent or not (that is, what the demonstrative pronoun actually refers to); the same goes for the question of whether only one or more than one interpretation is given for the same biblical text.[150] A further link to dream interpretation is made when specific rabbinic techniques (or at least their terminology) are taken to grow out of

[146] Hasan-Rokem addresses biblical verses in folklore both in their role as proverbs and as quotations (ibid. 54 ff.). The wider functional similarity of biblical quotation and proverb is taken for granted by Hasan-Rokem, but it stands in need of explanation, certainly for the case of rabbinic hermeneutics.

[147] Cf. Boyarin, *Intertextuality*, ch. 8 (the *mashal* as manifestation of 'ideological codes' and 'carrier(s) of values and ideology in the culture', p. 92).

[148] See Oppenheim, 'The Interpretation of Dreams in the Ancient Near East'. On the link to the *Petirah*, see Alexander, 'Bavli Berakhot 55a–57b: The Talmudic Dreambook in Context'; Niehoff, 'A Dream Which is Not Interpreted is Like a Letter Which is Not Read'; Alexander, 'Pre-Emptive Exegesis: Genesis Rabba's Reading of the Story of Creation', 242 f.; Patte, *Early Jewish Hermeneutic in Palestine*, 300–8 (on Qumran *Pesher*); Silberman, 'Unriddling the Riddle', 332 f.; Alexander 'Quid Athenis et Hierosolymis?', 117–19. See also Fraade, *From Tradition to Commentary*, 3–6. In his ' "Comparative Midrash" Revisited', Fraade briefly lists a number of surface differences between Qumranic *Pesher* and rabbinic *Petirah* (pp. 6 f.).

[149] For the biblical evidence, see Fishbane, *Biblical Interpretation*, 447 f.

[150] Cf. Fraade, *From Tradition to Commentary*, 5 f., 13 (on the apparently puzzling simultaneous presence of 'deictic' and 'dialogic' features). The study of Qumranic exegesis in particular seems to suffer from an insufficient separation of underlying hermeneutic movement on the one hand from presentational feature on the other. One cannot *assume* that there is a one-to-one correspondence between literary format and hermeneutic function; and such an exclusive correspondence would in fact be surprising.

a common Mediterranean[151] or specifically Greek tradition of explaining dreams.[152] But what is relevant in the present context is the claim that dream interpretation accounts for the hermeneutics of the *Petihah* (that is, the mechanism as we can actually observe it in rabbinic literature, not as it might have been before). Explaining the hermeneutic movement underlying many *Petihot* (the *Petirah*) in the light of dream interpretation is an alternative—probably an incompatible one—to explaining it as Use3/4. My hypothesis is that the *Petirah* is often fully intelligible on the basis of a re-utterance of a general fixed formulation (tenor verse) about a unique event represented by a second fixed formulation (event verse), with the presence of the event verse opening up the hermeneutic operation to accommodate further, intrinsically metalinguistic, resources of the type discussed in other parts of this study. (Whereas the Qumranic *Pesher* is often best understood as a re-utterance of a general fixed biblical formulation about a unique event in the sect's past and present, that is, Performance2.) On the other hand, to say that the *Petirah* is like dream interpretation must, it seems to me, imply that its regularities are governed by the associative or image-led thought of the unconscious (although I have not found this claim spelled out boldly);[153] or alternatively, that it has no regularities, but is arbitrary.[154] It seems that the field on which to test these alternatives is the empirical investigation of (many) *Petihot*, and very likely a differentiation of types of *Petihot*. However, before the model of dream interpretation can be successfully applied to the *Petirah*, some conceptual requirements need to be met. There is first the point that the dream is not, *as such*, a fixed linguistic formulation. But for the *Petirah*, the rigidity of biblical wording (which is paralleled not by the dream, but by the proverb) is constitutive. Also, the rabbinic reader has to find the correct context of the new utterance from among the biblical events; that is how the hermeneutic work is performed. By contrast, the meaning of the dream, at least if the conventions represented in the biblical and rabbinic dream texts are anything to go by, is bound to the situation of its occurrence; the interpreter does not have to scan the centuries or continents to find the situation or personage to which the dream's message applies. The dream, unless it becomes Scripture (like Nebuchadnezzar's dream, Dan. 2:31 ff.), does not *keep*. Far from the interpretation of the text coming after (*logically* after) that

[151] Cf. Oppenheim, 'The Interpretation of Dreams'.

[152] In particular with the *Oneirocritica* of Artemidorus. Cf. Lieberman, *Hellenism*, 70 ff. (also quoting the earlier literature); Finkel, 'The Pesher of Dreams and Scriptures'; Alexander, 'Quid Athenis et Hierosolymis?', and cf. the next note.

[153] An exception is Güttgemanns in a fast-paced (and extremely illuminating) article, 'Die Semiotik des Traums in apokalyptischen Texten'; but he is not concerned with the *Petihah*.

[154] The demonstration that rabbinic hermeneutics somehow anticipates Freud (as well as Derrida), makes it *the* historical alternative to the Western reading tradition of 'logocentrism' for some. Cf. Boyarin, *Intertextuality*, 93 f.; Niehoff, 'A Dream Which is Not Interpreted Is Like a Letter Which is Not Read'.

of the dream, the evidence points in the other direction: the practice of interpreting linguistic signs is *presupposed* in important aspects of dream interpretation.[155]

[155] It seems to me that the semiotic complexities of dream interpretation (both in the ancient cultures *and* in Freud) are insufficiently appreciated in recent attempts to apply it to the *Petihah*. For an orientation, cf. Malcolm, *Dreaming*, in particular ch. 12 (on the contemporary convention of 'having' or 'telling' a dream); Boyarin, *Intertextuality*, 91 (*meshalim* 'must be made into fictions before they can signify'—this is equally true of dreams); Faur, *Golden Doves With Silver Dots*, pp. xviii, 82, 122 f.; Handelman, *The Slayers of Moses*, 142 f.; Said, *Beginnings*, 264 (on Freud's dreams being constituted as texts); Blumenberg, *Die Lesbarkeit der Welt* (chapter 'Die Lesbarmachung der Träume', on Freud). Güttgemanns, 'Die Semiotik des Traums in apokalyptischen Texten' (pp. 18 ff., 40 ff.), deals with the dream's textuality. For the representation of biblical dreams, see now Jackson, *Studies in the Semiotics of Biblical Law*, sec. 8.1.

6

Biblical Events Illustrating Normative and Descriptive Schemata

The Mishnah may take a biblical action as instance of a halakhic norm. In such normative generalizations, certain features of the narrative situation are de-emphasized. At the same time, fresh features are provided by the Mishnaic framework in which the norm finds its place among other norms. Mostly, a narrative biblical segment is quoted whose contribution is defined by the specific point at which it appears in the Mishnaic discourse. This imposes on it a perspective different from that imposed by its narrative setting in Scripture. The Mishnah may also take biblical happenings as instances of how the world is governed (rather than how man should behave). Frequently, the presence of the biblical quotation produces a conspicuous repetition of reports of the same biblical event. This repetition could indicate a hermeneutic distinction between biblical happenings on the one hand, and their (selective) representation in the biblical text on the other. Events of biblical times actually presented in the biblical narrative would thus be marked out for lasting and therefore contemporary relevance to the rabbinic reader.

IMPOSING A PRESCRIPTIVE SCHEMA ON BIBLICAL NARRATIVE

The Mishnah can make biblical events its topic without recourse to the very words in which they are reported in Scripture. We have seen this for events which are treated as known, and whose rabbinic evaluation proceeds from a summary or 'name' (Topic3).[1] Also for the USE resources,[2] the event for which the tenor verse comes into play is evaluated—but no quotation of its Scriptural report is necessary (and the tenor verse itself, whose wording is

---

[1] See Ch. 3 above.   [2] See Ch. 5 above.

quoted verbatim, does not come under scrutiny). We now come to another way of investing biblical events with meaning: their treatment as providing an *example* of behaviour (and also as instantiations of the order of reality). We shall name this group of resources NORM. Through the NORM resources, biblical events or happenings are foregrounded (as in some of the USE resources). However, these events are not investigated for their intrinsic meaning in the situation or narrative in which they appear (although the situation may be used to limit their function). Instead, they are employed as evidence for something outside that biblical framework, namely, the behaviour expected from the users and makers of the Mishnah. And, in contrast to the Mishnaic USE passages, an explicit quotation from Scripture is usually presented.

Let us first deal with the biblical examples for behavioural norms, reserving for later biblical instances of the laws of reality. Often, the reference to the biblical event is introduced by the particle -שׁ, 'for'. It forms part of the formula ב- מצינו שכן, *'for* thus we find it with . . .'.[3] Two further phrases starting with -שׁ precede the Scriptural quotation in the most elaborate passages, of which the following is an example:

[52a] = [6] mSan 2:3 I (2)[4]   2 Sam. 3:31

If a relative of his [the king] dies, he may not go out of the door of his palace. R. Yehudah says: If he wants to leave after the bier he may leave. For (-שׁ) thus we have found it with David, who (-שׁ) went out after the bier of Abner, as (-שׁ) it is said, 'And king David walked after the bier'. They said to him: The thing happened only to appease the people.[5]

The format is: . . . שׁנאמר . . . שׁ . . . ב מצינו שכן. The five elements linked by this structure are: (a) the norm (Yehudah's version): the king may go out after the bier if he wants to; (b) the reference to the biblical event instantiating the norm: for thus we have found it with David (שׁכן מצינו בדוד); (c) the Mishnaic event report: [David], who went out (שׁיצא) after the bier of Abner; (d) the link of the Mishnaic event report to a Scriptural wording introduced by שׁנאמר;[6] (e) the Scriptural event report as quotation: 'And king David walked after the bier.'

The structure is punctuated by the three occurrences of the particle -שׁ: after the norm meaning 'for', before the Mishnaic event report meaning 'he who', and before the Scriptural quotation meaning 'for'. Immediately noticeable is the redundancy produced by this: the action is encapsulated by the norm, reported twice, and pointed to a fourth time in the demonstrative *ken*, 'thus' (כן). The unit, although barely three lines long, contains *two* signals for an argument or warrant: the first and the last -שׁ ('for') are of

---

[3] Bacher, i. 114, says little about the function of שכן מצינו for this type of resource; it is also used to introduce analogies (which I treat in Ch. 8 below).

[4] • ¶N1T2.

[5] This passage served in Ch. 2 as an example for the use of co-text (Cotext5).

[6] Not all biblical events used as exempla have quoted biblical wording; see below n. 47 and passage [59].

this kind. The suggestion seems to be that of a *hierarchy* of reasons. I shall propose the explanation that while the norm is supported by the event's having happened, the event's relevance to the rabbinic discourse is proven from the fact that a biblical *report* of it exists (see next section).

However, the quotation also identifies a textual area in Scripture in which the larger narrative context can be ascertained. In case **[52a]** the presentation of an example is followed by an objection which challenges R. Yehudah's position on the basis of the narrative setting of David's behaviour:

They said to him: The thing (דבר) happened only to appease the people.

It is important to note that this objection uses *davar* ('word, thing, matter') to refer to the event, not its biblical formulation. The biblical narrative leaves little doubt of the motivation of David. Verse 37 reads: 'So all the people and all Israel understood that day that it had not been the king's will to slay Abner the son of Ner.' But this passage is not quoted to support the objection, nor is any other. Knowledge of the events in their narrative interdependence is presupposed and unproblematic, and is directly relied upon to say that it was exceptional circumstances that led to David's behaviour. The explicit quotation can also be absent from the proposal of an exemplum itself (not merely an objection to it, as here). The introductory formula 'for thus we have found' need not lead to a quotation formula and quotation: in mMen 4:3 I (2) the behaviour of Israel in the wilderness is proposed as exemplary with regard to certain types of offerings. While the Mishnaic event report is introduced with the words . . . שכן מצינו ישראל כשהיו במדבר, that is, with the formula also used in **[52a]**, the claim is not supported by any quotation.

If we now compare the two event reports in **[52a]**, we can see that there is plenty of semantic overlap, but the wording is by no means the same: where the Mishnah uses יצא, Scripture has הולך; the bier is identified explicitly as Abner's in the Mishnah but not in Scripture (although his name is mentioned before and after the quoted sentence). These differences between the quotation and its explicit paraphrase are one manifestation of the Mishnaic perspective. The biblical event has been stripped down to its essentials in R. Yehudah's use of it, and what is essential is dictated by the Mishnaic discourse at this point. David's behaviour is transposed into the new discourse setting by supplying both a summary (incorporating Abner's name) and an assimilation to the wording of the *norm* appearing earlier in **[52a]**. That norm mentions the king *leaving* (יצא) *his palace* to follow the bier, and there is nothing corresponding to this detail in the Scriptural text. Alongside the paraphrase is given the biblical passage which it paraphrases. This means that the biblical wording is not used expressively (π), but reduplicated in Mishnah's own words.[7] As I said before, this

---

[7] See Kern, 'Die Verwendung von Schriftversen in rabbinischen Texten'.

reduplication characterizes the midrashic unit, and is well suited to a format which presents evidence for a discursive position. Further aspects of the perspectivization are that not David the individual, but David in the institutional role of king is emphasized. The Mishnaic norm also imports a theme which is absent from the biblical narrative: the problem of impairing the king's dignity by him following a bier.[8] The detailed biblical account of David's manifestations of mourning gives no hint that a norm of royal behaviour might be violated (2 Sam. 3:31–5). The narrative is quite compatible with the interpretation that there was an *obligation* for David to express his grief, and that abstention from mourning would have been wrong even if there had been no suspicion among the people that he was implicated in Abner's murder. If we now reconsider the answer given to R. Yehudah, it reveals the possibility of an apologetic function. David *had* to impair his royal dignity (that is, break a norm whose rationale exceeded his individual status), because more important things were at stake. In this context it may be relevant that Abner was no relative of David, and thus does not really fit one of the norm's operative assumptions (namely, that only for a close relative would the king even wish to show himself mourning in public).[9] All in all, the midrashic unit provides considerable positioning or perspectivization in order to fit the biblical event into the Mishnaic norm. We can set out the main points in the format which norms often have in the Mishnah, as a protasis–apodosis unit:

(1) If a person is an Israelite king
(2) and if a relative of his dies
(3) and if he wishes[10] to follow the bier
(4) thereby leaving his palace
[(5) and impairing his dignity]
— Then he may do so (R. Yehudah)
— Then he may not do so (anonymous Mishnaic voice and objectors to R. Yehudah).

Of the five parts of the protasis here explicated in our own paraphrase, one (2) is inapplicable and one (4) is absent from the biblical narrative. This shows the *schematism* of the hermeneutic operation. The biblical account is made to contribute its evidence in a structure which is not its own; it is being summoned like a witness.[11] It can only answer the questions the

---

[8] This seems to be the point of the norm (see Bertinoro and Tif'eret Israel ad loc.). Note that R. Yehudah uses the biblical events to argue for the *absence* of a constraint on behaviour (there is no prohibition regarding the king's following the bier): the events show *e silencio* that there is no such prohibition.

[9] The norm begins, 'If a *relative* of his dies'. David's action could be taken to prove (arguing for R. Yehudah) that the public display of royal distress is permissible even for a non-relative, let alone a relative (see next chapter on the *a fortiori*).

[10] R. Yehudah's position seems to follow a pattern in allowing the king's preferences (cf. mSan. 2:2, again using David as exemplum).

[11] Cf. Goodrich, *Languages of the Law*, 193 ff.

Mishnah puts to it, and in the manner in which they are put; the segment which serves as evidence does not shape those questions. The most important format in which the Mishnaic perspective is brought to bear on the biblical message is the casuistic norm or hypothetical case schema (often consisting of a protasis–apodosis unit).[12] It is the Mishnaic case schema which carries out the *schematizing of the biblical narrative* with regard to prescriptive norms. We have already encountered other resources which tie Scripture to a Mishnaic protasis–apodosis unit. In interpretations of the Topic2 type an unconditional Scriptural clause is used to support a Mishnaic apodosis (and see also Performance3). There, the biblical and the Mishnaic syntagmas are both normative, and do not depend on a specific instance or individual. By contrast, our current group of resources has to impose a *normative generalization* on the biblical event before it can be used to support the apodosis of a Mishnaic case schema. The reason for this is that the biblical sentence contains a narrative report, not a norm. The normative generalization consists of interpreting the reported event as embodying the behaviour *incumbent* on *everyone* in the same circumstances.[13]

A number of distinctions need to be made here. There is first that between prescription and description. Is the biblical narrative taken as an illustration of the validity of a certain behaviour, or of the truth of a proposition? About an event, such as David's marrying Saul's widows, one may say: we see here that it is *obligatory or permissible* for a king to marry the widow of a king (cf. mSan 2:2). This is concerned with the behaviour that is *required* of a king. But when deducing from the fact that in a certain biblical battle the Israelites started to flee and were then defeated a general truth, namely that flight (for Israel!) is a *cause* of military defeat (cf. mSot 8:6 II (2)), one is concerned with how things *are*. This statement formulates a law or regularity of reality. Such military insights or psychological laws are—in the Mishnah at least—usually descriptions of how the world is governed by God, and *thereby* incorporate also values. But they are still descriptive of reality, not prescriptive of behaviour. So, while the first class of hermeneutic operation supports a prescriptive schema from a biblical instance, the latter supports a descriptive schema.

I will use the labels Norm1–Norm5 for the prescriptive types of schematization, while reserving Norm8 for the descriptive ones. Interpretations of biblical instances as prescriptive can be divided further according to whether Scripture records the action of a human protagonist (Norm1 and Norm2) or of God (Norm3 and Norm4); and whether the

---

[12] The word 'hypothetical' used here has nothing to do with this particular case (a Jewish king at the time of the Mishnah) being hypothetical: all norms of the Mishnah, insofar as they are expressed in a format which is conditional on certain situational factors, are hypothetical in this sense. See below.

[13] The *normative* character of the generalization is important for Norm1–5. The inference is not that everyone *behaved* (or behaves) like that, but that everybody *should* behave like that. See presently.

starting-point is the fact that someone *did* something (Norm1, Norm4), or that a protagonist (in particular God) *told* someone else to do something (Norm2, Norm3). From biblical speech which is taken to presuppose a norm we shall separate biblical speech whose *speech acts* are taken as exemplary in themselves (Norm5). I shall also use the numeral 1 as second digit of a NORM resource code to identify biblical instances which are seen by the rabbis to have *institutional* significance in that they concern the *first* action of a whole class of actions commanded for repetition (i.e. Norm*.1). This produces double-digit codes such as Norm1.1 and Norm2.1. My case **[52a]** comes under the resource Norm1.

Norm1: Identification of an action reported in Scripture of a human protagonist as conforming to a behavioural norm formulated by the Mishnah.

Where the exemplary event is a verbal act of a biblical hero, there seems to be a hermeneutic assumption that the speech has the status of a judgement (of an individual case) or an imperative, and incorporates a norm in this fashion. The following passage is an illustration.

[53] mSheq 1:5[14]   Ezra 4:3

If a non-Jew or Samaritan wishes to pay the [temple] *Sheqel*, one does not accept it from them. And one does not accept from them the bird offerings for a man or a woman who has had a flux, or for women who have given birth; sin offerings and guilt offerings one does not accept from them. (But what is vowed or volunteered one does accept from them.) This is the rule (כלל): Any [offering which is] vowed or voluntarily offered one accepts of them, and every [offering which] is not vowed or voluntarily offered one does not accept of them. And so it is explicated by Ezra,[15] for it is said, 'You have nothing to do with us in building a house unto our God'.

The biblical utterance is quoted to support either the opening Dictum on the *Sheqel* contribution, or the 'rule' (כלל). If the latter, this is based on the technical Mishnaic distinction between voluntary and mandatory offerings.[16] The 'explication' (the term מפורש) of this rule is ascribed to Ezra as author of the biblical book (cf. bBB 15a), while the voice speaking in the biblical narrative is that of Zerubbabel and the other chiefs who address the 'people of the land' (verse 4) wishing to contribute to the temple. The biblical narrative gives a very specific perspective to the utterance, for the request to contribute to the temple comes from of the 'adversaries of Judah and Benjamin' (verse 1), and is followed by an account of their attempts to sabotage the building work. But for the Mishnah Zerubbabel's answer is not dictated by unique circumstances. Instead, it is taken to be the pronouncement of a judgement in one concrete halakhic instance and as presupposing a *rule* (כלל). In other cases of this type, it is the *command* of a

---

[14] ΔC5L3N2T2T3.

[15] וכן הוא מפרש על ידי עזרא שנאמר; MS Kaufmann omits שנאמר, as well as the text in round brackets.

[16] The same distinction is made e.g. in mMeg 1:10, also introduced as general rule.

biblical protagonist as embedded into a narrative situation which is understood to apply a norm (e.g. mShab 9:3 I (3)).

Norm2: Identification of human speech reported in Scripture and set in a narrative context as applying a behavioural norm formulated by the Mishnah.

It is God in particular whose utterances are taken to incorporate general norms, even where they are embedded in narrative situations.

Norm3: Identification of divine speech reported in Scripture and set in a narrative context as example of the application of a behavioural norm formulated by the Mishnah.

Perhaps all Mishnaic cases in this category, Norm3, relate to utterances which can also be taken to be narrative 'firsts' and may thus be interpreted as laying the foundations for an enduring institution or repeatable ritual. A good example is the creation of a council of elders to help Moses 'carry the burden of the people' (Num. 11:17). This is taken by the Mishnah to be the first Sanhedrin, that is, the rabbinic supreme court. God's command to Moses to take seventy elders is thus understood to identify the constitutive number of the—greater—Sanhedrin for all time.

[54] mSan 1:6 I (5)[17]   Num. 11:16

The greater Sanhedrin was made up of seventy-one [judges] and the lesser one of twenty-three. And whence do we learn that the greater Sanhedrin should be made up of seventy-one? For it is said, 'Gather unto me seventy men of the elders of Israel [. . . and let them take their stand there with you]', and Moses over them—behold, seventy-one. R. Yehudah says: Seventy.

In the biblical narrative God's utterance is presented as response to a specific complaint by Moses (in verse 11). However, the Mishnah interprets it as establishing a rule, indeed as the founding proclamation of an institution with contemporary (that is, Mishnaic) relevance. I will mark the fact that the Mishnah considers a divine utterance as embodying a norm which is constitutive for an enduring institution (determining its shape in some way), by the addition of a second digit '1' to the resource code.

Norm3.1: Identification of divine speech reported in Scripture and set in a narrative biblical context as the initial and constitutive creation of a Mishnaic institution or ritual.

For some other resources of the NORM family a similar variant seems to exist (all of them are represented by a separate resource definition with the added second digit '1' in Appendix I). For human action (Norm1), such an interpretation was encountered earlier, in passage **[48]**. Here is its text again:

---

[17]   ¶®ΔC5N3.1T3.

[54a] = [48] mSot 7:6 = mTam 7:2[18]   Lev. 9:22

The priestly blessing—how? In the country they say it as three blessings, and in the sanctuary as one blessing; in the sanctuary they say the Name as it is written, and in the country by circumlocution; in the country they raise their hands to the height of their shoulders, and in the sanctuary over their heads, except for the high priest who does not place his hands higher than the forehead-plate. R. Yehudah says: The high priest too places his hands above the forehead-plate, as it is said, 'And Aaron raised his hands towards the people and blessed them'.

In my earlier discussion of this passage[19] I accepted as plausible the notion that the Scriptural verse is meant to link up with the position that the high priest does *not* place his hands higher than the forehead-plate. This means that the quotation belongs to the anonymous Dictum and not R. Yehudah's negation of it. If so (but equally if the verse belongs to Yehudah's position), it is clear that the interpreter takes the event about which the verse speaks to embody a norm which is attached to a specific but repeatable cultic act. Lev. 9:22 is taken to report a unique event, namely, one of the actions performed by Aaron at his induction (a 'first'); but it is also seen as the model of a ritually repeated action, namely the pronouncement of the 'priestly blessing' (which is a Topic3 term) by any high priest after Aaron. It is therefore the 'inaugural performance' variant of the resource Norm1:

Norm1.1: Identification of an action reported in Scripture of a human protagonist as the initial and constitutive performance of a Mishnaic ritual or procedure.

At the beginning of this chapter I drew attention to a formula which introduces biblical events as arguments in the Mishnaic discourse starting with שֶׁ־, 'for'. This 'for' ties the hermeneutic movement, not just for NORM resources, into the fabric of the Mishnah as a persuasive or probative discourse (see next chapter, and Chapter 12). We find a further formula above in [54], namely, the question 'whence that?', מִנַּיִן שֶׁ־ . . . . ?. This question is answered by a Scriptural quotation introduced by 'for it is said' (שֶׁנֶּאֱמַר). The question has to be understood as elliptic, probably involving a verb of saying.[20] It is an epistemic interrogative, asking, in effect: Whence do we know? In other words, just like the phrase 'for thus we *find* with . . .', it allocates argument function to the Scriptural event, the event serves as *evidence*. This is how Bacher describes the function of the מִנַּיִן-question: it is 'applied constantly in tannaitic midrash, be it to ask for the biblical origin of a thesis, of a halakhah, be it to ask in the course of a discussion for evidence for the

---

[18] Δ¶C5N1.1(T0)T3T5.
[19] See [48] in Ch. 5.
[20] For the rare full form 'Whence do you say?', see Bacher, i. 106. Cf. the counterpart formula, 'From here they said' (מכאן אמרו) coming after a Scriptural quotation. Mishnaic examples include mNeg 12:6 III (3) (resource Use6); mMS 5:14 (Performance4/8); mSan 10:5 II (2); mSan 10:6 II (6); mEduy 5:6.

extension of a thesis which itself can be concluded directly from the biblical text.'[21]

The question 'whence?' appears about twenty times in the Mishnah in hermeneutic contexts, but only in some of these is the answer derived from Scriptural examples, that is, involves NORM resources. More often, information implied in a biblical wording provides the answer, that is, resources which have nothing to do with the idea of example. 'Whence?' tends to appear in clusters: mShab 9:2–3, mSan 1:6, and mAvot 3:6 together account for thirteen of its Mishnaic occurrences. In these clusters, in particular in mShab 9:3, questions to which the response is a biblical example are found alongside other types of answers (that is, resources), and no distinction is signalled. The interrogative form itself underscores that the knowledge ostensibly supported or even derived from the biblical example is already *available*, and not in itself problematical. Although 'whence?' presents evidence for a statement or norm, that norm/statement is characterized not as doubtful, but as presupposed. These two faces of the quotation are in fact a manifestation of the underlying imposition of a hermeneutic perspective. Imposition of perspective is constitutive where unique narrative events are integrated into a normative or conceptual *schema*. The schema or generalization is on the one hand prior, or presupposed, thus shaping the view of the text; on the other, its validity is subject to a demonstration from biblical evidence.

Returning to the NORM resources, we come to Norm4, a divine deed set in the narrative and taken as exemplary. We find that there is only one Mishnaic passage which identifies a divine act as exemplary in this sense, and even that is open to an alternative reading:

[55] mYeb 6:6 II (3)[22]   Gen. 5:2

No man may set aside [the obligation of] 'fruitfulness and multiplication' unless he already has children; the House of Shammai say: two males. And the House of Hillel say: A male and a female, for it is said, 'male and female he created them . . . [and he called their name *Adam*] . . .'.

We are concerned here with the second half of the argument. The Hillelites support their idea that the norm requires one child of each gender by reference to what God *did*, or at least that is one way to construe the hermeneutic operation. There is, however, an alternative, namely to stress the fact that God called both of them together 'Adam', that is, 'man'. This implies that only male and female together count as one 'man', and thus as minimal fulfilment of the obligation to be fruitful and multiply: one 'Adam', that is, one male and one female child. I am inclined to favour this interpretation of the *mishnah*, in which case divine speech, not divine action, would embody the norm, making this an example of Norm3 rather than Norm4.[23] This

---

[21] Ibid. (my translation).

[22] ◊•¶πN4.1orN3.1(N8)O1.4O9W1.

[23] Cf. Albeck, *Einführung*, 85.

renders doubtful the only case of the hermeneutic employment of *imitatio dei* in the Mishnah. I shall provide a definition of the relevant resource, as Norm4. But I shall mark by square brackets the fact that the Mishnah does not provide unequivocal testimony to its availability in early rabbinic Judaism.

[*Norm4]: Identification of a divine deed reported in Scripture and set in a narrative context as exemplifying a behavioural norm formulated by the Mishnah.

The question to what extent God's actions are considered to be different in nature or essentially the same as man's, and therefore may be imitated by him, is of some importance for this resource.[24] Any use of God's acts as model presupposes that divine and human actions are comparable. This is obviously problematic for some deeds, such as creating a man from dust, and so on.[25] Perhaps this is why **[55]** prefers evidence from a divine utterance over the direct report of the deed ('male and female he created them'). But even for divine deeds which seem more amenable to direct comparison a problem remains. Consider the case of God burying Moses, taken as exemplary in bSotah 14a. Is burying a person really considered *the same* when God performs it as when man performs it? In mAvot 5:6 Moses's grave is categorized as one of the miracles of creation and the Bavli passage also stresses its supernatural status. But, the Bavli continues, man can at least 'follow' the *middah* ('rule') of God.[26] This formulation is precise: not the divine deed, but its 'rule' or 'measure' (*middah*) is to be followed (*halakh*). This really implies that the norm has priority to or independence from God's behaviour exemplifying it: divine deeds do not, through their facticity, *set* a norm—they *follow* one or conform to it. One could say that the deed is conceptualized as mediated by a divine *middah*, and that *middah* corresponds to the halakhic norm (cf. the word *halakh*) ascertained by resource Norm4. And the biblical deed is *mediated* again for the human interpreter: through *language* (in Scripture's report), using words which also describe human deeds.[27] The point which affords access to the norm (*middah*, *halakhah*) of the divine deed is, for man, Scripture's report on it. This is how one could explicate the theological background of the Norm4 resource in a rabbinic context. We shall address the importance of the Scriptural mediation of biblical deeds again in the final section of this chapter.

---

[24] Cf. Schechter, *Aspects of Rabbinic Theology*, 201 ff. (pp. 199–205). Further on the *imitatio dei* in rabbinic Judaism, Marmorstein 'Imitatio Dei', in id., *The Old Rabbinic Doctrine of God*; Maier, *Geschichte der jüdischen Religion*, 155 f. (link to Exod. 34: 6–7); Abrahams, *Studies in Pharisaism and the Gospels*, 138–82; Kadushin, *The Rabbinic Mind*, 201 ff.; id., *Organic Thinking*, 246 f. Cf. also Soloveitchik, *Halakhic Man*.

[25] The most direct imitation of the actual execution of this divine deed is not the act of having children, but the creation of a *golem*—i.e. an act not required by a halakhic norm.

[26] The expression is: .לֵילֵךְ אַחַר מִדּוֹתָיו שֶׁל הַקָּבָּ"ה

[27] In mAvot 5:22 the Torah is called the best *middah* a man can have.

Numerically speaking, the most important type of exemplary behaviour concerns the *way* in which biblical protagonists *speak*. It is not the subject-matter of the utterance which is taken to presuppose the norm (as in Norm2, see [53]). Rather, it is the speech act itself which is taken as a model, even though it occurs in a narrative setting, and not in a biblical ritual involving performed speech (such as the *Sotah* and *Halitsah* rituals). Thus, Boaz's using the name of God in a greeting (Ruth 2:4) is identified as an exemplary speech act in the Mishnah (in ΩmBer 9:5 III (6)). Likewise, David's calling Ahitophel his master, because he learned from him, is interpreted as giving a model of *verbal* behaviour in [mAvot 6:3 I (3)] [52]. And the utterances of Joshua and Achan receive a similar treatment in the following passage:

[56] = [57b] mSan 6:2 I–II (2)[28]   Josh. 7:19–20

When he was ten cubits away from the place of stoning they say to him: Make confession, for thus is the way of all who are condemned to death to make confession, for everyone who makes confession has a share in the world to come. For thus we find it with Achan, for Joshua said to him: '[And Joshua said to Achan:] My son, give now honour to the Lord the God of Israel and give him confession [or: thanks, *todah*] and tell me now what you have done; do not hide it from me. (20) And Achan answered Joshua and said: In truth I have sinned against the Lord the God of Israel and thus and thus I have done: . . .'. And whence that his confession brought atonement for him? For it is said: 'And Joshua said: Why have you troubled us? The Lord shall trouble you on this day'—this day you will be troubled, but you will not be troubled in the future to come.

There are two claims here which receive Scriptural support: that those condemned to death *should* be asked to make confession, and that this confession *has* an atoning effect. Both the prescriptive claim (what ought to happen) and the descriptive one (what is the case) are supported by reference to the same unique biblical situation. Postponing the treatment of the descriptive aspect, I am here concerned with the prescription derived from Joshua's exemplary utterance which precedes Achan's execution (verse 25). The interpreter identifies the biblical *todah* exclusively, and not without cost for co-textual cohesion,[29] as meaning 'confession of sins' (an instance of the Word1 resource). And, as is usual for the NORM resources, there are some narrative circumstances which are too specific or not specific enough to fit exactly into the halakhic schema in whose support the Mishnah quotes the biblical case. The Mishnah links the request for confession to a position 'ten cubits away from the place of stoning'. There is no indication of distances in verses 19–20, certainly no sign of a distance measured in cubits. By contrast, the Mishnah links distance *systematically* to

---

[28] C1(*todah*)C5C9N5×2 T3(*widuy*)W1(*todah*).

[29] In particular the parallel position of 'honour' in the verse is affected, see BDB, 392b–393a; yet, BDB include the idea of 'acknowledging and abandoning sin'. See now Grossfeld, 'The Biblical Hebrew ידה'.

stages of the proceedings: *mishnah* 6:3 specifies that the undressing of the condemned has to take place at four cubits' distance. Scripture gives no indication at this point of a movement from a place of sentencing to a place of execution (but cf. verse 24). At the narrative junction defined by the quoted verse 19, Joshua really asks for a confession as part of the reconstruction of the crime, not as part of a procedure setting in after a human court has passed sentence. Verses 19 and 20 tell how Joshua and Israel caught up with God's knowledge of the nature of the crime and the identity of the criminal; Achan's punishment is already divinely ordained (verse 15), and his uncovering is divine work. From all of these narrative circumstances the Mishnah abstracts the one element in which it is interested at this point in its halakhic discourse: that a person, Achan, was asked to confess his sins before execution. It is this one aspect which finds its (new) place in an otherwise Mishnaic structure for the judicial procedure of capital cases. The biblical event's place in the Mishnaic procedure is *fixed*: 'ten cubits' defines a distance but, more importantly, it defines a point in the Mishnaic sequence of actions.[30] The interpretation thus *distinguishes in the first place* which features of the biblical situation belong to the unique setting, and which are the expression of a norm with regard to a predetermined halakhic topic. The other narrative features may, of course, be exemplary for other topics, but they are de-selected for this one.

Norm5: Identification of the speech reported in Scripture of a biblical protagonist as conforming to a norm of verbal behaviour formulated by the Mishnah.

Using the neutral word 'protagonist', we allow for the application of the resource to both human and divine speech. Among the cases of verbal behaviour which the Mishnah considers exemplary are speech acts appropriate in certain situations, such as imperatives (see [56]), greetings (the case of Boaz in mBer 9:5 III (6) mentioned above), or terms of address (case [52]). The difference between Norm2 (protagonist's utterance) and Norm5 (verbal example) is important. The former deals with cases where the behavioural norm happens to be expressed in the speech (as imperative or judgement), but does not concern a verbal behaviour. For Norm5 cases, on the other hand, the speaking *is* the behaviour whose generalization constitutes the norm. There are even cases where the details of the textual constitution of the verbal act are taken as exemplary, in particular for the format of legally effective rabbinic speech or texts. In Num. 32:29 f. Moses sets out the terms of an agreement with the tribes settling east of Jordan. The Mishnah, in mQid 3:4 I (2), takes this as a model for the *format* of conditional agreements in general (האי, see passage [110] in Chapter 11). In the following passage the textual constitution of Scripture itself is taken as

---

[30] Cf. the resource Topic2 discussed in Ch. 4 above.

embodying a norm (presumably the divine author is the person whose verbal behaviour is taken to exemplify the norm):

[57] = [131a] mYad 4:8 I (2)[31]   Exod. 5:2

A Galilean heretic[32] said: I raise a complaint against you, O Pharisees, for you write the [name of the] ruler together with [the name of] Moses in a bill of divorce. The Pharisees say: We [raise a complaint] against you, O Galilean heretic, for you write the Name [of God] together with [the name of] the ruler on [one] page, and not only that, but you [plural] write the ruler above and the Name beneath, (as it is said),[33] 'And Pharaoh said: Who is the Lord that I shall listen to his voice to let go Israel? [I do not know the Lord and also Israel I shall not let go].' And when he was smitten, what does he say? 'The Lord is righteous [and I and my people are the wicked ones].' (Exod. 9:27)

Ignoring the last sentence,[34] we can see that the argument is derived from the fact that anybody who copies the text of the Torah is forced to write the name of Pharaoh before writing the name of God in the utterance ascribed to Pharaoh (which utterance itself is derogatory).[35] An *a fortiori* argument (see next chapter) proceeds from this observation: if the divine author had no qualms about producing such structures in Scripture, then the presence on the same page of the ruler's and Moses's names in a rabbinic legal document cannot constitute a problem. Although the hermeneutic operation here is quite complex, it starts from the existence of *one single instance* (not a norm, and not a regularity) of a textual phenomenon, and thus requires the sort of generalization from an example which is characteristic of the NORM resources. Interpretations that rely on the very *format* of Scriptural text (whether or not they are reported direct speech[36]) can be distinguished as a sub-category of Norm5:

Norm5.2: Identification of the textual format of a passage in Scripture, or of the format of a speech reported in Scripture of a protagonist, as conforming to a Mishnaic norm for the formulation of a legal document or speech act.

FROM INDIVIDUAL CASE TO CASE SCHEMA

Let us look a little closer at the structure *into which* the biblical event is integrated, and which in turn singles it out as exemplary from the flow of biblical events. This structure does not merely tell us which events are

---

[31] ΩΔ•¶A4.2M1N5.2T9.

[32] Variant reading for 'heretic' in the printed texts: 'Sadducee' (cf. Lisowsky, *Jadajim*, 79).

[33] Absent from Kaufmann and other MSS, but found in a Genizah Fragment (Taylor-Schechter, Cambridge, E1 / 151), and in the MSS Oxford (MS Heb. c 17 No. 15) and Parma (de Rossi 138) as well as the popular prints; cf. Lisowsky, *Jadajim*, 91.

[34] Classed as secondary in Epstein, *Mavo*, 975.

[35] On the question of the resource used here (Map1) and the terms 'above' and 'beneath', see my discussion in Ch. 13 below, case **[131a]**.

[36] A Mishnaic example of the latter type of Norm5.2, mQid 3:4 I (2) **[110]**, is discussed in Ch. 11.

exemplary and which are not (there are probably no events told in Scripture which cannot become exemplary for the rabbinic reader if the correct question is applied to them). It tells us what, in the flow of happenings told in the biblical text, *constitutes* a significant event-unit, namely, an exemplary action. Where does it start; where does it end? Where, in a regulated sequence of other actions, is its place? Through the narrative summary, the normative generalization, and the boundaries of the quotation, the Mishnah selects certain aspects of the biblical action, and de-selects others. If the hermeneutic move is accepted, the selected features become part of the self-contained action, the de-selected ones become part of the background or the unique situation. The unique factors, however, are precisely that which is cancelled in their importance, otherwise no generalization would be possible. That is the meaning of the objection used in **[52a]**. It claims that the situational factor 'popular suspicion that David had Abner killed' is part and parcel of David's action of following Abner's bier; one cannot consider the latter in isolation from the former. A generalization of this newly defined action is presumably also possible (if David's actions are, in principle, exemplary). For instance: a king is allowed to suspend the prohibition to follow the bier for the good of the country, and so on. But such a norm would include in the generalization the factor 'popular suspicion that David had Abner killed', instead of ignoring it. This shows that some interest or question needs to come from the rabbinic reader to the biblical text *before* an 'example' can be *found* in the unique biblical events. So Scripture provides examples, but the Mishnah determines what they are examples of. Again we encounter another form in which a perspective is imposed on Scripture, namely the schema of a commandment imposed on narrative events.

Is there a constant shape to the normative schemata thus imposed? All the Mishnaic norms which integrate biblical examples are either formulated as protasis–apodosis units or can be so recast. Let us use passage **[54a]** as an illustration:

> *If* a person is the high priest
> and *if* he performs the priestly blessing in the sanctuary (protasis)
> *then* he should not raise his hands above the forehead-plate (apodosis).

We have addressed in Chapter 4 the manner in which the protasis–apodosis unit can be used to engage the Scriptural text on a level more specific than that suggested by its wording and co-text. The protasis–apodosis unit is schematic in that it is not about a *unique and specific* case: it is hypothetical, and therefore general.[37] *Any* person condemned to death by a rabbinic court needs to be asked to make a confession—ideally, ten cubits

---

[37] On the important link between the hypothetical or conditional and the generalization, see e.g. Frawley, *Linguistic Semantics*, 358. See further Ch. 9 (text to n. 83).

away from the place of execution. It is this schema, the generalizing power of saying 'if–then', which is addressed to the biblical event.[38]

The usual word for systems of law which proceed from a large number of general case structures is 'casuistic', and Mishnaic and biblical law are examples of it.[39] This means that, although many individual situations are treated by rules, these situations are not individual cases, but define situational features under which individual cases can be subsumed. Does the use of a biblical example in connection with such a casuistic norm (as in our NORM cases) amount to treating the individual case as 'precedent' in the modern technical sense,[40] that is, more than, say, evidence of custom? In a system such as English law judges scrutinize earlier judgements in individual cases to find their decision in the case at hand. Their point of reference is the earlier case in all its unique complexity, the facts of the case,[41] the line of reasoning taken in the earlier judgement,[42] the distinction of those parts of the judgement which constitute *obiter dicta*[43] from those which contain a 'principle of law' or *ratio decidendi*.[44] The hermeneutic procedure of 'precedent' thus depends on a wealth of factual information about that earlier case, and a report on the reason for the judge's decision.[45] It seems that the word 'precedent', if taken in this highly defined sense, cannot be applied to the NORM family of resources. Resources which treat reports regarding the *conduct* of a biblical protagonists (Norm1, Norm3, Norm5) are clearly different in type. But even where an earlier 'judgement'

---

[38] Calum Carmichael has suggested that certain biblical norms were formulated specifically so as to justify or respond to the behaviour of protagonists of biblical narrative; see his *Law and Narrative* and *Biblical Laws of Talion*. This would make the hermeneutic moves here called NORM resources a factor in the production of legal biblical texts. Cf. Jackson, 'The Original Oral Law'.

[39] For the casuistic and apodictic law in biblical studies (as well as protasis and apodosis), see the excellent overview by Clark, 'Law', 105–16; cf. also Gerstenberger, 'Covenant and Commandment'; Patrick, *Old Testament Law*, 21 ff. See also the literature quoted in n. 82 in Ch. 9 below.

[40] Cf. Walker, *Oxford Companion to Law*, s.v. 'case law': 'The general term for principles and rules of law laid down in judicial *decisions*, for generalizations based on past *decisions* of courts and tribunals in particular cases . . . What is fundamental about case law is . . . that the previous *decisions* are treated as normative and looked to for principles or rules which by convention should, and in some circumstances must, be followed and applied' (p. 190, emphasis mine).

[41] 'Precisely the same set of facts as were before the court in a precedent never recur, and it is always a question whether or not the different facts which have arisen in a later case are sufficiently similar to those of the precedent to make the decision in the precedent a guide to the decision in the present case' (ibid. 978).

[42] 'The use of precedents as a source for a rule of law to be applied to the decision of a later case depends on the long-standing custom of judges of the superior courts, when deciding cases, giving judgments which review the relevant law, including any relevant previous decisions, and give their legal reasons for the decision reached; on the equally long-standing custom of reports being published of interesting and important cases, setting out the judgments in full . . .' (ibid. 977).

[43] Cf. ibid. 897.

[44] 'A precedent is binding or persuasive in a later case only in respect of the principle of law, if any, on the basis of which it was decided, and which can be extracted from it for subsequent use. This is termed the *ratio decidendi*' (ibid. 979). Note his use of the word 'extracted'.

[45] 'It is for the subsequent court to determine what the *ratio* [see preceding note, A.S.] of a precedent is. A case may yield no useful *ratio*, if decided on a point of pleading or of fact, or entirely on its own facts, or it may be so ill-reported, or the judgments may be so obscure, that the later court cannot discover on what basis the previous court decided the precedent' (ibid. 979).

or decision is taken as the starting-point, this is not subjected to the type of scrutiny which the examination of an earlier—written and voluminous—judgement involves in English law. In most biblical passages the amount of information available from Scripture is less, not more, detailed than that from the Mishnaic discourse itself: rather bare and basic points taken from the narrative flow are embedded into a richly detailed and diversified Mishnaic structure.[46] This is particularly obvious when the exemplary action stands already in a 'legal' context in Scripture, as in our case [56]. The procedural specifics of the Mishnaic discourse exceed anything that is visible in or around the wording of the biblical report on an exemplary event. Also, there is no claim made that those specifics are to be found in Scripture at this location or in some other verse. The 'ten cubits' of passage [56] are a case in point. But this tendency is visible in most other cases as well: there is no mention of a palace in the biblical account of David and Abner [52a], nor of the priestly blessing in the report on Aaron's induction [54a]. In general, the amount of detail available from narrative accounts in Scripture is famously sparse. It seems that none of the Mishnaic interpretations characterized by NORM resources can be construed as allowing the distinctions necessary for the modern hermeneutic procedure of 'precedent' summarized above. In some cases there is no quotation from Scripture at all.[47] What Scripture offers is subjected to a refraction, and the Scriptural segment delimited as a result is integrated into a different, and highly articulated structure. The segment's function and meaning is determined by its place in that structure, not by the biblical structure from which it was isolated.[48] Or, at least there is no indication of a procedure for or intention of making its function *also* dependent on the biblical structure of which it is part. Decisions about what constitutes the exemplary features of the event, what constitutes the boundaries of the event itself, and whether any of its situational factors need to be taken into account, are not, as in the modern precedent, part of the hermeneutic question; they are not treated as problematic. We can understand this, on a more abstract level, as a manifestation of the fact that the Mishnaic division of Scripture into segments does not become the object of a hermeneutic question: it is presupposed in the formulation of the question or project. It seems thus that the *technical* aspects of the modern term 'precedent' can make no direct contribution to our understanding of the use of biblical examples in the Mishnaic legal discourse. This means that terminological reference to 'precedent' can create

[46] See my discussion of Topic2 in Ch. 4.

[47] There are at least four examples of NORM cases where no Scriptural wording is quoted at all: mSan 2:4 I (4), mMen 4:3 I (2), mNed 3:11 VII (10), and mSan 4:5 III (5). There is also mBB 8:3, for which see below, [59].

[48] This does not deny that elements of the Mishnaic structure, or the whole of it, could in some way be derived from Scripture whole or piecemeal. However, there is no attempt being made in the Mishnah to show that this is the case, or to demonstrate that the fragment of Scripture is part of a Scriptural whole which is isomorphic with the Mishnaic whole of which it becomes part. The segment is not acknowledged to be a fragment.

an unwarranted impression of conceptual precision. This picture is broadly confirmed when the use of non-biblical 'precedents' in Mishnaic discourse is examined. These short narrative units, called *ma'aseh* ('work, happening' in the sense of 'real case'),[49] are also not presented within hermeneutic structures similar to the modern law of precedent outlined above.[50]

I shall now turn to interpretations which take Scripture to provide examples, not of correct behaviour, but of the nature of 'reality'.

IMPOSING A DESCRIPTIVE SCHEMA ON BIBLICAL NARRATIVE

It is characteristic of rabbinic literature that observations on nature or observable 'laws' of reality, insofar as evidence for them is adduced, are supported by reference to Scripture and not by reference to perception or experience. Insofar as support for such general truths takes the form of a biblical *instance*, they belong to the NORM family of resources and will be labelled Norm8. Among these, causal schemata which are an implicit expression of God's governance of the world, that is, *theologoumena*, assume a prominent place. I have already pointed this out in my discussion of the rabbinic *mashal*.[51] Here is a definition of the Norm8 resource, followed by a passage we already know:

Norm8: Identification of an event or speech reported in Scripture in a narrative context as illustration of a general Mishnaic statement articulating a regularity governing nature or the world.

[57a] = [3] = [130a] mShab 9:3 II (3) = mShab 19:3[52]   Gen. 34:25

Whence [do we know] that one bathes a child[53] [even] on the third day [after circumcision] that falls on the Sabbath? For it is said, 'And it came to pass on the third day when they were in pain . . .'.

It is not the information that the wound is permitted to be bathed on the Sabbath which is derived from this unique narrative instance (that would make it a Norm1). Rather, it is the fact that the circumcised person is in pain on the third day. This, together with the assumption that alleviating

---

[49] Cf. the expression *halakhah le-ma'aseh*, on which see n. 62 in Ch. 11.

[50] Cf. Goldberg, 'Form und Funktion des Ma'ase in der Mischna', 34 f., 38. See also Elon, 'Ma'aseh and Precedent'. H. Ben-Menahem writes, 'More generally, there is no strict system of precedent in Jewish law: if a *posek* decides to publish his decision in an actual case, the authority of his published judgment will derive from the authority it enjoys, or acquires, as a "responsum", rather than from the judicial determination', 'Postscript: The Judicial Process and the Nature of Jewish Law', 430. Cf. also Urbach's linkage between the *ma'aseh* and the act of testimony, *The Halakhah*, 77 ff., and Segal's account of the distinction between 'halakhah' and 'ma'aseh' ('Jewish Law during the Tannaitic Period', 106 ff.). On the *ma'aseh* as a literary form which provides redundancy in the Mishnaic discourse, see my 'Delaying the Progress from Case to Case'.

[51] See my discussion of resource Use5 in Ch. 5 (cf. n. 71 there).

[52] C5N8S5.2T2T3.1.

[53] The popular prints have here 'the circumcision', i.e. the wound of circumcision.

such pain is allowed on the Sabbath,[54] and that bathing amounts to such alleviating, provides the warrant for the Dictum. As in other cases of exemplary biblical happenings, the Dictum is introduced by 'Whence that ...?' (... מנין ש). Although this midrashic unit stands in an extended sequence of 'Whence . . .?' questions, its topic is not pursued further in the Mishnaic co-text at mShab 9:3.[55] Circumcision provides its own, thematic, series of midrashic units at mNed 3:11, on which more presently. First, another example for Norm8, a passage which is quoted as part of [56] above. Note that the earlier introductory formula, 'for thus we find', is here followed up by 'and whence?'

[57b] = [56] mSan 6:2 II (2)[56]   Josh. 7:25

And whence that his confession brought atonement for him? For it is said: 'And Joshua said: Why have you troubled us? The Lord shall trouble you on this day'— this day you will be troubled, but you will not be troubled in the future to come.[57]

Achan's case illustrates a general truth here: that the confession of the person condemned to death provides atonement for him (in conjunction with his execution). '*Everyone* who makes confession has a share in the world to come' is the Dictum to which this relates, in [56] above. Achan's share in the world to come is taken to be proclaimed by Joshua by the somewhat conspicuous words 'this day' (an Opposition1 combined with Topic3). The dependence of that announcement on Achan's confession, which ended in verse 22, is perhaps taken to be implied in the fact that Joshua's words are, if not a direct response to Achan, then at least the next utterance reported after that verse (Cotext9).

The regularities of reality captured by such rabbinic maxims are largely based on notions of God's retribution or mercy in the world, and are thus value concepts. This is most obvious in passages where the Mishnaic voice assumes the mood of praising or lamenting, for which one signal is the exclamation—for instance, 'Great is the circumcision!' in mNed 3:11 VII (10). There is also a small group of midrashic units which establish from biblical examples the regularities of seasonal changes. These are of some importance for the timing of prayer, *shofar*-blowing, and fasting; they are found scattered throughout the tractate Taanit.

Here is a passage whose general observation belongs to a very interesting class of maxims, in that it compares groups of norms, that is, is meta-halakhic:

[54] Cf. mShab 19:2: 'They may perform on the Sabbath all things that are necessary for circumcision.' The indirectness of the link between Lemma and Dictum seems thematized at bShab 134b with the formula '. . . an allusion to the matter' (see n. 76 of Ch. 8, and list VI.1 in Ch. 12, final section); cf. Epstein, *Mavo*, 650.

[55] But it is embedded into the theme of mShab 19:3, its second occurrence (where it is ascribed to R. Eleazar ben Azariah and where there is no 'whence . . . ?' question).

[56] ®C1C9N8O1T0T3×2.

[57] This expression (לעתיד לבא) is found in MSS Kaufmann, Cambridge, the *editio princeps*, and the Venice print of the Yerushalmi (Venice 1523/4); other texts have לעולם הבא (Krauß, *Sanhedrin-Makkot*, 392). On the terminology, see Schäfer, *Studien zur Geschichte und Theologie*, 246–56.

[58] mArak 3:5 II (2)[58] Num. 14:22

'Regarding the one who "brings an evil name" [the law] may deal leniently or stringently' [cf. *mishnah* 3:1]—how so? [Regardless whether] one brought an evil name against a great woman from among the priesthood or against an insignificant one (from among Israel)—he gives a hundred *Selas*. One finds that the one who speaks with his mouth [is treated] more severely than the one who does a deed. For thus we find that the decree of judgement was only sealed against our fathers in the wilderness because of slander, as it is said, '[None of the men who have seen my glory and my signs which I wrought in Egypt and in the wilderness] and have tempted me these ten times, and have not hearkened to my voice [shall see the land . . .]'.[59]

The principle 'the one who speaks with his mouth [suffers] more than the one who does a deed' is linked to a comparison of the two case schemata here and in *mishnah* 3:4: the man who slanders a woman pays a hundred *Selas*, while the man who violates a woman pays fifty (also regardless of the social status of the woman). In other words, the principle is presented as a (meta-halakhic) generalization from two Mishnaic case schemata, and it is presented with the evidential expression 'it is found' (נמצא).[60] Only afterwards is the general observation linked to an instance from the biblical narrative, again introduced by 'find', this time in the familiar formula of שכן מצינו ש . . . שנאמר. God condemns the generation of the wilderness for their slander, while alluding to 'ten' earlier provocations. In order to follow the line of argument of the midrashic unit, we have to assume that those unspecified earlier transgressions were by deed, not by utterance, thus illustrating harsher punishment for the latter than for the former.

In case **[49]** above we find the rabbinic principle 'measure for measure' in a hermeneutic application to the manner of Absalom's death. In that Mishnaic passage the narrative is freshly constituted on the basis of the rabbinic maxim: the link between Absalom's taking pride in his hair and that hair being entangled is established by the Mishnah (not as such in the biblical narrative). And it is established *as* a special case of a more general norm. These features belong to the resource Use6. But the elements involved are also similar to the Norm8 resource. It is the direction of the hermeneutic movement which is distinct. Where the maxim is presupposed and the narrative is being explained, we have a Use6; where what happens is taken for granted (and stands for nothing but itself, so to speak), and its regularity is being explained, we have a Norm8. In both hermeneutic operations a general rabbinic formulation is brought into contact with a unique instance of Scriptural origin, and it is not always easy to decide for

---

[58] πC5(slander of the land)N8O8(ten times)T3.1.

[59] Cf. on the substance, mAvot 5:4 II (2); for the significance of 'ten', cf. mAvot 5:2. See also Towner, *The Rabbinic 'Enumeration of Scriptural Examples'*.

[60] On the various types of 'to find' used in hermeneutic contexts in rabbinic literature, see Bacher, i. 113–15. In mZeb 7:6 II (2) the expression מה מצינו בשחיטה is used to identify a feature to be transferred in a normative analogy (a case of Analogy0; see Ch. 8 below).

a given unit of interpretation which of the two hermeneutic movements is being performed, or whether they are perhaps even performed both at the same time. There is always the interpretative option to reverse the perspective, that is, to turn the narrative structure which has been uncovered with the help of a rabbinic maxim into an *example* for that maxim. This ambiguity is pronounced for some cases,[61] and almost absent from others (which are clearly either Norm8 or Use6). In order not to separate out too early the evidence into mutually exclusive groups, I am including the Norm8 code in the hermeneutic profiles for all Mishnaic Use6 cases. I shall attempt to define a criterion of distinction below.

When reviewing the descriptive generalities which the Mishnah presents as being exemplified by biblical events, one is reminded of the considerable thematic spread of the wisdom sayings of tractate Avot. They are all in some way connected to values of rabbinic Judaism, and therefore indirectly, of course, to norms of behaviour as well. It is thus not wholly surprising that in all our sample passages the Norm8 observation happens to stand in the service of clarifying a norm of *behaviour*.[62] It may be useful to think of these generalities as 'rabbinic wisdom' in analogy to biblical wisdom. One difference between the approximately fifteen Mishnaic Norm8 cases on the one hand and the material in tractate Avot on the other is the absence in the former of sayings concerned specifically with the conduct of judges. Table 6.1 offers a summary of the relevant Norm8 passages, including all Use6 cases (in italics).

Clusters of passages appear in Sotah and Avot, mainly but not exclusively because of our automatic inclusion of the Use6 cases. Let us look at the themes. The repeated occurrence of the topic 'warfare' in mSot 8 is accounted for by the fact that all of these passages are part of a verse-by-verse interpretation of the speech of the 'anointed for battle' in Deut. 20:2 ff. (Σ).[63] The maxim concerning the soreness of circumcision appears to be used like a 'scientific' fact, while the observations on the timing or location of rainfall are really about patterns of divine punishment[64] and the appropriate human acts of entreaty. Circumcision as a value is proclaimed in mNed 3:11, while the 'measure by measure' principle, when used to evaluate narrative facts, and insofar as it constitutes a Norm8 structure at all, is about reward and punishment.[65] The reward of Torah in old age (as well as for youth) is stressed in mQid 4:14, and the awfulness of murder in San 4:5. The other topics are similar; they fall broadly within the ('aggadic')

---

[61] Thus, mSot 8:1 VI (8) seems to oscillate between Use6 and Norm8: a maxim contrasting human strength in war with that of God is used to bring out narrative structures in 1 Sam. 17:46 and 2 Sam. 10:16–18, while these episodes also serve as examples for the maxim. Cf. also mAvot 6:6.

[62] Cf. my remarks on the relationship of 'aggadah' and halakhah in Ch. 1 above (at n. 87).

[63] More on the *sigma* format Σ in Ch. 12.

[64] Cf. for this mAvot 5:7 ff.

[65] For the case of mArak 3:5 II (2), cf. mAvot 2:1. See the next chapter for degrees of normative severity in Mishnaic comparison.

TABLE 6.1 *Summary of Norm8 passages*

mShab 9:3 II (3) = mShab 19:3	The wound of circumcision hurts on the third day
mTaan 1:7	Rainfall after the end of Nisan is a curse (not a blessing to be prayed for)
mTaan 3:3	It can happen that one city alone receives no rain
mNed 3:11 VII (10)	The importance of circumcision brooks no delay (Great is the circumcision)
mSot 1:7	*Symbolic correspondence of sin and punishment (the Sotah's punishment) Use6*
mSot 1:8 I–IV (4)	*Symbolic correspondence of sin and punishment Use6*
mSot 8:1 IV (8)	Israelite warriors treat their brethren with mercy even in war
mSot 8:1 VII (8)	*The strength of the human allies of Israel's foes fails, the strength of God as Israel's ally does not Use6*
mSot 8:6 II (2)	With a beginning in flight comes defeat (in the case of Israel)
mQid 4:14 III (4)	Keeping Torah protects/gives hope to a person in old age
mSan 4:5 I (5)	The guilt of killing a person includes the destruction of his/her prospective progeny
mSan 4:5 III–VII (9)	A person's life is worth a full world; no one's father is greater than another; only one power is in heaven; God's power is manifest in differentiating one man from another (also Use5); the whole world is created for every man's sake
mSan 6:2 II (2)	A person condemned to death atones for his sins (through his death) if he confesses to them
mAvot 5:1–6	*Things happen in bundles of 10 Use6?*
mAvot 5:17	*Controversies for God's sake are of lasting worth Use6*
mAvot 5:18 I (2)	The person through whom many are virtuous is protected from sin
mAvot 5:18 II (2)	There is such a thing as the sin of the many depending on one man, *or*: the person through whom many sin is cut off from repentance
[mAvot 6:3 I (3)]	*He who learns a halakhah from someone must honour him Use8 and Use5*
[mAvot 6:6]	*Teaching in the name of one's teacher brings salvation into the world Use6*
mArak 3:5 II (2)	The punishment for a verbal sin is/can be more severe than that for a deed
[mNeg 12:6 III (3)	Woe to the wicked, woe to his neighbour (אוי לשכנו . . .)!]

area of the rabbinic concern with the ethical, the meta-halakhic, and divine justice.[66]

We have seen that where a biblical event is taken to provide an instance of a norm of behaviour, that event acquires a 'timeless' quality. The same happens to the narrative, temporal quality of biblical happenings in the Norm8 resource. Although their narrative connectedness is investigated up to a point (for example, in order to uncover causal links), their uniqueness in time and place is played down: they are taken to follow a *pattern*, and to manifest a truth unaffected by unique circumstances. This may help solve our earlier difficulty in understanding how Norm8 and Use6 interpretations differ from each other. The Use6 treatment of biblical events also brings to bear a general, timeless truth. But, in contrast to Norm8, it does so in order to identify the significance of the one thing that happened; the timeless pattern (for instance, 'measure for measure') is used to uncover mechanisms of narrative meaning which are not found on the surface of the biblical text.

THE SCRIPTURAL QUOTATION

To return now to a question asked earlier: why, given the Mishnah's own report on the biblical event, is there also a quoted Scriptural report? We here encounter the drill of the midrashic format, the regular quoting and reformulating of Scripture, that is, the explicit separation of biblical message from biblical wording. In other words, the hermeneutic movement NORM is presented in the format of the midrashic unit (discussed in detail in Chapter 12). There are some exceptions to this.[67] There are references to biblical examples which are simply presupposed as known; the biblical story to which they belong is neither introduced as such, nor is the wording quoted. The contrast between such unstressed use of biblical material and the passages which quote Scripture is quite marked. Here is an example of Scripture being used tacitly, which occurs in a co-text concerned with the halakhah of inheritance:

[59] mBB 8:3[68]   Num. 27:1 ff., in particular 27:7

The daughters of Zelophehad took three portions in inheritance: the portion of their father who was with those that went out from Egypt; and his portion among his brothers in the possessions of Hepher, and since he was a first-born he took two portions.

Fairly detailed knowledge of the events is presupposed here, without

---

[66] The final passage in the Table, mNeg 12:6 III (3), arises from a biblical case schema, not an individual biblical occurrence. Cf. mAvot 1:7 (הרחק משכן רע), and mAvot 2:9 (Yose, שכן טוב). For the exclamation and its format cf. mEduy 4:9.

[67] See above, n. 47.

[68] C5T0T5U6.

Scripture being quoted. It may be of importance that in this case the biblical event itself is heavily marked as constituting a legal decision and inaugurating law (cf. verses 5 ff.), and *generalized* law at that. Yet the point made in the above *mishnah* is not contained in these generalizations, but is part of the individual occurrence. So the hermeneutic movement which is our concern here, namely, linking a biblical instance to a Mishnaic norm, is still present. This shows that there is nothing automatic about the quotation of the biblical event report. Furthermore, where it is quoted the resulting conspicuous repetition of wording is not eliminated (for example, by ellipsis; see for instance [52a]).[69] So why is there the Scriptural quotation at all? Was there a need to distinguish biblical events in other versions from biblical events as reported in Scripture itself? Although retellings of biblical stories abound in pre-rabbinic Judaism and could well have been known to the rabbis, it is unlikely that participants in the technical discourse of the Mishnah would be prone to mix those up with the biblical text's own version. Was there a need to prove that a certain event indeed took place? Presumably (but see below), what makes an action or utterance exemplary for the rabbis is that it happened, and that it happened in the biblical past. So it is conceivable that Scripture is quoted to confirm that certain events happened. But who doubted that among the participants of the Mishnaic discourse? And who, if they doubted the facticity of these biblical events, would not also doubt the veracity of the biblical account? More promising is the following answer: Scripture was thought to make a difference to the representative character of these events. The quotation showed not so much that things of a certain nature had taken place, but that Scripture wanted to *make known* that they had taken place. The fact that the divine author had *included* an account of them in Scripture might have been seen as creating their exemplary status. Not certainty of knowledge, but of the informativeness of a communication would be the moving hermeneutic factor. The inclusion of events in the text would be seen as vouchsafing their *relevance* for the future. A passage in mSan 4:5 offers a striking illustration. It claims that man (Adam) was created alone in the world in order to *teach* (ללמד) that each life is worth a 'full world'. Here the 'why' of the event is *equated* with its 'teaching', but without its *report* in Scripture there could be no teaching.

So, if the mere inclusion of an event in Scripture can imply its relevance,[70] rabbinic hermeneutic competence in each new context would consist in selecting the matching concern, in finding the issue(s) to which the events are meant to be relevant. The exemplary character of biblical happenings

---

[69] The presentational redundancy of NORM resources is merely a special manifestation of the redundancy of any proof-text structure; cf. my, 'Delaying the Progress from Case to Case'.

[70] It is interesting to note that such a notion may have a parallel in the biblical narrative itself. With regard to the precedent status of the case of the daughters of Zelophehad (cf. Num. 27:7), B. Jackson writes: 'The authority of the casuistic paragraph derives not from the decision *per se* but rather from God's command to Moses to proclaim it', 'Law, Wisdom and Narrative', sec. 3.

would be merely one manner in which to read Scripture as relevant. The specific format of the question of relevance is: what is the correct behaviour in situation X? Conversely, once an event has been identified as exemplary, the fact that it is reported in Scripture could be seen as sanctioning its exemplary character. This (its appearance in Scripture) is presumably only one such criterion. Others include the qualities of the biblical protagonist or the *role* in which he or she can be placed or is placed by the narrative. Thus, David is 'king' (not poet, lover, prophet, sinner, and so on) in **[52a]**. Biblical villains can thus become examples also, for instance with regard to retribution, or with regard to psychological regularities.[71]

What does it mean to say that Scripture, in reporting the event, caters for its future relevance to the rabbinic reader? Rabbinic hermeneutics probably implicitly held that there is not only one way to report an event; and that even where one event is reported, another might not be. In some cases there may even be in the background of the NORM resource an implicit comparison of the biblical narrative containing that specific event report which yields the example, with the same overall narrative without it.[72] The amount of detail provided by Scriptural narrative is generally small— rabbinic interpretation makes use of this sparseness in a number of ways. The rabbinic picture of biblical events is richer in detail: this implicitly acknowledges that some of the things which 'happened' alongside the reported biblical events must have gone unreported, and are not represented in the text or are presupposed there. In other words, for the rabbis events represented in Scripture are there by way of *selection*. This could be reformulated in the following way: by presenting some actions of biblical protagonists, but not others, and by presenting them in a particular way, and by including or not including certain details, the divine author has *perspectivized* the events. And selecting from the Scriptural text and perspectivizing it is precisely what we see the Mishnah do with Scripture. In taking these two together, I propose the following heuristic formulation of a fundamental assumption of rabbinic hermeneutics:

with regard to biblical exempla, the text of Torah achieves total relevance by a correspondence between the perspectives in which the biblical events are selected and, to some extent, recounted in Scripture on the one hand, and the perspectives or concerns of the rabbinic discourse, that is, the discourse of Torah, on the other.

My thesis is the following: the biblical quotation in NORM cases does not

---

[71] BerR 55:8 ad Gen. 22:3, to quote just one example, takes the behaviour of Balaam and Pharaoh as examples of the truth that proper conduct (שורה) is liable to be set aside by hatred (ed. Theodor-Albeck, ii. 593 ff.).

[72] In such a case, the narrative as a whole is treated as a syntagma, and is contrasted with a shorter syntagma (from which the account of the event is missing) to probe the specific contribution made by the event. Cf. resource Opposition8 (Ch. 11), which allocates separate relevance to apparently superfluous elements. However, I cannot find among the Mishnaic NORM cases an overt expression for the view that a biblical event is in some sense superfluous to the narrative in which it occurs, unless treated as yielding an exemplum.

confirm the facticity of a biblical event, but the intention of the divine author for the rabbinic reader to *know* about it, therefore in principle its relevance qua example. We find a text in the Mishnah (at least, in the tractate Avot) which has some bearing on this question. It is not concerned with biblical exempla; but it makes a hermeneutic distinction between God's actions on the one hand and their being *told* in Scripture on the other.[73]

[60] mAvot 3:15 I–III (3)[74]   Gen. 9:6; Deut. 14:1; Prov. 4:2

He [Aqiva] used to say: Beloved is man that he was created in the image [of God]; greater abundance of love is that it was made known to him that he was created in the image, as it is said, '. . . for in the image of God he made the man'.

Beloved is Israel because they are called children of God; greater abundance of love is that it was made known to them that they were called children of God, as it is said, 'You are children to the Lord your God'.

Beloved is Israel because given to them was the instrument with which the world was created;[75] greater abundance of love is that it was made known to them that to them was given the instrument with which the world was created, for it is said, 'For a good teaching have I given you; my Torah do not forsake'.

The rabbinic voice asserts three facts: that man was created in God's image; that Israel is called God's children; that Israel was given the '(precious) instrument' = Torah. The quotations, however, are explicitly introduced not as confirmation of these facts (they are that too, of course), but as confirmation that the facts are *mentioned* in Scripture.[76] The result is a highly repetitive text: each of the three units contains the asserted fact three times: as Mishnaic report ('Beloved . . . that'); as dependent clause of the phrase 'made known'; and in the quotation. This is reminiscent of the redundancy of such passages as **[52a]**:

norm + 'for thus we have found it with . . . who . . .' + quotation.

In **[60]**, the act of making known is contained in Scriptural reports on God or a voice assuming his perspective speaking directly.[77] The Mishnaic unit

---

[73] Note the difference between two recensions of the text of mSan 10:1: denial of resurrection is specified as the transgression in some texts, while others speak of denial that (knowledge of) resurrection is '*from the Torah*'. Note also mAvot 5:1, 'By ten utterances was the world *created*. And what does Scripture *teach* thereby?' Here the meaning of an event is directly equated with the meaning of Scripture's report of it. The question is expressed as: ?ומה תלמוד לומר.

[74] •T1(known)T7(U6).

[75] Other Mishnaic texts, including the version of Avot in *Mahzor Virtry* and MS Munich have here 'a precious instrument' (כלי חמדה), cf. Marti and Beer, *Abot*, 82. This is a biblical expression from the semantic field of treasures; see Hos. 13:15, Nah. 2:10 (E 9), Jer. 25:34, 2 Chron. 32:27, 36:10 (precious vessels of the Temple), Dan. 11:8. See also Taylor, *An Appendix to Sayings of the Jewish Fathers*, 152.

[76] In MS Kaufmann the three Scriptural quotations together with their introductions, are absent from the main body of the text, and added in the margins; see Marti and Beer, *Abot*, 191.

[77] Such an assumption is necessary to read the emphatic sense of 'my *Torah*' (as opposed to 'my teaching') in Prov. 4:2. This construction of Prov. 4:2 also shows that God's 'making known' is not only to be sought in narrative divine speech, but includes God as speaker or author of Scripture. For Prov. 4:2 is not spoken as part of the encounters of God and Israel in history (as are the other two

celebrates the three facts, but it also celebrates the fact of their being revealed. The passage thus makes just the sort of distinction we have found relevant in our reflection on the use of biblical examples in the Mishnah. Here the distinction is merely a preliminary step in an argument that understands revelation as an act of love, and an abundance or additional love (חבה יתרה), separate and further to the acts of love it reports. This is a somewhat paradoxical but typically rabbinic shift of emphasis. It allows us to take one step further the idea of the Scriptural quotation adding *relevance* to the event it reports. Compared to whether or not an event is mentioned in Scripture, the question whether it *took place* pales into insignificance. What makes these items of information relevant is their occurrence in Scripture. If a wholly incongruous supplementary revelation were to proclaim that some of the biblical events did not take place, but are *only* contained in Scripture to make a relevant point—would that change much for the rabbis? The question does not seem to fit into a serious historical agenda; yet it puts a spotlight on the centrality of the hermeneutic project for the rabbis. It may be heuristically appropriate to say that, for them, the intentions of God and the relevance of his communication for a life of Torah make Scripture what it is, not historical accuracy.[78] There is cumulative evidence in different areas of rabbinic literature pointing in this direction. For the topic at hand, in any case, it seems clear that the Mishnaic discourse attaches importance to the fact that God *wished* Israel *to know* about the biblical events taken as exemplary.

quotations); it is spoken as part of Scripture first and foremost (even requiring Cotext1, in order to be identifiable specifically as God's speech).

[78] This dichotomy is not rabbinic. Its terms are situated in *our* academic discourse (intention and relevance of the text on the one side, historical accuracy or the facts on the other). Yet the rabbis do, in the course of their very different discourse on history and textual meaning, touch upon the topic. Thus the idea can be expressed that the events related in the book of Job *never happened*, and that Job was a *mashal* (bBB 15a). In such a context at least, 'example' (משל) becomes a word for what in modern terminology is narrative *fiction*.

7

Analogical Resources I:
The a fortiori Inference

The Mishnaic *a fortiori* inference, or *qal wa-homer*, consists of an analogical transfer between subjects which need not be represented by or linked to biblical wording. Its function in the Mishnaic discourse is often explorative rather than apodictic. The mechanism of the inference involves an assignment of (mostly halakhic) categories to the two subjects; a ranking of these categories in a dimension of comparison; and the transfer of what is known about one of them to the other based on its higher rank in the comparison of categories. It is this differential of ranks which leads to the claim that for the second subject the validity, certainty, or reasonableness of the inferred proposition is even *greater* than for the subject from which it is inferred.

Devices which are based on the comparison between specific entities, be they objects or norms or events, are of some importance in the Mishnaic discourse. Insofar as hermeneutic work is done with them we shall refer to them as analogical resources. They need to be distinguished from generalizations, of which the classification of biblical events as exemplary is one type.[1] Other resources of generalization are discussed in Chapter 9. Analogical resources, in their Mishnaic employment, are largely concerned with exploring norms. The first analogical resource to be examined is the *a fortiori* inference. The *a fortiori* is presented with and without involvement of Scriptural wording. The two types are closely related,[2] but the *a fortiori*

---

[1] The use of Scriptural (or non-Scriptural) examples (NORM) is *not* analogical in the following sense. The unique event is linked to a generalized hypothetical case of which it is understood to be an instance. This is different from comparing two individual cases with each other (even if such comparison might involve a preliminary generalization, see below). Aristotle, in his *Rhetoric*, treats the example ('paradigma'), which he classifies as an induction, in close proximity to other analogical devices, including the *a fortiori* argument (B20, 1393a–b); cf. Lloyd, *Polarity and Analogy*, 407–13, and see n. 41 below. But Aristotle's examples of 'example' make it quite clear that orientation for a specific situation is sought, and no generalized situation is formulated from the 'example', as it is in the NORM resources. We shall return to the terminology of analogy in Ch. 8.

[2] The same is not true for the other types of analogical inference to be discussed in Ch. 8.

without Scripture is more frequent. Where biblical wording is involved, the space provided for it is additional, that is, optional. The overall form of the *a fortiori* is not: 'Scripture *says* x, *a fortiori* does it *say* y', but rather: 'x is the case (as Scripture says . . .), *a fortiori* is y the case.'

The borderline status of the *a fortiori* with regard to the involvement of biblical wording is typical for analogical resources (see next chapter), and requires a clarification in the context of Mishnaic hermeneutics. This is all the more important as, under its name *qal wa-homer*, this resource belongs to the core of hermeneutic techniques in rabbinic tradition, if the lists of hermeneutic *middot* are anything to go by. By including the *a fortiori* in our discussion of hermeneutic resources it is also recognized that it would be difficult to draw a clear and universal distinction between hermeneutic reasoning on the one hand, and other kinds of informal, culturally embedded reasoning on the other; furthermore an absolute separation would be historically inappropriate in the case of the rabbis, whose aim is pragmatic as well as theoretical.

Since the *a fortiori* argument, as well as other analogies, can be thought of as having, logically speaking, premisses and conclusions, Scripture can be involved as support of one or more of the premisses (qua Dicta). However, where this happens there is a distinct hermeneutic movement in addition to the *a fortiori*. The provision of a Scriptural support for one of the premisses is in principle no different from the relationship between any rabbinic Dictum and its supporting Scriptural Lemma. It is not the *a fortiori* as a whole which accounts for their hermeneutic relationship, but separate resources. There is an incidental hermeneutic effect, though. Since the Dictum is a premiss, the whole of the logical structure of the *a fortiori* contributes to the imposition of a perspective on the Scriptural wording which is being drawn upon. The second manner in which Scripture can play a role is by providing counterparts for the two main subjects of the *a fortiori* (see below). In that case, the relationship between two Scriptural subjects is determined. The *a fortiori* inference is based on a comparison or statement of similarity. When both subjects are from Scripture, a hermeneutic relationship between them is thus established by the inference.[3]

For the most part, the various resources of *a fortiori* discussed in the following treat whole norms, functional parts of norms (for example, protasis, apodosis), or propositions. Thus they deal with the *contents* of biblical clauses or sentences (insofar as biblical links are established at all).[4] They are therefore parallel to the primary focus of the NORM resources; they

---

[3] By contrast, for other types of analogy it is usually a textual structure which determines which objects are similar (not necessarily what the similarity consists of). This makes analogies which use Scriptural starting-points quite different from those which do not; while the *a fortiori* argument is structurally the same whether or not it makes use of Scriptural wording.

[4] Hirschfeld, for example, treats the *qal wa-homer* under the general heading 'Die Behandlung des objektiven Inhalts' (*Halachische Exegese*, p. xii, *re* p. 168).

too focus on the substantive contents rather than the linguistic form of the biblical words, namely, the events they report.

THE *A FORTIORI* ARGUMENT IN MISHNAIC DISCOURSE

The *a fortiori* argument treats norms as units which, through their relationship to other norms, allow further norms to be inferred.[5] However, in anticipation of some of my results, it can be said that the Mishnah uses the *a fortiori* more for probing the consistency of a normative position, or for exploring its consequences, than for categorically determining it.

I shall refer to the *a fortiori* by the resource names Analogy4 and Analogy5, also speaking occasionally of the 'Mishnaic *a fortiori* argument'. I use these artificial names despite the fact that there appears to be a rabbinic name for the resource: *qal wa-homer*. The reason for this is that the hermeneutic argument known in rabbinic literature and in modern scholarship as *qal wa-homer*, while potentially accounted for by our Analogy4/5 definitions, is not clearly defined. The terminology from which this name derives, the metaphors 'light' (קל) and 'heavy' (חומר),[6] appear in some Mishnaic Analogy4 passages. But, as usual, there is no one-to-one relationship between resource and rabbinic terminology. We find passages not using these terms which conform to the same structure as those which do, and the most widespread terminology employs דין, 'judgement' or 'inference'.[7] More importantly, although the Mishnah does not seem to use the terms *qal* and *homer* in conjunction with any hermeneutic resource other than Analogy4, the possibility of that happening somewhere in rabbinic literature cannot be ruled out. It is therefore important, for the time being at least, to use a name which connotes exclusively the resource as defined by the Mishnaic examples and is independent of the rabbinic terminology.

The *qal wa-homer* and its logical structure has attracted more scholarly attention than many other topics in rabbinic hermeneutics.[8] Its position at

---

[5]   Kneale and Kneale, *Development of Logic*, 42; cf. 111. I use the expression *a fortiori* in a wide sense, such as the one defined by Burchfield: 'introducing a fact that, if another fact already accepted is true, must also and still more obviously be true, i.e. with yet stronger reason, more conclusively' (*New Fowler's Modern English Usage*, 32). He also gives an example: 'It could not have been finished in a week; *a fortiori* not in a day.'

[6]   I am following 'careless popular usage' in speaking of *qal* rather than *qol* (Wiesenberg, 'Observations on Method in Talmudic Studies', 18). Cf. Bacher, i. 172–4; ii. 189.

[7]   Bacher, i. 21 ff.; cf. Jastrow, 301b; but, as Bacher points out, this word is also used for other types of inference, a Mishnaic example being mBQ 2:5. For the traditional terminology naming parts to the argument, see Lauterbach, 'Talmud Hermeneutics' and Mielziner, *Introduction to the Talmud*, 132.

[8]   Jacobs, *Studies in Talmudic Logic and Methodology*, 3–8; see also his 'Hermeneutics', col. 367; Mielziner, *Introduction to the Talmud*, 130–41. Cf. further Elon, 'Interpretation', col. 1421; Lauterbach, 'Talmud Hermeneutics', 32; Bialoblocki, 'Hermeneutik', cols. 1185–7; Schwarz, 'Hauptergebnisse der wissenschaftlich-hermeneutischen Forschung', 7–10. Schwarz's work is adversely affected by his assumption of schematic stages in the historical development of rabbinic hermeneutics, and by the confusion of synchronic and diachronic lines of enquiry.

the top of the two earlier rabbinic lists of hermeneutic rules or *middot* may partly account for that.[9] This prominence in the lists is a manifestation of the apparent general importance accorded it by the rabbis themselves. We have probably more explicit information on the rabbinic understanding of this argument (and its limits as the rabbis saw them) than for other hermeneutic rules. However, another reason for the amount of scholarly attention this argument has received is its apparent amenability to a 'logical' explanation (rather than a hermeneutic one). A 'logical' argument such as the *qal wa-homer* seems to hold out the best hope for showing that rabbinic hermeneutics was, despite its generally messy appearance, strictly logical (tacitly identified with 'rational').[10] While the Mishnaic *qal wa-homer* material is partly very germane to these questions, it cannot be assumed to be representative enough to settle them. Settling these issues depends, in any case, just as much on conceptual clarification as on empirical investigation.

It will be useful to arrange the discussion of the Mishnaic *a fortiori* argument under the following three points: 1. the core of the argument is a graded comparison; 2. Scripture is no necessary part of the argument; 3. the halakhic *a fortiori* is used heuristically, not apodictically.

---

[9] It occupies the first position in the *middot* ascribed to Hillel and Ishmael. It forms numbers 5–6 in *Mishnat R. Eliezer* (ed. Enelow, 17–18). See Stemberger, *Introduction*, 18; Alexander, 'The Rabbinic Hermeneutical Rules'. Hirschfeld, *Halachische Exegese*, 217 ('Der Schluss des Gegensatzes'), was perhaps the first explorer of the *qal wa-homer* to attempt a symbolic representation of its logic. The formula he devised, for one main version of the argument, is: 'A–α = A + x :: B + α = B + x' (p. 227; the original has a roman 'a', I assume by mistake, in place of the second *alpha*). But the reduction of complex conceptual relationships within the *qal wa-homer* to the meaning of the arithmetic signs of minus and plus offers no adequate analysis of the argument's structure. Modern symbolic logic is certainly in a better position to capture the dynamics of the *a fortiori* argument, and Koch and Rüßmann, *Juristische Begründungslehre*, 259 f. and Klug, *Juristische Logik*, 132–7, attempt to provide formulas. In an informal conversation with me in July 1984 the Oxford logician Jonathan Cohen once worked out the following representation of the *a fortiori*, according to my notes:

$$(n) \; [(x)(y) \; (F(x,y) = n \to G(x,y) = ^m) \to (a)(b) \; (F(a,b) > n \to G(a,b) > ^m)].$$

Jacobs offers the following formalization: 'If A has x, then B certainly has x', and 'If A, which lacks y, has x then B, which has y, certainly has x'. These formulas correspond to what Jacobs distinguishes as the simple and the complex type of the inference (*Studies*, 4; 'Hermeneutics'). The first of these reproduces the grammar of the 'simple' *a fortiori* argument, but not its logical form, since for the logical form some comparison between A and B is always necessary. And the comparison at the centre of the argument is in any case not accurately represented by the idea of 'lacking' or 'having' y, but rather by 'having y in varying degrees'. See further Hallaq, *Law and Legal Theory in Classical and Medieval Islam*, 289–96, 300–2.

[10] It is precisely the 'rationality' of the *qal wa-homer* which, for A. Schwarz, constitutes proof that the Jews share the same logic with the rest of mankind ('Hauptergebnisse', 8). Schwarz's work is grounded in an apology for rabbinic hermeneutics as 'logical' (e.g. 'Hauptergebnisse', 31). Cf. Elman, 'Towards a History of *Ribbuy* in the Babylonian Talmud', 87.

THE CORE OF THE ARGUMENT IS A
GRADED COMPARISON

In most of its Mishnaic occurrences the argument has a general structure consisting of three or four statements whose validity is presupposed, and one statement whose validity is concluded from them. According to the type of item which appears in the structure, I shall distinguish two kinds: those that deal with whole norms (Analogy4.2), and those that deal with units within norms, such as protases and apodoses (Analogy4.1). Here is the definition of type Analogy4.2:

Analogy4.2: Inference by analogy that norm m possesses predicate A, in the following manner: if norm n which belongs to the category N, which category is lower on scale X, has predicate A; then norm m which belongs to the category M, which category is higher on scale X, logically also has predicate A (or: logically must have more of the quality A).

One, several, or none of the norms and terms presupposed in the Analogy4.2 argument may be found to be tied to Scripture; this does not affect the argument's form, but its hermeneutic function.

It may be useful to present the inference in a layout which distinguishes the various levels of dependency and pairing, representing the main clause in bold type:[11]

> **If norm n**
> which belongs to the category N
> which category is lower on scale X
> **has predicate A, then norm m**
> which belongs to the category M
> which category is higher on scale X
> **logically also has predicate A.**

At the centre of the whole operation there is a graded or scalar comparison of the two categories N and M to which the two norms are being allocated: 'which category is lower/higher on scale X.' The norms are compared in the dimension of X, and it is the *difference* within that dimension which is the mainspring of the argument. It is this element which suggests that the conclusion (that m has predicate A) can be intensified or catapulted beyond the starting-point (that n has predicate A). This provides for the alternative conclusion 'logically must have *more* of the quality A'—where the subject-matter of the inference allows such intensification. The mutual comparison is represented in our definition by the concept of grade and

---

[11] But the structure cannot be *reduced* to the parts presented in bold print, for that would leave the mechanism of the argument wholly unexplained. See my criticism in n. 9 above of the formula given by L. Jacobs.

scale; depending on the dimension X used in any concrete Analogy4 passage, different words expressing the quantitative relationships must replace these concepts, such as 'higher/lower', 'more intense/less intense', 'larger/smaller', 'graver/lighter', 'more stringent/less stringent', and so on.[12]

For parsing concrete rabbinic passages which we suspect to contain an *a fortiori* argument, I shall use the following five-point structure, which takes the argument to have four premises and one conclusion:

1. there is a norm *n*; there is a norm *m*;
2. *n* belongs to norm type N, *m* to norm type M;[13]
3. compared in dimension X, type M (norm *m*) has a higher grade, type N (norm *n*) has a lower grade;
4. to type N (norm *n*) applies feature A;
5. *therefore: To norm* m *feature A should apply even more.*

Consider an example. Here is one of the few Mishnaic Analogy4 passages to incorporate a Scriptural quotation:

[61] mMak 3:15 IV (4)[14]   Deut. 12:23–5

R. Shim'on ben Rabbi says: Behold (הרי) it says: 'Only be firm not to eat the blood, for the blood is the life . . .'. And if the person who separates from the blood, from which man recoils, receives a reward; then the person who separates from robbery and forbidden sexual relations, which man covets and desires, how much more so (על אחת כמה)[15] will he acquire merit for himself and his generations and the generations of his generations until the end of all the generations!

The description of the reward for the second set of norms is couched in terms of reward throughout the generations. This is modelled on the biblical reward for abstaining from blood found in the biblical co-text, verse 25: 'You shall not eat it; that all may go well with you and with your children after you . . .'. This verse is clearly taken into account (the Cotext5 resource), but the Mishnah first sums it up by saying 'for separating from the blood . . . man . . . receives *a reward*'. The Mishnaic unit comes hard on the heels of a passage which makes a related point, and is ascribed to R. Shim'on. *Mishnah 3:15* is concerned with the expiating effect of the punishment of scourging, and is thematically parallel to chapter 10 of the tractate Sanhedrin. If we paraphrase the text of the *a fortiori* argument and

---

[12] There may be an irreducibly metaphorical element in all comparisons of qualities.

[13] Hirschfeld, following the lead of the traditional expression גזו, identifies the *qal wa-homer* as an inference from *opposition* ('Gegensatz', *Halachische Exegese*, 217 f. and 224). It seems to me that the relationship of opposition, or even difference, cannot be the basis of the inference (cf. also Schwarz, 'Hauptergebnisse', 8). However, while the opposition or difference expressed in point 2 is always available from the surface format of the argument (at least in the Mishnah), the graded comparison or ranking in point 3 is not. See below.

[14] ◊•A4.1C5, several T3.

[15] So MSS Kaufmann and Parma (de Rossi 138). The other texts add a וכמה (thus making it formulaic), which could be rendered as: '. . . how much more so! [So] that he will acquire merit . . .'. See Krauß, *Sanhedrin-Makkot*, 406; Albeck, *Einführung*, 178.

distribute its operative elements to our heuristic five-point structure, we obtain the following:

1. do not eat blood (*n*); do not commit robbery/incest (*m*);
2. *n* forbids what one does not want to do anyway (norm type N), *m* forbids what one wants to do (norm type M);
3. compared for ease of fulfilment (dimension X), type M is more difficult to fulfil than type N;[16]
4. abstention from blood (*n*/N) carries a reward (predicate A), that is, the welfare of a person and his/her children (Deut. 12:23–5);
5. *therefore, there should also be a reward for abstention from robbery/incest and it should be even greater, for example, by being extended further into the future.*

In parsing the Mishnaic text of [61] in this way, a number of textual features have not been represented. The biblical quotation is omitted from this schema. The structure of the text which orders the components in the sequence *n*–N–A and *m*–M–A (as does our resource definition) is not reproduced, but transformed into a pairing of the different types of concepts (norms, categories of norms). Stylistic features, such as the duplication 'covets'–'desires' and the repetition of 'generations', as well as the format of exclamation,[17] are not represented.

Something has also been added, in point 3: I am spelling out one of the possibilities for the dimension of comparison (X), namely, by calling it 'ease of fulfilment'. This is not merely a question of choosing a suitable wording. The dimension of comparison is not usually explicated in our texts (nowhere in the Mishnah, at any rate), and that means that choices have to be made when explicating the texts. There is bound to be a plurality of possibilities for point 3 in each case. There is no obligation to guess the 'right' one—there clearly never was one 'right' one, because it was not articulated. The hermeneutic obligation is to choose a strong point 3 from among the historically appropriate ones, in order to represent—to us— the possibilities of the argument. But it seems to me that *some* point 3, undeclared or otherwise, is necessary for the argument to work.[18] Without it, the *grading* of the two categories M and N remains unmotivated, and point 2 only provides us with their mutual definition. We can define different categories as long as we wish, but no grading results without a shared dimension in which the one is a 'more' and the other a 'less', or to use

---

[16] One could formulate this point as: The reward is proportionate to the exertion, or: Comparing the distance between the desired and the commanded, in the case of M (*m*) that distance is greater than in the case of N (*n*).

[17] Cf. also the 'behold', הרי, which introduces the quotation.

[18] Many modern interpreters are concerned with the precise difference between *qal wa-homer* arguments starting from the 'light' and those starting from the 'heavy', respectively. But what does it mean that the argument has such a directionality in the first place? Point 3 in our schema is where this directionality is made explicit.

the metaphors of the *qal wa-homer*, in which one is the 'heavy' (חמור) and the other the 'light' (קל). Point 2 makes clear that the two norms *n* and *m* are separated (namely, by belonging to two different categories); but something that *unites* them has to be found as well, otherwise there is no conduit by which the predicate A can travel from *n* to *m*. Categories M and N are different but not *disparate*, they can be compared and ranked in respect of a shared dimension—the dimension X, one possible interpretation of which is brought to the surface in point 3. So, while the argument does not work without an assumed point 3, it works quite well without an *explication* of point 3. In this regard it resembles the metaphor, whose *tertium comparationis* may be impossible to pin down in a paraphrase, for its illuminating potential cannot be exhausted once and for all for all readers and users.[19] And yet metaphors have information content and communicative function, in fact they belong to the most effective linguistic devices.[20] So, in explicating point 3 of the argument's schema it is important not to be too rigid and thus do injustice to the supple instrument for conveying ideas and arguments that the *a fortiori* is. And one should certainly avoid 'translating' a rabbinic argument so that it fits into a predetermined, 'known' logical format, in particular if that leads to the 'discovery' of Greek logic in the rabbinic procedures.[21] In most cases a translation of this type does indeed succeed in reducing the ambiguities of the original argument. But the price that has to be paid for this is high, because the new language, 'logic', is so much poorer. A century of intense investigation of the relationship between logic and ordinary language has resulted in an attitude of extreme caution towards such translations even within a contemporary setting,[22] let alone for arguments from culturally or historically distant contexts.

Explicating point 3 in our schema of the Mishnaic *a fortiori* is an exercise in historical interpretation, not a matter of endowing with the sanction of formal logic an argument that could not carry conviction without it. Point 3

[19] Cf. Sharpe, 'Metaphor', 555 ('invites us to join in an exploration of points of similarity and difference'); Lakoff and Johnson, *Metaphors We Live By*; Taylor, *Linguistic Categorization*, 130 ff.; and see the influential article 'Metaphor' by Black, in his *Models and Metaphors*, 25–47. It may be argued that the links between the *a fortiori* argument and metaphor (and also other forms of analogical reasoning and metaphor) are substantial. In that case, Black's critique of the view that one can substitute a non-metaphorical expression for metaphors without loss of 'cognitive content' (*Models*, 46) would also apply to the *a fortiori* argument. He explicitly criticizes attempts to articulate the point of similiarity for metaphors with the help of a formula such as 'Is A more like B than C on such and such a scale of degrees of P?' (p. 37, but see pp. 46 f.), i.e. a formula whose second half is very similar to our point 3 for the *a fortiori* argument. And yet the *a fortiori* is, after all, an argument of sorts; so such an explication is in fact more appropriate for it than it is for metaphors. Yet both have a playful side (see below). See also Ashley, 'Arguing by Analogy in Law: A Case-Based Model'.
[20] We have drawn attention to the metaphorical nature of the *qal wa-homer* terminology, and technical terms are often metaphorical in origin (cf. the language of computing and the internet).
[21] The work of A. Schwarz on rabbinic hermeneutics suffers from such circularity; see below.
[22] Wittgenstein and Grice are prime examples of scholars interested in logic whose work has helped to bring about an explosion of research into the way language is tied to the situations of its use (i.e. its illogicality, in a manner of speaking).

is meant to capture one possibility for that non-formal force of the argument. It is a good test of whether the terms of the argument have been given their correct function in the overall structure. And it is a lead into the vast and silent world of the presuppositions of the Mishnaic discourse. A fortiori arguments in rabbinic literature are points at which deep-seated assumptions come to the surface. While they are also not fully explicated in that argument, they can be grasped through the effect they produce.[23] But since formulating point 3 involves the modern interpreter directly in constructing the argument, and thus depends on our knowledge of the Mishnaic universe of discourse in general, the dimension of comparison is labelled X, that is: 'unknown.'

The absence from the text surface of any definition of point 3 is not a special feature of the Mishnaic a fortiori argument. The argument appears also in Aristotle's list of 'enthymemes',[24] and the examples he uses are of the same type as those found in the Mishnah, except that they are not about norms. Thus he presents the following inference from a 'more/less' relationship: a person who strikes even his father will also strike his fellows. The personal or moral characteristic, however, whose required measure is higher in the case of parents than in the case of others is not identified. What exactly is it that 'striking one's parents' has 'more' of than 'striking others': disdain for divine punishment, or loss of self-control? It seems that it is this 'incompleteness' in articulating the argument's assumptions which gives it a rhetorical, as opposed to an analytical, flavour (to use the categories of Aristotle's oeuvre). There is something of the appearance of a paradox, as well as of the surprise effected by a punchline, in the a fortiori argument.[25] It shall be seen later that the Mishnah's use of the a fortiori suggests that the rabbis thought of it as a figure of rhetoric as well as logic, insofar as these terms can apply to them.

Let us first consider the second thematic type of a fortiori inference in the Mishnah.

[62] mYad 4:7[26]

The Sadducees say: We raise a complaint against you, O Pharisees (for you say: If my ox and my donkey have caused damage they are culpable [making me liable]; but if my slave and female slave have caused damage, they are free [causing no

---

[23] For examples of a careful drawing out of concepts and values embedded into rabbinic discourse (rather than articulated by it), see Goldberg, 'Schöpfung und Geschichte', and 'Der einmalige Mensch'.

[24] Rhetoric, 1397b (bk. ii, ch. 23.4); cf. Topics, 114b37–115a14 (bk. ii, ch. 10): ἐκ τοῦ μᾶλλον καὶ ἧττον; for a list of all Topics passages, see Kneale and Kneale, Development of Logic, 42, n. 4. According to Kneale and Kneale, Aristotle speaks about the a fortiori argument as a 'well-recognized theme' (ibid.). For passages in Homer which combine a fortiori with the idea of example, see Lloyd, Polarity and Analogy, 386, and n. 1 above. Cf. also Ellis, 'Biblical Interpretation in the New Testament Church', 700.

[25] It may be noted that the Petirah of the rabbinic homily has often been likened in its effect to the punchline of a joke. See Lenhard, Die Rabbinische Homilie, 31; Goldberg, 'Versuch', 34.

[26] ◊∆•¶A4.1.

liability for me]).[27] Just as with regard to my ox and my donkey, concerning which I am not liable through commandments (מצות), behold I am liable for damage, is it not logical (אינו דין) that with regard to my slave and my female slave, concerning whom I am liable by commandments, I should be liable for damage?

In this passage the *a fortiori* argument serves as an attack on the position of the Pharisees. The main elements are: the two kinds of possessions which have the potential to cause damage, animals and human beings; two types of liability arising from owning them (which is the point under discussion); and two categories into which the possessions fall: possessing them is subject to commandments (humans) or it is not (animals). Using the five-point structure, we can lay out the steps of the argument as follows:

1. Oxen/donkeys may be owned by me and can cause damage (n); slaves may be owned by me and can cause damage (m).
2. I am subject to commandments (M) concerning my possession of slaves (m), but not subject to commandments (N) concerning my posession of oxen/donkeys (n).[28]
3. Compared for the degree of responsibility imposed on me (X), that responsibility is greater for items for which I am subject to commandments (M) than for items for which I am not (N).
4. To damage caused by an ox (n, N) applies liability of the owner (A).
5. *Therefore: to damage caused by a slave (m) liability of the owner (A) applies also/even more.*

It can be seen that this argument is not about norms as whole units, but about functional parts of norms. We shall distinguish it as the Analogy4.1 sub-type of the Mishnaic *a fortiori* argument. The substance of one of the norms is in question, in the following way: which apodosis belongs to the protasis: 'If my slave has caused damage'? Is it the apodosis: 'I am liable', or the apodosis: 'I am not liable'? The norm concerning animals, whose substance is not in contention, is split up into a protasis appearing in point 1 and an apodosis appearing in point 4—that apodosis is the clincher of the argument, once the graded comparison between the two protases is set up. There is no element of increase overtly suggested in this Analogy4.1 example, although it appears in other passages. Here is the general shape of the Analogy4 argument when used to determine the identity of an *apodosis*:

Analogy4.1: Inference by analogy that the protasis of norm m has the apodosis A, in the following manner: if the protasis n which belongs to the category N, which category is lower on scale X, has apodosis A; then protasis m which belongs to the category M, which category is higher on

---

[27] The words in round brackets are absent from MS Kaufmann and others but found in the popular prints (cf. Lisowsky, *Jadajim*, 77).

[28] A very similar point 2 is found in the *a fortiori* at mShebu 3:6, concerning oaths involving the performance of commandments. But in that passage, the same point 2 leads to a different point 3, because the commandments themselves are treated as a kind of oath, i.e. a comparison is drawn between two types of oaths.

scale X, logically also has apodosis A (or: logically must have an intensification of the apodosis A).

One, several, or none of the norms and terms presupposed in the Analogy4.1 argument may be found to be tied to Scripture; as for Analogy 4.2, this does not affect the argument's form, but its hermeneutic function. This is how Analogy4.1 looks using the five-point schema:

1. protasis *n*; protasis *m*;
2. an element of the protasis *n* belongs to category N; the same element of the protasis *m* belongs to category M;
3. compared in dimension X, category M has a higher grade than category N ;
4. the apodosis belonging to *n* is A;
5. *therefore: the apodosis belonging to* m *should also (even more so) be A.*

In **[62]** the category M is simply a negation of the category N (possession subject to/not subject to/commandments). Our next example shows that other types of relationship can also hold between these two categories:

[63] mYeb 8:3 II (2)[29]   Deut. 23:4 (E 3)

'An Ammonite and a Moabite' are prohibited [to marry an Israelite] and their prohibition is an everlasting prohibition [cf. verse]. But their females are allowed right away. An Egyptian and Edomite are only prohibited for three generations, males as well as females. (R. Shim'on allows the females right away.)[30] R. Shim'on said: The things are the light and the heavy (קל וחומר): If in a place where it [Scripture] forbids the males with an everlasting prohibition, it allows the females right away; then in a place where it forbids the males only for three generations, is it not logical that the females are also allowed right away?

In question stands again the apodosis of a case schema or norm. This is the gist of the argument:

1. Ammonite/Moabite women's availability for marriage (*n*); Egyptian/Edomite women's availability for marriage (*m*);
2. Ammon/Moab are in the marriage category 'never' as far as their males are concerned (N); Egypt/Edom in the category 'after three generations' (M);
3. Comparing the severity of restrictions on intermarriage by nation (X), those applying to Ammon/Moab (N) are severer than those applying to Egypt/Edom (M) due to the treatment of the men;
4. (Nevertheless) the women of Ammon/Moab (*n*) are allowed right away (A);
5. *Therefore: the women of Egypt/Edom* (m) *should also be allowed right away* (A).

---

[29] •¶A4.1≈O1.5.

[30] This sentence, and a similar one, are only found in the *editio princeps* of the Bavli (Venice 1522) and in MS Munich. See Rengstorf, *Yebamot*, 230.

As in the previous examples, the actual formulation of the graded comparison (point 3) is not found in the Mishnah. This means: no *general* principle of comparing norms is formulated, and yet one is presupposed. The Mishnah does not speak about the ease of the fulfilment of commandments **[61]**, the degree of responsibility **[62]**, or the severity on marriage restrictions **[63]** in so many words. And yet, in order to claim the 'even more so' or the 'at least as much as' of the conclusion, some such common measure must be taken for granted. The movement of overarching, of catapulting the conclusion *beyond* the point at which the premiss number 4 is found, seems always present and is often expressed explicitly, for example, in the phrases קל וחומר and על אחת כמה וכמה.[31] This is the case even where the nature of the subject-matter does not allow for any quantification, but is presented as a yes–no decision.[32] Thus, there is nothing quicker than 'right away' **[63]**. Similarly, the principle of liability which is the topic in **[62]** allows no increase as such. But sometimes, and where there is room to express the increase, it receives dedicated expression. Thus, the apparently two generations of Deut. 12:25 ('you and your children after you'), tacitly presupposed in **[61]**, become a rather extravagant (and eschatological) 'himself', 'his generation', 'the generations of his generations', and 'the end of all the generations'![33]

What exactly is increased in the argument? The impression of a quantitative increase is sometimes due to the fact that the categories of point 2 are defined in terms of quantitative differences,[34] for example, when monetary value is the defining moment (e.g. mHul 12:5). But if one looks around for something that can be increased in all the cases, whether or not any of the subjects as such allow for quantification, one is only left with two possibilities it seems: an *epistemic* increase, and a *deontic* increase. In this context the curious resilience of the *qal wa-homer* is of interest. In the Mishnah it is often used for positions that are actually considered doubtful, and then have an air of saying: if this *is not* correct, it really *ought* to be! This points in the direction of a concern with what the logic of the normative system

---

[31] It is one of the effects of Schwarz's identification of the *qal wa-homer* with the Aristotelian syllogism ('Hauptergebnisse', 8 f.) that the element of increase is eliminated from the argument. (Cf. Jacobs, *Studies*, 5 f., and id., 'Hermeneutics', col. 367.) He holds that the difference between the syllogism and the *qal wa-homer* is 'purely formal' (p. 8). Since in logical operations everything depends on the formal structure, the strangeness of this statement is rivalled only by his declaration that the syllogistic structure was too 'boring' for the Hebrew mind (p. 9). His translation of the Aristotelian example 'All humans are mortals; Socrates is a human—Socrates is a mortal' into a *qal wa-homer* reads: 'Socrates is a human—how much more so is he mortal!' (p. 9). This is of course nothing like a *qal wa-homer*, but it could be the concluding half of one, as follows: If Adonis, who is a god, is a mortal, how much more so is Socrates, who is a human, a mortal. Once we have restored a genuine *a fortiori* form to the argument its difference from the syllogism becomes very clear.

[32] The term קל וחומר appears in the following units whose subjects do not admit a quantitative interpretation: mYT 5:2; mYeb 8:3 II (2) **[64]**; mSot 6:3 III (4); mEduy 6:2; analogous case for the formula על אחת כמה וכמה: mMak 3:15 II (4).

[33] It could, however, be argued that the very use of such hyperbole means that any identification of the increase in *real* terms is avoided.

[34] Cf. Hirschfeld, *Halachische Exegese*, 226 f.

requires. Where the *a fortiori* is subsequently rejected, the Mishnaic discourse reveals that law is convention or divine commandment, not logic.[35] It seems that the increase suggested is thus one of epistemic and normative certitude.[36]

Perhaps this is the reason for two famous rabbinic hedges limiting the force of the *a fortiori*. The first restriction is found, among other places, in mBQ 2:5, in the context of a dispute between the sages and R. Tarfon. Although formulated in general terms, it is not presented as a rule accompanying the 'rule' called *qal wa-homer*; but used to decide a specific instance of *a fortiori* 'increase'. In a situation which according to the majority of the rabbis calls for the payment of half damages, R. Tarfon argues for full damages. His two *a fortiori* arguments are both countered with the so-called *dayyo* maxim: דיו לבא מן דין להיות כנדון, 'It suffices for the conclusion to be like the premiss'. The text explains how this is meant to apply in the case against Tarfon, but the sentence itself is general, and is marked in the course of the dispute as formulaic by being repeated word for word. There is a second rabbinic restriction for the application of the *qal wa-homer* which stipulates that the measure of a punishment is not to be determined from an 'inference' (דין). The co-texts of the passages in which this maxim appears suggest that an inference of the Analogy4 type is meant.[37] The actual purpose and effect of such hedges are not easy to determine.

Here is an example of an *a fortiori* argument not concerned with norms.

[64] mSan 6:5 II (2)[38]   Deut. 21:23

R. Meir said: At the time when a man is troubled [punished], what does the [common] language say? I am lighter than my head, I am lighter than my arm. If thus (כך/כן), says God [MS Kaufmann: 'Scripture'], I am pained[39] at the blood of the wicked (which is shed), how much more at (קל וחומר על) the blood of the righteous (which is shed)![40]

---

[35] See below on the position of Neusner, and n. 53.

[36] Cf. Jacobs's suggested formula for the argument which ends in *'certainly* has x', *Studies*, 4 (emphasis mine).

[37] Sifre Num. 1 (ad Num. 5:1); Mekhilta Ishmael ad Exod. 21:33 (Lauterbach, iii. 91); bMak 5b: שאין עונשין מן הדין. On biblical redundancy operations and Analogy4 as rival sources of halakhic information, see below. On the two restrictions see Mielziner, *Introduction*, 134 f.; Bacher, i. 22 (where the Sifre passage is erroneously cited as Sifre Deuteronomy).

[38] (•)A5.

[39] מצטער, lit. 'to suffer'; see also Jastrow, 1294b ad. loc.

[40] The passage presents a number of linguistic and textual problems (cf. Krauß, *Sanhedrin-Makkot*, 201), and only some of the textual variants are presented in our translation (see ibid. 393). Yet, all versions seem to presuppose the following basic hermeneutic structure. A fixed idiomatic phrase from ordinary language, such as 'I am lighter than my head', makes use of the word קל to express pain. This word is then linked to the biblical 'curse', קללה in Deut. 21:23, so that the expression קללת־אלהים can be understood as implying that the executed person pains God, i.e. that God has pity for the executed person. Some such mechanism provides the central element (namely point 4 and part of point 1) of the *a fortiori* inference. Text corruption could then arise from two factors: euphemistic tendencies interfering with an ascription of pain to God; and the fact that the wording of the idiomatic phrase current at the time of the Mishnah is grammatically or semantically opaque and therefore unrecoverable for later scribes.

These lines are found in a passage dealing with capital punishment. The biblical injunction not to let the executed person linger overnight is taken to show that God grieves about the death of the wicked. It is not as straightforward as before to apply the five-point schema to this argument. Some reflection is necessary to see what the assumptions actually are, in terms that have meaning within the rabbinic discourse. They could be presented as follows:

1. The shedding of the blood of the unjust causes suffering (or, destruction of creation); the shedding of the blood of the just causes suffering (or, destruction of creation);
2. The suffering of the unjust (or, the destruction of unjust creation) is an expression of God's just punishment; the suffering of the just (or, the destruction of innocent creation) is not;
3. Compared in the dimension of God's compassion, the suffering caused by (God's) just punishment is less grievous then the suffering caused by injustice;
4. Nevertheless, the shedding of the blood of the unjust grieves God;
5. *Therefore, the shedding of the blood of the righteous must grieve God even more.*

It is impossible to feel entirely comfortable with having to flesh out the argument to this extent. However, the alternatives are either to reduce the schema to fewer points or to reject the idea that this is an *a fortiori* argument. The latter is clearly wrong; not only is it a Mishnaic *a fortiori* argument by logic and terminology, it is actually a strikingly effective one (not a decisive point, but also not irrelevant). As for the option to reduce the structure to, say, three points: that would not change the level of implicitness of the passage, and thus the ambiguities with which we are faced; it would merely mask them. To take just one component of the argument: it is clear that the shedding of the blood of the wicked does not refer to just any demise, but to execution (by the human court, in the Mishnaic co-text and in the biblical Lemma). Point 2 thus forms an integral part of the argument, even though it is not explicated inside the *a fortiori* sentence. The same goes for the idea of suffering or destruction of creation formulated in point 1; this idea is not named in the text, but is in some form necessary, for the shedding of blood as a *physiological* process is not what grieves God. And so for other points. Still, explicating Analogy5 clearly involves us deeply in hermeneutic decisions on co-text and cultural and historical context.

I shall now modify my earlier definition of the *a fortiori* argument to fit inferences not dealing with norms; I shall nevertheless retain the functional letters n, m, N, M, and A in their respective slots.

Analogy5: Inference by analogy that predicate A applies to subject m, in the following manner: if subject n which belongs to the category N, which category is lower on scale X, has predicate A; then subject m which belongs to the category M, which category is higher on scale X, logically also has predicate A (or: logically must have more of the quality A).

One, several, or none of the terms presupposed in the Analogy5 argument may be found to be tied to Scripture; as before, this does not affect the argument's form, but its hermeneutic function.

SCRIPTURE IS NO NECESSARY PART
OF THE ARGUMENT

The discussion of passage [61] shows that the Scriptural quotation contributes nothing to the logical form of the argument of the resource Analogy4. In other words, the resource is not, as such, directed towards the wording of the biblical text. This is parallel to the use of biblical events as exemplary, the NORM family. The latter does not depend, as such, on the way in which the events are told in Scripture, but has to be deliberately connected to it. Of the four first points of the *a fortiori* argument, all could in principle be tied to a biblical support text, and a whole biblical norm in the role of item n will cover point 4 wholly and point 1 partly. If that is the case it only means, however, that information which the argument *relies upon* is separately linked to biblical evidence. As part of the argument these points are treated as premises, that is, as valid 'for the sake of the argument' in any case. But for the most part the elements of Analogy4 in the Mishnah are not given such Scriptural ties at all. Of c. twenty Analogy4 passages, three quote Scriptural wording[41] and three use it allusively (π)[42] within the Mishnaic passage setting out the argument. A further six are linked by cohesion to a Scriptural quotation in the co-text.[43] All the others make no effort to bind any part of the *a fortiori* argument to Scripture, and there is no attempt to validate from Scripture *all* assumptions of any one *a fortiori*. Where a quotation is given, its gist is *represented again* in the formulation of the argument. In other words, there is a duplication of the relevant part of the Scriptural message in Mishnah's own words, summed up in the subordinate clauses of the complex sentence that presents the inference. Thus in passage [61] the summary ('and if for separating from the blood . . . man receives a reward') represents Deut. 12:23–5 distributed over two places

---

[41] They are: mMak 3:15 IV (4): points 1 (n), 4; [mAvot 6:3 II (3)] [52]; mHul 12:5: points 1 (n), 4; mYad 4:8 I (2) [57] = [131a]: points 1(n), 4(?). The Avot 6 passage is not included in the total. It is a special type of Analogy4, containing the behaviour of a biblical hero as point 4 (i.e. a NORM resource). The mYad 4:8 passage also has an exemplum, with Scripture as a textual format providing the model for a rabbinic legal document (see on this Ch. 13). Cf. also the Homer passages discussed by Lloyd (n. 24 above).

[42] They are: mYeb 8:3 II (2): point 3; mHul 10:1 II (2): point 2(?); mNeg 10:2 I (2): point 1 (n)(?).

[43] They are: mSot 6:3 I (4): points 1 (n), 4; mSot 6:3 III (4): points 1 (n), 4; mSan 6:5 II (2): parts of points 1 (n), 4; mMak 1:7 VI (6): point 1 (n), perhaps also point 4; mMak 3:15 II (4): points 1(n), 4; mNeg 12:5 IV (4): points 1(n), 4.

in the sentence. And [64] contains a paraphrase ('if thus God is pained at the blood . . .') of a paraphrase ('I am lighter . . .') of a Scriptural quotation, using the deixis כן to point to that dependency.[44] This transposition from Scriptural quotation into Mishnaic Dictum tends to have a contribution from hermeneutic transformations, in particular generalizations. Thus the person executed by a specific method mentioned in the Scriptural quotation of [64] becomes the wicked person whose blood is shed *par excellence*. In mMak 1:7 VI (6), Deut. 17:6 is taken to refer to a person being an accessory in giving false testimony. This is generalized to an accessory in *any* transgression, and in this general form becomes the element *n* of an Analogy4.2 operation. But also, taken as a whole, the *a fortiori* argument incorporating biblical wording imposes a hermeneutic perspective on that wording. Any terms rooted in the discourse of the Mishnah used in the *a fortiori* have the same perspectivizing effect as the Topic3/Topic4 resources for the biblical Lemma. Of central importance in this function is the pair 'light–heavy', which provides one basic formula for the *qal wa-homer* terminology. The unexpressed dimension of comparison, on the other hand (dimension 'X' in our point 3) is very similar to a tacit assumption of the Topic0 type: necessary for arriving at the interpretation and therefore imposing a perspective on the Lemma, but not made explicit. But all these hermeneutic effects are peripheral. The raw material for the logical mechanism are not the signs of Scripture as signs; they are what the signs of Scripture refer to, and that is also what we found for NORM resources. Any hermeneutic operation necessary in order to identify what people did, for the NORM resources, or what the biblical norms or values are, for the Analogy4/5 resources, is preliminary to the analogy actually performed in the *a fortiori*.

An examination of which points of the argument are usually linked to Scripture (see the preceding footnotes) shows that where Scripture is quoted, it tends to serve as support for the elements *n* and A (points 1 and 4 in the schema). For the Analogy4.1 cases this means the protasis and apodosis of the *known* norm. In some cases it is not easy to determine which point of Analogy4 is actually supported by Scriptural wording (partly because of mediating hermeneutic transformations). Nevertheless, all nine cases of dedicated biblical quotation seem to fall into this category. This is only what one would expect: where Scripture is quoted it can be employed as a warrant, and the obvious point at which to support an *a fortiori* argument by a warrant is the first element of its premiss, points 1 and 4 (in fact, its *n*–A axis). On the other hand, where Scriptural terms are used for the Mishnah's own expression (π, three cases), they concern either point 1, 2, or 3. Where a Mishnaic *a fortiori* argument proceeds without any recourse to Scriptural wording (the majority of cases), we must assume that its premisses have the same authority as that of any unsupported Dictum in

---

[44] The same expression is used in mMak 1:7 VI (6).

Mishnaic discourse, that is, are considered unproblematic unless or until challenged.

THE EXPLORATORY USE OF THE *A FORTIORI* ARGUMENT IN THE MISHNAH

Although not syllogistic in nature, the *a fortiori* argument has the potential for being presented in an apodictic and formal manner. Here is an illustration, made up for the purpose:

Consumer groups in individual commercial sectors have shown that they can successfully exert pressure to influence specific business and government decisions (for example, Brent Spa, genetically modified foods).[45] There is thus no doubt that consumer concern mobilized across *several* commercial sectors would have an even bigger impact.

This is still persuasive rather than apodictic in tone ('no doubt', but also 'would'). And yet, even this level of firmness is absent from our passages.[46] The following points emerge from an examination of the Mishnaic evidence. (a) The format of the argument is the hypothetical conditional. The argument is presented in a complex sentence and has the grammatical structure 'if . . . then'. (b) Most units have a clearly marked *question* format. The hypothetical is combined with a negated, rhetorical question (anticipating the answer 'yes'): If y is the case, is it not logical to assume that x is the case? (c) About three-quarters of all *a fortiori* arguments appearing in the Mishnah are either introduced as the argument of one voice involved in a dispute with other voices (including passages **[62]** and **[63]** above), or they are presented as preliminary positions set up in order to be ultimately rejected (by the same voice that proposed them).[47] In the coded profiles for individual passages these two discourse structures are represented symbolically as ¶ and as 'non'-sign (¬), respectively.[48] The frequent appearance of *a fortiori* arguments within dispute structures is not in itself surprising, for it is an instrument of persuasion. What is more remarkable is the fact that fairly often *two a fortiori* arguments are pitted against each other in disputes. This means either that the same *n* and *m* components are

[45] Note that the examples given in brackets fulfil a function similar to that of Scriptural quotations in some Mishnaic Analogy4/5 units. They provide factual backing for the opening premiss, which itself is a generalization of concrete instances.

[46] Although we need to make allowances for cultural differences in the way in which convictions are put across. For example, understatement is certainly a feature of British English (at least in certain types of discourse) when compared to, say, German. Such differences may affect our perception of the degree of conviction visible in the stylistic choices for the Mishnaic *a fortiori* argument listed presently.

[47] Mielziner, *Introduction*, 136, in an attempt to generalize over a much larger literary corpus than the Mishnah, says: 'We sometimes find there very problematic and even sophistical inferences set forth merely as suppositions or hypotheses; these are, however, finally refuted.' See also 139 ff.

[48] The sign ¬ is often used in symbolic logic to represent negation.

allocated to different categories N and M by the two opposed voices, or that the categories are placed in rival dimensions of comparison resulting in reversed rankings. In other words, the dependency of the force of the argument on the choice of suitable points 2 and 3 is *exposed* in such disputes, the choice is shown to depend to some extent on the position one has set out to defend.[49] The question of graded comparisons of legal objects, and the possibility of determining the outcome of their ranking by a suitable choice of perspective, is of some concern to the Mishnah and is not restricted to *a fortiori* contexts. A dispute at mSan 9:3 about the severity of different kinds of capital punishment is a good example, and it shows the pervasive use of the 'light/heavy' terminology for such purposes:

R. Shim'on said to them: If burning were not more severe (חמורה), the priest's daughter who committed adultery would not be punished by it. They said to him: If stoning were not more severe, the blasphemer and the idolater would not be punished by it. (cf. mSan 7:1)

Generally speaking, terminology connected with the roots חמר and קול is prominent in the Mishnaic discourse on the level *above* that of the individual case schema. This is also the context in which its use in the normative *a fortiori* has to be seen: the interrelationship of casuistic norms. The grading or comparison of norms by severity is an occasional but regular feature of Mishnaic discourse; it can even generate Mishnaic lists. It sometimes serves as an objection (or an anticipated objection) to a Mishnaic interpretation of Scripture, quite independent of the *a fortiori*. The concern seems to be with explaining cases where the ranking between norms somehow violates expectations; this seems to have been an issue.[50]

On one occasion the wide choice involved in the graded comparison of an *a fortiori* seems to be articulated in the Mishnah. Following on from unit [63], anonymous opponents of R. Shim'on ask him if he holds his position on the basis of having a 'halakhah', or on the basis of the inference. If the former, they would accept his position, but if the latter, 'there is an answer' (ואם לדין יש תשובה). This can obviously refer to any type of counter-argument, but the use of the word דין suggests an attack on the choice of premises for the *a fortiori* argument specifically. Insistence on a tradition ('halakhah') is something of a rabbinic topos for the limits of the certainty of logical or hermeneutic reconstruction.[51] Another type of refutation of the *a fortiori* argument is not usually distributed to two different voices, but is presented anonymously. It consists of simply overriding the logic of the argument by

[49] Cf. Mielziner, *Introduction*, 136 f. for this and other counter-arguments.

[50] Cf. case [58] in the preceding chapter, where the biblical example supports a statement about the ranking of deed and word; see also mArak 4:4 discussed in the next chapter as [75]. For a mere mention of the ranking, without controversy, see e.g. mArak 3:2. B. Jackson draws attention to the 'axiological' nature of halakhic analogies, i.e. the link between reasoning and values expressed in the terminology of *qal* and *homer* ('On the Nature of Analogical Argument in Early Jewish Law', in particular 158 ff.).

[51] See above, text beginning after n. 36.

factual reference to a Scriptural quotation which says the opposite, often introduced by תלמוד לומר.[52] This type of refutation shows up the limits of the argument, at least if applied in the area of law (or perhaps specifically divine law). Seizing upon this aspect, J. Neusner has claimed that the relationship between Sifra and Mishnah is defined by Sifra's insistence that reasoning (in particular *qal wa-homer* reasoning) is insufficient for ascertaining the halakhah.[53] But the Mishnah itself contains this procedure too often for it to mark an ideological difference between the makers of the Mishnah and the makers of Sifra (or the Gemaras).[54] Such refutations also have another effect: they show that a given segment of Scripture is not *redundant*.[55] Quite regularly the *a fortiori* engages with the Scriptural segment quoted for its refutation in such a way that an unstressed biblical expression becomes emphatically relevant, namely, as saying the *opposite* of the proposition presented by the *a fortiori*. This type of concern with Scriptural redundancy belongs to the core of rabbinic hermeneutics in the Mishnah.[56] Showing that the *qal wa-homer* leads astray is to justify that God the author used so many words in his communication to Israel. But perhaps most revealing are those adversarial *a fortiori* arguments which refute the opponent's position (usually also an *a fortiori*) by confronting him with another, clearly unwanted, consequence of his own method of reasoning. The *a fortiori* argument is here used to expose consistency problems in the opponent's position, and is a type of dialogical[57] *reductio ad absurdum*.[58] There is an astonishing passage, mEduy 6:3, in which an anonymous group

---

[52] mSot 6:3 I (4), mSot 6:3 III (4), mBek 9:1 II (2). The phrase is also used to reject positions other than those presented as Analogy4 argument, but does not appear very often in the Mishnah. Cf. Bacher, i. 190 ff.

[53] Neusner explains the use of the *rejected* para-logical argument (often the *a fortiori*) in Sifra as a reaction to the 'autonomous autocephalic authority' of the Mishnah (*Judaism*, 218, 219 f.; cf. *History of the Mishnaic Law of Purities*, part 7, *Negaim*). With regard to mSot 6:3, he says: 'M. 6:3 then goes through the exercise of claiming that the propositions of M. 6:2 can be proved only through exegesis of Scripture, since simple logic will have yielded a contrary and false result . . .' (*History of the Mishnaic Law of Women*, part 4, *Sotah. Gittin. Qiddushin*, 60).

[54] Other tannaitic works have this routine also, cf. e.g. the sequence of interpretations in Mekhilta Ishmael ad Exod. 21:32 f. (ed. Lauterbach, iii. 89–92).

[55] This point was articulated clearly in Maccoby's review of Neusner's *Uniting the Dual Torah* (*Journal of Theological Studies*, 1993). See also text to n. 35 above.

[56] For mechanisms which employ opposition in stressing biblical words, see Chs. 11 and 12 below; for redundancy through repetition see Ch. 13.

[57] The hypothetical argument is personalized by the use of second person verb forms, 'Would you declare unclean . . .?' See also the second part of mYad 4:7. Note that much current research in analogy concentrates on its link to processes of *learning* (cf. Helman (ed.), *Analogical Reasoning*; Vosniadou and Ortony (eds.), *Similarity and Analogical Reasoning*).

[58] Jacobs devotes one of the chapters of his *Studies* to the *reductio ad absurdum* in rabbinic literature. He quotes C. S. Peirce's definition: 'The disproof of a proposition by showing that among its consequences there is one which is impossible or simply false' (see Jacobs, *Studies*, 38). However, Jacobs's inclusion of cases where a norm is rejected because of the *practical* problems of iteration (e.g. p. 39, dealing with mYom 1:1), confuses the issue. Logical and normative impossibility are not the same: the rabbis had the option (not taken in mYom 1:1) of imposing pragmatic limits even when accepting a potentially infinite regress (see e.g. the iteration of the 'added fifth' in mBQ 9:7 [39]). Cf. also Wiesenberg, 'Observations', 29 f.; Honderich (ed.), *Oxford Companion to Philosophy*, 750; Hallaq, *Law and Legal Theory*, 296–9, 302–6.

('they') challenges two named opponents in turn by suggesting an *a fortiori* argument that seems to follow from their position and is yet incompatible with it.[59] While this text is unusual in its literary features as well as in the format of its argument, it highlights what is implied in most *a fortiori* passages. The *a fortiori* seems to be employed mainly to probe and explore, to experiment with certain links, or to examine inconsistencies. Analogy4 does not so much lead to a categorical result as it implements a heuristic procedure, and the rhetoric of increased epistemic or deontic certainty goes hand in hand with the gestures of questioning, hypothesizing, and persuading.[60] These speech acts are characteristic for the Mishnah as a whole: the giving of reasons or the consideration of alternatives is pervasive in it.[61] The Mishnah problematizes to a conspicuous extent the force of the *a fortiori* in its application to concrete problems. But that merely highlights the status of *all* hermeneutic resources insofar as they appear in the format of the midrashic unit, as part of a discourse of reasons and of persuasion. Whereas passages containing Analogy4.1 often have the format of the rhetorical question, Analogy4.2 seems to be more compatible with an exclamation format (emphasizing the idea of increase). Overall, one receives the impression that the *a fortiori* belongs to the generally quite prominent dimension of the Mishnah which supplements authoritative solutions by heuristic probing and didactic presentation.

[59] The exclamation 'no!' (לא) marks the beginning of the counter-argument; it is also found in mYad 4:7.

[60] Some 'heuristic' aspects of analogy are explored in Agassi, 'Analogies Hard and Soft'. Particularly apt is Agassi's notion that understanding analogies involves the explication of tacit (i.e. contextually presupposed) assumptions: 'The presentation of an analogy often alludes to a context not explicitly described. The worth of the analogy depends on the context and is not examinable without it' (p. 417). It is quite easy to see that, in proposing or refuting halakhic analogies, the rabbis explore and bring to the surface assumptions of the halakhah they have already accepted.

[61] On the classification of the Mishnah as 'persuasive communication', see Úchelen, *Chagiga*, 62 f. (and see Ch. 12 below).

8

Analogical Resources II: Transfer Within and Between Co-texts

The Mishnah may base analogical transfer between two subjects on specifically linguistic or textual information in Scripture. The manner in which Scripture *speaks* about the subjects thus becomes relevant to analogy. Of importance are, in particular, the following textual relationships: proximity, recurrence of the same term in different co-texts (*gezerah shawah*), and redundancy implied between a subject expressed once in more specific and once in more general terms. The feature to be transferred is either selected by the Mishnaic perspective or provided by its discourse. The directionality of the transfer is also open to the Mishnahic choice, that is, does not depend directly on the biblical sequence of the two terms.

In the Mishnah the biblical exemplum and the argument *a fortiori* are both only indirectly concerned with the biblical wording. The linguistic signs of Scripture are used to establish the facticity or the significance of a biblical event, and one or the other premiss of the *a fortiori* inference. But scrutiny of the biblical wording is extraneous to the application of the resource: the resource can be defined and therefore has to be defined without recourse to a specific semiotic constellation in the biblical text. The hermeneutic analogy, several types of which will concern us in this chapter, is different. Textual relationships as such become constitutive for the analogy; and a key concept once more is the notion of co-text. The following parameters may play a role in Scripture-based analogies: (i) whether there is a multiple occurrence of the same biblical lexeme; (ii) whether there is only one co-textual environment involved or more; (iii) whether the subjects of the analogy are given a similar linguistic treatment in Scripture (for example, parallel position in the sentence); and (iv) whether a substantive, text-independent similarity is ascribed to the two subjects. The first section of this chapter is devoted to the hermeneutic analogy whose two subjects are defined by their textual proximity (Analogy2, Analogy3), that is, their presence in each other's biblical co-text. We shall contrast it in various ways with dominant forms of analogical reasoning outside the rabbinic context, as well as with the example of a Mishnaic analogy not based on Scriptural wording at all (for which we shall use the label Analogy0). The second section deals with the hermeneutic analogy between a more specific and a more general Scriptural term (Analogy8). All these will share the resource name ANALOGY. Of a different kind, but still constituted by the semiotics of Scripture, is another type of analogy to be discussed in the third section of this chapter. This analogy is based on the occurrence of the same term in two different biblical co-texts (Keying2, Keying3). The chapter will end with an attempt to spell out what relationship between biblical words and analogical subjects must be assumed to hold for the ANALOGY and KEYING resources to be applicable. I shall use the word 'subject(s)' throughout when speaking of the two elements between which an analogical transfer holds, somewhat in the manner in which one speaks of the 'subject' of a sentence.

TRANSFER OF A FEATURE BETWEEN CO-TEXTUAL SUBJECTS

Just as in the *a fortiori* argument, analogical inferences appear in the Mishnah with and without explicit links to Scriptural wording. The ones which have such links fall into different categories: there is not only *one* basic type of hermeneutic analogy. However, there is no clear demarcation on the text surface separating the types, for example, terminology. The core of the analogical mechanism is a comparison of two distinct subjects, as in resources Analogy4/5. But in contrast to the *a fortiori*, the analogical comparison of the ANALOGY and KEYING resources may take as its starting-point, and sole *raison d'être*, the *textual* relation in Scripture of the two subjects. The analogy becomes *wholly* a textual resource, so to speak, in a way in which the Mishnaic *a fortiori* argument never does. The core of the analogy cannot be summed up or rephrased in a formulation which is independent of Scripture, for it depends on certain linguistic aspects and on the inter-relationships of the words Scripture uses. I shall distinguish two main groups according to whether the operative textual relationships hold within the same biblical co-text (Analogy2/3, Analogy8), or concern the co-textually different meanings of the same word appearing in two separate biblical environments (Keying2/3).[1]

---

[1] Cf. the distinction of Schwarz between 'juxtapositional' and 'isorhemic' analogies ('Hauptergebnisse', 3 f.).

In speaking about analogy, a terminological problem is encountered. The modern disciplines concerned with the logical, rhetorical, linguistic, computational, and psychological aspects of analogy do not offer a common definition of the term. The main reason for the lack of consensual definition, it seems to me, is that *all* of these disciplines are today interested in the analogy.[2] This has moved analogical modes of reasoning away from their position on the margins of logic, where their status was that of defective syllogisms. Of particular importance in this is the theory and history of science. These disciplines have provided evidence of the decisive connections between scientific thought on the one hand and non-scientific, pre-scientific, or philosophical modes of discourse on the other. This includes the role of informal arguments, among them metaphors, in the genesis of the modern scientific outlook.[3] Although there has sprung up a vocabulary for describing analogy which is united by the use of such words as 'transfer', 'mapping', 'domain', 'storage', and 'retrieval', the main context in which the term analogy has a stable meaning seems still that of traditional logic and rhetoric.[4]

Some authors reserve the word analogy exclusively for a similarity of *relationships*, that is, *ratios* or proportions. In this usage, its meaning is today perhaps more easily recognized under the word 'model'.[5] It is Aristotle whose influence is still visible in the modern formulations of this type of analogy.[6] It can be presented as follows: 'As A to B, so C to D.' To quote the example Aristotle uses in the context of speaking about metaphors(!):[7] as old age is to life, so evening is to day, therefore one can call old age the 'evening of life', or the evening 'old age of the day'. This type of analogy is

---

[2] Johnson-Laird, 'Analogy and the Exercise of Creativity', is good on the interdisciplinary angle. Artificial intelligence research drives much of the research, and computing provides many of the metaphors (such as storage, retrieval, accessing); see presently.

[3] See e.g. Max Black in *Models and Metaphors*; Mary Hesse, *Models and Analogies in Science*. See also the work of Hans Blumenberg on cultural metaphors accompanying and shaping the emergence of modern natural sciences (*Paradigmen zu einer Metaphorologie; Die Lesbarkeit der Welt*).

[4] But this verdict may be no more than a reflection of my inability to 'translate' the technical language of contemporary psychology and computing sufficiently to apply it to the Mishnaic material.

[5] Cf. Black, 'Models and Archetypes', in his *Models and Metaphors*, 219–43 ('use of a dominating system of concepts to describe a new realm of application by analogical extension', p. 240). Stimulating is Holyoak and Thagard, *Mental Leaps*, where 'isomorphic' analogies are treated pp. 28 ff. and 56 ff.; examples from the history of science are given pp. 185–97; a quick orientation is offered by Edge, 'Metaphor in Science' and Bhaskar, 'Models'.

[6] λόγων ὁμοιότης, rendered as 'resemblance of ratios' in Whately, *Elements of Rhetoric*, 81. Cf. Perelman, *The New Rhetoric and the Humanities*, 91 ff.: 'The typical schema of the analogy is the affirmation that A is to B as C is to D.' For the Aristotelian example Perelman uses (pp. 92 f.), see presently. Cf. also Gentner, 'The Mechanisms of Analogical Learning', 199–241 (analogical reasoning concerns relations or 'structure-mapping', not attributes or similarity of features).

[7] *Poetics* 1457b 7 ff. Analogy and metaphor are terms often used interchangeably (see the examples used throughout Vosniadou and Ortony (eds.), *Similarity and Analogical Reasoning*). Cf. also Gentner, 'Mechanisms', 235, n. 12. Similes in the explicit format of 'equality of relationships' are found often in certain types of poetic language ('They love not poison that do poison need | Nor do I thee . . .', Shakespeare, *Richard II*, v. vi).

not central to the analogical resources of the Mishnah, although it does occur (see below, Analogy3.5).

A second notion of what is now called analogy is also found in Aristotle, although he uses the word παράδειγμα, 'example', for it.[8] This is an inference which starts with an individual instance, case, or object and transfers one of its features to a second individual instance, case, or object. Aristotle thinks that this presupposes a tacit generalization,[9] and classes it as a kind of induction. Somewhat aligned with the difference between these two types of analogy is another difference: that between analogies comparing objects that are heterogeneous or 'domain-incongruent', and those comparing objects that are homogeneous or identical in some respect. Some researchers would exclude close similarity, such as in the following example, from the realm of analogy: 'This '82 Buick is like this '83 Buick: you can use it to drive across town.'[10] Our Mishnaic cases of analogical reasoning tend to be very much like this,[11] for they transfer information between two items that are considered to be very similar or identical in some respect. Here is another example: in order to ascertain if a video casette with the visible tape wholly on the left hand side is rewound or at the end of the tape, I look at one which I remember rewinding yesterday: since it has the tape on the left, I know that the other tape is also at the beginning.

Mishnaic analogies without Scriptural wording tend to start from an assumption that two subjects fall in the *same* category with regard to some halakhic feature, so that a different halakhic feature can be transferred from one to the other. And although the hermeneutic analogies of the Mishnah

---

[8] *Prior Analytics*, 68b38ff (bk. ii, ch. 24), where he says that it is a relation from part (of a whole) to part (of the same whole); *Rhetoric* 1393a22–1394a18 (bk. ii, ch. 20). See Lloyd, *Polarity and Analogy*, 407–13, 418. Cf. also the distinction in Holyoak and Thagard, *Mental Leaps*, 43, between objects-sameness and relations-sameness.

[9] Davies, 'Criteria for Generalization', provides an attempt to formalize this generalization (without reference to Aristotle); his hypothesis is that 'the criteria for reasoning by analogy can be identified with those for the induction of a rule from one example' (p. 229).

[10] Used in Gentner, 'Mechanisms', 220. She comments: 'By Holyoak's criterion this is an analogy, because a specific goal is under consideration; yet to my ear the two Buicks are literally similar whether or not a goal is involved' (cf. Holyoak and Thagard, *Mental Leaps*). Davies, 'Criteria for Generalization', takes *common properties* as the starting-point of analogy (pp. 228 f.). Cf. Perelman, *New Rhetoric and the Humanities*, 92 f., on the uses of heterogeneity in the 'equality of relations' analogy. Vosniadou, 'Analogical Reasoning in Knowledge Acquisition', 414–17, speaks of the difference between 'within-domain' analogies and 'between-domain' analogies. A pragmatic approach is taken by Walton, *Informal Logic*, 256–60, dealing mostly with subjects that are essentially alike. Important is Turner's pragmatic definition ('Categories and Analogies', 5): 'analogy makes a bid to establish or influence category structures', i.e. the habits of categorical ordering. I think this is a very fruitful way to look at the arguments from analogy presented in the Mishnaic discourse. Cf. Jackson's point that 'classification . . . involves the making of analogical claims' ('On the Nature of Analogical Argument in Early Jewish Law', 162), and Neusner's explanation of the 'logic' of Mishnaic *Listenwissenschaft* in terms of 'the logic of analogy and contrast' ('The Mishnah's Generative Mode of Thought', 319).

[11] Except that they are obligation-oriented instead of being goal-oriented. An important difference, but one that affects the whole of the Mishnaic discourse, not merely its analogical reasoning.

do not start from such an assumption alone, shared normative classification still seems to play an important subsidiary role in them.[12] It may be useful to illustrate some of these conceptual issues by first looking at an
analogy which works without recourse to Scriptural wording (Analogy0):

[65] mZeb 1:1[13]   [cf. Lev. 5:14 and 4:2; 7:7]

All animal offerings that were slaughtered not under their proper [offering's] name
are valid—except that [in the case of an offering of the individual] they do not count
towards [the fulfilment of] their owner's obligation—apart from the passover and
apart from the sin offering. The passover in its [proper] time, and the sin offering at
any time. R. Eliezer says: The guilt offering also. [Therefore: apart from] the
passover in its time and the sin offering and the guilt offering at any time. R. Eliezer
said: The sin offering comes for sin (חטא), and the guilt offering comes for sin. As the
sin offering is invalid if it is not [offered] under its name, so the guilt offering is
invalid if it is not [offered] under its name.

Eliezer's argument does not seem to be an analogy qua equality of relationships. If one tries to express it in a manner which conforms to the schema of
ratios, one obtains not four independent terms, but only three. The feature
'invalid if offered under the wrong name' is transferred from the sin offering to the guilt offering because *both* are brought for 'sin'. In other words,
the observation on which the transfer is based is a statement of shared class
membership: both guilt offerings and sin offerings belong to the class of
offerings brought for sin. It is a native halakhic category that is shared, not
some secondary, or ad hoc, or extrinsic class feature.[14] That makes it like the
comparison of an '82 Buick with an '83 Buick cited above. One might continue from this observation of shared class membership as follows: *and
since the case of the sin offering suggests that all offerings for sin are invalidated by
using the wrong name*, the guilt offering too is invalidated by the wrong
name. This seems to do the argument justice, except of course that the
Mishnah does not spell out the generalization articulated in the last sentence, and marked by the use of italics. As in the case of 'point 3' of the
a fortiori inference, we cannot transform the argument into a 'complete'[15]

---

[12] Cf. the distinction between Analogy2 and Analogy2.1 made below.

[13] •¶A0; cf. mSheq 6:6 I (2); mYad 4:2.

[14] Cf. the discussion in mYad 4:3 (involving a transfer between countries which share membership
in the class 'outside Israel'). Cf. also mShebu 3:1.

[15] The word 'enthymeme' is traditionally used for an incomplete logical argument in the sense
that some of the premisses necessary for the conclusion are not explicitly stated. However, this is
presumably strictly true only for arguments which are amenable to a transposition into the
'premisses–conclusion' format. Even where this holds true, problems of interpretation arise that are
by no means trivial. Cf. Walton, *Informal Logic*, 115. He also rejects the idea that, in order to be valid,
the analogy has to be based on an induction (pp. 258 f.); cf. Holyoak and Thagard, *Mental Leaps*, 154.
Outside certain types of theoretical or scientific discourse, analogies might best be treated as communicative forms whose potential cannot necessarily be taken into full view even by its author.
I may well propose the following analogy; but can I exhaust its meaning *in one go*? The relationship
of a person to a sacred text defining his/her culture is like the relationship of an animal to its eco-
logical niche' (one aspect of this topic is treated by Patzig, *Tatsachen, Normen, Sätze*, 35–9). One final
example: 'But thought's the slave of life, and life time's fool' (Shakespeare, *1 Henry IV*, v. iv).

one without supplementing information not explicit in the Mishnah.[16] The Mishnaic co-text actually shows that '. . . all offerings *by the individual* for sin are invalidated . . .' might be a more accurate generalization—if the distinction between individual and communal offerings is relevant to the position defined by the name 'Eliezer'. In order to find the range of appropriate generalizations one would need to think through all the connected halakhic and conceptual issues, and not just from the perspective of the anonymous Mishnah, but also from that of the voice speaking at this point in the text ('Eliezer'). It is thus clear that the information available from the Mishnaic text in most cases could not wholly determine the outcome of such a transformation of the logic of the argument.

To sum up, in **[65]** there is an analogy whose two subjects are taken to be similar to each other, and no 'equality of relationships' is proposed. Further, the analogy appears to transfer a feature between two subjects (of similar generality) on the basis of a tacit generalization involving a second, shared, feature. If one distributes the elements of the operation to a five-point schema, one gets the following for **[65]**:[17]

1. subject n,[18] subject m;[19]
2. n is known to have the two (normative) predicates B and A (that is, n belongs to the classes B and A);
3. tacit generalization from n: not only n, but every subject that has B also has A;[20]
4. subject m is known to have predicate B;
5. *therefore, subject* m *also has predicate A.*

Here are the items for **[65]** *in concreto*:

1. subject *sin offering*, subject *guilt offering*;
2. the *sin offering* is known to have the two (normative) predicates 'coming for sin' and 'invalidated if offered under another name';
3. tacit generalization from the *sin-offering's* case: not only *sin offering*, but every offering coming for sin is invalidated if offered under another name;

---

[16] This Aristotelian idea persists in research into analogical reasoning. Thus Johnson-Laird ('Analogy', 323) uses it when presenting a step-by-step analysis of the following 'analogy' (!): 'The Westland helicopters affair has transformed Mrs. Thatcher into the Richard Nixon of British politics.' The third step is explicated as follows: 'The information that is retrieved must then be given a *superordinate characterization*. The Westland affair can thus be characterized: "A politican commits a misdemeanor and then attempts to cover it up"' (emphasis mine).

[17] Walton's much less cluttered (and less specific) schema for an argument from analogy can be gleaned from the following example: 'The right thing to do in S1 was to carry out A. S2 is similar to S1. Therefore, the right thing to do in S2 is to carry out A.', with S standing for 'situation' and A standing for 'action' (*Informal Logic*, 257).

[18] The subject of the analogy which is the tributary element, the so-called 'phoros'.

[19] The subject which is the receiving element, traditionally called 'theme'.

[20] Put differently: n is merely an *example* of the coincidence of predicates B and A. Cf. Aristotle's above-mentioned use of the word παράδειγμα for the analogy.

4. subject *guilt offering* is known to be 'coming for sin';
5. *therefore, subject* guilt offering *also is invalidated if offered under another name.*

Three points seem characteristic of this kind of analogy. The first two I have already noted: (a) the two subjects are not heterogeneous but are members of the same class, and (b) what is transferred is not a relation or a feature that needs transposition into another concept, but a normative class membership. The third is that (c) since the subjects *m* and *n* share a whole raft of legal features, there seems to be no wide choice of potential *n* subjects of the same degree of similarity. The *n* subject is thus not used to *illustrate* a general link between two features; it could not be added to, or easily replaced by, other illustrations equally as apt. Instead it is intrinsically and substantively connected to *m*. Compare with this the following—Aristotelian—example of an analogy:

Choosing a statesman by ballot is analogous to determining by ballot who is the best athlete.

The choice of subject *n* (the athlete) in the analogy is to some extent arbitrary for the author of the analogy; other analogies making the same point are easily found and Aristotle envisages a plurality of them in rhetorical support of the same opinion.[21] Basically, only rhetorical adequacy or factors of economy limit the *number* of analogies (or metaphors) that could be adduced in making the same point. But there seems to be no comparable dimension of choice or open-endedness in our Mishnaic analogy concerning the subjects 'sin offering' and 'guilt offering', and the legal categories into which they fall. To speak in terms of an analogy: the sin offering is to the guilt offering as the '82 Buick is to the '83 Buick. Again, the feature which is transferred from *n* to *m*: ('invalidated if offered under another name') is not modified or transposed in any way in order to be applicable to the new subject. It is a legal category, or an *apodosis*, which remains rigidly unchanged whether applied to the guilt offering or the sin offering. As a legal category, it is literally the same for both types of offerings, and the concepts it presupposes are not more 'at home' with the sin offering than with the guilt offering.

Consider now the format of **[65]**. Two parallel clauses are combined in a complex sentence (of paratactic structure), asserting the same feature (predicate B) of the two subjects appearing in the different norms: בא החטאת בא החטאת על חטא והאשם בא על חטא. This is followed by another complex sentence with the structure 'just as . . . so also' (. . . מה חטאת . . . אף האשם), which assigns an apodosis clause (invalidity in case of wrong name) to the first norm's

---

[21] *Rhetoric* 1393b (bk. ii, ch. 20). Aristotle himself gives not just one but two analogies for the above argument, the second being the election of a ship's captain by vote among the crew members. Walton rejects the idea that analogies are necessarily open to a multiple example structure, *Informal Logic*, 258.

protasis by way of summarizing known information, and then assigns the same apodosis to the second norm's protasis by way of inference.

It is useful to examine the relationship of this analogy to Scripture. Apart from the sacrificial terminology itself, which Scriptural and Mishnaic discourse share, there is no sign of recourse to Scriptural wording. But Scriptural passages could have been used fairly easily, and in two interestingly different ways. The identification of the point of similarity between the two types of offerings could have been supported by quotation of Lev. 5:14 and 4:2, where they are each mentioned in conjunction with the word 'sin' (אשם). The similarity itself, on the other hand, could have been supported by a quotation used in Cotext1 fashion:[22] Lev. 7:7 places the two types of offerings on an equal footing, although with specific regard to the dues to the priest. And use of Lev. 7:7 would have changed the nature of the argument, in the manner I shall explain presently. But it is clear that the Mishnah assigns no function to Scriptural wording whatever, unless one identifies as two instances of Scripture *use* the Mishnaic words 'sin' (π of Lev. 5:14) and 'sin' (π of Lev. 4:2).[23] As it is, Eliezer's analogy is based on the (normative) facts of the matter, treated as shared knowledge.

If one now examines what is different when Scriptural wording forms the basis of the analogy, one finds that what is called 'predicate B' in the five-point schema above is replaced as the pivot of the argument by some co-textual relationship between the subjects *n* and *m*. The two subjects are *textually* constituted in some way, and the resources which achieve this and endow the textual relationship with meaning are independent from the analogy itself. They are accordingly identified separately, for example, as Cotext5 or Extension9, in the hermeneutic operation's code.

[66] mHul 8:4 II (3)[24]   Deut. 14:21

R. Yose Ha-Gelili says: It is said, 'You shall not eat any carrion', and it is said, 'You shall not cook the kid in the milk of its mother'—that which is forbidden because of 'carrion' is [also] forbidden to cook in milk.

This statement is presented as a response to R. Aqiva and concerns the status of wild animals and birds with regard to the prohibition to cook the young in the mother's milk. The position taken by Yose leads in principle to the inclusion of these two categories, which are subject to the law of carrion.[25] He transfers the feature 'forbidden to cook in milk' from the sentence which actually contains this prohibition to the sentence which contains a different prohibition entirely. It is clear that no substantive link

---

[22] Which is what happens in mZeb 8:11, where Lev. 7:7 is used to support the view that the restrictions concerning the sprinkling of blood which apply to the sin offering also apply to the guilt offering (R. Eliezer).
[23] One would expect some signal of this in the case of a common biblical word (e.g. adaptation of a slightly larger biblical segment to allow identification of the two relevant verses).
[24] •¶πA2.1C6 (¬O1).
[25] For birds this consequence is subsequently rejected, see case [89] in Ch. 10.

can be the reason for this, the two normative themes being quite incompatible. However, they appear in consecutive sentences (part of the same verse in the Masoretic division) and share the same apodictic format.[26] This then, must provide the basis for the transfer: that they form each other's co-text,[27] and perhaps also that they share a common format. The interpreter selects a feature to be transferred between the two, and the *direction* of the transfer: in our case, from the subject mentioned in first place to the one mentioned second. The rabbinic term *semukhin*, in some of its uses, may apply to such a resource.[28]

It may be useful to attempt some overview presentation of the terms and relationships. I shall represent the two terms as carrying each other as an index (indicating the analogical comparison), the textual proximity as a double arrow, and the feature to be transferred in square brackets:

$$\text{no carrion}_{(\text{no kid in milk})}: \text{animal class X} \Longleftrightarrow \text{no kid in milk}_{(\text{no carrion})[\text{animal class X}]}$$

In order to illustrate the difference, the non-Scriptural analogy of [65] can be represented in a similar way, replacing the arrow which indicates co-textual relationship with a similar one indicating substantive similarity or identity. The indices are the two subjects of the analogy.

$$\text{sin}_{(\text{sin offering})}: \text{invalidated by wrong name} \longleftrightarrow \text{sin}_{(\text{guilt offering})[\text{invalidated by wrong name}]}$$

Although other Mishnaic interpretations identify subjects for analogy which belong to the same case schema, and are therefore substantively connected, case [66] shows that the co-textual analogy works even in the absence of such substantive connections.[29] This marks a decisive difference to the non-hermeneutic analogy also found in the Mishnah. Clearly, in [66] no attempt is made to point to a substantive connection between the subjects, apart from the neighbourhood of signs representing them. There is no generalization of substantive features that could be articulated, even by way of speculation, on the basis of such a relationship. The interpretation spells out what is taken to be implied in the textual proximity,[30] not implied in some analogical structure of the subjects considered apart from the textual position in which their names appear. It is like saying: 'This Martin Jones here in the telephone book is like our grocer Matt Jones listed next to him in the book: we can infer that one can buy fruit from him.' And yet it is clear from a measure of terminological overlap that the Mishnaic

---

[26] The verse runs: 'You shall not eat any carrion; to the sojourner who is in your gates you shall give it and he shall eat it, or sell it to the foreigner, for you are a holy people to the Lord your God. You shall not cook the kid in the milk of its mother.'

[27] See Ch. 2 on the resources Cotext5, Cotext6 which utilize co-textual proximity.

[28] See Mielziner, *Introduction*, 177 f. (the legal 'juxtaposition'). Cf. Ch. 2, text to n. 51.

[29] The Analogy2.1 resource shares this feature with the *gezerah shawah*. See below on Keying2/3.

[30] The shared format, although perhaps of subsidiary importance, cannot explain the selection of these two verses from all the many other biblical verses in the same format.

authors saw a link between analogy without Scripture and transfers on the basis of semiotic constitution such as [66],[31] [67], and [68]. This can only be explained if some items in the Mishnah's universe of discourse were thought to be affected in their very constitution or definition by their representation in the Scriptural text. Under such an assumption, textual proximity ceases to be extraneous to the subjects referred to. From this angle the transfer of features on the basis of textual position becomes indeed a special type of analogy.[32]

Since [66] is the only Mishnaic example of a hermeneutic analogy which *must* be taken to rely on co-textual proximity alone, it may be useful to keep it separate from the more common resource in which other linguistic features, such as semantic overlap or similar syntactic position, may contribute to the basis of the inference. The more comprehensive ANALOGY resource could be defined as:

Analogy2: Selection and transfer of a substantive feature between two subjects defined as related on the basis of the textual proximity of their biblical representations, with Scripture also providing a shared or parallel linguistic treatment for them.

The same resource, where it relies on proximity alone, may be defined as follows (the asterisk indicates the presence of only one certain Mishnaic example):

*Analogy2.1: Selection and transfer of a substantive feature between two subjects defined as related on the basis of the textual proximity of their biblical representations.[33]

Analogy2 as defined above is often referred to by the name *heqqesh* in the literature.[34] As far as the Mishnah is concerned, this terminological choice lacks good support; there is one, doubtful, case of Analogy2 involving the infinitive להקיש, mMak 1:7 I (6);[35] the other three occurrences of להקיש in hermeneutic contexts belong to Analogy8 (see below).

Let us now look at some examples for Analogy2, that is, textual

---

[31] It must be said that [66] itself does not exhibit any terminology typical for the analogy (e.g. the ... מה ... אף ... format). However, there is no one, stereotyped way to present analogy in the Mishnah in any case.

[32] I shall explore the implications of this in the final section of this chapter. Cf. Jackson's hypothesis that 'the justification of the choice of comparanda lies within some conception of the uniqueness of the canonical text, a uniqueness deriving from the perfection of the Torah as the product of divine, rather than human, draftsmanship' ('On the Nature of the Analogical Argument in Early Jewish Law', 137).

[33] Mielziner defines the so-called *semukhin* in the following way: 'A peculiar kind of analogy which has some similarity to *Heckesh* . . . is that called סמכין, *contiguous passages*, or the *analogy* made from the *juxtaposition* of two laws in Scripture' (*Introduction*, 176). See Ch. 2 above and resource Cotext5 for 'another kind of סמכין' distinguished by Mielziner (*Introduction*, 178 f.).

[34] See e.g. Mielziner, *Introduction*, 152 ff.; Bacher, i. 44 ff. Bacher also draws attention to the fact that the nominal form ('heqqesh') is not found in tannaitic sources.

[35] This *mishnah* can be interpreted as either using Analogy2 or Analogy8; only a larger corpus with a regular distribution of להקיש could settle this question.

proximity combined with shared or parallel linguistic treatment. The latter usually indicates substantive similarities of some sort. That substantive shared features are thus also caught in the net of a procedure which starts from co-textual relationships alone is of course not surprising: Scripture is a book that is to some extent *thematically* organized.

[67] mSan 1:4 II (2)[36]   Exod. 21:29

The ox that is to be stoned [that killed a person], [is judged] by twenty-three [judges], as it is said, 'The ox shall be stoned and its owner also shall be put to death'—in the same manner in which the owners are put to death [that is, after sentencing by twenty-three judges] is the ox put to death.

Here we have a parallel structure in the two halves of a biblical sentence, including a lexeme indicating similarity (גם, 'also'). However, the feature that is being transferred is not selected by the grammar of the sentence but by the reader, and so is the directionality of the transfer: from the second subject (the more general 'be put to death', said of the man) to the first ('be stoned', said of the ox). Here is a schematic representation:

$$\text{owner}_{(ox)}: \text{by } 23 \Longleftarrow\Longrightarrow \text{ox}_{(owner)[by\ 23]}$$

This passage should be seen in conjunction with the one that precedes it:

[68] mSan 1:4 I (2)[37]   Lev. 20:16; 20:15

Cases involving capital punishment [are judged] by twenty-three [judges]. The beast that commits or suffers human connection [is judged] by twenty-three [judges], as it is said, '[And the woman who approaches any beast to lie with it,] you shall kill the woman and the beast; [they shall be put to death . . .]' (Lev. 20:16), and it says, '[And the man who gives his copulation to a beast shall surely die] and the beast you shall kill' (Lev. 20:15).

The first verse quoted establishes that the beast committing a sexual act with a human is to be killed, the second shows the same for the animal that suffers an act. In both cases the verses place in parallel the execution of the human and that of the animal. Furthermore, the word used with regard to the woman ('kill') is the same as that used with regard to the animal in the other verse, although it is not clear if that plays a role in the hermeneutic argument. This produces the linguistic as well as substantive basis for the transfer of a feature which is quite absent from the biblical text: namely, the constitution of the court by twenty-three judges, here as in **[67]** brought into play as an unproblematic item of rabbinic information (Topic3.1). In both verses, the directionality of the transfer is from the second term to the first: from the human participants, mentioned first, to the animal. For the animal committing the act, the schema for **[68]** looks like this:

---

³⁶ ℞≈A2C1T3.1.   ³⁷ Twice: ≈A2T3.1.

$$\text{woman}_{(\text{beast})}: \text{by } 23 \Longleftrightarrow \text{beast}_{(\text{woman})}[\text{by } 23]$$

In [67] and [68] the hermeneutic analogy is based on co-textually parallel structures. Viewed from the point of necessary information, this textual configuration might be called *redundant*. The biblical passages treated in [68] are fairly explicit and repetitive in their provisions, while the biblical quotation in [67] stands in some tension to the subsequent verse which allows for payment of ransom, as well as to rabbinic halakhah which does not allow for the owner of the ox to be executed.[38] In a way in which [66] does not, these two cases then provide for the possibility that the co-textual elements render each other in some way redundant, either by being repetitions, or even by being inconsistent. I shall return to the questions of redundancy and conspicuousness later.[39]

What exactly is different when Scripture is involved in the analogy? We still have two subjects, *n* and *m*; we still have a feature A which is known of *n* and transferred to *m* (for example, 'judged by twenty-three judges'). But how exactly are points 2 and 3 in the five-point schema to be construed now? Or have they disappeared? The suggestion that follows here is structured as far as possible in parallel to the non-Scriptural analogy so as to show how different the two actually are.

1. Subject *n*, subject *m*;
2. *n* is known to have predicate A;
3. at least in some Scriptural locations, an A-suitable subject is placed in *n*'s co-text to show that it also partakes in predicate A;
4. *m* is an A-suitable subject and appears in *n*'s co-text in Scripture;
5. *therefore, subject m may be meant to have predicate A.*

The problem here is, of course, that one cannot generalize point 3 without doing an injustice to the rabbinic approach to Scripture. There is no rigid rule in Mishnaic hermeneutics that *any* A-suitable subject placed in *n*'s co-text is meant to partake in predicate A. Rather, there are other, extra-textual factors which make it likely or certain for the rabbinic reader that the co-textual relationship implies shared features for some subjects (but not others).[40] This has the consequence that point 5 cannot be formulated as a universal conclusion; it does not necessarily *follow* from the first four points in the sense in which a conclusion follows from its premises. The format

[38] Cf. Chajes, *The Student's Guide Through the Talmud*, 6, 12; cf. bSan 15b. See, however, Geiger, *Urschrift*, 448–50, and Krauß, *Sanhedrin-Makkot*, 75, who assume that this *mishnah* does indeed imply that the owner is also executed.
[39] For a rather one-sided view of the link between redundancy and the analogy, see Schwarz, 'Hauptergebnisse', 4 f. Schwarz claims that the later rabbinic insistence on biblical redundancy for the application of this resource marks a regression in the development of the resource; for him, maxims restricting the application of hermeneutic techniques generally indicate a demise in the logical competence of the rabbis.
[40] Cf. my explanation of why the terms 'method' or 'rule' are inappropriate, in Ch. 1 (text preceding n. 33).

premiss–conclusion of ordinary (non-deontic) logic is inapplicable, since we are dealing with rules whose application depends on contexts and goals. The five-point schema is therefore inapplicable to Analogy2. Another important point emerges from the above. The author of an analogy who is engaged in persuasive discourse may highlight, in order to prepare the transfer of another feature, the similarity between m and n. But the author's freedom to select is here replaced by a given fact of textual relationship. The basis of the transfer thus becomes *another voice's* responsibility, namely, Scripture's. Not only does textual proximity take the place of a known substantive similarity between the two subjects, as we said above. We do not have an *argument* from analogy any more, although we still have something that can be called analogy. Insofar as the proximity of Scriptural terms self-selects the subjects of the analogy (as in Analogy2.1), there is no construction of a persuasive argument. The interpreter of Scripture is not the creator of the analogy, because he is not responsible for finding that subject n (in the above scheme) which supports the view that the subject m has indeed feature A.[41] And Scripture, which *does* determine (through placing in proximity) which subjects stand in an 'analogical' relationship, does not guess or persuade. For the rabbinic reader it speaks from a position of knowledge, not of inference. It would be difficult to say that Scripture is taken to *argue* for the accuracy or validity of a certain position. If there is a disagreement, it is not about the properties or features of subjects m and n, that is, the suitability of the analogy; but about the textual features which are said to convey the analogy: are they correctly interpreted as analogy, and if so, is the point of the analogy correctly identified? This distinguishes hermeneutic analogies from the non-Scriptural analogy in the Mishnah (case **[65]**) on the one hand, and on the other from the *a fortiori* argument.

It may be useful to summarize the results of my analysis of Analogy2. (a) The two subjects need not be heterogeneous but may be closely related; (b) the transferred feature may be a substantive category, equally germane to both subjects; (c) in the Scriptural basis of the analogy the defining moment is the textual relationship of the two subjects; that is, the substantive relationship mentioned in (a) is not necessary as the basis of the analogy and need not be highlighted or rephrased separately; (d) Scripture contains the two subjects and some textual trace of their analogical status, but not the feature to be transferred, nor need the feature be indicated in any way; (e) the sequence of subjects in the Scriptural text need not be taken to determine the directionality of the transfer from the one to the other; (f) the argument from co-textual position as implying analogy is not in itself analogical; (g) analogies contained in Scripture are strictly informative,

---

[41] As in the following argument: 'What makes you think that we can use a '83 Buick to drive across town?' 'Because it is like a '82 Buick which we used before for that purpose' (on the Buick analogy, see above).

not probative: while their correct interpretation may be in question, the validity of the information does not depend on an *argument* from analogy; (h) Scripture is taken to define some substantive features through textual structures alone, that is, in ways that are distinct from the meaning of its words.

In addition to Mishnaic analogies whose subjects are drawn from co-textual relationships, we find analogical transfers based on the explicit mention in Scripture of some similarity of subjects. Occasionally these are biblical metaphors or comparisons. Their interpretation may result in a transposition to partial *identity*. Where Scripture likens the two subjects to each other in some unspecified manner or as irreducible wholes, they may be taken to be *the same* in a defined respect. Such an interpretation I shall label Extension9.[42] On the basis of such partial identity, another feature may be transferred between the two subjects in a manner not very different from Analogy2. I shall call this transfer Analogy3. Where the biblical formulations which form the basis of Analogy3 draw on the figurative potential of the terms compared,[43] the *analogical* reading of such comparisons also has the effect of endowing biblical metaphors with their literal sense (which is a resource related to lexemes, Word6.1).[44] The following passage is an example of the combination of Analogy3, Extension9, and Word6.1:

[69] mShab 9:1 = mAZ 3:6 II (2)[45]   Isa. 30:22

R. Aqiva said: Whence [do we know] of an idol that it conveys uncleanness by carrying like a woman menstruating (כנדה)? Because it is said, '[And you will defile your silver-covered graven images and your gold-plated molten images;] you will scatter them like a menstruous thing (כמו דוה), [you will say to it: Go forth]'. As a woman menstruating conveys uncleanness by carrying so an idol conveys uncleanness by carrying.

The type of analogical transfer accomplished here can perhaps be captured by the following resource definition:

Analogy3: Selection and transfer of a substantive feature between two subjects linked by a biblical expression of a common feature, comparison, or metaphorical similarity.

Insofar as this means that a biblical comparison or simile is taken as implying specific and non-figurative similarity, it may be useful to define separately a further resource here, whose home is the EXTENSION family:

Extension9: Interpretation of a biblical comparison, simile, or metaphor as implying a substantive and specific similarity or shared class membership

---

[42] Defined presently. More on this resource is found in my discussion of passage [129] in Ch. 13.

[43] A clear instance of the analogical treatment of the literal meaning of a biblical metaphor is mAZ 3:6 I (2): idolatrous objects (Deut. 7:26) are placed in the same technical category as creeping things for their ability to convey uncleanness. This *mishnah* forms the co-text of passage [69], quoted presently.   [44] See Ch. 14.

[45] ®•¶C1≈A3E9T1T3.

between the two subjects; this similarity is thus incompatible with a purely illustrative or stylistic purpose of the biblical construction.

There are also in the Mishnah examples for the analogy which compares relationships ('ratios'), for which I used above the Aristotelian illustration of old age as the evening of life. The following passage, in accounting for what is taken to be a biblical comparison, produces something like an analogy of relations. As it happens, it also involves the idea of the day:

[70a] mSan 10:3 IX (10)[46]   Deut. 29:27 (E 28)

The Ten Tribes shall not return again, for it is said, '[Therefore the Lord uprooted them from their ground in anger and fury and great wrath] and he cast them into another land like this day'. As 'this day' goes and returns not, so they go and return not—these are the words of R. Aqiva.

The particle כ in כיום ('like this day') is unlikely to be one of comparison in the biblical co-text,[47] but is taken as such by Aqiva (resource Word1.2) and here translated accordingly. The Mishnaic explication of a selected *tertium comparationis* can be presented, after some considerable transposition, in form of the schema, 'A is to B as C is to D':

As return is to the expulsion of the ten tribes, so reversibility is to the day: as reversibility is impossible for a day that has passed, so return is impossible for the expelled tribes.

The Mishnah also gives a second view, using the same comparison to achieve the opposite Dictum, but also based on an analogical explication of the comparison:

[70b] mSan 10:3 X (10)[48]   Deut. 29:27 (E 28)

R. Eliezer says: As the day darkens and [then] lightens, so the ten tribes, as darkness fell on them, so light will shine upon them.

Here is Eliezer's explication recast as an equality of relationships:

As expulsion is to the ten tribes, so darkness is to the day: as the darkness of the day is followed by the light of the day, so the expulsion of the tribes is followed by their return.

It may be noted in passing that this interpretation takes for granted that night-time precedes daytime (Topic3.1); the Greek idea of the day (embodied in the metaphor of old age as the *evening* of life) could not be used for this explication.[49]

---

[46] ≈•¶A3.5C5E9O8(R2.1)T3T3.1W1.2.

[47] Its meaning being rather 'at this day', 'as today'; cf. BDB, 453b, 454b, 400b ('as it is at this day'); cf. Clines, iv. 347 f.

[48] ≈•¶A3.5C5E9T3T3.1W1.2.

[49] Fraenkel (*Darkhey*, i. 217 ff.) suggests there is a common cross-cultural fund of metaphors on which the rabbinic interpreters draw; but he opens his account with the Aristotelian example of old age as the evening of life.

I allocate a separate resource code to the employment of an analogy of this type, designating the second digit 5 to mark the equality of relations for any of the types of analogy distinguished up to here. Cases **[70a]** and **[70b]** are thus evidence for the resource Analogy3.5: equality of relations (Analogy*.5) based on the presence of biblical comparison (Analogy3). By reserving the second digit '5' for 'equality of relations', I prepare for the possibility of additional resources such as Analogy2.5 existing outside the Mishnah. The following 'infix' text is used to specify that an ANALOGY resource (with the exception of Analogy4/5) works as an equality of relations:

Analogy*.5: Selection and transfer, *on the basis of an equality of relationships*, ...

Here is the corresponding version of Analogy3, which explains passages **[70a]** and **[70b]**:

Analogy3.5: Selection and transfer, on the basis of an equality of relationships, of a substantive feature between two subjects linked by a biblical expression of a common feature, comparison, or metaphorical relationship.

At this point a further type of analogy needs to be addressed, in which only one of the two subjects comes from Scripture, while the other is supplied by the reader. The subject supplied is usually a case schema (i.e. Topic2), and the Scriptural subject is taken to provide, by analogy, the apodosis for the Mishnaic case schema. I define the resource in the following way:

Analogy1: Selection of a situational or substantive similarity (or dissimilarity) between a biblical subject and a non-biblical subject (in particular Topic2) in order to determine the apodosis of a Mishnaic protasis–apodosis unit.

In the following case, the type of Analogy1 used is that of *relationships* defined as above, i.e. an Analogy1.5:

[71] mAZ 3:5 I (2)[50]   Deut. 7:25

If the gentiles worship mountains and hills—these are permitted, but what is upon them is forbidden, as it is said, 'You shall not covet the silver and gold upon them (עליהם) and take it for yourself, lest you be ensnared by it'.

What is the object 'upon' which the gold and silver are found in the biblical text? It is mentioned in the first half of the verse, 'The carved images (פסילי) of their gods you shall burn with fire . . .'. The gold and silver *upon* the carved objects is what Scripture speaks of here; the Mishnah therefore transfers the relation of 'being on' from the gold and silver being 'on'

---

[50] ¶A1.5C1C5O1(upon)T2.

idolatrous objects, to idolatrous objects being 'on' mountains and hills: they, too, should not be coveted or taken (this is the biblical norm, taken as the apodosis of the Mishnaic case schema: Topic2). The analogy takes us only so far, however: for the idolatrous objects upon which the gold and silver are found are prohibited too; while in the case of mountains and hills the prohibition is taken to single out what is *upon*, in contrast to that upon which it is (Opposition1). In a rival interpretation to support the same Dictum following our passage above, R. Yose Ha-Gelili uses the verse Deut. 12:2, which also employs the word 'upon' but actually speaks of mountains. This second interpretation may be quoted precisely because it avoids the need for a somewhat incomplete analogical transfer as in [71].

TRANSFER OF A FEATURE BETWEEN SUBJECTS OF DIVERGENT GENERALITY

Analogical reasoning seems to be involved not only when a feature is transferred between two subjects of the same level of generality, that is, subjects which can be construed as being fellow hyponyms of a common superordinate. The Mishnah also uses Scripture-based analogy to extend a specific normative feature found in a subject of lesser generality to a class of which it is a member. Where the more specific subject, i.e. the hyponym, is taken to represent in some way a whole category, but the larger category is not identified as also being mentioned in Scripture, the mechanisms involved are basically semantic or paradigmatic. They belong to the EXTENSION family of resources and will be discussed in the next chapter. The case where analogical reasoning seems to come into play is where the superordinate (or class) as well as the hyponym is identified as coming from Scripture. Thus, the more general term may appear in the same sentence or norm as the more specific one. Or, two norms appear separately in Scripture which are considered as basically identical except that the one contains the general, the other the specific, expression. In other words, although the presence of the operative terms in each other's co-text is not required (which is essential for Analogy2), it seems still important to the mechanism that they are found in the same text (either the Pentateuch or some larger unit), thus rendering each other partially redundant. Passage [72] is an example of the first type (same sentence or contiguous text), [73] of the second (separated occurrences).

The verse whose wording is presupposed in [72] reads (the specific term is underlined, the generalized expression represented in capitals): 'And so you shall do with his ass; so you shall do with his garment; so you shall do with ANY LOST THING of your brother's, which he loses and you find; you may not withhold your help.' Here is the Mishnaic passage:

[72] mBM 2:5[51]   [Deut. 22:3; cf. Exod. 22:8]

The 'garment' also was included amongst all these things[52] [which must be proclaimed so that their owner can claim them]. Why was it mentioned separately (למה יצאת)? To compare [something else] to it: to teach you that as a particular garment has both special marks and persons that lay claim to it, so everything must be proclaimed which has both special marks and persons that lay claim to it.

The text preceding this unit speaks of items which either need not be returned by the finder, or must be advertised in order that their owner can claim them (that is, the norm contained in Deut. 22:1–3 and Exod. 22:8). Our unit follows on from these lists and gives something of a general rule regarding the type of item falling in either class, but how the rule is related to each of the items mentioned by the Mishnah in the lines leading up to [72] is not obvious. It starts from the observation that, within the same biblical verse, a general expression 'any lost thing' (לכל־אבדת אחיך) is found alongside two specific items, namely, the ass and the garment. Ignoring the case of the ass, the Mishnaic discourse generalizes two features of the 'garment', special marks and a claimant, to the whole class of 'lost thing' (which have to be proclaimed). These two features are not treated as problematical, and they are not derived from this passage. They may well be linked, however, to Exod. 22:8, which deals with items deposited for safekeeping but also mentions 'any lost thing, about which one says: This is it'.[53] It also contains the word 'garment' (spelled שלמה, not שמלה). So, in adding features to the subject of an obligation, the class of lost thing for which a proclamation must be made is narrowed down: from an apparently all-inclusive 'any lost thing', to 'any lost thing that has special marks and a claimant'.

Whether the sequence in which the two terms are mentioned in Scripture—first the more specific, second the more general—plays any role here is not clear. The fifth *middah* in the list ascribed to Ishmael says that if the sequence is *perat ukhelal* (as here), the general form of words 'adds' (מוסיף) something to the meaning of the individual items.[54] I shall deal with a resource of this type later (Extension3, in the next chapter). Without going into the details of what 'adding' means and how this rule is actually employed,[55] it is clear that this is not what happens in [72]. There is, how-

[51] πA8[K2?]O8T1.

[52] אף השמלה היתה בכלל כל אלה.

[53] See on this Epstein, *Mavo*, 1132.

[54] Introduction to Sifra (ed. Finkelstein, 3, 6). Cf. Stemberger, *Introduction*, 19 f.; Bacher, i. 80 Mielziner, *Introduction*, 165 f., who translates the rules as: 'In the case of Particulars and General, the general term adds to the contents of the particulars, and we include everything (belonging to this general)'. Cf. my 'Between Scripture and its Rewording', 47, and resource Extension3 as well as case [79] in Ch. 9 below. Windfuhr (*Baba meßia*, 27) claims that our passage [72] illustrates *perat ukhelal*, which he rephrases as 'Näherbestimmung des Allgemeinen durch das Spezielle' (!).

[55] Mielziner, *Introduction*, 165 f., says that the particulars are, under this rule, regarded 'merely as illustrative examples of that general'. Mielziner, followed by Handelman, *Slayers of Moses*, 226, also speaks of *middah* 8 as being a *modification* of *middah* no. 5. However, the two *middot* seem to me of a quite different nature. Both of these modern authors use our case [72] as illustration of *middah* 8,

ever, another *middah*, number 8, which seems applicable to **[72]**. A literal translation of it runs: 'Every item which was in the general goes forth from the general (that is, is mentioned separately) in order to teach; not in order to teach about itself does it go forth, but to teach about the general as a whole.'[56] The rule does not explicate the textual relationship of the particular and general in Scripture. Presumably they are both in Scripture; are they close to each other, does it matter in which sequence they come?[57] Whatever the precise meaning of this rule, or of the other *middah* mentioned, they certainly constitute evidence for the perception that a norm which receives Scriptural expression on two different levels of generality poses a hermeneutic task, and such evidence is broadly compatible with the resource here discussed. Depending on the actual meaning of *middah* number 8, it could also apply to the next passage, **[73]**.

This Mishnaic unit again deals with the wording of biblical passages that are not actually quoted, similar to case **[72]**. But here the general and particular term are distributed to two different locations in Scripture, in what is *de facto* taken to be a repetition of the same norm. I first quote the relevant verses, thereafter the Mishnaic passage:[58]

> If it is an animal such as men offer as an offering to the Lord, all of such that any man gives to the Lord is holy. He shall not substitute anything for it or exchange it, a good for a bad, or a bad for a good; and if he makes any exchange of beast for beast, then both it and that for which it is exchanged shall be holy. (Lev. 27:9–10)

> And all the tithe of herds and flocks, every tenth animal of all that pass under the herdsman's staff, shall be holy to the Lord. A man shall not inquire whether it is good or bad, neither shall he exchange it; and if he exchanges it, then both it and that for which it is exchanged shall be holy; it shall not be redeemed. (Lev. 27:32–3).

[73] mTem 1:6 III (3)[59]   [Lev. 27:9 f.; 27:33]

> Bird offerings and meal offerings do not create substitutes [for something else], for it is only said, 'cattle'. The congregation and the joint owners cannot create substitutes, as it is said: 'He shall not substitute it'—only an individual can create a substitute, the congregation and the joint owners cannot create a substitute. Offerings for the 'temple upkeep'[60] cannot create substitutes. R. Shim'on said: And was not the

---

while Sifra (ed. Finkelstein, ii. 7) ties the rule to a different illustration. See further, Jackson, 'On the Nature of Analogical Argument in Early Jewish Law', esp. 154 ff.

[56] כל דבר שהיה בכלל ויצא מן הכלל ללמד לא ללמד על עצמו יצא אלא ללמד על הכלל כולו (Sifra, ed. Finkelstein, ii. 4); but already the second formulation in Sifra, tied to the example (ibid. 7), is different from this wording. Mielziner translates a text divergent from both of these: 'When a single case, though already included in a general law, is expressly mentioned, then the provision connected with it, applies to all other cases inlcuded in that general law' (*Introduction*, 170).

[57] Mielziner's other example for illustrating this rule (bSan 67b ad Exod. 22:17 and Lev. 20:27, using the terminology of analogy, להקיש) features two *separate* biblical passages, as well as the mention of the general *preceding* that of the particular. See, however, Jackson, 'On the Nature of Analogical Argument in Early Jewish Law', 156.

[58] The translation is RSV.

[59] (®)•πA8.1O8T3.

[60] The expression בדק הבית, literally 'fissure of the House', is used in rabbinic literature to refer to

'tithe' [of cattle contained] in the general (בכלל) [formulation of the norm in Lev. 27:9 f.]? And why was it mentioned separately (ולמה יצא) [in Lev. 27:33]? To compare [something else] to it: As the tithe [of cattle] is an offering of the individual, the offerings of the congregation [are thereby] excluded, as the tithe [of cattle is an offering] to the altar, the offerings for the 'temple upkeep' [are thereby] excluded.

I am concerned here with the inference by R. Shim'on. It is actually elliptic, possibly because two analogies are proposed at the same time. Here is an expansive paraphrase, restoring the אף-clause ('so . . .') to the argument:

As the tithe of cattle is an offering of the individual, so the whole class of substitutable offerings is restricted to the individual, excluding the congregation; and as the tithe of cattle is an offering to the altar, so the whole class of substitutable offerings is to the altar, thereby excluding the temple upkeep.

We have a similar analogy from the less general to the more general as in [72]: the features that can be 'read off' the case of the tithe of cattle are generalized to the whole class of substitutes—with the effect that the boundaries of that class become narrower or are more sharply defined. This is also what happens to the lost objects requiring proclamation in [72]. However, the two biblical expressions between which the features are transferred are not in each other's immediate textual neighbourhood; they are separated from each other by a considerable number of verses. I shall thus distinguish two versions of this resource: Analogy 8 (for cases such as [72]), and the subtype Analogy8.1 (for [73]).

Analogy8: Transfer of a (substantive) feature from the more specific to the more general of two Scriptural subjects mentioned in norms or statements which are substantively identical or receive a shared or similar linguistic treatment in Scripture, and are textually contiguous.

Analogy8.1: Transfer of a (substantive) feature from the more specific to the more general of two Scriptural subjects mentioned in norms or statements which are substantively identical and receive a similar linguistic treatment in Scripture.

Three formal features are of interest. (a) As it happens, neither of the passages [72] and [73] contains a quotation of the relevant Scriptural passage and none is to be found in their Mishnaic co-text. Knowledge of Scripture is assumed. But it is not some vague awareness of the biblical origin of these norms (of sacrificial substitution, or of the return of lost property) that is presupposed. Rather, the exact wording of the norms is drawn upon, namely, the fact that Scripture 'brings out' (יצא)[61] a certain

---

the monetary fund from which both sacrifices and other expenses of the temple were paid. Its wording derives from 2 Kings 12:8 (cf. Jastrow, 141b). See Mekhilta Ishmael, Pisha 18 (ed. Lauterbach, i. 161 f.) ad Exod. 13:13, where the term is employed in retopicalizing Num. 18:15 (cf. Halivni, *Peshat and Derash*, 62 f.). See Schürer (ed. Vermes *et al.*), *History of the Jewish People in the Age of Jesus Christ*, ii. 270 ff.   [61] Bacher, i. 74, 80, 153.

item, that is, mentions it specifically. This observation on the biblical formulation is encapsulated in the 'why'-question. The specific term is used expressively (π) in the Mishnaic passage; the more general term is neither mentioned nor used, but named as 'the general' (כלל). This shows that even a resource which is concerned specifically with the biblical wording can be applied without a quotation of the Scriptural evidence. (b) The phrasing of the interpretation employs in both examples the infinitive להקיש,[62] 'to compare', which has given analogical operations one of their traditional names, *heqqesh*. The two subjects of the analogy are regularly—although not in [73]—introduced by מה and אף ('just as . . . so . . .'). This is also true for Analogy2. And usually—but here Mishnaic Analogy2 differs—the Analogy8 inference will contain the word כל ('all' or 'every'). (c) Case [73] illustrates the fact that Analogy8 (as well as Analogy2) is often introduced by an explicit hermeneutic question, and the textual feature pinned down by that question is the *redundancy* of the more specific item.[63]

TRANSFER OF CO-TEXTUAL FEATURES BETWEEN TWO OCCURRENCES OF THE SAME LEXEME

The ANALOGY resources discussed hitherto, insofar as they are based on the presence of both subjects in the Scriptural text, depend at least partly on textual contiguity and proximity (Analogy2, Analogy3, and Analogy8), or mainly on a presumed thematic identity of two separated passages (Analogy8.1). By contrast, the next resource to be examined achieves analogical transfer on the basis of textual structures which are in principle independent of thematic overlap as well as of textual proximity. Instead, the link is created by the recurrence of the same lexeme in two different co-texts. The meaning of the term in one co-text is being 'keyed' (or: unlocked) according to the other co-text, in a manner of speaking. I shall refer to this group as KEYING resources. In rabbinic literature this resource is linked to the name *gezerah shawah*,[64] counted among the Seven, Thirteen, and Thirty-two *middot*.[65] The subjects of the ANALOGY resources are represented by

---

[62] As I said above, in mMak 1:7 I (6) the term could be linked to either Analogy2 or Analogy8, while in mBM 2:5, mMen 7:6, and mTem 1:6 III (3), the operations are of the Analogy8 type. See Bacher, i. 44–6, and n. 33 above. The analogy called *heqqesh* ascribed to Hillel in yPes 33a14 is structurally identical with my Analogy0 example, [65] (Bacher, i. 46).

[63] The following Analogy8 passages seem to have this 'why'-question of redundancy: mBM 2:5; mMen 7:6 (where contradiction to another Scriptural segment plays a role); mArak 8:6 III (3) (?); mTem 1:6 III (3); mKer 4:3(?); also mBQ 5:5 I (2), although the item cannot be construed as redundant from the Mishnah's perspective. See also mMak 1:7 I (6).

[64] In the Mishnah the term is used only once in connection with the Keying2 resource, at mArak 4:4 III (3), quoted as [75] below. It occurs in mYT 1:6 applied to an analogy without Scriptural wording (Analogy0). Cf. Faur, *Golden Doves*, 178.

[65] Cf. Lieberman, *Hellenism*, 58 ff.; Bialoblocki, 'Hermeneutik', cols. 1187 ff.; Zeitlin, 'Hillel and the Hermeneutic Rules', esp. 165 ff.; Daube, 'Alexandrian Methods of Interpretation and the Rabbis' and 'Rabbinic Methods of Interpretation and Hellenistic Rhetoric'; Alexander, 'Quid Athenis et

different words but mostly in the same co-text. For the KEYING resources the two subjects are represented by the *same word* occurring in two different co-texts. One of the two co-texts provides the thematic framework for the other, while the analogical feature to be transferred travels in the opposite direction. The feature to be transferred is basically the second co-text's contribution to the meaning of the duplicated lexeme. The following passage will illustrate the procedure.

[74] mSot 6:3 IV (4)[66]   Deut. 24:1; 19:15

There is an inference to be drawn from the less to the more stringent concerning the first testimony from this very fact [that only one witness is necessary]: Just as the last testimony which renders her forbidden for ever, behold, is established by one witness [only], should not the first testimony which does not render her forbidden for ever also be capable of being established by one witness [only]? In this regard it is instructive that Scripture says: 'For he has found in her the indecency of a *matter* [and he writes for her a bill of divorce]', and above (להלן)[67] it says: 'According to two witnesses [or according to three witnesses] shall the *matter* be established'. Just as the 'matter' enunciated above is [established] according to two witnesses, so the 'matter' enunciated here (כאן) is according to two witnesses also.

The first half of this unit contains an *a fortiori* argument. The analogy which follows it is meant to refute that *a fortiori*. The introduction תלמוד לומר ('in this regard it is instructive that Scripture says') makes clear its function as counter-argument.[68] The Mishnaic topic at this point is the halakhah of the wife suspected of adultery (the *Sotah*), and most of its biblical links come from Num. 5:11 ff. Deut. 24:1 is elsewhere in the Mishnah related to the halakhah of divorce and its reasons;[69] this midrashic unit takes the difficult phrase 'indecency in a matter' to include adultery, thus linking this passage to the *Sotah* topic.[70] Deut. 19:15 deals in general with the requirement of two or three witnesses for the prosecution of any sinful act. The link between these two verses from Deuteronomy is established by the occurrence in both of the word 'matter' (דבר). The transfer of the feature 'according to the testimony of two witnesses' is based solely on this textual fact; there is no direct thematic link between the two passages. Deut. 24:1 does not mention

Hierosolymis?'; Mielziner, *Introduction*, 142 ff.; Stemberger, *Introduction*, 18 f.; Jacobs, 'Hermeneutics'; Fraenkel, *Darkhey*, i. 179.

[66] (A2)E1.0K2(O1?)T1.

[67] This discourse deixis points to another passage in Scripture. The English 'above' and 'below' are functionally similar, except that להלן does not indicate the direction. On this term and its counterpart כאן, or כן (in codex Kaufmann, Bietenhard, *Sota*, 106), see Bacher, i. 76 f., 15 f. Jastrow's translation of the pair as 'here' and 'there' (354a) obscures its text-deictic function.

[68] My elaborate rendering of *talmud lomar* is meant to represent its three main discourse functions: taking up a previously mentioned thesis, refuting that thesis by explicit evidence (instruction, taken as correction), and pointing to the fact that this evidence comes in the form of Scriptural wording (saying). Cf. Bacher, i. 200.

[69] As e.g. in mGit 3:2 and mGit 9:10 I–II (3), where the meaning of 'indecency of a matter' becomes thematic without mention of the witness analogy.

[70] This interpretation of the phrase ערות דבר is specifically linked to the House of Shammai in mGit 9:10 I (3).

witnesses (although Num. 5:13 does), and Deut. 19:15 or its co-text are free from any reference to divorce, marriage, sexual behaviour, or even women. Moreover, whatever thematic link may be constructed between the topics of Deut. 24:1 (divorce) and Deut. 19:15 (testimony),[71] it must rest on the topic-defining words 'witness' and 'indecency', and neither of these two themes is semantically connected to or synonymous with the word 'matter'. This means the word 'matter' can *absorb* the topical specificity from its co-text at the one location and *release* it into its second co-text at the other. That, in a metaphorical nutshell, is the nature of the resource. The two locations stand in communication with each other through the presence of the same lexeme: the co-textual topic at location A gives location B its theme; the co-textual specificity determining the recurrent lexeme at location B gives location A the transferrable feature.

To speak about the case at hand: the meaning of the word 'matter', as defined by its use in the phrase 'according to two witnesses . . . shall the matter be established' (Deut. 19:15), could perhaps be summed up as, 'two-witness-proven matter'. This ad hoc definition of the meaning of the word *davar* does not enlarge its lexical meaning; and I do not think that this is what the rabbis would have offered in answer to the question, 'What does the word *davar* mean?'[72] But it is treated *as if* it was part of the semantic range of the word 'matter', in this one respect: that it can travel together with the word itself to a different co-text, the target location. In [74] that target location is Deut. 24:1, and that provides a different thematic focus for the word 'matter': a woman's indecency in a marital relation. The meaning of *davar* as defined by its co-text in Deut. 19:15 travels to Deut. 24:1, as it were on the back of the word *davar* itself. The resulting meaning for Deut. 24:1 is something like this: for he has found in her the indecency of a two-witness-proven matter. The thematic focus of the location Deut. 24:1 (marital indecency) now *surrounds* that of Deut. 19:15 (two witnesses), in the same way in which it surrounds the word 'matter' itself. An alternative

---

[71] It is often easy enough to find *some* link between different areas of halakhah, which is sustained by an organic network of shared concepts. But that is quite different from saying that the biblical text offers non-midrashic evidence for such a link. The interpretation in [74] makes no attempt to understand adultery simply as a member of the general class of transgressions ('any iniquity . . . or wrong'/לכל־עון ולכל־חטאת) dealt with in Deut. 19:15, so that its general provisions simply included the case of adultery.

[72] There is some indirect evidence in the Mishnah for saying that the feature to be transferred is not considered to be part of the constant meaning of the lexeme. Thus, the Hebrew word 'congregation' (עדה) is used twice in interpretations of this type (mSan 1:6 II (5); mHor 1:4), but a different feature is transferred in each case. This does not clinch the argument, however, for the Mishnah might simply be inconsistent. Quite diverse things happen to the word *davar*, the operative lexeme in [74]. It is placed, as verbal act, in opposition to a deed, in mSheb 10:8 I–II (2) (= mMak 2:8), and mBM 3:12 I (2); it is taken to imply an utterance in mMak 2:5 II (2); and it is put into opposition to 'the whole' of a thing in mHor 1:3. Cf. also the remark of H. S. Hirschfeld, made in connection with *asmakhta* and *zekher*: 'Die Schaffung einer neuen Bedeutung für ein Wort gehört in jeder andern Exegese in das lexicalische Gebiet . . . in der talmudischen Exegese ist die Bezeichnung zufällig, nur für eine Stelle. Sie gehört nicht in das Lexicon. Der Sinn des Wortes ist eigentlich nur an dieser Stelle gewaltsam verändert' (*Halachische Exegese*, 445 n.).

way to present the logic of this resource is to say: a word's meaning is the sum of all its uses in Scripture; these uses and their individual meanings are defined by the Scriptural co-text with which it is surrounded; any one of these co-texts can become a meaning *index* of the word, and can be attached to it in another—suitably selected—occurrence in Scripture.[73] The following schema represents some of these features:

2 witnesses necessary in (sinful) **matter**

> **matter**, (sexual) indecency of, necessary for divorce [and *Sotah* procedure]

The information from the biblical co-text of 'matter' which is selected for transfer is 'two'; the topic 'witnesses in the *Sotah* procedure' is given by the Mishnaic co-text; and the link between it and the information to be transferred is created by Deut. 24:1 with its partial textual overlap with Deut. 19:15.[74] It is clear that, while the feature to be transferred does indeed come from the co-text of the (B) occurrence of the recurrent lexeme, it is *selected* from that co-text due to the perspective of the Mishnah, and the whole chain of passages depends on this. It is not just any aspect of the *Sotah*, but specifically the question of how many witnesses are necessary, which is the theme of the Mishnaic discourse at this junction, and this provides the perspective in which the Scriptural wording is viewed. One could almost say that the information from Deut. 19:15 is not so much transferred to Deut. 24:1 as to the discourse of the Mishnah at the point mSot 6:3, with Deut. 24:1 serving as a relay station. Here is a definition of such a hermeneutic movement:

Keying2: Transfer of a feature linked to the co-text of a lexeme at one Scriptural location (location B) to the same lexeme's occurrence in a different co-text at another Scriptural location (location A).

It should be noted that the sequence in which the two passages are mentioned in the midrashic unit is A–B. Thus the first verse mentioned is the one that contains the direct thematic link to the Mishnaic discussion, so that the hermeneutic reasoning involves something of a 'round trip': starting with A, visiting B to collect the co-textual feature of the lexeme, and returning to A to implant it there.

It is important to see how this resource is actually employed. The above definition suggests, and is meant to suggest, that the two occurrences of the lexeme can be quite far apart. Although there is sometimes room for doubt, as the verses involved in the operation may not be uniquely identified

---

[73] For formal modern attempts to bind co-textual meaning into lexicography, see the summary in McCarthy, 'Lexis and Lexicology' (the COBUILD project). Cf. also Longacre, 'Items in Context: Their Bearing on Translation Theory'.

[74] This verse *could* be taken as a general rule (three occurrences of the word 'all') subsuming divorce/Sotah as a special case (i.e. an Extension resource). But that is not how the hermeneutic operation is presented in the Mishnah. See n. 71 above.

by the phrase quoted, Table 8.1 makes an attempt to list the 'distances' between the two main verses among the Mishnaic examples.[75]

The distances seen here seem to range from neighbouring chapters (to take a very rough measure of textual closeness) to separate books, or even separate divisions of the Bible (mSan 8:2).[76] Most conspicuous is perhaps the case of neighbouring verses, and a plurality of them, in mArak 4:4. This seems to violate the notion of 'different' co-texts in my Keying2 definition above. Indeed, this midrashic unit exhibits *all* of the features which we listed at the beginning of this chapter: a repeated lexeme, textual proximity, parallel linguistic treatment, and unity of topic. And it is the one place in the Mishnah where the term *gezerah shawah* occurs in a hermeneutic function.[77] Let us take a closer look. I have marked its units by the roman letters I to III.

[75] mArak 4:4 I–III (4)[78]   Lev. 27:7; 27:3; 27:5; 27:6

(I) 'And the valuation at the time of [the vow of the] valuation' (quotation from *mishnah* 1)—how? . . . When he was thirty days, [he gives] like younger than that. When he was 5 years old, and when he was 20 years old, [he gives] like younger than that, as it is said: 'And if from among the 60-year-olds and upwards, if a male'— there we learn for all of them from the case of the age of 60. As the age of 60 is [treated] as [belonging to the age] below it, so the age of 5 years and 20 years [is treated] as [belonging to the age] below it.

(II) But how?—If [Scripture] makes the 60-year-old like the one younger, thereby rendering more stringent [the ruling], can the 5-year-old and the 20-year-old be made like the younger ones, thereby rendering [it] more lenient?

(III) In this regard it is instructive that Scripture says 'year', 'year', for [use in] a *gezerah shawah*. As the 'year' that is enunciated in '60 years' [means] like younger than it, so the 'year' that is enunciated in '5 years' and '20 years' [means] like younger than it—regardless of whether the effect is to render [the ruling] more lenient or more stringent.

Lev. 27:3–7 details the different *Sheqel* sums attached to persons whose value was the subject of a cultic vow, distinguishing according to age

[75] The interpretation of Num. 35:24 contained in mHor 1:4 listed in Table 8.1 does not conform clearly to the Keying2 definition given above, in that its co-text requires its own hermeneutic resource (in fact something like an Analogy2) to yield the feature to be transferred.

[76] This passage contains a rabbinic phrase which seems to express doubt about the sufficiency of biblical evidence: זכר לדבר ('[the Lemma is merely] an allusion to the matter'). Note that it is precisely the link between biblical words and Mishnaic topic which is at stake here. It is not clear if the doubt has to do with the textual distance between the two locations (which is linked to the potential absence of thematic unity, in a thematically organized book). The term *zekher* is sometimes also used where only one biblical location is involved, as in mShab 8:7 I–II (2) (Isa. 30:14), mShab 9:4 (Ps. 109:18). Yet, in passages such as mShab 6:4 (Isa. 2:4) and mShab 9:2 I–II (2) (Prov. 30:19; Isa. 61:11), which seem comparable, it is not used. See also mTaan 1:2 (Joel 2:23), where the subject-matter of the Mishnaic discussion (and a related verse from the Pentateuch) is explicitly mentioned in the prophetic verse. The first passage listed in Table 8.1, mNaz 9:5 [93], combining two passages from the prophets, is concerned prima facie with a non-halakhic question. Bacher, i. 51–5, offers an extensive treatment of *zekher*, listing 48 tannaitic examples (including Baraitot).

[77] As mentioned above (see n. 64), in mYT 1:6 it appears in connection with resource Analogy0; cf. Bialoblocki, 'Hermeneutik', col. 1189.

[78] I: §¶A8(A2)K3; II: ¶A0/A4.2?(¬K3)T0; III: A8(A2)K3.

TABLE 8.1 *Locations for resource Keying2*

1 Sam. 1:11 and Judg. 13:5	mNaz 9:5 I–II (2) **[93]**
Deut. 24:1 and Deut. 19:15	mSot 6:3 IV (4), passage **[74]**
Deut. 26:5 and Deut. 27:14	mSot 7:3
Deut. 25:9 and Deut. 27:14	mSot 7:4 I (2)
Deut. 11:30 and Gen. 12:6	mSot 7:5 I (5)
Num. 35:24 f. and Num. 14:27	mSan 1:6 II–III (5)
Deut. 21:20 and Prov. 23:20	mSan 8:2
Lev. 4:13 and Num. 35:24	mHor 1:4
Lev. 27:7; 3; 5; 6	mArak 4:4 I–III (4), see **[75]**

bracket and gender. The values increase with age, except for the last one (60+) which goes down in price. The analogy offered in part I of **[75]** determines to which age bracket those persons belong who are of the age actually mentioned in the text. The rule adopted has the effect of making the borderline case 60 (to go with 59) more expensive then otherwise, while making the borderline cases 20 (to go with 19) and 5 (to go with 4) less expensive then otherwise. This effect forms the basis of the objection, in II, which assumes that a principle which in Scripture's own explicit application leads to greater strictness cannot *by analogy* be applied to cases where it leads to lesser strictness. This objection is highly interesting. It seems to make the 'stringent–lenient' distinction (which we know to be linked by terminology to the substantive comparisons of Analogy4)[79] the yardstick by which to measure an analogy of purely textual constitution. However, the point is answered by what seems merely an elaborate repetition of the original analogical resource, in III; and it is at this point that the term *gezerah shawah* makes its appearance, and textual analogy wins the day.

All the elements which distinguish various forms of analogical resource appear here together. We have the recurrence of a lexeme ('year'), which we defined as the characteristic element of Keying2. Yet we encounter its two selected occurrences in *contiguous* verses, which is a defining feature of Analogy2/3 and Analogy8. At the same time, Scripture offers parallel linguistic treatment of the subjects compared, and very substantial text-independent similarities, which is also typical for these latter resources: the different age categories belong to what is substantially the same norm.[80]

[79] See Ch. 7 (text to n. 50) for an observation on the discourse function of this categorization.

[80] Cf. Mielziner, *Introduction*, 147: 'The external analogy (the parity of expression) from which the argumentation proceeds, is there generally of such a nature as to imply also an internal or real analogy which justifies the conclusion to be drawn from it.' Mielziner introduces further types of *gezerah shawah* (distinguishing 'constructional' from 'exorbitant'), and claims there is an 'exegetical' *gezerah shawah* which is devoted merely to ascertaining the Scriptural usage of a certain word (pp. 143 f.). As the 'exegetical' *gezerah shawah* seems defined only by its results coinciding with those of modern philology, all of these categories remain external to (and apologetic of) the rabbinic material.

And yet we have enough difference within this textual proximity to allow the transfer of co-textual information typical for the Keying2 resource: the word 'and upwards', which is *only* used in conjunction with the word 'year' in the case of the 60-year-old, is taken to travel *together* with the word 'year' to all the other occurrences of that lexeme in verses dealing with the other ages. Finally, we seem to have a generalization of the feature attached to 'year' to the one age in regard of which the word 'year' is not used at all: the thirty-day-old child.[81] I take this to be a separate operation. Here then is the definition of the recurrent lexeme resource found in [75] (marked for single occurrence in the Mishnah by the asterisk):

*Keying3: Transfer of a feature linked to the co-text of a lexeme at one Scriptural location (location B) to the same lexeme's occurrence in a different co-text at another Scriptural location (location A) which is in close proximity to location B or exhibiting thematic links with it.

It is clear that for identifying this resource the way in which it is presented is crucial. In the absence of an indication that the *occurrence of the same lexeme* is taken to be the basis of the analogy, midrashic units which would otherwise qualify for Keying3 might be understood as examples of the transfer of features on the basis of textual proximity and parallel linguistic treatment (including thematic similarity or unity), that is, as Analogy2. And [75] shows that the two resources can coexist with each other in the same passage; also, that there need be no attempt to separate them at all. This also means that that passage cannot be used as unequivocal evidence as to the meaning of the term *gezerah shawah* in the Mishnah. We cannot be sure, on the evidence of this one occurrence, whether this term is restricted to our resource Keying3, or can cover both Keying2 and Keying3 (and more besides), or whether it might even be restricted to the very combination of resources here encountered: Keying3 *plus* Analogy2 (for the thirty-day-old), although that is perhaps unlikely.

Since the term *gezerah shawah* is not explained here while also not being self-explanatory, it is likely to be used as part of a terminology. It may have a legitimizing function in the context of rejecting the objection in part II of the unit, but it merely labels a repeated application of the same procedure.[82] Yet the use of the metalinguistic term 'said, enunciated' (האמורה) within the format 'Just as . . . .so' distinguishes III from I. It could thus be that, through use of this term and the label *gezerah shawah*, the metalinguistic nature of the procedure is stressed, highlighting the concern with the *wording* of Scripture (see below).

Both Keying2 and Keying3 effect the transfer of substantive (in most cases halakhically relevant) features on the basis of a linguistic recurrence

---

[81] This is presupposed clearly in the Mishnaic ruling itself (the thirty-day-old is treated like a younger infant) and from the phrase 'there we learn for *all* of them from the case of . . .' הרי אנו למדים) (בכלם משנת ששים.

[82] This is the terminology: תלמוד לומר שנה שנה לגזרה שוה מה . . . . אף . . . בין להקל בין להחמיר.

in the *same* text. The identity and unity of the Scriptural text, its borders, perhaps even its internal divisions, are presupposed by the resource. These resources allocate to textual similarities in Scripture the same function as to substantive similarities between the subjects of analogy for the Mishnaic discourse. Taking the two clearest cases, Analogy2.1 and Keying2, it seems that either close textual proximity or recurrence of the same lexeme are minimal textual conditions for such transfer. It is, by the way, quite hazardous to try to impose a scheme of developmental logic on these resources. One might feel that resources which are based on substantive similarities or shared textual topic are earlier while the more 'abstract', namely purely textual ones, are later. But whether or not such a development took place needs to be studied in a separate examination of the evidence (Mishnaic and extra-Mishnaic) from a diachronic perspective, and for this perspective no specific 'logic' of development, regardless of how plausible it may seem to the modern scholar, should be assumed *a priori*.

As for the Keying2/3 resources in particular, it is important to note that they differ from the Analogy2/3/8 resources not only in the fact that they start from lexemic recurrence. They also differ in that the feature to be transferred is defined by suitably selected Scriptural segments, that is, has a presence in the text. This makes a difference for the 'feel' of the midrashic passages based on the two resource families, and also helps structure one's investigation when faced with a midrashic unit of uncertain analogical nature.

THE USE OF SCRIPTURE IN ANALOGICAL RESOURCES: SOME GENERAL OBSERVATIONS

Here I will pull together some of the strands emerging from the material of this chapter with respect to the way Scripture's wording is employed. In two passages Scripture is expressively used (π), but in a manner which makes clear that Scriptural wording is referred to also. Thus, 'garment' in [72] is both the word the Mishnah needs to use to talk about its subject-matter *and* marked as coming from Scripture, namely, in the question 'Why was it mentioned separately?' The same is happening in [73] with 'tithe' ('of cattle'—from Lev. 27:32). Apart from these examples for Analogy8 and Analogy8.1 respectively, the other midrashic units contain explicit quotations. They are mostly introduced by שנאמר or נאמר, except for the Keying2/3 cases. These are more elaborate, using (also) *talmud lomar* and singling out the recurrent lexeme for an interesting combination of use and mention. That is achieved, for example in [75], by employing the operative word twice, once in expressive use, and once quoted as part of a relative clause introduced by the verb 'to say' (here: 'enunciated'): מה שנה האמורה

... בשנת ששים—'As the "year" *that is enunciated in* "60 years" ...'. This achieves a very close alignment of the Mishnaic discourse on the topic on the one hand and the textual structures in Scripture which are being quoted as support on the other.

Here follow some further issues emerging from the cases analysed in this chapter.

1. The case of the 'absent' quotation in [72] and [73] seems to show that the Mishnaic co-text can make up for an explicit quotation of the verses in question (or at least of one of them). To take [73] as an illustration, the word 'tithe' occurs many times in Scripture. And as for the second biblical location involved, its wording is not represented at all, but only referred to by the term 'the general' (כלל). It would be difficult in the extreme to find the verse in question, were it not for the Mishnaic co-text identifying sacrifice substitution as the general topic. Mishnaic co-text replaces the Scriptural co-text of a segment in its effect of narrowing down the meaning of the Scriptural words.[83] In the above cases [72] and [73] it is largely the overlap of the theme of the Mishnaic co-text with the theme of the original Scriptural co-text which ensures that the location of the Scriptural quotation can even be identified. But for resources where there is perhaps no thematic overlap between Mishnaic and Scriptural text (in particular, of the B location in Keying3), the identification of the biblical location can be precarious. An illustration is afforded by [74], which quotes the frequently occurring word 'matter, word' simply from 'elsewhere' (להלן).[84] Much depends, of course, on the choice of the B location for constructing the resource—it provides the co-text from which the transferable feature is extracted. In their identification of that B verse most modern commentators, translators, and editors—including myself—depend on traditional exegesis of the Mishnah. This dependency can hardly be avoided with our current state of knowledge. We do not know enough about the resources and their differences and their different employment in various states and documents of rabbinic Judaism to achieve verification of the traditional choices or independence from them.

The case of the absent quotation is noteworthy for another reason also. It seems to mark one pole in the formulation of midrashic units, while the quotation of biblical event reports in the NORM passages seems to mark the opposite pole. NORM units tend to offer dedicated biblical quotations in connection with a resource which, as such, is not based on the Scriptural wording but on a fact of Israelite 'history'; while the above-mentioned Analogy8 passages are wholly predicated on certain textual relationships, yet do not provide a separate mention of Scriptural text.

2. In Chapter 3 I attempted to explain that the Mishnaic co-text expresses

---

[83] See pages 69 f. above.

[84] Cf. also mHor 1:4, simply quoting the word 'congregation' as coming from the B passage.

the perspective in which the Scriptural wording is read, and that this narrows down the meaning of the quoted or used segment in a way which is explicitly or tacitly different from the original co-text of the segment in Scripture. The very act of dividing Scripture into units small enough to receive such striking redefinitions of topic or perspective is fundamental to rabbinic hermeneutics as manifest in the Mishnah. We also alluded to the fact that, rather than imposing such perspective by new rabbinic co-text, the interpreter can employ text coming from elsewhere *in Scripture* for the purpose. This is almost exactly what happens in the Keying2 resource and in many cases of *gezerah shawah* in rabbinic literature outside the Mishnah. One segment is read in the light of another segment, and that other segment narrows down the meaning of the recurrent lexeme to a very specific point, exactly as Mishnaic co-text can. But it is ostensibly not the interpreters' words, but biblical ones, which achieve this effect by surrounding the biblical wording. The interpreter disappears behind the Scriptural wording itself—he remains invisible until the moment when the selection of the second verse, the one which co-textualizes the first, is focused. Scripture itself comments on Scripture. This phenomenon has been encountered before: in the use of tenor verses as evaluation of biblical events (Use1–4, Use8). Here, in the Keying2 resource, the mechanism is quite different, and the interpreter also remains very much present in that he must use his own voice to quote Scripture and point out the textual relationships. But Keying2 obscures the interpreter's choices even better, allowing the interpretation to emerge as inevitable and automatic. For the second passage of a *gezerah shawah* selects itself, so to speak—by virtue of the appearance of the same lexeme in it. The Keying2/3 passages seem to carry much conviction in the Mishnah; hardly any is disputed, and none is suggested only so as to be refuted, as is the case with a number of Analogy4 interpretations (marked by the '¬' sign). Case **[75]** is one of only two passages[85] which contain an objection to the use of KEYING, and a clear and well-developed one at that.[86] Yet it is defended, apparently successfully, by nothing more than a more detailed explanation (and naming) of its mechanism.

3. There is another link between the analogical resources on the one hand, and the USE and PERFORMANCE families on the other, although it is very abstract and I am not sure of its consequences. Where a tenor verse or rabbinic maxim employed to speak about a biblical event is metaphorical (as many proverbs are), the selection of a suitable subject to be elucidated by its use depends on the same faculties of *analogical* reasoning as those relied upon in ANALOGY and KEYING resources. I. A. Richards has called the metaphor a 'transaction between contexts'.[87] Now we know that the

[85] The other passage is mNaz 9:5 I (2) **[93]**.

[86] How significant for its lack of impact is the fact that it is based on the same concepts as the Analogy4 resource?

[87] '(Metaphor) . . . fundamentally . . . is a borrowing between and intercourse of *thoughts*, a transaction between contexts', *Philosophy of Rhetoric*, 94; cf. Black, *Models and Metaphors*, 38.

mobilization of co-texts in the service of perspectives (that is, contexts) is characteristic for Mishnaic hermeneutics. This allows us to make rabbinic sense of Richards's phrase with a small but crucial modification: as 'transaction between *co*-texts', it becomes a description of the resource Keying2.[88]

4. I should clarify a little further the phenomenon of resources which base an analogy on purely textual relationships. I drew attention, apropos case **[66]**, to the fact that analogies *can* be based on textual relationships which do not as such imply extra-linguistic, substantive links between subjects; and what is true of Analogy2 is also true of Keying2. This probably means that Scripture is taken not to be external, or secondary, in relation to the subjects it speaks about. But that only works on the further assumption that the textual positions occupied by these subjects in Scripture are different from those in other texts (for example, the Mishnah). Other texts, in the view of the rabbis, come *after* their subject-matter, and speak *about* it. But Scripture is different: its textual features become part and parcel of the things it speaks 'about'—it seems to shape these things, or some of their defining features, in the way it speaks about them.[89] The way these subjects are presented in the Scriptural text becomes a part of what they are.

5. There are also some issues of redundancy.[90] For some of the analogical resources we raised the question how important initial observations of redundancy might be. It is possible that an interpretation such as **[67]** makes partial use of the presence of the word 'also' (גם) in its verse, which furthermore contains two synonymous verbs, as do the Scriptural texts of **[68]**. Passages **[69]** to **[71]** deal with comparisons, which could be seen as having their own inherent redundancy. In none of these examples, however, is there an indication that biblical redundancy is relevant to the analogy.[91] The Analogy8 cases **[72]** and **[73]** are different: the very question they ask is why the same subject should be covered *twice* in Scripture, once as specific item and once as subsumed in a general class.[92] As for Keying2, its observation of the recurrence of a linguistic sign in a large text hardly

---

[88] But what does that mean? That the co-textual information taken from biblical location B is treated like a *metaphorical* meaning for the lexeme in question? But 'matter' surely cannot be a *metaphor* for '2-witness-proven matter'. So, maybe, this line of thought simply peters out.

[89] Employing the language of the rabbis, one might say that Scripture comes *first*: Torah was created before creation. Rabbinic statements on the Torah such as this one, whose exact import in their historical context is difficult to assess, have exerted an indirect but quite powerful influence on the contemporary discourse on reading and hermeneutics. Goldberg makes an attempt to integrate them into a theory of rabbinic hermeneutics in 'The Rabbinic View of Scripture'. For the textual nature of rabbinic analogy, see Jackson, 'On the Nature of Analogical Argument in Early Jewish Law'.

[90] See Ch. 11, and esp. Ch. 13.

[91] Cf., however, the Analogy2 operation in mMak 1:7 V (6), which is introduced by the statement: לא בא השלישי אלא להחמיר עליו.

[92] Cf. the question asked in mMak 1:7 I (6), למה פרט הכתוב בשנים למה מתקימה העדות בשנים? אם, which directly addresses redundancy (introducing either Analogy8 or Analogy2). Redundancy as linked to an internal contradiction is found in mMen 7:6, introducing Analogy8 by the words: אם כן למה נאמר . . . ? See next chapter, text before n. 26.

constitutes redundancy in itself; but this changes when Keying3 is considered, since the recurrent lexeme is actually repeated at close range— very conspicuously so in the case of 'year' in [75]. Still, no observation on redundancy as such is offered as part of this Keying3 passage. In post-Mishnaic literature the *gezerah shawah* is linked to observations on redundancy quite emphatically,[93] and explicit rules limit its application to redundant Lemmas. There is a considerable number of resources (for example, REDUNDANCY, DIFFERENCE, Opposition8) which are directly concerned with biblical redundancy. I shall deal with these resources in later chapters. Among the analogical resources, it is those which deal with some kind of repetition in the immediate textual neighbourhood (in particular Analogy8.1 and Keying3) which are most likely to incorporate a subsidiary focus on redundancy in their operation.

[93] The expression used is מופנה; on this, see Ch. 2 above (text to n. 33), and the literature quoted there; see also Ch. 13. Cf. Mielziner, *Introduction*, 150 ff.; Chajes, *The Student's Guide*, 9 (bKet 38b and bYeb 24a); further Gilat, 'The Development of the Gezerah Shawah', in his *Studies in the Development of the Halakhah*, 366 and 372.

9

Taxonomic and Paradigmatic Extensions. Logical Constants

The Mishnah may probe concrete Scriptural expressions for their potential to become extended to a more general class, or to be supplemented by further terms of similar generality in Mishnaic lists. In such interpretations, ready-made Mishnaic lists of items (paradigms) play an important role, as well as verses which contain a group of co-ordinated terms. The Mishnah may also read the presence of certain other words in the biblical co-text, for example, 'all' or 'also', as effecting a generalization of concrete expressions. The word 'all' itself, as well as biblical particles of negation, may be emphasized for their universal ('logical') scope. The Mishnah may treat the meaning of biblical 'and' and 'if–then' as similar to the corresponding logical conjunctions.

BIBLICAL HYPONYMS EXTENDED TO MISHNAIC SUPERORDINATES, LISTS, OR CLASSES

We now stand at a crossroads for the presentation of resources in this book. The ANALOGY resources discussed in the preceding chapter point to the hermeneutic importance of biblical redundancy. However, I shall leave this topic until Chapter 13. I will first pursue another aspect noticed in some ANALOGY resources, namely, the generalization of features from one item mentioned in Scripture to a whole class. A second group of resources to be introduced here concerns specific biblical words, in particular 'and', 'all', and 'no' / 'not', and their Mishnaic interpretation in ways which recall their function as logical constants in modern formal logic.[1]

The hermeneutic device labelled Analogy8 in the preceding chapter allows the interpreter to transfer a feature from a less to a more general

---

[1] The word 'constants' covers both connectives and quantifiers in logical terminology (cf. Allwood *et al.*, *Logic in Linguistics*, 27, 62). See below n. 62.

subject. The transfer is analogical, and based on both subjects being mentioned in Scripture. We shall now turn to resources which provide for extensions (or restrictions) of biblical expressions *without* reference to more general terms found in Scripture treated in an analogical manner. Our basic procedure will be to investigate passages where a Mishnaic companion term differs in generality or inclusiveness from the Scriptural Lemma, either conspicuously or explicitly. Some companion terms align the biblical text with the specific terminology of the Mishnah (Topic3). The biblical Lemma's scope may be extended by being reformulated using a superordinate term, a class, or additional similar terms. Sometimes, however, a biblical expression is paraphrased by a more *specific* term (a hyponym). All of these (including the last one) shall be labelled resources of EXTENSION. Of central importance for my descriptive task are the concepts 'hyponym-superordinate', which will serve in the articulation of several EXTENSION resources. For two words, such as 'animal' and 'donkey', the former is termed the superordinate, while the latter is the hyponym. To express the fact that a hierarchical relationship of inclusion holds between lexemes of different generality I shall use the term 'taxonomic'.[2] I shall distinguish types of biblical Lemmas on the one hand, and types of companion term on the other. The variations of the former are represented by the first digit in the EXTENSION code, while variations of the latter are indicated in the second digit. Table 9.1 gives a summary of these types of resources and their relevant codes.

Among the relevant combinations found are the following: Extension1.1 links a series of Mishnaic lexemes to one biblical lexeme of similar generality (see case [77] below); Extension1.2 links a superordinate Mishnaic term to one biblical expression; Extension2.1 means that a list in the Bible is matched by an (extended) list in the Mishnah. Not all theoretically possible combinations exist in the Mishnah and I shall not provide an example for all the ones that do. I shall concentrate instead on cases which are either quite frequent (such as Extension1.1 or Extension2.1), or conspicuous in a way that throws light on the Mishnaic attitude to taxonomic relationships in general.

What unites most interpretations of this type is that the Mishnah determines that the biblical lexeme stands for a *more general* meaning than that suggested by an exclusive emphasis on the lexeme actually occurring.[3] We know this because in the Mishnah's restatement of the biblical message the lexeme's place is taken by an expression which has a wider meaning. The clues in Scripture which the Mishnah is following up in cases of semantic extension are often not easy to see. On the one hand we need to ask the

---

[2] Cf. Cruse, *Lexical Semantics*, 136 ff.; for hyponyms and superordinates, see 88 ff. The fact that not *all* taxonyms are also hyponyms (pp. 144 f.) seems to be of no consequence for our material. See also McCarthy, 'Lexis and Lexicology'; Ilson, 'Lexicography'.

[3] Such exclusive emphasis being another hermeneutic option (the OPPOSITION resources), to be dealt with in Ch. 11. See also below, on case [77].

TABLE 9.1 *Extension resources*

Types	Resource name
Of Lemma	
One lexeme	Extension1
Two (or more) lexemes of similar generality	Extension2
A name or singular referring expression	Extension4
One or two lexeme(s) plus a subsequent, more general	
category, or 'all'	Extension3
Of Dictum	
A general class defined by a phrase using constructions	
such as 'all', or 'things which . . .'[a]	Extension*.2
Two (or more) lexemes of the same level of generality as	
the biblical lexeme, with or without repeating the Lemma	Extension*.1
A superordinate lexeme	Extension*.2
The biblical lexeme used as a term for a whole class[b]	Extension*.3
Dictum more specific than Lemma	
A proper name or singular referring expression	Extension*.4
One hyponym or more	Extension*.0

Notes: [a] For the latter, mShebu 3:5 II (3) is the only example I have found. See [79] below.
  [b] The foundation case for this category is mBQ 1:1 [24] (the four 'fathers' of damages). As I explained in Chapter 4, this *mishnah* involves expressive *use* of Scriptural wording, accompanied by a definition of some sort; it also has the automatic effect of treating the original passage from which each Lemma comes as a special case within a larger category, even where it is biblically presented as the only category of its type (resource Topic5). Passages such as mBQ 1:1 are regularly classified as examples of the rabbinic *middah* of *binyan av* in the secondary literature. See below.

following question: what linguistic or textual mechanisms might allow the Mishnah to create such extensions?[4] On the other hand, we need to investigate the following points: are there discourse structures which indicate the wider relevance of such extensions? What is the nature of the extensions, which paradigms are used to construct them, and in which perspective are they selected?

Here are some possible answers to the first question, namely, which linguistic or textual factors the Mishnah sees as implying the extensions.[5]

  [4] Stress on *Mishnah*. Here it is particularly important to keep separate the evidence of the Mishnah from that of the Gemara, because the latter often offers explicit procedures where the Mishnah is silent in connection with EXTENSION structures. We should keep in play the various answers suggested in the following until conclusions based on the systematic comparison with extra-Mishnaic material become available.
  [5] I am excluding here ANALOGY mechanisms. Some the passages classed as using an EXTENSION resource could in fact be interpreted as using one of the ANALOGY resources, but that does not affect the conceptual distinction between the two types.

Extension1: This is the most basic case of one biblical term being understood or applied on a level of generality different from that suggested by the term's meaning alone. If combined with Extension*.1–3, this amounts to an extension of scope, effectively *generalizing* the biblical term in a certain perspective. If the Mishnaic generalization can be linked to other features of the biblical text, one of the other EXTENSION resources defined here will be used as label instead of Extension1. If combined with Extension*.4/ Extension*.0 this resources amounts to a *superordination* or to an *application* of the biblical term.

Extension2: Here, two or more biblical lexemes of the same type are contained alongside each other in the same sentence and in parallel syntactic position in Scripture (usually linked by 'or' or 'and'). That fact itself may be taken by the Mishnah to indicate that the categories are extendable, and that their upper limit is a comprehensive class containing the biblical elements as members, but also others. The biblical enumeration is understood as an *open* list, and the Dictum continues or completes the list according to a paradigm relevant to the Mishnaic discourse. Open lists of a type which tacitly call for active extension by the receiving audience seem to occur in face-to-face conversation.[6] Extension2 can be found combined with Extension3. It can also be allied to the Mishnah's focusing of a more general term in a biblical parallel for the same norm or statement (see the example of Exod. 23:4/Deut. 22:1–3, relevant to **[76]** below).

*Extension3: In quite a few cases the biblical listing of two items is followed in the same sentence by a general phrase containing the word 'all'. Thus, the general phrase or 'all' may motivate an extension in meaning for the individual items found earlier in the biblical sentence. (This stands in contrast with the Analogy8 resource.) Although this seems to suggest a link to the rabbinic *middah* of *perat ukhelal*,[7] that *middah*'s terminology is not used in the only Mishnaic example (see case **[79]** below). Extension3 or Extension2 interpretations are identified in the secondary literature as representing another rabbinic *middah* altogether, the *binyan av*. However, most modern accounts of this rabbinic hermeneutic 'rule' distil its principles from a mixture of very diverse sources. No attempt is usually made to review systematically midrashic units that tacitly apply the *middah*, while systematic weight is often given to purely etymological considerations concerning the *middah*'s terminology. It is too early to say how direct is the link between the EXTENSION resources and the *binyan av* (the same goes for the ANALOGY resources). It is clear in any case that the name *binyan av* is used by the rabbis for several quite distinct procedures.[8]

---

[6] Cf. Sacks, *Lectures on Conversation*, ii. 499 ff. See the discussion of **[76]** below.

[7] See Ch. 8, text to n. 54. On that *middah*, cf. Chernick, 'The Formal Development of כלל ופרט וכלל'.

[8] The name is linked to rules number 3 and 4 in R. Ishmael's list (cf. *Sifra*, ed. Finkelstein, ii. 3 and 5), number 8 in *Mishnat Rabbi Eliezer*. A clear example of an interpretation linked to the *binyan av* terminology is found in Mekhilta Neziqin 9 (ad Exod. 21:26 f.; ed. Lauterbach, iii. 72 f.). Cf.

*Extension4: The interpretation of a proper name in the biblical text as standing for a general concept or class of items. There is only one example of this, namely, the interpretation of 'Molekh' as 'heathendom' in mMeg 4:9. However, it could be that names of pagan deities are not treated by the rabbis as proper names at all; so this resource's representation in the Mishnah is doubtful (it is also explicitly rejected and ascribed to a Targumic rendering).

Extension5: Any expression of arguably general meaning found in the co-text of the Lemma, or any expression which is unrestricted in its own syntactic slot, may serve to broaden the Lemma's range. These elements are usually found in the same sentence as the Lemma, but the mechanism is *independent* of the syntactic links between the relevant biblical words,[9] and the generalizing expression does not need to include the expression whose extension is stated in its scope.[10] Instead, the resource is based on textual proximity within the sentence. It is sometimes also based on an additional mechanism such as the distribution of redundancy.[11]

*Extension5.5: Where such broadening of a Lemma's range is also based on the presence of certain particles such as גם, אף, or את, these may either be found in syntactic positions where they govern the Lemma, or further away in the sentence.[12] The presence of these particles in the biblical verse seems to be a popular choice in the Gemara's attempts to account for Mishnaic operations of EXTENSION, and the term *ribbui* often appears with operations involving these particles. (For the only clear Mishnaic occurrence, involving גם, see below **[80]**.)

*Extension6: Within the framework of an explicit Mishnaic taxonomy, a biblical expression is classified as standing in for a larger class due to its frequency or commonness. We find an explicit claim to this effect in passage **[76]**; how we would otherwise know that this is the mechanism by which the extension is hermeneutically supported, I do not know. Compare the next resource, which is similar also in other respects.

Stemberger, *Introduction*, 19. Birnbaum, *Encyclopedia of Jewish Concepts*, 332, identifies the millstone case in mBM 9:13 IV (4), an Extension3.2 case, as an example of the *binyan av* (I do not know his source for this). See also Elon, 'Interpretation', col. 1421 f.; Jacobs, *Studies in Talmudic Logic and Methodology*, 9–15. The modern confusions seem to start with the evidence usually relied upon for clarification, namely, the rabbinic lists of *middot*. See Finkelstein's note on the *binyan av* in Sifra (*Sifra on Leviticus*, vol. IV: *Commentary*, 3 ff.); also the literature quoted in n. 54 in Ch. 8, n. 8 in Ch. 7, and n. 54 below.

[9] It therefore excludes cases in which a more general expression and a more limited one refer to the same subject. See below, case **[76]**.

[10] On the notion of scope, cf. Frawley, *Linguistic Semantics*, 472–5; Crystal, *Dictionary of Linguistics and Phonetics*, 271.

[11] See the Redundancy9 resource explained in Ch. 13.

[12] These are the particles linked to the *ribbui* resource (see below) in later rabbinic literature. These elements are also in some sense potentially 'superfluous', see the second section of Ch. 11. The case of a *restriction* of generality by other types of particles (e.g. אך) occurs outside the Mishnah and I have reserved the resource name Extension5.6 for it (cf. *mi'ut*, see Stemberger, *Introduction*, 23).

[Extension7]: This mechanism depends on the relationship of certain 'prototypical' lexemes to their superordinates. Here we would understand the Mishnah to identify the biblical term as semantically representative of the larger class (without pragmatic reasons, as in Extension6). The origin of the semantic theory of prototypes lies in modern philosophy of language (Wittgenstein's 'family resemblances') and more recent psychological research.[13] Contemporary speakers of English, for example, identify 'pigeon' as being more representative of the category 'bird' than 'ostrich';[14] and they consider the chair a more central example of the class 'furniture' than the refrigerator, and so on.[15] These observations are based on repeatable, controlled experiments with native speakers; they are supported by differences in the processing time it takes native speakers to verify statements of various types.[16] This makes it very difficult to use the idea of a 'prototype' in historical hermeneutics. One would have to claim that the rabbis, on the basis of their native-speaker competence for (rabbinic) Hebrew, recognized certain lexemes in Scripture as particularly central, or prototypical, for a more general category. This would amount to saying that, in the absence of the other resources here listed which could have similar results, it is in particular such 'prototypical' lexemes that receive the EXTENSION treatment in the rabbis' interpretation. However, as long as there is no evidence for which terms the rabbis would consider 'prototypical', *apart* from their explanations of Scripture, this would clearly be a circular procedure. But what could constitute other evidence, since the above-mentioned experiments cannot be repeated with native speakers of rabbinic Hebrew?[17] Moreover, it would be naive to assume that rabbinic Hebrew emerged or developed outside the sphere of influence of Scripture as a text. As a result, some of the rabbis' native-speaker intuitions about which hyponyms are prototypical for their superordinates could have been formed under the impact of precisely those biblical passages which they explain exegetically as pointing to a superordinate when only the hyponym is used. Clearly, prototype theory could be very relevant to the many instances of the use of EXTENSION we find in rabbinic literature. But the methodological problems posed by a transfer of this theory to material which is historically remote, cannot be subjected to experiments, and is explicitly exegetical, are formidable.

There are also cases where the Mishnah *defines* the class of items which it takes to be designated by a biblical expression. I have introduced this

---

[13] See Taylor, *Linguistic Categorization*. Taylor explains Wittgenstein's influence (pp. 38 f.), and the impact of cognitive psychologist Eleanor Rosch since the 1970s (pp. 42 ff.); see also Hesse, 'Theories, Family Resemblances and Analogy'.

[14] Cf. Cruse, *Lexical Semantics*, 148.

[15] Cf. Taylor, *Linguistic Categorization*, 44.

[16] Cf. ibid. 45.

[17] I am leaving aside (but not because I consider it settled) the issue of whether there were 'native speakers of rabbinic Hebrew' in the sense in which there are native speakers of English.

resource as Topic8 in Chapter 4: a certain predicate (for example, a physical measurement) is stipulated as limiting or extending the biblical expression's scope. There is no claim that the stipulation is dependent either on the expression's meaning or on its co-textual relationships in Scripture; instead, the dynamics of the halakhic concepts of the Mishnah play the decisive role here.[18] Hand in hand with the stipulation goes the adoption of the biblical expression into a Mishnaic technical use. Topic8 has the effect of determining the generality or inclusiveness of a biblical expression. This is particularly clear from a case such as mBQ 5:5 I (2) [5]. This passage stipulates that the norm for which Scripture uses only the word 'pit' is applicable to a number of separately listed holes in the ground (Extension1.1); and the continuation of that passage defines the legal category by the ability of the cavity to cause death, linking it to a specified depth of ten handbreadths.[19]

Consider now some of the Mishnaic passages which the EXTENSION resources ought to help describe.

[76] mBQ 5:7[20]   Exod. 21:33

Equally treated are the ox with all the cattle, regarding (i) the 'falling into the pit' and (ii) the separation from Mount Sinai, and (iii) the twofold restitution, and (iv) the return of 'a lost thing', (v) the unloading, (vi) the 'muzzling', (vii) the 'diverse kinds', and (viii) the Sabbath. And so is the wild animal and the bird. If so, why is it said, 'an ox or an ass'? Simply because Scripture speaks [only] of that which actually happens (or: is usual).[21]

In this tremendously condensed passage two steps of generalization take place, and they are applied across eight different biblical norms. One is the identification of the word 'ox' with its superordinate 'cattle' (בהמה); the second is the addition of the classes 'wild beast' (חיה) and 'birds'. The category expansion is spelled out for one norm (Exod. 21:33), while the other seven are merely listed. Here are the likely biblical passages concerned, with the operative words given in bold print:[22]

(i) Exod. 21:33   'When a man leaves a pit open . . . and an **ox or** an ass falls into it . . . and the dead shall be his'.
(ii) Exod. 19:12   'whoever touches the mountain . . . . whether **beast** (בהמה) or man, he shall not live'.
(iii) Exod. 22:9   'for every breach of trust, whether it is **for ox, for** ass, for sheep, for clothing, or for any kind of lost thing, of which one

---

[18] Cf. Albeck, *Einführung*, 87 ff.
[19] 'Just as a pit which is deep enough to cause death is ten handbreadths deep, so any [cavity] deep enough to cause death [must be] ten handbreadths deep.' The measurement of ten handbreadths provides the cut-off point for a number of norms belonging to quite different halakhic themes in the Mishnah. See also Ch. 11 (first section).
[20] ◊πE2.2E6T3.1.
[21] The concluding maxim reads: אלא שדבר הכתוב בהווה.
[22] I am assuming that, insofar as interpretative work on individual biblical passages is presupposed, it concerns the extension from ox and ass to cattle, not to wild beasts and birds.

		says "This is it", the case of both the parties shall come before God'.
(iv)	Deut. 22:1–3	'You shall not see your brother's **ox or** his sheep go astray, and withhold your help . . . and so you shall do with his ass; so you shall do with his garment; so you shall do with any lost thing of your brother's, which he loses and you find . . .' cf. Exod. 23:4: 'If you meet your enemy's **ox or** his ass going astray, you shall bring it back to him'.
(v)	Exod. 23:5	'If you see the ass of one who hates you lying under its burden . . .' (cf. Exod. 23:4).
(vi)	Deut. 25:4	'You shall not muzzle an **ox** when it treads out the grain'.
(vii)	Deut. 22:10	'You shall not plough with an **ox** and an ass together.' Lev. 19:19: 'You shall not cause your cattle (בהמתך) to breed with a different kind . . .'
(viii)	Deut. 5:14	'. . . you shall not do any work, you and your son and your daughter and your manservant and your maidservant and your **ox and** your ass and all of your cattle and the sojourner . . .' Exod. 20:10: 'you and your son and your daughter, your manservant and your maidservant and your **cattle** (ובהמתך), and the sojourner . . .'

It emerges that the different Lemmas are not at all homogeneous: in most of the verses the term 'ox' appears in the Extension2 manner, that is, alongside one of two or more similar items (i, iii, iv, vii, viii); in one it occurs alone (vi), and in two it does not occur at all, but instead its fellow term 'ass' (v) or its superordinate 'cattle' (ii). In two cases the parallel biblical passage has only the superordinate 'cattle' (vii, viii), and in three cases the word 'ox' is followed by a superordinate, be it 'lost thing' (iii, iv)[23] or 'cattle' (viii). Conspicuous are the cases where the ox is not even mentioned; they show that the overarching purpose of the Mishnaic list is to point out the common application range of these norms, not to present a key for interpreting all the biblical passages involved. The one biblical passage whose wording is quoted, Exod. 21:33, is quite typical and belongs to the Extension2 verses.[24] All in all, there seem to be three structures in particular which would support the extension to 'cattle' in these passages. The first is the potential open-endedness of the list format itself, that is, Extension2; the second and third are the appearance of the superordinate either in the same passage as the list (Extension3) or in a parallel biblical passage. But none of these seem to provide a criterion for the extension to wild animals and birds, categories which are of similar generality as 'cattle', but not linked to the hyponyms 'ox' and 'ass'. This seems to be precisely the point raised by the question 'If so . . .?' The answer confirms this: if the whole class of cattle, including sheep and goats,[25] is taken to be what Scripture is talking about,

---

[23] Which phrase receives an analogical treatment in case **[72]** above.

[24] It is also linked to the first case in the Mishnaic list, and thereby to Mishnaic co-text.

[25] They are presumably just as likely to fall into pits, move too close to Sinai, be lost, etc., as the ox and the ass. In any case, the word בהמה includes both large and small cattle (cf. Jastrow, 142b).

then its silence about wild animals and birds could be accounted for by
the criterion of frequency or likelihood, and thus relevance. So the question
does not ask: why do we say cattle when Scripture says ox and ass? It asks,
why do we say wild animals and birds when Scripture says ox and ass, that
is, cattle?[26] And to *that* the answer is: because Scripture only mentions what
actually happens, that is, the more frequent cases. If this interpretation of
our *mishnah* is correct, then the reference to frequency as motivation for
mentioning something, which is elsewhere in the Mishnah found in
connection with *rabbinic* sayings,[27] is not used as justification for the bulk of
the EXTENSION resources. But it does articulate a hermeneutic expectation,
namely, that the biblical treatment of some halakhic topics is more prag-
matically oriented than that of the Mishnaic discourse, and less concerned
with defined conceptual boundaries. Scripture is expected to pose the
hermeneutic task of transforming information from the specifics of what
'actually happens' to more abstract categories with clear limits.

We have pointed to a number of additional factors which may facilitate
the Mishnaic perception that Scripture's words are to be taken in a general
manner. These include the occurrence of a more general term close by, or
in a parallel biblical passage. But clearly Mishnaic expansions are not
dependent on such textual circumstances. Extension2 also works when
Scripture offers merely a plurality of same-level items, and it is independent also from the fact whether the biblical list is presented with 'or', 'and',
or as an asyndetic construction.[28] How can we understand this as a hermeneutic phenomenon?

It seems that a similar phenomenon can be observed in face-to-face
conversation. In one of the taped oral exchanges analysed by Harvey Sacks,
a woman says (apropos Christmas gifts): 'When's that guy gonna learn that
I don't want an electric skillet, I wanna coat, or I wanna sweater.' Further on
in the same conversation, it is reported that the gentleman in question has
presented her with a cigarette lighter. The response to this by one of the
earlier interlocutors is: 'At least it was for her use.' Having just looked at the
Mishnaic handling of same-level items in Scripture, it will be natural to
recognize this response as providing a general category ([something] for
her use) for the two items mentioned earlier (coat, sweater, as opposed to
skillet). Here is how Sacks explains the structure:

One thing is noted as not wanted and two things are noted as wanted, with their
status being alternative . . . A question is, why does she have two things that she
wants, and what will people make of that? At least an initial suggestion is that if she

[26] The Gemara (bBQ 54b) takes its cue from the question so understood; but it does not stop with
the Mishnaic answer. Instead, it looks for answers from the relevant verses by way of procedures
which cannot be described in terms of taxonomic semantic relationships (as can the ox–cattle link).

[27] The maxim is also found at mShab 6:6 and 9, mErub 1:10, mYeb 15:2, mNed 5:5, and mEduy 1:12,
applied throughout to what 'they' or 'the Sages' said. The meaning seems to be 'example from real
life' (in mYeb 15:2 it is linked to the expression מעשה שהיה).

[28] Cf. Gesenius–Kautzsch, *Hebrew Grammar*, sec, 154, n. 1; sec. 104.

says 'I want a coat' then presumably she wants a coat. But if she says 'I want a coat or I want a sweater', then it isn't that she wants one or both of those, but giving two things, it may be that she's thereby locating a *sort* of thing she wants, where something else would also satisfy that, in a way in which something else might not satisfy 'I want a coat'.

The presentation of what she wants is, then, to be treated as instantial by virtue of the alternatives.[29]

It is suggestive that fairly ordinary conversational mechanisms should allow a mini-list to provide an efficient and communicable description of a whole class of objects which are not otherwise defined, and which might turn out to be quite difficult to *define* at all.[30] Sacks takes the fact that people can present such a list as a category, and be *understood* in doing so, as an illustration regarding 'the most obvious topic in the study of communication, i.e. do people understand each other? How do they understand each other?'[31]

Sacks goes on to consider another potential similarity of the list items as determined by the sentence in which they occur: that they are reasonably affordable (a new car does not figure). This leads on to another important feature of the Mishnaic expansion of specific categories: the choice of a superordinate. Taken on their own, the words 'ox' or 'ass' could be subordinated to a whole range of different classes, for example 'four-legged animals', 'domestic animals', 'hoofed animals', simply 'animals', 'mammals', 'things under the sun', 'expensive items of property', or 'animate objects'. Each of these is located on a relative level of generality ('mammal' is more specific than 'animal', which is more specific than 'animate objects').[32] And they also express different contexts or perspectives: in a context in which 'mammal' is highly informative, 'things under the sun' or 'four-legged animals' may be quite irrelevant. The choice of superordinate 'cattle'[33] also reflects the thematic orientation of the Mishnaic discourse. The hermeneutic perspective imposed by the choice of companion term is even clearer when it is not a superordinate (Extension*.2), but a list of items (Extension*.1). Here is an example, coming from a section of the Mishnah which offers a verse-by-verse treatment of an extended biblical passage (marked by Σ)[34] and which contains several EXTENSION interpretations:

[29] Sacks, *Lectures on Conversation*, ii. 500 (the chapter is entitled 'The Workings of a List'). Although the list quoted uses 'or' to link the items, Sacks clearly does not consider that to be the decisive characteristic, but their list character.

[30] In this regard, open-ended lists may be like metaphors or analogies, i.e. not subject to exhaustive reformulation. Cf. Cruse, *Lexical Semantics*, 148. Cf. n. 19 in Ch. 7 and nn. 3 and 5 in Ch. 8.

[31] *Lectures on Conversation*, ii. 500.

[32] Languages differ of course in the degree to which they lexicalize such taxonomies.

[33] Jastrow has 'cattle, quadruped domestic animal (mostly of the horned race)', 142b.

[34] See Ch. 12.

[77] mSot 8:2 I (3)[35]   Deut. 20:5

(continued from *mishnah* 8:1) 'And the officers shall speak to the people saying: What man there is who has built a new house and has not dedicated it, he shall go and return to his house . . .'—It is all one whether he builds a house for straw, a cattle house, a house for wood, a house of storage;[36] it is the same for the one who builds, and for the one who buys, and for the one who inherits, and if it was given to him as a gift.

The Mishnaic list of things that are to receive the same treatment under the law is structured by the use of the expression 'it is one/the same if he . . .' (. . . אחד ה). 'One' may introduce all the additional items in a series at once (this is the case for the types of house in our passage), or introduce each of them with its own 'one' (this is what we find in the second part of **[77]** and the opening phrase of **[76]**).[37] The biblical lexeme 'to build', on whose interpretation I shall concentrate here, is extended in the direction of other types of *acquisition*. Other ways to obtain possession of a house, apart from 'to build', are listed: to buy, to inherit, and to receive as a gift. This is the Extension1.1 structure: one biblical item is taken to point to further items, given in list form. No exegetical reason is signalled for this in **[77]**, although the Gemara identifies it as a type of Extension5.[38] I shall use the notion of *paradigm*, or 'axis of selection', for speaking about these options for extension.[39] The notion of a paradigm is contrasted to that of a *syntagma*, or the 'axis of combination'.[40] It is, of course, my contribution to provide a general term for the paradigm along which the Mishnah extends the meaning of 'to build', namely, 'acquisition' in my explanation of **[77]**. The terms which make up the Mishnaic list are readily transposed into a series of halakhic case schemata. Perhaps the use of an abstract term (whose link to individual case schemata would require its own interpretation) is precisely what the Mishnah wishes to avoid by adding terms of the same generality as the biblical one.[41] How is the paradigm, or the perspective in which the

---

[35] ΣπE1.0E1.1(E5?)T3.

[36] The Munich MS and the first print of the Mishnah start the list of items with the biblical 'house' (or 'new house').   [37] אחד שׁור ואחד כל בהמה.

[38] Cf. bSot 43a. The prominent generality with which the subject of the sentence is expressed (. . . מי־האיש אשׁר) is taken to provide an extension of the verb. However, that subject phrase could not determine the Mishnaic paradigm (which still depends on 'to build', see presently), nor does it explain the specific selection of a paradigm of acquisition. See also n. 42.

[39] A very simple example for a paradigm are the numerals, 1, 2, 3, 4, etc. In mMak 1:7 IV (6) we find that the biblical phrase 'two witnesses or three witnesses' (Deut. 17:6) is explained as 'even a hundred'. The rabbinic expression 'a hundred' seems to point to the following hermeneutic move (Extension2.1): the biblical 'two witnesses or three witnesses' implies an open list, extendable to 'four', 'five', 'six' . . . 'one hundred' (cf. Krauß, *Sanhedrin-Makkot*, 325, n. 4). See also case **[101]** in Ch. 11.

[40] These formulations are Jakobson's, e.g. in his 'Linguistics and Poetics', 358. See Lyons, *Introduction to Theoretical Linguistics*, 70–81; Cruse, *Lexical Semantics*, chs. 2 and 3 (esp. pp. 72 ff.). Cf. Malmkjaer, *The Linguistics Encyclopedia*, 437, and also 441; McCarthy, 'Lexis and Lexicology', 299 f., 301 f.; Krampen, 'Ferdinand de Saussure and the Development of Semiology', 73 f.; Lyons, *Semantics*, i. 240 ff.; Crystal, *Dictionary*, 299 f. (s.v. 'syntagmatic').

[41] It is worth recalling that lists are extremely important for the construction of the Mishnaic dis-

Mishnah extends the biblical lexeme, determined? In the present case, it may well be limited by the *legitimacy* of the action—the usurping of property by occupation, for example, is not mentioned—but that is not a prominent semantic aspect of the word 'to build'. On the other hand, certain aspects of the word's meaning are actually suppressed or cancelled: according to the Mishnah, there is no need to have *built* the house in the sense of constructing it, or even to have paid someone else to *build* it. In other words, the semantic facet of 'construction' is eliminated. This means that an interpretation by emphasis and contrast which stresses the word in its semantic limitations is specifically rejected. The above interpretation is the exact opposite of saying: since Scripture chose the word *build* explicitly, it means to exclude *buy* (and *inherit*, and *receive as gift*), because buying is not building.[42] This method of dealing with the boundaries of lexemes (the topic in Chapter 11) is found in the Mishnah much more often than the semantic extension, and it gives a very precise picture of the hermeneutic route not taken in EXTENSION interpretations. In a text such as [77] it is assumed that, by using one term, Scripture includes a whole paradigm of which the term is a member. In defining that paradigm, the slot which the term occupies in the biblical syntagma (be it the sentence, or be it a larger section of the text) is clearly taken into account, and several of these slots can be treated for extension in turn, as is the case in the present passage. What is interpreted is the whole phrase 'to build a house', not merely 'to build'. If the object of 'to build' were not a house,[43] but a bridge or a wall, the paradigm 'build–buy–inherit–receive' would be odd. Clearly, it is put together with the whole biblical sentence (syntagma) in mind. Here is an extreme case where the lexeme to be extended makes no semantic contribution at all. What is extended is the syntactic slot in which it occurs, as such:

[78] = [110b] mBM 9:13 II (4)[44]   Deut. 24:17

A widow, be she poor or be she rich, one does not seize a pledge (ממשכנין) from her, as it is said, 'You shall not [pledge-] take a widow's garment.'

Several things are going on here. The biblical word for taking a pledge (חבל, binding a person by taking a pledge)[45] is replaced by the technical Mishnaic

---

course itself. Neusner's work in particular makes this point repeatedly (e.g. 'The Mishnah's Generative Mode of Thought'). In listing items, rather than defining the class to which they belong, the Mishnah keeps open the lines of communication with the protasis–apodosis units or case schemata. It is their 'casuistic' level which is the main level of discourse for the Mishnah. For this reason alone, the tendency to work with *abstract* companion terms for Scripture could be limited.

[42] Note that in such a case of OPPOSITION the paradigm 'build–buy' could still be the same paradigm, only the relationship of the members would be one of hermeneutic exclusion, not inclusion.

[43] A glance into the biblical concordance shows that the verb 'to build' occurs frequently, but in severely limited collocations: mostly its object is the house (the large majority), the city, and the altar.

[44] ◊C5?L3O9T3.

[45] BDB, 286a; Clines, iii, 149.

one (Topic3); the norm's application to widows is taken to be 'absolute' in a sense that allows no normative distinction between poor or wealthy widows (Opposition9, see Ch. 11); and the word 'garment' *disappears* in the Mishnaic paraphrase. The notion of 'pledge' contained in the Mishnaic verb is not a hyponym of the word 'garment'—they are not linked semantically in the way in which 'ox' and 'cattle' are. In other words, this is not an EXTENSION resource. But it is instructive to see what receives the generalizing treatment here: it is the negated (Logic2) verb חבל, that is, the syntactic slot which the word 'garment' occupies in the verse, with the resulting sense: you cannot take *any* pledge from a widow. I shall return to such cases below when dealing with interpretations of biblical negatives.

The basic classification of the EXTENSION resources revolves around the taxonomic relationship between the lexemes appearing in the Lemma and the Dictum, that is, a semantic relationship. However, when we look at the biblical structures which the Mishnah treats to a semantic extension, the clue often seems to lie in co-textual relationships *within* Scripture: as is clear from a case like **[78]**, the syntagmatic slot is potentially very important in determining the direction of expansion (the paradigm selected by the Mishnah). Also, the group of interpretations dealing with biblical segments containing more than one similar term, that is, the open list, is numerically significant: at least five biblical segments interpreted as allowing extensions are of the Extension2 type,[46] and nine if the passages alluded to in **[76]** are counted.[47] There is a third group of cases which seems to take account of co-textual factors: those where the more specific term is followed by a more general one, or by an all-inclusive statement of some sort (Extension3).[48] The following text illustrates this:

[79] mShebu 3:5 II–III (3)[49] Lev. 5:4

It is all one whether the matters [of the oath] concern himself or others, and whether they regard things that are material or not—how so? If he said: I swear that I will give this to such a man, or: That I will not give it, or: That I have given it, or: That I have not given it . . . R. Ishmael says: He is only liable for [an oath regarding] the future, as it is said, 'To do evil or to do good'. R. Aqiva said to him: If so, I have nothing but [oaths regarding] matters of evil or good—whence [oaths regarding] matters other than evil or good? He said to him: From the extension of Scripture (מרבוי הכתוב). He said to him: If Scripture has extended (רבה)[50] in this regard, it has extended also in the other.

---

[46] mShab 6:4, mBQ 5:7 = **[76]** for Exod. 21:33, mBM 9:13 IV (4), mSan 11:1, mShebu 3:5 I (3), to be discussed presently **[79]**.

[47] Additional verses connected to the **[76]** interpretation: iii (Exod. 22:9), iv (Deut. 22:1), vii (Deut. 22:10), and viii (Deut. 5:14).

[48] Including the following **[76]** cases: iii (Exod. 22:9), iv (Deut. 22:3), viii (Deut. 5:14).

[49] II: •¶¬E2.2(or ¬E3.2)O0(good, bad)T1T3; III: •¶E3.2(good, bad)E3.2(past, future)T1T3.

[50] So the prints. MSS Kaufmann and Cambridge have here, and again in the next clause, the nominal construction ריבוי הכתוב, as does the Sifra parallel ad Lev. 5:4, (ed. Finkelstein, ii. 179). The Gemara (also Bacher, i. 180) simply assumes that there is a switch of speakers, so that the initial claim that there is a *ribbui* is allocated to Aqiva, not Ishmael, and that the last sentence is said by Aqiva. This

The Mishnah's topic are oaths whose violation bring into operation the norms of Lev. 5:6 ff., where confession and offerings are prescribed. The four types of oath given in the opening sentence of [79] reflect the types distinguished in *mishnah* 3:1. Ishmael argues that the words quoted from Lev. 5:4 exclude oaths concerning the past. Here is that verse, in a literal English transposition: 'Or if one swears, to utter with his lips rashly, to do evil or to do good, any rash speaking that men do by oath and it is hidden from him, when he comes to know it he shall be guilty in any one of these.' Two extensions are at stake in this dispute: that from the future sense, expressed in the infinitives,[51] to the past; and that from oaths regarding evil/good to oaths regarding any topic. Ishmael wants to admit the latter, but not the former; Aqiva insists that by admitting the latter through a reading called *ribbui* ('enlargement'), Ishmael also has admitted the former. What is this *ribbui*? The term takes on a very specific meaning in later rabbinic literature, and becomes the opening *middah* or rule of interpretation in the collection *Mishnat R. Eliezer*. I have allocated to this type of *ribbui* the code Extension5.5 above, defining it as dependent on the presence of certain words found in the co-text of the Lemma, such as 'also' (גם).[52] But there seems nothing suitable for the Extension5.5 resource in this verse, Lev. 5:4.[53] On the other hand, there is an 'extension' coming up in the second half of the verse: the word כל (all), translated above as 'any' (that is, Extension3). That seems all that is necessary for Aqiva to include oaths concerning the past and for Ishmael and Aqiva to include oaths concerning any topic.[54] Basically, Scripture could be seen to *provide* the generalization by using 'all', insofar as what comes later in the text constantly modifies the reader's understanding of what came before: readjustment of meaning in the light of later information in the same text is the very substance of textuality and textual consistency.[55]

removes the problem that tradition links the *ribbui* method with Aqiva, not Ishmael; but neither the accepted Mishnah text (including the testimony of Kaufmann) nor the close parallel in Sifra as represented by codex Assemani (ed. Finkelstein, ii. 179) warrant this. See also n. 53 below.

[51] In mMak 1:6 II (3) also, the infinitive seems to be taken as implying future action.

[52] Mielziner, *Introduction*, 124 ff.; Stemberger, *Introduction*, 23; Bacher, i. 180 f.; cf. Elman, 'Towards a History of *Ribbuy* in the Babylonian Talmud'.

[53] The Gemara at bShebu 26a makes some suggestions; they have the disadvantage (or advantage) of robbing the word *ribbui* of any meaning linked to the interpretation of specific types of words (see next note). The resource suggested by the Gemara is what I shall label Redundancy9 (Ch. 13).

[54] Passage [79] could be read as a *perat ukhelal* (see n. 54 in Ch. 8), but it is not *this* rule that is invoked in the text, if any rule is invoked. The Gemara (bShebu 26a) allocates to the two rabbis neatly symmetric and mutually exclusive hermeneutic operations (*ribbui-mi'ut-ribbui* for Aqiva, *kelal-ufrat-ukhelal* for Ishmael). But our Mishnaic text shows no trace of these very involved hermeneutic operations. Also, as we said above (n. 50), this talmudic interpretation allocates the *ribbui* to Aqiva, cf. Albeck, *Einführung*, 62. Our *mishnah* also depicts the two rabbis as agreeing, at least for the sake of the argument, on the method of extension and the name of this method. The easiest explanation is that the word *ribbui* did not have a very specific technical meaning, or the meaning later linked to it. See Ch. 13, case [126].

[55] Which is why reading a text a second time is so important for successful reading; it extends the mechanism of consistency from the back to the front. Cf. also my 'Between Scripture and its Rewording', 47. See also the resources of consistency (DIFFERENCE) discussed in the next chapter.

There seems to be only one Mishnaic example of 'also' (*gam*) being specifically selected by a hermeneutic operation. It is found as part of an operation which distributes biblical segments (irrespective of their syntactic function) to a paradigm of Mishnaic companion terms, that is, a Redundancy9 resource.[56] But, although it thus appears in the larger context of a hermeneutic operation of different nature, the *gam* is clearly taken to extend the meaning of the biblical wording *in the dimension determined by its immediate co-text*. Its effect can be accounted for within the syntactic framework of the biblical sentence as it is, aligning it with other EXTENSION resources. And one can conjure up conversational situations in which 'also' could have such a function, as we shall see below. Here is the Extension5.5 passage in question; the two segments of special interest are given in bold print:

[80] = [126a] mMS 5:10[57]   Deut. 26:13

At the time of the afternoon offering on the (last) day of the festival they used to make the declaration [regarding the clearing out of the tithes]. How was the declaration [made]? 'I have removed the holy thing from the house'—this is the second tithe, and the fourth-year planting; **'[also] I have given it to the Levite'—this is the tithe of Levites; 'also (גם) I have given it'—this is the heave offering and the heave offering of the tithe;** 'to the sojourner, to the orphan, and to the widow'—this is the tithe for the poor, the 'gleanings', and the 'forgotten' [sheaf] and the *peah*— even though their absence does not invalidate the declaration; 'from the house'— this is the *Hallah*.

There is no semantic link between 'also' and the heave offerings; there is also no direct linguistic connection between 'house' and the *Hallah*. The passage as a whole applies a distributive approach: items from a Mishnaic paradigm are allocated to members of a Scriptural sentence with varying syntagmatic and semantic functions (see on this Chapter 13). It is in this context that we encounter the particle *gam* (גם) which later rabbinic literature links to the *ribbui*. The allocation of (two types of) heave offering (תרומה) to 'also' cannot be explained as a one-to-one correspondence of these two words. It needs to be framed by the co-textual link between 'also', 'given', and 'Levite'. For the heave offering and the heave offering of the tithe[58] go to the priests, that is, a special group of Levites. The term 'priests', whose inclusion *gam* is taken to indicate, is semantically connected or parallel to one of the terms to which *gam* belongs in the syntactic structure, Levites.[59] The priests thus fulfil the hermeneutic double function of being in

[56] Our topic in the second section of Ch. 13.

[57] Σ ΔπC1(*gam*)D2E5.5(*gam*)P4R9(from the house). There may be a second case of E5.5 in mSot 5:1 II (3) (Aqiva).

[58] Rashi, who otherwise follows this *mishnah* quite closely in his explanation of the verse, has at this point: 'to include (לרבות) heave offering and *first fruits*', i.e. not the heave offering of the tithe.

[59] It is theoretically possible to apply the *gam*-resource (Extension5.5) to 'give' instead of to 'Levite'. The semantic extension would then fall into the dimension of other verbs relevant to the Mishnaic discourse at this point.

the semantic orbit of the biblical wording and of locking on to an item from the relevant Mishnaic paradigm: the priests receive their own categories of agricultural dues. The 'also' is thus not interpreted as defining the relationship between members *present* in the same sentence. Instead, the 'also' points to *unexpressed* information. In this reading, 'And I have *also* given to the Levites' works like the 'also' in the following exchange:

A: 'What did you buy?'
B: 'I *also* bought us a newspaper'

—enunciated with a stress on 'also'. There is *no* other item mentioned in the co-text to which the 'also' can apply in this utterance. In such an exchange, the 'also' would convey the message that the speaker bought something else in addition to the newspaper, which is not being mentioned.[60] If the verse is read in such a construction, 'I *also* have given to the Levites', the *other*, tacit, part of the information would be sought as thematically connected in some way to the giving to the Levites, and that seems to have happened with the Mishnaic choice of heave offerings (to the priest).[61]

In contrast to passage **[79]**, the name *ribbui* is not used here in **[80]**. Whether **[80]** is an example of a *ribbui* as understood in some of the rabbinic sources which regularly mention the name is not clear. It is quite possible that it is a *peripheral* example, for many of the interpretations called *ribbui* do not seem to admit the type of close syntactic and semantic integration of *gam* that I have just provided for **[80]**. The *ribbui* seems often closer to an asemantic and distributive procedure; and our case of 'also' in **[80]** is in fact combined with such a procedure (Redundancy9). My uncertainty about the role of syntactic integration in the resource is reflected in the ambiguous definition of *Extension5.5 above, which is not quite satisfactory. In due course, when a larger corpus of examples from outside the Mishnah has been reviewed, it may be possible to separate procedures involving *gam*, and so on, into two groups: one where they have effect purely through their presence in the co-text; and a second where they presuppose the syntactic integrity of at least the immediate linguistic environment.

THE MISHNAIC INTERPRETATION OF BIBLICAL WORDING AS LOGICAL CONSTANTS[62]

Extension1.0: All the EXTENSION resources discussed so far provide for a biblical lexeme being semantically subsumed under a Mishnaic expression or list. I shall now briefly look at the reverse, that is, a Mishnaic term being

---

[60] Cf. Maimonides's *Commentary* on this passage (trans. Qafih, *Zeraim*, 232), and also on mTem 1:1 (p. 167); see also Bertinoro's Mishnah commentary.
[61] Thus the exclusive linkage of *gam* to 'given to the Levites' presupposes a neutralizing of co-textual links (Cotext1), for Deut. 26:13 *mentions* the other items to which the 'also' applies.
[62] Cf. Allwood *et al.*, *Logic in Linguistics*, for the terminology. 'And' and 'if–then' are treated as

subsumed under a biblical one. Where the Mishnaic term used in the reformulation of one biblical word is a hyponym of the biblical one (say, 'donkey' being subsumed under 'animal'), this is a case of Extension1.0. The general label (leaving open which biblical structure is so interpreted) is Extension*.0, although all the examples I am aware of relate to the occurrence of only one biblical term (that is, Extension1). An instance of this is found in [77] above: the Mishnaic terms 'house for straw' and 'house for cattle' are likely to be considered as falling under the more general biblical 'house'. But this is a special form of Extension1.0, in that the two terms are related as a simple word ('house') and genitive compound ('house of . . .').[63] On the whole, the Extension*.0 resource is rare in this corpus, that is, Mishnaic passages employing or quoting biblical wording. It may be of much greater importance, however, for Mishnaic statements which lie beyond the scope of this investigation: passages which betray no hermeneutic link to Scripture on the Mishnaic text surface. Passage [77] is interesting in that the Mishnaic co-text (*mishnah* 8:3) also provides information on what it considers *excluded*, namely the gatehouse, the portico, and the balcony/gallery.[64] Here is a slightly different example. Scripture is credited with choosing a superordinate ('flock') when it could have used the two words which are the relevant hyponyms ('sheep', 'goats'):

[81] mBek 9:1 II (2)[65]   Lev. 27:32

Tithe applies . . . to sheep and goats, and they can be tithed one from the other . . . It could have been a [correct] inference [to say]: If the old and the new breed, which are not diverse kinds for each other, cannot be tithed one from the other, should sheep and goats, which are diverse kinds for each other, not all the more be forbidden to be tithed one from the other? In this regard it is instructive that Scripture says (תלמוד לומר), 'and the flock'—the whole of the meaning of 'flock' is as one.[66]

The two terms 'goat' and 'sheep' exhaust the superordinate 'flock' (צאן). The overall structure of this passage is familiar; several times in Chapter 8 an *a fortiori* argument has been encountered which is presented as being only a preliminary position (¬Analogy4), and whose refutation is introduced by תלמוד לומר. The *a fortiori* here suggests a distinction between goats and sheep regarding the substitution of tithe of cattle. This is rejected on the basis of Scripture in the relevant verse using a superordinate that covers both simultaneously. The word 'one/the same' is again used as indication that items share the same class, as in passages [76], [77], and [79]. Here it is used

logical connectives (pp. 26 ff.) and so is negation (p. 30); 'all' is a logical quantifier (p. 62); for the word 'constants', covering both connectives and quantifiers, see pp. 27, 62. Cf. Frawley, *Linguistic Semantics*, 465 ff. (links between logical quantifiers and demonstratives and articles).

[63] There is a remarkable exploration of taxonomic relationships in non-biblical Hebrew usage in mNed 7:1.

[64] בית שער/אכסדרה/ומרפסת. The first of these terms also shows that the inclusion or exclusion does not depend on the presence of the word 'house' in the Mishnaic compound.

[65] E1.0O9.

[66] The concluding phrase in Hebrew is: כל משמע צאן אחד.

to say that the hyponyms of 'flock', sheep and goat, are 'as one', that is, can be tithed one from the other.

Interpreting Biblical 'all'[67]

In the next category of resource the Scriptural intention to include a whole is not located in its choice of lexeme, but in its employment of the word 'all'. The Mishnah *emphasizes* the inclusive, or 'absolute', character of the Scriptural 'all, every'.[68] These interpretations could be said to pick up the *rhetorical* dimension of 'all', probing the difference it makes to the clause or sentence in which it occurs—what is *added* when compared to the same sentence without 'all'. This is manifest mostly by the Mishnah's identification of an extreme[69] or unexpected element. This element shows which *paradigm* the Mishnah has identified as being completely included in the 'all' of Scripture. Perhaps the most famous example is the following passage, which includes the sinners of Israel in the life of the world to come:

[82] mSan 10:1 I (2)[70] Isa. 60:21

All of Israel have a share in the world to come, for it is said, 'And your people all of them are righteous ones, forever they shall inherit the earth, branch of my planting, work of my hands that I may be glorified'.[71]

It is clear from the co-text that the Mishnaic theme here is the life of those who were condemned to death by a human court.[72] It is the sinners which the Mishnah identifies as being called 'righteous'—by virtue of being members of Israel. Why? Obviously because it says 'your people are *all* righteous'.[73] If we look at this passage from the point of view of the 'axis of selection', it is clear that the word 'righteous' simply defines the paradigm applied to which 'your whole people' also includes the other end of the spectrum: the sinner (although no such antonym to 'righteous' appears in the Mishnaic text). This is quite typical: 'all' is emphasized by presenting a paradigm of opposites whose *two end-points* are included. Recall here passage [13] mBer 1:5 I (2); in the biblical phrase 'all the days of your life' the

---

[67] Cf. Allwood *et al.*, *Logic in Linguistics*, 61 ff.; Quine, *Methods of Logic*, sec. 16; Frawley, *Linguistic Semantics*, 466. On the grammatical aspects of כל, see Gesenius–Kautzsch, *Hebrew Grammar*, secs. 127b, c, 146c; also secs. 117c, 152b.

[68] Our first taste of this was [13] mBer 1:5 I (2), in Ch. 3.

[69] Occasionally the Mishnah uses a word to signal the presence of such an interpretation: 'even', אפילו. See n. 93 below and Ch. 12, text at passage [114a] (Opposition6/7).

[70] L1O7(forever)T3W1(*olam*)W7(earth).

[71] So MS Munich and the Naples print, except that the latter has a shorter quotation. However, this opening of the tenth chapter of Sanhedrin is not found in all texts, and even where it is found it does not always have the Scriptural quotation. The whole is absent from MSS Cambridge and Kaufmann, while Parma (de Rossi 138) does not have the quotation, cf. Krauß, *Sanhedrin-Makkot*, 397 f. See also Goldin, *Studies*, 31; Urbach, *The Sages*, 991 f. Finkelstein suggests that this passage once belonged to tractate Avot to which it is still linked in its liturgical usage (*Mavo le-Massekhtot Avot we-Avot de-Rabbi Natan*, 104, 212 ff.; also pp. xxi f.).

[72] Cf. the thematically connected unit [57b] in Ch. 6, and also mMak 3:15.

[73] Although the Mishnah goes on to specify exceptions, these are not what one might call 'regular' sinners and criminals—for the latter, the inclusive effect of the 'all' holds.

word 'all' is understood to *add* the nights to the days, making them complete 'days'. Similar again is the way in which the following midrashic unit brings into play the rabbinic concept pair of good and evil inclination:

[82a] = [15] = [114a] mBer 9:5 I (9)[74]   Deut. 6:5

Man is obliged to perform blessings over evil just as he performs blessings over good, as it is said, 'And you shall love the Lord your God with all your heart and with all your soul and with all your might'. 'With all your heart'—with your two inclinations, with the good inclination and with the evil inclination.[75]

The biblical metaphor 'heart' is taken in its figurative sense, understood by the Mishnah as the seat of the will or the inclinations[76] or the appetites. But its two opposite directions (Topic3, as assumed by rabbinic views on humanity) are yoked together by the word 'all'. This meeting of opposites in the biblical 'all' is no less effective when biblical norms are the topic, as the following passage shows:

[83] mBek 8:1[77]   Exod. 13:2

A man who has no children and marries a woman who has already given birth; [a woman who] was still a bondwoman and was then freed, [a woman who] was still a non-Jew and then converted, and she gave birth after she became an Israelite: [her son] is [deemed] 'a first-born for inheritance and not a first-born for the priest['s dues]'.[78] R. Yose Ha-Gelili says: He is a first-born for inheritance and for priest['s dues], for it is said, '[Holy to me be every first-born], opening of [every] womb among the children of Israel . . .'—as long as they open the womb in Israel.

The second halakhic category of first-born is defined by the father's obligation to redeem every first-born by payment to the priest. The verse in question contains *two* appearances of 'all, every': קדש לי כל־בכור פטר כל־רחם בבני ישראל. And it seems that it is the second occurrence which serves R. Yose to make his argument: if 'womb among the children of Israel' means every Israelite woman's womb—what does '*every* womb among the children of Israel' mean? As in the case of the 'righteous' in [82], the paradigm is taken to be determined by a term occurring in the phrase itself, namely, the phrase 'among Israel'. And, again as in passage [82], it is at the *opposite* end of the spectrum so defined at which the additional meaning is located: outside Israel. Brought into the range of the norm by the word כל are women

[74] ΩL1O6T3(two inclinations).

[75] See the literature cited in n. 52 of Ch. 3. The use of the concept of the two inclinations for interpreting 'with all your heart' could be influenced by the interpretation of the subsequent 'with all your might' (namely as בכל מדה ומדה). However, the overall structure of the Mishnaic passage is three-fold, distributing separate themes to the three occurrences of 'with all your . . .'.

[76] 'Inclinations' is one of the choices offered by BDB (523b), especially for the occurrences in the books of Chronicles.

[77] •¶L1O8(in)T3W2(*peter*).

[78] The opening sentence of this *mishnah* introduces a distinction between two concepts of 'first-born': the first-born whose inheritance is the double portion, and the first-born who, as holy to God, requires redemption money to be paid to the priest. A person may be a first-born under one definition but not the other. The main hand of MS Kaufmann omits the 'all' from the subsequent biblical quotation, as do other witnesses.

whose womb had been opened before, but *outside* Israel. The stress on '*every womb among* Israel' then produces the result that the (first) opening of the womb *inside* Israel is meant, even if that is not the (first) opening for the woman concerned.[79]

This is the taxonomic effect which the Mishnah achieves by placing a hermeneutic focus on the biblical universal quantifier (to give it its name in logic):[80]

Logic1: Interpretation of the effect of biblical 'all, every' as including all members of the lexeme governed by it. The totality can be identified as a universal class, or as including even the eccentric members of a paradigm partly selected according to the lexeme governed by 'all', or as uniting the two poles of an opposition whose terms are hyponyms of the lexeme governed by 'all'.

Why should the biblical כל be considered to *add* anything at all?[81] Why not simply say that the sentences in which 'all' occurs are universal, and those in which it does not are not? It seems that the answer must be sought in the normative speech act performed by or ascribed to biblical verses. If we consider for a moment the distinction introduced by Albrecht Alt between casuistic and apodictic legal sentences,[82] we see that both types require a universal reading. The parts of verses listed above for our passage **[76]** may serve as a reminder of the formal traits. To take Exod. 23:5 (v) as an example, it is clear that the very use of the word 'ass' in that sentence requires the interpretation 'any ass'. The 'if–then' structure is a generalizing format, and all conditional structures like it (containing a protasis and apodosis) are formats for generalizations. Among other things, this is clear from the alternative formulations we can give them by using such words as 'whenever' and 'whoever' (cf. the translation of Exod. 19:12 as verse (ii) of **[76]**). So, hypotheticals create generalizations,[83] and this is a feature that gives the Mishnah itself much of its character, for it is dominated by this format. But the apodictic format too requires a general interpretation of its terms: 'You shall not muzzle an ox when it treads out the grain' does not mean: you may not muzzle the next ox you come across treading grain, but the one you meet thereafter you may muzzle. One is not done fulfilling the

---

[79] It should perhaps be conceded that the same result might have been achieved by exclusive stress on the phrase 'womb among the children of Israel' alone. One thus cannot be *certain* that the presence of the 'all' was decisive for the operation, in particular in view of the MS situation (see preceding note). The very same paradigm is the basis for an OPPOSITION operation in mBek 1:1, despite the appearance of 'all' in the verse: the unborn first-born of an animal bought from a non-Jew is not subject to the law of the first-born.

[80] See the literature quoted in n. 62 above.

[81] Cf. Albeck, *Einführung*, 84.

[82] Alt, 'The Origins of Israelite Law'; cf. Westbrook, 'Biblical Law', 6; Noth, *The Laws in the Pentateuch and Other Studies*, 7 f.; Jackson, *Studies in the Semiotics of Biblical Law*, sec. 2.3.1 f.

[83] See Frawley, *Linguistic Semantics*, 358 and 405 f., where conditionals and generics are treated together: 'Whoever has any time lifts a finger to help' and 'Should he have any time, he will lift a finger to help'.

norm after once fulfilling it. It means *any* ox. The English phrase 'an ox' in the translation of that verse is not like the same phrase in 'Yesterday I saw an ox with a blue ribbon tied around its neck'. It is not a narrative ox; it is a normative one. So the moment the Mishnah has decided that something in Scripture is a norm, not the report of some singular fact, happening, or act, it has to impose a generalizing reading on the terms of the text.[84] This is understood throughout, and is sometimes obvious from the appearance of a Mishnaic 'all, every' in the Dictum where there is none in the Lemma.[85] And where the expectation of a deliberate crafting of the text is as high as it is in rabbinic hermeneutics, which assumes a divine legal draughtsman, the presence of a word like 'all' becomes a conspicuous, namely initially redundant, *addition* of generality.

Before I turn to another manifestation of generality, negation, these interpretations of 'all' should be put into perspective. The Mishnah gives to many biblical verses containing an 'all' a meaning which is incompatible with Logic1, that is with its interpretation as universal inclusion or as adding information for inclusion.[86] It can receive a wholly pragmatic interpretation, as the next unit shows, which deals with the rebellious elder:

[84] mSan 11:4[87]   Deut. 17:13

They do not put him to death in the court which is in his city, and not in the court which is in Yavneh, but they bring him up to the great court which is in Jerusalem. And they guard him until the pilgrim festival, and put him to death at the pilgrim festival, as it is said, 'And *all* the people shall hear and shall fear [and not act presumptuously any more]'—these are the words of R. Aqiva. R. Yehudah says: One does not delay the sentence of such a one, but puts him to death immediately, and they write and send messengers to *all* places: The man so-and-so was found liable to death in court.

The requirement that *all* the people should hear and see the punishment receives two solutions, but only R. Yehudah reflects the 'all' of the verse directly. R. Aqiva's solution is totally pragmatic. The large number of Jews gathered in Jerusalem during the three pilgrim festivals is perhaps an approximation to reaching them 'all'—but clearly not if read with strict emphasis. But there may be a stress on 'shall hear' here (Opposition0: no *seeing* required, for example). And if the pilgrims are assumed to bring back rumour of the execution to their homes and villages after their return, perhaps 'all' will indeed hear of it. Yet there may be places which do not

---

[84] This is the reason why similar norms can be seen as incompatible with each other on the basis of slight differences between them. See next chapter. Cf. Hirschfeld, *Halachische Exegese*, 191.

[85] These cases are numerous, see e.g. mMen 10:4 II (2). But where this happens with verses which are not norms, such as Isa. 10:13 in mYad 4:4 II (4), we are forced to look for other reasons for the generalization.

[86] To take just one example, mSan 10:6 II (6): the expression 'all its spoil' in the norms for the apostate city in Deut. 13:17 (E 16) is contrasted with the spoil 'belonging to God' which is thus seen as lying outside the scope of the 'all'. So, as in the case of taxonomic relationships, the paradigm can be used to limit as well as to expand.

[87] • ¶¬L1O0(hear only?)T5.

hear of it, and here R. Yehudah is different with his insistence that *all* places be informed. So Aqiva's reading of the verse could be described partly by the *non*-application (¬) of resource Logic1.

Interpreting Biblical Negation[88]

Negating a sentence can have a similar effect to generalizing it. Compare 'Some animals lay eggs' with 'No mammal lays eggs'. The word 'some' signals that no generalizing is possible: some animals lay eggs, others do not. The word 'no', on the other hand, allows generalization across all members of the class 'mammal': none of them lays eggs, and therefore the statement is true of *all* of them.[89] The emphatic or 'literal' interpretation of negation is illustrated in the following midrashic unit. There is again a refutation of an *a fortiori* argument by way of a Scriptural interpretation introduced by תלמוד לומר:

[85] mSot 6:3 II (4)[90]   Num. 5:13

[*mishnah* 2] If one witness said: 'I have seen her, that she was defiled', she does not drink [the *Sotah* waters], and not only thus, but even a slave, even a handmaid, behold these are believed . . . Her mother-in-law, the daughter of her mother-in-law . . . behold these are believed . . . [3] It could have been a [correct] inference [to say]: If the initial testimony, which renders her not forbidden forever [to her husband], cannot be established by less then two witnesses, should not the later testimony which does render her forbidden forever, [also] be established by a minimum of two witnesses?[91] In this regard it is instructive that Scripture says, 'and there is no witness against her'—any testimony regarding her.

The negation found in the biblical phrase quoted at the end, ועד אין בה, is given a generalizing interpretation to extraordinary effect. If only the *total absence* of witnesses is a necessary condition of the *Sotah* ordeal, then even one witness is enough nullify that condition. One witness is not 'no witness', despite the otherwise entrenched Mishnaic notion of a minimum of two witnesses (cf. Deut. 19:15).[92] And the extension goes further: persons who in other contexts are ruled out as witnesses can give testimony in this case—'even'[93] they are enough to falsify the '*no* witness' condition. Two different paradigms have been chosen in succession: the number of

---

[88] Cf. Gesenius–Kautzsch, *Hebrew Grammar*, sec. 152.

[89] Of some importance in explaining this is the notion of scope of negation; see Frawley, *Linguistic Semantics*, 399 ff.

[90] ¶L3O1.4O7.

[91] The two types of testimony seem to relate to the wife's hiding (with another man, after being warned by her husband) on the one hand, which testimony launches the *Sotah* ritual; and on the other hand to her committing adultery, which testimony renders the *Sotah* ritual superfluous. Cf. ySot 6:3 (ed. Krotoshin, 27b); see Bietenhard, *Sota*, 107. This means that the phrase 'no witness' is taken to the immediately preceding 'has defiled herself' and not the earlier 'has hidden herself' in Num. 5:13. See also Epstein, *Mavo*, 655 ff.

[92] Cf. the discussion in bSot 2a–b; see Jackson, '*Testes Singulares* in Early Jewish Law and the New Testament', who does not mention our passage; however, see ibid. 186, n. 46.

[93] The word used in *mishnah* 2: אפילו. See n. 69 above.

witnesses, and the status of the witnesses, and at least for the former, and perhaps for both, the presence of the negation is taken to mean inclusion of extreme cases[94] or borderline cases.

Logic3: Interpretation of the effect of a biblical negation as including all members of the lexeme governed by it. The totality can be identified as a universal class, or as including even the eccentric members of a paradigm partly selected in accordance with the lexeme governed by the negation, or as uniting both poles of an opposition whose terms are hyponyms of the lexeme governed by the negation.

That negation can be construed as defining a whole class is clear from an example like mPeah 7:7 I (3),[95] where the prohibition to take the defective clusters when harvesting the grapes (Lev. 19:10) is understood by Aqiva to hold '*even* if they are *all*' defective clusters.

Interpreting the Biblical Conjunction Waw[96]

If the above treatment of biblical 'all' and 'not' is considered, it can be seen that it resembles the interpretation given to these signs of natural language in the context of formal logic. That is why I have chosen the name LOGIC for this resource family. In formal logic, negation is taken to invert the truth value of the term governed by it. As far as 'all, every' is concerned, it is classed among the logical constants, as I said before. There is another biblical construction which the Mishnah sometimes interprets in the same way in which formal logic treats certain signs occurring in natural language. This is the biblical use of the conjunction 'and'. In formal logic, a proposition put together from two clauses joined by 'and' is only true if both of its clauses are true.[97] This *defines* the logical connective 'and'. Thus, the whole sentence 'The sun is a star and the sun was first discovered by Galileo', is not true unless Galileo was the first to discover the sun, even if it is true that the sun is a star. This logical interpretation is by no means divorced from the use of 'and' in ordinary language. But there are cases where the import of 'and' is quite different, as for instance in the sentence: 'The grass is green, the sun is shining, and I am happy.' Clearly, the treatment of 'and' as logical connective has its limits for natural language.[98] But the Mishnah contains interpretations which show that the formal logical qualities of 'and' were part of its hermeneutic horizon:

[86] mZeb 12:1[99]   Lev. 7:33

. . . [priests] with a blemish, be it a permanent blemish or a transitory blemish, have

---

[94]   In the case of the number, the limiting case is the smallest integer: one.
[95]   Quoted in its entirety as **[115]** in the next chapter.
[96]   Cf. Gesenius–Kautzsch, *Hebrew Grammar*, sec. 154.
[97]   Allwood *et al.*, *Logic in Linguistics*, 32 ff.
[98]   The Mishnaic treatment of 'and' also has another dimension, see the Syntax5 resource defined in Ch. 13.   [99]   (E1.2)L7T2.

a share and eat [of the priestly food], but they do not offer sacrifices. And anyone who is not fit for [sacrificial] service has no share in the flesh [of the sacrifices], and anyone who has no [share] in the flesh has none in the hides. Even (אפילו) he who was unclean at the time of the sprinkling of the blood and clean at the time of the burning of the fat pieces has no share in the flesh, as it is said, 'He who offers the blood of peace offerings and the fat among the sons of Aaron, his shall be the right thigh for a portion.'

The opening sentence of this *mishnah*, not translated here, speaks of a priest for whom the sunset completes his period of purification. That is the perspective imposed on the biblical verse: a priest who makes the transition from unclean to clean *during* the time of the sacrifice (Topic2). Of such a priest it is said that he has not, by being ritually pure at the time of the offering of the fat pieces alone, acquired the right to the sacrificial portions, because of the 'and' (*waw*) connecting the blood and fat in the conditional clause. Only of the person who would be fit to offer the blood *and* fat does Scripture say: 'his shall be the right thigh for a portion.' The word 'to offer' is understood as 'to offer validly' (Habit4), which in the selected perspective means specifically 'ritually clean'; the verse's message is also generalized to any priest who *potentially* offers, that is, is eligible to offer. Interpreted as logical connector (and perhaps seen to be emphasized by the presence of the *nota accusativi*), the 'and' produces a decision on a borderline case: the person who fulfils one condition, but not the conjunction of conditions, falls outside the limit. In our passage, the borderline perspective is expressed by 'even', אפילו. The same word is used to mark the inclusion of extreme members of a paradigm in the above passages illustrating the resources Logic1 and Logic3. A conjunction of conditions as highlighted for Lev. 7:33 in **[86]** is quite frequent in biblical law, and so rabbinic interpretation could often have had occasion to make a decision (tacit or otherwise) about the force of the connector 'and'.

Logic7 Interpretation of the effect of biblical 'and' (*waw*) as making a Mishnaic or biblical apodosis dependent on simultaneous fulfilment or applicability of all the biblical elements conjoined by it.

Here is another example of such an understanding of 'and':

[87] mBQ 4:9 II (3)[100]   Exod. 21:29

If its [the ox's] owner had tied it with reins, and shut it in properly and it got out and caused damage, be it accounted harmless or an 'attested' danger, he is liable—the words of R. Meir. R. Yehudah says: For the ox accounted harmless he is liable, and for that accounted an 'attested' danger he is free, for it is said, '[And if . . .] and he does not guard him . . .'—and this one [the ox under discussion] is guarded. R. Eliezer says: There is no guarding for it but the knife.

[100] ◊ • ¶πL7O7T2T3.

The biblical verse here used by R. Yehudah reads: 'And if (וְאִם) the ox was accustomed to gore in the past and warning had been issued ("attested") to its owner and he does not guard it and it kills a man or a woman, the ox shall be stoned and its owner also shall be put to death.' For R. Yehudah, and perhaps also for R. Meir, the condition 'he does not guard it' is as necessary as the other conditions to which it is linked by 'and' in the protasis (attestation, killing). In other words, if the owner *has* 'guarded' it, the apodosis becomes inapplicable. The presence of 'and he does not guard him' in the rule regarding the ox which is an attested danger therefore has the effect of limiting liability; a somewhat paradoxical effect, as for the ox accounted harmless no such limitation exists in R. Yehudah's view. The *waw* is taken to have 'absolute' meaning, making a difference for the special hypothetical case (Topic2: ox guarded, but able to free itself).[101]

HERMENEUTIC EVIDENCE AND HALAKHIC EFFECTS; THE ELEMENTS OF CATEGORY EXTENSION

In using the notions of extension or exclusion it is important to distinguish the description on the level of the sentence and its semantic relationships from the level of halakhah: what is an extension in semantic terms can, depending on the construction in which it occurs, turn out to be a restriction in halakhic terms. This is in fact quite common. The application of Analogy8 in [72] affords an example. The whole class of property to be proclaimed by the finder is *restricted* to those items which have a distinct mark and a claimant through analogically *extending* the characteristics of 'garment'. Among the factors which determine the halakhic effect of a semantic expansion are the syntactic slot in Scripture, as well as the overall meaning of the sentence: is it affirmed or negated, does it regulate an obligation or a permission?[102] In passage [76], the subject of the norm is generalized (from 'ox' to 'cattle', to take the simplest case), therefore the halakhic scope is extended. Similar are [77], [79], and [83]. The question of scope needs in turn to be kept separate from the question of leniency or stringency, for the expansion of a 'lenient' norm may mean that a case otherwise subject to a more stringent norm is treated as less severe, and so on. Also, what is lenient for one party in a legal relationship may be disadvantageous (and thus 'stringent') for the other. The effect of [86] is to exclude more priests from theoretical benefit, because the elements in the conditional clause are read in strict conjunction; in [87] the effect is—in the opinion of R. Yehudah—similar, leading to an exclusion of liability for the owner of the ox. By speaking about these effects of the hermeneutic work

---

[101] A close parallel in the Mekhilta to the above passage [87] is discussed in Jackson, 'On the Nature of Analogical Argument in Early Jewish Law', 162 ff.

[102] Cf. Frawley for the semantic aspect (*Linguistic Semantics*, 421 ff.).

performed with the biblical texts I am moving on to totally unfamiliar ground in this study. This alone shows how absent observations of *this* kind are from the hermeneutic argument of the Mishnah. Halakhic outcomes as such, whether in terms of advantage or disadvantage, leniency or stringency, values of practicality or fairness, or similar considerations do not, as such, become routinely part of the hermeneutic procedure. Something similar is true of 'theological' convictions or values in the non-halakhic ('aggadic') hermeneutic discourse. All sorts of priorities or preferences that may have played a role in interpreting the biblical wording in one way rather than another, or in favouring a particular version of a biblical norm over another, or in applying a resource which 'extends' in preference to one which 'excludes', are absent from the midrashic units quoted above and are generally rare. They may well be presupposed, however, and occasionally become visible in substantive assumptions entering the hermeneutic process (e.g. Topic3/Topic3.1). They sometimes also enter the argument in the case of disputes. Thus, the practicability of a halakhic consequence drawn from an interpretation is questioned in mYom 1:1 (with the words, 'if so, the matter would have no end'—אם כן אין לדבר סוף). There is certainly no watertight separation of formal and pragmatic arguments in the Mishnaic discourse in any case, and that includes hermeneutic arguments. And yet, it happens only very occasionally that the non-hermeneutic or 'motivational' element clashes directly with the results of observations on the biblical text (but see resource Topic8.5).[103] This almost certainly means that most interpretation results which were in practice quite unacceptable to the rabbis are simply not suggested in the first place (at least in the Mishnah).

To review the different resources by which the level of generality of a biblical expression can be determined: there is the taxonomic substitution of a hyponym by its superordinate or a class (Extension1.2, [Extension7], Analogy8). There is also the option to interpret a biblical sentence which contains a generalizing expression (either a superordinate, or 'all') that governs or supplements a lexeme with narrower meaning as extending that narrower meaning, that is, Extension3. All other EXTENSION resources rely on mechanisms of textual *proximity* which operate even in the absence of syntactic dependency or semantic overlap, usually in the same sentence. These proximity resources include:

- the presence of further items of the same level of generality (understood as an 'open' list, Extension2);
- the presence of a universal quantifier or generalizing expression (such as 'the/any man who') governing a lexeme other than that whose range is expanded (Extension5);

[103] For Topic8.5 see Ch. 12 below. What seems to happen more often is that a hermeneutic observation is countered by another hermeneutic observation first (so that they cancel each other out), and thereafter an argument of different *type* is brought to bear.

- the presence of redundant items in the co-text (Redundancy9, see Chapter 13 below); and
- the proximity of certain particles of inclusion (*Extension5.5).

It is with special regard to these resources that the investigation of some of the rabbinic *middot* seems most promising. It seems worth asking whether the presence of one or several of these resources could trigger use of the names *heqqesh*, *ribbui*, *perat ukhelal*, or *binyan av* in rabbinic literature, and in which parts of rabbinic literature.

10

Biblical Presupposition and Canonical Meaning. Biblical Contradiction and Biblical Constrast

The Mishnah may address explicitly information which is merely presupposed in biblical formulations. Such presuppositions can be turned into conditions for the application of a norm. The Mishnah may also address biblical expressions on the level of their semantic 'normality' (canonicity), deriving from them a 'suitability' restriction in the scope of norms. In construing the meaning of Scripture, the Mishnah is guided by an underlying search for coherence and thus avoids inconsistency. Where inconsistency is tacitly avoided or becomes an explicit hermeneutic problem, the most frequent solution is the *distributive* allocation of topics, meaning, or reference to two biblical segments. Such distributive allocation may also be used to endow with special significance structures of linguistic or textual discontinuity which are not open 'contradictions' on a propositional level. In such cases, Mishnaic paradigms or lists play an important role.

INVESTIGATING THE BIBLICAL PRESUPPOSITION OF EXISTENCE

Almost constantly when using language we take for granted the existence of certain things without explicitly asserting or addressing their existence. The utterance 'We are going to meet in the town square at six o'clock' makes no claim that there is a town square, and yet its validity would be severely affected if it turned out that there was no square in that town. Such indirect and unavoidable commitment to the existence of certain items mentioned in an utterance is usually referred to as presupposition, or existential presupposition.[1] The sentence 'There is a town square in that town', which asserts its existence, would simply be false if there were no town square. But an utterance which *presupposes* the town square's existence, while still affected, is apparently not invalidated in the same way. There are several stock illustrations for presuppositions, among them 'Have you stopped beating your wife?'[2] and 'The present king of France is bald'.[3] The 'town square' is not a stock example, but appears (in a manner of speaking) in a biblical norm which is of interest to the Mishnah. Deut. 13:12 ff. commands the destruction of an idolatrous city, and the city's 'open space' plays a role:

[88] mSan 10:6 I (6)[4]　　Deut. 13:17 (E 16)

'And all its spoil you shall bring into the midst of its open space [and you shall burn with fire the town and all its spoil, a complete-offering to the Lord your God, and it shall be a ruin forever, it shall not be built.]' If it does not have an open space, they make an open space for it; if its open space was outside it, they bring it into it, for it is said, 'into the midst [of] its open space'.

What is of interest to us in the present context is the interpretation required by the first Dictum in particular. The biblical norm *presupposes* that the city will have such an open space, and the Mishnah isolates this presupposition as such. It answers the question: how is the validity of the norm affected if this presupposition is not fulfilled? In other words, it tacitly rejects a treatment of this presupposition as irrelevant or unimportant. In the Mishnaic view, the biblical wording disallows that the spoils can be burned elsewhere, or need not be burned at all, and so on. Specifically, two ways are addressed in which the presupposition may be unfulfilled: the city may not have an open space, or it may lie outside the town.[5] In either case the Mishnaic solution involves those charged with the application of this norm in *creating* the existentially presupposed item: the open space is necessary for the fulfilment of the norm. On the other hand, its existence is not taken to be presupposed as from *before* the commencement of the punitive action commanded in the sentence—were this so, its lack could not be remedied. Here is an example of how the same attitude to presupposition, namely,

---

[1] Allwood *et al.*, *Logic in Linguistics*, 150 f. distinguish three types of presupposition: existential, factive, and sortal (or categorial). Although there is at least one example of a categorial presupposition being clarified in the Mishnah (mHag 1:7 III (3)), most of them seem to be existential.

[2] Ibid. 149; cf. Levinson, *Pragmatics*, 181 f. (no. 4); Walton, *Informal Logic*, 35 ff.; see also Sperber and Wilson, *Relevance*, 202–17, esp. 202 f., 213–15; Coseriu, *Textlinguistik*, 171 f. Cf. also Austin, *How to Do Things with Words*, 20, 48–51, 149.

[3] Object of a famous pair of papers in modern logic: Bertrand Russell's 'On Denoting' and Peter Strawson's 'On Referring'. See Black, *Models and Metaphors*, 48–63; Cruse, *Lexical Semantics*, 110–11 (n. 20); Levinson, *Pragmatics*, ch. 4 (pp. 167–225); Walton, *Informal Logic*, 28–59; Sperber and Wilson, *Relevance*, 202–21; Brown and Yule, *Discourse Analysis*, 28–34; Frawley, *Linguistic Semantics*, 22 f., 41 f.; Kempson, *Semantic Theory*, 139 ff.　　　　　　[4] ΣπH6.

[5] BDB, s.v. רחוב (932a), take Nahum 2:5 to imply that the open space was outside Nineveh's city walls; and Dan. 9:25 to list it as an apparently essential part of a city. The concluding biblical quotation is missing from popular prints (cf. Krauß, *Sanhedrin-Makkot*, 399). It works well, by suggesting a reading of אל־תוך רחבה as: 'in(to) the middle, its open space'. Hoenig discusses the significance of the 'open space' in 'The Ancient City-Square'.

that it affects the application of a norm, works when there is nothing to be done[6] about the existence of the item presupposed:

[89] mHul 8:4 III (3)[7]   Deut. 14:21

A bird, which is forbidden because of 'carrion', is it not an inference that it is forbidden with regard to cooking in milk?[8] In this regard it is instructive that Scripture says: 'in the milk of its mother'—[this] excludes the bird, for it does not have mother's milk.

This midrashic unit follows on from passage **[66]** mHul 8:4 II (3). In that unit Yose Ha-Gelili argues that the proximity of the two norms on carrion and on cooking the kid mean that the range of subjects of the former is the same as that of the latter. The voice speaking here in **[89]** (also Yose Ha-Gelili?) seems to accept that position with the exception of birds: the bird is excluded because the term 'milk of its mother' cannot be applied to it. In other words, the fact that one of its existential presuppositions is not fulfilled is accepted as excluding birds from the range of the norm as a whole. Here is the hermeneutic mechanism in a nutshell:

Habit6: Explication of one of the existential presuppositions of a norm as possible or definite condition of its application.

The resource is defined inclusively ('possible or definite') so as to capture all cases in which an existential presupposition is explicated by the Mishnah, regardless of whether or not it is adopted or rejected as a criterion for the application of the norm. The same goes for the resources Habit4 and Habit7 to be defined below.

I will shift perspective for a moment and look at the halakhic effect of this (cf. the final section of the preceding chapter). It will be obvious that the Habit6 resource can be handy to make the application of a biblical norm, or a punishment, more difficult than it might otherwise be: the existence of every element in the norm's wording can be turned into a necessary condition for its application, thus reducing the actual number of instances for which the norm takes effect.[9] There is patently much freedom in choosing to which norms to apply the presupposition question, and which semantic elements of a given norm to select for it. However, as far as the semantic mechanism itself is concerned, there is much less choice: the presuppositions connected with linguistic items seem to be determined strongly by the identity of that item itself.[10]

---

[6] Practical difficulty encountered in bringing about an existential presupposition is used as argument in mYom 1:1. See the final section of Ch. 9 above.

[7] •πH6.

[8] The terminology of 'inference' (דין) is used in MS Kaufmann and Maimonides' text (*Commentary*, trans. Qafih, *Qodashim*, 142); other witnesses have 'could it be . . .?'

[9] A very clear example is mSan 8:4 **[91]**, using the related resource Habit7 (explained below). According to a voice in bSan 71a this norm, the stubborn and rebellious son, has no application, its sole purpose being to allow the acquisition of merit through Scriptural exegesis (דרוש).

[10] Cf. the list of linguistic phenomena triggering presuppositions in Levinson, *Pragmatics*, 181–5.

Fulfilment of the presupposition need not be made a condition of the application of the relevant norm, and the Mishnah contains at least one passage which explicitly rejects the biblical norm's dependency on one of its existential presuppositions. The biblical verse in question deals with a girl who is discovered not to be a virgin only after the wedding has taken place: 'And they shall bring the girl out to the door of her father's house and the men of her town shall stone her with stones and she shall die, for she has done an abomination in Israel to whore while in the house of her father and you shall eliminate the evil from your midst.' The Mishnah, after showing that the words 'in Israel'[11] and 'door of her father's house' affect the applicability of this norm (prescribing stoning) to the daughter of a proselyte, continues as follows:

[90] mKet 4:3 III (3)[12]   Deut. 22:21

If she does have a 'father' but does not have a 'door (of the father's house)', if she does have a 'door of the father's house' but no 'father', behold, she is [nevertheless] punished by stoning. It is said, 'door of her father's house' only for a *mitswah* (= 'commandment').[13]

The concluding statement explicitly rejects the idea that the biblical expressions preclude the application of the norm to girls without a 'father' or 'father's house', that is, where the existential presuppositions of these terms are found not to be fulfilled. The rejection introduces a distinction between a part of the apodosis which contains a *mitswah*, namely, the venue of the stoning, and a main part which prescribes the stoning. The word *mitswah* means 'commandment', and is here used in the sense of a non-essential element of a norm: a requirement that can be dispensed with if necessary.[14] This presupposes the division of the norm into separable parts, and it is really this question of divisibility which is decisive for the hermeneutic operation. The notion that a norm becomes inapplicable because the existential presupposition of one of its terms is not fulfilled implies that the norm has to be taken as a whole or not at all (compare Logic7).

The normative use of biblical presuppositions is only one of a group of resources which give hermeneutic significance to what is understood as the normal, the regular, or the ordinary, and therefore taken to be tacitly assumed in the biblical word choice. In order to express this, I shall name these resources as forming the HABIT family; my choice of this name is also partly determined by the fact that the first letters of other suitable terms are already taken by larger resource groups (see Appendix I below).

[11] Cf. case [83] mBek 8:1 in Ch. 9.

[12] π¬H6¬O6T3.

[13] The format of this phrase, לא נאמר פתח בית אביה אלא למצוה is similar to the question–answer structure, 'If so, why is it said? Because . . .'. The latter is found in some Mishnaic disputes; see list item I.7 in the final section of Ch. 12.

[14] Cf. Jastrow, s.v. מצוה (823b), and the contrasting term עיכוב, defined by Jastrow as 'a circumstance which makes a religious act invalid' (1069a). The latter, used as a verb, does in fact occur in mYeb 12:3 I (2), expressing a distinction between indispensable and dispensable elements of a norm.

Habit6 is applied in most Mishnaic cases either to the apodosis of
a casuistic law or to an apodictic law. This can be understood on the
following basis: since the casuistic norm puts into explicit hypothetical
mode the conditions of the norm, any investigation of the terms of its protasis becomes automatically an investigation of the range of phenomena or
situations to which the norm as a whole applies. A norm starting with 'If
a woman conceives and bears a male child'[15] makes its apodosis explicitly
dependent on there being a woman, childbirth, and a male child. Thus, in
the conditional clause at least some of the existential commitments are
already explicitly presented as conditions for the application of the norm.
But not all terms are equally explicitly included in the conditional structure,
and there seem to be Mishnaic interpretations which make a norm dependent on the existential presupposition of a protasis, not an apodosis.[16]

The question of existential presupposition was encountered in Chapter 3
in the context of introducing the resources Topic3, Topic3.1, and Topic4/
4.1. There I asked: to the existence of what is the Mishnah committed by
giving the biblical text a certain interpretation? And it was discovered that
Mishnaic terms which are offered as companion terms to biblical Lemmas
presuppose, in the very act of explaining the biblical meaning, the existence
of certain items, for example, 'the world to come' or 'the wicked'. In
other words, when investigating what other commitments, apart from the
validity of interpretation, the Mishnah made when interpreting Scripture,
I investigated the *existential presuppositions* of the sentences in which the
Mishnah repeated what it considered to be Scripture's meaning.

There is a resource which is in some respects quite similar to Habit6 but
seems to be based on a different mechanism. It deals with existential presuppositions contained in words as they are on their own, even where used
in isolation. An illustration given by linguists is the word 'kick', which
semantically presupposes the organ with which one performs the action
of kicking: the foot. The technical expression for such a relationship is
'semantic encapsulation'.[17] It seems that such semantic encapsulation is
also occasionally identified by the Mishnah as creating a condition (or
additional condition) for the application of a biblical norm. This is what
appears to happen in the next passage. It deals with the biblical case schema
of the 'stubborn and rebellious son':[18]

<hr>

[15] Cf. Lev. 12:2.
[16] There are two, somewhat doubtful, cases in mZeb 14:1 and mBQ 4:7 (the 'owner' is mentioned
both in the protasis and the apodosis).
[17] Cruse, *Lexical Semantics*, 123 f., 105 f. Other examples are 'finger' encapsulating 'hand', and
'glove' encapsulating 'hand'; 'to drink' encapsulating 'liquid', or 'uncle' encapsulating 'male'. Lyons
(*Semantics*, i. 262) has 'bite' encapsulating 'teeth'. Cruse proposes a 'but'-test for deciding whether a
given pair of words stands in the relationship of semantic encapsulation. If the 'but'-sentence is odd,
the relationship of encapsulation is confirmed, as it is in 'He kicked me, *but* with his foot'.
[18] It is the only *clear* case of semantic encapsulation that I have found in the Mishnah. Accordingly,
at the point of its definition the resource code will be marked by an asterisk.

[91] = [126b] mSan 8:4 I–III (4)[19]   Deut. 21:19 f.

If his father wants [to accuse his son] and his mother does not; [or if] his mother wants it and his father does not want it, he is not deemed a 'stubborn and rebellious son'—only if they both want it. R. Yehudah says: If his mother was not suitable (ראויה) for his father, they do not deem him a 'stubborn and rebellious son'. If one of them has a cut-off hand (נדם), or is lame, or mute, or blind, or deaf, they do not deem him a 'stubborn and rebellious son'; as it is said, 'And his father and his mother shall seize him'—and they do not have a cut-off hand; 'and bring him out'—and they are not lame; 'and they shall say'—and they are not mute; 'our son, this one'—and they are not blind; 'he does not listen to our voice'—and they are not deaf.

Concentrating for the moment on the opening member of the list of physical impairments, we can see that it is parallel to 'kicking requires the existence of a foot'. The biblical word for 'to seize' (תפש) is taken to presuppose somehow the existence of a functioning hand—one might say, it is taken to encapsulate the functioning hand semantically.[20] From such an observation it is concluded that the person with a maimed hand is excluded from charging his/her son as 'stubborn and rebellious'. In other words, information encapsulated in the apodosis of the biblical law is separated out and put as explicit condition—as in the Habit6 resource. Here is the resource of semantic encapsulation:

*Habit7: Explication of an expression's semantic encapsulation as possible or definite condition of the application of the biblical norm in which it occurs.

But this is not all that happens in **[91]**. I have taken the Mishnaic word נדם as 'cut-off hand', that is, in its widest sense, instead of opting for a more restricted 'maimed in the hand' (Danby's translation). But even so, the parent may still be able to 'seize' the son unless the damage concerns both hands at the same time. Something similar holds for the other items in the list: a lame person may still be able to 'bring out' the child; a blind person may still be able to verify both the identity and position of the child, even pointing and saying 'this one'. And if the Gemara's construction (bSan 71a) of the final item in the list is accepted, namely, that the parent has to hear the son's verbal response in order to be sure that he does indeed not *listen-obey*, it is conceivable that a lip-reading deaf person achieves this too, or that written communication also counts. In other words, none of these items have the strict and necessary relationship that 'kick' and 'foot' have (or that governs the extraction of existential presuppositions). In order to achieve

---

[19] Part III: πD6H4H7R9T1T2T3.

[20] The Mishnaic word used here, נדם, seems to refer to the stumping of the hand or the fingers, although not all fingers need to be affected (cf. Jastrow, 213b, 235b). If we apply the 'but'-test to this case (see n. 17 above) by using the word 'hand', it works: 'He seized me, but with his hand' is strange in the sense required by semantic encapsulation. However, the Mishnaic Dictum, while depending on semantic encapsulation, does not use the word 'hand' at all. For the other items in the list the nature of the biblical Lemmas is different and the relationship between the impairment and the affected organ less direct than required by Habit7.

such strict pairings, the biblical items would have to be explained in the following way: 'shall seize him'—and they have no hands; 'and bring him out'—and they cannot move; and so forth. In other words, there is something else in the selection of exclusions here which moderates pure semantic encapsulation. There are a number of suggestions which one might make as to the identity of this source of moderation. One is to say that the Mishnah selects the most *common* reasons for people not being able to 'seize', 'bring', 'say' and so on. Another is to say that the Mishnah envisages these actions as they *properly* are. Thus, a father may just be able to drag out his son in some manner even if lame, but that is not *properly speaking* 'to bring out'. This leads in a very important direction: a tendency of Mishnaic exegesis to interpret words (at least when they appear in biblical norms) as implying *normality*, or even *legality*. This, too, can be linked to a semantic observation, as shall be seen in a moment.

Before examining a little more the semantics of this 'properly speaking', it is necessary to look at the ability of the HABIT resources to link into Mishnaic paradigms. It can hardly be an accident that the semantic prerequisites of the various biblical expressions in Deut. 21:19 f. are moderated in such a way that they yield this particular list of impairments: maimed in the hands, lame, mute, blind, deaf. These are stock disqualifications from legal obligations and/or cultic priestly duties. In various combinations these disqualifications occur in several halakhic contexts in Mishnaic discourse, and are prefigured by Scripture.[21] In this context it may also be noted that the execution of (capital) punishment is sometimes compared to the performance of a sacrifice.[22] This means that the accuser/witness (who is also involved in the execution) may have been considered subject to the same physical disqualifications as the priest. In other words, we have something of a *paradigm* of disqualifications here, or a combination of several such paradigms.

And yet, it is important that the dependency on the semantics of the biblical verse is not broken too early: the interpretation clearly explores the existential prerequisites of performing all these acts too. And in sticking to the normal or proper way in which these are performed (seizing by using the hands, bringing out by moving on foot, pointing to what one's eyes can see), the Mishnaic interpreter selects for most words what are known as *canonical* semantic traits. Certain aspects of the meaning of a word are clearly indispensable; for a triangle not to have three sides is impossible. But for many words some semantic features are more central than others. For a dog to have four legs is not necessary; it is still a dog after losing a leg in an accident. And yet having four, not three, legs seems to form part of the regular meaning of the word 'dog'; in the absence of some signal to the

---

[21] Cf. the list of blemishes disqualifying priests in Lev. 21:18 ff.

[22] As when the destruction of the idolatrous city is depicted as an *offering* to the Lord, Deut. 13:17 (E 16), a point not lost on the Mishnah in mSan 10:6 III (6).

contrary, we would expect a dog mentioned in conversation or a text to have four legs, not three or five.[23] In semantics, the trait 'four-legged' is therefore said to be *canonical* for the word 'dog'. A. Cruse defines canonical traits as semantic features 'whose absence is regarded as a defect'.[24] Going back to passage **[91]**, it is clear that the idea of canonical traits seems very helpful in understanding the assumptions under which the Mishnah interprets the biblical words 'seize' and the others. The interpretation does not identify the hidden existential claims of these words by taking them to their semantic boundaries (for example, 'no hands at all'). Rather, it locates their existential claims in their middle ground, in their canonical traits. The habitual, canonical act of seizing, the canonical trait of bringing, these are the Mishnaic starting-points for identifying disqualifying impairments. And, for the Mishnah, a *legal* impairment can be just as important as any physical dysfunctionality—in fact, in our example the physical impairments *are* legal disqualifications because of the normative context. Let us consider an example where legal normality as such is treated as the *canonical*[25] trait of a biblical lexeme, and therefore as a condition for applying the norm. This is how Scripture regulates the relationship between a man who violated a virgin who was not betrothed: 'And the man who lay with her shall give to the father of the girl fifty silver *sheqels* and to him she shall be for a wife, because he has violated her; he shall not send her away all the days of his life.' The following *mishnah* relates to this verse:

[92] = **[110a]** mKet 3:5 II (2)[26]   Deut. 22:29 (Deut. 24:1)

How does he [the violator] 'drink out of his pot' (*mishnah* 4) [by marrying the woman he violated]? Even if she is lame, even if she is blind, and even if she is afflicted with skin-disease [he must marry her]. Should there be found in her some 'indecent matter' (cf. Deut. 24:1),[27] or if she is not suitable (ראויה) to marry into Israel, he is not permitted to keep her, for it is said: 'And to him she shall be for a wife'— a wife that is suitable for him.

Our signal here is the (double) occurrence of the word 'suitable', or 'fit' (ראויה). The marital obligation imposed on the violator operates under the

---

[23] As it happens, the Mishnah disqualifies as firstling any animal which has three or five legs (mBek 6:7).

[24] See his treatment of the question in *Lexical Semantics*, 18 f.

[25] The legal connotations of the word 'canonical' are of course particularly apt in our present context, suggesting a 'canon' as a source of law. However, the term's definition as quoted above ('trait whose absence is regarded as a defect') is not limited to the realm of the normative. It is important to keep the idea that a semantic trait is canonical (whether or not it has to do with legality as a topic) separate from the idea here ascribed to the Mishnah that, for some words, the legal status they connote constitutes a canonical semantic trait. For the lack of a clear distinction within the Mishnah of features that are 'unusual' from those that are 'reprehensible', see Jackson, 'Maimonides' Definition of *Tam* and *Mu'ad*', 174 ff. For the idea that legal rules are contextualized by what one might call their 'narrative' meaning, see Jackson, *Making Sense in Law*, 177 ff. (see also the index, s.v. 'narrative').

[26] π_j(Deut. 24:1)O8T2W1.

[27] MS Kaufmann has here דבר זמה ('wicked matter', or 'lewd matter'), instead of the biblical דבר ערוה. See n. 84 in Ch. 11.

general constraints governing any marriage to an Israelite; when Scripture speaks of her as being 'to him for a wife', it speaks of the *canonical* 'wife', suitable to *him* in the emphatic sense of his legal status as an Israelite. The paraphrase of the biblical expression shows that the presence of the biblical *dativus ethicus* plays a role in this interpretation. The ethical dative is often the target of a hermeneutic question of redundancy; in the verse used here it also has a conspicuous position at the beginning of the clause. As for assuming that the status of 'wife' implies legality, we have encountered the very same assumption in **[91]** above, and the word 'suitable' also occurs there.[28] This term ראוי, expressing the modality of appropriateness, seems to be the most frequent label for the canonical meaning of a biblical lexeme.[29] The following is an attempt to define the hermeneutic resource:

Habit4: Explication of one of the canonical semantic traits of a lexeme as possible or definite condition of the application of the biblical norm in which it occurs.

Behind this resource stands the assumption that parts of a norm which describe and refer are just as 'normative' in their intention as its main subject. It may be useful to put this into contrast with the Norm1–5 resources discussed in Chapter 6. They transform the biblical 'is' (or 'was') into a Mishnaic 'ought', that is, derive what should happen from what did happen. In the HABIT resources, on the other hand, we have a link of what ought to happen to what *normally* happens. And the Habit4 resource also stands in contrast to a number of resources which probe the *limits* of biblical words. Most of the LOGIC resources discussed in the last chapter are of this sort, and we shall encounter more later (e.g. Opposition7). In contrast with such probing of the extreme meaning boundaries of a word, the Habit4 resource restricts the biblical meaning to the ordinary and normal. In the other resource groups (NORM, LOGIC, and OPPOSITION), biblical information may be understood as *expressing* canonicity, while Habit4 takes the biblical text to *presuppose* that the canonical meaning is known to the reader.[30] The identification of the canonical traits of a biblical expression has particularly far-reaching effects when those are traits directly connected to legal definitions, such as the concept of marriage. As in the case of Habit7, it seems that the biblical normative context of many of the Scriptural texts discussed in the Mishnah forms here part of a perspective of reading for Habit4. Certain interpretation results achieved by way of Habit6–7 and Habit4 could have a further grounding in the transfer of

---

[28] The Gemara for mSan 8:4 II (4) (bSan 71a) assumes that Yehudah must mean something else apart from 'legally suitable', namely physical resemblance (because of the absence of a term such as 'wife' from the verse?).

[29] Apart from passage **[92]**, it is used in the following Habit4 passages: mSot 4:3, mSan 8:4 **[91]**, mHor 1:4, mZeb 14:2 and mArak 7:5. Other phrases are used in mYeb 12:6 I (5) (הוגנת, 'fitting'), and mBM 2:10 IV (4) (יכול). Cf. also mZeb 12:2 I (2) (זכה) and mMen 6:7 (כל צריך).

[30] This resource too is used in the Mishnah to treat non-biblical wordings (usually prayers or vows), see e.g. mTaan 1:1 (R. Eliezer).

information between diverse biblical locations, for example, as selected according to thematic priorities. Elsewhere in the biblical system the Mishnah might have found a source for the legal definition of 'x', and that definition is assumed to be applicable to the biblical location at hand, for there is a hermeneutic presumption that the system is consistent. To this presumption I now turn.

DISTRIBUTING TOPICS, MEANING, AND REFERENCE: BIBLICAL INCONSISTENCY

The impression that there is an inconsistency between two segments of the same text is a common and productive mechanism of the activity of reading itself. It is part of the process of generating initial hypotheses for the meaning of a complex textual structure, which are thereafter constantly getting revised or confirmed in the course of reading a text or rereading it. Information coming later in the text is used in this way to throw light on, or revise, the meaning hypotheses formed on the basis of the earlier parts. And the earlier parts shape expectations and projections for the parts not yet read.[31] Two segments which are experienced as contradictory draw the attention on to each other, and are focused together, in order to ascertain if the wording of one of them can be construed in such a way that the inconsistency disappears. Consistency is the notion which *guides* the process of constructing meaning for any sustained utterance or text (and also in conversation). The expectation of consistency can, under normal conditions, be disappointed if evidence for inconsistency accumulates; but it is not abandoned easily—other assumptions of reading are probably modified first.[32] The assumption of consistency is particularly important where what is said is surprising or unusual; in that case, the attempt to read the text as a consistent whole is vital for ensuring that inapplicable conventional opinions employed as initial projections of the text's meaning *founder*. Sometimes the expectation of consistency is removed or substantially weakened in the service of the hermeneutic task, as when the message is suspected or known to be esoteric or produced under the conditions of censorship. In that case the message of any segment of the text becomes doubtful because its meaning does not receive guidance or confirmation

---

[31] Of importance is here the notion of the 'hermeneutic circle'. See Gadamer, *Truth and Method*, 167 ff., 235 ff., 258 ff. (*Wahrheit und Methode*, 194 ff. [178ff], 270 ff. [250 ff.], 296 ff. [275 ff.]). Ultimately, the point is that the dimension of *time* cannot be excluded from the process of reading and that, when meaning is construed, something takes place that eludes repetition and full representation.

[32] This includes preconceived ideas of the reader about the topic at hand. In other words, the expectation of consistency is one of the main mechanisms by which a text can 'correct' or disappoint tacit reader prejudices after they have already entered the construction of meaning. This is the case unless there is evidence from the situation, e.g. the identity, or youth, of the speaker, or previous experience with him/her, pointing in the direction of a low consistency in her or his linguistic production.

from its coherence with the rest of the text. Suspending the expectation of direct textual consistency without firm knowledge in what dimension to look for new, underlying consistency, undermines the very mechanism of feedback and revision which establishes meaning: for a time, *anything* goes in the construction of meaning in that text.[33] This shows how important the expectation of consistency is for the process of reading.

In the case of Mishnaic exegesis, there is some evidence that the reading hypothesis of consistency for Scripture is much stronger even than in ordinary communication,[34] due to the identification of God as the direct author of at least certain parts of the text. This could well have the effect of suppressing, in the presentation of interpretation, any initial hypotheses of inconsistency which actually made a contribution to an interpretation whose effect is (also) to establish consistency. As we said, experimenting with the notion that there might be a contradiction is often, even in ordinary reading, just a transitory stage in establishing the text's message; in rabbinic reading the possibility might well be excluded *per definitionem*. But that does not mean that consistency (and its opposite) is absent from the process of constructing meaning—on the contrary. Yet it can very easily be absent from the presentation of the reading result. Mishnaic passages which contain the presentation of an initial inconsistency between two biblical segments could be just the tip of the iceberg for the hermeneutic fecundity of the search for (in)consistency. There might well be many more units of interpretation in which the removal of an initial appearance of Scriptural inconsistency is a contributing hermeneutic mechanism. But once the interpretative solution is achieved the problem disappears— because the interpreter is satisfied that it was an *apparent* inconsistency, as indeed is required by the basic assumptions of rabbinic reading. It must, of course, be assumed that for any literary formulation of a midrashic unit the results of the interpretation are known at the start. Therefore, the presentation of an opening hypothesis of inconsistency is not the spontaneous manifestation of a chronology of hermeneutic steps, but a literary conceit— in this case, an indication of the hermeneutic operation qua argument for the interpretation, for example. I shall return to this question below, after having defined the resource Difference2.

How is an initial hypothesis of inconsistency falsified? Mostly, to judge from the Mishnaic passages, by *differentiating perspectives*. This is an important resource also in the treatment of apparent redundancy (see Chapter 13). Basically, what happens is that the perspective imposed on a segment's topic, meaning, and reference is determined in the light of the perspective

---

[33] The word used in historical scholarship for such texts is 'esoteric', supplemented by the term 'censored'. Jewish literature knows of examples for both. Leo Strauss has argued that for two major Jewish voices, Maimonides and Spinoza, the expectation of consistency needs to be suspended (see his *Persecution and the Art of Writing*); cf. Gadamer, *Truth and Method*, 524, n. 196 (*Wahrheit und Methode*, 300 [278], n. 224). See also Samely, *Spinozas Theorie der Religion*, 15 ff., 77 ff.

[34] See my 'Scripture's Implicature'.

imposed on *another segment's* topic, meaning, and reference. However, since perspective is merely a name for the operative expectations of relevance with which the reader approaches a given segment of the text, it is clear that the apparatus which removes the inconsistency is identical with the apparatus which formulates the initial meaning hypothesis for both segments. The construction of the initial inconsistency problem is itself partly or substantially dependent on the perspectives or interests of the reader. To mention just one example, a chemist reading a crime novel may feel inclined to examine in passing the consistency as well as accuracy of the text's depiction of the mechanisms of a poisoning, even when consistency in this regard is quite unimportant to the author and most readers.

The importance of the expectation of consistency for the construction of meaning is very clear from the following Mishnaic passage. Its hermeneutic question concerns a lexemic ambiguity, clarification of which provides the first step in a transfer operation (the Keying2 resource). Inconsistency is not in the frame; but in answering the hermeneutic question the avoidance of inconsistency plays a critical role:

[93] mNaz 9:5 III (3)[35]   1 Sam. 16:2, 1:11; Judg. 13:5/ 16:17

Samuel was a Nazirite[36] according to R. Nehorai, as it is said, 'And a razor (מורה) shall not ascend on his head' (1 Sam. 1:11). About Samson it is said 'razor' (מורה, Judg. 13:5/16:17), and about Samuel it is said, 'razor': as the 'razor' which is enunciated in connection with Samson [means] Nazirite, so the 'razor' which is enunciated in connection with Samuel [means] Nazirite. R. Yose said: But does this מורה not simply mean that the fear (also מורה, or מורא) of flesh and blood (shall not ascend on his head)?[37] R. Nehorai said to him: And is it not already said, 'And Samuel said: How shall I go? If Saul hears it, he will kill me' (1 Sam. 16:2)?—so that it is already [clear] that the fear (מורא) of flesh and blood did indeed come upon him.

The first half of this passage performs a transfer of co-textual information between two separate biblical locations (i.e. the Keying2 resource discussed in Chapter 8), namely, from Judg. 13:5 to 1 Sam. 1:11. But the term מורה in the 1 Sam. passage is linked by R. Yose not with 'razor', but with מורה/מורא[38] 'fear, terror'. Thus, as a preliminary step towards the transfer the meaning option 'fear' must be removed by R. Nehorai. This is done by reference to the second 1 Sam. passage. It is the compatibility of the propositional contents of these two verses which provides the clarification. On the 'fear' reading, the verse in 1 Sam. 1 says: Fear shall never come upon Samuel (and the fulfilment of this vow of Hannah is taken for granted).[39]

---

[35] Ω•¶C5D4L1L3T0T3.

[36] A person who has bound himself with vows of abstinence and refraining from cutting his hair.

[37] This is in fact close to the sense which Targum Jonathan provides for the phrase in 1 Sam. 1:11, 'dominion'.

[38] The spelling with *he* is used in Ps. 9:21, but the link with מורא is not certain, see BDB 432a. For the wider issues see Boertien, *Nazir*, 200–7.

[39] This is in itself a characteristic hermeneutic procedure: since the vow is reported without later narrative qualification, it is taken to have been fulfilled.

But 1 Sam. 16 is taken to indicate that Samuel was afraid at least on one occasion, producing a contradiction. So, in order to preserve Scripture's full consistency one of these two locations needs to be interpreted in a different manner. The alternative is already provided for in the two senses of *morah*—one, but not the other, produces the inconsistency. Once the idea of 'fear' is removed from 1 Sam 1:11, the way is clear for the transfer of the feature 'Nazirite' between the appearance of *morah* in that verse and in Judg. 13:5.

In text **[93]** the criterion of consistency with one biblical verse is clearly used as a gauge for establishing the meaning of a second one, but inconsistency is not presented as the hermeneutic problem. The meaning of text segments receives constant adjustment in the light of the meaning of other text segments—this is the ground rule of the game of textuality, of textual coherence. How exactly is the clash of statements regarding Samuel avoided? By allocating to the two verses *different topics*.[40] If the suitable, consistency-preserving, meaning of *morah* is chosen, the two verses concern two disparate aspects of the life of Samuel, and there is no room for contradiction. I shall label hermeneutic mechanisms which address internal textual differences (whether initially presenting them as inconsistency or not) as DIFFERENCE resources. Here is a pair of them, with Difference4 accounting for the example **[93]**.

Difference4: Narrative or propositional compatibility with one biblical segment (segment B) is used as the guiding principle in narrowing down meaning possibilities in another biblical segment (segment A). The result is a mutual differentiation of topics, referents, or meanings for the two passages.

Difference3: Narrative or propositional compatibility with one biblical segment (segment B) is used as a guiding principle in determining the nature or identity of an event or fact mentioned in another biblical segment (segment A).

Difference3 and Difference4 mark out certain districts in the rather large phenomenon of rabbinic 'harmonization' of Scripture (which, as we explained above, merely radicalizes the underlying importance of textual consistency in all construction of meaning). The specific formulation of Difference3 is meant to capture cases such as mEduy 2:9. In that *mishnah*, two biblical statements about the length of the Egyptian exile (one expressed in generations, the other in years) are reconciled with each other by claiming that a generation's life is of a certain length.

It may be remembered that the very first Mishnaic passage quoted in this

---

[40] It may be noted that the avoidance of inconsistency by *introducing conceptual* distinctions was, for the area of philosophical thought at least, a methodological maxim in the Middle Ages. See Coseriu, *Textlinguistik*, 5, n. 1, with reference to W. James, *Pragmatism*, 44 ('whenever you meet a contradiction you must make a distinction').

study injects the alien topic of the Sabbath limit into a verse concerning the Levitic cities and their outskirts. I shall now look at the inconsistency problem which gives that interpretation its presentational framework:

[93a] = [1] mSot 5:3 I (2)[41]   Num. 35:5 and 4

That same day R. Aqiva expounded, 'And you shall measure outside the city for the eastern side two thousand cubits . . .' and another verse says, '. . . from the wall of the city and outward a thousand cubits round about'. It is not possible to say, 'a thousand cubits', for it is already said, 'two thousand'; and it is not possible to say, 'two thousand', since it is already said, 'a thousand'. (How so?) A thousand [constitutes] the 'outskirts' and two thousand the Sabbath limit.[42]

Here is how that passage continues:

[94] mSot 5:3 II (2)[43]   Num. 35:5 and 4

R. Eliezer ben Yose Ha-Gelili says: 'A thousand cubits'—the outskirts; (and) 'two thousand (cubits)'—fields and vineyards.[44]

Both answers to the inconsistency question, by Aqiva and Eliezer, are based on the same mechanism. They allocate to the two measurements two different topics. One number specifies the outskirts, while the other number specifies either the Sabbath limit (Aqiva) or the area of fields and vineyards (Eliezer). Both suggested distinctions remove the same inconsistency. This type of answer, the allocation of two different subjects to two Scriptural segments or of two different referents to two biblical words, is the most frequent mechanism by which apparent inconsistency is put to use in the Mishnaic determination of Scriptural meaning.[45] It is incidentally also used, already in the Mishnah, for contradictions between units of rabbinic tradition.[46]

Consider the terminology for presenting the second quoted segment. In both [93] and [93a] the second quotation, the one which contradicts the first segment in that segment's initial interpretation, is introduced with the expression 'it is already said'. This curious 'already' (כבר) has nothing to do with the biblical sequence of the verses involved.[47] It seems to stress the

---

[41] • ¶C1≈D2T1T3.
[42] The text is articulated by the following phrases: אי אפשר לומר . . . שכבר נאמר . . . אי אפשר לומר . . . אי אפשר לומר . . . שכבר נאמר . . . הא כיצד? . . . The hermeneutic question הא כיצד? is found in the Bavli text of the Mishnah, Venice 1522, and in popular editions, including Albeck (*Shishah Sidrey Mishnah, Seder Nashim*, 245). MS Kaufmann has instead: ולמה נאמר אלף אמה ולמה נאמר אלפים באמה; see Bietenhard, *Sota*, 96. This is Maimonides' text (*Commentary*, trans. Qafih, *Seder Nashim*, 178). See further two notes on passage [1] in Ch. 2.
[43] • ¶≈C1≈D2T3.
[44] The word 'cubits' is missing in MS Kaufmann and other text witnesses; the word 'and' is absent from MS Cambridge (cf. Bietenhard, *Sota*, 190).
[45] This way of handling apparent inconsistency, namely by differentiating topics, ties in with a general tendency in rabbinic hermeneutics to increase the number of distinct subjects about which Scripture is taken to speak. Cf. Ch. 2 above, and my 'Scripture's Segments and Topicality'.
[46] Examples are found in mPes 9:6 and mYeb 8:4.
[47] Bacher, i. 77 merely records its use, but offers no explanation. Jastrow also gives the meaning 'once' (609b). In biblical Hebrew it is only attested in Ecclesiastes (meaning 'already').

historical priority of the quotation itself: the biblical text of which the quotation forms part *precedes* all speaking about it and about its topic—the answer to a rabbinic (human?) question may need to be *found*, but it has *been* there all along. In other midrashic units 'already' is used to introduce a quotation which in some way contradicts, or proves wrong, a rabbinic position which precedes it.[48] In the present case, however, its use has an added acuteness: the 'already' of a Scriptural segment for another Scriptural segment. The meaning of the one cannot be established in the absence of the other because it is already there—they are all simultaneously given in the text of Scripture.[49] In other words, the 'already' in this usage may point to the fact that meaning *at any point* in the text must be construed under the assumption of textuality, that is, an assumption of the consistency of its different parts. The expression may thus signal the intuition that the totality of the text precedes the construction of meaning for any one of its individual components.[50]

Difference2: Differentiating two closely related or similar biblical segments by allocating to each a separate subject-matter or referent in the light of a difference in their wording, thereby removing the potential for textual inconsistency.

Of special importance in the *contrastive* identification of the subject-matter or referent of two related biblical segments are subjects which are linked to each other as members of the same Mishnaic category or paradigm, in particular *oppositions*. I introduced the hermeneutic category under which such oppositions can be subsumed as pairs of Mishnaic companion terms, labelled Topic4 (see Chapter 3). Here is an example of the combination of Topic4 and Difference2:

[95] mArak 8:7[51]   Deut. 15:19; Lev. 27:26

The first-born, be it perfect or blemished, may be devoted. How is it redeemed? They estimate[52] how much a man would want to give [in payment] for this first-born, to give it to the son of his daughter, or to the son of his sister. R. Ishmael says: One verse (כתוב) says, 'you shall sanctify', and one verse says, 'he shall not sanctify'.[53] It is impossible to say 'you shall sanctify', for it is already said 'he shall

---

[48] It is found, e.g. in mSan 4:5 IV–V (5), mMak 1:6 II (2), mMen 11:5, mArak 8:7, mTem 1:1 III (3). Apart from mArak 8:7, case [95] below, only mMen 11:5 seems to be linked to the DIFFERENCE family of resources.

[49] In a manner of speaking, the two biblical segments are in dialogue *with each other* all along, 'already'. Cf. Ch. 5 on the impression of Scripture interpreting itself.

[50] Compare with this the temporal adverb 'still, yet', used in the phrase ועדיין הדבר שקול in mSot 5:5 I (2), which serves to highlight an ambiguity *before* its resolution is achieved by aligning the meaning with another passage. [51] • ¶C1D2.1T4.

[52] Most texts have here אומרין ('they say'); however, the reading אומדין of MSS Oxford 408.409 and the Bavli print (Venice, 1528) seems the correct one; see Krupp, '*Arakin*, 116.

[53] Here and in the other quotation of Lev. 27:26, the Mishnaic text quotes the biblical wording as אל תקדיש instead of the Masoretic לא יקדיש איש. The grammatical person of Lev. 27:26 (third person, prohibition) is adapted to that of Deut. 15:19 (second person, positive command). See below on syntagmatic similarity.

not sanctify', and it is impossible to say 'he shall not sanctify', for it is already said, 'you shall sanctify'. Say from this (מעתה) [observation]: you may sanctify it for valuation [עילוי, of money], and you may not sanctify it for the altar [i.e. an offering].

The two verses here quoted employ similar phrasing and are about the firstlings of cattle. Deut. 15:19 reads: 'All the firstling males that are born of your herd and flock you shall consecrate to the Lord your God; you shall do no work with the firstling of your herd, nor shear the firstling of your flock.' The second verse, from Leviticus, reads: 'But a firstling of animals which as a firstling belongs to the Lord, no man may dedicate; whether ox or sheep, it is the Lord's.' Looking at the whole of these verses, it is clear that the word 'sanctify' appearing in both is equivocal. In the case of the first-born animals, no individual dedication is necessary; they belong to God by virtue of being first-born, and the owner can only ratify the fact by fulfilling the norm.[54] The second (Lev.) passage, on the other hand, speaks of voluntary offerings, and rules that no one is allowed to dedicate the same animal twice, by designating an animal as a voluntary offering which, by virtue of being first-born, is already 'the Lord's'. The substance of the norm in Deut. is in fact explicitly recapitulated in the Leviticus passage. In other words, these two norms cannot be seen to contradict each other unless the co-text which removes the ambiguity of 'sanctify' is neutralized first. Only then do they appear to be mutually exclusive, the one commanding and the other prohibiting the sanctification of the first-born animal. Yet this is the way the hermeneutic question is framed (and note the use of 'already', discussed above). This inconsistency question is answered with the help of a new difference: that between offerings dedicated to the altar, and offerings whose monetary value is paid to the temple.[55] This is a Mishnaic opposition within the category 'sanctification' which has no direct counterpart in the biblical text (i.e. a Topic4 pair of terms). As such it is used to differentiate the two senses of 'to sanctify'. In effect, the Mishnah says: the prohibition in Lev. 27:26 only prohibits voluntary sanctification of that very animal as individual, not its monetary value. Which makes possible the voluntary dedication of the same first-born animal, by separating the two manners in which it becomes 'the Lord's'. The two manners in which it becomes 'the Lord's' are part of a paradigm, the two biblical norms being thematically allocated to contrastive members of the same Mishnaic paradigm.

It is of some interest that the construction of the inconsistency problem depends to some extent on a prior neutralization of the co-text that actually serves to differentiate the senses of the two segments in Scripture. For they can be read in their co-text as differentiated along the lines of

---

[54] This is the understanding bArak 29a ascribes to Ishmael's position. As alternative, Deut. 15:19 is taken to imply a specific act of dedication on the side of the owner.

[55] The technical term is בדק הבית (taken to exclude offerings 'for the altar' or sacrificial portions going to the priests, cf. mArak 8:6 I (3)). See [73] mTem 1:6 III (3), also interpreting the substantive similarity of norms harbouring a difference. Cf. further the case of Num. 18:15 discussed in Halivni, *Peshat and Derash*, 62 f.

'obligatory'–'voluntary' sacrifices, which is elsewhere also attested in the Mishnaic discourse. A differentiation along this paradigm is tacitly rejected here. Instead, a deliberately constructed inconsistency is resolved within a paradigm ('for the altar'–'for monetary valuation') which is *not* available from the Scriptural co-text. There could be no better illustration of the fact that the inconsistency observation is already the result of a construction, and no more spontaneous or automatic, than its solution. The hermeneutic apparatus required to construct coherence is in principle the same apparatus necessary to construct inconsistency as an initial problem.[56]

A critical component of that apparatus is the paradigm of contrastive or differentiated items that can make their appearance in otherwise similar norms. Terms that belong to the same paradigm are defined precisely by their ability to take each other's place in the same syntagma. Thus, the word 'window' can take the place of the word 'door' in the sentence 'Please shut the door'. However, the word 'doormat' could not take the place of 'door'. It is crucial for the type of hermeneutic treatment found in [95] that it is capable of reducing the difference between two segments to one point in otherwise similar structures, that is, to the choice of one rather than another of the terms of the *same* paradigm. In the present case the similarities of the norms or syntagmas are actually accentuated by a *misquotation*: the prohibition in Leviticus is assimilated formally to the commandment in Deuteronomy by being put into the second person.[57] Here is an example of closely related syntagmas, constructed for the present purpose with exaggerated formal similarity:

On Nisan 14 you shall slaughter a lamb.
On Nisan 14 you shall slaughter a bullock.
On Nisan 15 you shall slaughter a lamb.
On Nisan 14 you shall eat a lamb.
On Nisan 14 you shall offer a lamb.
On Nisan 14 you shall give a lamb to the priest.

If Scripture contained such similar norms, their collocation would yield a paradigm each for the *date point* (containing two members, namely, Nisan 14 and Nisan 15), for the *ritual act* (four members), and for the *ritual animal* (two members).[58] These paradigms can simply be 'read off' segments corresponding to the same syntagmatic slot in each line. This is possible because the norms are very similar syntagmas. And it is their similarity which gives rise in the first place to the idea that they may be meant to contain *the same* norm—in which case they are mutually exclusive versions

---

[56] Cf. Jackson's examination of the distinction in modern jurisprudence between 'hard' and 'easy' cases (*Making Sense in Jurisprudence*, 239 ff.).
[57] See n. 53 above.
[58] The first two lines allude to Deut. 16:2 (Exod. 12:21) and Exod. 12:5. The inconsistency between these verses is treated in Mekhilta Ishmael Pisha 4 (ed. Lauterbach, i. 32), often used to illustrate the 13th hermeneutic *middah* of R. Ishmael; cf. also mMen 7:6. See n. 65 below.

of that norm, that is, the most striking case of inconsistency. Although biblical norms can provide the raw material for hermeneutically functional paradigms or prefigure them in some way, it is the reader of Scripture who controls, selects, or creates them for application in reading. Thus, it has been seen in [95] how a difference provided for in the Scriptural co-text is ignored in favour of a paradigm creating differentiation in *another* perspective, namely, the perspective of relevance to the Mishnaic discourse. The importance of such paradigms for the way in which the rabbinic reader's perspective actually interacts with the biblical text can hardly be overestimated. They have been seen at work in the resources of category EXTENSION (Chapter 9), and will be encountered again in the resources of OPPOSITION (Chapter 11) and REDUNDANCY (Chapter 13). Here is an attempt to capture their essence in the context of the DIFFERENCE resources. As in some other resource families, I use the second digit '1' to provide for special combinations. In this family Difference*.1 is meant to be a component to be combined with Difference2 or Difference4, to produce the more detailed resources Difference4.1 or Difference2.1.

Difference*.1: Complementary distribution of the members of a binary Mishnaic paradigm to two closely related biblical segments, thereby identifying their difference in meaning.

The term 'complementary distribution' is used as shorthand in this definition for the fact that the two terms are related in such a way that the appearance of the one excludes the appearance of the other in the same syntagma. The term comes from structuralist linguistics, where it is used in particular in phonetics and semantics.[59] However, I am using it here not in the description of the intrinsic semantic relationships of the two terms used by the Mishnah—it is not the language system which 'distributes' the terms. Rather, I ascribe the distribution to the rabbinic reader as part of a deliberate hermeneutic procedure. I claim thereby that the Mishnah considers the two biblical terms as mutually exclusive in that particular syntagmatic slot. If we cast our net quite widely, including the examples for the differentiation of potential inconsistency (marked with an asterisk), and also passages used earlier in this book to illustrate other resources, it is possible to find a number of examples where Mishnaic paradigms are applied in the service of interpretation (Table 10.1); in the hermeneutic profiles belonging to those passages their presence is marked mostly by the code Topic4.[60]

Since the effect of such complementary distribution is for two biblical segments to have distinct meaning, any inconsistency is banned. But as the

---

[59] Crystal, *Dictionary of Linguistics and Phonetics*, 60 f.; Cruse, *Lexical Semantics*, 198 ff.; Vachek, *The Linguistic School of Prague*, 52 f.; Lyons, *Introduction to Theoretical Linguistics*, 70; Lyons, *Semantics*, i. 279.

[60] In the hermeneutic profiles 'Topic4' (T4) will be separately mentioned even when the sign Difference*.1 (or Difference5–7, see below) is already present.

TABLE 10.1 *Mishnaic paradigms with distributive effect*

*Dedication to the altar–dedication of monetary value (עילוי)	[95] mArak 8:7
*The 'outskirts' of a city–the fields and vineyards of a city	[94] mSot 5:3 II (2)
*Serving God from fear–serving God from love	mSot 5:5 I–II (2)ᵃ
Evil–good; evil inclination–good inclination	[15] [82] [114a] mBer 9:5 I (9)
Sheep–goats	[81] mBek 9:1 II (2)
The future–the past	[79] mShebu 3:5 III (3)
Rich–poor	[78] mBM 9:13 II (4)
Offerings to the altar–offerings to the 'Temple upkeep'	[73] mTem 1:6 III (3)
Offerings of the individual–offerings of the congregation or joint owners	[73] mTem 1:6 III (3)
Doing a deed–making it known	[60] mAvot 3:15 I–III (3)
A great priestly woman–an insignificant Israelite woman	[59] mArak 3:5 II (2)
Doing a deed–speaking a word	[59] mArak 3:5 II (2)
Voluntary or vowed offerings–(obligatory) offerings	[53] mSheq 1:5
Rise from the dead to stand in judgement–have a share in the world to come	[50] mSan 10:3 IV (10)
Proselyte–Israelite	[47] mBik 1:4
Norm binding inside the land of Israel–norm binding outside the land of Israel	[26] mHul 12:1
This world–the world to come	[21] mSan 10:3 VI (10)
(Ox of a) neighbour–(ox of the) Temple	[18][118] mBQ 4:3 I (4)
Unblemished–blemished	[14] mTem 1:2 I (2)ᵇ
Days–nights	[13] mBer 1:5 I (2)
Non-capital cases–capital cases	[7] mSan 4:1

Notes: ᵃ This passage seems to be the only example of Difference4.1 in the Mishnah: it also explores, as does [93], a homophonic alternative: that between לא (the *ketiv*) and לו (the *qere'*) in Job 13:15.
ᵇ Cf. [95] above, where this pair of terms appears in the opening line but is not used in hermeneutic function.

above list shows, the same distribution may be found employed in connection with other hermeneutic questions, and one important field of application has yet to be discussed (see next chapter). And as I have said before, the framing of an explicit inconsistency question is a matter of presentation, among other things. The midrashic unit is no record of some mythically pure and unmediated encounter between reader and text.[61] Since we do not know whether a given pair of passages posed a consistency problem or a redundancy problem; and since a second biblical segment may not be

---

[61] Cf. Ch. 3, first section.

quoted separately, or not quoted at all when it is actually being allocated a distributive role, it is often not possible to gauge the extent to which the avoidance of inconsistency leads to the employment of a distributive mechanism. On the other hand, passage [95] shows that the presentation of inconsistency may itself be the result of another part of the hermeneutic operation—in this case, a neutralization of co-text (Cotext1). I therefore have to allow for the following two possibilities. There may be hermeneutic operations employing the distributive mechanism Difference*.1 in which the avoidance of inconsistency plays only a secondary role. And conversely, the distributive mechanism may be the only trace left of an initial inconsistency problem, in particular if the unmentioned second passage is part of the same verse or contiguous with it.[62]

One of the *middot* in the lists of Ishmael (no. 13)[63] and Eliezer (no. 15) calls for a decision between two conflicting biblical passages on the basis of a third passage agreeing with one of them.[64] This rule, *sheney ketuvim*, is clearly concerned with a special case of contradiction, and suggests a special kind of solution for the hermeneutic problem, namely, a rejection of the information acknowledged to be contained in one of the three segments.[65] In the light of the pervasive importance of consistency for the establishment of textuality, this solution is actually uncharacteristic: it consists of an arbitration procedure which renders the observation of contradiction hermeneutically unproductive.[66] This could be an essentially *incomplete* treatment of the passages involved. Perhaps the biblical segment whose meaning is left unaccounted for should be considered as always receiving a new meaning as part of the same operation.[67] In any case, I could not find an example of this in the Mishnah.[68] There seems to be, however, one passage in the Mishnah which implicitly acknowledges an inconsistency problem, but leaves it hermeneutically unresolved. In mSot 3:2 the conflicting biblical messages of Num. 5:24–35 and Num. 5:26 (regarding the

---

[62] Passage [13] mBer 1:5 I (2) may serve as an example. Deut. 16:3 mentions 'day' twice: the seven-*day* period of unleavened bread, which is linked to the remembrance of the exodus '*all the days* of the your life'. In linking this last phrase (see Gemser, 'Motive Clauses') to the wholly separate topic of the recitation of the *Shema*', the intepretation *also* neutralizes any potential tension between these two time-spans (seven days, all days). But there is no acknowledgement of an *inconsistency* problem being addressed in [13] mBer 1:5 I (2). Until we know how often this happens (and what it means), it is best to make sure that any incidental removal of inconsistency is made explicit in resource profiles.

[63] Cf. Sifra, Introduction (ed. Finkelstein, ii. 4, 9 f.). In the illustration of the *middah* (ibid. 10 f.), the problem is framed as in passages [93a] and [95]: 'it is impossible', 'already', and מעתה (found only in [95]).

[64] Bacher, i. 86 f., 77, 90 ff.,170 f.; Mielziner, *Introduction*, 175 f.; Stemberger, *Introduction*, 21.

[65] Mekhilta Pisha 4 ad Exod. 12:5 usually serves as illustration; see n. 58 above.

[66] Cf. Samely, 'Between Scripture and Its Rewording', 66. For a formula allowing inconsistency to be solved otherwise than by arbitration, see Bacher, i. 171; cf. Mekhilta Ishmael Pisha 14 ad Exod. 12:40 (ed. Lauterbach, i. 111). See also n. 72 below.

[67] In mMen 7:6 we do not find the operation of arbitration, but we find a *compensating* operation for those segments which need to be rejected in the arbitration (see nn. 58 and 65). See also Halivini, *Peshat and Derash*, 194, n. 26.

[68] Kasovky's condordance lists *ketuvim* only for mSheq 6:6 (also in mYad 3:5, as the name for the third division of the *Tanakh*).

sequence of actions) are simply translated into two conflicting Mishnaic positions (Dicta). I shall reserve the code Difference0 for interpretations in which a biblical contradiction is noted or implied but not defused.[69] In other cases a very interesting interaction can be found between Difference2 and the Mishnaic dispute format (marked throughout this book by the sign ¶). Where two obviously related (but discontinuous) biblical segments are used to support two mutually exclusive rabbinic positions, either the second party to the dispute or the Mishnaic editor presenting their dispute sometimes provides a new interpretation for the segment first quoted and 'refuted' by the rival position. I found this in mBer 1:3, mMak 1:6, mArak 8:6, and mPeah 7:7,[70] where the following happens: position A is stated by one voice, supported by the first Lemma; position B is stated by the second voice, supported by the second Lemma; and then there follows a third midrashic operation which allocates a new topic, meaning, or referent to the first Lemma. The first and last midrashic unit are thus concerned with the same biblical segment, but allocated to two distinct voices and mutually exclusive Dicta. It is interesting that the provision of an alternative meaning concerns the first Lemma only. This may mean that the first rabbinic voice assumes that both relevant biblical passages support its position. Alternatively, it could lend a historical or narrative directionality to the dispute, in the following way. The first voice, employing only one biblical segment, does not 'know' of an inconsistency problem; it is only after the second position has been stated and supported by a quotation of its own that a new hermeneutic problem appears and that an obligation has been created to seek a new function to the first Lemma. But this can also be looked at from another angle. Perhaps one motive for disagreeing with the first Dictum is the very fact that if its interpretation of the first Lemma were right, two closely related biblical norms would say *the same*. If this is the genesis of some of these disputes, the underlying hermeneutic problem would not be one of inconsistency but of redundancy (see further Chapter 13), and it would not be a consequence of the dispute, but a reason for it.

There are faint but sufficient traces of another procedure for handling potential Scriptural contradictions in the Mishnah. This consists not in a distribution of themes, but in the *fusion* of various aspects. The same subject-matter is acknowledged to be treated in two different biblical segments; the segments are also acknowledged as not saying exactly the same. However, the two segments are taken to be complementary, that is, to refer to different *parts* of the same subject. Thus, mYoma 3:4/6 f., 7:1/3 f. speak of two sets of garments for the high priest at different times during the Day of Atonement, possibly thus harmonizing the use of two different

---

[69] See Appendix I. In mSot 3:2 we find the question of practice decided, but not linked to the question of meaning. The solution is to give priority to one practice, but allow the other as valid once performed. There are other Mishnaic examples of accepting as a *fait accompli* an otherwise rejected option; they do not seem to be linked to Scripture.

[70] See passages [115] (Ch. 12) and [130b] (Ch. 13).

biblical words for the garments in Exod. 28:39 and 39:27–9 on the one hand, and Lev. 16:23 on the other.[71] But the only explicit Mishnaic case of such an internal differentiation of a subject-matter is mSheq 6:6. It ascribes to Yehoyada' the high priest a practical procedure which allows a sacrificial animal to belong 'to the Lord' at the same time as belonging 'to the priest', thus reconciling the wording of Lev. 5:19 with that of Lev. 5:15. In this type of harmonization, some notion of the spatio-temporal togetherness of a physical object seems important, as the example attached to the thirteenth *middah* of R. Ishmael also suggests.[72]

Difference8: Identification of two aspects of one subject treated by two divergent or contradictory wordings in Scripture. These aspects are such that relationships such as harmony, union, cumulation, or combined spatial or temporal presence hold between them. As a result, both wordings can be applied to the same subject without inconsistency.

THE PARADIGMATIC DIFFERENTIATION OF BIBLICAL CONTRAST AND CO-TEXTUAL DISCONTINUITY

There are a number of further resources highlighting a biblical contrast or an incongruence between biblical passages. The biblical text is taken to set up a deliberate contrast or difference, either in contiguous segments (Difference5, Difference6), or in segments separated by further text (Difference7). The Difference6 resource may take any linguistic discontinuity between neighbouring segments to *imply* a difference or contrast. These resources are not linked to the explicit presentation of an inconsistency problem, and the biblical segments concerned are not usually similar enough to suggest that they concern the very same subject-matter. However, in explicating the difference or contrast found in the biblical wording by way of these three resources, paradigmatic structures of the same type as those employed in defusing Scriptural inconsistency are often involved. They also tend to allocate a clear structural opposition to biblical segments whose wording or co-text favours merely diffuse or undefined difference.

Difference5: Projection of a narrative or thematic contrast between contiguous or close Scriptural segments onto two (or more) contrasting members of a Mishnaic paradigm.

Difference6: Distribution, to two (or more) contrastive members of a

---

[71] A detailed discussion is offered in Sanders, *Judaism*, 100 ff.
[72] Sifra, Introduction (ed. Finkelstein, ii. 9). In the explanation of this rule *sheney ketuvim* the two conflicting aspects are fused, not one chosen over the other: God spoke *both* from heaven and from the mountain, by lowering the heavens.

Mishnaic paradigm, of co-textual biblical segments set off against each other or distinguished by some linguistic or textual discontinuity.

Difference7: Distribution of two (or more) contrastive members of a Mishnaic paradigm to two discontinuous biblical verses, creating a contrastive relationship between them. By creating this link, the interpretation also increases biblical coherence.

All of these resources involve some account of the relationship of segments to their co-text. They also involve, *per definitionem* ('members of a Mishnaic paradigm'), the use of Mishnaic expressions as Scriptural companion terms which have their own firm place in the Mishnaic discourse (Topic3). Here is one example for each of them:

Difference5
[96] mTaan 4:8 I/II (3)[73]   Prov. 31:30–1

R. Shim'on ben Gamliel said: Israel had no better holidays than the fifteenth of Av, and the Yom Kippur, for on them the daughters[74] of Jerusalem used to go out in white garments . . . And the daughters of Jerusalem used to go out and dance in the vineyards. And what were they saying? Young man, lift your eyes and see what you choose for yourself. Do not set your eyes on beauty, set your eyes on family.[75] 'Charm is deceitful and beauty is vain, it is the woman that fears the Lord who shall be praised!' And it says, 'Give her of the fruits of her hands and let her works praise her in the gates'.

The subject shift in the *eshet hayil* passage, from charm and beauty on the one hand (verse 30), to the fruits of the woman's hand and her works on the other (verse 31) is understood to set up an opposition. This opposition is explicated by repeating the idea of beauty with a different word (זי), and providing 'family' as its contrast term. This gives a very specific and concrete nuance of meaning to the metaphor of 'fruits' and the word 'works' of verse 31. It also downplays the importance of the other main contributor to a definition of meaning for these terms: the fear of the Lord, which actually provides a more direct contrast with 'beauty' in the biblical sequence of themes.[76] The Mishnaic pair of values, 'beauty' and 'family', in their application to and ranking of female virtues, serves to refocus a contrast signalled by the biblical wording itself.

[73] ΩΔπD5P8W6.2W7. Cf. also **[51]** in Ch. 5 above. Pettit, *Shene'emar*, 205 ff., analyses the distribution of voices in our text; see Epstein, *Mavo*, 686 f.
[74] MS Kaufmann here reads 'sons' or 'children'; see passage **[51]**.
[75] The biblical quotations now following are found in the prints, but absent from the MSS (Correns, *Taanijot*, 128, 137).
[76] The Mishnah probably assumes a direct link between the woman's fear of God and her fertility, which serves to justify the apparent shift in focus.

Difference6

[97] mNeg 12:6 III (3)[77]   Lev. 14:42 a + b

[And they shall take other stones and put them in the place of those stones, and he shall take other mortar and shall plaster the house'] . . . From here [this verse] they have said: Woe to the wicked, woe to his neighbour! Both of them take out the stones, both of them scrape the walls, both of them bring the stones; but he alone brings the earth, for it is said, 'And he shall take other earth and plaster the house'— his fellow does not join him in the plastering.

The biblical text offers a prescription of what ought to happen after stones of a house affected by scale disease have been removed. The interpretation hinges on the shift from plural to singular in the biblical verb forms. According to the endings of the verbs in the Masoretic text, more than one person performs the taking and bringing of new stones, but only one person takes the earth and plasters the house. The Mishnah translates this grammatical difference[78] and textual discontinuity into a precise normative contrast of two stages in the rebuilding, one involving an obligation on the side of the neighbour to participate, the other not.

Difference7

[98] mMQ 3:9 I–II (2)[79]   Jer. 9:19 (E 20) and Isa. 25:8

I. On the first days of the months, on Hanukkah and on Purim, they may sing lamentations and (do not)[80] clap their hands. On neither may they 'wail'. After the corpse is buried they do not sing lamentations and do not clap their hands. What is a lamentation? When all answer like one. And a 'wailing'? When one sings (lit. speaks) and all answer after her, as it is said, '[Hear, O women, the word of the Lord and let your ear receive the word of his mouth,] and teach your daughters a lament, and each (lit. a woman) her companion a wailing. [(20) For death rose up in our windows, he came into our palaces, cutting off the children from the street, the young men from the squares. (21) Speak, Thus says the Lord: The dead bodies of men shall fall like dung upon the open field, like sheaves after the reaper and none shall gather them]'.

II. But for the time to come, it says: 'He has swallowed up death for ever, and the Lord God has wiped away tears from all faces, [and the reproach of his people shall he take away from upon the whole earth, for the Lord has spoken].'[81]

The midrashic unit starts from a 'definition' question: what is the difference between lamenting and wailing, two terms used in the Mishnah in the preceding sentences? The answer is linked to Jer. 9:19 by other resources; but the topic of death, implied in the opening sentence of the *mishnah*, and

---

[77] Σ®D6O1.4T3.1T4.

[78] The singular–plural opposition in the grammatical paradigm is an independent element in Mishnaic hermeneutics (Opposition1.4, Ch. 11).

[79] I: Ω§πC5D7O1.4R4.1; II: ΩπC5D7P2T4.

[80] 'Do not' is found in MS Kaufmann, which also creates a different period, namely: 'and do not clap their hands on the one or the other, and they do not "wail".'

[81] This end-unit (Ω) is suspect according to Albeck, *Einführung*, 183, n. 12 (but see p. 91). Epstein considers only our part 'II' as secondary (*Mavo*, 975).

elaborated in the biblical verse of which the quotation is part, is then pursued in its own right: the picture of death painted in Jer. 9:19 is contrasted with 'the time to come' (אבל לעתיד לבוא הוא אומר) in which death will vanish. It is the Mishnah which provides the contrasting elements, the present on the one hand, and the eschatological future on the other. In the perspective of salvation chronology, the two verses are allocated to different ends of the same spectrum or paradigm. The opposition between the present (and it is the Mishnah's present, not Jeremiah's present) and some eschatological time also provides the perspective in which the second biblical segment is selected in the first place, for it is not found in the co-text of Jer. 9:19. The contrast drawn here between the unredeemed and the redeemed world is constitutive for the type of midrashic units placed at the ends of rabbinic homilies (the so-called *Hatimah*).[82] It is probably no accident that this midrashic unit is found at the end of a Mishnaic tractate (signalled by the sign Ω).[83] It is also interesting that the thematic boundary of the *mishnah*, that is, the question of which expressions of grief are allowed on Hanukkah and Purim, is irrevocably breached by this end-unit: the subject-matter has very clearly changed and that change is 'frozen' into the text by the fact that the tractate ends there, and no attempt can be made to link it to something following. Here the Mishnah seems to take up what might be termed the meaning *surplus* of a biblical text—surplus to the Mishnah's own discourse requirements at this point, which provide the initial reason for the presence of the biblical quotations.[84] This stands in stark contrast to the usual precise barriers; normally the biblical quotations are shut into a very limited space of Mishnaic discourse, allocated only a narrow function and specific contribution to the Mishnaic discourse. But even in those cases the *surplus* may be at work, or may retain its latent power.

[82] Goldberg, 'Die Peroratio (Hatima) als Kompositionsform der rabbinischen Homilie'; Lenhard, *Rabbinische Homilie*, 61–9. The Hebrew phrase cited above is typical for homiletic *Hatimot* (cf. *Rabbinische Homilie*, 62 f.), and so is the contrast it creates (p. 63).

[83] See Ch. 1, text after n. 60; n. 81 above.

[84] There are a few other cases like this in the Mishnah, such as mSan 6:4 III (3), mTem 1:2 I (2) [14], and mYad 4:8 II (2) (on which see Maimonides' *Commentary*; Noy, 'Aggadic Endings', 56). The rarity of this phenomenon in the Mishnah may be typical for the document, or rabbinic hermeneutics; my impression is that Paul, for example, uses the 'surplus' of Scriptural proof-texts quite often to structure his own discourse.

11

The Perspectives of Opposition[1]

In stressing a certain biblical word, the Mishnah may take other words to be deliberately excluded. The item identified as excluded as well as the biblical item may be a member of a list known from other places in the Mishnaic discourse. These *paradigms* thus constitute perspectives for the interpretation of biblical word-choice. In normative contexts such interpretations, while based in the semantics of biblical expressions, often tie in with the Mishnaic division of a larger halakhic theme into a number of distinct legal cases or protasis–apodosis units. The Mishnah also puts longer biblical sentences or phrases into contrast with similar but shorter alternatives, with the result that apparently superfluous words are emphasized and allocated specific information.

CASUISTIC PARADIGMS IN THE MISHNAH

The topic in this chapter is the way in which the Mishnah creates a perspective for the biblical text by determining the *axis of selection* belonging to biblical syntagmas.[2] In doing so, the Mishnah identifies paradigms for specific Lemmas. Examples of such imposition of perspective have been seen in Chapter 9 (EXTENSION resources). In particular, I drew attention to mBQ 5:5 I (2) **[5]**, in which the 'pit' (בור) is taken to stand in for a whole paradigm of holes in the ground: cistern/pit, trench, cavern, ditch,

---

[1] A first account of this resource in the Mishnah, including a list of over 70 contrast terms and their biblical Lemmas, may be found in my 'Stressing Scripture's Words', (list 226–9). See also my 'What Scripture Does *Not* Say'. For a summary on Neusner's work on Mishnaic lists, which is one of literary formats for halakhic paradigms, see his 'The Mishnah's Generative Mode of Thought'.

[2] Neusner speaks of the 'subordination of Scripture to the classification-scheme', saying that Scripture makes no 'categorial contribution' to that scheme ('The Mishnah's Generative Mode of Thought', 319). On the terminology of paradigm and syntagma (not used by Neusner), see the literature quoted in n. 40 of Ch. 9; also Coseriu, *Einführung in die Allgemeine Sprachwissenschaft*, 141 ff. The distinction between paradigm and syntagma (or 'syntagm') can be 'established at all levels of analysis' (Crystal, *Dictionary*, 299 f.). Following widespread usage in literary studies, we shall employ the notion of 'syntagma' to refer also to units larger than the grammatical sentence where necessary.

channel.[3] But much more frequent than the *inclusion* of the other items in a paradigm determined by the Mishnah is the assumption that the biblical word-choice stands in opposition with them. Before I investigate the resources connected with such contrastive paradigms, I need to put the notion of a Mishnaic paradigm into context. It seems that the most important function of paradigms in the Mishnah is to generate groups of halakhic case schemata which are distinguished against each other by their conditional sentences or protases.[4] The importance of such groups of case schemata for imposing a perspective on Scriptural wording has already been encountered in Chapter 4, and the following passage was used as an illustration:

[98a] = [35] mHag 1:5[5]   Deut. 16:17

He who has many eaters and few possessions brings many peace offerings and few whole offerings; [he who has] many possessions and few eaters brings many whole offerings and few peace offerings; [he who has] few of these as well as those, about him they said [cf. *mishnah* 1:2]: a *meah* of silver, and: two pieces of silver; [he who has] many of these as well as those, about him it is said: 'Each man (shall give) according to the gift in his possession, according to the blessing of the Lord your God which he has given you.'

The biblical ruling is allocated firmly to *one* member of the paradigm, despite the fact that the absence of further differentiations from the biblical co-text seems to suggest that it is meant to cover the whole theme. Although this manner of allocation is not very frequent, it is fairly typical for the Scriptural wording to be linked to a point of fine halakhic detail when its wording and co-text suggest that it concerns a broader topic.[6] In sum, insofar as the Mishnaic discourse generates ramified paradigms of case schemata differentiated against each other along the lines of additional conditions or sub-conditions,[7] Scripture is often linked to a member of a paradigm appearing on the level of sub-condition even when the biblical norm is concerned with the main framework to which all individual case schemata belong.[8]

In the modern linguistic idea of a paradigm, the framework for any paradigm is created by a syntagma: a paradigm in the narrower sense are the terms which are excluded by a choice of a term in a certain syntagmatic position. Consider the following syntagma:

---

[3] The list of cavities may even be a somewhat standardized paradigm with regard to the collection of rainwater: cf. the three expressions שיחין, בורות מערות in mTaan 3:2, repeated in a narrative context in mTaan 3:8. If so, that would go some way towards explaining why 'pit' is taken to represent them rather than exclude them.

[4] In other words, the term which the Mishnah takes to be excluded by Scripture can often be seen as standing for a whole protasis coming from a paradigm of protases, i.e. a group of interrelated case schemata.

[5] πC5P3R4.1T2.1.

[6] A further illustration is mGit 3:2, discussed below as **[109]**.

[7] I make an attempt to describe this in more detail in 'From Case to Case'.

[8] See on resource Opposition8 below; cf. Opposition6 in the next chapter.

My brother picked a flower yesterday.

Alternatives which are excluded by 'yesterday' in this syntagma comprise, for example, 'earlier today'. 'Earlier today' can occupy the same slot as 'yesterday'—but in any one sentence only one of them can appear. This is why they belong to the same paradigm, in the narrow sense of that word as used in modern linguistics.[9] The phrase 'for my mother' could also occur in the spot now occupied by 'yesterday'. But 'yesterday' and 'for my mother' do not exclude each other (one could combine them in 'My brother picked a flower for my mother yesterday'), and thus do not belong to the same paradigm in that linguistic definition. But even within the paradigm itself there are further restrictions. Certain items from the same paradigm as 'yesterday' could not take its place, for example, the word 'tomorrow': the tense of the verb disallows it. There are other constraining factors. As impossible as 'tomorrow' is 'in the year 34 CE', but for a very different reason: people do not live that long (assuming the utterance is made today). Here extra-linguistic factors are decisive; clearly, 'world knowledge' or encyclopaedic knowledge also enters the construction of paradigms, and so do expectations of relevance. Some linguists distinguish the paradigm as defined by the linguistic options from the narrower paradigm of what is relevant or possible by calling the latter an 'existential paradigm'.[10] Alan Cruse suggests that certain types of words have a higher 'degree of implicit contrastiveness' than others. He says: 'A major function of a term like *spaniel* is to exclude certain other closely related items, such as *alsatian*, *collie*, etc.'[11] But much will always depend on the concerns of the listeners or readers, or on what degree of contrastiveness the audience expects (compare an audience of dog-breeders with one of management consultants for the example just mentioned). As the discussion in the next section will show (in particular, the examples for the resource Opposition2), paradigms of a fairly narrow constitution are crucial to a description of the Mishnaic operations of contrast, opposition, and emphasis. But these cannot be predicted by reflection on some inherent, semantically abstract features of the word in question. We know of these paradigms *only* through the Mishnah

---

[9]   According to Coseriu it is a *defining* moment of a paradigm that its members exclude each other (*Einführung in die Allgemeine Sprachwissenschaft*, 144 f.; see also 148 f., 'Inhaltsparadigma'). For an account of logical and semiotic relationships of opposition and negation (the 'semantic square') in a legal context, see Jackson, *Semiotics and Legal Theory*, 75 f.; *Making Sense in Law*, 149 f.

[10]   Coulthard, *An Introduction to Discourse Analysis*, 103 f., using the following example: The question, '*Cup* of coffee?', delivered with stress on 'cup' and in a situation where the addressee is known to drink only coffee anyway, 'implies a choice from an existential paradigm consisting of "cup" and "mug" '. (Note the use of the word 'implies'.) Cf. Coseriu, *Einführung in die Allgemeine Sprachwissenschaft* (definition of paradigm, p. 143). See also Lyons, *Introduction to Theoretical Linguistics*, according to whom the paradigmatic and syntagmatic relations that words can enter into are 'of various kinds' (p. 74). Thus, they can be determined with or without regard to the following: meaningfulness; situational features for actual utterances; dependencies of sentences in connected discourse. Lyons's paraphrase for the paradigmatic relationship is: 'potentiality of occurrence' in the same context.

[11]   *Lexical Semantics*, 266.

(usually several places in the Mishnah, not just the passage containing the interpretation) and later rabbinic literature. They depend very specifically on the historical context of the discourse, and we have no direct access to that context—it is not shared by us. One could define the very idea of historical distance with the help of this phenomenon: being historically (or culturally) distant means having no direct, full, and intuitive knowledge of the 'existential' paradigms which inform the linguistic choices.

PARADIGMS OF SEMANTIC OPPOSITION

The interpretation of a choice of words[12] with the help of the choices it is taken to exclude is one of the most frequent resources in the Mishnah. I am going to reconstruct that resource group with the help of the notion of paradigm,[13] in the following way: the paradigm is what the Mishnaic reader uses to contextualize the information available from Scripture. The reader's identification of the item (or items) taken to be excluded by a certain choice of words shows what makes the text *relevant* in the context of reading. At the same time, the linguistic structures of the text are necessary to determine the paradigm—the Lemma is construed as being a *member* of it and, by virtue of that membership, to exclude the other members. The basic hermeneutic movement is that of trying out what happens to the meaning if an expression is substituted by a different one, while its sentence environment is left unchanged.[14] All members of the same paradigm are fit to appear in the same syntagmatic position, and the paradigmatic members not chosen are represented *in their absence*. Insofar as the choice of one of them is taken to show that the others are not meant to be included, this interpretation takes a course exactly the reverse of that of some of the EXTENSION resources. As may be recalled, in case [77] the Mishnah took the biblical 'to build' as also implying 'to buy', 'to inherit', and 'to receive as a

[12] Choice, or selection from a set of alternatives, is a necessary condition of communication. 'A linguistic unit . . . has no meaning in a given context if it is completely predictable in that context', Lyons, *Introduction to Theoretical Linguistics*, 89.

[13] Linguistically speaking, the notion of paradigm is wholly dependent on that of opposition. Thus members of a paradigm stand in a relationship *'in absentia* . . . die Nicht-Identität in semiotischer Hinsicht, m. a. W. [= mit anderen Worten] eine *Opposition'* (Coseriu, *Textlinguistik*, 168). The distinction between relationships *in praesentia* and *in absentia* in modern structuralism goes back to Saussure. Because of its intrinsic connection to opposition, the linguistic idea of paradigm is ideally suited to explain the rabbinic procedure of OPPOSITION.

[14] Cf. Coseriu, *Textlinguistik*, who says that an intuitive 'test of substitution' is always at work when exploring the full meaning of a focused expression. 'Wir fragen uns, was geschehen würde, wenn ein Segment des Textes durch ein anderes ersetzt würde, und diese meist unbewußt an den Text herangetragene Fragestellung ist ein Teil der komplexen Operation des Verstehens' (pp. 121, 114). Coseriu goes on to demonstrate the application of the test of substitution on the narrative level (i.e. treating a whole narrative as syntagma): how would the meaning of Kafka's *Verwandlung* change if Gregor Samsa turned into an Arab stallion instead of an insect? See the final paragraph of the present section for Mishnaic contrasts of biblical *events*. Cf. the traditional *argumentum e contrario* (see e.g. Hallaq, *Law and Legal Theory*, 297, n. 37).

gift'. Employment of an OPPOSITION resource would here lead to the inverse result, namely, that 'to build' is meant to *exclude* these other ways of acquiring possession of a house. I shall use interchangeably the terms 'contrast' or 'opposition' when referring to the resources of this group.[15] Here is an introductory example:

[99] mSot 8:1 III (7)[16]   Deut. 20:3
[continued from earlier quotation of Deut. 20:2] 'And he [the priest anointed for battle] shall say to them: Hear, oh Israel, you are today drawing near for battle against your **enemies**'—against your enemies and not against your **brethren**, not Judah against Simeon and not Simeon against Benjamin, so that if you fall in their hands they will have mercy upon you, as it is said . . .

Ignoring all other aspects of the passage, I simply note the terms in bold print: 'enemies' is supplied by Scripture,[17] 'brethren' is supplied by the Mishnah. I shall occasionally refer to the biblical expression as 'base term', while using 'contrast term' for the Mishnaic one. The latter places the former in perspective, by identifying what 'enemies' *excludes*. One can see that this indeed imposes a perspective if one thinks of all the other possibilities which, according to the context of speaking, might be excluded by the word 'enemies'. For example: 'enemy' (in the singular, a grammatical paradigm), 'allies', 'neutrals', 'friends', 'neighbours', 'arch-enemies', and so on. Each of the latter is excluded in the above sense by the occurrence of 'enemies'—and that biblical word assumes a different colour and significance for each of these exclusions. And of course, no implied message may be here at all: the word 'enemies' need not be stressed, and therefore not be *meant* to exclude anything specific.[18]

As with most other hermeneutic resources, there are certain strong analogies to be found in the conversational use of language. In a situation where both participants in the conversation know that the door as well as the window of a room are open (at opposite ends), the request 'Please shut the door' may often be intended and understood to mean, 'Please shut the door, not the window'. It will be almost certainly understood in this way if

---

[15] Neusner, in explaining how the Mishnah relates to (unmentioned) Scripture in mZab 5:2, takes for granted that the biblical expression 'under him' (Lev. 15:10) was subjected to a contrastive comparison with 'above him'. He calls this strategy 'the rule of opposites' ('The Mishnah's Generative Mode of Thought', 320), or the rule 'like follows the like, and the unlike follows the opposite' (p. 319). But for Neusner the Mishnah's engagement with the signs of Scripture is no different from its classification of objects in the world: 'Scripture supplies *facts*' (p. 319; emphasis mine).

[16] Σπ‡O1(O2)(O8). Another section of this continuous exposition (Σ) of Deut. 20:2 ff. is discussed in Ch. 13 below as **[121]**.

[17] For the second time at this point: it also appears in the report introducing this direct speech, verse 1. This, together with the fact that 'drawing near for battle' virtually predicts a word like 'enemy', may have given rise to the question 'why do we have this word here at all?' (the Opposition8 question, see below).

[18] A careful modern interpreter of Scripture constructs a context or historical perspective first before arguing that a certain biblical word-choice excludes one specific other member of the same paradigm; see e.g. J. Goldin's interpretation of Exod. 15:18 in *The Song at the Sea*, 42 ff., and esp. 47 f. (and see 57 f.).

the word *'door'* is stressed heavily. Such stress in itself can create a contrastive meaning, foregrounding a subject or marking the topic of the utterance.[19] One can conjure up further contextual factors making the intended meaning even clearer. Thus, if the addressee was already on her way to close the window and the utterance 'Could you please shut the *door?'* is being made, the addressee will assume that the speaker was aware of her intention to close the window. In such a case the strength of the implied message 'door, not window', can be as clear as if it had been put into these very words.[20] The phenomenon in spoken language is one of *stress* and intonation; more generally, it is one of *emphasis*, and information implied by emphasis. The notions: emphatic reading and probing of the text for *implied* information, could serve as a heading for the whole group of OPPOSITION resources. For the information contributed by the term selected for an operation of opposition is taken to be *new*, or focused. The Habit6/7 and Habit4 resources discussed in the preceding chapter derive maximum relevance or information from parts of the biblical segment that are unstressed or presupposed. The OPPOSITION resources, by contrast, derive maximum relevance or information in particular from parts of the biblical segment taken to be emphatic, or foregrounded.[21]

But what is characteristic for rabbinic interpretation is a fusion of the movements of emphasizing on the one hand and decoding emphasis on the other. The author of Scripture is understood to have implied this information. But the author is not currently speaking, so no pattern of intonation can be directly perceived. Nor is the text short, such that its application to a situation would be unambiguous and immediate. Also, the context of text production is not identical with the context of reception, and indeed the context of reception changes constantly. Thus a somewhat paradoxical situation arises, at least compared to face-to-face conversation. The text is read *as if stressed* potentially *at any point*;[22] and this means that it is potentially relevant at all times and in all situations. But this also means that the reader becomes partly originator of the message. Because the text cannot be stressed at all points *at the same time*, the reader has to make decisions that

---

[19] This phenomenon of stress and intonation is even referred to as 'topicalization' by some linguists, see Coseriu, *Textlinguistik*, 12.

[20] A Targumic example of treating background knowledge implied in conversation hermeneutically can be found at Pseudo-Jonathan, Gen. 26:2, discussed in my *The Interpretation of Speech*, 58 f. A film scene I remember gives a variation on this theme: the heroine is being released by her kidnappers and starts running in the direction of her rescuer standing at some distance. He shouts, 'Walk!' and she slows down. Cf. also Coseriu, *Textlinguistik*, 18 f.

[21] Allwood *et al.*, *Logic in Linguistics*, 153 f.: The sentence 'Mr Jones is sober today' is processed under the assumption that it has a point, or newness, of information; so much so that from its utterance in a suitable situation it will be concluded that Mr Jones is usually intoxicated. Cf. Sperber and Wilson, *Relevance*, 202 ff. The so-called 'topic' or new information (as opposed to so-called 'comment' or known information) of an utterance is the stressed or foregrounded part; it is to these that the contrasts in ordinary conversation are linked (but for the rabbis any part of Scripture can carry stress).

[22] The implications of this statement are going to be explored in the next chapter.

are, in spoken language, taken by the author. The reader has to test the text for emphasis, and to find the points in the text which engage with his own situation; those points are the ones that need to be stressed and thus exclude what they exclude in the reader's own time. This makes the reader something of a co-author, and provides a further manifestation of the tendency of the rabbinic reader to take over functions of the author.[23] It should probably be understood in terms of the committed *use* of the ready-made biblical text as rabbinic utterance discussed in Chapter 5. The main direct evidence pointing to such a parallel with USE resources is found in the most common formula employed to mark the presence of an OPPOSITION operation, the phrase 'and not'. This expression (ולא) and the Mishnaic wording it introduces can at least sometimes be read as grammatically continuous with the biblical quotation, thus turning biblical words into Mishnaic speech.[24] The next passage is an example where the biblical base term is used in that way, that is, forms a necessary part of the Mishnaic expression. It also takes us further into the mechanisms of OPPOSITION.

[100] mYeb 3:9[25]   Deut. 25:5

If three brothers were married to three unrelated women, 'and one of them died', and the second [brother] betrothed her [his widow] and then died, behold this one [widow][26] must perform *Halitsah* and is not taken in levirate marriage, as it is said, 'and **one** of them died . . . her brother-in-law shall go in on her' upon whom there is a levirate tie to **one** brother-in-law, and not upon whom there is a levirate tie to **two** brothers-in-law.

The biblical link is very likely meant to account only for the notion that the first widow need not remarry; the reason why the widow of the second brother is not to be married by the surviving third brother is separate. For the ruling concerning the widow of the first brother, the Mishnah takes the biblical phrase 'and one of them' to be decisive. That phrase contains the word אחד ('one'), and it is this 'one' which is stressed for the purposes of this interpretation. It is placed into opposition with 'two', and this opposition is understood to mean that the widow is not bound successively to two different brothers-in-law. Thus אחד is taken as a member of the paradigm of cardinal numbers, 'one, two, three, four', and so on. The word can only stand in a relationship of contrast with these other numerals, if it is a numeral itself.[27] This is perhaps one of the most obvious cases of a paradigm, because it is a numeric series, and one can easily understand that

---

[23] Compare with this the hypothesis that for the rabbis there is a 'correspondence between the perspectives in which the biblical events are selected . . . in Scripture on the one hand and the perspectives or concerns of the rabbinic discourse' (formulated in Ch. 6 above, text preceding passage [60]).

[24] More on this peculiarity of the phrase 'and not' can be found under point 4 in the final section of Ch. 12 (the reprise format, ®).

[25] ®¶πO1T2.1.

[26] So the *editio princeps* (Rengstorf, *Jebamot*, 42); some witnesses, including MS Kaufmann, read 'these [widows]', and thereafter the plural of the verb forms (on which see ibid. 43, 225).

[27] For the use of the paradigm of numerals as *extending* an open biblical 'list', see mMak 1:7 IV (6), explained in n. 39 in Ch. 9.

where one number is specified, all the others might be excluded. A recipe
requiring two tablespoons of sugar cannot be said to have been followed if
one tablespoon was used, or three. A signal agreed as consisting of five
knocks is not successfully transmitted by knocking four or six times.[28] But
by saying that the biblical 'one' excludes 'two' the Mishnah does not merely
provide a semantic contrast between two terms. It claims that the 'one' of
the biblical text is *of the sort* to have 'two' as a contrast term in the first place.
For there are other types of 'one'/אחד. The word may connote wholeness,
or internal indivisibility, thus being opposed to 'fragment'[29] or 'having
parts'.[30] And in a phrase such as 'one of them', the meaning might well be
'any one of them', that is, the indeterminate nature of the occurrence—
'regardless which of them'.[31] This is in fact a privileged reading for our
biblical verse, in the absence of any indication from the co-text that the 'one'
is especially stressed. In such a reading there is no stress on the numeral
(one as opposed to two); instead, the effect of 'one' is to leave unspecified
the identity of the brother who died. We could invent a new contrast to
express the information thus: 'if one of them died—and not only if the
eldest of them died.' Such a contrast paradigm would not support the
halakhic position expressed in the Dictum in [100]. It would imply that, if
two die in succession, further information or decision is required. What
happens to the widow would under this reading not be determined by the
use of the expression 'one'. In sum, identifying 'two' as excluded by 'one'
does not merely provide an opposition, it fixes the meaning dimension of
the 'one' in a certain paradigm. This amounts to choosing one from the
(usually) several meaning nuances available for a biblical word—if viewed
in isolation. I shall return to the topic of different meaning nuances for the
same word in Chapter 14 (the Word1 resource).

This is the double nature of the hermeneutic operation of OPPOSITION: on
the one hand, it affirms the biblical syntagma by emphasizing that the
identity of one of its members excludes similar members (that is, other
members of the same paradigm). On the other hand, the interpretation
changes the syntagma by narrowing it down in selecting one of the several

---

[28] In mTem 6:3 II (3) the Mishnah takes the word 'the *two* of them' to exclude the numeral four.
And in his commentary on mYeb 1:1 (trans. Qafih, *Nashim*, 7), Maimonides explains the singular of
'house' as excluding the number *two* (two houses), showing that the stress on *grammatical* number
can also lead to such results (see resource Opposition1.4 below).
[29] This is precisely what happens to a biblical 'one' in mMen 7:2 I (2), where it is contrasted
with פרוס, 'as pieces'. Again the Lemma, from Lev. 7:14, singles out one item from a group of items
(והקריב ממנו אחד מכל קרבן תרומה לה); cf. Clines, i. 181b. On wholeness as the meaning of biblical אחד, see
ibid. i. 179b.
[30] The interpretation of the theologically important אחד in Deut. 6:4 immediately comes to mind.
For Maimonides, important exclusions of this 'one' concern themes in philosophical discourse
which were forged without reference to Deut. 6:4 (*Mishneh Torah, Hilkhot Yesodey Ha-Torah* 1:7; cf.
also Kadushin, *Organic Thinking*, 236 f.). The paradigm of oppositions 'makes sense' of the text by
binding it into the network of sense that holds together the world of the reader.
[31] For the function of אחד as indeterminate article in biblical Hebrew, cf. BDB 25b; see also 580b (s.v.
מן); Clines, i. 181a (with מן, 'almost as indefinite article').

possible paradigms. The surface manifestation of this modification of the syntagma is the phrase 'and not . . .'. As I said above, this addition can be construed as grammatically *continuous* with the biblical sentence to which it is attached. In such construction it presupposes that sentence, and the Mishnah is involved in *using* that sentence expressively when asserting the exclusion.[32] But that means that a syntagma which does not contain the phrase 'and not . . .' is replaced by one which does. The biblical 'and one of them died . . .' becomes 'and if one, but not two, of them died'—a different syntagma.[33] In the first syntagma the word 'one' can be contrasted with 'two' as well as, say, 'the eldest'; in the second syntagma, 'the eldest' has become impossible, because the meaning of 'one' is already determined as belonging to the paradigm of numerals. Other numerals, on the other hand, could in fact be added. It is perfectly possible to extend the contrast terms along the same paradigm: 'and one of them, but not two or eight or fifteen, died.' There are quite a few such multiple oppositions in the Mishnah (summarized in Table 11.1), and that is how they work: they employ as contrast terms *several* members of the *same* paradigm with the one biblical base term.[34]

Here is a definition of such provision of multiple contrasts:

Opposition2: Explication of the meaning of a biblical expression in the light of its opposition to several other expressions. The other expressions would fit the same biblical syntagma and are members of a paradigm of Mishnaic relevance. By taking these expressions to be excluded, the perspective of the Mishnaic paradigm is imposed on the meaning of the biblical expression.

The usefulness of the idea of paradigms in analysing Mishnaic *extensions* of the meaning of a single biblical term (EXTENSION resources)[35] shows, among other things, that contrast terms are not employed to highlight purely *stylistic* features;[36] nor are they chosen so as to put into perspective different stages of the Hebrew language, or regional variations, or register, or vowel quality, or poetic metre, or even the grammar of the sentence.[37] We also do not find the following type of contrast: 'Bill slapped the wall all over with cheap whitewash, he didn't *paint* it.'[38] Instead, we find this type:

---

[32] The phrase 'and not' can be used to structure a series of Mishnaic case schemata; therefore it appears also in non-hermeneutic contexts, but nevertheless tied to paradigms (see e.g. mBB 8:1; cf. also my 'From Case to Case').

[33] This replacement of syntagmas is what happens when contrast terms become incorporated into the Targumic versions of Scripture. See my 'What Scripture Does *Not* Say', and 'Scripture's Segments and Topicality'.

[34] A similar treatment of non-biblical language is found in mNed 6:1.

[35] See Ch. 10; see also my discussion at passage [96] in Ch. 11.

[36] Cf. my remarks on the absence in the Mishnah of any independent hermeneutic interest in stylistic or artistic features of Scripture in Chs. 1 and 14.

[37] Rashi offers such contrasts; see e.g. his commentary on בראשית in Gen. 1:1, placing it in grammatical opposition to בראשונה.

[38] The example is adapted from Frawley, *Lexical Semantics*, 431.

TABLE 11.1 *Multiple oppositions*

mMS 5:14	Persons with no inheritance in the land
mBik 1:2 II (2)	Types of control over fruit-producing land
mBik 1:5	Persons with restricted legal or personal status
mYeb 8:2 III (3)	Types of marriage partners according to ethnic criteria
mSot 2:4 I (2)	Types of writing materials
mSot 2:4 II (2)	Types of writing instruments
mSot 4:1	Types of ties binding a woman to a husband or future husband (see **[108]** below)
mSot 8:3	Types of buildings
mSot 8:3	Types of invalid marriage
mSan 10:5 I (2)	Types of non-permanent residents in towns
mMak 3:13	Bodily postures
mZeb 9:5 II (2)	Body-parts that are neither 'flesh' nor 'blood'
mMen 7:4	Types of stand-ins for sacrifices
mArak 9:1	Types of years without crop
(mBek 2:9 II (3)	Types of births, Opposition6)
mTem 1:6 I (3)	Types of sacrifices
mNeg 14:2	Directions defined by landscape features

'Bill plastered the wall, he didn't *paint* it.' The Mishnah does not subject the biblical word-choice to an experimental substitution with words whose variation of meaning is *thematically irrelevant* or, to use a different characterization, whose truth conditions are the same as the base term's.[39] The Mishnaic oppositions always seem to probe for difference in propositional meaning or implied information; I have not found contrasts which keep the *meaning* more or less the same from the perspective of the Mishnaic discourse at this point (but see passage mBek 9:1 II (2) **[81]**, mentioned below).

We also find that oppositions are drawn from the same base term in two different semantic directions. Multiple contrast terms (Opposition2), as in the passages just listed, are given in enumerative format (only one 'and not . . .' governs all contrast terms). This is not what happens when two different paradigms are brought to bear. In such cases, the phrase 'and not . . .' itself seems to be repeated for each contrast term. A good example is mSan 8:1, which makes use of two distinct paradigms for the same biblical base term, and therefore provides two disparate (incompatible) contrast terms:

---

[39] What is denied by saying that Bill didn't 'paint' the wall when he only slapped it all over with cheap whitewash is, paradoxically, not that he painted it—he did. But 'to paint' is rejected as a proper characterization of what he did—a 'metalinguistic' negation, as Frawley says (*Lexical Semantics*, 432). Cf. the idea of canonical meaning (Habit4) used in Ch. 10 above.

[101] mSan 8:1[40]   Deut 21:18

'A stubborn and rebellious son'—From when can he be deemed a 'stubborn and rebellious son'? From the time that he produces two hairs until he grows a beard—the lower one and not the upper one, but the Sages spoke in modest language—for it is said, 'If a man have a son'—a son and not a daughter, a son[41] and not a man; a minor is [in any case] exempt, for he does not come within the scope of the commandments.

The first contrast goes along a gender paradigm, the second along an age paradigm; these are in fact common Mishnaic paradigms for persons, in addition to a third paradigm which is ethnically defined (inside/outside Israel). Thus mBQ 4:3 puts the biblical word 'neighbour' first into contrast with 'temple', that is, uses the axis 'profane–holy' or 'priest/levite–Israelite' (see passage **[118]**), and then into contrast with 'non-Jew', that is, along the axis 'Israel–outside Israel'. The word 'Israel' is treated repeatedly as implying both of these different paradigms: sometimes taken to convey a contrast to other *ethnoi*,[42] sometimes a contrast with priests and levites.[43] Of interest here is also mHul 8:4 I (3), in which the various kinds of presuppositions of the biblical prohibition to cook the kid in the mother's milk provide the implicit basis of contrasts in three different paradigms of animals: mammal versus non-mammal (bird); clean versus unclean (unclean cattle); and domestic versus wild (wild animals). But these exclusions are linked (by R. Aqiva) to the *three* separate occurrences of the norm in Scripture (Exod. 23:19; 34:26; Deut. 14:21). While also solving a redundancy problem, this may well be a reflection of the fact that the contrast terms do not belong to the same paradigm: the interpreter might have felt that, for three different paradigms of opposition, three occurrences are necessary. Here is a definition of the basic resource of OPPOSITION when only one contrast term is used.

Opposition1: Explication of the meaning of a biblical expression in the light of its opposition to another expression. The other expression would fit the

---

[40]   §π®O1×2 T3.1T8(W1 son = child).

[41]   Rabbinic halakhah allocates to the stubborn and rebellious son only a brief period between the coming of age as a *bar mitswah*, and the coming of age in the sense of showing physical signs of sexual maturity; yStan 8:1 mentions a maximum period of six months, bSan 69a one of three months. The word 'son' connotes of course also a relationship between two adults, and as *such* could not be opposed to 'man'; so implied in the opposition is a meaning 'child', rather than 'filial relationship'. This is marked by Word1 (see Ch. 14) in the resource profile of the passage. Note that both Gemaras oppose the word 'son' not to 'adult man' directly, but to 'father', i.e. the son as a father or potential father (sexual maturity).

[42]   Cf. mKet 4:3, mBek 1:1, 3:4; 8:1.

[43]   Cf. mArak 9:8, where Israel functions as the contrast term to the biblical 'Levite'. Different semantic mechanisms may be involved in multiple oppositions for the same Lemma, see Cruse, *Lexical Semantics*, chs. 9–11; specifically for Hebrew, see Bochorovski and Trommer, 'A Semantic-Pragmatic Study of the Sense Relation Called "Opposition" '. The Hebrew title of this article alludes to Ben Bag-Bag's hermeneutic imperative in mAvot 5:22: *'turn* it [= Torah]!' (הפוך בה). In the the light of the hermeneutics of opposition, this maxim should perhaps be translated as, 'interpret Torah by looking for the opposite!'

same biblical syntagma and is a member of a paradigm of Mishnaic relevance. By taking this expression to be excluded, the perspective of the Mishnaic paradigm is imposed on the meaning of the biblical expression.

In some cases, the Mishnaic contrast terms are either standard terms of Mishnaic discourse (Topic3), or of distinctly greater specificity than the biblical base terms, such as Topic2 (or both). Thus, in mSot 9:2 I (2) the expression 'in the land' from Deut. 21:1 is contrasted with the more specific 'hidden in a heap', and the word 'lying' with the very conspicuous 'hung on a tree' (cf. Deut. 21:22).[44] Here the contrast resource is combined with a number of perspectivizing mechanisms, which we have encountered separately, into a complex package: a treatment of biblical expressions of more general meaning on a specialized level linked to case schemata (Topic2), a use of terms whose function in the Mishnaic discourse is highly defined (Topic3), a decision on the paradigm to which a biblical term belongs, and a selection of one contrast term from that paradigm (Opposition1). In one Mishnaic case, the contrast is metalinguistic, in that it puts into opposition two linguistic alternatives for referring to the same class of animals. In mBek 9:1 II (2) [81], the fact that Scripture chooses the term 'flock' over the pair of terms 'sheep and goats' is taken as halakhically significant.

The decision in which particular paradigm to locate the opposition may sometimes make use of paradigms in the narrow grammatical sense. An example is the paradigm of grammatical persons, as realized in personal pronouns, object suffixes, prepositional suffixes, or verbal affixes in Hebrew. These can be interpreted in their mutually exclusive sense, as in the following passage.[45]

[102] mYeb 6:6 III (3)[46] Gen. 1:28

The man is commanded 'fruitfulness and multiplication', but not the woman. R. Yohanan ben Baroqa says: About both of them it says: 'And God blessed **them** and said to them (להם): Be fruitful and multiply'.

In Ben Baroqa's interpretation an emphasis on 'to them' leads to the inclusion of the woman; in other words, the suffixed preposition 'to them' (להם) is implicitly contrasted with 'to him'.

Opposition1.3: Explication of a biblical personal pronoun or personal affix in the light of its opposition to another member of the paradigm of grammatical persons.

More often, however, the personal pronoun or suffix is interpreted along a paradigm established for the term it stands in for, and not restricted to the

---

44 Cf. my 'Stressing Scripture's Words', 215.
45 Cf. my 'What Scripture Does *Not* Say', 264 f.
46 π•¶C5O1.3P3R6.4.

grammatical paradigm of pronouns.[47] Of some hermeneutic importance in the Mishnah is the grammatical paradigm of singular and plural (the dual seems to play no role),[48] applied to conspicuous effect where the biblical co-text suggests a collective use of the singular.

[103] mTem 1:6 II (3)[49]   Lev. 27:10

The congregation and joint owners can not create a valid substitute [sacrifice], as it is said: 'He shall not substitute it'. The individual (יחיד) can create a substitute, the congregation and joint owners can not create a substitute.

The biblical verse (despite the negation) is understood to permit sacrifice 'substitution'.[50] On the basis of this understanding, the grammatical singular of the verb form (ימיר) is taken to restrict that permission to individuals, which restriction is then made concrete by two contrast terms, the 'joint owners' and the 'congregation'.

We also find the plural stressed to exclude the singular. The following passage could also have been used earlier as an illustration of the inclusive interpretation of 'all':

[104] mNeg 2:3[51]   Lev. 13:12

A priest who is blind in one of his eyes or the light of whose eyes is dim may not view the scale disease, as it is said, 'in all the sight of the eyes of the priest'.

The plural of 'eyes' is taken to exclude the case of a priest whose vision may be perfect, but only in one eye. Here is another example:

[105] mSan 4:5 I (5)[52]   Gen. 4:10

In capital cases, his [the wrongfully condemned person's] blood and the blood of his seed [that should have been born to him] hangs upon him [the false witness] until the end of the world,[53] for this is what we find regarding Cain who killed his brother, as it is said, 'The bloods of your brother cry out'. It does not say 'the blood of your brother', but 'the bloods of your brother'—his blood and the blood of his seed.

This passage, whose central component is the emphasis on the plural of 'bloods',[54] explicitly opposes the singular and the plural. Its formulation is

---

[47] As e.g. in mTem 6:3 III (3), where 'they' is contrasted not with other pronouns, but with 'their young'. The expression 'its young' belongs to a Mishnaic paradigm 'sacrificial animal—its substitute—its replacement—its young'.

[48] For the role of paradigm in linguistic analysis, see Bloomfield, *Language*, e.g. 222 f.; Coseriu, *Einführung in die Allgemeine Sprachwissenschaft*, 142 f.

[49] ®O1.4T2. The continuation of this passage, and a hermeneutic link established to a nearly identical Dictum by way of resource Analogy8, is given in passage [73] above.

[50] Cf. the concluding part of the verse, 'And if he substitutes . . .'.

[51] I: O1.4T2(eyes) II: L1R4.4 or H7.

[52] ◊¶®N8O1.4T1T3.

[53] MS Parma (de Rossi 138) as well as the Yerushalmi prints have here: 'until the end of all the generations'; cf. Krauß, *Sanhedrin-Makkot*, 389, 161 f. MSS Kaufmann and Munich do not have the clause 'who killed his brother' in the following sentence.

[54] Cf. BDB, 196b: 'of . . . blood shed by rude violence, and of bloodstains'. This is the line taken in an alternative interpretation offered in the Mishnah after [105] ('because his blood was cast over the trees and stones').

of interest, for it contrasts the actual words of Scripture with a hypothetical alternative: אינו אומר דם אחיך אלא דמי אחיך. The implication is that, had the singular been used, no additional responsibility for hypothetical future generations would have been ascribed to the murderer by Scripture (at this point).

Opposition1.4: Explication of the number of a biblical expression in the light of its opposition to another grammatical number.

Of special importance is the interpretation of the grammatical plural as implying the minimum quantity of two. In some midrashic units this minimum of two is also treated as a fixed maximum of two, as in the case of the number of judges in courts of different constitution (e.g. in mSot 9:1 II (2) **[19] [121a]**). In such cases there may be a question whether the biblical plural is really interpreted by opposition, namely, as 'not (only) one'. Perhaps the plural is taken to imply 'two' as a canonical trait; or possibly, the plural as a *dual* is involved. The specific number 'two' for the plural can in any case not be the result of a plural–singular contrast alone, as that would include numbers greater than two. An additional hermeneutic component is required to account for the upper limit 'two'. That could be a tacit assumption that no higher number is appropriate to the subject under discussion (i.e. Topic0).

Similar to the binary singular–plural contrast is the grammatical gender contrast, of which one also finds examples in hermeneutic application. As in the case of the singular collective, this procedure is most conspicuous when a masculine ending, which the biblical co-text suggests is generic, is taken to exclude the female.

[105a] = [63] mYeb 8:3 II (2)[55]   Deut. 23:4 (E 3)

'An Ammonite and a Moabite' are prohibited [to marry an Israelite] and their prohibition is an everlasting prohibition. But their females are allowed right away.

The Mishnaic Dictum repeats precisely the biblical form of words as found in the relevant verse, which excludes members of these two peoples 'until the tenth generation', or 'for ever'. This employment of the biblical wording relates the Mishnaic differentiation between the two sexes to the biblical use of the masculine form; for both nations biblical feminine forms exist.[56]

Opposition1.5: Explication of the gender of a biblical expression in the light of its opposition to the other gender in the grammatical paradigm.

Another type of contrast needs to be investigated which, while stressing the semantic limits of the biblical word-choice, does not say which other word could have been used and is thus excluded. One is not given contrast term(s), and therefore no identification of a paradigm. *All* other

---

[55] •¶A4.1≈O1.5.   [56] Cf. bQid 75a; Elon, 'Interpretation', col. 67.

possibilities are excluded in such cases, usually by putting 'only' or 'unless' in front of the base term, or by supplementing it with 'no other', or by negating it in its *negated* form.[57] Yet, although these cases need to be distinguished from Opposition1, they too seem to make tacit use of comparisons within a paradigm delineated in the Mishnaic co-text. At first sight such interpretations create very general categories. For example, the biblical phrase 'And the man who does wantonly' (Deut. 17:12) is translated into a normative condition in this manner: 'he is *not* culpable *unless* he teaches practice' (see below). Such a sentence is totally open in what it excludes. It stresses the one specification to the exclusion of *all* others. Uncountable other actions lie beyond the application of the biblical prohibition;[58] the all-embracing negative excludes an infinite list of *irrelevant* alternatives. But infinity, resulting from a purely semantic or logical operation, is not what the Mishnah is after: in every Mishnaic paraphrase using an indeterminate exclusion of this type, a named instance can be found close by. While the format of the Mishnaic rewording suggests a universal operation of exclusion, the discourse function and the paradigmatic constitution usually show that a *specific* item or concept in which the Mishnah is interested is taken to be excluded by the Scriptural term. The result is thus similar to Opposition1.[59] Here is the example alluded to above:

[106] mSan 11:2 III (3)[60]   Deut. 17:12

If he [the rebellious elder] returned to his town and **taught** (ולמד) again[61] the way in which he used to teach, he is not culpable; but if he taught to **do** (הורה לעשות), he is culpable, as it is said, 'And the man who **does** (יעשה) wantonly'—he is not culpable unless he teaches to do.

The contrast runs along the path 'teach' versus 'do', the latter paraphrased as '*teaching* to do'. This sets up a very clear opposition between two types of teaching, one for halakhic theory and one for practice.[62] The two are reflected in two distinct words for teaching,[63] and by co-opting the infinitive of the biblical 'does'. The paraphrase following on from the quotation[64] merely provides a universal negative ('not . . . unless'). However, the Dictum leading up to the quotation identifies the specific item

[57] Cf. mYeb 10:3.

[58] There are infinite possibilities contained in statements which negate that a subject has a certain predicate (e.g. 'The cat is *not* on the mat' leaves open infinite possibilities as to where it actually is). Cf. Kant, *Kritik der reinen Vernunft*, 111 f. (Akademie-Ausgabe, 70–3).

[59] Combinations of reformulation with 'only' and the grammatical paradigms are found also, see e.g. [34] mBik 1:2 I (2), and mParah 3:7.   [60] ®ΣO0O1T3.

[61] Krauß (*Sanhedrin-Makkot*, 299) argues that the expression ושׁנה should not be translated as 'again' but as the technical 'to learn'.

[62] On this distinction, see Urbach, *The Sages*, 616 f.; Urbach, *The Halakhah*, 127–30; see also 388 f., n. 49; Zlotkin, *The Iron Pillar Mishnah*, 130, 216 (with reference to our passage [106]); Halivni, *Peshat and Derash*, 105 f. (he erroneously suggests that the Mishnaic text uses the term פסק), and 133. For a modern interpretation of the 'ideal' character of halakhah, see Soloveitchik, *Halakhic Man*, 24 ff., 64 f.

[63] Cf. the use of the root ירה in the text and title of the Mishnaic tractate *Horayyot*. Cf. Albeck, *Einführung*, 321 ('eine Entscheidung für die Praxis treffen'; the entry is s.v. ירה!)

[64] We shall look at such post-lemmatic paraphrases in the next chapter.

which is taken to be excluded by the biblical 'do': a different type of teaching, teaching halakhic theory. Thus the universal exclusion is in effect limited to a concrete exclusion, producing the Opposition1 effect of defining a paradigm for the meaning of the biblical term. In such cases, that is, where a specific contrast term is found alongside a universal exclusion, this will be indicated by a combination of one of the resources Opposition1–5 with the following resource:

Opposition0: Explicating the meaning of a biblical expression by stressing its exclusive effect in a paraphrase using, for example, 'not . . . unless' (עד ש . . .),[65] 'only' (בלדב) or אלא . . . אין),[66] or employing it in a negated phrase.[67]

Oppositions also appear on the level of the patterns of action and of narrative, in addition to the level of semantic choices. Very important for rabbinic literature in general is the contrastive comparison between the ways of God and the ways of man. Many rabbinic parables put the king 'of flesh and blood' in opposition to the divine king. An example of the God–man contrast is found in mSot 8:1 VI (8). In that passage the somewhat redundant biblical expression 'for the Lord your God is he that goes with you' from Deut. 20:4 is paraphrased as 'they come in the strength of flesh and blood, but you [Israel] come in the strength of the Almighty'. This is illustrated with examples from the biblical narrative.[68] The antithetical comparison between God and man is also a recurrent theme in the rabbinic discourse on biblical narrative or biblical values.[69] It furthermore plays a direct role in rabbinic halakhah, in the distinction of punishments by the human court from *karet*, premature death, and other heavenly sanctions (used as hermeneutic OPPOSITION in mSan 11:5). Similar oppositional comparisons in hermeneutic application are found for 'Torah'. Thus, mQin 3:6 I (2) contrasts the mental faculties of the ageing elders of the halakhically indifferent or ignorant (the *am ha-arets*) with those of the ageing 'elders of Torah'. And mQid 4:14 I (4) puts the effects of learning Torah into opposition to those of learning the worldly crafts.[70]

OPPOSITIONS FOR SYNTAGMAS

The resources to which I now turn could be characterized, at a first approximation, as oppositions for *whole syntagmas*. The contrast structure is different from the comparison with and exclusion of items belonging to the

---

[65] e.g. mBik 1:2 I (2). Cf. my 'Stressing Scripture's Words', 216 f.
[66] e.g. mBQ 7:1 and mHul 10:1 II (2), respectively.
[67] e.g. mBek 2:9 II (3).
[68] 1 Sam. 17:46; 2 Sam. 10:16–18.
[69] I once compiled a list of approximately 50 instances of contrastive comparison of man and God found in Tanhuma (ed. Buber); and of 15 instances in the first 12 chapters of BerR ed. Theodor-Albeck. The task was set me by Arnold Goldberg.
[70] Using the contrastive phrase . . . אלא כן אינה התורה אבל.

same paradigm in that the biblical syntagma itself, not merely one of its members, is put into the hypothetical mode. It is viewed as one of *several possible* syntagmas. The hermeneutic operation focuses on elements of the wording which do not constitute the nucleus of the sentence. The significance of such linguistic elements is then emphasized by comparing the biblical sentence containing them with a similar sentence that does not. This amounts to a comparison of two syntagmas, one of which represents the actual text of Scripture, while the other represents a leaner, more 'economic' version. *Ex hypothesi*, the operation results in investing with emphatic significance the apparently dispensable or negligible textual element. The question of whether it is dispensable serves merely to identify the precise point of relevance.[71] Our first example below has been chosen for explicating the hermeneutic operation rather fully. The reason for this full explanation is that the biblical verse is to be uttered in the performance of a Mishnaic commandment (a Performance4 case):

[107] mNeg 12:5 I (4)[72]   Lev. 14:35

How is the viewing of a house [for scale disease done]? 'And the one whose house it is shall come and tell the priest, saying: It seems to me that there is the like of scale disease in the house'. Even if he is a disciple of the Sages (*talmid hakham*) and knows for sure that it is scale disease, he may not decree (יגזור) [it] and say: It seems to me that there is scale disease in the house, but 'It seems to me that there is **the like** of scale disease in the house'.

The biblical particle כ, 'the like of', is stressed as a result of the specific situation that the Mishnah suggests could arise. *Even* (אפילו) if the person reporting the problem is a rabbinically trained student of Torah, this particle in his report ensures that the pronouncement proper (גזר) is left to the priest. It therefore also goes hand in hand with the note of uncertainty in the verb 'it seems to me', instead of being rendered redundant by it. Choosing a different vantage-point, one can also say: the Mishnah supplies a situation in which the particle כ has a *necessary* function in advertising the fact that the initial report of the owner of the house is different from the priest's final verdict: namely, when the owner has the *competence* to make the final announcement, that is, could be misunderstood as taking the decision himself.[73]

---

[71] See n. 85 below. In allocating *necessity*—i.e. the relevance—to every textual element in this way, rabbinic hermeneutics seems to presuppose a compositional ideal of *economy*, as does any modern writer checking a draft for words that can be deleted; cf. the notion of *efficiency* in Sperber and Wilson, *Relevance*. But economy is not a universal ideal for texts, as a perusal of the texts collected in the Buddhist Pali canon will confirm.

[72] Σ πO6?O8(like)O9P4T3.

[73] Cf. mNeg 3:1, stating that everyone may inspect the signs in persons, but only the priest may make the declaration. A skilled person inspecting signs of scale disease may tell the priest to say 'Unclean' or 'Clean', thus ensuring that it is the priest (even if unskilled himself) who performs the pronouncement.

[108] mSot 4:1[74]   Num. 5:29

The betrothed woman and the woman waiting to be married by her deceased husband's brother do not drink [the *Sotah* waters] and do not receive the *Ketubbah*, for it is said, 'when a wife turns aside, being under the authority of her husband . . .'—[Scripture] details [as excluded] the betrothed woman and the woman waiting to be married by her deceased husband's brother.

The verse (and thus the *Sotah* ritual) is taken to deal with women who are under the authority[75] of a husband, thus excluding two borderline cases of women who are bound to a specific man by ties of merely near-marital strength. The widow waiting for levirate marriage to be performed and the betrothed woman are tied by a legal tie that is expected to lead to full marriage, but they are not yet fully married. These wives presumptive are taken to be excluded by the somewhat redundant biblical phrase 'being under her husband'. The hermeneutic operation is best understood as the result of comparing the actual biblical syntagma, containing the phrase תחת אישה, with a virtual or alternative syntagma that does not contain these two words but is otherwise the same. Such a test of substitution shows that the phrase gives added emphasis, beyond the word 'wife', to the married status of the woman, and for this emphasis the Mishnah finds two suitable subjects. The metalinguistic terminology is of interest here. The verb translated as 'to detail' above is פרט. In one, very common, rabbinic usage the root expresses the idea of something being specific, as opposed to it being general. Paradoxically, it is used in the above passage and similar extra-Mishnaic ones for something that Scripture is *silent* about—the opposite of specification, one might think.[76] The difficulty of two apparently unconnected meanings for פרט could be solved by reference to a rabbinic intuition that contrast terms are *present* in Scripture *in absentia*, namely, through the paradigm.[77] This would explain how Scripture can be said to *specify* them.

One syntagmatic element which the Mishnah repeatedly tests for its contribution by imagining its absence is the dative object, including but not restricted to the *dativus ethicus*. The following passage provides an illustration, and also shows how very different levels of generality can be made to meet (Topic2.1):

---

[74] ®O2O8T2.1T3.

[75] For this sense of תחת, see BDB 1065b. According to Bietenhard (*Sota*, 81) the word is understood as implying intercourse (i.e. consummation of the marriage).

[76] Bacher, i. 153, is puzzled and suggests that a different base meaning might be involved here ('aussondern, ausscheiden (vgl. פרד)'). Alternatively, one could approach this problem from the word's opposition to כלל—the latter taken in its meaning of 'inclusion' rather than 'general'. Cf. also Jastrow, s.v. 1224b. The function of the word in this usage is exactly the same as that of להביא, 'to bring in', in other rabbinic texts (and see e.g. mBer 1:5 II (2)).

[77] On relations *in absentia*, see n. 13 above.

[109] mGit 3:2[78]   Deut. 24:1

He who writes out copies of bills of divorce needs to leave space for the man, and space for the woman, and space for the time . . . [here other legal documents are listed], because of the benefit [of having ready documents]. R. Yehudah declares all of them invalid. R. Eleazar declares them all valid, except for the bills of divorce, as it is said, 'and he shall write for her' (לה)—for her in particular (לשמה).

The situation to which the biblical 'for her' is made relevant is: a scribe preparing bills of divorce in advance by writing out the standing formula with spaces left empty for the later addition of the specifics of each divorce. The question of whether or not it is admissible for scribes to prepare bills of divorce in this way is on a totally different level of generality from the basic norm as expressed in the biblical sentence, namely, that there should be something like a written divorce document in the first place (and the subject of 'he shall write for her' is, grammatically speaking, the husband). In other words, the apparently superfluous preposition with suffix is taken to make a contribution to the halakhah of divorce not on the level of basics (as the biblical sentence as a whole), but on a level of fine detail. This is a method of imposing perspective which I have labelled Top2.1 previously (Chapter 4), and which I have linked to the phenomenon of paradigms in the opening of this chapter. However, the Lemma can make this contribution only because it is not necessary for establishing the *gist* of the biblical sentence in which it appears; it is, viewed from the grammatical sentence, not necessary. Again, we can thus understand the operation on the basis of a comparison of the same biblical sentence *without* לה.

Confirmation that a comparison of syntagmas, or a 'superfluity' in the biblical text, is involved in this hermeneutic move is sometimes available from the co-text of the midrashic unit, as in the following passage:

[110] mQid 3:4 I–II (2)[79]   Num. 32:29–30

R. Meir says: Any stipulation of conditions[80] which is not like the stipulation of the children of Gad and the children of Reuben is no stipulation, as it is said, 'and Moses said to them: If the children of Gad and the children of Reuben pass over etc. . . .' (and it is written:)[81] 'And if they do not pass over armed . . .'.[82] R. Haninah ben

---

[78] • ¶O8(O1.4)T2.1. Cf. my 'Stressing Scripture's Words', 210 f.

[79] I: • ¶πN5.2O6O8T1T3; II: • ¶(¬)N5.2O8T1T3.

[80] The word תנאי is a technical term of rabbinic contract law; see e.g. Jastrow, 1680a ad loc.

[81] The text in brackets is not found in MS Kaufmann; in other recensions it constitutes one of the very rare appearances of the Aramaic כדב in the Mishnah.

[82] Here are the relevant portions of Scripture, in the RSV version: 'And Moses said to them: If the sons of Gad and the sons of Reuben, every man who is armed to battle before the Lord, will pass with you over the Jordan and the land shall be subdued before you, then you shall give them the land of Gilead for a possession; but if they will not pass over with you armed, they shall have possessions among you in the land of Canaan' (Num. 32:29–30). There is, however, a second version of the agreement: 'So Moses said to them: If you will do this, if you will take up arms to go before the Lord for the war, and every armed man of you will pass over the Jordan before the Lord, until he has driven out his enemies from before him and the land is subdued before the Lord; then after that you shall return and be free of obligation to the Lord and to Israel; and this land shall be your possession before the Lord. But if you will not do so, behold, you have sinned against the Lord; and be sure your

Gamliel says: It was necessary for the matter to be said (צורך היה הדבר לאמרו), for otherwise it could be understood (יש במשמע) that even in the land of Canaan they should not inherit.

R. Meir's position seems to be that the agreement made between the two tribes of Gad and Reuben and the other tribes concerning the conquest of Canaan is a halakhic model (i.e. Norm5.1) for any contract, in that it stipulates both what happens if the condition is met and what happens if it is not met. Stating both sides of an alternative is, of course, intrinsically an uneconomic procedure. However, in the legal context redundancy can have the function of excluding ambiguity, and that seems to be the effect R. Meir wants to achieve. The hermeneutic question is in fact also one of redundancy, and the longer, two-pronged syntagma is being compared with a briefer syntagma stating only what happens if the two tribes do meet the condition. That is clear from the objection of R. Haninah. This objection takes the form: since the double formulation removes the possibility that the two tribes might be allocated no land at all, it cannot be taken as redundant and therefore also not as a model of the sort of legal redundancy R. Meir envisages.[83] Haninah's objection directly addresses the meta-linguistic issue by saying that the extra 'word' (הדבר) was *necessary*. Here is a general formula for such an interpretation:

Opposition8: Allocation of a separate meaning, subject-matter, or referent to a biblical expression or clause on the basis of contrasting the biblical syntagma with an alternative syntagma which is identical except for not containing that expression or that clause. This tacit comparison points to the meaning surplus or meaning differential provided by the apparently redundant expression or clause.

One important feature of this resource is aptly illustrated by [110], namely, that it can be applied to linguistic signs on several levels. For what is at stake in [110] is the necessity or superfluity of a complete complex sentence (the negative version of a conditional sentence, including its apodosis). In other words, the framework of comparison lies on the linguistic level above the sentence, it comprises the whole textual unit called 'conditional agreement' (תנאי), consisting of two such complex sentences. Most of the Mishnaic operations of this type, however, target the level of phrases, as in [108], words, or suffixed prepositions as in [109]. As

sin will find you out' (Num. 32:20–23). See on this Brin, 'The Problem of Sanctions in Biblical Law', 359 f.

[83] As the preceding note shows, there are other redundancies in the biblical text, and their function is difficult to link to the format of legal agreements. The Gemara on this *mishnah* (bQid 61a–62a) does not address these questions either. It does, however, use the two positions imputed to Meir and Haninah to explore a long series of biblical 'double stipulations' and how they can be read on the one hand as redundant (i.e. conforming to Meir's idea of a conditional agreement), and on the other as non-redundant (according to Haninah, who is taken to find such redundancy in legal agreements unnecessary). Other formal aspects of the biblical passage, and their model character for legal documents, including bills of divorce, are discussed in bGit 75a–b.

was said before, prepositional constructions in the dative are several times the target of a Mishnaic Opposition8 operation, of which the following is another illustration:

[110a] = [92] mKet 3:5 II   Deut. 22:29 (24:1)

. . . Should there be found in her some 'indecent matter' (cf. Deut. 24:1)[84] or if she is not suitable to marry into Israel, he is not permitted to keep her, for it is said: 'And to **him** she shall be for a wife'—a wife that is suitable for him.

The result of the hermeneutic operation is that the wife has to be 'suitable': while the theme of this extra condition is due to the perspective chosen by the Mishnah, it homes in on the elaborate biblical construction which employs the dative. The expression 'for him', לו, in comparison with the simpler 'his wife', is uneconomical and thus conspicuous. Conspicuous, however, in rabbinic hermeneutics means by definition important and relevant, even if it is conspicuous to begin with precisely because it looks irrelevant. One might say, if it looks unnecessary it must be necessary. The expectation of relevance turns what might be negligible into what is emphatically important—one only has to know the topic or perspective in which it is important. And that topic must lie in all cases of potential redundancy *beyond the subject-matter* already treated explicitly in the biblical sentence (or beneath its level of generality). We find again, as for the resources of contradiction (DIFFERENCE) a differentiation of topics. In passage [110] the new topic which the vacuum of redundancy attracts is the question of marriage restrictions. For the rabbinic reader the information flow only *seems* to slacken in a redundant or uneconomic part of the sentence; in reality, it continues apace, but the topic has shifted, needs shifting—away, for example, from what the violator *has* to do towards what the violator is *forbidden* to do even as compensation for his transgression. Where the result of a comparison of Scripture with a slimmed-down version of itself shows that the main topic of the overall syntagma is not affected, the resource assumes that the 'uneconomic' biblical segment must be necessary in respect to some other topic.[85]

As I have said, the test of substitution works on all linguistic levels. The resource is also found on the level of particles or enclitics, putting their effect into co-textual relief. This includes grammatical signs, such as the *nota accusativi*, whose employment or absence is open to choice in biblical Hebrew, and particles of limitation, extension, or addition with independent meaning such as גם and אף or the conjunctive *waw*.[86] In its application

[84] As noted at the first occurrence of this passage, MS Kaufmann reads דבר זמה ('wicked matter', or 'lewd matter'); it also has לא instead of לו in the quotation from Scripture. The hermeneutic profile is πᵢ(Deut. 24:1)O8T2W1.

[85] Cf. the notion of Scripture being true about *something* (just as the proverb)—but its topic has to be found (see Ch. 5, n. 32). Here the unnecessary is being treated as necessary for *something*, and again the hermeneutic competence consists in identifying the topic.

[86] Cf. mSot 5:1 I (3), where I am not sure about the resource, but which is taken in this sense in bSot 28a.

to these signs in particular, the Opposition8 resource seems an integral component of the rabbinic hermeneutic rules of *ribbui* and *mi'ut*.[87]

As so often when observations of a 'purely' textual nature are built into the resources, the impression that an element of the biblical text is extravagant, or superfluous to the main thrust of the sentence, lies to some extent in the eye of the rabbinic beholder. What I said about the initial perception of a biblical inconsistency[88] also holds, *mutatis mutandis*, for the perception of superfluity: the very same Mishnaic interest which guides the discovery of relevance for the chosen segment (the extra topic or referent), may already be part of the initial suggestion that the Lemma has no relevance for the larger syntagma's topic.[89] The concern which drives the recognition of a 'problem' also drives the construction of its 'solution'— they are two sides of the same hermeneutic move. It is possible to invert, up to a point, the manner in which the Opposition8 resource is described. Instead of saying that the text offers a conspicuous—namely, redundant— structure, to which the reader brings a new topic, one could say: the reader recognizes that the biblical expression speaks of a topic of concern to him *before* establishing that this expression's contribution to the overall topic of the verse is negligible.[90] But by the time one is presented with a midrashic unit in a rabbinic text, these distinctions are irrelevant. The textual ground has been tested, and the decision has been taken that it can carry the weight of the idea hermeneutically connected to it. One does not learn which other avenues were explored and rejected because the textual or linguistic structures of the biblical wording were found insufficient to bear the burden of the argument. And of the hermeneutic ideas that might have been tried but found wanting for a given Lemma by their own authors, one knows almost nothing.[91]

Let me clarify some of the implications of my description of Opposition8 as a comparison of syntagmas. I am really saying that there must be a paradigm of syntagmas,[92] within which the comparison takes place. Where are the examples of syntagmas which provide the standard of comparison for

---

[87] See Ch. 9 (Extension5.5; and n. 12 there). On *plene* spellings as the source of *ribbui*-like extensions, see Elman, 'Towards a History of *Ribbuy* in the Babylonian Talmud', 89 f.

[88] Cf. Ch. 10, text preceding passage [93].

[89] It is a manifestation of our own blinkers as historians that we can mistake the rabbinic probing for relevance as 'a type of source criticism', i.e. by way of a category that happens to be ever-present in *our* practice of reading (see e.g. Lightstone, *The Rhetoric of the Babylonian Talmud*, 151, on bBek 2a ff.); the same goes for the application of the label 'folk *etymology*' to rabbinic hermeneutics (see Ch. 14, n. 39, and Ch. 1). A related type of erroneous 'updating', committed by the present author, is discussed in the next chapter.

[90] Cf. the idea of an attitude 'topical alignment' discussed in Ch. 3 above.

[91] As far as resources are concerned, there seems to be no principal difference between interpretations which the Mishnah marks as rejected or disputed ('¬' and '¶' in our codes) and others. This could mean that it is primarily not the hermeneutic appropriateness, but the resulting Dictum which is disputed or rejected. Certainly, the study of hermeneutic disputes in the Mishnah cannot be separated from the study of non-hermeneutic ones (see Ch. 15 below). Cf. also the commitment to Dicta, as distinct to the commitment to the interpretation, discussed in the next chapter.

[92] Cf. Coseriu, *Einführung in die Allgemeine Sprachwissenschaft*, 147.

the rabbinic reader? Is it the rabbinic interpreter's own use of language in smaller or larger texts? But even if this were so, is rabbinic linguistic or stylistic intuition not likely to have been influenced in some measure by Scripture? It seems plausible to assume that Opposition8 is at least sometimes based on an intuitive or even systematic comparison of biblical syntagmas with other *biblical* syntagmas. Several ways to define the biblical 'control group' come to mind: other biblical occurrences of the same type of sentence, or the same type of function (that is, normative), or the same topic; other sentences in the same biblical section, or belonging to the same 'style' or genre, as perceived by the rabbis. Behind some cases of Opposition8 may be the intuition that a biblical formulation is conspicuous because it contains extra elements, compared *with similar biblical formulations*.[93] Some of the examples for the related resource Opposition9, to be discussed presently, add credence to this possibility. It certainly seems worth keeping in mind that the biblical text itself might provide the reservoir or *paradigm* of syntagmas used in these two resources, Opposition8 and Opposition9.

One can also find in the Mishnah comparisons which reverse the Opposition8 procedure. They show that some expected specification, that is, a position in the syntagma, is *missing* from a biblical syntagma. In this hermeneutic operation the importance of the reader's assumption and anticipation of what is relevant is even more manifest than in the case of Opposition8.

Opposition9: Explication of a biblical syntagma in terms of a syntagmatic position not provided by it (that is, a tacit contrast with a richer or more complex syntagma). The absence of the position is taken to imply the exclusion of a member (or members) of a Mishnaic paradigm which could occupy that position.

Here the interpreter's room for manoeuvre is considerable. The reader selects the 'absent' syntagmatic slot, of course with a relevant paradigm in mind, as well as the individual item from that paradigm determined as excluded. However, due to the Mishnah's basically thematic orientation, one can usually discover additional constraints which reduce the seemingly limitless freedom of choice offered by the Opposition9 resource. These constraints come either from the co-text of the biblical Lemma (as thematically relevant),[94] or from thematic parallels elsewhere in Scripture. It may be useful to start with an example in which the choice of an

---

[93] See Ch. 10 above (text on *dativus ethicus* after case [92]).

[94] e.g. mSot 9:5 II (3), which deals with Deut. 21:3. That verse specifies that an animal which had borne the yoke is disqualified from serving in the ritual of the heifer whose neck is broken. The Mishnah concludes from this and (I think) also from the fact that no *further* disqualification is mentioned that a blemish does *not* disqualify it. It seems to me that this is not a mere Opposition1 case, but a combination of Opposition1 and Opposition9: cultic disqualifications are expected to come in clusters, not just one at a time, so that the *absence* of a very common disqualification regarding 'blemish' is emphasized in this interpretation.

'absent' syntagmatic slot is not fully explicated. I return to a passage discussed earlier:

[110b] = [78] mBM 9:13 II (4)[95]   Deut. 24:17

A widow, be she poor or be she rich, one does not seize a pledge (ממשכנין) from her, as it is said, 'You shall not [pledge-]take a widow's garment'.

The interpretation takes as *absolute* the prohibition not to hold a widow's garment, in this one respect: the widow's wealth. Irrespective of where between the two extremes of rich and poor (. . . ש בין . . . ש בין) a woman's possessions are located, the prohibition applies. This conclusion seems to be derived, to judge from the verse selected, from the lack of qualification in this commandment, given in apodictic format. Since the wealth of the widow is only one of many situational factors that can change from case to case and about which Scripture is silent, a *selection* is made by the rabbinic interpreter: of all the things this syntagma is silent about, wealth is chosen. This means that there was an *expectation* of relevance for this point. Only because of its latent importance can Scripture's silence about it be taken to imply deliberate rejection. The two defining extremes of the paradigm (rich–poor) are taken to be rejected by Scripture as criteria for the workings of the norm. But it is not the *poor* widow which is the problem case included by Scripture's silence, it is the rich one. The question of wealth is pertinent if one looks at the biblical co-text of the Lemma. The expectation could well have been formed, on the basis of that co-text, that the norm only applies to the poor widow, for poverty is one of the factors that bind together the various laws in Deut. 24. They embrace the prohibition to take essential possessions as debt security, regulations ensuring the fair treatment of hired servants, sojourners, orphans, and widows, and provisions for letting the sojourner, the orphan, and the widow(!) collect agricultural produce left in the field after a harvest (the latter in verses 19–22). However, although the biblical co-text could well have prompted the Mishnaic selection of the wealth paradigm as potentially relevant to the norm, there is no overt indication that this is so. The next case is slightly more transparent on the question of choice of topic for the absent slot:

[111] mBM 9:12 II (3)[96]   Deut. 24:14 f.; Lev. 19:13

To the resident alien (גר תושב), 'in his day you shall give him his hire' applies; and, 'do not keep the wages of a hired servant with you overnight until the morning' does not apply.

The Mishnaic inclusion of the alien in the law of the hired servant in Deut. 24:14 f. is not explained. This textual unit does not have a midrashic format, using instead both biblical sentences directly as part of a Mishnaic utterance (π). However, Deut. 24:14 contains an explicit stipulation, 'be he from your brethren or from your sojourners . . .', and awareness of this is certainly presupposed in the Mishnaic Dictum. In the Leviticus passage, on the other hand, one finds no qualification with regard to the hired servant.[97] Although one cannot be sure, I think that the unit **[111]** means to set up a contrast in the formulation of the two closely related biblical laws (a variation of the Difference7) which provides for the following argument: since in Lev. 19:13 the alien is not explicitly included, as he is in Deut. 24:14, he is meant to be excluded. There would be a comparison of the actual syntagma of Lev. 19:13 on the one hand with the same syntagma hypothetically enlarged after the model of Deut. 24:14 ('be he from brethren or from sojourners') on the other. This comparison highlights the *empty space* in Deut. 24:14, the space in which the alien would find mention had his inclusion been intended. It is such a comparison which makes the *absence* in the Leviticus law meaningful, implying an exclusion, as in case **[110b]**.[98] Even such a comparison of biblical structures would, however, probably still presuppose a Mishnaic paradigm whose members include casual labourers or persons of restricted social and legal rights.

[97] On the contrary, in the same verse a general injunction not to oppress 'your neighbour' is found. This could have provided the basis of a co-textual analogy (cf. case **[66]** mHul 8:4 II (3)), i.e. an application of the Analogy2.1 resource. This is how the Gemara seems to reconstruct this part of the hermeneutic argument (bBM 111b). However, the close and emphatic juxtaposition of Deut. 24:14 and Lev. 9:13 in our *mishnah* suggests to me another resource, namely Opposition9.

[98] In other biblical sentences the absence of a qualification might well be interpreted as absence of an *exclusion*, so that Scriptural silence would be taken to indicate the inclusion of every member of a paradigm not explicitly excluded. But here the 'missing' bit is itself a biblical formula of *inclusion*.

12

Projecting Commitment Through Scripture. The Midrashic Unit

The separation of Scripture as a text from the Mishnah's own voice is not to be interpreted as implying a 'historical' attitude to Scriptural meaning. Instead, the hermeneutics of appropriation amount to a direct commitment to Scripture's validity and relevance. This commitment is projected onto the biblical text both through the Mishnaic reformulation (in the case of the midrashic unit) and through the expressive use of biblical words (π). There may even be cases of biblical quotations where little more than Mishnaic commitment is added to the words of Scripture. The midrashic unit, consisting of a quotation and a Mishnaic reformulation, is thus not a device to place responsibility for the validity of norms or propositions onto the biblical text, thereby reserving for the Mishnaic voice merely the commitment to the validity of the *interpretation*. Rather, the midrashic unit as a hermeneutic utterance commits its speaker to the validity of the interpretation as well as to the validity of the statement or norm expressed in duplicate.

THE PROJECTION OF COMMITMENT

I have dealt in the last chapter with a phenomenon central for an understanding of the rabbinic interpretation: emphasis. In this chapter, I shall investigate it further, but link it in particular to the question of how one can best understand the type of speech act with which interpretations of Scripture are typically tied up in the Mishnah. This involves some historical speculation on a very general level. Turning away from what happens to the biblical words—they are pronounced emphatically—to what happens to the interpreters, I shall say that they *commit* themselves. The emphatic repetition of Scripture as the rabbis' own utterance *binds* the rabbis, in ways similar to how any utterance, but in particular the promise, binds its speakers. This binding does not come after the act of interpretation is completed, attaching itself to its result, the rabbinic Dictum. The rabbinic voice's commitment to the Dictum is *identical* with the emphasis the rabbinic interpreter places on the words of the biblical Lemma. The commitment to what Scripture says operates on principle and does not depend on the concrete results of interpretation. And the commitment to the Dictum precedes the interpretation in a manner of speaking, but not in the sense that the interpretation is adjusted in the light of the acceptability of the Dictum.[1] The commitment to the Dictum precedes the interpretation because the Dictum *is* the rabbinic utterance of Scripture.[2]

Direct commitment to the words of Scripture is obvious where those words become part of the Mishnaic utterance. I have discussed this phenomenon in Chapters 4–5: the format π, and the resource families PERFORMANCE and USE. It is worth recalling the phenomenon by way of example. Lev. 4:13 prescribes an offering for a sinful error committed by the whole congregation. It has the following protasis: 'And if the whole congregation of Israel commits an error (ישגו) and the thing be hid (ונעלם דבר) from the eyes of the community and they do (ועשו) one of all the [things] which the Lord has commanded not to be done, and they incur guilt . . .'. The elements of this passages are combined into a new, Mishnaic, statement in the following passage:

[112] mHor 2:3[3]   Lev. 4:13

They are liable only concerning 'something hid' (העלם דבר) together with (עם) an 'erroneous' 'act' (שגגת המעשה).

It is clear that the authors of the Mishnah create their own expression of obligation, the utterance by which they bind themselves and their audience, with the help of the words of Scripture. The Mishnaic formulation employs the biblical lexemes for 'hide', 'thing', 'error', and 'act', while making clear that the different aspects of the conditional clause need to apply simultaneously. But such direct commitment to the words of Scripture, in a meaning whose link to the biblical meaning is transparent, is not restricted to the format of expressive use. That commitment is just as present in the midrashic format which juxtaposes biblical quotation and Mishnaic formulation. To make it easier to spot the commitment, I shall begin with a case in which the difference between Mishnah and Scripture is minimal.

---

[1] That may well also occur, but is a different phenomenon, and we mostly never see the midrashic units that took a 'wrong' turn (cf. text between nn. 90 and 91 in Ch. 11 above; Ch. 10, text preceding case [93]).

[2] See below in the second section of this chapter. The will to accept Scripture as divine communication and demand logically precedes this kind of hermeneutic work, and the hermeneutic work cannot fully justify that will, nor can the text 'falsify' it. See my 'Scripture's Implicature', 195; Ch. 2 above on Torah (text to n. 87).

[3] πL7x2 O6.

[113] mBM 9:13 I (4)[4]   Deut. 24:11

The person lending to his fellow does only exact a pledge from him through the court. And he does not enter (ולא יכנס) his house to take his pledge, as it is said, 'Outside shall you stand (בחוץ תעמד) [. . . and he shall bring outside to you the pledge]'.

Note the very close reformulation of the verse by the Mishnah: the biblical phrase speaks of standing 'outside' (בחוץ תעמד), the Mishnah speaks of 'not entering' (ולא יכנס).[5] There is certain to be some semantic difference between the two formulations which, in suitable circumstances, is capable of generating additional information from the Mishnaic rephrasing.[6] But their difference is not stressed, and there is nothing in the Mishnaic co-text to show what work the difference could have been meant to perform. As the two formulations are presented, the main distinction between Dictum and Lemma is that the former is speech of the Mishnah while the latter is speech of Scripture. This means that the main difference is the directness (i.e. presentation) of the commitment: the Dictum is a repetition of Scripture, in slightly different words but mainly with the Mishnah's *commitment* added to them. Scripture's message is *affirmed*, that is, presented as ratified by the Mishnah. The Mishnaic gesture of making Scripture its own which so obviously underlies the *expressive use*—for example, in [112]—is here performed also, and made conspicuous by the closeness between the two formulations.[7] Scripture's words are not an utterance that could commit the rabbis unless they produced a new utterance with it—passages [112] and [113] show two formally distinct but essentially similar ways to do just this.

Topic 7: Provision of a close rephrasing of a Scriptural expression, clause, or norm. The semantic difference of this rephrasing to Scripture is minimal and not exploited for the allocation of a separate topic or function in the Mishnaic discourse. Thus, the resultant adjustment of links within the biblical co-text is also negligible or imperceptible.

---

[4] ◊πC5R6.4?T7.

[5] The object 'house' is also biblical, mentioned in Deut. 24:10. The opposition 'inside–outside' is of general importance in Mishnaic discourse. An operation of opposition like [113] is found in mNeg 12:6 I (3), concerning the stipulation in Lev. 14:38 that the priest go 'to the *entrance* of the house' for inspecting it. Passage [88] mSan 10:6 I (6) above is concerned with the case of the open space of the apostate city lying *outside* it. The paradigm 'inside/outside the Land' is frequently invoked (e.g. mHul 12:1), and sometimes (e.g. mBek 9:1 I (2)) combined with the temporal 'before–after' of the sanctuary. On the semantics of the more general terms פנים/חוץ in Hebrew, see Bochorovski and Trommer, 'A Semantic-Pragmatic Study of the Sense Relation Called "Opposition" ', 240.

[6] The presence of the Mishnaic word will, for *some* contexts, exclude meaning possibilities inherent in the biblical word taken on its own. Something of a '3D' effect is achieved by synonymous expressions; and in socially embedded language use they tend to be differentiated against each other (see Ch. 9 above, n. 84; Ch. 10, text succeeding n. 56). Linguists are inclined to deny that true (or 'absolute') synonyms exist; see e.g. Cruse, *Lexical Semantics*, 270; Pope, *The English Studies Book*, 380. Lyons (*Semantics*, i. 202) defines 'same sense' as holding 'over a certain range of *utterances*', i.e. not sentences (emphasis mine).

[7] Cf. B. Kern, 'Paraphrasendeutung im Midrasch'. The role of repetition as *recognition* is explored in the semiotics of A. J. Greimas and utilized for biblical and legal studies in the work of B. Jackson, see esp. his *Studies in the Semiotics of Biblical Law*, chs. 8–9; *Making Sense in Law*, 144 ff.

Of some relevance here is the separation of the propositional content or propositional meaning of a sentence on the one hand from the speech act— promise, question, warning, statement, and so on—which may be performed 'with' it on the other.[8] In quoting a text while withholding a decision on its validity, one treats it somewhat similar to a propositional contents of which one does not know if it belongs to a statement or a question or a warning, threat, promise, or prediction. When Gottlob Frege devised a formal conceptual language, inaugurating in the process the modern study of logic, he felt the need to distinguish the representation of the content of a sentence from its affirmation as true, that is, from the *commitment* of the speaking voice (for which he used the sign ⊢). The format which he chose to express the fact that the speaker's commitment is *withheld* was the indirect *quotation*.[9] By contrast, the direct use of a clause or concept (as in the Mishnah's expressive use of Scriptural wording), commits the interpreter.

Viewed from this angle, the midrashic format does in fact allow one to put a distance between the quoted wording and its truth or validity. One can, after all, emphasize the verb of saying when introducing a quotation in order to express *doubt*, as in the following case: 'The engineer *said* it could be done in a day, meaning it would be finished before Friday.' (But the speaker doubts he can do it.) Yet although the format allows such distancing, this is not how the midrashic unit is employed. The Topic7 category points in a quite different direction, namely, that of a very direct commitment to the words of Scripture, since the Mishnah's own words are so very close in meaning. But the key is that the Mishnah, in being committed to its *own* words, is committed to words *which rephrase Scripture.* The quotation is not introduced in the following mode:

(a) If the report is reliable, the ship reached Surabaya in July 1835.

but in this mode:

(b) Since the report is reliable, the ship reached Surabaya in July 1835.

From this last sentence the first half can be eliminated without changing the strength of commitment. The person uttering (b) shoulders the burden of truth, even while giving a source of information. And the most appropriate parallel is in fact something like the following:

(c) Since the law says that you can't sell fixtures of listed buildings, you (or: we) are not allowed to sell the paintings.

---

[8] See e.g. Levinson, *Pragmatics*, 245: The propositional content of the following utterances is said to be the same: (a) I predict that you will go home; (b) Go home!; (c) Are you going to go home?; (d) I advise you to go home, etc.

[9] Such as, '*The circumstance that* e.g. opposite poles of a magnet attract each other . . .' or the '*The sentence that* opposite poles of a magnet attract each other . . .' (Frege, *Begriffsschrift*, 2; cf. *Conceptual Notation*, 111 f.; emphasis mine).

This last example is closer than (a) or (b) to cases where the Mishnaic interpretation of Scripture provides for the formulation of *norms*. In sum, the Mishnah is committed to the rephrasing it offers of Scriptural wording, even though the quotation format *could* signal the withholding of commitment. And the commitment of the Mishnah to its own words qua reformulation of Scripture is just as strong in cases where a distance in generality or perspective or topic is noticeable between Scripture and the Mishnah (that is, in the large majority of—non-Topic7—passages). For otherwise there would be no reason to remould Scripture's message in the form of the Mishnaic discourse.

One can now add a new dimension to the phenomenon of emphasis. Take, for example, the Opposition8 resource. It allocates to an apparently unnecessary part of the biblical syntagma a relevant topic and thus confirms its importance. But how do we know it is important to the Mishnah? Because it is being linked to *a Mishnaic utterance*, the Dictum. Let us look at some of the examples of Dicta which we have encountered in the last chapters:

[107] Even if he is a disciple of the sages and knows for sure that it is scale disease, he may not decree [it] and say: It seems to me that there is scale disease in the house, but 'It seems to me that there is the like of scale disease in the house'.

[108] The betrothed woman and the woman waiting to be married by her deceased husband's brother do not drink [the *Sotah* waters] and do not receive the *Ketubbah*.

[109] R. Eliezer declares them all valid, except for the bills of divorce.

[110] R. Meir says: Any stipulation of conditions which is not like the stipulation of the children of Gad and the children of Reuben is no stipulation.

[110a] If she is not suitable to marry into Israel, he [the violator] is not permitted to keep her.

These Dicta *commit* the Mishnah, or the individual to whom they are ascribed. They express what the Mishnah or these individuals find right and proper, they promise to treat certain actions in a certain way, they *bind* the Mishnaic judge or rabbi. The people uttering these words *can be held to them* in a way in which they *cannot be held to the words of Scripture* (unless used expressively). But the Dicta are meant to express commitment, and that commitment cannot be separated from the process of interpretation. The voices speaking these Dicta are not committed to them *to the exclusion* of the Scriptural quotations to which they are attached—the commitment includes the meaning of Scripture because the Dicta *identify meaning for Scripture*.

Since the Opposition8 resource makes emphatic and important what in Scripture seems incidental or superfluous, it has the effect of *spreading* emphatic commitment to unstressed parts of the biblical text.[10] And this constitutes a third distinct phenomenon of commitment, in addition to expressive use of Scriptural wording (π, e.g. [112]) and near-synonymous rephrasing (Topic7, e.g. [113]). The reason for this is that the Mishnaic Dictum shifts the weight of full commitment onto parts of Scripture which, in the Scriptural co-text, are not so weighted. This means that the Mishnaic imposition of commitment becomes more visible than when dealing with parts of Scriptural syntagmas for which an 'emphatic' reading is already given by the biblical arrangement of words. Consider the differences in commitment which can exist even within the space of one sentence, if that sentence is used as a promise:

(a) At six o'clock I shall come to the entrance of the park with my friends.

Clearly, if the person making this promise does not turn up on the agreed day at all, she or he has not kept the promise. But what if the person were to turn up at five past six? Or at five to six? Or brings only one friend? Or comes not to the entrance of the park, but waits on the opposite side of the road? Or has been at the entrance all day long, and so did not 'come' to it at all? It will depend on the situational circumstances, and on the context of the conversation of which this promise is part, how important these differences are. But there is clearly a centre and a periphery to the commitment made by this promise. If it makes no material difference to the purposes of the person to whom the promise is given, then turning up at five past six with only one friend and on the opposite side of the street is likely still to count as having fulfilled the promise. And if any of these things made a difference, we would in most circumstances expect the utterance to highlight them in some way, as when saying:

(b) **At** precisely **six o'clock**, not a minute earlier or later, **I shall** *arrive* **at the entrance of the park**, exactly by the gate, *and bring* no less than two **friends**.[11]

This is a quite different promise, and if it were followed by the kind of lackadaisical performance pictured in the preceding paragraph, it could not be considered as fulfilled. In a manner of speaking, this new utterance is not so much a promise as the text of a contract, since we tend to ascribe to *legal* language such elaborate nailing down of a commitment.[12]

---

[10] We shall discuss the spreading of a topic from one or two items in a Scriptural unit to all of its members regardless of semantic or syntactic function in Ch. 13 (resource Redundancy9).

[11] The text in bold marks words identical with (a), while italics show parts which are modfied by (near-) synonymous rephrasing. This is how Targumic differences from the biblical original are often marked in modern scholarship. The version (b) could indeed be called a Targum of (a); cf. Shinan, ' "Targumic Additions" in Targum Pseudo-Jonathan', as well as my 'Is Targumic Aramaic Rabbinic Hebrew?' and 'Scipture's Segments and Topicality'.

[12] Its characteristic is to leave as little as possible unexpressed of the contextual circumstances which give the words their full meaning or importance; cf. Goodrich, *Languages of the Law*, 193 ff. But in perceiving such an attempt as typically 'legal' we are the children of our time. Documents consti-

Mishnaic interpretation offers many examples of a biblical sentence of the type (a) being read as if it had the meaning of (b). The OPPOSITION resources in general constitute key elements in this approach. Thus, Opposition9 reads the silent spaces of the syntagma as absence of specific provisions or qualifications; and Opposition1.4 highlights that 'friends' is not the same as 'friend'. Other resources directly connected with this type of emphasis are the LOGIC family, and also Habit6/7 (see below). But the term 'legal interpretation' does not so much analyse the phenomenon as merely label it.[13] Let us see what contribution the idea of commitment can make to an analysis of the phenomenon. One can describe what happens in (b) in the following way: the level of commitment of the promise in its shape (a), in the strength with which it attaches itself to the syntactic 'core' of the sentence, is spread out to all its parts. The (b) version imposes an emphasis on the plural 's' of 'friends', and highlights the fact that the phrase 'six o'clock' in (a) is not qualified by some expression such as 'approximately', or the like. The Mishnah repeats as utterance with full commitment the biblical silences, syntagmatic gaps, plural 's', and terms whose *absence* is expressed by the *presence* of certain expressions, as well as the biblical presuppositions. It is not so much that the emphatic interpretation imposes commitment on Scriptural words as utterances, but that it imposes commitment to parts of Scripture which are unstressed. And that is the point at which the Mishnaic commitment becomes visible as something on which the whole of the hermeneutic operation rests. Consider two more of the resources which extend the burden of obligation from stressed parts of the biblical text to unstressed parts. The following passage says, in effect, that any commitment to an utterance in which the word 'Nisan' figures includes the very last day of Nisan.

[114] mTaan 1:2[14]   Joel 2:23

Until when does one ask [for rain in prayer]? R. Yehudah says: Until Passover is over. R. Meir says: Until Nisan has ended, as it is said, '[Be glad, O sons of Zion, and rejoice in the Lord, your God; for he has given the early rain for your vindication], he has poured down for you the rain, the former rain and the latter-rain in the first'.

The biblical expression 'in the first'[15] is understood to refer to the point of

tuting legal wills, for example, used to contain much more context-sensitive information in earlier times, see Danet and Bogoch, 'Orality, Literacy, and Performativity in Anglo-Saxon Wills', 119–23. Cf. the characterization of promises as 'loose' in Finnis, *Natural Law and Natural Rights*, 308 f. On the question of the 'negotiability' of promises, see Sbisà and Fabbri, 'Models (?) for a Pragmatic Analysis'.

[13] Cf. Rosenblatt's formulation (*Interpretation*, 3) that 'One of the principles observed in the interpretation of *legal instruments* is that their stipulations cannot be made to exceed the narrowest meaning of the phraseology' (emphasis mine). The reference is to a maxim ascribed to Aqiva, פשטה המרובה לא תפשה; תפשה המועט תפשה (e.g. in Sifra on Lev. 15:25); cf. also Bacher, i. 110 f. More on the problems of such a view is found in Ch. 1 above.

[14] •¶[C5G2(*bet*)N8O7O8T0T1(W3).

[15] Some ancient versions, followed by RSV, read 'as at first'; JPS has, '[as] formerly' instead; cf. BDB s.v. ראשון, 911b.

the last rain in the season, namely, the first month (of Aviv/Nisan, also the month of Passover) according to the biblical counting. So the expression is understood to refer to Nisan, and furthermore the prophetic utterance is taken to express (or to presuppose) the regular timing of the rainy season.[16] On that basis, the concept of 'in the first' is then taken to its limits of commitment by saying that the *very last day* of Nisan is also included.[17]

These interpretations probe the outer boundaries of an expression, the limits of what a speaker can be taken to be committed to when the words are emphasized. One of the terminological signals for such interpretations is the word 'even', אפילו. I have drawn attention to its signalling function in connection with the resources allocating total scope to 'all' (Logic1) and to the negation (Logic3).[18] The word 'even' can appear wherever there is an emphasis on Scriptural words which leads to an 'absolute' reading. However, the extension of commitment to the outer limits is most striking when it is combined with a focus on existential presupposition (Habit6). One of the most famous interpretations in rabbinic literature belongs to this group:

[114a] = [15] = [82a] mBer 9:5 II (9)[19]   Deut. 6:5

Man is obliged to perform blessings over evil just as he performs blessings over good, as it is said, 'And you shall love the Lord your God with all your heart and with all your soul and with all your might'. 'With all your heart'—with your two inclinations, with the good inclination and with the evil inclination; 'and with all your soul'—even if he takes away your soul; 'and with all your might'—with all your wealth.

I have earlier scrutinized the above treatment of the word 'heart'.[20] Now I am concentrating on the interpretation of *nefesh*, 'soul/life'. This interpretation is elsewhere in rabbinic literature found embedded in a narrative of R. Aqiva's martyrdom, that is, a narrative about the extremes of a commitment.[21] It takes the emphasis on 'soul/life', partly through an emphasis on the total scope of 'all', to an extreme with regard to its existential presupposition. 'Even (אפילו) if he takes away your soul/life', means: at the cost of your life; the obligation to love God with 'all your soul qua life' extends up to the point at which its existential presupposition, life itself, is removed.[22] A similar effect is achieved in the following interpretation for a halakhic theme:

[16] The Mishnah tends to allow only that which *can* happen as a legitimate topic for petitionary prayer (or vows), not the miraculous.

[17] The other end of the limit, irrelevant at this point in the Mishnaic discourse, is of course Nisan's *first* day. See below.

[18] In Ch. 9, at n. 95, and the text leading up to the definition of resource Logic7.

[19] Ω®¬H6L1O6W1(*nefesh*)W1.2(*bet*).

[20] In Ch. 3 above I explain the perspectivization achieved by the rabbinic terminology of the two inclinations: [15]; in Ch. 9 the reading of 'all' as including two opposites: [82a].

[21] It is found in bBer 61b, i.e. the Gemara dealing with our *mishnah*. See Goldberg, 'Das Martyrium des Rabbi Aqiva'; Boyarin, *Intertextuality*, 125 ff.

[22] There is a somewhat similar interpretation in mSot 5:5 I (2) linked to the question of whether Job served God from love (!) or from fear (Job 13:15 and 27:5).

[115] = [130b] mPeah 7:7 I–II (3)[23]   Deut. 24:21; Lev. 19:10

A vineyard which is all defective clusters—R. Eliezer says: [They belong] to the owner. R. Aqiva says: To the poor. R. Eliezer said: 'When you [grape-] gather your vineyard you shall not take the defective clusters' (Deut.). If there is no [grape-] gathering whence defective clusters? R. Aqiva said to him: 'And from your vineyard you shall not take the defective clusters' (Lev.)—even though (אפילו) it is all defective clusters.

Eliezer holds that the use of the verb here translated as 'grape-gather' has the existential presupposition that there are regular grapes, not merely defective clusters, to gather. Aqiva, on the other hand, using the apodictic version (Lev. 19:10) of the same biblical norm, gives an 'absolute' interpretation which implies that the obligation to leave the defective clusters to the poor is valid even when its existential presupposition (in the Deuteronomy formulation) is not fulfilled.[24]

There are here two types of going to the *limit* of meaning with commitment, which I shall distinguish as Opposition6 and Opposition7. Opposition6 goes to the outer limit of the Scriptural sentence, colonizing its peripheral members, unstressed parts, or words which do not stand in the service of new information. Opposition7, on the other hand, probes the limits of the semantic information contained in any one biblical expression. A favourite way of implementing Opposition6 in the Mishnah is to join an unstressed element of a Scriptural segment to the apodosis of more specific case schema (i.e. resource Topic2).

Opposition6: Extension of the full commitment attaching to the grammatically central parts of a biblical period to its periphery or to elements which are unstressed, presupposed, incidental, or absent.

Opposition7: Inclusion of the extreme quantitative, spatial, temporal, or numerical limits of a biblical expression through emphasis. Where appropriate, limiting or oppositional members of a subordinate paradigm are named. (Cf. Logic1.)

The formulation of Opposition7 makes clear the potential link to reader paradigms. For even where only one limiting point is mentioned, the whole of the paradigm must be intended. Thus, in passage **[114]** 'Nisan' can only be emphasized to include the *last* day of Nisan if the *first* day (albeit irrelevant to the Mishnah's point) is included also. We do in fact find interpretations of the Opposition7 type which are interested in articulating *both* limiting points of meaning. They do not employ 'even' (אפילו), but constructions such as 'be it X or Y' (. . . בין . . . בין),[25] or 'it is all one whether X or Y'

---

[23] I (Eliezer): ®•¶πH6T2W1(grape-gather); II (Aqiva): ®•¶πL3O9R3.1T2.

[24] He continues the argument by allocating a new topic and function to the Deuteronomy verse, i.e. removing the appearance of biblical inconsistency. See on this Ch. 10, text to n. 72.

[25] e.g. mRH 2:9 I (2); see also mArak 4:4 III (4), discussed earlier as case **[75]**, which is of particular interest since it combines this construction with the 'light/heavy' terminology of Analogy4, בין להקל בין להחמיר.

(. . . ה אחד . . . ה אחד).²⁶ The passage quoted as **[110b]** above, mBM 9:13 II (4), containing the phrase 'be she poor or be she rich', is an example of this.

As regards Opposition6, there is a considerable number of passages in which one finds a movable focus on items of the Scriptural text which are best understood as reading the text emphatically, thereby justifying units of rabbinic commitment (i.e. Dicta). Regularly used in this way are the OPPOSITION resources, the LOGIC resources, and Habit6/7. It may be helpful to look at this also from the reverse perspective: as the focus moves from one item to the next in the Scriptural text the items call up units of commitment which have the effect of producing emphatic readings of them. Here is an application of resource Opposition1 in which the focus can be observed as moving:²⁷

[116] mYeb 12:3 I (2)²⁸   Deut. 25:9

If she took off [the shoe] and spat, but did not say [the prescribed words], the *Halitsah* is valid. If she said [the prescribed words] and spat, but did not take off [the shoe], the *Halitsah* is invalid. If she took off [the shoe] and said [the prescribed words], but did not spit—R. Eliezer says, The *Halitsah* is invalid; R. Aqiva says, The *Halitsah* is valid. R. Eliezer said: 'Thus shall it be **done**'—everything that is a deed invalidates [the *Halitsah* if omitted]. R. Aqiva said to him: From that [same verse] there is proof [of my opinion]: 'Thus shall it be done *to the man* [who does not build the house of his brother]'—everything that is a deed [done] *to the man* [invalidates the *Halitsah* if omitted].

Aqiva's position on the role of spitting in the ceremony of the *Halitsah* seems to presuppose that the act is not in fact directed at the man's face;²⁹ the widow spits on the ground in front of the man.³⁰ We can read the two alternatives offered by Eliezer and Aqiva as the movement of a focus through the biblical phrase כּכה יעשה לאיש, 'thus shall it be done to the man'. Eliezer emphasizes the part 'thus shall it be *done*', accounting for this whole phrase by extracting from it the very specific information that the physical acts, but not the verbal acts, are of vital necessity. Aqiva expands the focus, and accordingly narrows down the realm of what is absolutely necessary: first 'done' excludes speech, then 'done *to the man*' excludes acts not done to the man. And in mSot 7:4 II (2) (see passage **[127]**), R. Yehudah is reported to put a stress on the next word in the same biblical phrase, 'thus'. He thereby extracts additional specific information from the last unstressed member of this biblical clause.³¹ Thus, from Yehudah to Eliezer and Aqiva the focus can be seen to move along the words of Scripture, until each of the

---

²⁶ A case in point is mArak 9:4; mostly, however, this formula is used to express inclusions (i.e. Extension1 and Extension2 resources).   ²⁷ Cf. my 'Stressing Scripture's Words', 203.
²⁸ I: •¶C5E1.2O1(P4)T2.1; II: •¶C5E1.2O6(P4)T0T2.1T3W7?.
²⁹ The biblical בפניו.
³⁰ Cf. Chajes, *The Student's Guide Through the Talmud*, 6: 'before his face' is taken to mean 'on the ground' not 'upon his face'.
³¹ Namely, that the language of the declaration has to be Hebrew, the overarching topic at this point of mSotah.

three words can be stressed and, in being stressed, be made to generate or support a specific commitment.[32] In the biblical text, on the other hand, this whole phrase, uttered by the widow at the end of the ceremony, is unstressed except for 'thus'. By its very nature—being the speech that points to the preceding act—the phrase should be quite redundant with regard to the *specifics* of the act to which it points. At this point in the text one would not expect the biblical voice to supply *new* information on the act itself. But this is how Yehudah, Eliezer, and Aqiva read the segment. The three hermeneutic operations ascribed to them show therefore very clearly how the focus of commitment is *extended* by the Mishnaic reading to include unstressed biblical elements, and how a level of commitment and emphasis belonging naturally to the core of a biblical message is transferred to its periphery; Opposition6 is meant to capture this hermeneutic move.

We also find, from time to time, cases where the Mishnaic commitment is explicitly withheld, or weakened. The significance of a given expression in Scripture may well be acknowledged and spelled out. Thus, mSot 9:5 III (3) first acknowledges explicitly that Deut. 21:3 requires the heifer whose neck is broken to be brought down a 'rugged' valley, and then goes on to say the Mishnaic norm has no such requirement (and cf. mKet 4:3 III (3) **[90]** above; and see the list of abrogated biblical norms in mSot 9:9). One Mishnaic way to put this is to say 'what he has done is done' (מה שעשה עשוי, see e.g. mTer 3:6). I shall use the code Topic8.5 (see Appendix 1) for the Mishnah's withholding its commitment from what it acknowledges to be the biblical meaning of an expression or clause.

THE MIDRASHIC UNIT: A HERMENEUTIC UTTERANCE

The Hermeneutic Speech Act

What sort of commitment is being expressed in the Dicta which are tied to Scripture in the midrashic unit? As far as the Mishnah is concerned, most of them belong to the halakhic discourse, which means that they express norms or 'the law' of rabbinic Judaism.[33] There are two ways to look at such norms: on the one hand, the voice of the Mishnah, in determining the halakhah, prescribes how others should act; on the other hand, in accepting the biblical word as halakhah, the voice of the Mishnah accepts and

---

[32] I have discussed such a moving focus, and the total shift of topic that can go with it, in its Targumic manifestation in 'Scripture's Segments and Topicality'.

[33] Commitment is by no means restricted to utterances which make a promise or accept a norm. Every type of speech act carries commitments of one sort or another, including the 'mere' statement. Cf. Austin, *How to Do Things with Words*, 154, 156, 157 f., 161 (regarding the commitments of 'verdictives', 'exercitives', 'commissives', 'behabitives'). The 'expositives', to which belong the 'constative' verbs such as 'affirm, state, describe, class, testify, report', are not explicitly compared for commitment in that chapter; their assimilation to performatives is central to Austin's book as a whole (e.g. pp. 52, 148, and 152: 'all aspects are present in all my classes').

confirms an obligation coming from elsewhere. In both respects the collective or individuals behind the voice of the Mishnah commit *themselves* to these norms. The Mishnah's voice, the collective of the rabbis, is committed to the validity of the norms both as a legislator on the one hand and as addressee of divine legislation on the other. The persons responsible for the utterance 'Mishnah' apply these norms to themselves, they commit themselves to abide by these rules; as judges, as peer group, or as individuals they promise to support others in accepting them, or to sanction their infringement. They will be *bound* by them; *after their utterance* it will be appropriate to measure their actions against these norms. And, despite the assumed divine origin of the norms, it would be misleading to define the rabbis wholly as the subjects of the law, in contrast to a totally autonomous giver of law (who is not bound by his own laws). Even many types of autonomous legislation involve the self-commitment of the legislator. And rabbinic literature contains distinct traces of the idea that, although the divine legislator is in principle totally autonomous, the law is worked out with the co-operation of Israel. One could perhaps say that the existence of the Mishnah *alongside* Scripture is the most striking if implicit manifestation of such a view. And there are some important explicit statements to this effect, for example, the famous interpretation of the phrase 'It [the Torah] is not in heaven' from Deut. 30:12.[34] There was clearly room for the view among the rabbis that the halakhah is to some extent *their responsibility*; that the process of finding, developing, and applying the halakhah is not 'in heaven'; and it is not a merely mechanical task of tracing what God had written. In any case, with the expression of halakhah, the commitment of the participants in the discourse of halakhah is not to someone else's words but to their own. It is not merely (if it is at all) an *imperative* addressed to someone else (the readers of the Mishnah, the Jewish people), but a kind of *promise*.[35] And the biblical words are being made the rabbis' own in the Mishnaic discourse, they are appropriated. In this regard, there is no difference between the *use* of a biblical sentence as rabbinic utterance (that is, the phenomenon discussed in Chapters 4–5) and the reduplication of meaning in the midrashic unit. The biblical text is adopted for commitment; it is uttered again as a speech act of the rabbis, not as a speech act of God. The imperatives become commitments, promises, confirmation, and acceptance of commandments. The Mishnah *speaks* those parts of the biblical wording which occur in it, but not in the way in which an actor speaks a part.

---

[34] The discussion is in bBM 59a/b (oven of Akhnai). See e.g. Boyarin, *Intertextuality*, 33 ff.

[35] In emphasizing the self-commitment of the rabbinic lawgivers or legal guardians I find myself furnishing historical support for a theoretical stance taken by some contemporary jurisprudents on the question of legal commitment. They consider the self-application or 'reciprocity' of legal norms an essential element of the notion of law (cf. Finnis, *Natural Law and Natural Rights*, 6 ff.). However, it needs to be stressed that in our context this interpretation flows from the nature of the hermeneutic utterance, and the nature of the utterances in rabbinic literature, not from an independent notion of law. In fact, it may ultimately flow from a notion of *utterance*.

In an earlier reflection on what sort of speech act the midrashic unit is, I maintained that the 'exegete is explicitly committed only to the validity of interpretation . . . We may *assume* for midrash that, given the belief in the truth of Scripture, the truth of . . . [the Dictum] is (usually) also tacitly claimed.'[36] I thus made a distinction between a commitment to the validity of the interpretation on the one hand, and a commitment to the truth of either the Scriptural segment or the Dictum linked to it on the other. I used this distinction to draw attention to specific material assumptions or existential presuppositions which form part of the hermeneutic operations and to whose validity the interpreter is automatically committed. These formally identifiable components (for example, 'this world–the world to come') I now understand as Topic3 and Topic4 resources. The distinction furthermore helps to see that the midrashic utterance is about meaning, not directly about law or fact. The commitment to the validity of interpretation is necessary for constituting the midrashic unit in the first place.[37] But how useful is a formal separation of commitment for understanding the function of midrashic units in a text like the Mishnah? The answer is that it misses the point by a mile. It describes the opposite of what we find in the Mishnah. In fact, it articulates our own ideal of objectivity, the attitude of disengagement for which we use terms like 'philology', 'historical-critical approach', or 'historical scholarship'. Of course, one *can* read the midrashic units—at least in isolation—in such a framework of reading: namely, as *only* committed to the validity of interpretation. This possibility resides in the duplicating format of the midrashic unit, as I said before: the interpreters may have meant to distance themselves from the text's validity. The rabbinic readers *might* have said: this (the Dictum) is what Scripture says, and we can reserve our thinking about its truth or relevance. But this is not how the midrashic units are used in the Mishnah, or how the reading is actually done, as the resources discussed in this book show.

Thus, we cannot in fact separate the commitment to the validity of interpretation from the assumption of the truth of Scripture on the one hand, and the self-commitment to the norm which appears as reformulation of Scripture on the other. Their *unity* characterizes the hermeneutic speech act in the Mishnah. The commitment is not three different speech acts one after the other, one confirming the truth of the Lemma, one confirming the truth of the Dictum, and one confirming the truth of the hermeneutic operation. The midrashic unit as employed in the Mishnah is a commitment to *one* truth covering three different aspects. One might say that it is the absence of this unity of commitment which distinguishes philological from hermeneutic interpretation.

[36] 'Scripture's Implicature', 201. Cf. Goldberg, 'Die funktionale Form Midrasch', 38: 'Propositionen in "D[ictum]" können daher niemals falsch sein, "D[ictum]" kann nur negiert werden, sofern nachgewiesen wird, daß "L[emma]" nicht "D[ictum]" meint.'
[37] See presently on the hermeneutic operation as functional component of the midrashic literary form.

The Functional Components of the Midrashic Unit

In this study I have consistently employed three terms for the parts of the midrashic unit, but I have yet to address their terminological status. I have used 'Lemma' for the Scriptural text focused by the hermeneutic operation, 'Operation' for that operation, and 'Dictum' for the rabbinic formulation linked to the Lemma by way of the operation. These terms were introduced as technical terms in the publications of Arnold Goldberg from the early 1970s.[38] It is important to understand that these terms are meant to name the *functions* which textual components within the midrashic unit have. In other words, they name the relationships necessary for any midrashic form, but do not prejudge the question whether every text containing a midrashic unit has separate parts corresponding to every one of them, in what sequence they are arranged, what is their size, and so on. The functional nature of these terms is very clear from the fact that the quoted biblical words at times do not even include the Lemma (but only an early part of the verse in which it occurs). The Lemma is determined by the whole of the unit, that is, including an understanding of the operation as defining the relationship between the Dictum and the Lemma, not only by the words quoted.[39] The Mishnah even provides examples for a midrashic unit *without* a Lemma textually realized as quotation. The passages cited above in Chapter 8 as [72] and [73], mBM 2:5 and mTem 1:6 III (3), address the meaning of specific and identifiable biblical segments without reduplicating them.[40] The Operation itself only rarely receives articulation as a textual component of midrashic units in the Mishnah. Most midrashic units are silent about it, and in others the operation only surfaces in form of an additional rephrasing of the Lemma alongside the Dictum (see below). But the assumption of a hermeneutic operation is an indispensable element in speaking about a midrashic unit. It makes it the hermeneutic animal it is, and distinguishes the relationship between Dictum and Lemma from the relationship between any other regular pair of textual items, for instance, a person's name and the number found next to it in a telephone book.

Thus, the degree to which the functional units of the midrashic unit are textually represented is fairly variable, and so is their sequence. If one ignores the position of the hermeneutic operation, there are basically two ways in which the midrashic syntagma is ordered sequentially: the Dictum precedes the Lemma, or the Lemma precedes the Dictum. For the internal functionality of the midrashic unit, there is no difference between these two forms.[41] But for the functionality of the midrashic unit within the larger textual environment or genre of literature in which it is found, the

---

[38] His functional analyses of rabbinic literature are now collected as Volume 2 of his *Gesammelte Studien*. Most of them appeared first in *Frankfurter Judaistische Beiträge*, the annual he founded in 1973.

[39] See my observations in Ch. 2 above (text starting at n. 109) and Ch. 14 (text following n. 26).

[40] See also text to n. 83 in Ch. 8.

[41] See Goldberg, 'Die funktionale Form Midrasch', 27.

difference is very important. I shall refer to the sequence of Dictum followed by Lemma as the D-L form; where the Lemma comes first, I shall speak of the L-D form. For the Mishnah, the sequence Dictum-Lemma is most characteristic. This has consequences for the way the midrashic units are integrated into the flow of the Mishnaic text. The Dicta belonging to a midrashic unit usually share the form of Dicta found in the Mishnah in general, and those found in the co-text of the midrashic unit in particular, whether anonymous or assigned to a named rabbi. In other words, the Dictum accompanied by a Lemma can be viewed on the one hand as component of the syntagma 'midrashic unit', on the other hand as component of a progressive series of Dicta making up a larger Mishnaic entity.[42] In most cases, the position of the midrashic unit in the larger Mishnaic unit will be determined by its Dictum and that Dictum's thematic *fit* with other Dicta. However, there are also cases where the Lemma precedes the Dictum. And in some cases this reversal of sequence from D-L to L-D goes hand in hand with a larger literary unit whose structure stands in a special relationship to an extended unit of biblical text. In such structures, an L-D unit is not surrounded by a number of individual Dicta, but by other L-D units or by Scriptural text used expressively. And the sequence of these midrashic units (or π-wordings) mirrors the sequence of their Lemmas in Scripture. For this format I shall use the Greek capital *sigma*, the sign of summation in mathematics;[43] I shall refer to it for short as *lemmatic chain* or *sigma* chain.

Σ: Juxtaposition of two or more midrashic units (with the Lemma preceding the Dictum) or two or more instances of expressive use (π) of biblical wording in such a way that their sequence corresponds to the sequence of the segments in their Scriptural co-text.

This phenomenon is sometimes referred to as 'midrash' in the Mishnah,[44] and is clearly somehow related to the formal features typical for the genre of 'exegetical midrash'. I can see the following rationale for it. The biblical sequencing of sub-topics belonging to a larger theme (that is, going beyond one sentence or verse) is adopted as the Mishnah's subdivision of its own treatment of the same larger theme, that is, as its own principle of arrangement. In other words, for a given topic the Mishnah perceives the biblical treatment of a subject (in particular its division into smaller topics) as congruent or isomorphic with its own agenda concerning that subject. This allows the Mishnah to express itself by either quoting and reduplicating or expressively using the Scriptural wording (or a combination of these two formats).

If this is correct, then the hermeneutic utterances contained in lemmatic

---

[42] Cf. e.g. on this my 'From Case to Case'.
[43] See e.g. Gullberg, *Mathematics*, 105.
[44] See e.g. Danby's introduction to his translation (*The Mishnah*), p. xxiv. Fishbane (*Biblical Interpretation*, 274 and n. 76) is correct in stressing the *topical* orientation of such structures in the Mishnah. For the 'commentary' format, see Fraade's definition in *From Tradition to Commentary*, 1 f.

chains (Σ) are not in principle different from those found elsewhere in the Mishnah. In particular, they are no less specific in imposing a thematic framework on the appearance of Scriptural wording on the text surface of the Mishnah. They do not constitute a different genre of Mishnaic discourse, 'commentary on Scripture'. The biblical segments are used at a point wholly circumscribed and predetermined by the flow of the Mishnaic (not Scriptural) discourse. This is, among other things, clear from the extent and the position of lemmatic chains. Their boundaries are *thematically* defined—and the relationship to neighbouring themes needs to be ascertained through the Mishnah's text, not Scripture's. Also, the 'density' of interpretation is clearly dictated by the Mishnaic perspective. Thus, in some lemmatic chains the Mishnah provides a word-by-word interpretation,[45] while in others certain verses belonging to a biblical sequence otherwise adopted are left out.

There is a continuum of formats for the relationship of the Mishnaic discourse to the sequential integrity of Scripture. One finds everything from the *occasional* quotation/use of verses selected from *anywhere* in Scripture at one end of the scale,[46] to the extended sequence of contiguous biblical Lemmas here under discussion at the other end.[47] Between these two extremes one finds in particular: (a) Mishnaic passages which occasionally quote verses from a thematically unified and parallel Scriptural account in the biblical sequence, but the quotations are separated from each other by Mishnaic material; (b) a number of contiguous verses employed in the same Mishnaic passage, but *out* of sequence;[48] (c) a sequence of biblical verses employed to structure a sequence of Mishnaic Dicta, but with much Mishnaic material between each quotation and not all verses present.[49] Occasionally one finds some or all of the intermediary forms *alongside* a lemmatic chain in the treatment of the same halakhic topic in the same Mishnaic chapter or neighbouring chapters.

A number of Mishnaic topics treated by way of lemmatic chains concern rituals which involve the halakhic performance of speech acts using biblical verses (that is, the Performance4 resource). For these, the list of things that need to be said 'in the holy tongue' given in mSot 7:4 functions as something of a Mishnaic index; the individual items (that is, the

---

[45] e.g. mSan 10:6. See above on the 'movable focus' exemplified in passage [116]; but that does not mean an exhaustive treatment (see Ch. 2 above, text before n. 102).

[46] This is the most common case. Cf. Ch. 1 (text by n. 74).

[47] Texts with *sigma* format (Σ) include: mMS 5:10–14 (tithing declaration, Deut. 26:13 ff.); mYeb 12:6 III–IV (5) (*Halitsah* ritual, Deut. 25:9 f.); mSot 8:1–3 (exemptions from military service/speech of the priest anointed for battle, Deut. 20:1–7, see passage [121]); mSot 8:5–6 I (2) (same topic, Deut. 20:8 f.); mSot 9:1 I–II (2) [19] [121a] (ritual of the heifer whose neck is broken, Deut. 21:1 f.); mSot 9:6 I–V (5) [125] (same topic, Deut. 21:8); mSan 10:6 I [88]–VI (6) (punishment of apostate city, Deut. 13:17); mNeg 12:5 I [107]–IV (4) (procedure for inspecting a house with scale disease, Lev. 14:35 f.).

[48] e.g. mSan 2:4.

[49] An example is found at mSot 2:3 ff. The arrangement of information between mSot 2:3 and mSot 4:3 II (2) [23] follows (or at least makes use of) the approximate verse sequence Num. 5:23/22 to Num. 5:26.

lemmatic chain which contains the text for the prescribed speech act) are here, as often in the Mishnah, introduced by the interrogative, 'how?', כיצד.[50]

At the core of the midrashic unit as a functional component of the rabbinic discourse is the *duplicating expression of Scriptural meaning*. However, on reviewing the Mishnaic evidence it becomes clear that the textual realizations of the midrashic unit can vary quite a lot. That flexibility seems related to the way in which the midrashic units are integrated into the flow of the Mishnaic discourse, as I said before. This is of some relevance for the prehistory of the Mishnaic text, which is not the present topic. Suffice it to say that, if the midrashic units now in the Mishnah had an independent previous life as fixed textual units,[51] Mishnaic authors felt free to modify them to adapt them to the new discourse environment. There are even passages which, to all intents and purposes, are midrashic units, but do not represent the wording of the Lemma by so much as a quoted word, simply making clear that *some* biblical passage is intended.[52] Some idea of the formal variety of the midrashic unit can be gleaned from the textual transitions between the Dictum and the Lemma.[53] That transition, frequently managed by linking formulas, often gives a clue also for the resource family or resource, although there is no one-to-one correspondence. Linking formulas can thus be an intimation of that elusive third element in the functional unit of midrash: the hermeneutic operation—not through their intrinsic meaning but through repeated pairing of formula and resource. This points to the existence of *some* literary conventions holding for the work Mishnah. We have met quite distinct formulas linked to the *a fortiori* argument (Chapter 7), the analogy (Chapter 8), and the biblical exemplum (Chapter 6). More specific links can be observed, such as between Topic2 and the question 'whence?' or between Opposition1 and the phrase '. . . and not . . .'. But for the majority of linking formulas, to be considered below, there is no trace of a regular connection to a specific resource. The list below contains expressions found in the Mishnah which either link the opening element of the midrashic unit (whether D or L) to the preceding text or the various parts of the midrashic unit to each other. It should be stressed that the list is not complete, but gives examples for the major groupings. Groups I and II are devoted to the L-D form, while VI deals with the form D-L. The

[50] See also mNeg 12:5; cf. item IX.1 in the list of formulas below, and Ch. 4 on the reiteration format §.

[51] For the special case of a text actually known to us, Sifra, this idea has now been revived by Reichman's *Mishna und Sifra*.

[52] See above, text by n. 40.

[53] 'Quotation formulas' for Scripture have been studied in particular in the context of Qumran and the New Testament: Metzger, 'The Formulas Introducing Quotations of Scripture in the NT and the Mishnah'; Bernstein, 'Introductory Formulas for Citation and Re-Citation of Biblical Verses in the Qumran Pesharim'; Fitzmyer, 'The Use of Explicit Old Testament Quotations in Qumran Literature and in the NT'; Fishbane, 'Use, Authority and Interpretation of Mikra', 347–56. See also Gordis, 'Quotations as a Literary Usage in Biblical, Oriental and Rabbinic Literature'. On almost all of the expressions given below valuable material can be found in Bacher, *Exegetische Terminologie*, i.

expressions belonging to III, IV, and V occupy an intermediary position in that the Dictum comes after the Lemma but is anticipated to varying degrees by the words introducing the Lemma. Groups VII, VIII, and IX show ways in which Scripture is integrated into a Mishnaic sentence or larger textual unit without being duplicated, that is, in expressive use (π); for this expressions found in I.1–3, II.7, and II.9 are also used.

I. *Expressions linking the Lemma to the preceding text (Dictum post-lemmatic)*

   (1) no expression (e.g. in cases of a lemmatic chain (Σ), see VII–IX below)

   (2) Rabbi X says: 'L' (e.g. רבי אליעזר אומר);[54] cf. V.5 below

   (3) Rabbi X expounded: 'L' (e.g. בו ביום דרש ר' עקיבא)[55]

   (4) הרי הוא אומר[56]

   (5) הכתוב אומר[57]

   (6) for quoting two biblical locations: כתוב אחד אומר . . . וכתוב אחד אומר;[58]
נאמר . . . ונאמר;[59] נאמר ב . . . ונאמר ב . . . וב . . . ללמד ש . . .;[60]
תלמוד לומר . . . ולהלן הוא אומר . . .;[61]

   (7) אם כן למה נאמר[62]

   (8) כיוצא בדבר אתה אומר, introducing a further midrashic unit starting with a quotation of the Lemma[63]

   (9) דבר אחר, introducing the lemma for a second time with the Dictum in post-lemmatic position[64]

   (10) embedded within a narrative as direct speech: כתוב בתורתכם[65]

   (11) לא היו צריכין לומר ונכפר להם הדם אלא רוח הקודש מברשתן אימתי . . . —introducing the next lemma in a lemmatic chain[66]

---

[54] From mShebu 2:5 I (3), and similar in mMen 11:4; cf. mBQ 6:4 II (2), for which see group V below. Case mYad 4:3 II (2) [41] is different in that there is no duplication of Scriptural meaning, i.e. no midrashic unit; cf. mAvot 4:19, which quotes a rabbi uttering Scripture pure and simple (but it is probably no accident that the verse is a proverb, cf. Ch. 5 above). In some passages where the context makes it clear that a text is quoted, the Mishnah puts prayer wording directly into the mouth of rabbis, e.g. mBer 6:8 (Tarfon); mPes 10:6 (Tarfon, Aqiva); cf. MS Kaufmann discussed in Zuidema, 'Changes in Meaning and Evolution of Meaning', 45.

[55] mSot 5:4.

[56] Found at mMak 3:15 IV (4) as an introduction of the biblical quotation in connection with an Analogy4.1 resource, and followed by . . . ש וכמה כמה אחת על . . . הדם אם ומה.

[57] mYad 4:4 I (4).

[58] mArak 8:7 [95].

[59] e.g. mMen 13:11, found in a tractate-final position (henceforth indicated by Ω).

[60] e.g. mHul 8:4 II (3) [66].

[61] mSot 6:3 IV (4) [74], a Keying2 resource employed to reject another opinion.

[62] e.g. used in mPes 9:1 II (2), not constituting an attack on an earlier Dictum.

[63] mMak 2:8 [12]; mRH 3:8 II (2).

[64] e.g. mBer 9:5 IV (9), mSan 4:5 II (5), mMak 1:9 II (2).

[65] mAZ 3:4 Ia&Ib (2).

[66] mSot 9:6 IV (5) (lemmatic chain, henceforth indicated by Σ).

II. *Expressions linking the Dictum to a preceding Lemma*

(1) no expression[67]
(2) grammatical continuity between the Lemma and the Dictum or part of the Dictum; [68] see also II.7, below
(3) the deictic term זה, or its plural or feminine forms[69] (cf. VI.4, below)
(4) מכאן אמרו[70]
(5) כמשמעו[71]
(6) . . . אלא ללמד ש . . .[73];תלמוד לומר[72]. . . מלמד ש . . .
(7) לא . . .[74]
(8) כלומר . . . ונמצא שם שמים מתחלל[75]
(9) אפילו[76]
(10) כיצד[77] ? (see IX.1, below)
(11) . . . ואם כן ענש הכתוב[78]

III. *Questions introducing the Lemma which presuppose all or part of the proposition of a post-lemmatic Dictum*

(1) מנין שאף במשא? תלמוד לומר . . .[80];ומנין אפילו . . . ? . . . שנאמר . . .[79]; . . . ? מנין?[81]
     מנין ל . . . שמטמאה במשא כנדה? שנאמר . . .[82];ומנין? שנאמר . . . מלמד ש . . .[83]
(2) בזקנתו מהו אומר?[84]
(3) על מה היא אומרת אמן אמן?[85]
(4) על מה חסה התורה?[86]

---

[67] e.g. mYeb 12:6 III (5) (Σ), mSot 9:1 (Σ), mSan 2:4 I (4) (Σ). There is also a group of passages which append two competing Dicta to a Lemma preceding, e.g. mNeg 12:5 III (4).
[68] e.g. mSot 8:6 I (2) (Σ).
[69] e.g. mMS 5:10 (Σ), mYoma 5:5, mSot 8:1 I (8), mSot 8:1 VIII (8) (perhaps a Use6 resource), mSot 8:4 I (5), mSot 8:4 V (5) (a Redundancy9 resource, multiple זה); mBQ 9:7; זה can also indicate a USE resource as in mTaan 4:8 III (3) [51]; cf. Ch. 5 above.
[70] e.g. mMS 5:14; mSan 10:5 II (2) (Σ); mNeg 12:6 III (3) [97] (Σ).
[71] e.g. mSot 8:5 I (3) (Σ), mSot 9:5 III (3) (Σ).
[72] mKer 6:9 I (4).
[73] mRH 2:9 II (2).
[74] e.g. mYeb 3:9 [100], can be used to continue the Lemma grammatically; also used in the *reprise* format (®) defined at the end of this chapter.
[75] mSan 6:4 III (3).
[76] mNeg 12:5 II (4) (Σ).
[77] mNed 11:9; the expression follows the quotation, and is followed by a case schema and a general rule. On this interrogative in the Mishnaic text, see Epstein, *Mavo*, 1032–9.
[78] mMak 1:7 VI (6), the opening of a complex sentence offering an Analogy4 argument.
[79] e.g. mShebu 3:5 I (3).
[80] mAvot 3:6.
[81] mHul 9:5.
[82] mBik 1:9 [117].
[83] mShab 9:1 = mAZ 3:6 II (2).
[84] mQid 4:14 II (4).
[85] mSot 2:5 I (4) [9] [124]; on the question format, see Goldberg, 'Questem'.
[86] mNeg 12:5. III (4).

IV. *Other introductions for the Lemma which presuppose all or part of the Dictum's proposition, including Lemmas occurring in two different locations*

(1) עובר בלא תעשה שנאמר[87]

(2) סדר נחלות כך הוא: איש כי ימות[88] . . .

(3) כיוצא בדבר אתה אומר[89]

(4) אלו הן מעמדות לפי שנאמר[90]

(5) introducing two biblical locations: שנאמר כאן עדה ונאמר להלן עדה[91]

V. *Introduction of a Lemma whose Dictum is (partly) presupposed by standing in a relation of exclusion to a preceding Dictum (¶)*

(1) תלמוד לומר[92]

(2) אי אפשר לומר . . . שכבר נאמר . . . הא כיצד[93] . . . והלא כבר נאמר?[94]

(3) אם כן למה נאמר[95] . . .?

(4) הרי הוא אומר[96]

(5) Rabbi X says: 'L' (π)[97]

(6) כל מקום שצריך לומר הפוך אמר הפוך[98];צורך היה הדבר לאומרו[99]

(7) קיימת[100] . . . ולא קיימת . . . איזה זה (cf. VI.10 below)

(8) משם ראיה[101]

VI. *Expressions linking the Lemma to a preceding Dictum*

(1) שנאמר;משום שנאמר[102];לפי שנאמר[103];עד שדרשה בן זומא שנאמר[104][105]

וכן הוא מפורש על ידי עזרא שנאמר[106];אע׳ ף שאין ראיה לדבר זכר לדבר (שנאמר)[107]

---

[87] mMen 5:2 I (2).

[88] mBB 8:2 (cf. also mTaan. 3:1); note the similar biblical phrase, 'This is the *torah* of . . .'. I find the semantic link with the meaning 'to order, arrange' not wholly convincing for this usage of סדר (e.g. Albeck, *Einführung*, 220; Jastrow, 958b).

[89] mRH 3:8 II (2).

[90] mTaan 4:2.

[91] mHor 1:4.

[92] e.g. mMen 8:5; cf. mSot 6:3 IV (4) **[74]**, where this phrase is followed by another Scriptural quotation introduced by ולהלן הוא אומר, in the service of a Keying2 operation.

[93] e.g. mMen 7:6, mMen 11:5, mTem 1:1 III (3), mNaz 9:5 II (2) **[93]** (Difference1). On the hermeneutic significance of 'already' in this formula, see Ch. 10 (text after **[94]**).

[94] mSot 5:3 I (2) **[1] [93a]**.

[95] mArak 8:6 III (3), after a Difference2 resource; also mBer 1:3 II–III (3); in mSan 1:6 V (5) the phrase is preceded by a question beginning with שמע אני ש . . .?.

[96] mNed 10:7.

[97] mBQ 6:4 II (2).

[98] mQid 3:4 II (2) **[110]**.

[99] mNeg 10:2 II (2).

[100] mBQ 3:9 III (4).

[101] mYeb 12:3 II (2).

[102] The most common signal of the presence of a biblical quotation in midrashic units in the Mishnah, with *c*.335 occurrences.

[103] e.g. mParah 3:7, mBik 1:2 I (2) **[34]**. See also n. 54 in Ch. 4 above.

[104] mTaan 4:2.

[105] mBer 1:5 I (2) **[13]**.

[106] mShab 8:7 I (2) (the שנאמר is not in all texts); mShab 9:4 [see 9:1].

[107] mSheq 1:5; for וכן in the Mishnah, see Epstein, *Mavo*, 1043 ff.

(2) ¹¹⁰ועליו הוא מפורש על ידי יחזקאל ¹⁰⁹;ועליו הכתוב אומר ¹⁰⁸;על זה נאמר

(3) ¹¹²שהיא זונה האמורה בתורה ¹¹¹;הוא גבן האמור בתורה

(4) ¹¹⁴הרי זה מושב לצים שנאמר ¹¹³;הרי הוא

(5) ¹¹⁶;וכן בדויד הוא אומר . . . ¹¹⁵;שכן מצינו ש . . . אלא על לשון הרע . . . \הוא אומר שנאמר

¹¹⁷וכן הוא אומר בשאול

(6) ¹¹⁸מפני הכתוב שבתורה

(7) ¹¹⁹דכתיב

(8) ¹²⁰ממשמע שנאמר . . .

(9) ¹²¹מעלה עליו הכתוב כאלו . . . שנאמר

(10) cumulative Lemmas relating to the same Dictum: ¹²²שנאמר . . . ואומר

¹²⁶;דכתיב ¹²⁵;ובקבלה הוא אומר ¹²⁴;נמצאו שני כתובים קיימים . . . ו ¹²³. . . ;. .ונאמר

¹²⁷משום . . . ומשום

VII. *Expressions for referring to a Scriptural norm (π, Scriptural wording in bold print)*

(1) ¹²⁸וחייב באותו **ואת בנו**

(2) ¹²⁹עובר על **לא תעשה**

(3) ¹³¹והלא מן התורה הוא אסור? שנאמר . . . ¹³⁰;מצוה מן התורה לפרוק

---

¹⁰⁸ e.g. mSukkah 2:6; mPeah 7:3 II (2), cf. 5:6, mYeb 9:6; in mHag 1:5 **[35]** **[98a]** it is used for the Topic2 resource, cf. also mYoma 3:11 **[40]**. See also next note.

¹⁰⁹ For mPeah 8:9 I (4), some texts have עליו הכתוב אומר while others (including MSS Munich and Kaufmann) have על זה נאמר; cf. Bauer, *Pea*, 71; some versions of mQid 1:10 have ועליו הכתוב אומר, others שנאמר.

¹¹⁰ mTam 3:7, see mMid 4:2. For the use of על, see Bacher, i. 174 f. (s.v. קרא).

¹¹¹ mBek 7:2 II (4); cf. the phrase ומה אם מצוה קלה שהיא כאסר אמרה תורה למען in mHul 12:5 (Ω); mNeg 9:2, and see below list VII.

¹¹² mYeb 6:5, used in connection with Topic2 resource. In mYeb 3:7 a slightly different formula (זו היא שנאמרו) is used to allocate a case schema to a more general rule mentioned earlier (in mYeb 1:1). Thus, the hermeneutic movement is analogous to Topic2.1, but concerns a non-biblical text.

¹¹³ mSot 8:5 III (3) (Σ and ¶); similar mKet 5:6, used for a Topic8 resource.

¹¹⁴ mAvot 3:2 I (3).

¹¹⁵ mArak 3:5 II (2).

¹¹⁶ mAvot 3:7.

¹¹⁷ mNed 9:10.

¹¹⁸ mHallah 4:10 and mBik 1:3.

¹¹⁹ mTaan 3:3 (¡); this Aramaic equivalent of שנאמר is likely to be secondary (Epstein, *Mavo*, 685); see below VI.10.

¹²⁰ mSan 1:6 IV (5), answering a מנין-question.

¹²¹ mAvot 3:9 I (2).

¹²² mSheq 3:2; mNed 3:11 II (10); ואומר in mYoma 8:9 II–III (3) (Ω) stands at the point of transition between two midrashic units of different form (D-L and L-D).

¹²³ In mEduy 2:9 it introduces the third quotation.

¹²⁴ mSheq 6:6 I (2).

¹²⁵ mTaan 2:1.

¹²⁶ Introducing the second biblical location in mQid 3:4 I (2) **[110]**.

¹²⁷ mMak 1:3.

¹²⁸ mHul 4:5, 5:1.

¹²⁹ e.g. mNeg 7:4, mNeg 9:2.

¹³⁰ mBM 2:10 III (4).

¹³¹ mMen 10:3.

(4) נדונים[134] כעור הבשר[133]; איזהו מחיר כלב?[132] שלוח הקן נוהג בארץ ובחוצה לארץ

(5) לא נאמר בל תוסיף אלא כשהוא בעצמו[135]

(6) אחר[136] הפסח בלא יחל דברו

(7) כדי[137] לקיים בו מצות קלוי באש

(8) שניהן[138] אינן בכור—הראשון משום שאינו פטר רחם

(9) יש בו משום . . . ויש בו משום . . . (see below IX.4)[139]

VIII. *Expressions for the manner in which Scripture formulates a subject-matter (not used to introduce quotations)*

(1) אם[140] מתקימת העדות בשנים למה פרט הכתוב בשלשה?

(2) העופות[141] והמנחות אינן עושין תמורה—שלא נאמר אלא בבהמה

(3) והלא[142] המעשר בכלל היה? ולמה יצא? להקיש אליו . . .

(4) שנאמר[143] . . . ולמה לא נתפרשו . . . אלא ללמד ש . . .

(5) אלא[144] שדבר הכתוב בהווה

IX. *Expressions which introduce a Scriptural quotation (marked or unmarked) for use as Mishnaic utterance (π)*

(1) חליצה[146] כיצד?[145]; כיצד ראית הבית? . . .

(2) מהו אומר?, embedded in a retelling of biblical events (biblical speaker)[147]

(3) אבל[148] לעתיד לבוא הוא אומר

(4) יש בו משום . . . ויש בו משום . . . (see VII.9 above)[149]

This list offers some information on the manner in which the rabbis saw their hermeneutic task. I shall point to some pertinent themes.

1. There is the construction of Scripture (or one verse) as if it were a person speaking or writing (I.4, 5, 6; III.2; V.4; VI.2, 5), sometimes even as a person 'punishing' (II.11), 'reckoning' (VI.9), or 'taking thought' (III.4). This ties in with certain hermeneutic resources, and culminates in Scripture

---

[132]   mHul 12:1.
[133]   mTem 6:3 I (3); similar e.g. mBek 7:3.
[134]   mNeg 6:8.
[135]   mZeb 8:10 II (3).
[136]   mNed 7:9.
[137]   mMen 10:4 I (2).
[138]   mBek 2:9 II (3); mMak 1:3.
[139]   mBM 9:12 I (3). In such usage, משום can be an indication of the presence of the Performance3 resource, as it is in the cited passage.
[140]   mMak 1:7 I (6).
[141]   mTem 1:6 I (3).
[142]   mTem 1:6 III (3) **[73]**.
[143]   mRH 2:9 II (2).
[144]   mBQ 5:7 **[76]**.
[145]   mNeg 12:5 I (4) **[107]** (Σ).
[146]   mSot 7:4 I (2) and in several of the subsequent *mishnayyot*.
[147]   mYad 4:8 II (2) (Ω).
[148]   mMQ 3:9 II (2).
[149]   mBM 9:12 I (3).

being presented as *performing an utterance* about events as they happen.[150] The exact nature of the relationship between this terminology and the hermeneutics of PERFORMANCE and USE requires further investigation.

2. There is a wide variety in the terminology, and certain phrases appear, suitably modified, in both of the basic forms of the midrashic unit (L-D and D-L). As was said before, this points to very comprehensive compositional control or intervention by the Mishnaic authors in adapting the form of any pre-existing midrashic units (and see next point).

3. The meaning of expressions used for linking the Lemma to a preceding Dictum (VI) is of some importance. Many of them strongly suggest a warrant, or support, and thus imply a *discourse* setting such as the one in which they are now found, the Mishnah. This presumably also implies a thematic orientation. The formulas include conjunctions of reason or ground (ד-/ש-, משום, שנאמר, מפני, שכן, שהיא); phrases pointing to an origin (VI.9 מ-, מנין? III.1), combinations of the terminology of origin with that of reason (שנאמר in III.1, and see [117] below), deictic terms (הוא, זה, הרי), expressions of finding (מצינו) or confirming (וכן). This is particularly significant in the light of the fact that the form D-L predominates in the Mishnah. It means that the very link between D and L as articulated by these formulas points to a thematic and discursive context. The nature of the Mishnaic text as a discourse, rather than a command, or a proclamation, or a statement, comes to the fore in this. The link between L and D is one of *reason* or warrant; and the way in which midrashic units are embedded into processes of questioning, probing, suggesting of alternatives, or rejecting (see Chapter 7 above) shows that they form part of a fabric of persuasive communication.[151] This means that hermeneutic resources, as the heuristic principles that link the D to the L, form a pool of *arguments*, and that this characterization cannot be separated from their format in the midrashic unit—the reduplication (see Chapter 4). This confirms a result reached in Chapter 5 by a different route: the resources of the PERFORMANCE and USE family cannot be classified as arguments; their function is different from probative discourse, and their claim to validity is not *conditional*. In this context, it is important to note that the Scriptural quotations actually used as warrants (as opposed to those being used expressively) are, on the whole, verifiable and unmodified quotations. Although alterations do occur, I know of no case where the wording of the biblical quotation in the Mishnah is modified *in the point which requires proof.*[152]

---

[150] See esp. the text succeeding n. 128 in Ch. 5 above.

[151] See Uchelen, *Chagiga*, 62 f.; Goldberg, *Rabbinische Texte als Gegenstand der Auslegung*.

[152] For this procedure in pre-Mishnaic Jewish hermeneutics, see now Lim, *Holy Scripture in the Qumran Commentaries and Pauline Letters*. If the Mishnah had originally contained modified quotations, these could (and very likely would) have been adapted to the Masoretic text in the centuries following its composition. In that case one dimension of the early rabbinic treatment of Scripture would now be missing from our evidence. Are some of the Mishnaic interpretations of this kind which stubbornly resist explanation? Instances of quotations which are modified, though not in the rabbinic point at issue, are found in the Mishnah; see n. 53 and text to n. 57 in Ch. 10 above.

4. The manner in which the various components of the midrashic unit interact with other Mishnaic forms is of interest, in particular, its interaction with the dispute (¶) and the Mishnaic *question* (which helps to organize the Mishnaic discourse in general). The interaction can produce a characteristic modification of the midrashic form, namely, a full or partial *doubling* of the Dictum through an anticipation of its content (lists III and V). Quite a number of midrashic units already quoted in this study have this form, which I shall refer to as *reprise* of the Dictum.[153] Here is a fresh example for the *reprise* form, marked by the sign ® in the hermeneutic profiles:

[117] mBik 1:9[154]   Exod. 23:19

Whence [do we know] that a person is liable for their value [with his possessions] until he has brought them [the first-fruits] to the temple mount? (cf. *mishnah* 8). For it is said, 'The first of the first-fruits of your ground you shall bring to the house of the Lord your God'—this teaches that he is liable for their value [with his possessions] until he has brought them to the temple mount.

The terminology structures the different parts of this unit in the following way: ש מלמד—שנאמר—?ומנין. Three components are clearly demarcated: the מנין-question whose propositional content is identical with the Dictum; the quotation given in answer to the question (the 'origin'); and a reformulation as Dictum of the Lemma's 'teaching' which wholly coincides with the wording of the question.[155] The topic of this midrashic unit is already treated in *mishnah* 8, where concrete instances of the loss of first-fruits on the way to the temple are enumerated. In other words, the presupposition of the Dictum as *known* (attached to the question 'whence') has cohesive function here.[156] But even if the overlap with *mishnah* 8 is discounted, the degree of repetition resulting from a *reprise* of the Dictum is conspicuous, since coherence in the Mishnah is so often achieved by the opposite of redundancy, namely, ellipsis.[157] Here is another case, in which the *reprise* (marked in bold print) can be construed as grammatically continuous with the biblical quotation to which it is appended:[158]

[118] = [18] mBQ 4:3 II (4)[159]   Exod. 21:35

The ox of an Israelite which gores that of the sanctuary, or that of the sanctuary which gores the ox of an Israelite[160]—[the owner] is not liable, for it is said, 'the ox of his fellow'—**and not the ox of the sanctuary** (של הקדש).

---

[153] They are: mBQ 4:9 II (3) **[87]**, mSan 1:4 II (2) **[67]**, mSan 4:5 I (5) **[105]**, mSan 8:4 III (4) **[91]**, mSan 11:2 III (3) **[106]**, mArak 4:4 I (3) **[75]**, and mTem 1:6 II (3) **[103]**.

[154] ®O6T1T3.

[155] The main resource is an emphasis on the unstressed element '[to] the House of the Lord', i.e. Opposition6.

[156] This is not always the case for מנין-questions in the Mishnah, see e.g. mShab 9:2 I–II (2).

[157] See my 'Delaying the Progress from Case to Case'.

[158] See in the above lists under II.2 and II.7.

[159] ®O1T2T3.

[160] Some prints of the Bavli have here the word 'commoner', הדיוט, instead of 'Israelite'; cf. Windfuhr, *Baba qamma*, 89.

There is no signal here, in the reprise, of where the quotation ends and the rephrasing begins. Among the expressions which produce such ambiguous cases of reprise are 'even' (אפילו) and the phrase 'and not' (which introduces the contrast terms for some OPPOSITION resources, as here).[161] If one counts all midrashic units which exhibit partial or full overlap between the Dictum and another rabbinic reformulation of the Lemma, there are about 120 reprise passages in the Mishnah. In cases such as [117] above it is difficult to detect a specific functional difference between the two Mishnaic Dicta (except that of framing the Lemma on opposite sides), since they are identical. But in other passages the two Dicta are quite unlike each other, that is, they exhibit a specific hermeneutic difference. Where this applies, the second formulation tends also to be *closer* to the wording of the Lemma, while still reflecting the point of the pre-lemmatic Dictum. The reprise Dictum can occupy an intermediary position between the Lemma and the pre-lemmatic Dictum, and thus between the perspectives of the Scriptural discourse and that of the Mishnaic discourse, bridging (part of) the gap between them. Sometimes the reprise is a direct paraphrase of the Lemma (like a Topic7 formulation), while the pre-lemmatic Dictum is not, or is less so.[162] This suggests an intriguing possibility, namely, that the reprise does duty for a hermeneutic operation on the text surface of the midrashic unit, even in the absence of a metalinguistic terminology or explanation.[163] On the other hand, post-lemmatic Dicta in *reprise* format can also be more general than the pre-lemmatic Dictum (for example, where this provides Topic2 cases, e.g. mZeb 14:1 f.), in which they resemble Mishnaic sentences of the type זה הכלל. Now the *reprise* format seems to presuppose a thematic setting for the interpretation of Scriptural wording. If so, the rabbinic genre of 'exegetical' Midrash (in which the Scriptural quotation comes always first and in the biblical sequence of Lemmas) should not be the natural home of reprise passages. A question for future research arises from this: do the Dicta in such Midrashim tend to resemble the pre-lemmatic or rather the post-lemmatic Dicta of the reprise passages in the Mishnah?

---

[161] See passage [100] in Ch. 11 and the text immediately preceding it.

[162] The implications this has for the 'directionality' of the midrashic unit as it relates to the surrounding Mishnaic discourse is a question worth pursuing.

[163] For which mSan 1:4 II (2) [67] is an example. One would have to investigate further the information which the reprise Dictum might contain for the hermeneutic resource.

13

Appropriating Redundancy.
Clause Relationships

In the Mishnaic treatment of apparent biblical repetition, the use of complementary distribution is important, and in this Mishnaic paradigms, in particular of *pairs* of related concepts, again play a role. In some cases the link between biblical terms and their paradigmatic counterparts can be predicated on the basis of their semantic relationship to each other. But overall quantitative correspondence between the number of biblical items and the number of paradigmatic members is also important. Sometimes the quantitative correspondence carries the interpretation as a whole, because one-to-one correspondences can only be established for some, not all, of the biblical elements. In such cases the segmentation of Scripture interacts in a numerical manner with the substantive paradigms of Mishnaic discourse. There are further resources which address the division of biblical sentences into smaller units, or the syntactical relationship between neighbouring or conjoined clauses. Paratactic biblical constructions may be interpreted as temporal, or temporal conjunctions as implying causal relation. Textual relationships may also be translated into relationships of time and space by way of figures of speech.

THE DISTRIBUTIVE TREATMENT OF REPETITION

Affirming the relevance and validity of Scripture in its unstressed parts, of peripheral members of a sentence, or of information presented as incidental, is clearly an important hermeneutic concern in the Mishnah. A number of resources which achieve this have been encountered in the preceding two chapters, in particular Opposition8 and Opposition6. I have explained these resources as treating apparent redundancy. Redundancy here refers to an unnecessary, conspicuously elaborate, or generally uneconomic way to express something, for example, spelling out what is already implied elsewhere in Scripture. I will call such lack of economy the *redundancy of explicitness*. I now turn to redundancy which is the result of a biblical *doubling* of meaning. Examples of apparent duplications include the biblical use of the same expression twice, or of semantically related expressions in similar function close to each other. This I shall refer to as *redundancy of repetition*, and to the relevant resource family as REDUNDANCY. For both types of redundancy the most frequent hermeneutic mechanism is *distribution*. A separate topic, referent, speech act, phase of the action, or case schema is identified for the redundant expression. Such treatment of the redundancy of repetition will be labelled Redundancy*.1, that is, carry the number 1 as second digit in a REDUNDANCY code. Such complementary distribution of biblical signs has been encountered already in the avoidance of biblical inconsistency (the Difference*.1 resource in Chapter 10), and a similar provision of distinct themes can be found in Opposition6/Opposition8 interpretations. Among the passages interpreting the redundancy of repetition, distributive differentiation accounts for approximately half of the total.[1] But there are also other resources which can endow repetition with the value of additional information. Linguistic repetition can be taken to imply repetition of action, accumulation, or iteration (Redundancy*.2).[2] It may furthermore be treated by the Mishnah as pointing to semantic modification or cross-fertilization of the meaning of the two expressions (Redundancy*.3).[3] This resource is difficult to define satisfactorily (see below). Also available is the option to read repetition as emphasis (Redundancy*.4). Another mechanism which is not easy to pin down is a link of Scriptural repetition to the idea of simultaneity, or completeness, or wholeness (Redundancy*.5). Finally, one finds that in the context of quoted direct speech repetition is sometimes eliminated by distributing it between two distinct speakers (*Redundancy*.6).[4] All of these hermeneutic mechanisms will be represented by the *second* digit in the resource code starting with the prefix 'Redundancy'. The first digit of the REDUNDANCY codes will indicate which linguistic type of redundancy is targeted by the operation.[5] There is also a somewhat separate mechanism of distribution (Redundancy9) which is probably triggered by the presence of some redundancy (of explicitness *or* repetition). It allocates to *all* members of a biblical syntagma, whether redundant or not, and whether of the same semantic status or not, the members of a Mishnaic paradigm (of open or fixed number). I shall devote the second section of this chapter to this

---

[1] Accounting for at least 40 of approximately 80 cases using Redundancy2–8.

[2] About 10 cases, with three each linked to Redundancy7 (infinitive absolute) and Redundancy3.

[3] About 10 cases, of which 4 are found linked to Redundancy4.

[4] The only convincing example for Redundancy3.6 is mSot 9:6 V (5), quoted below as [125]; hence the asterisk preceding the resource name.

[5] As in the case of the EXTENSION and DIFFERENCE families, this allows us to combine information on hermeneutic mechanism and biblical structure in the same resource name. Not all possible combinations occur in the Mishnah.

important resource. The third and final section deals with resources which endow certain syntactic structures with specific significance (the SYNTAX family).

Here is a list of the linguistic and textual structures in Scripture which attract the interpretations summarized above as Redundancy*.1 to Redundancy*.6.

Redundancy2: Explication of the occurrence of two (or more) synonymous expressions or clauses in similar syntactic function in the same biblical sentence or in each other's co-text as differentiated from each other.

Redundancy3: Explication of the occurrence of two biblical sentences with similar (or identical) propositional meaning as differentiated from each other.

Redundancy4: Explication of the employment of two (or more) biblical expressions from the same lexical field in a similar syntactic function in the same biblical sentence or in each other's co-text as differentiated from each other.

Redundancy5: Explication of the employment of two (or more) biblical expressions from distinct lexical fields in a similar syntactic function in the same biblical sentence or in each other's co-text as differentiated from each other.

Redundancy6: Explication of two occurrences of the same biblical expression in the same sentence or co-text in a similar or different syntactic function as differentiated from each other.

Redundancy7: Explication of a biblical collocation employing two different word-forms belonging to the same root (for example, infinitive absolute) as differentiated from each other.[6]

Redundancy8: Explication of two contiguous and asyndetic occurrences of the same biblical expression as differentiated from each other (see below, case [124]).

These codes for textual and linguistic structures of repetition found in Scripture can be combined with any of the Redundancy*.1 to Redundancy*.6 codes mentioned above to form specific resource descriptions. Not all possibilities are realized in the Mishnaic material; there are no instances of Redundancy2.4, Redundancy4.4, Redundancy3.4, or Redundancy6.3, for example. Here is a list of their definitions. They are meant to continue from the final words of any of the Redundancy2–Redundancy8 definitions, indicated here by an overlap of words:

---

[6] The term 'word-form' refers to the shape of a word as actually found in a given instance of use (i.e. with signs of inflection or derivation, etc.), as opposed to the abstract lexeme to which all the different forms belong. Thus the word-form 'went' belongs to the lexeme 'Go'. See Bauer, *English Word-Formation*, 11–13. More on this in the next chapter.

Redundancy*.1: . . . differentiated from each other in respect of their topic or case schema (Topic2), action, speech act, or referent.

Redundancy*.2: . . . differentiated from each other in terms of a repetition of an action, an iteration, or an accumulation.

Redundancy*.3: . . . differentiated from each other in terms of a semantic extension, or mutual modification.

Redundancy*.4: . . . differentiated from each other in terms of extra emphasis.

Redundancy*.5: . . . differentiated from each other in terms of their separate contribution to a whole of complete or simultaneous parts.

Redundancy*.6: . . . differentiated from each other in terms of a switch of speaker.

Resources Redundancy2, Redundancy4, and Redundancy5 cover manifestations of what modern scholarship calls biblical parallelism. As the list of hermeneutic mechanisms actually defining the relationship shows, the most common Mishnaic treatments are not compatible with interpreting parallelism as a *stylistic* phenomenon, for any 'open' poetic effect of the redundancy is rejected in favour of specific and new information, that is, non-redundancy. This is perhaps the most obvious manifestation of the fact that Mishnaic hermeneutics contains no resources which seem to acknowledge what Jakobson called the 'poetic' function of language (on which see below).[7] An apparent exception is the reading of redundancy as emphasis (Redundancy*.4); however, even Redundancy*.4 cases are far removed from the appreciation of an emphatically meaningful correspondence of form and content which is typical of the modern approach to artistic texts.[8]

Let us reflect for a moment on the underlying assumptions of the REDUNDANCY resources. Where fresh information is expected from every new occurrence of a sign, even if the sign itself is identical (e.g. Redundancy8), the hermeneutic mechanism must be specifically *textual*. That is to say, it is ultimately the textual position which is taken to be the carrier of information, not the identity of the sign—at least in cases where it is repeated.[9] The textual position itself *cannot* be repeated, and this uniqueness provides the maximum standard of non-redundancy. That maximum standard is: as many new items of information as there is capacity for carrying information. The 'point in the text', which changes from sign to sign (and

---

[7] For some problems with Jakobson's view, see Coseriu, *Textlinguistik*, 57.

[8] As we said before, the rabbinic treatment of the different linguistic and semiotic levels of a given biblical passage need not, and usually does not, form a unified picture of its meaning. See Ch. 2 (text by n. 96) and below.

[9] The hermeneutic importance of textual space in rabbinic interpretation is indirectly confirmed by the Map1 resource explained below.

occasionally that may mean: from letter to letter),[10] is taken to define the meaning of each occupant as *new* (for that co-text at least) and nonredundant.[11] Note that the textuality of rabbinic hermeneutics as embodied in these REDUNDANCY resources is quite different from the notion that a given passage has to be seen in its co-textual relationships. These relationships may be suspended, that is fundamental to the hermeneutic approach of the Mishnah. So the textual or positional quality of Scripture as seen by the rabbis must be understood as consisting of an irreducible *quantity* of mutually distinct points of information, not a quality of sequence or progression.

Such an expectation of fresh information (and that means, in the Mishnah, relevant information) being tied to textual position could explain also why there is a very strong *quantitative* aspect to the REDUNDANCY resources. This is most obvious where the Mishnaic companion terms expressing the meaning, topic, or referent of the biblical text form a (Mishnaic) paradigm with a *fixed* number. There are several examples of units of interpretation in which the overall *numerical* match of biblical signs with Mishnaic signs carries the burden of the hermeneutic operation, while the individual semantic links are weak. There is a tendency for this to happen in particular with some of the Mishnaic paradigms consisting of two oppositional members.[12] Pairs of opposites are employed, for example, to separate the meaning of semantic parallelism. Synonymous or near-synonymous phrases or clauses are thus allocated to two Mishnaic opposites. In the following example, numeric correspondence is achieved for the biblical pair 'finish'–'die' with the Mishnaic pair 'world to come'–'judgement'. However, only one of the biblical expressions has a direct semantic link to its Mishnaic counterpart—the other one is carried along on the strength of the relationship of pairing within the paradigm.

[119] mSan 10:3 VII (10)[13]   Num. 14:35; Ps. 50:5

The generation of the wilderness has no share in the world to come, and they do not stand in judgement, as it is said, 'In this wilderness they shall finish and there they shall die'[14]—words of R. Aqiva. R. Eliezer says: About them it says: 'Gather to me my pious ones, partners of my covenant over sacrifice.'

---

[10] Cf. the resources exploring the larger semiotic possibilities of the text (section two of Ch. 14), and the dimension of inexhaustibility addressed in Ch. 2 (text before n. 102).

[11] Cf. my 'Scripture's Implicature', 192 f., and 'Between Scripture and its Rewording', 42. Since the information gleaned from that non-redundancy can sometimes be found spelled out more clearly elsewhere in Scripture, this method of dealing with it is perhaps more an *exporting* of redundancy than an *elimination* of redundancy. Clearly, redundancy in the immediate textual environment is the more urgent hermeneutic problem for the Mishnah.

[12] I describe here one important application for the Topic4 resource, first introduced in Ch. 3 and elaborated upon for the distributive treatment of inconsistency in Ch. 10 (see Table 10.1). See also my 'Between Scripture and its Rewording'.

[13] Aqiva: •¶≈R2.1T1T4.

[14] The MS Munich has here: ' "In this wilderness they shall finish"—in this world; "and there they shall die"—for the world to come.' See Krauß, *Sanhedrin-Makkot*, 398. Cf. bSan 110b.

We have to assume that there is a link being made between the idea of the biblical 'finish' and the Mishnaic notion of 'world to come', while the biblical 'die' is taken to imply 'no life for the day of judgement'. The word 'there' (שם), as suggested by the biblical sentence and its surroundings,[15] is co-referential with 'this wilderness': it represents 'this wilderness' again in the second half of the verse. But the distributional pair 'world to come–judgement [day]' requires a different referent for 'there', namely, the standing in judgement. But, while it is clear that the first verb used, meaning to end or finish, refers to an event taking place in 'this' world, with possible lasting effect for the 'world to come', there is no independent semantic connection between 'die' and 'standing in judgement'. That Aqiva takes the second 'dying' to show that no resurrection for judgement will take place is clear only from the numerical distribution of the two redundant biblical verbs to two members of a Mishnaic paradigm. In fact, there is no organic connection between the verbs (תמם and מות) and the two Mishnaic items, except by way of the idea of resurrection.[16] That means that their duality and opposition, not the individual semantic identity of the items, is important for Aqiva's hermeneutic option. Even once this perspective is accepted, no *semantic* reason to link 'world to come' to יחמו emerges. If the verbs appeared in a different sequence in the two halves of the sentence, the operation could still proceed as before (but 'this wilderness' would be the constraining factor for the allocation of 'this world' in the Munich version, see n. 14). So, there seems to be no strong one-to-one connection of terms here at all: two Mishnaic items are linked to two biblical ones only as a *pair*. The Mishnaic paradigm as a whole, not each of its members, is matched against the biblical items, and the only absolute precondition of the match is the same *number* of items on both sides.[17] To see exactly what is absent from the operation in [119], I shall examine how a related pair of Mishnaic terms does its distributive work for another biblical verse:

[120] mAvot 4:1 III (4)[18] Ps. 128:2[19]

[Ben Zoma says: . . .] Who is rich? He who is happy with his portion, as it is said, 'The

---

[15] There is no other place mentioned in the co-text to which it could refer; instead, the word 'wilderness' is repeated several times (Num. 14:2, 29). In Num. 14:35 JPS does not translate the duplication of expression, but renders: 'in this very wilderness they shall die to the last man.' There is one, remote, alternative to the reference of 'there' as the wilderness: the land of Egypt, mentioned in Num. 14:2.

[16] There is no reason why the link of Mishnaic and biblical items could not be reversed apart from the temporal sequence of events. For such an inversion constituting a variant of the same midrashic unit, see my 'Scripture's Implicature', 183, n. 19.

[17] Very similar is mSan 10:3 VI (10), quoted as passage [21] in Ch. 3. The biblical phrase 'died of plague before the Lord' (Num. 14:37) is distributed in the following manner: ' "died"—in this world; "of plague"—in the world to come.' For such structures, now explicable as Cotext5–Redundancy8.1–Topic4, see my 'Scripture's Implicature', 173. Passage [119] appears in a series of similar and perhaps mutually reinforcing units of interpretation (i.e. ≈Redundancy2.1).

[18] (•)C5R2.1S5.1T4.

[19] This is how the verse reads when no attempt is made to represent the semantic dividing-lines in which the midrash is interested: 'You shall enjoy the fruit of your labors; you shall be happy and you shall prosper' (JPS). Cf. Ch. 1, text by n. 30.

toil of your hands when you shall eat, you shall be happy and it shall be well with you'. ('You shall be happy'—in this world; 'and it shall be well with you' (טוב לך)—for the world to come.)

I am interested in the explanation of the Lemma succeeding the quotation, that is, the text in brackets.[20] Here the semantics of 'world to come', that is, the element of the conceptual pair which carries the specific rabbinic meaning of reward, have a very clear overlap with the notion of well-being. Being well is what happens, in the rabbinic view, in the world to come: it is the ultimate reward. In other words, even without the dynamics of the binary pairing (Topic4), it would be possible to link 'it shall be well with you' with the notion of the world to come. Thus, here the semantic link reinforces the numeric correspondence. But cases such as [119] show that numeric correspondence on its own can also be acceptable in the Mishnah.

Here is an explication of the Redundancy2.1 resource, combining the Redundancy2 and Redundancy*.1 features introduced separately at the beginning of this chapter:

Redundancy2.1: Explication of the occurrence of two (or more) synonymous expressions or clauses as differentiated from each other, in the following way: the expressions (clauses) occur in a similar syntactic function in the same biblical sentence or in each other's co-text; and they are differentiated from each other in respect of their topic or case schema, action, speech act, or referent.

Below is an example for the use of Redundancy2.1 which does not seem to be connected to a Mishnaic paradigm with fixed membership, yet still provides a distinct adverbial supplement for each of the four biblical predicates.

[121] mSot 8:1 V (7)[21] Deut. 20:3

['And he said to them: Hear, oh Israel, you are today drawing near for battle against your enemies.] Do not be weak of heart, do not fear, and do not be alarmed, etc. [and do not tremble because of them].'[22] 'Do not be weak of heart'—because of the neighing of horses and the brandishing of swords; 'do not fear'—because of the rattling of the shields[23] and the stamping of the shoes;[24] 'do not be alarmed'—at the sound of the horns; 'do not tremble [because of them]'—because of the sound of their shouts.

The Mishnaic provision of potential causes of fear is lavish and detailed. The perceptions are with one exception auditory, and, for the first two

---

[20] The bracketed part is not found in MS Kaufmann, but is otherwise well represented in the textual evidence, including Maimonides' text as given in Qafih's edition (*Commentary*, *Neziqin*, 286); cf. Marti and Beer, *Abot*, 91, 192. The Dictum defines richness as contentedness. It is even possible that the original Dictum was expanded in two stages: first by the biblical quotation, then by the explanation of the biblical quotation.   [21] Σπ‡C2R2.1(T0).

[22] This initial quotation of the whole biblical period is absent from MS Munich.

[23] The Hebrew is הנפת תריסין; Jastrow (s.v. הנפה, 332a) translates 'fastening of the cuirasses'.

[24] Cf. Jastrow 1372a; also Bietenhard, *Sota*, 126 ('Krieger') and the manuscript variants listed by him, 193.

Lemmas, come in pairs. They are vivid, and conjure up a comprehensive picture of battle despite the dominance of mere sounds; and they are also depersonalized—no word for a human agent, not even 'enemy', appears here. What we have here is something of a catalogue of (conventional or experienced) battle features.

The Mishnaic reformulation provides detail and perhaps rhetorical vividness. Apart from that, its overall effect is to give each of a number of synonymous or semantically related biblical expressions a separate function and information. They are interpreted as not rendering each other superfluous because each is given something distinct to say.[25]

The format of this unit is of great interest. The Scriptural sentence (in this case a unit smaller than the verse) is first quoted in its entirety. It is part of a thematically bounded lemmatic chain (the Σ format) found at this point in the Mishnah.[26] This first quotation is followed by a second one of the same segment, but broken up into smaller pieces, each of which is followed by a rabbinic formulation. This formulation is grammatically continuous with the biblical reference (mostly linked by מפני or מ־) and narrows it down. The structuring thus achieved is a clear manifestation of the distributive nature of the hermeneutic operation—the *textual* separation of independent segments corresponds to and to some extent determines[27] the separate allocation of *points of information*.

There is no term or phrase articulating the transition from the quotation of the entire sentence to its repetition in segments. We also have no linking expression tying the smaller segments to their Mishnaic supplements, presumably because the supplements are grammatically as well as thematically adapted to the biblical text; they are offered in the form of a continuation or completion of the biblical words. Note that it is nevertheless impossible to read the textual units, each consisting of the biblical words together with the Mishnaic ones, as overall Mishnaic formulations (that is, as expressive use of the Scriptural segments, i.e. π). The reason for this is that the Scriptural text is represented twice,[28] and that the final Mishnaic phrase, 'because of the sound of their shouts', *replaces* the biblical 'because of them' and cannot be combined with it. So the unit has to be read as separating the two levels of text, Scripture and Mishnah. However, this metalinguistic presentation is achieved without any dedicated metalinguistic terms[29]—merely through the repetition of Scriptural wording, and the alternation of its reiterated parts with non-biblical wording. It seems to me that one condition for the success of this format is the fact that

---

[25] Cf. the (Palestinian) Targumic treatment of Exod. 14:13 f. (another battle situation), discussed in my *Interpretation of Speech*, 63. See the 'Amen, Amen' case in [124].

[26] See Ch. 12 for the definition of this format.

[27] Only to some extent, because some segments are given not one but two Mishnaic points, as noted above, and in contrast to passages [119] and [120].

[28] See Ch. 12 for such repetitions in cases of *reprise*, and their possible relationship to the operation.

[29] This point is of some importance in view of the functionality of the demonstrative pronoun זה; see below, and Ch. 5 (by n. 149). My translation adds signals, though: dashes and quotation marks.

the Lemma comes first. That seems to be enough in cases such as these to mark any additional words as supplement or paraphrase, revealing their metalinguistic orientation.

To complement these three examples for resource Redundancy2.1, here is an illustration of Redundancy4 (two terms drawn from the same lexical field), taken to convey an iteration or accumulation (= Redundancy4.2):

[121a] = [19] mSot 9:1 II (2)[30]   Deut. 21:1

(The [ritual of the] heifer whose neck is broken [is performed] in the holy tongue, as it is said 'If a slain person is found in the ground . . . and your elders and judges shall come forth [and measure towards the cities which surround the slain person] . . .'). Three [judges] from the great *Bet Din* which was in Jerusalem used to come forth. R. Yehudah says: Five, for it is said, 'your elders'—two; 'and your judges'— [another] two; and no *Bet Din* is even-numbered, [so] they add to them one more.

The topic of interest to the Mishnah at this point of its discourse is: how many members should a court have which deals with the case of the unknown victim of a killing? R. Yehudah's answer, specifying (unusually) five judges, is supported by Scriptural wording. Two biblical terms from the same lexical field, namely, 'elders' and 'judges', are taken to make the same contribution to that question, how many? They both yield the minimal quantity 'two', once their plural form is emphasized (i.e. the Opposition1.4 resource).[31] The contribution of this information is taken as separate for each word, so that the numbers are added up to make four.[32] So we have a repeated occurrence of the same information (the grammatical plural) being evaluated as independent items of significance, cumulative answers to the same question. Thus the two meaning-related terms 'elder' and 'judge' receive each their own weight in the scales of relevance: they are not redundant.[33]

Redundancy4.2: Explication of the occurrence of two (or more) biblical expressions from the same lexical field in a similar syntactic function in the same biblical sentence or in each other's co-text as differentiated from each other in terms of a repetition of an action, an iteration, or an accumulation.

The idea of accumulation or iteration can also be applied to biblical collocations which consist of two word-forms belonging to the same Hebrew verbal root, such as the infinitive absolute or the cognate object.[34] Here is an example:

[30] •¶ΔO1.4O7R4.2T0T1T3.1.

[31] See Ch. 11 (text succeeding the definition of Opposition1.4) regarding the fact that 2 is also the *maximum* assumed in such interpretations.

[32] At this point the auxiliary Mishnaic principle (Topic3.1) that no court can be allowed to be even-numbered is adumbrated with the practical consequence that another judge is added.

[33] In mSan 1:6 (5) a very similar interpretation is found.

[34] In addition to the case [122] found also in mBM 2:9, mBM 2:10 I (4).

[122] mHul 12:3 IV (5)[35]   Deut. 22:7

If he 'let it [the dam] go' and it returned, he 'let it go' [again] and it returned, even four (and five) times—he [still] is obliged [to let it go], as it is said, 'you shall surely let go [the dam]'.

The biblical phrase שלח תשלח את האם contains the lexeme שלח twice, once inflected and once in the infinitive absolute.[36] The Mishnah interprets this double structure as providing for the halakhic eventuality (Topic2) that the bird comes back after being released. An idiomatic construction in biblical Hebrew which involves semantic redundancy is thus translated into the specific information that the action denoted by the verb is to be repeated (if necessary).

Redundancy7.2: Explication of a biblical collocation employing two different word-forms belonging to the same root as differentiated from each other in terms of a repetition of an action, an iteration, or an accumulation.

We find iteration also with whole norms (that is, in the combination Redundancy3.2); thus in mMak 1:3 the double occurrence of a norm dealing with false witnesses[37] is taken by R. Meir to imply that the punishment for false testimony is doubled in certain cases.

At the beginning of this chapter I explained the second-digit category Redundancy*.3 as signalling a 'modification' of the meaning due to the repetition. As we indicated above, this is a very tentative definition; one really has to wait for extra-Mishnaic examples to provide a firmer basis for this resource in due course. To illustrate the need for *some* such resource, here is an example of the combination Redundancy3.3:

[123] mBek 1:2 I–II (2)[38]   Exod. 34:20; 13:13

A cow which gives birth to a young as of ass-kind, and an ass which gives birth to a young as of horse-kind, is free from the obligation of firstlings, as it is said, '(and) the firstling of an ass (you shall redeem by a lamb)', '(and) . . . the firstling of an ass'— ('ass') two times: as long as what gives birth is an ass and what is born is an ass.[39]

We are to understand from this unit that the *double* occurrence of 'firstling of an ass' (פטר חמר) implies that the norm in which these words occur applies only to cases where both the mother and the young are of the species ass. How are the biblical phrases construed to achieve this result? One could say that the doubling serves to dissolve the hypotactic collocation of the two terms in the genitive compound.[40] Or, the double occurrence is taken to

[35] πR7.2T2.

[36] Cf. Gesenius–Kautzsch, *Hebrew Grammar*, sec. 113 l–x; Bergsträsser, *Hebräische Grammatik*, 2. Teil: *Verbum*, 61–7. See Fraenkel, *Darkhey*, i. 119 ff. The text in round brackets is absent from MS Kaufmann.   [37] Exod. 20:16; Deut. 19:19.

[38] I: ®R3.3T2.1; II: A8.

[39] The words in round brackets are found in MS Kaufmann, but not in other versions of the text.

[40] See the definition of Cotext2 below. In our passage **[123]** this would allow us to read one of the

indicate an amalgamated sense, in the following way: 'the ass, firstling of an ass' (חמר פטר־חמר), perhaps even: 'the firstling, ass of an ass'.[41] The hypotactic relationship would still be suspended, this time to import a paratactic element into the hypotactic construction. The midrashic unit itself shows no interest in unpacking the operation beyond making clear that the double occurrence is crucial, and there are bound to be further possible explanations which I have failed to find.

Redundancy3.3: Explication of the occurrence of two biblical sentences with similar (or identical) propositional meaning as differentiated from each other in terms of a semantic extension, or a mutual modification.

The next passage combines the resources of Redundancy8 and Redundancy4. Its main concern is the immediate asyndetic repetition of the word 'Amen' in the response of the woman suspected of adultery, that is, a Redundancy8 phenomenon. This Mishnaic passage as a whole is something of a medley of REDUNDANCY resources, for it offers five alternative solutions to the question (one of which we already encountered in Chapter 2).[42] I shall distinguish them by lower case roman numerals.

[124] = [9] mSot 2:5 I–V (5)[43]   Num. 5:19–22

Why[44] does she say, 'Amen, Amen' (verse 22)?

(i) Amen to the 'curse' (האלה, verse 21), Amen to the 'oath' (השבועה, verse 21).

(ii) Amen because of this man, Amen because of another man.

(iii) (And) Amen that I have not 'defiled' myself, and [that] if I have 'defiled' myself they [the waters/curses] shall come into me.[45]

(iv) Amen that I have not 'turned aside' as a betrothed woman and as a married one, or as a woman waiting for levirate marriage and as a woman brought home [in levirate marriage].

(v) R. Meir says: Amen that I was not 'defiled', Amen that I shall not be 'defiled'.

Solution (i) separates the meaning of 'Amen' by giving each a specific object of response (i.e. Redundancy8.1; similar solutions iii, iv, and v). At the same time this implies that the significance of 'curse' and 'oath', which terms come from the same lexical field, are separate (Redundancy4.1), since they

two occurrences of the genitive compound as an apposition: חמר, פטר (= 'firstling, ass'), while the other would retain its reference to the mother beast as being of ass kind. But this suggests that the norm applies if *either* the mother beast *or* the young is of ass kind, which is excluded by the Dictum.

[41] An analogy would perhaps be: when keying in quickly the numbers '2', '2', the computer screen shows not '22', but '4'.

[42] These alternatives are organized as successive answers to a question which spells out shared presuppositions (in this case that there *is* something specific about which the woman says 'Amen, Amen'). See Goldberg, 'Questem'.

[43] I:Σ?¶C9P4R4.1(oath/curse)R8.1(*amen*); II: Σ?¶P4R8.1T1; III: Σ?¶C9P4R6.1(defiled)R8.1 (*amen*)T0; IV: Σ?¶C9P4R4.1R6.1(turn aside)R8.1(*amen*)T4; V: Σ?•¶C9P4R6.1(defile)R8.1(*amen*)T1.

[44] MS Munich and the *editio princeps* of the Babylonian Talmud (Venice 1522) have על מה instead of the למה here translated. Cf. Bietenhard, *Sota*, 188.

[45] Thus Kaufmann and other MSS. Other texts have this sentence after unit (iv), not before (also Albeck, *Shishah Sidrey Mishnah, Seder Nashim*, 239). MS Munich does not have the sentence; cf. Bietenhard, *Sota*, 188.

are separately confirmed. (However, the difference in meaning for these two words does not become thematic.) Solution (ii) separates the referent of an implied sentence confirmed by the 'Amen'. One 'Amen' concerns the lover who is the explicit cause of the charge; the second 'Amen' makes sure that, even if the charge is false for this particular man, she cannot deny it if there was some other man involved (another Redundancy8.1 resource). Suggestion (iii) has her imply with the first Amen that she did not defile herself, and affirm with the second the consequences in case she did, thus making explicit the conditional structure and taking up the multiple mention of the word 'defile' in the preceding text.[46] (I take it that here too, the second half is meant to belong to the second Amen, so that we have again a distributive perspective.) Answer (iv) is rather conspicuous in its wordiness. It applies the double Amen to four different halakhic categories, meant to form two groups: regular marriage on the one hand, and levirate marriage (again Redundancy8.1) on the other; this also picks up the two occurrences of 'turning aside' in the preceding text (Num. 5:19 f.). The widow remarried says 'Amen' for the marriage-like period between the death of her husband and the consummation of remarriage with his brother, as well as for the period after that. And the woman married for the first time says 'Amen' for the betrothal period as well as the period after consummation. The four categories, given in a sequence that makes chronological sense,[47] form a paradigm of marriage-like states[48] to be covered by the norm: these are the types of woman who are to be treated by the *Sotah* procedure.[49] Two of the members of the paradigm used here also appear in mSot 4:1 [108], but in the hermeneutic function of contrast terms. A comparison of answer (iv) with answer (i) is useful. It shows that, functionally speaking, a Mishnaic paradigm of halakhic categories (iv) is equivalent to the biblical co-text, utilized in (i). The same hermeneutic purpose is achieved in both interpretations, namely, the distribution of redundancy. Solution (v) is interesting in that it uses a binary structure available from non-specialist discourse: the distinction between past and future. The use of the same pair of terms has been encountered in mShebu 3:5 II (3) [79]; and similar pairs are in use for the OPPOSITION resources, such as day-time and night-time,[50] and youth and old age.[51]

The 'Amen, Amen' case is quite instructive with regard to what is assumed in the expectation of non-redundancy. There is *nothing* that

---

[46] Spelling out the consequences of the negative version of a conditional sentence is of importance for the rabbinic concept of ראי, also relevant to passage [110] mQid 3:4 II (2) in Ch. 11.

[47] I owe this observation, which underscores the possibility that 'narratives' of (everyday) life play an important role in law, to Bernard Jackson.

[48] A paradigm of quasi-marital ties is found in passage [108] above, mSot 4:1.

[49] In this regard (iv) takes the opposite view from an opinion encountered earlier in mSot 4:1 [108], which reads the biblical phrase 'under the authority of her husband' as limiting the norm to full marriage. Perhaps (iv) is meant to say that, while the *Sotah* procedure can only be *started* for full marriage suspicions, the woman's answer nevertheless also covers her pre-marital behaviour.

[50] See mBer 1:5 I (2) [13].

[51] As in mQid 4:14; cf. also mQin 3:6, where the process of ageing itself is addressed.

separates the two signs 'Amen' in semantic constitution, outward shape, speech perspective, or any relationship in the co-text. The only difference in their co-textual embeddedness is sequence: the second 'Amen' has a *preceding* co-text which contains the word 'Amen', the first 'Amen' has a *subsequent* co-text which contains the word 'Amen'. But whatever semantic information may be obtainable from this co-textual difference, it is not used in this passage. One might argue for the resource in (v) being an iconic projection of the dimension of time, or a generalization of the temporal movement of reading, like this: textual position n = past, position $n + 1$ = future. However, I favour a less specific explanation, as outlined above in general form. It is that, in principle, *any* position in the Scriptural text, regardless of whether or not the sign which occupies it is different from the sign that occupies the preceding position, carries *new* information for the rabbinic reader. Cases such as [124] show this with great clarity because the sign itself happens to be identical.

It is perhaps worthwhile to spell out in full the two REDUNDANCY resources encountered in [124].

Redundancy8.1: Explication of two contiguous and asyndetic occurrences of the same biblical expression as differentiated from each other in respect of their topic or case schema, action, speech act, or referent (apropos 'Amen, Amen').

Redundancy4.1: Explication of the occurrence of two (or more) biblical expressions from the same lexical field in a similar syntactic function in the same biblical sentence or in each other's co-text as differentiated from each other in respect of their topic or case schema, action, speech act, or referent (apropos 'curse', 'oath').

A very interesting solution to the repetition of messages (usually contained in clauses) is their distribution to more than one biblical protagonist as quoted speech. The result can be that the new speaker[52] *confirms* the truth of the preceding utterance, as is in the following example:

[125] mSot 9:6 IV (4)[53]   Deut. 21:8b

And the priests say: 'Forgive your people Israel whom you have redeemed, O Lord, and do not set guilt for innocent blood into the midst of your people Israel'. And it was not necessary [for them] to [also] say, 'And the blood guilt shall be forgiven for them',[54] but rather the holy spirit announces it to them: Whenever you do thus, the blood guilt shall be forgiven for you.

The whole biblical verse, in a translation which does not strive to eliminate

---

[52] In rabbinic literature this is usually some *deus ex machina* such as the Bat Qol or the holy spirit whose appearance requires no explanation. Cf. e.g. Samely, *Interpretation*, 127 f. (Neofiti on Gen. 27:33). See also Ch. 5 above, n. 126.

[53] ΣΔR3.6(*Bat Qol* versus priests)T3T3.1.

[54] MS Munich has an explicit hermeneutic question here, together with a repetition of the biblical segment: ומה ת(ל/למד) ל(ו/מר) ונכפר להם הדם; cf. Bietenhard, *Sota*, 195.

the repetition,[55] runs: 'Forgive, O Lord, thy people Israel, whom thou hast redeemed and set not the guilt of innocent blood in the midst of thy people Israel; but let the guilt of blood be forgiven them' (RSV). It is clear that allocating the segment after the colon to a new voice does eliminate the repetition, after a fashion. What the second speaker says is confirmation that the request is granted, not merely repetition of the request—and it also limits the text which is to be spoken as part of the ceremony. This is, by the way, already the second switch of speaker: the first sentence of this biblical direct speech (starting Deut. 21:7) is allocated by the Mishnah to the elders of the town concerned; the second to the priests (here in [125]), and the third to the holy spirit, as discussed. The introduction of the priests as speakers is due to the contents of the speech and the distribution to a Mishnaic paradigm of participants (both priest and elders play a role); it seems not to be connected with a phenomenon of redundancy.[56]

Redundancy3.6: Explication of the occurrence of two biblical sentences with similar (or identical) propositional meaning as differentiated from each other in terms of a switch of speaker.

For some of the REDUNDANCY resources (Redundancy6, Redundancy5, Redundancy*.4, Redundancy*.5) I am not going to quote at length any of the Mishnaic examples. They shall, however, at least be mentioned here. In mSan 1:6 II (5), the two similar clauses 'the congregation shall deliver' and 'the congregation shall judge' (Num. 35:24–5) are taken to imply an *aggregate* of two 'congregations' (determined by another hermeneutic operation as consisting of ten judges), that is, twenty judges. This provides an example for the Redundancy6.2 resource. The same passage reads the biblical terms 'deliver' and 'judge' as meaning 'condemn' and 'acquit', respectively.[57] It thus separates two expressions coming from distinct lexical fields but employed in similar syntactic function, distinguishing them along the lines of Mishnaic paradigm of opposites (example of a Redundancy5.1 interpretation). For the use of Redundancy*.5 (wholeness) we may have an example in mQid 4:14 IV (4) quoted as [17]. If the biblical accumulation of terms such as 'charge', 'commandment', and 'Torot' is taken by the Mishnah as reference to the *whole* Torah (which is possible but not the only explanation for that interpretation, because of the presence of the plural *Torot*), then it is a case of Redundancy4.5. A Mishnaic passage using Redundancy*.4 (extra emphasis) seems to be mBM 9:13 I (4) [113]: the double occurrence of the biblical word 'outside' is apparently understood

---

[55] As does JPS, by ending the direct speech earlier: ' "... and do not let guilt for the blood of the innocent remain among your people Israel". And they will be absolved of bloodguilt.' It thus achieves a similar result (confirmation) as our Mishnaic passage.

[56] Cf. Bietenhard, *Sota*, 149, n. 1. Distribution of one speech to a plurality of speakers (three) is made an explicit topic in tSot 9:2 ff. (ed. Zuckermandel, 312). TSot 9:3 reads: שלשה דברים זה בצד זה מה שאמר זה לא אמר זה.

[57] Which interpretation is not made explicit subsequently, in mSan 1:6 V (5).

as an emphatic reinforcement of the prohibition to enter the house of the debtor. Redundancy6.4 can account for such a hermeneutic move. However, insofar as the 'emphasis' is visible only in the fact that the Mishnah repeats a biblical norm in Redundancy*.4 cases, the resource stands in need of a larger supporting corpus of midrashic units from outside the Mishnah.[58]

NON-SEMANTIC DISTRIBUTION AND THE USE OF DEMONSTRATIVES

I now come to a resource which, although still connected to phenomena of redundancy, seems to extend the movement of distribution to nonredundant parts of Scripture. It takes the procedure of dividing Scripture into parts and matching them with Mishnaic paradigms into the realm of the purely numerical. When discussing [119], I drew attention to the weakness of the link between the biblical word 'to die' and the Mishnaic 'standing in judgement'. That correspondence is clearly forged not by a one-to-one relationship but as part of a distributive movement which also involves 'finish' from the biblical, and 'world to come' from the Mishnaic side. The following passages will show that semantic links between individual matched items may not just be weak—they may be wholly absent. Consider first the biblical text belonging to our next interpretation, Deut. 24:5: '[If a man has taken in marriage a new woman, he shall not go out with the army, and shall not be assigned to it regarding any matter,] he shall be exempt for his house for one year and make happy his wife (or: woman) whom he has taken.'[59] Concentrating on the second half of the verse, we find little sign of conspicuous repetition or semantic parallelism, although there is some redundancy in the final relative clause ('he has taken'). Also, בית, if taken in the sense of 'household' (JPS) rather than 'at home' (RSV), perhaps overlaps somewhat with the meaning of 'make happy the wife'. Be that as it may, the Mishnah has far-reaching divisions in store for this halfverse:

[126] mSot 8:4[60]   Deut. 24:5

And these do not move from their places [in case of war]: the person who built a house and dedicated it; the person who planted a vineyard and used its fruits; the person who marries the woman betrothed to him; the person who weds his

---

[58] In mBek 8:8 and mBM 8:1 II (2) (cf. [37]), redundancy is apparently taken to add emphasis qua financial liability for loss (Redundancy7.4).

[59] As often (see Ch. 1, by n. 30), my English translation stresses the semantic boundaries of individual expressions more than is necessary for, or indeed compatible with, understanding the sense of the whole period. The rendering of JPS reads: 'When a man has taken a bride, he shall not go out with the army or be assigned to it for any purpose; he shall be exempt one year for the sake of his household, to give happiness to the woman he has married.'

[60] ®C2R9T3W1(wife?)W5(household).

brother's widow, as it is said, 'He shall be exempt for his house for one year'. 'For his house'[61]—this is his house; 'he shall be'—this is his vineyard; 'and make happy his wife'—this is his wife; 'whom he has taken'—to bring into it the widow of his brother.[62]

This is the segmentation the Mishnah imposes in **[126]**:

   (i) he shall be [exempt]
  (ii) for his house [for one year]
 (iii) and make happy his wife
  (iv) whom he has taken.

And it allocates the following companion terms to these segments:

   (i) his vineyard
  (ii) his house (cf. Deut. 20:5)
 (iii) his own wife
  (iv) his brother's widow

One can see that the companion terms in (ii) and (iii) have a direct meaning connection to their biblical counterparts: the one takes 'house' in the sense of the concrete house (as opposed to household);[63] and the other allocates the meaning 'wife' to 'wife/woman' in the verse. But the other two matched pairs are of a quite different order. The biblical terms are both verbal expressions (יהיה and אשר־לקח). The biblical verb 'to take' is clearly understood in the sense of 'to marry'; its duplication here at the end of the verse is perhaps understood as pointing to a second type of marriage (namely, levirate marriage). That would make the identification with the nominal phrase 'his brother's widow' explicable, if still not straightforward. But I cannot see how the phrase 'he shall be' (with or without 'exempt'), taken on its own terms semantically, could be directly linked to the vineyard. One must conclude that the link is not meant as one-to-one correspondence. Rather, the *whole* of the Mishnaic set is projected onto the *whole* of the biblical sentence, and some of the segments match merely as members of their respective sets, not individually. In this context it should be noted that the sequence in which the segments are explained in the Mishnah does not correspond to the sequence of the segments in the verse (and as given above), but is as follows:

  (ii) for his house [for one year]—this is his house
   (i) he shall be [exempt]—this is his vineyard
 (iii) and make happy his wife—this is his own wife
  (iv) whom he has taken—to bring into it his brother's widow

---

[61] This is the Lemma as found in MS Parma (de Rossi 138) and the *editio princeps* of the Yerushalmi (Venice 1523/4). Others (e.g. MS Kaufmann) give no repeated quotation for this item, but 'house' is the word coming immediately before 'this is his house'. Bietenhard's suggestion for the Lemma ('exempt', נקי) has no MS support (*Sota*, 132 f., 194).

[62] Cf. Neusner, *A History of the Mishnaic Law of Women*, part 4: *Sotah, Gittin, Qiddushin*, 78 f.

[63] A Word5 operation; see the final section of the next chapter.

In other words, we start with a semantic link that can stand on its own, and are thereafter presented with a semantic link in alternation with a 'distributive' link.[64] The format is that of a one-to-one match, but only two of the four items can be tied to their opposite numbers as single items. It seems clear that the operation must be understood as a whole, that is, as one of segmentation and distribution whose criteria do not reside within the meaning of the individual biblical items, nor in the fabric of their biblical relationships.

There is an alternative way to account for passages such as [126], and that alternative needs to be considered on its merits in any similar rabbinic interpretation. It is the claim that there are conventions in the rabbinic reading of Scripture which provide individual and ready-made but non-semantic associations between items involved in such distributions. The possibility that 'and he shall', for example, is bound by some fixed convention or nexus of ideas to 'vineyard' cannot be excluded on principle (although I do not know of such a nexus). But I think it is quite unlikely that even a sizeable proportion of cases such as [126] can be explained by finding rabbinic evidence of conventionalized links for each and every one of the biblical segments involved. In other words, that possibility is unlikely to put into doubt the existence of a purely distributive resource. It is quite possible, however, that later rabbinic discourse looked with a certain unease on this fundamentally non-semantic mechanism, and strove to provide alternatives.

Here is another passage illustrating the same resource, quoted earlier.

[126a] = [80] mMS 5:10[65]   Deut. 26:13

At the time of the afternoon offering on the (last) day of the festival they used to make the declaration [accompanying first fruits]. How was the declaration [made]?

   (i) 'I have removed the holy thing from the house'—this is the second tithe, and the fourth-year planting;

   (ii) '[also] I have given it to the Levite'—this is the tithe of Levites;

   (iii) 'also (וגם) I have given it'—this is the heave offering and the heave offering of the tithe;

   (iv) 'to the sojourner, to the orphan, and to the widow'—this is the tithe for the poor, the 'gleanings', and the 'forgotten' [sheaf] and the *peah*—even though their absence does not invalidate the declaration;

   (v) 'from the house'—this is the *Hallah*.

As in the preceding passage, the sequence in which the segments are presented is different from the biblical one, in two places: the segment 'and also' precedes 'I have given it'; and the segment 'from the house' belongs to the opening clause. This is how the verse reads as a whole, with the five Mishnaic segments identified in brackets: 'I have removed the holy thing

---

   [64] Alternatively, the sequence follows the opening sentence of the *mishnah*, where it could reflect systematic ordering, e.g. importance or frequency.

   [65] ∑ΔπC1(*gam*)D2E5.5(*gam*)P4R9(from the house).

(i) from the house (v); also (iii) I have given it to the Levite (ii) and the sojourner, the orphan and the widow (iv), according to all your command- ments . . .' The text of the declaration extends from Deut. 26:13 to 15, and all of it is given a similar treatment in the Mishnah (ending in *mishnah* 13). In this passage the Mishnah works its way through a paradigm of agricultural dues. Some of the terms are a match with clear semantic overlap (for example, tithe of the Levites, poorman's tithe). Others can be understood to be linked by mechanisms of taxonomic relationships; thus 'the holy thing' (הקדש) can be made to serve as superordinate for a number of temple dues in the Mishnah's book, and the passage makes a selection from them.[66] The 'sojourner, orphan, and widow' are, as a set, linked elsewhere in Scripture to one of the Mishnaic items, the forgotten sheaf.[67] There is no direct semantic link between the 'house' and the *Hallah*, except by associa- tion with the *domestic* setting of the baking. The link between 'also' and the heave offerings is also not direct, but has to do with an extension of the semantics of 'given it to the Levite' as explained in Chapter 9.[68] So, one can find some sort of one-to-one connection for most of the correspondences. And yet there are strong signs of a distributive approach: items which have a homogeneous status (as nouns and types of dues) and come from a Mishnaic paradigm are matched up with Scriptural units whose syntactic function or semantic value is only partially taken into account.

On the whole, it seems to be a question of degree whether the hermen- eutic distribution can be effected without reference to the semantic content or syntactic function of the individual segments. None of the passages above lack semantic one-to-one correspondence for *all* of its members. Having one or several such links seems a necessary condition for linking further members of the same biblical syntagma to further members of the same Mishnaic paradigm. There seem to be all varieties of such matching. It may be useful to recall a passage discussed in Chapter 10, mSan 8:4 III (4) **[91]**. Here it is again:

[126b] = **[91]** mSan 8:4 III (4)[69]   Deut. 21:19 f.

If one of them has a cut-off hand, or is lame, or mute, or blind, or deaf, they do not deem him a 'stubborn and rebellious son'; as it is said, 'And his father and his mother shall seize him'—and they do not have a cut-off hand; 'and bring him out'— and they are not lame; 'and they shall say'—and they are not mute; 'our son, this one'—and they are not blind; 'he does not listen to our voice'—and they are not deaf.

[66] Maimonides in his *Commentary on the Mishnah* points out that both these dues are specifically called 'holy', in Lev. 19:24 (fourth-year fruits) and Lev. 27:30 (all tithes in general); cf. *Zera'im*, trans. Qafih, 232, and 230 (on *mishnah* 3).
[67] Deut. 24:19. There are other partial links in Scripture: Lev. 23:22 connects the poor and the sojourner to the *peah* and the gleanings; somewhat similar in Lev. 19:9.
[68] I have there explained this as Extension5.5 case. For the present context it is relevant that this interpretation of *gam* presupposes that the wider co-text is neutralized (so that the *also* can refer to something unmentioned; Cotext1).
[69] πD6H4H7R9T1T2T3.

We find here various sorts of one-to-one link explicable partly by concepts such as existential presupposition or canonicity. And yet the force of the whole is vastly greater than that of any of the individual links, and that is so because a sufficiently homogeneous Mishnaic paradigm of disqualifications and blemishes is projected onto the biblical syntagma. This becomes quite clear when one looks at what happens to the temporal sequencing of actions in this interpretation. The biblical verse has a very clear progression of events: one thing happens after the other (seize, bring, say). The Mishnaic counterparts, on the other hand are qualities, not actions; they are all simultaneous with each other.

Reading the biblical syntagma as a simultaneous paradigm often destroys essential syntactic cohesion. But it also adds to it the coherence of items *which belong to the same paradigm*. It seems as if the fact that these disqualifications or blemishes belong together and form a coherent set can, in the Mishnaic view, substitute or compensate for the syntactic coherence which is suspended in the process. As in **[126]** and **[126a]**, the Mishnaic terms in **[126b]** provide a new unifying topic for the whole biblical sentence. All the segments say something distinct, but they all speak to the *same* theme, be it disqualifications **[126b]**, types of exemptions from military service **[126]**, or agricultural dues **[126a]**. In some cases, as in **[126a]**, this links up with the overall biblical topic of the sentence; in others, such as **[126]**, this is only partially true.[70] In other interpretations again, of which **[126b]** is an example, there is not even a trace in the biblical wording of the overall theme as determined by the Mishnah. But since at least some of the items in each case have a semantic link, however tenuous, this imposition of a new, unified topic on all segments together can also be interpreted as a *spreading* of that topic, achieved through one or two direct links, to all neighbouring biblical segments within the chosen limits.[71] Thus, the separation of the segments in meaning goes hand in hand with their *mutual* modification. Where the biblical items are peripheral or redundant, it can be difficult to tell the distributive mechanism with which we are concerned here from a type of analogy called *heqqesh*. The idea of redundancy is frequently attached to that analogy in rabbinic literature. Passage **[126]** mSot 8:4 V (5) above is actually explicated with *heqqesh* terminology in the Tosefta, and the idea of a topic 'spreading' among members of a biblical syntagma seems central to such constructions.[72]

Here is a definition of the resource embodied in the last three passages:

---

[70] The exemption from military service effected by building a new house or planting a vineyard is not part of the biblical surface message at Deut. 24:5, but it is in Deut. 20:5 f.

[71] Cf. with this the idea of a midrashic 'metaphora continuata' in Fraenkel, *Darkhey*, i. 198 f.

[72] The Tosefta (tSot 7:20, ed. Zuckermandel, 309) reads: אף זה היה בכלל ולמה יצא להקיש אליו. Neusner translates this as follows: 'This matter was covered by the general principle, and why has it been explicitly stated? To allow for the imposition of an analogy on its basis, so teaching you . . .' (*History of Mishnaic Law of Women*, 4: 78). However, there follows a more specific Dictum than any of the Dicta found in our Mishnaic passage. Cf. Ch. 8 above, text to n. 57; Ch. 2, n. 33.

Redundancy9: Explication of the significance of a biblical syntagma through the numerically matched pairing of each of its members or subdivisions with one member of a Mishnaic paradigm. Some, but not all, pairings need to be explicable by way of a subsidiary hermeneutic resource producing a one-to-one link, and not all of the links need to involve the same hermeneutic resource.

The manner in which the segmentation is represented in Redundancy9 passages varies. In **[126]** and **[126a]** the segmentation is signalled by use of the demonstrative 'this' (זה). In **[126b]**, on the other hand, the segments are simply 'continued' in Mishnaic words, as is also the case in passage **[121]**. The difference in presentation is not linked to the presence of a full, uninterrupted citation of the whole biblical sentence; such a full citation is found in **[121]**, but not in **[126b]**. There may, however, be a link between use of the demonstrative pronoun and the extent to which individual matches are separately justified or justifiable. Where the match of the paradigmatic set can be individually confirmed, the continuation format may be easier to employ, or simply preferred to the use of a demonstrative pronoun. It could also play a role in these choices whether *one* resource, or resources related to each other, can account for all the individual links between matching items. In interpretations such as **[121]** or **[126b]**, the overall distributive effect for the Mishnaic paradigm can be achieved by applying *the same basic hermeneutic move* to one segment after another. It is worth investigating if the use of the demonstrative pronoun in interpretations of this type is rare, or rarer. I mentioned in Chapter 5 the idea that there is a link between the use of demonstrative pronouns in dream interpretation and in rabbinic hermeneutics. My observations in the present context seem to keep open the possibility of such a link. In any case, the Redundancy9 resource is clearly the pièce de résistance for establishing a historical dependency of rabbinic procedures (rather than certain themes or motifs) on ancient dream interpretation.

Regarding the presence of biblical repetition, it is not clear how essential it is as trigger for a Redundancy9 treatment of its wording. Almost all examples offer some degree of redundancy, although not much redundancy of repetition. Also, the procedure itself, by giving new function to *each* segment, suggests that while some segments are considered necessary in their biblical surface function, others are seen as superfluous if not examined for extra information. Thus, 'whom he has taken' is a repetition of sorts in **[126]** and 'also' is redundant in **[126a]**. The verse belonging to **[126b]** gives a list of actions which may have provoked the question: Why are we told all this? But there is no parallelism or any other structural redundancy. Among the remaining Mishnaic Redundancy9 passages, some have no sign of redundancy at all,[73] while others have some, accord-

---

[73] e.g. mSan 10:3 I (10) ad Gen. 6:3 (לעלם) לא־ידון רוחי באדם); mSan 10:3 VI (10) **[21]** ad Num. 14:37 ('died—of plague').

ing to midrashic standards.[74] The distributional mechanism treats the segments as equals, without any distinction between redundant and non-redundant ones. It is, in fact, an essential element of this resource that it can swallow up all manner of different parts of speech from the same sentence. This alone is sufficient indication that redundancy through parallel syntactic function can play no decisive role. In sum, one might say that the application of this resource often, if not always, presupposes that some redundancy is in fact perceived in the verse; but that, once at work, the distributive mechanism is designed to spread to all segments, including patently non-redundant ones.

For some of the segments created in the above passages, Redundancy9 presupposes not merely a general suspension of co-textual relations, but the separation of elements which are syntactically interdependent. The most obvious example is probably the expression 'he shall be' in [126] which, selected on its own, is linked to the vineyard. In mPes 5:5 [10] the hypotactic collocation כל קהל עדת ישראל ('the whole assembly *of* the congregation *of* Israel') is dissolved in favour of a paratactic structure, which is then translated into a temporal sequence (namely of the three groups slaughtering the Passover sacrifice).[75] The separation of items which in the biblical text stand in syntactic (in particular hypotactic) relationships is presupposed in many Mishnaic interpretations, not only of the Redundancy9 type. Since this dissolution of syntactic relationships can be seen as a special case of the neutralization of the co-text, I shall label it Cotext2:

Cotext2: Explicit or tacit analysis of the meaning of a syntactic collocation in terms of a paratactic, additive, or sequential relationship between its constituents.

I said above that the distributional mechanism of Redundancy9 projects a (Mishnaic) paradigm onto a (biblical) syntagma. This echoes a famous structuralist definition of poetics, formulated by Roman Jakobson, which speaks of the projection of the paradigmatic axis onto the syntagmatic axis.[76] Do I mean to claim that the hermeneutic procedure Redundancy9 shows that the rabbinic reader reconstructs the poetic function of the biblical text? No. The explanatory work of this REDUNDANCY resource is performed in a totally different context, which is given in my discussion above and throughout this book. Can it nevertheless be connected, as a parallel on the abstract level, or as a heuristic tool of further analysis, with Jakobson's idea of the poetic function? I am not sure. Jakobson speaks of a generative principle or option in the composition of texts. Also, the paradigms whose projection Jakobson envisages are of a different order

---

[74] e.g. mSan 10:3 II (10) ad Gen. 11:8 ('from there—to the face of all the earth'); mPes 5:5 [10] ad Exod. 12:6.   [75] Exod. 12:6 as explained in mPes 5:5.

[76] Jakobson, 'Linguistics and Poetics', 358: 'The poetic function projects the principle of equivalence from the axis of selection into the axis of combination.' Cf. also Coseriu, *Textlinguistik*, 133 f.; Lotmann, *The Structure of the Artistic Text*, 80 ff. (esp. 86 f.).

altogether; they belong to the linguistic system (not, say, a halakhic system). And yet, it is possible that there are some, perhaps very general, points of contact. There are certainly some parallels between rabbinic resources of interpretation and the type of analysis structuralist linguistics applies to language, in particular in defining meaningfulness as a result of functional opposition.[77] There is perhaps also a connection between the idea that artistic prose or poetry has a particularly high density of information on the one hand[78] and the rabbinic expectation of very high information density in Scripture on the other.

And yet, to our eyes, the midrashic reading of Scripture ignores the biblical text's poetic qualities. To say, 'In this wilderness they shall finish and there they shall die' (Num. 14:35) contains a repetition, no doubt; but it nevertheless has that brutal directness of biblical expression which is incompatible with mere repetition or tired rhetoric. To us there seems to be no need to explain its message, as the Mishnah does in [119] above, by saying that two neatly distinct types of 'death/finishing' are referred to.[79] Stylistic appreciation of biblical language and the characteristic *informativeness*[80] of its redundancy take a very different route from the approach visible in the Mishnah.

CLAUSE RELATIONSHIPS

The Redundancy9 mechanism allows for the nearly complete suspension of syntactic interdependency on the text surface of Scripture. A sentence whose predicate 'he shall be exempt' can be interpreted to denote or point to the newly planted vineyard must have been dissolved into parts whose function or mutual relationship can no longer be explained by the rules of grammar. The interpreter's replacement of all the more complex syntactic relationships provides, basically, a list structure; hypotaxis is transformed into parataxis. I now turn to other resources which address the interdependency of the parts of a biblical syntagma. For the most part, they accept the grammatical framework as given by the biblical phrase or clause, but target the relationship between syntactical units larger that these. I will begin with the least conspicuous form this can take. It concerns the way the interpreter connects a word or phrase whose function in the sentence is ambiguous. As in the following case, the rabbinic reader may choose a syntactic alignment which is not privileged by the biblical co-text.

[77] See e.g. Trubetzkoy, *Grundzüge der Phonologie*, 30 ff., 59 ff.; Coseriu, *Einführung in die Allgemeine Sprachwissenschaft*, esp. chs. 6–8.

[78] See Lotmann, *The Structure of the Artistic Text*, esp. ch. 4 (57 ff.), and the section on 'entropy' in ch. 1 (pp. 25 ff.). See also Ch. 2 above (section on 'Topical diversity and segment size').

[79] As often, JPS transforms the repetition and thus preserves its informativeness in other ways: 'In this very wilderness they shall die to the last man.'

[80] Some main accounts of the literary qualities of biblical prose include the opening chapter of Auerbach's *Mimesis*, Alter's *Art of Biblical Narrative*, and Sternberg's *The Poetics of Biblical Narrative*.

[127] mSot 7:4 I–II (2)[81]   Deut. 25:9

[*mishnah* 2: The following are said in the holy tongue: the first-fruit declaration, the *Halitsah*, the Blessings and Curses, the priestly blessing . . .] The *Halitsah*—how so? It says here, 'and she shall answer[82] and say . . .' and it says elsewhere, 'and the Levites shall answer and say'. As the answering and saying there is in the holy tongue, so it is here in the holy tongue. R. Yehudah says: 'She shall answer and say thus (ככה)'—as long as she speaks in this tongue.[83]

I am not interested at this point in the first interpretation contained in this passage (resource Keying2), but in R. Yehudah's alternative confirmation of the same Dictum. The biblical sentence details what the widow says as part of the *Halitsah* declaration. Taken in context, the word 'thus' is a demonstrative referring to the actions the woman has just performed (spitting, pulling the man's sandal off),[84] and is the beginning of her speech: 'his brother's widow shall go up to him in the presence of the elders, pull the sandal off his foot, spit in his face, and begin and say: *Thus* shall be done to the man who will not build up his brother's house!'[85] R. Yehudah, however, takes the 'thus' as the last word of the speech report, rather than the first word of the utterance: '. . . spit in his face, and begin and say *thus*: It shall be done to the man who will not. . .'. By so doing he gains the special emphasis that the speech *in precisely this form* is what the woman has to say—including its language, Hebrew.[86]

In taking *kakhah* to belong to the words that precede it rather than those that follow, R. Yehudah makes a decision on what, judged merely from the point of view of grammatical relationships, is a possibility for construing the sentence. In fact, the two options are not quite equal even on purely syntactic grounds. But the important point is that the hermeneutic operation leaves no unmanageable fragment in its wake: abrupt beginnings or transitions are by no means rare in the biblical text. This manner of perceiving and deciding between options of syntactic construction (even when it leaves some rough edges), is what the resource definition below is about. There is, however, a neater Mishnaic example. In mYoma 8:9 I (3) the clause, 'From all your sins before the Lord you shall be clean' (Lev. 16:30) is taken as, 'From *all your sins before the Lord* [as opposed to fellow-man] you shall be clean'. This takes the place of the link favoured by the biblical co-text, which knows nothing of the topic of fellow-man: 'From all your sins, *before the Lord you shall be clean*.'[87] Also, where a link is extended across the

---

[81] II (Yehudah): •¶C5S3T3W1.2.

[82] The same verb (ענה, cf. BDB 772b f.) could also mean 'to sing', or 'to raise one's voice' (explained in BDB 777a, but not with reference to Deut. 25:9). Perhaps this is important for the link to the 'holy tongue'.

[83] This unit in the name of R. Yehudah is absent from MS Munich.

[84] This is how it is taken in mYeb 12:3 II (2) (ascribed to R. Aqiva). Cf. my discussion of [116] in the preceding chapter.   [85] JPS translation, slightly adapted.

[86] Cf. Fraenkel, *Darkhey*, i. 104. Maimonides, *Commentary* (trans. Qafih, *Nashim*, 181), explains it as a meaning inherent in the word *kakhah* or *koh* in all its biblical occurrences.

[87] JPS translates: 'For on this day atonement shall be made for you to cleanse you of all your sins;

boundary of the Masoretic verse (Cotext7), it may be this resource which reconstructs the grammatical relationships (see mMak 3:10 **[8]**).[88]

Syntax3: A textual direction is chosen for the syntactic dependency of a biblical expression, phrase, or clause which is not supported by the wider co-textual relationships, in the following way. The biblical unit is capable, from a grammatical point of view, of being connected to the preceding or to the subsequent text. Either the rabbinic choice selects the direction not privileged by the co-text, or it selects only one direction when the co-text privileges neither.

Another type of ambiguity arising from syntactic structures is the manner in which genitive constructs are interpreted. The following resource identifies the mechanism connected to this:

Syntax4: Construing a genitive collocation as *genitivus objectivus* when the co-text privileges the *genitivus subjectivus* meaning or vice versa.

An example for this can be found in mBM 2:7 I (2), quoting Deut. 22:2. Its phrase 'inquiry of your brother' (דרש־אחיך) is understood as an inquiry whose *object* is the brother (to see whether he is the rightful owner), instead of the brother's inquiry after a thing lost.

I have treated in some detail above a number of Mishnaic options for interpreting biblical parallelism. They all share the assumption that, in most of the biblical structures addressed by the Mishnah in this way, both syntactic parallelism and some semantic overlap is present (see Redundancy2, and Redudancy4–8). It is therefore of special interest that, in places where the syntactic similarity is present, but the semantic overlap is absent or de-emphasized, the Mishnah may choose to relate the two terms to the same subject or referent. This amounts to a resource which is the *opposite* of Redundancy*.1. In the example below the biblical syntagma offers two items fulfilling the syntactic function of adverbial amplification of the same verb, 'passing through'. The Mishnah concludes from this that the two expressions refer to the same place:

[128] mSot 7:5 I (5)[89] Deut. 11:30; Gen. 12:6

The Blessings and Curses—how? When Israel had crossed the Jordan they came to Mount Gerizim and Mount Ebal in Samaria, by the side of Shekhem, which is close to the 'terebinths of Moreh', as it is said, 'Are they not beyond the Jordan, [behind the west road that is in the land of the Canaanites who dwell in the Arabah, near Gilgal by the terebinths of Moreh]' (Deut. 11:30). And elsewhere it says, 'And Abram passed through the land to the place Shekhem, to the terebinth of Moreh' (Gen. 12:6). As the 'terebinth of Moreh' which is enunciated there is Shekhem, so the 'terebinth of Moreh' which is enunciated here is Shekhem.

you shall be clean before the Lord.' Epstein argues for treating this passage as secondary in the Mishnah (*Mavo*, 1306 f.).

[88] See also the literature on הכרע quoted in n. 68 of Ch. 2 above.
[89] (K2)S2.

In the verse from Genesis the expressions 'place Shekhem' and 'terebinth of Moreh' are presented in parallel position: each is an adverbial phrase for the same occurrence of the verb 'to pass through'; both introduced by the same preposition, and juxtaposed to each other asyndetically. This is the basis of an identification of the referent of the one with the referent of the other: they are taken to refer to the same geographical location. (This is the first step in a transfer between two co-texts of the occurrences of the 'terebinth of Moreh' , i.e. a Keying2 procedure.)

Syntax2: Identification of a common or partially common referent for two expressions linked paratactically or asyndetically and fulfilling the same syntactic function in Scripture.

The use of Syntax2 in preparing the ground for a transfer operation (Keying2 or Keying3), as in **[128]**, is quite plausible. The resource achieves the *total* determination of an item from its co-text—its referent is simply identified as the *same* or partially the same as that of an expression in the co-text.[90] It is thus an extremely effective way to fix the meaning of a biblical word by way of its co-text. And this, a meaning firmly defined by the co-text in one biblical segment, forms the basis for all such transfer resources. Moreover, taking two signs (namely in the same co-text) to refer to the same thing at the same time also implies that there is repetition in the biblical syntagma. From here it is only a short step to the explicit rabbinic demand that resources such as Keying2 and Keying3 should *only* be applied where an item is redundant (*mufneh*) at one of the biblical locations involved—co-textual definition and redundancy imply each other to some extent.[91] It is, however, important to note that the technical hermeneutic term *mufneh* is not used here or anywhere in the Mishnah.

Of some importance to the Mishnah is also the syntactical construction of comparison. In some respects the Mishnaic treatment of biblical comparisons (also of identity statements) is similar to its treatment of metaphors (see next chapter, in particular Word6.2).[92] Biblical similes or comparisons are not taken as indicating some overlap of features, or a mixture of similar and dissimilar features. Instead, the biblical comparison or simile is pinned down to a relevant area in which the similarity is total, amounting to shared membership of a class. In the Mishnah's interpretation, as far as this one aspect is concerned, the two subjects are not *alike*; they are identical. We have already encountered an example of this when discussing ANALOGY in Chapter 8, passage **[69]**. The link to analogy is almost automatic for cases of halakhic categories—they are conceptual and ideal, and seem to admit no similarity, only identity or non-identity. If something 'counts as' something else, it is that something else for legal purposes. And although in the

---

[90] As in mMiqw 9:2, quoted as **[30]**; from the fact that 'miry clay' stands in syntactic parallel to 'pit' it is concluded that it is the type of clay found in pits.

[91] See text belonging to n. 33 in Ch. 2, as well as point 5 at the end of Ch. 8 (succeeding n. 90).

[92] The two can be presented as rival strategies, as in mAZ 3:6 I (2).

Mishnah all interpretations of a biblical comparison are linked to *halakhic* analogy, I shall nevertheless formulate the resource without specific reference to halakhic categories. There may be other types of class membership which are constructed by interpreting biblical comparisons, even if they are not found in the Mishnah. In addition to case **[69]**, which may also be consulted as an illustration of this resource, the next passage shows how this works. The Lemma contains a double simile, and the Mishnah is interested in the two terms of comparison, not the item which is compared to them (namely, the cursing):[93]

[129] mShab 9:4[94] Ps. 109:18

Whence [do we know] that anointing is like drinking on the Day of Atonement? Although there is no proof for the matter, there is a mention (זכר) of the matter, as it is said, 'And may it come like water into his body and like oil into his bones'.

The double simile is read as applicable to the halakhic situation of what is or is not forbidden on the fast day of Yom Kippur: is anointing prohibited? The answer, as ascribed to this verse, is: yes. And the prohibition of anointing for Yom Kippur conveyed by this verse is not *like* the prohibition of drinking; it is not similar, or related, or partial. None of these words apply. Drinking is forbidden and this biblical comparison tells us that anointing is also (cf. Yom 8:1). The perspective imposed is so narrow as to reduce the comparison to an observation of identity, because the perspective itself (Topic2) supplies a yes–no alternative for class membership (actions forbidden on Yom Kippur). The effect of this seems strong enough to produce by itself a transfer of features, that is, the result otherwise achieved by resources of ANALOGY. We do not seem to have two steps here, the first being the interpretation of the comparison as implying shared class membership, and the second being an additional analogical transfer. It might therefore be preferable to say that in cases of this type, which I have labelled Extension9 (see Chapter 8), the Analogy3 resource simply becomes superfluous or is implied. I have, however, chosen to include Analogy3 in the hermeneutic profile of such midrashic units, so that all of these passages can be easily included in any future assessment of the ANALOGY resources in general.

Returning to the question of how clauses relate to each other, some Mishnaic reformulations target the asyndetic juxtaposition (cf. the Cotext6 resource for individual expressions). But where there is a biblical conjunction explicitly linking the two parts, one needs to make a decision on how to interpret these interpretations. Is the Mishnah concerned with the meaning of the conjunction (that is, a decision on the meaning of one word) and the syntactic relationships are adjusted accordingly? Or is the interpretation interested in the relationship of the propositions contained in the two

[93] 'May he be clothed in a curse like a garment, may it enter his body like water, his bones like oil' (JPS).   [94] •?A3C1E9T1T2.

biblical parts, defining that relationship (sometimes) in disregard of the limits imposed by the meaning of the conjunction? In the relevant passages, the Mishnah shows no special interest in tying the interpretation to the meaning of the conjunction; its meaning is never addressed as such. Mostly one is dealing with the paratactic 'and' (*waw*). From this one should perhaps conclude that, although an adjustment for the meaning of the 'and' (and other conjunctions) is at times possible and thus required as part of a general adjustment of co-textual relationships, it is those relationships directly which are addressed.[95] But one cannot exclude the possibility that some of these passages are also meant to make a claim about the semantics of 'and' (of which there are traces elsewhere in the system of resources).[96] Here is an example:

[130] mSan 6:4 I (3)[97]   Deut. 17:7

One of the witnesses pushed him [down the place of stoning] onto his loins. If he turned onto his heart, he turns him [back] onto his loins.[98] If he died from this, the obligation is fulfilled. And if not the second witness takes the stone and puts it on his heart. If he died from this, the obligation is fulfilled.[99] And if not, his stoning is [performed] by all Israel, as it is said, 'The hand of the witnesses shall be against him at first in order to kill him and the hand of all the people at last [and you shall eliminate the evil from your midst]'.

The biblical sentence is taken to apply to the specific case when both witnesses have followed the rabbinic procedure of stoning but the condemned person is still alive (Topic2). The relationship of the two parts of the sentence each side of the 'and' is read as: The hand of the witnesses shall be against him *at first*, so that he be killed—only if that is not the case, *at last*, is the hand of all the people against him. The opposition between the biblical 'at first—at last' is stressed in this also.[100] The very first Mishnaic interpretation cited in this book reads the relationship of the two parts of Jer. 17:7 in a related manner: Blessed is the (needy) person trusting in God (as opposed to *Peah*), *for* God will provide for his security [trust].[101] Here is the general formulation of the resource, followed by a similar resource.

Syntax5.1: Construing a biblical syntagma consisting of two paratactic or asyndetic biblical units (clauses or expressions), as indicating a temporal sequence, or as a hypotactic dependency (causal, final, concessive, or conditional).

[95] For this distinction see also the difference between the resources Word1/3 on the one hand and Word2/4 on the other (Ch. 14).

[96] See resource Logic7, discussed in Ch. 9.

[97] (D6)O1O8S5.1T2.

[98] For the problematic sense of this passage, see Krauß, *Sanhedrin-Makkot*, 191 f.

[99] In some texts the first witness puts the stone on the condemned, and only if that does not kill him is the action repeated by the second witness; ibid. 190–2 and 392.

[100] An Opposition8 case. The *editio princeps* separates the two parts of the quotation by introducing the second half by an additional ראמר, thus emphasizing the pairing of expressions, see ibid. 195 (n. 10).

[101] The interpretation is found in mPeah 8:9 I (4), which I cited in Ch. 1 (text to nn. 18, 49).

Syntax5.2: Construing a biblical syntagma consisting of two paratactic clauses for whose relationship the co-text privileges simultaneity or temporal sequence, as indicating cause, consequence, purpose, concession, or condition.

For the latter resource, the following passage may serve as illustration. We have seen it already in Chapter 2:

[130a] = **[3]** = **[57a]** mShab 9:3 II (3) = mShab 19:3[102]   Gen. 34:25

Whence [do we know] that one bathes a child[103] [even] on the third day [after circumcision] that falls on the Sabbath? For it is said, 'And it came to pass on the third day (ביום) when they were (בהיותם) in pain . . .'

The link with the event narrated earlier in Scripture—namely, that the male population of Shekhem submitted to circumcision—is presupposed here (Cotext5). In the light of this link, the sentence is read as: 'And it came to pass when they were in pain because it was the third day (after circumcision) . . .'

One also finds that the conditional כי can be taken as a temporal conjunction—albeit only in one case. This interpretation is found as continuation of a passage encountered before, as **[115]**. I repeat that material in smaller print:

[130b] = [115] mPeah 7:7 III (3)[104]   Deut. 24:21 (Lev. 19:10)

A vineyard which is all defective clusters—R. Eliezer says: [They belong] to the owner. R. Aqiva says: To the poor. R. Eliezer said: 'When you [grape-]gather your vineyard you shall not take the defective clusters' (Deut.). If there is no [grape-]gathering whence defective clusters? R. Aqiva said to him: 'And from your vineyard you shall not take the defective clusters' (Lev.)—even though (אפילו) all of it is defective clusters. If so, why is it said: 'When (כי) you [grape-]gather [your vineyard] you shall not take the defective clusters'? The poor do not have [a right] to the defective clusters before the gathering.

Aqiva (or some voice continuing on his behalf), after rejecting Eliezer's Dictum with the help of Lev. 19:10, still has to explain the function of the second and conditional version of the norm (Deut. 24:21).[105] His answer depends on reading the two parts of the sentence, not as conditional (as used by Eliezer), but as temporal: once the time has come to grape-gather, do not collect the defective clusters (not even if the vineyard is all defective clusters). In this passage it is possible to concentrate the weight of the hermeneutic argument in the meaning of the conjunction. Perhaps the conjunction כי is read as 'at the time when' instead of its usual range of

---

[102] C5N8S5.2T2T3.1.

[103] The popular prints have here 'the circumcision', i.e. the wound of circumcision. (Nowack's *Schabbat*, 143, gives no clear idea of the variants.)

[104] •¶R3.1S6T1W1.2(*ki*).

[105] For this need to go back to find a function for the other party's Lemma in a dispute, cf. Ch. 10 (text to n. 70).

meanings[106] (making this a case of Word1.2). If so, the resource defined presently would have to be removed from the Mishnaic configuration of resources, because [130b] is the only passage providing evidence for it.

*Syntax6: Construing a biblical period consisting of two clauses in causal, final, concessive, or conditional relationship as indicating an exclusively temporal relationship.

Some of the resources just discussed, in particular Syntax5.1, read a paratactic sequence as some more specific type of interdependence. Of some interest is the transformation of textual sequence into temporal relationships. Where the thing first mentioned is taken as prior in temporal terms, one has something like a semiotic transfer from the process of reading (the sign that is encountered first in reading) to the events described. Even clearer is that semiotic transfer where it is not restricted to the realm of time. In the following passage, the sequence of items in the text is taken to indicate *ranking*, that is, an abstract quality not directly connected to time.

[131] mKer 6:9 I (4)[107]   Lev. 4:32

R. Shim'on says: Lambs precede goats everywhere [in Scripture]. Could it be because they [the lambs] are preferred over them [the goats]? In this regard it is instructive that Scripture says: 'If he brings a lamb as his offering for a sin offering'—it teaches that both of them are equal.

The biblical verse does not mention goats, but they are dealt with in Lev. 4:28–31, so goats do in fact precede lambs in the text. The argument presupposes that textual sequence *could*, in theory, imply ranking or (divine) preference, in two ways. First, as a hypothesis of meaning expressed in the question. And second, in the way the assumption is refuted: it is not rejected in general terms, but on the basis of evidence of the same kind: *both* sequences occur in Scripture. This unit is part of a series of three interpretations, all using the same resource. The second passage deals with the sacrificial pair turtle doves/young pigeons and the third with father/mother.[108]

The next passage, quoted earlier in Chapter 6, takes the semiotics of

---

[106] BDB 473: 'if, whenever'; Clines (iv. 386b) has 'introducing conditional clause (sometimes with temporal aspect)', 'if, supposing that, in the case that, when'. See bGit 90a, and mGit 9: 10 III (3) [2].

[107] $\Omega \bullet \approx$ M1T1. The concluding lines of this *mishnah* at least (not quoted here) are textually suspect; they are marked as addition in some manuscripts, and are absent from MS Munich (Albeck, *Einführung*, 180). However, all of it is found in MS Kaufmann.

[108] The latter reappears in a conspicuous series of MAP interpretations in the opening section of Mekhilta Ishmael (ed. Lauterbach, i. 2–3). The subjects there are: Moses/Aaron, heaven/earth (*temporal* sequence in creation, not direct ranking), the three patriarchs, father/mother, and Joshua/Caleb. In all cases preference is rejected on the basis of the inverse sequence of mention also being found in Scripture.

textual position one step further still; here the topography of the text, seen in the dimension 'above–below', is seen as providing a metaphor of rank:

[131a] = [57] mYad 4:8 I (2)[109]   Exod. 5:2

A Galilean heretic[110] said: I raise a complaint against you, O Pharisees, for you write the [name of the] ruler together with [the name of] Moses in a bill of divorce. The Pharisees say: We [raise a complaint] against you, O Galilean heretic, for you write the Name [of God] together with [the name of] the ruler on [one] page, and not only that, but you (plural) write the ruler above and the Name beneath, (as it is said), 'And Pharaoh said: Who is the Lord that I shall listen to his voice to let go Israel? [I do not know the Lord and also Israel I shall not let go]'. And when he was smitten, what does he say? 'The Lord is righteous [and I and my people are the wicked ones].' (Exod. 9:27)

Scripture serves here as direct *model* for the writing of legal documents (Norm5.2). The answer of the Pharisees gains extra force by the relative position of the names of Pharaoh and God in the verse quoted: Pharaoh comes to stand *above* God's name (מלמעלן, as opposed to מלמטן). Although this could simply mean that the one precedes the other[111] and implies rank in this manner, I am inclined to take the spatial categories literally, in particular as they provide a specific contrast with the *get*. This in turn probably means that it is the second occurrence of God's name in the verse, not the first, which is intended (see the continuation of the verse in square brackets, above). That second occurrence is sufficiently far away from 'Pharaoh' virtually to guarantee that it comes to be written in the subsequent line, that is, beneath, in any manuscript. The fact that ranking is implied here is clear from the wording ('and not only that') and the thrust of the argument as a whole: if any disrespect were implied by Scripture's using these names on the same page, it would be even greater for the fact that the divine name appears *under* that of the ruler.

In both **[131]** and **[131a]** the linguistic metaphors[112] of ranking ('precede' and 'above–below') are taken to be iconically conveyed in the spatial relationships of the signs in the biblical text. Ranking is perhaps one of the more important but not the only figurative usage linked to spatial relationships; therefore, the formulation of the resource should not be too specific:

Map1: Interpretation of the relative textual position of signs in Scripture in terms of sequential or spatial figures of speech, taken in their conventional figurative meaning.

---

[109] ΩΔ•¶A4.2M1N5.2T9.

[110] Variant reading 'Sadducee'; for this variant and the quotation formula given in brackets, see our textual notes for **[57]** in Ch. 6.

[111] This seems to be Maimonides' opinion (*Commentary*, trans. Qafih, *Tohorot*, 443).

[112] Lakoff and Johnson, *Metaphors We Live By*, 14, recognize an area of metaphorical organization they call 'orientational metaphors', with regard to which they explore the ramifications of 'up–down' orientation for ranking or values. See also Taylor, *Linguistic Categorization*, 136 ff.; Johnson, 'Some Constraints on Embodied Analogical Understanding', 30 ff. (regarding the 'path').

It may be noted that, in explicating a hermeneutic resource such as Map1, one is also involved in interpreting the linguistic metaphors on which they rely. That would be difficult if those linguistic expressions were to be treated as problematic in their own right. Therefore the above definition stresses their conventional character.

14

Constructing Words and Word Meaning. Metaphors

The Mishnaic treatment of word meaning frequently depends on the licence to separate a biblical segment from its co-text. This opens up the full range of lexical meaning, and allows a fresh narrowing down of meaning possibilities, this time by the Mishnaic concern (visible as the difference between biblical and Mishnaic co-text for the word). As a result, the lexical meaning allocated to the biblical word may be that of a different semantic nuance, or that of a different word of the same appearance (homonym), or that of some semantic extension of these. Mishnaic interpretations of biblical word-forms can be achieved indirectly, by the imposition of a perspective elsewhere in the biblical co-text. The extent of such co-textual adjustments defines the outer limits of the Scriptural segment created or presupposed by the interpretation. The Mishnah offers no support for the idea that the determination of lexical meaning is meant also to clarify the *historical* relationship of the biblical word-forms (etymology). The Mishnah may provide semantic analyses of idiomatic biblical phrases, opaque compounds, or proper names by dividing the Scriptural text into segments smaller than the word or fixed collocation. The biblical text may also be analysed in its wider semiotic (as opposed to narrowly linguistic) constitution. Finally, the concrete meaning of a biblical metaphor may be reactivated in the service of the very same theme to which its figurative meaning points in the biblical text. At times biblical expressions which carry concrete meaning in their co-text are allocated a figurative meaning by the Mishnah.

USING OR EXTENDING THE FULL SEMANTIC
RANGE OF A LEXEME OR HOMONYM

The resources discussed in the present chapter are all concerned with the Mishnaic allocation of meaning to words in the biblical text. The Mishnah quite often suggests that a biblical word has a meaning nuance that calls for an adjustment of the meaning of the whole sentence in which it occurs. Or, it links the word with another form of similar but not identical appearance. Or, it discovers special meaning in biblical metaphors. These will be the main hermeneutic phenomena discussed in the three sections of this chapter. For these resources, the need to uncouple rabbinic hermeneutic resources from the assumptions of modern biblical scholarship is, if anything, stronger than for others. But, as for all the resources, uncoupling cannot achieve separation. In the field of word meaning, the concrete results of modern biblical scholarship stand in direct rivalry to Mishnaic hermeneutics; but they also provide the immediate background to it.[1] The following—simplified—principles of modern scholarship determine the framework in which we see the results of the rabbinic treatment of word meaning. And as they provide the framework, it is precisely these principles which should not be ascribed to the rabbis without supporting evidence:

1. The acceptance that the *history* of a word as reconstructed with the methods of philology, comparative linguistics, and etymology has to make a contribution in determining the meaning of a word in earlier documents.

2. The assumption that the sentence-environment and the wider *co-text* are an indispensable part of the constitution of word meaning.[2]

3. The (usually tacit) assumption of modern biblical (and other) lexicography that meaning can be allocated to and collected in abstract entities which subsume a variety of linguistic forms. These abstract entities are called *lexemes* in contemporary linguistics; thus, 'gone' and 'went' are said to belong the *same* lexeme despite their very different word-form or appearance (see below).

4. The concomitant assumption that there is, *in principle at least*, a clear distinction between multiple meanings inside the lexeme (called *polysemy*) on the one hand and multiple meanings between distinct lexemes represented by the same word-form (called *homonyms*) on the other.[3] An example of polysemy is the meaning difference between 'leg' in 'leg of a man' versus

---

[1] See Ch. 1 on the general features of this hermeneutic situation.

[2] Cf. Coseriu, *Einführung in die Allgemeine Sprachwissenschaft*, 179: ' "Kontextbedingte Determinierung" (wobei wir die außersprachlichen Kontexte unberücksichtigt lassen) bedeutet . . . daß die in einem Redeakt oder "Diskurs" realisierten Einheiten sich wechselseitig bestimmen.' This mutual determination is what is suspended when the contribution of the co-text to meaning is neutralized (as explained in Ch. 2 above).

[3] Cf. the excellent account of the problems in Kempson, *Semantic Theory*, 79 ff.

'leg of table'. An example of homonymy is the meaning difference between 'bank' in 'river bank' versus in 'robbing a bank'.[4]

The only way to lessen the surreptitious influence of these assumptions on modern descriptions of the Mishnaic interpretation of word meaning is to declare it. One cannot ignore them, for without them one would not have anything to describe, as is particularly clear in the case of word meaning. Implicit decisions on word meaning are present in all interpretations, for the biblical text is made up of 'words'. If one made no prior selection, *every* description of a rabbinic interpretation should contain an account of the treatment of individual words. But even then the question would be, which words? All words of the verse, or all those contained in the quotation, or just a few of them, or just one, and if so which one? And even if one offered a description of word-meaning choices for every case of rabbinic interpretation and for each biblical word affected, what sort of description could be offered? If there is nothing *conspicuous* about the Mishnah's treatment of a word, all one could say is that the meaning *tacitly* allocated to it matches, *as far as one can see,* the meaning allocated to it by our dictionaries. But this is obviously pointless. It emerges that one needs to define rabbinic mechanisms of interpretation first and foremost in those cases where the meaning prima facie allocated to the biblical word can *not* be accounted for by the historical methods of reading of Scripture. The WORD group of resources shows clearly that one perceives rabbinic hermeneutics, at least initially, only in those parts which cannot be assimilated to the results of historical and philological scholarship or similar approaches.[5] Thus the assumptions whose tacit intrusion into the definition of the resources I intend to avoid are already constitutive for the resources' very existence or selection.

All the more important to acknowledge at the outset the central importance of etymology, co-text, and the very notion of 'word' (as in 'lexeme') in the modern scholarly construction of biblical word meaning. For reasons that will become clearer as I go through the WORD resources individually, I shall deal with the four points raised above in the following manner:

1. *History*: I shall construct the WORD resources as *making no automatic claim* about word-history. I thus allow for a separation of synchronic from potential diachronic rabbinic procedures, and create room for one or more separate resources in which diachronic claims are made or presupposed,

---

[4] For the two English examples, see *Shorter OED* (i. 153 f., and 1196). Homonymity is of some conceptual importance to the notion of 'word'. See Matthews, *Morphology*, 27 ff.; Lyons, *Introduction to Theoretical Linguistics*, 405 f.; Cruse, *Lexical Semantics*, 80. For the gap between linguistic theory and practical lexicography, see Matthews, *Morphology*, 31 ff. Clines's *Dictionary of Classical Hebrew* remains quite traditional in its approach to the idea of 'word' or 'root' in biblical Hebrew.

[5] Our perception of the *whole* of rabbinic hermeneutics is thus likely to be affected by an imbalance in the direction of what is *different*. This imbalance is not quantifiable, and we can never catch up fully with its distorting effects even as we refine our reading, because that presupposes taking a view of the *whole* of our own reading assumptions.

should there be evidence for them (see below, apropos the resource Cotext3).

2. *Co-text*: I shall make explicit the fact that the Mishnaic licence to choose from an unrestricted range of semantic nuances for a word's meaning depends to some degree on the suspension of its relationships to the biblical co-text. See below, on passage **[133]**. As a convenient model for that unrestricted range of meanings I shall use a word's dictionary entry.

3. *Lexeme*: I shall avoid speaking of the lexeme when referring to a biblical word chosen as the focus of the rabbinic interpretation. Instead, I shall use the term 'word-form' (explained presently). This allows me to distinguish potential resources, which commit the rabbinic interpreter to an allocation of lexemes to word-forms, from resources which involve no such allocation.

4. *Homonymy*: The primary evidence for saying that the meaning for the same word actually varies is the difference of the contexts and co-texts in which it can be used. Since this is the decisive factor, common to both polysemy and homonymy, and since the role of co-text also defines a major difference between the rabbinic and the historical interpretation of biblical words, the distinction between polysemy and homonymy does not provide a solid criterion for the description of the hermeneutic mechanisms as found in the Mishnah (more on this in my discussion of **[132]** below).

As a general precaution against importing too much of the modern lexicography into the rabbinic resources, I shall refer to the biblical entity whose meaning we see the Mishnah determine as the 'word-form'. In this I follow a current terminological distinction between 'word-form' (sometimes also 'linguistic form', or simply 'word') on the one hand and 'lexeme' on the other.[6] Put simply, the word-form is the concrete shape in which the word is found when in use, including any signs of declination, inflection, or compounding—such as the English forms 'gone' and 'went'; while the lexeme is a more abstract entity to which a number of word-forms are assigned or from which they are said to be 'derived'. Thus the English word-forms 'gone' and 'went' are said to be realizations of the lexeme 'Go',[7] and their meaning is found under the entry 'Go' in a dictionary. When speaking about the rabbinic interpretation of biblical words, I shall characterize the Lemma as 'word-form', not as 'lexeme'. This means that I can explicate any rabbinic *allocation* of a word-form to a lexeme (bounded meaning) as a distinctive part of certain WORD resources but not others (see e.g. Word4).

---

[6] Lyons, *Introduction to Theoretical Linguistics*, 196 ff.; Bauer, *English Word-Formation*, 11 ff.; Matthews, *Morphology*, 24 ff.

[7] It is important to note that 'go' is both the name for the lexeme 'Go', and one of the word-forms of that lexeme (as in the imperative 'go!'). The selection of the word-form which gives the whole lexeme its name (called 'citation form' by Bauer) may be different from language to language, cf. Bauer, *English Word-Formation*, 12.

Here is a simple example for the variation in meaning of one and the same word-form according to its use in context (that is, for the purposes here, co-text).[8] The meanings listed in our dictionaries for the biblical Hebrew noun דָּבָר (i.e. consonants and vowels together, distinguishing it, for example, from *dever*, 'pestilence') include 'speech', 'thing', and 'manner', among many others.[9] In the following passage the Mishnah presupposes the meaning 'speech' for דָּבָר as occurring in Deut. 15:2. And yet this is the 'wrong' meaning as far as the dictionaries are concerned, because of the biblical co-text.[10]

[132] mShebi 10:8 I (2)[11]   Deut. 15:2

If someone repays his debt in the seventh year, he [the creditor] says to him: I grant release. If he [the debtor] says to him: Even so!, he may accept it [the repayment] from him, as it is said, 'And this is the *davar* of the release (דבר השמטה): [every creditor shall release the due that he claims from his fellow]'.

One finds here no explicit matching of the biblical *davar* with the meaning 'speech', as expressed in the protasis, 'he [the creditor] says to him' (יאמר לו). However, it is clear that the link between the quotation and the Mishnaic text can only be understood on the basis of the occurrence of a word in the biblical text which *may* mean 'speech'.[12] The Mishnaic case schema implies that the duty imposed by the biblical norm is not the actual cancellation of the debt but only the *offer* of such cancellation, whether or not this leads to cancellation.[13] If the biblical segment is to support that, *davar* has to be read as 'speech' rather than, say, 'matter'. (JPS translates it as, 'This shall be the *nature* of the remission'.)

In narrowing down the meaning of the 'polysemic' (or 'homonymous') דָּבָר in this biblical passage, our dictionaries and this Mishnaic passage use different criteria. The dictionaries depend on the larger phrase in which the

---

[8] Cf. Fraenkel's section on 'semantic difference', *Darkhey*, i. 94 ff.

[9] BDB 182 f. offers the following main sub-entries relevant to our discussion: I. speech, discourse, word; IV: matter, affair, thing about which one speaks, act, events, things; IV.7: way, manner (183b), ad Deut. 15:2, with reference to the first line of the Siloah inscription and other passages in this meaning with demonstrative pronoun (in the phrase כדבר הזה); Clines, ii. 397–411 lists the following main meanings: 1. word, speech; 2. thing (matter affair, cause, case, deed, event, something, anything, everything); 3. way, manner; 4. reason, cause. Our passage Deut. 15:2 is again allocated to the meaning 'way, manner' (repeated in 11QMelch₃).

[10] *Davar* is interpreted in this manner by the Mishnah on several occasions: mShebi 10:8 II (2) = mMak 2:8 (Deut. 19:4); the same Lemma as in [132] is addressed with similar results in mMak 2:5 II (2) [11]. The Gemara (bBM 43b–44a) ascribes to the Mishnah a similar interpretation also at mBM 2:5 I (2) (Exod. 22:8). On *davar* as an example of polysemy treated in rabbinic interpretation, see also Fraenkel, *Darkhey*, i. 99 f.

[11] ◊C1O1O6T2≈W1(*davar*).

[12] Since the quotation is presented as backing the specific case (Topic2) of the debtor offering to pay, the reader's attention is moved back to the Mishnaic mention of the creditor's obligation to *say* something. Thereafter, things fall into place: *davar* can be taken in this phrase as 'speech' rather than 'matter', which results in a different function for the demonstrative this/זה and requires some neutralizing of the co-text.

[13] The halakhic concern here should be seen in the context of the rabbinic mechanism of *prozbul*, cf. mShebi 10:3 ff.

word-form occurs (and its parallels in other biblical passages), while the Mishnah does not. However, since the meaning suggested by the Mishnaic 'he says' is taken to be *one* of the meanings of *davar* by the biblical dictionaries, it is indeed found in the entry for the word. Only, the biblical passages quoted in the dictionaries for the meaning 'speech' do not include this biblical passage Deut. 15:2, while that verse is allocated to the meaning 'manner, way'.[14] In other words, even within the same dictionary entry one finds the biblical Lemma allocated to a *different* sub-entry. However, the biblical dictionaries are by no means unanimous in separating multiple meanings. Quite often, what in one is classified as a meaning variant belonging to the same lexeme is separated out as constituting the meaning of a different, homonymous lexeme in the other.[15] Does this affect in any way the hermeneutic mechanism? Is there reason to think that the nature of the rabbinic resource depends on whether it allocates to the word-form another meaning from the same lexeme, or the meaning of another lexeme altogether, namely, a homonym? I suggest that we have no evidence on this point, which in itself mitigates against imputing the distinction to the rabbinic exegetes. In the Mishnah at least, there is no trace of a distinction corresponding to that between polysemy and homonymy. Indeed, as example **[133]** will show, the flexibility of word-form meaning includes semantic extensions which cannot necessarily be captured in dictionaries at all, or for which no biblical sample passage can be found. In other words, it goes beyond the limits even of the polysemy-homonymy variations. Also, since there is no consensus on the treatment of individual biblical words in Hebrew lexicography, it is impossible to make resource distinctions depend on this pair of concepts without reference to specific modern dictionaries.[16]

Thus the following factors play a role in an interpretation such as **[132]**:

(a) The meaning identified by the rabbinic reader is either allocated to a different biblical reference (i.e. co-text) in one and the same entry in our

---

[14] See n. 9 above.

[15] Scholarship in the last hundred years has tended to widen the range of homonyms. Although the entry for *davar* is not an illustration of this trend (while the treatment of the *verb* דבר is), Clines lists many meanings as homonyms which in BDB were treated as polysemes. According to Clines, ii. 10 f. this tendency 'destabilizes' the lexicon; cf. also Richardson's review of Clines's dictionary in *Journal of Semitic Studies*. Of about 10,000 words of 'classical' Hebrew 1,500 are 'well-recognized homonyms', i.e. there is 'an extreme situation of homonymy' (Clines, 'The Postmodern Adventure in Biblical Studies', 1609). If there ever was a common lexicographic standard by which to measure the rabbinic treatment of polysemy versus homonymy, it seems to have disappeared. See also next note.

[16] A mixture of theoretical and pragmatic factors influence lexicographers' decisions on whether a meaning is polysemous or homonymous. In the words of John Lyons (*Introduction to Theoretical Linguistics*, 406): 'The distinction between homonymy and multiple meaning is, in the last resort, indeterminate and arbitrary . . .' Kempson (*Semantic Theory*, 81 f.) has argued for the automatic treatment of *any* substantive meaning difference as homonymous; for the opposite position, see Coseriu, *Einführung in die Allgemeine Sprachwissenschaft*, 185 ff.

biblical dictionaries; or is allocated to a different, homonymous entry; or is not found in the dictionary at this point at all, because it provides a productive extension of meaning.

(b) This means that the choice of semantic nuance for the biblical word-form is not restricted by the biblical co-text at this point in Scripture (as it is for modern biblical lexicography), but embraces potentially the totality of meaning of the word-form when taken in isolation (for which the complete entry in a dictionary, or a cluster of neighbouring entries, may serve as an approximate representation).

(c) The meaning intended for the word-form may occur in the Mishnaic co-text of the biblical wording (e.g. as part of the Dictum), as is the case with the word 'says' in **[132]**; or it is presented as explicit paraphrase or synonym. A less direct manner of identifying word meaning than either of these is defined below as resource Word2.

(d) The overall meaning or message determined by the hermeneutic operation may depend on a weakening of the links to the biblical co-text; it may not be possible or particularly meaningful to readjust the co-textual relationships in the light of the new meaning given to the selected word-form, and **[132]** is an illustration of this. But there are other interpretations where the readjustment of the whole phrase or sentence in which the word-form appears is essential for understanding the overall dependency of the Dictum on the biblical quotation. This phenomenon will be encountered in passage **[133]** below.

Here is an attempt to identify the critical features of the resource:

Word1: Explication of a biblical word-form by choosing a meaning from the full range of polysemous, homonymous, or extended semantic possibilities for that word-form. The word-form is thus taken in independence from its limitations in the biblical co-text, and in turn calls either for an adjustment of the co-textual relationships or for their active suspension.

Does the rabbinic interpreter in **[132]** 'misunderstand' the biblical phrase of which *davar* is part in Deut. 15:2? Is the co-textual effect overlooked, or does the rabbinic reader always approach the text without taking account of the co-text? I suggest that this is not the case, but that the Mishnaic reader makes a hermeneutic choice; or, put differently, that neutralizing the co-textual contribution to word meaning is wholly compatible with a background acceptance of the force of the co-text. That this is so is in fact clear from a number of hermeneutic phenomena. I will start with cases where the meaning determined for a specific biblical word-form is only known to us because of Mishnaic meaning choices for lexical items *in its textual neighbourhood*. In such a case, the co-textual relationships *re-define* the meaning of the word-form for any user of the Mishnah. And they do so by moving its meaning away from its *original* co-textual meaning, but towards a *new* co-textual meaning represented by the very same biblical co-text. Here is an example:

[133] mMak 3:16[17]   Isa. 42:21

R. Hananyah ben Aqashya' says: The Holy One, Blessed Be He, wished to justify (לזכות) Israel, therefore he increased for them Torah and commandments (ומצות), as it is said, 'The Lord was pleased for the sake of his righteousness to make great (יגדיל) Torah and to make it glorious'.

The biblical quotation is very heavily perspectivized by the accompanying rabbinic technical terms (Topic3) in the Dictum: זכה 'to justify, to allocate merit', and 'Torah', whose rabbinic sense is made clear in turn by מצות 'commandments'. These terms have the effect of moving the meaning of the biblical 'righteousness' (צדק) in the direction of 'declare (Israel) righteous (in judgement)', and the general sense of the sentence becomes now: 'The Lord was pleased, in order to be able to justify Israel in judgement, to increase the commandments of Torah (and thus the opportunities for Israel to acquire merit)'.[18] Pivotal for the new sense of the sentence is the meaning of 'make great' (יגדיל). This word needs to be understood as 'make numerous' or 'increase in number', rather than 'magnify' or 'elevate-praise', which is the meaning privileged by the parallel with 'make glorious'/יאדיר in the same verse. (The reward for fulfilling *even one* commandment is the topic of the preceding lines in the Mishnah.) And it is this shift in the meaning of the verb which makes this an example of a WORD resource.[19]

What is important here is that in building the co-textual relationships which allow the meaning 'multiply the number of Torah-commandments', one needs to put the words together *without neutralizing the co-text*. All semantic choices need to be enacted simultaneously, otherwise they become an obstacle to each other through their co-textual links; but once they are enacted together they manifest co-textual links that *reinforce* the individual Mishnaic meaning choices. To read the sentence as an emphatic unit[20] is essential for producing from the isolated words a new proposition, a complete message: that of the Dictum. The Scriptural sentence structure as reinterpreted (not neutralized) is what carries the freshly selected meaning 'make numerous' to its point. And it is the point of the sentence as a whole, not the meaning possibilities of 'make great', which is the *raison*

---

[17] Ω•C1O7(for the sake of)T3W1(righteousness)W2(make great).

[18] Maimonides gives the following rephrasing of the verse in the Dictum's perspective: ה' חפץ לצדק את ישראל למען כן יגדיל תורה ומצות ויאדיר (trans. Qafih, *Neziqin*, 165). For the history of this unit, see Finkelstein, *Mavo le-Massekhtot Avot we-Avot de-Rabbi Natan*, English summary, p. xix; Epstein, *Mavo*, 977 f.

[19] BDB 152b; 'make great' seems to be used only with uncountables in Scripture (*pace* Rosenblatt, *The Interpretation of the Bible in the Mishnah*, 9). See below.

[20] Up to a point: now the link between יגדיל and יאדיר is weak, while that link is strong under the reading favoured in the biblical setting of the verse. There is a trade-off here between the strength of the newly created links of cohesion and their limited scope—if they could extend into ever wider co-textual regions they would be identical with the preferred reading of modern scholarship.

d'être of this interpretation in the first place. Only as a whole sentence with this proposition does the verse connect with what matters to the Mishnah, has relevance, and thus ultimately justifies the interpretation. But where exactly does the new meaning for יגדיל become visible in the Mishnah? How is it selected from the possibilities of the lexeme to which it is thought to belong? The answer is that it is the Mishnaic Dictum which *acts as the new co-text* in selecting the new meaning for יגדיל. The Dictum provides the sense in the light of which the biblical verse as a whole is to be read and the meanings of the individual word-forms are adjusted and integrated accordingly, or where that is not possible or necessary, they are ignored (as with יאדיר). It is part of this adjustment of the whole sentence which imposes the new meaning on יגדיל. And this happens by way of adjusted co-textual relationships. How important adjustment within the sentence can be is shown by this very example. For in the case of יגדיל, this adjustment stretches the semantic boundaries of the word beyond its attested meanings, even if these are considered in isolation, that is, as a complete dictionary entry. For the meaning 'to make numerous', which is here imposed on יגדיל, is not a regular meaning option for this verb—either in biblical or rabbinic Hebrew.[21] It cannot be verified from the dictionaries, which means that it works in the same manner in which any *productive* semantic effect, for example a metaphor, is encoded and decoded.

In effect, one only knows from adjusting יגדיל in the light of the new meaning of the biblical co-text that the Mishnah takes it to mean 'to make numerous' at this point. We are offered dedicated reformulations for the sense which the Mishnah identifies for צדק and תורה, but not for יגדיל. No *one* Mishnaic word or phrase can be identified as segmented equivalent of the biblical word. There is thus the need to make explicit one's own hermeneutic contribution as a reader of midrashic units, which is to allow a convergence of sense between the Mishnaic Dictum and the Scriptural quotation.

Here are the key elements of this resource:

Word2: Tacit selection of a meaning from the full polysemous, homonymous, and extended semantic range of a biblical word-form as part of an adjustment of co-textual relationships within a biblical sentence; that adjustment is called for by the Mishnaic explication of another word-form in the same sentence, or the convergence of sense between the Scriptural segment and its Mishnaic co-text.

Readers of this book will not be surprised to be told that the phrase 'convergence of sense between the Scriptural quotation and its Mishnaic co-text' in this definition is meant to describe the imposition of perspective,

---

[21] On the hermeneutic option of using the historical meaning difference between the two types of Hebrew (biblical and rabbinic), see Fraenkel, *Darkhey*, i. 98. Fraenkel is right in comparing this rabbinic procedure to the deliberate, hermeneutic use of the difference between Hebrew and other languages (ibid. ii. 590, n. 47), on which below.

and is also meant to describe it in such a way that cases of expressive use (π) are included. Returning to the question of the background importance of co-text, Word2 marks out cases where the meaning selected for the biblical word-form, although in one sense *not* privileged by the original co-text, totally depends on the freshly adjusted co-textual relationships. It is quite clear here that the construction of cohesion continues to work in the background even where some neutralization of co-textual relationships is required for the hermeneutic operation. The *suspension* of co-textual relationships stands in parasitic relationship to the constant *construction* of such relationships. Consider another manifestation of the underlying importance of co-textual relationships for Mishnaic hermeneutics:

[134] mMen 11:5[22]   Lev. 24:7; Num. 2:20

And two handbreadths of space was in between [the two sets of loaves of shewbread], so that the wind could blow between them. Abba Shaul says: That is where they used to place the two dishes of frankincense of the shewbread. They said to him: And is it not already said: 'And you shall place *upon* (על) the row [of shewbread] pure frankincense'? (Lev. 24:7) He said to them: And is it not already[23] said, 'And *by* him (עליו) the tribe of Manasseh' (Num. 2:20)?

Abba Shaul implies that the על in Lev. 24 should be interpreted in the sense of 'next to' or 'by', instead of 'upon'. The quotation of Num. 2:20 does not show that this is the sense required at Lev. 24:7. What it shows is that the mere occurrence of the word על in Lev. 24 does not settle the matter one way or another. For על is polysemous with regard to spatial relationships: 'by' is as much a meaning for this word-form as 'upon' (although the latter is much more common), so simply quoting Lev. 24:7 constitutes no counter-argument to Abba Shaul's position. How exactly is the evidence from Num. 2:20 construed? The verse demonstrates that על can have the meaning 'next to' only because of the *co-text* which it provides for that word. That co-text compels the reader—at least the reader who wishes to understand the sense of the whole phrase—to give על a meaning different from 'upon', because 'upon' is simply impossible for these linguistic surroundings.[24] If it were legitimate to neutralize the effect of the environment on על in Num. 2:20, the verse could prove nothing for its meaning possibilities. In other words, the full integration of co-textual relationships is necessary at this point in the hermeneutic argument, and indeed accorded ultimate persuasive force.

There exists, then, some *dependency* of specific and limited suspension of co-textual relationships on a background assumption that such relationships do in fact hold (e.g. **[133]**); and occasionally there is explicit recourse, in a hermeneutic context, to the force of the co-text in narrowing down the

---

[22] Num.: •¶ΔC5T5W1.2(al)ΔO7T5.

[23] This second 'already' is missing in MS Kaufmann.

[24] The Babylonian Gemara attached to this part of the Mishnah (bMen 98a) offers a similar treatment of the על appearing in Exod. 40:3, ascribed to Rabbi.

meaning possibilities of a biblical word-form (as in [134]). It is also clear that in some hermeneutic operations the co-textual sense of words is presupposed, or even underscored (embodied in the resource Cotext5). But these considerations can be widened considerably further. Does not the Mishnaic interpreter presuppose, every time one item in the flow of a text is selected for focusing on, that the other items in the sentence will be reinstated into their co-textual relationships at least to some degree?[25] Would it be possible to cancel all force of collocation and still retain a *meaning* for the text? Is it not always presupposed that *as many co-textual links* as possible are in fact maintained under the new interpretation? It seems, indeed, that the reader of rabbinic interpretation is expected to be ready at any point to reinstate, re-create, maintain, or readjust the integrity of the biblical co-text as far as possible, once she or he has taken on board the meaning chosen for one of its members. This is often necessary to see the link between Dictum and biblical quotation at all. So the suspension of co-textual relationships is selective, occasional, and most interestingly, regulated by the *reader of the midrashic unit*—it is part of the contribution made by the user of rabbinic texts, part of the interpretation of interpretation. From this vantage-point another observation finds its explanation. I said earlier that it is ultimately the reader of the Mishnah who, in understanding the rabbinic interpretation, determines the *segment* of Scripture that is being explained.[26] It is not the extent of the quoted words, which may have been abbreviated or restricted to the beginning of the verse, which marks the boundaries of the segment of Scripture. The rabbinic interpretation itself (namely, the hermeneutic operation) defines the limits of Scriptural segments, and thus the segments into which the rabbinic interpreter divides Scripture are constructed by the interpreter of rabbinic interpretation. This gives us something of a definition of the word 'segment' as used in this study: the segment is defined *by the point in the biblical text up to which the co-textual relationships need to be adjusted to reinforce the rabbinic interpretation.*

Passage **[134]** also throws some light on the question of whether Mishnaic hermeneutics presupposes an abstract notion of the unity of a word in the sense of 'lexeme'. As far as it goes, the case of על seems to show that it does. For in order to conclude anything from Num. 2:20 for the meaning of Lev. 24:7, the two word-forms *al* and *alaw* must be recognized as belonging to a semantically unified linguistic entity (i.e. the lexeme *al*).[27] Compared as word-forms alone they are not identical. One may take this passage as an indication that the 'lexeme' approach to biblical word-forms is available in principle, even if it is not exclusive (see the second section of this chapter).

---

[25] Cf. my 'Scripture's Implicature', 194 (human Hebrew as the 'background code').

[26] See Ch. 2 (text starting at n. 109).

[27] Or, alternatively, that they belong to two different words (homonyms) which yet would have the same linguistic *base* (namely *al*) to which both *al* and *alaw* can be traced back.

Passages [133] and [134] point in the direction of an acceptance of co-textual meaning, and of an assumption of entities similar to the 'lexeme'.[28] But the significance of these principles is different within Mishnaic hermeneutic practice from their role in the historical approach. For the Mishnah they constitute only options; options that can be supplanted by their opposite. But in historical reading this is not the case; the co-textual approach cannot be suspended, except perhaps by text-critical arguments, and the most recent tendencies of biblical scholarship tend to restrict such moves to a necessary minimum. In the context of modern philology or linguistics, it would be illegitimate to apply the notion of the lexemic identity of Hebrew words to only some passages, or only some words. As underlying assumptions of *all* reading in modern scholarship, these principles have no counterpart in the hermeneutic practice represented in the Mishnah. And this means that one needs to ask for each resource if it presupposes either of these principles or not; if they were imputed auto-matically, certain features of rabbinic interpretation would become invisible.

The interpretation seen in [134] opens up the meaning of a word which is neither a noun, nor a name or verb, but a preposition. It is quite convenient to have a special resource for slight shifts in meaning for such functional words, which can be a highly effective way to impose a fresh perspective on the whole sentence in which they occur, because of their transmission or 'keying' function.

Word1.2: Explication of a biblical word-form representing a particle, preposition, conjunction, and the like, by choosing a meaning from the full range of polysemous, homonymous or extended semantic possibilities for that word-form. The word-form is thus taken in independence from its limitations in the biblical co-text, and in turn calls either for an adjustment of the co-textual relationships or for their active suspension.

The semantic reshaping of word meaning is very common in the Mishnaic treatment of Scripture. Very often it is clear from the use of contrastive terms (Opposition1, Opposition2) that a certain semantic facet has been chosen over others. Thus, in mSan 8:1 [101] the meaning of the biblical word 'son' is placed into opposition to the adult man, not to other types of kinship relation such as daughter, or the absence of kinship.[29] The same is true of the meaning of 'one of them' as focused in [100] mYeb 3:9. The opposition interpretations are probably the most important evidence for the Mishnaic determination of lexical meaning, for one can recognize them regardless of whether or not they lead to *conspicuous* choices in the sense discussed above. Variations of meaning within one and the same lexeme may even

---

[28] Coseriu, *Einführung in die Allgemeine Sprachwissenschaft*, 185, 188, speaks of 'zones' as opposed to 'points' for the sort of (functional) unity of meaning which defines the lexeme.

[29] Cf. the observation by Leech, *Semantics*, 92, that the opposites to 'woman' include 'girl' as well as 'man'; McCarthy, 'Lexis and Lexicology', 300.

stand in a relationship of functional opposition (at least from the point of view of structuralist linguistics). We have also encountered examples of Word1 in combination with other oppositions. Thus נפש is taken as 'life' rather than 'seat of the will'[30] in mBer 9:5 I (9) **[15] [82a] [114a]**. In mSot 7:6 = mTam 7:2 **[48] [54a]** one perhaps finds a reading of אל in terms of על, that is, the linguistic reverse of Word1.2 passage **[133]** above. In mSan 6:2 I (2) **[56]** the interpreter requires the very specific meaning 'confession' for the biblical *todah*, despite the parallelism with 'to give honour' in the same verse. The meaning of the particle כ is identified as 'like (this day)' rather than 'at (this day)' in mSan 10:3 IX–X (10) **[70]** and **[71]**. In passage mMak 3:10 **[8]** we encounter the biblical phrase '*by* number 40' being interpreted as meaning 'approximately 40'.[31] We have also met a case where the semantics of a formative[32] linguistic element, namely the 'infinitive', was at stake: R. Ishmael's choice of the future as part of the meaning of the infinitive form in mShebu 3:5 II (3) **[79]**.

Of some importance for an understanding of the treatment of the biblical words in the Mishnah and beyond is the rabbinic *analysis* of a complex expression into its constituent semantic parts. Such analysis, a routine part of all linguistic processing as well as linguistic description, is conspicuous where it focuses individual elements in a complex expression whose combined meaning is not merely a regular combination of the meaning of their elements. Opaque compounds are an example. In such compounds, for instance, the word 'blackmail', the semantic elements from which they are made up (here: black, mail) do not account for the meaning of the compound. There are of course also compounds whose meaning is directly related to the meaning of their constituents, for example, 'airmail'. These are said to be transparent.[33] For biblical Hebrew, the expression לחם פנים may serve as an example. Although its two constituents have meaning, the meaning of the whole expression ('bread of display' in the JPS translation) cannot be predicted on the basis of the two constituents. This is very obvious from the clearly conjectural as well as uninformative translation given by BDB (537a) as 'bread of the face' (of the Lord), supplemented by the phrase 'i.e. in his presence'; Clines (iv. 536) translates 'bread of the presence'. But one cannot turn ordinary לחם into לחם פנים by 'looking' at it, or by allowing it to be present anywhere, or by displaying it in a shop, or by shaping into it the features of a face, and so on. It is exclusively one specific type of bread, used in a certain way in a specific context, which has this

---

[30] BDB 661a (7. mental acts, 8. acts of the will, and see entry no. 10). The meaning 'life' is listed on p. 659 (3.c).

[31] BDB lists the relevant verse under the meaning: '8. of a standard of measurement or computation, with, by' (90b). Parallels in the biblical text include Lev. 25:15, 50 ('according to the number of years'); Num. 1:2 ('according to the number of names').

[32] On this term, see Bauer, *English Word-Formation*, 16 f.

[33] The examples and terminology in Bauer, *English Word-Formation*, 19. For the difference between compound and idiom, see Matthews, *Morphology*, 94 ff.

name.[34] In other words, the combination has its biblical meaning as a whole and distinct expression, its meaning is not put together from its elements, as would be the case for an expression such as 'bread of wild wheat'. Where the rabbinic interpreter prefers to analyse the meaning of such a unified expression as a combination of its semantic elements, one thus has a hermeneutic decision worth pinning down. The following passage shows how the Mishnah reads the meaning of לחם פנים in the light of its two semantic components, taken as 'bread' and '(sur)face' respectively:

[135] mMen 11:4[35]   Exod. 25:30

. . . Ben Zoma says: 'And you shall set upon the table bread of the presence [before me continually]' (לחם פנים לפני תמיד)—so that it has a face (פנים).[36]

The meaning of the phrase here translated 'so that it has a face' is problematic. However, the account following in the next *mishnah* of how the corners of the shew-breads were doubled over on both sides so as to 'face' each other furnishes some idea of what might have been meant by this. Whatever the details, it is quite clear that this explanation of the expression לחם פנים rests first on reconstituting the single semantic elements ('bread', and 'face' or 'direction'), and second, on seeing the meaning of the complex expression as consisting of a transparent combination of the two. In other words, such an interpretation is like explaining the opaque compound 'blackmail' along the lines of the transparent compound 'airmail' (for example, 'mail which puts you in a black mood'). It rests on a decision to impose a segmentation along internal semantic lines on an expression whose ordinary usage or biblical co-text suggests that it functions as a semantic whole. This is merely a special case of looking at word-forms not from the point of view of their overall meaning (which is invariably the meaning relied upon in the sentence), but from the perspective of their semantic components, whether lexical or grammatical.[37] Modern linguistics performs such analysis, for example, to find the 'morphs', that is, the smallest carriers of meaning or information. Hebrew biblical lexicography and grammar presupposes such an analysis, as well interpreting the prefixes and suffixes as 'added' to a 'stem'. It is important to see that such an analysis relates, in the first instance, functional parts of the language system as it is at any given point in time, that is, synchronically. Claims about the history of word-forms do not follow necessarily from it, and evidence on the word's history does not enter the picture. Conversely, native speakers can make connections between semantic elements of

---

[34] Cf. on the historical and theological aspects, Dommershausen and Fabry, 'lehem' (in Botterweck *et al.* (eds.), *Theological Dictionary of the Old Testament*), 525–7, who translate 'face bread(s)' (German original 'Angesichtsbrote', 543).

[35] • ¶ΔC3T5W6.1(face).

[36] Danby (p. 508) translates the Dictum: 'it shall have [all] its surfaces visible.'

[37] For a very clear example of such analysis, and a clarification of the technical meaning of terms such as 'root', 'stem', and 'base', see Bauer, *English Word-Formation*, 19–22; also Lyons, *Introduction to Theoretical Linguistics*, 180 ff. and 202 f. Lyons (p. 181) speaks of the 'segmentability of words'.

the same language which are, historically speaking, 'inaccurate' (see below).

The neat separation of synchrony and diachrony is itself a hallmark of our modern discourse on language and may well have no equivalent in the assumptions of rabbinic exegesis.[38] So it may be better not to ascribe to the rabbis a 'synchronic' view of biblical language (despite certain theological pointers in that direction). Yet etymological claims are unnecessary for the hermeneutic use made of the rabbinic analysis of biblical words into semantic units. There is no trace in the Mishnah of any attempt to use word history as hermeneutic argument, quite apart from the Mishnaic tendency to read Scripture within the horizon of its own present, as documented throughout this study. The label 'etymology' has been applied to some aspects of rabbinic hermeneutics[39] with the bizarre consequence that it needed to be qualified by the word 'folk' (that is, *false*), a tendency also present in the more flattering phrase 'creative philology' (see Chapter 1 above). But it is really unacceptable to explain what the rabbis do in terms of etymology and thereafter to say that, regrettably, they got it wrong. If they got it wrong on such a scale, a more fruitful working hypothesis is surely that they were not trying to do it. This is generally true of attempts to describe a cultural activity as a *failed* attempt to do 'X'—in particular if 'X' happens to be what we consider *ourselves* to be successful at.

Here is a description of the resource of semantic analysis:

Cotext3: Explicit or tacit analysis of the meaning of a biblical word-form, compound, idiom, or fixed collocation into its semantic components (or in the case of compounds, its word-forms).

Within the analysis of word-forms according to semantic criteria (for wider semiotic criteria, see below) there is room for differences and variation.[40] Above, when introducing passage **[135]**, I used the sign '(sur)face'. In doing this, I was suggesting that the reader move away from taking 'surface' as an integral whole, and perceive it as a word made up of two components which can be recognized as meaningful in themselves, or at least as a word (surface) which also *contains* another independent word, namely 'face'. The linguistic or historical status of such a suggestion is quite unimportant: what counts is the appearance of further *meaning*. This is the hermeneutic effect which the Cotext3 resource helps to produce: a sudden change in the way in which one perceives the semantic make-up of words, just as when

---

[38] Matthews (*Morphology*, 78–80) argues that a conceptual separation of synchrony and diachrony may be impossible, although it is important for practical purposes.

[39] Yonah Fraenkel is among the more recent scholars to classify connections made on the basis of semantic analysis and division as 'etymology'. He is aware of some problems in using this word (*Darkhey*, i. 107). But he employs the term without ado in his explanations of individual passages (e.g. i. 224) and even speaks of the Notarikon as 'etymology' (i. 114). Cf. also Heinemann, *Darkhey Ha-Aggadah*, 110 ff.

[40] For some examples of non-standard or ad hoc analysis of English words, and pragmatic limits for the analysis in modern morphology, see Matthews, *Morphology*, 18.

an ambiguous picture changes, or there is a reversal in the depth of a three-dimensional drawing.[41] These changes are sudden or surprising—they can be used to make a new point—because the integrity and semantic composition of the larger unit is not questioned in ordinary use; the ordinary use *depends* on the ability to abstract from the meaning of the components. Thus, all semantic links that can be construed within a language system, regardless of whether they are 'correct' from a systematic or from a historical point of view, form latent functional elements for native speakers of that language.[42] It is therefore to be expected that the units so identified are at times very different from components selected by the specific grammatical tradition dominating biblical Hebrew since the Middle Ages.[43] I shall therefore avoid terms such as 'root' or 'radical', as well as the terms 'morph'/'morpheme' which are defined by the methodology of modern linguistics.[44] A more neutral term is 'formative',[45] but I shall mostly use the rather vague expression 'semantic components' when speaking about the word-parts separated by this type of rabbinic analysis.

The Cotext3 resource identifies semantic tributaries to a word-form's meaning, that is, 'formatives', whose information can be ascertained from the structure of the language. But one also finds some wider semiotic structures not tied to the specific linguistic meaning of Hebrew at all, or not to it alone. The segments identified for such semiotic information do not, therefore, depend on characteristically Hebrew formatives. Instead, what one finds is that they become carriers of information by virtue of their *graphic* separation and identity within the word-form, that is, as letters of the alphabet. Hermeneutic operations of this type presuppose an internal division of word-forms by grapheme or grapheme group.[46] While all

---

[41] The so-called Necker cube is perhaps the best-known example; cf. the use of analogies of reading in Gregory, 'Illusions', 339 f.; and the articles 'Gestalt Theory' (pp. 288–91) and 'Figure–Ground' (pp. 263 f.) in the same volume. Wittgenstein draws explicit attention to the interpretative nature of such perceptional switches in *Philosophische Untersuchungen*, part II, xi (pp. 308, 320).

[42] Coseriu (*Textlinguistik*, 70) cites the French example (from the writings of Paul Claudel) of the word 'connaître' (to know) being analysed into the (linguistically unrelated) word 'naître' (to be born) and the prefix 'co-' (meaning togetherness). No knowledge of the true etymology of these two words is required to understand Claudel's conceptual point. Notable among the modern texts which have to be read with a readiness to engage in synchronic analysis of word-forms are Heidegger's (see n. 79 below). Coseriu also quotes the example of a use of the name 'Apollon' in a line from Aeschylos (*Textlinguistik*, 134); see further Lyons, *Introduction to Theoretical Linguistics*, 407, on the effect of etymological knowledge on the native speakers of a language.

[43] Cf. Wout Jac. van Bekkum, 'Deutung und Bedeutung in der hebräischen Exegese'. Here is an example of the sort of anachronism we might wish to avoid: 'It is evident from such etymologies as שעמנז ונז ושזי שזע i.e. שז + ם + נז that exegetes of the Mishnah subscribed to the theory, that was maintained until the 11th century, of biliteral and even uniliteral roots' (Rosenblatt, *The Interpretation of the Bible in the Mishnah*, 6 f., regarding mKil 9:8). All the main descriptive terms here ('etymologies', 'theory', 'biliteral/uniliteral roots') beg the historical question. My analysis of that interpretation in mKilaim is ®πC4I3W3, by the way.

[44] It is in fact not even a condition of a 'morpheme' that it can be separated out from an existing word-form as a distinct segment; it is defined through opposition (cf. Lyons, *Introduction to Theoretical Linguistics*, 182 f.).   [45] Cf. Bauer, *English Word-Formation*, 13–17.

[46] On the grapheme as the smallest unit from which the message of revelation is construed by the rabbis, see Goldberg, 'The Rabbinic View of Scripture'.

resources of the Mishnah are compatible with a setting in which the written text of Scripture was available to the interpreter, these resources may have *required* such availability. The biblical word-form thus becomes merely the outer boundary of a cluster of consonants whose semiotic constitution and grouping depends on the new semiotic system imposed, be it iconic, numeric, alphabetic by permutation, acrostic, and so on. I have formulated the following separate resource for such a semiotic (as opposed to semantic) division of a word-form:

Cotext4: Explicit or tacit analysis of the meaning of a biblical word-form or expression according to the semiotic meaning (see GRAPHEME/ICON) attached to its constituent graphemes, individually or in groups.

This preliminary step of breaking down a biblical word-form into related components *below the linguistic level of the word*, that is, interpreted as mere graphemes or grapheme clusters, is of fundamental importance for resources which address wider semiotic (rather than narrowly linguistic) possibilities of meaning. Although there are some Mishnaic examples, this type of operation is of much greater importance in other works of rabbinic literature. A number of traditional *middot* or hermeneutic rules presuppose the Cotext4 resource. Among them are at least some of the operations going under the names *notarikon, gematria, al tiqrey*, and *atbash*. I will give a list of semiotic procedures in the next section.

The Cotext3 and Cotext4 resources are complemented by the dissolution of syntactic collocations (Cotext2) whose hermeneutic effect I discussed earlier in connection with the Redundancy9 resource (Chapter 13).

In the next passage an imposition of semantic analysis (Cotext3) is applied to a biblical *name*.

[136] mMid 4:7[47]   Isa. 29:1

And the sanctuary (ההיכל) was narrow at the back and wide at the front, resembling a lion, as it is said, 'Ho, Ariel, Ariel, city where David encamped'—as a lion is narrow at the back and wide at the front, so the sanctuary was narrow at the back and wide at the front.

This interpretation endows the biblical name 'Ariel' (lit. 'lion of God'), applied to the city of Jerusalem, with an iconic significance. Why the word should be taken to refer to the sanctuary building, rather than Jerusalem as a whole (or only the altar), is not clear to me.[48] The word Ariel (in the *qere'*) is applied to the altar hearth, for example in Ezek. 43:15 f. (cf. mMid 3:1), and so translated in the Targum of Isaiah, which renders the opening phrase here as, 'Woe O altar, altar which was built in the city in which David . . .'. Still, since the altar (hearth) is different from the sanctuary build-

[47] ®C1C3(S3?)T1W9.
[48] Cf. however, Abrahams, *By-Paths in Hebraic Bookland*, 362 f. On the various items referred to by the proper name Ariel, see Clines, i. 377b; all occurrences in Isa. 29 are given as 'place name Ariel, i.e. Jerusalem'; cf. BDB 72a.

ing, the *heykhal*, this does not solve the problem. The features which the object 'temple building' receives from the appellation Ariel are iconic; they have to do with the physical shape of a lion. But one only gets there by way of the *semantic* contents of the name, suitably subdivided into semantic components in this case (resource Cotext3). A proper name however functions differently from other words; its special characteristic is to denote 'rigidly', to use a formulation employed in recent philosophical linguistics.[49] This means it refers to items not by virtue of its meaning but by virtue of a naming convention. It seems that, from the point of view of their linguistic name-function, 'proper names do not have sense'.[50] The common noun 'carpenter' refers to a person by way of its meaning, as when one says 'The carpenter has just gone up to the second floor'. But the proper name 'Carpenter' identifies a person so named regardless of whether he is a carpenter; and a man may be called 'Israel' whether or not he wrestled with God, while many people called 'Petit' are taller than the average person. It is therefore a distinct hermeneutic movement to reflect on the *semantic* contents of biblical names,[51] and it is useful to define this movement as a resource in its own right.

Word9: Identification of a meaning for a biblical proper name in terms of the meaning of its semantic component(s).

Exploring in a narrative manner the meaning of proper names is one of the most frequent and important metalinguistic structures found within the Hebrew Bible, and plays a prominent role in rabbinic and targumic literature.[52] In the Mishnah, however, the biblical concern with names finds its most direct continuation not in the semantic analysis of names of biblical heroes, but of names of earlier sages or figures of rabbinic tradition. Our passage **[135]** is the only clear example of a biblical name being analysed semantically in the Mishnah, while there are at least five cases of such analysis for non-biblical names of persons or objects.[53]

---

[49] The expression 'rigid designator' is used by Kripke, *Naming and Necessity*, 48 ff.; see also Searle, *Speech Acts*, 162–74; Evans, *Varieties of Reference*, ch. 11.

[50] Lyons, *Semantics*, i. 198; Lyons explains the issues very clearly on pp. 216 ff. Cf. Kripke, *Naming and Necessity*, 26.

[51] For our Mishnaic case it may not be unimportant that Isa. 29:2 uses the word like a common noun, with the definite article ('you shall be to me like the Ariel').

[52] On naming as a performative act, see Lyons, *Semantics*, i. 218. For rabbinic literature, see Heinemann, *Darkhey Ha-Aggadah*, 110 ff.; Böhl, 'Name und Typologie'; id., 'On the Interpretation of Names'; Cashdan, 'Names and the Interpretation of Names in the Pseudo-Jonathan Targum to the Book of Genesis'. For the biblical cases, see e.g. Jackson, *Studies in the Semiotics of Biblical Law*, sec. 2.2.

[53] They are mSheq 5:1 (cf. Albeck, *Einführung*, 181); mSheq 6:3 I–II (2); mSot 9:15 I (2); mMid 2:6.

GRAPHIC AND SEMIOTIC DERIVATIONS
OF MEANING

The first section of this chapter was devoted to the manner in which the semantic range of a given word-form, if seen in isolation, is utilized by the Mishnaic exegete. We now turn to cases where the exegete establishes links between word-forms of different appearance, and thus extends the range of meaning to lexemes or roots which are, from the point of Hebrew lexicography, not linked. Here is an example:

[137] mMak 3:15 I (4)[54]   Deut. 25:3

All guilty of extirpation who have received lashes (שלקו) are saved from their extirpation, as it is said, '[. . . lest, if one should continue to beat him with more than these stripes, much] dishonoured (ונקלה) will be your brother in your eyes'—from when he has received lashes (משלקה), behold he is like your brother—the words of R. Hananiah ben Gamliel.

The previous verse speaks of the person receiving the lashes as 'wicked', while this verse calls him 'brother'. This is picked up as a significant shift in the word choice (Difference6, see Chapter 10). It goes hand in hand with an interpretation of the word-form נקלה in the light of the word-form לקה. The first means 'dishonoured, degraded', the second 'lashed'.[55] If we place the meaning which we are explicitly given as synonym into the sentence environment of 'dishonoured', ignore the fact that this is part of a clause containing a purpose, and adjust the co-textual relationships in the concluding part of the sentence, we obtain: having been lashed, he is (again) a brother for you. This is translated into the concrete thematic concern of the Mishnaic passage as saying: he again has, as all the brotherhood of Israel, a share in the world to come (cf. mSan 10:1 [82]; cf. mSan 6:2 I–II (2) [56]/[57b]). But how is the meaning 'lashed' linked to the word-form for 'dishonoured'? The answer is that there is some overlap *in appearance*. The two verbs share the same consonants (*qof, lamed, he* and *lamed, qof, he*), merely their sequence is different. The one can be obtained from the other by *metathesis*.[56]

There are several aspects to be distinguished here: the segmentation of the word-form along the lines of consonants (i.e. the Cotext3 resource defined above), and the matching of the pool of consonants (not their sequence) with that of an entirely different word. It is this partial matching

---

[54] ◊•¶®C3D6G1T1T3W3.

[55] For this rabbinic meaning of the word, see Albeck, *Einführung*, 216.

[56] There remains some doubt here, because the resource is not made quite explicit. It is just possible, as Krauß obviously thinks (*Sanhedrin-Makkot*, 375), that the identification of 'being disgraced' and 'being lashed' is considered so strong that the one is simply read as the other. The co-text of the above *mishnah* allows such an interpretation because it speaks of the condemned as 'being disgraced' (ונתקלקל) by his bodily functions while receiving the punishment. But is it really assumed that *every* condemned must become disgraced in this way?

of consonants which I shall take as the defining moment of the resource; but it has quite a variety of forms, apart from the metathesis illustrated in **[137]**. Here is the general mechanism, the umbrella-resource, so to speak:

Word3: Explication of a biblical word-form in the light of the meaning of a partially similar word-form (belonging to a different lexeme). The word-form is thus taken in independence from its limitations in the biblical co-text, and in turn calls for an adjustment of the co-textual relationships or for their active suspension.

The manner in which the word-forms are 'similar' can be described in more detail, and some of these distinct procedures have names in rabbinic literature. The following is a somewhat systematic differentiation into groups, whose codes indicate what *type* of Word3 resource applies. They form the GRAPHEME family of resources:

Grapheme1: metathesis of consonants, illustrated by **[137]** above.[57]

Grapheme2:[58] graphic similarity of consonants (e.g. *dalet* and *resh*).[59]

Grapheme3: partial overlap of consonants between the word forms (for example, two out of three consonants are the same).

Grapheme4: similarity or identity of sound (e.g. לא versus לו;[60] interchange of final *kaf* and *het*,[61] etc.).

Grapheme5: alternative vocalization of the same consonants producing a different word-form.[62]

The rabbinic term *al tiqrey*, usually rendered by the phrase 'Do not read X, but read Y', seems to cover both cases of Grapheme5 and of Grapheme3 outside the Mishnah;[63] in the Mishnah the term is not used. As far as vo-

---

[57]   See Geiger, *Urschrift*, 305 for an example of metathesis of letters as accounting for a change in the biblical text (linked to Lev. 18:21 and similar passages). The presence of the Grapheme1 resource in the Mishnaic configuration of resources does not depend on **[137]** alone; it also seems necessary for explaining mSukkah 4:5.

[58]   This resource is never spelled out explicitly in the Mishnah, and the same result could be achieved on the basis of a Word1.2 interpretation of the enclitics concerned. See mShab 9:2 I (2), mTaan 1:2 **[114]**, and mMak 3:10 **[8]**.

[59]   The role of such similarity of consonants in modifications of the biblical text (not in its hermeneutic treatment) is stressed frequently in Geiger, *Urschrift*; see e.g. 269, 302.

[60]   In mSot 5:5 I (2), contrasting the *ketiv* and the *qere* of Job 13:15. Whether or not this amounts to identity of sound, or merely its similarity, depends of course on the difference between speakers, regions, and periods of Hebrew. I have formulated the main resource as including both alternatives, identity and similarity; sub-categories of Grapheme4 can easily be introduced in cases for which firm evidence is available from the rabbinic formulation of the interpretation.

[61]   mBek 7:5 II (4), ascribed to R. Ishmael: the person characterized by the *hapax legomenon* אשך מרוח in Lev. 21:20 is identified as כל שנמרכו אשכיו.

[62]   mSot 5:2 is perhaps the only clear example.

[63]   See e.g. Bacher, i. 175 f.; as is clear from Bacher's examples, the formula covers at least three quite different equivalences: that between two different vocalizations of the same cluster of consonants; that between two words which—often depending on the phonetic distinctions between gutturals—sound alike or identical but are spelled differently (homophone); and that between words which use

calization is concerned, the name *al tiqrey* itself suggests that a prior vocalization exists which is being *altered*; and that may indicate that a vocalization (presumably often identical with the one now known as Masoretic) was accepted as default word-form, that is, as giving semantic unity and identity to the cluster of consonants. As was said before, often a whole range of phenomena is covered by one rabbinic term or *middah*. The different procedures can either be functional alternatives, or can appear together in clusters (in which case it may not be easy to see which resource is actually named by the rabbinic term).

There is another group of resources linking word-forms of disparate meaning. These, just as resources of the GRAPHEME group, take the cluster of consonants chosen as the Lemma as signs. However, they do not understand them as signs only in the defined language system Hebrew. Beyond the confines of language, or the confines of Hebrew, these consonants are endowed with wider semiotic significance in the following dimensions:[64]

[Icon1]: transformative alphabet (*atbash* or *gematria*).

[Icon2]: numerical value of the consonants transformed into a new word (*gematria*).[65]

Icon2.1: numerical value of the letters taken as number.[66]

Icon3: acronym (*notarikon*).

*Icon4: iconic value (i.e. shape of the letter).[67]

Icon5: symbolic representation (defined further below).

[Icon6]: language system other than Hebrew.[68]

These are some but not all of the semiotic transformations one finds in rabbinic literature (those not found in the Mishnah are again marked by the use of brackets). They have in common with each other (and are opposed to the GRAPHEME resources in this respect) that the mechanism by which the lemmatic word-form is taken to represent meaning is not specifically linguistic (or not with regard to Hebrew, in the case of Icon6). The basic

the same consonants, but in different sequence (and yet also sound similar). Bacher also cites an interpretation where the structure of the whole sentence is affected and yet it is introduced with this formula, p. 176 (Sifre Deut. ad Deut. 11:21).

[64] Cf. Lieberman, *Hellenism*, 70 ff.

[65] Cf. Fraenkel, *Darkhey*, i. 132–7.

[66] On the example in mUqtsin 3:12 I (2), cf. also Maimonides' *Commentary*, who employs the words 'gematria' and 'remez' ad loc. The textual status of this unit at the end of the tractate (Ω) is questionable, cf. Albeck, *Einführung*, 182.

[67] The relationship here labelled 'iconic' is quite complex, and not restricted to graphic signs (I have used the word above to explain the way in which the temple and the lion are linked in [136]). This is clearly an area that needs some further distinctions; see Samely, 'Between Scripture and its Rewording', 41. An orientation is offered by Lyons, *Semantics*, i. 102 ff.; also Coseriu, *Textlinguistik*, 82–8. The only Mishnaic example is mPes 9:2 II (2), where one of the *puncta extraordinaria* is endowed with topical meaning.

[68] See Fraenkel, *Darkhey*, i. 115–18.

function of the consonants as representing a *word* is dissolved—although the word-form is still usually respected as providing the *boundary* for the cluster of consonants. It is not that the biblical words are taken, *as words*, to be like some other words. Rather, the biblical word-form is first transformed into an entity consisting of a cluster of graphic signs, or numbers, or shapes, before meaning is attached to it (even if that meaning again is represented as a—different—word, as in the case of Icon1–2, Icon6).

The Icon3 resource treats a word-form as acronym, where each letter represents a full new word (or part of a word, or a phrase). This is known in rabbinic literature as *notarikon*.[69] This word is used in the Mishnah only in the meaning of 'abbreviation'.[70] It seems that Icon3 is explicitly applied in the Mishnah only once, in mKil 9:8.[71]

It is important to note that for this group of resources the Mishnaic passages do not provide *enough* material to decided which feature is central, which is necessary, or which is superfluous and plays no role independently. The relevant material in the Mishnah seems both scarcer and less differentiated than that which we see outside the Mishnah. This means that the distinctions within the GRAPHEME and ICON groups and their definitions (such as they are) need to be revisited in the context of resources emerging from a much larger corpus of this type of interpretation. By such comparison one should be able to see whether it is significant, in the Mishnah, that a high percentage of the few occurrences of the GRAPHEME and ICON resources is concentrated in the same interpretations. If this concentration in clusters is significant, it could mean that the separating out of independently operating resources came after the Mishnaic material received its shape.

ACTIVATING AND NEUTRALIZING METAPHORICAL MEANING

Metaphors have the power to convey linguistic messages which are fully adapted to the context of their use, and to convey them sometimes with a degree of irreducible implicitness.[72] The meanings which a word has when used metaphorically cannot be exhaustively listed, or even anticipated at

---

[69] See mKil 9:8 I (2) ad Deut. 22:11 (*sha'atnez*). Cf. Fraenkel, *Darkhey*, i. 125–31.
[70] Cf. e.g. Bacher, i. 125 ff. The expression occurs in mShab 12:5 (נוטריקון אחת אות כתב) in the sense of 'abbreviated word'.
[71] Depending on how narrow the definition of the Icon3 resource is taken, this passage contains one or two Icon3 interpretations (of the same Lemma). There is a second, doubtful, Mishnaic location: mSot 9:9 II (2).
[72] See on this the literature quoted in n. 19 of Ch. 7; see also ch. 7 in Taylor, *Linguistic Categorization* (pp. 122 ff.), and Lakoff and Johnson, *Metaphors We Live By*. Mary Hesse, speaking from a different perspective, says, 'Scientific concepts . . . can best be understood in terms of a more radical analysis of metaphoric meaning in language in general. I shall not here repeat the arguments for regarding metaphor as all-pervasive in language . . .' ('Theories, Family Resemblances and Analogy', 322); see also her 'Texts Without Types and Lumps Without Laws', 45 f.

all, by a dictionary.[73] They belong wholly to the productive side of language, another manifestation of which is that the number of possible sentences cannot be exhaustively listed. The meaning conveyed with such 'live' metaphors need not be capable of 'translation' into non-metaphorical language; the live metaphor can be interpreted, but it may remain inexhaustible in its meaning. As a latently productive source it is like a model or analogy: transcending its original 'point', it retains a potential to offer new insights, even to its author.[74] On the other hand, much of our vocabulary consist of words whose *main* and conventional meaning is in some way figurative. Such 'dead' metaphors, enshrined in many idioms and standing phrases, have a meaning which is conventionally circum-scribed and can be treated in regular fashion by lexicography. In many cases multiple meanings or polysemes within a 'lexeme' have a semantic nuance which can be understood as metaphorical in relation to other mean-ings in the same entry.[75] However, the very expressions 'live' and 'dead' incorporate a historical perspective (in addition to being metaphorical themselves). We tend to think of the concrete meaning as being there first, and the figurative meaning as a secondary development. Clearly, we feel, English could not have had the word 'leg of table' *before* using the word 'leg' of living things; table legs are so called because of an analogy to the legs of animals or men, not the other way round.[76] Yet the two types of 'leg' are now available in the language simultaneously. Their two meanings are dis-tinguished by the collocations (that is, co-textual relationships) they can enter into and their situational context of use, not by chronological priority. As for frequency of occurrence, priority often goes to the 'secondary' mean-ings.[77] There may in fact be no conventional 'primary' meaning for the particular word-form. We seem to encounter the term 'grass roots', for

[73] I. A. Richards makes this point with regard to the following lines: '(But) she looks like sleep, As she would catch another Antony, In her strong toil of grace' (from the last scene of Shakespeare's *Antony and Cleopatra*). He asks: 'Where, in terms of what entries of what possible dictionary, do the meanings here of *toil* and *grace* come to rest?' (*Philosophy of Rhetoric*, 49). Cf. also Levinas, 'Meaning and Sense' (in *Collected Philosophical Papers*, 75 ff.), who calls metaphor 'the reference to absence' (p. 77).

[74] See esp. Black, *Models and Metaphors*, 25–47. The link between metaphor and analogy is made in Aristotle, *Rhetoric*, 1411a f. It is of some interest that recent psychological research suggests that checking the 'metaphorical' option for any expression may be an automatic part of the processing of language. See Holyoak and Thagard, *Mental Leaps*, 218–19.

[75] The difference between the resource Word1 and the resources to be defined in this section (in particular Word6) does not reside in the word meanings as perceived by us; it lies in the aspect on which the rabbinic interpretations concentrates. If the interpreter selects from the polysemes of a word one which is different from that privileged in the co-text, and the one selected happens to be a conventional figurative meaning, this is a case of Word1. If the hermeneutic movement *links* concrete and figurative meaning for the same word, then we have a case of Word6, and similarly for the case where a figurative meaning is de-selected in favour of a concrete one. See below.

[76] Cf. *Shorter OED*, i. 1196 ('Something more or less like a leg in shape or function'). I. A. Richards also says of this particular metaphor, 'We call it dead but it comes to life very readily' (*Philosophy of Rhetoric*, 127). For the biblical רֶגֶל (on which see below) as used of tables, see Exod. 25:26, 37:13.

[77] But now Clines's *Dictionary of Classical Hebrew* lists the metaphorical meaning first if this is the word's most frequent use (i. 10, 19).

example, only in social or political contexts, not in horticultural ones.[78] This shows that connecting the term 'grass roots' with its literal meaning is a hermeneutic step, a treatment *sui generis*; it does not provide an account of the word's 'history' or 'original' meaning. But the same would be true *if* there was a horticultural (that is, 'literal') use for 'grass roots'; we would still be concerned with establishing a semantic link between two separate but simultaneous items of our vocabulary. We would go sideways, not back in time, in a manner of speaking. And for a case like 'grass roots', an explanation of its concrete meaning amounts to a *revival* of its metaphorical power. This is of particular interest when that revival is applied to the topic as defined by the *conventional* (that is, figurative) meaning of 'grass roots', i.e. defined by the meaning of the 'dead' metaphor. This is what happens in one of the main hermeneutic resources to be dealt with presently.[79] It explores a point of similarity between the object referred to by the conventional metaphor and the same object referred to by the metaphor's concrete sense.

Biblical language offers a considerable number of terms for which a lexicalized figurative and a non-figurative meaning co-exist, that is, 'dead' metaphors in the sense clarified above. Take the word 'house' (בית), used in co-texts where its meaning must be 'household, family' or ' slaves' (BDB, 109b); or the word 'foot', used only in the plural (רגלים, as opposed to the dual) with the meaning 'times' (BDB, 920a); or the idea of a 'burnt offering' (עולה) which shares its verbal realization with a word meaning 'going up', paralleled by the case of the 'heave offering' (*terumah*) whose 'other' meaning is linked to the idea of the physical movement of lifting. All these examples of conventionalized metaphorical meaning in biblical Hebrew receive hermeneutic attention in the Mishnah.[80] In most of these interpretations the metaphorical sense is not replaced by the concrete one, but is complemented by it. The hermeneutic movement consists of applying a concrete reading of the term *to the same subject* to which the figurative or abstract one applies. However, in sustaining both the conventional figurative meaning and the concrete meaning, the metaphorical power of the expression is revived. The procedure points to a sense[81] in which the

[78] The word did not exist before coming into use in its metaphorical meaning; the 1973 edition of the *Shorter OED* has it in the 'Addenda' section (ii. 2632). It is of course perfectly possible that native speakers of English will now adopt the meaning 'grass roots' also for horticultural purposes (along the lines of a transparent compound, such as 'airmail', see above).

[79] Cf. Fraenkel, *Darkhey*, i. ch. 8 (*Ha-Allegoristiqah*); issues of terminology (allegory, metaphor) are addressed on pp. 197 and also ii. 613, n. 1. He also has a section on the 'pun' (i. 436 ff.). Heidegger has the following aside on his use of 'literal' or etymological meanings: 'If we now translate *"aletheia"* not by "truth" but by "non-hiddenness", the translation is not merely more "literal", but contains the instruction to think and turn back, from the familiar concept of truth taken as the correctness of a statement, to that as yet ungrasped openness and opening of being' (*Vom Wesen der Wahrheit*, 15; my translation). This is very similar to the rabbinic procedure described here as Word6.1.

[80] That they receive attention in a concrete textual setting, and are not addressed as lexical items in isolation, is important.

[81] Again, it is necessary to avoid preconceptions about the etymologically 'correct' way being the only way to connect the meanings. Our example [138] is a case in point.

metaphor, *beyond* convention, hits the mark, or highlights a (specific) feature of the subject-matter. As in the resources discussed in earlier sections of this chapter, the biblical co-text's effect in narrowing these words down to their conventional meaning (their 'dead metaphor' meaning) is neutralized. The resulting larger meaning potential is utilized by the interpreter to make the word speak about the topic *in a different way*. But, in contrast to the Word1 resources, the overall topic of its biblical sentence environment is retained and built upon: the conventionalized meaning of the term, together with its co-text where necessary, is taken to identify the subject-matter of the sentence.

The hermeneutic revival of the metaphorical power inherent in conventional figurative usage can be shown with particular clarity in cases where the expression is allocated a *fresh* figurative meaning by the rabbis. The following passage provides extra meaning for the very common biblical word עולה,[82] which I mentioned above as being the name of one type of sacrifice, the burnt offering:

[138] mZeb 9:1 I (2)[83]   Lev. 6:2 (E 9)

The altar sanctifies that which is suitable for it. R. Yehoshua says: All that is suitable for the [altar] fires, if it has gone up (אם עלה), it does not come down, as it is said, '[This is the law of the burnt offering:] The burnt offering (העלה) itself shall be on the hearth upon the altar [all night until morning, while the fire on the altar is kept going on it]'.

We shall not deal with the analogical extension to all types of sacrifices suggested by R. Yehoshua (Analogy8); nor with the point of the subsequent dispute with Rabban Gamliel (not translated here).[84] We shall concentrate entirely on the interpretation presupposed by R. Yehoshua: that at least in the case of the burnt offering, Scripture *tells* us (no need for analogy here) that what goes up must stay up. The root עלה makes its appearance in this Mishnaic text in two ways: as a word for the concrete physical movement of the sacrificial parts onto the altar hearth (contrasted with their coming down from there) and as a noun for burnt offering. But it effects also a third meaning: the *elevation in sanctity*,[85] which is defined as irreversible. In the words of the anonymous opening statement, the altar 'sanctifies', and here as in other halakhic contexts sanctification is envisaged as a level which allows only upward, not downward, movement.[86] It is this meaning which explains why something that has 'gone up' cannot come 'down' again. The

[82] BDB (750a) gives the number of occurrences as 286.

[83] •¶≈C5.2C5E1.2O1O8T2W6.2 (A8?).

[84] As so often, it is not easy to disentangle the hermeneutic core in this passage from the issues actually thematic in it, and even less from the issues made thematic in the post-Mishnaic discussions on it. They are ramified indeed; see in particular the Gemara (bZeb 83a/b), Maimonides' *Commentary* (trans. Qafih, *Qodashim-Tohorot*, 46 f.), and Rashi ad bZeb 83a.

[85] Cf. Jastrow, 1081b (s.v. עלי). On this passage, see also Friedman, 'The Holy Scriptures Defile the Hands', 123, 128 f.

[86] Cf. the rabbinic saying, מעלין בקדש ואין מורידין.

semantic opposition of the concrete movements (going up/coming down) alone could not account for this, for the opposition does not disallow their occurring one *after* the other.[87]

So, what happens to the biblical word עולה is this: it is sufficiently isolated from its use in the biblical co-text to allow an activation of its concrete meaning ('going up'). This 'going up' is used in turn in a different figurative sense belonging to the language of the rabbis, namely, as applying to the one-directional movement of the degrees of holiness. The original 'dead' metaphor is read as a second metaphor with fixed conventional meaning, but by route of examining afresh the *concrete* sense for its metaphorical potential. And as in many cases of Word1, the fresh information thus unlocked[88] is applied *within the semantic framework* dictated by the conventional biblical meaning of the word, that is, by the original biblical co-text. (The relevant information on holiness—it only 'goes up'—is applied to the object—the burnt offering—as defined by the biblical *conventional* meaning of 'going up'/עולה.) Earlier I drew attention to the fact that there may be a connection between this treatment of metaphors and the interpretation of explicit biblical comparisons as indicating shared class membership, that is, total identity in a relevant perspective, rather than partial similarity.[89]

I shall distinguish two versions of this resource, according to whether the metaphorical potential is unlocked to apply in a *concrete* sense (Word6.1, of which the next passage is an illustration), or whether a different metaphorical sense is adduced, as in [138]:

Word6.2: Explication of a biblical word-form whose co-text suggests one figurative meaning as conveying a different figurative meaning, in the following manner: (1) the new figurative meaning applies to the subject-matter as determined by the figurative meaning privileged by the biblical co-text; (2) it is thus integrated into the sentence or wider co-text to some extent; (3) the new figurative meaning can only be derived from the biblical figurative meaning by way of a consideration of the concrete meaning of the word; (4) the concrete meaning cannot be focused unless the co-textual determination of the biblical word as figurative is initially or partly suspended.

Word6.1: Explication of a biblical word-form in terms of a concrete meaning whose biblical co-text privileges a figurative (or figurative-idiomatic) meaning. The word-form is thus taken in independence from the biblical co-text, but is nevertheless applied to the subject-matter as determined by

---

[87] BDB (740a) has here an elaborate and theological paraphrase, which links the dead metaphor to the concrete meaning ('ascent of the soul in worship')—a hermeneutic updating, in fact.

[88] The Prague School approach to poetics speaks of a 'de-automatization' of language by the artist. This concept may well be useful in pursuing further the nature of the resource Word6.2. Cf. Coseriu, *Textlinguistik*, 111 ('entautomatisierte Sprache'); Lotmann, *The Structure of the Artistic Text*, 69 ff.

[89] See Ch. 13 (definition of Syntax7) and Ch. 8 (definition of Analogy3).

the biblical co-text (and the figurative meaning); it therefore calls in turn for a partial adjustment of the co-textual relationships or their suspension.

For the latter resource an example is provided by the Mishnaic treatment of biblical רגלים, mentioned above as a 'dead' metaphor of Scripture. This biblical plural of foot (רגל), appears in the phrase 'three times', in a biblical sentence dealing with the three pilgrimage festivals. Although in this case the hermeneutic treatment in the Mishnah does not provide a *new* metaphorical dimension, its selection of the concrete meaning for the subject-matter of the sentence still has the effect of reviving the metaphorical force:

[139] mHag 1:1[90]   Exod. 23:14

All are obliged to 'appear' (Exod. 32:17; cf. Deut. 16:16) [in Jerusalem], except for a deaf-mute, an insane person, and a minor . . . (and) anyone who cannot go up on foot. Who is [considered] a minor? Everyone who cannot ride on the shoulders of his father so as to go up from Jerusalem to the temple mount—these are the words of the House of Shammai. And the House of Hillel say: Everyone who cannot hold on to the hand of his father and go up from Jerusalem to the temple mount, as it is said, 'three רגלים (times/feet/pilgrimages) [in the year shall you celebrate to me]'.

The concrete meaning ('foot') attached to the word רגלים ('times') appears in the opening sentence of this passage, in the phrase 'cannot go up *on foot*' (ברגליו) and in the opinion of the Hillelites the inability to walk on foot, even with support from the father, provides the defining point of minority with regard to this obligation. Although they do not use the expression 'on foot', the notion is implied in the use of the verb 'go up' in combination with the holding of hands, and in the use of the biblical quotation. The Lemma רגלים in the quotation now must be read as containing the idea of 'on foot', otherwise the Mishnaic passage is incoherent. We cannot read the Lemma as 'three feet', but we can construct something like this for the biblical clause: 'three foot-festivals in the year you shall celebrate to me.' But whichever is the exact construction, it is clear that the word רגלים is taken to be part and parcel of the topic 'pilgrimage'—in fact, in rabbinic Hebrew that is one of its meanings.[91] Thus its link with the topic as defined by the biblical sentence (and its co-text) is maintained, and that means its conventional meaning is also retained. (How the rabbis defined that meaning is not actually clear from this passage, but they are certain to have been aware of Exod. 23:17 employing פעמים in place of רגלים in Exod. 23:14.)[92] At the same time, the latent concrete meaning of רגלים, involving the notion of feet, is activated to

---

[90] •¶C1(H6)O0O1R3.1T1W6.1.

[91] For the rabbinic usage (also in the singular), cf. Jastrow, 1449a; Albeck, *Einführung*, 356.

[92] In Deut. 16:16, the word פעמים is also used instead of רגלים (it is also used, but without link to pilgrimage, in Num. 22:28, 32, 33). König, *Hebräisches und aramäisches Wörterbuch zum Alten Testament*, 431b, actually suggests a metonymical link between the appearance of the pilgrim in Jerusalem three 'times' a year, and the 'foot' meaning, producing the following chain of meaning extensions: foot—trace of foot—print—trace—indication of presence (presence).

contribute *further* information on the theme as given by the biblical sentence—but for activating the concrete meaning the co-textual relationships have to be selectively suspended, as in the Word1 resource.

It may be noted here that this hermeneutic movement (applying the concrete meaning to the topic as defined by the figurative meaning) is easily combined with an increase in specificity: the Mishnah may be concerned with only a sub-topic of the biblical topic, which makes this resource ideal for combination with the Topic2 resource, that is, the link to a case schema.

Among the Mishnaic examples for this hermeneutic resource is also mPeah 8:9 IV (4), where blindness of the eyes is ascribed to the bribe-taking judge (whose biblical 'blindness' is linked to his bias in judgement). But there are also interpretations which consider the concrete sense on its own, and as separate from the conventionalized figurative meaning. A case in point is the biblical expression 'pay of a dog', which, in parallel to the 'fee of a whore', is not to be used to finance the purchase of offerings. Here is the biblical verse in its setting, Deut. 23:18 f., in the JPS translation: 'No Israelite women shall be a cult prostitute, nor shall any Israelite man be a cult prostitute. (19) You shall not bring the fee of a whore or the pay of a dog[93] into the house of the Lord your God in fulfilment of any vow, for both are abhorrent to the Lord your God.' The co-text suggests quite strongly that 'dog' here has a meaning different from four-legged canine, and the modern dictionaries and translators follow its lead.[94] The Mishnah, on the other hand, reads the meaning as 'dog', and that means that there is no metaphorical dimension, no semantic comparison, and also no fresh interaction and adjustment of the co-textual relationships after initial suspension.

[140] mTem 6:3 I (3)[95]   Deut. 23:19 (E 18)

What is the 'price of a dog'? If someone said to his fellow, Here, take this lamb for this dog. And similar two joint owners who divided [their possessions], if one takes ten [lambs] and the other takes nine and a dog: the ones opposite the dog are forbidden, those together with the dog are allowed.

The question asked here concerns the meaning of a term which appears in a preceding Mishnaic list (§), where it was used as Mishnaic expression (π). It is here answered, as so often in the Mishnah, by a case schema (Topic2) which demonstrates how the concept is applied. But the case schema, although merely using and not defining the word 'dog', shows very clearly that the dog of the biblical norm is taken to be the four-legged animal. Accordingly, there is no metaphorical potential to be unlocked, as there

---

[93] The translators explain in a footnote: 'male prostitute' (p. 310).

[94] Clines, iv. 415: 'servant—sometimes temple servant, hierodule', translating our passage as 'hire of a (temple) servant'; BDB, 477a 'name given to male temple-prostitutes'. Margalith, 'Keleb: Homonym or Metaphor?', 494, argues that the word is not a metaphorical extension of 'dog', but a regular synonym for 'slave/servant'.

[95] §πC1R4.1T1T2W5(W1).

would be if the Mishnah understood 'dog' as an expression for a male temple servant or prostitute and applied the idea of a concrete dog *within that sphere*.[96] As for the links to the other words in the biblical sentence and beyond, they are grammatically sustained but thematically suspended; or, put differently, the two items 'pay of a dog' and 'fee of a whore' are made to speak to two quite different topics, instead of merely expressing the same idea twice to cover both genders (which double coverage is already available in analogy to verse 18 anyway). In other words, there is a distribution of redundancy (see Chapter 13) in the passage, in addition to a concrete interpretation of a word used as metaphor. Although perhaps more manifest in [140], redundancy is also a concern in the other two passages discussed above. In [138] the biblical sentence is full of repetitions, which include the word 'burnt offering' itself. And in [139] the verse (Exod. 23:14) is a 'heading' for a three-verse section which lists the pilgrimage festivals and ends in a 'summary'. That summary (verse 17) is quite similar to verse 14,[97] except that it uses the word פעמים, making the use of רגלים in verse 14 doubly conspicuous and redundant. Thus, all of these cases show that the neutralization of co-text which is necessary to gain access to the concrete sense of a metaphor can go hand in hand with increasing the number of topics in the biblical passage to forestall redundancy.

Here is a description of the hermeneutic move found in [140]:

Word5: Explication of a biblical word-form, in independence from the figurative (or figurative-idiomatic) meaning privileged by the biblical co-text, in terms of a concrete meaning without direct relation to the subject-matter as determined through the figurative meaning.

In other words, the application of this resource imposes a new perspective or topic on the biblical segment, as seen in [140] above.

Linking a metaphorical sense to a concrete sense is also presupposed where biblical words become the basis of some physical symbol or representation. For example, the Mishnah speaks of the symbolic representation of the bitterness of Egyptian bondage by the bitter herbs of the Seder (mPes 10:5 I (2)); in this case the hermeneutic move links the wording of two biblical passages (Exod. 12:8 and 1:14). The remaining Mishnaic passages of this type concern the Yom Kippur ritual of the scapegoat. There are brief reports of a strip of crimson having been tied to the animal (mShab 9:3 III (3)) and/or to the door of the sanctuary (mYoma 6:8). Both reports are linked to a promise in Isa. 1:18 that, even if the Israelites' sins were as red as scarlet/crimson, forgiveness will make them as white as snow/wool. In all

---

[96] The same can happen when only the larger co-text (not the immediate sentence environment of a word) shows that the usage is metaphorical, as in the case of Ezek. 23:48 ('And all the women shall take warning not to imitate your wantonness'). The links of this verse to its co-text are neutralized in mSot 1:6 in that the verse is taken to speak on the topic of adultery (Word5, Topic2).

[97] See the use of the word *inclusio* for such biblical structures, Fishbane, *Biblical Interpretation in Ancient Israel*, 30 (and index).

of these cases the representative act or thing is in turn presented by the words of the Mishnaic report. Such verbal formulation is of course crucial for bringing out the concrete-metaphorical relationship, for the physical object itself can be perceived or used without making any linguistic connection. The following is an attempt to extract the hermeneutic aspect of translating biblical words into symbolic representations, verbally expressed. It is allocated to the ICON family of resources because the representational relationships impute semiotic functions to objects.

Icon5: Description or prescription of a symbolic representation of the concrete sense of a biblical word-form whose co-text privileges a figurative (or figurative-idiomatic) meaning. (Cf. Word5.)

All of our resources linked to the hermeneutics of metaphor share two features. First, they make no distinction between 'live' and 'dead' metaphors in the biblical text. The reason for this may well be that, for the rabbinic readers of Scripture, there are no 'live' metaphors in the text, if such a distinction was made at all. Biblical Hebrew is a finite linguistic system, represented in a body of texts whose lexemes and collocations can be exhaustively catalogued and conventionalized by constant rereading. Even the most unusual poetic imagery must eventually become part of the passive, maybe even active, fixed vocabulary of the readers in a society which puts a high premium on constant study of the text. And there is, of course, no trace of an attempt to put the distinction into a historical context, as by asking: was this phrase already a cliché by the time biblical author X wrote? And the modern historical approach, which does ask this question, finds that its evidence is often quite insufficient to make a decision. Even if this were otherwise, however, the distinction may simply play no role for the rabbinic interpreters, or at least there is no evidence from the Mishnah that it does.

The second shared feature is that I have not attempted to separate metaphors on the one hand from idioms on the other. Quite apart from some intrinsic difficulties with this, again exacerbated by the historical distance and limited textual basis for biblical Hebrew, the point is that the net needs to be cast as wide as possible. These resources define hermeneutic procedures as they apply to figurative meaning; and in principle, any figurative expression in Scripture can become the target, whether it also has other characteristics (such as being a word put together from other words, or a fixed collocation) or not. Since the rabbinic procedure is hermeneutic, and addresses the figurative dimension for its additional information content on extra-linguistic issues without making systematic linguistic or etymological claims, such distinctions are unlikely to have played a role, and there is no sign of them in the Mishnaic passages. The main difference that I would expect between the treatment of a frozen metaphor as opposed to an idiomatic expression with metaphorical constitution is that the latter, but not necessarily the former, will also exhibit an analysis into parts as semantic constituents. In other words, any treatment of an idiomatic expression as metaphorical will also have the Cotext3 code in its hermeneutic profile, while those which deal with one-word metaphors may or may not have it (the latter being the more likely case, to judge from the Mishnaic examples).

There is a further phenomenon in the Mishnaic treatment of metaphorical meaning which requires description; it is the interpretation as figurative of an expression whose meaning is concrete in its biblical co-text. Before turning to this type of case, however, it is perhaps useful to note that the appreciation of a (conventional) metaphorical expression *as metaphorical* is sometimes very clearly visible in the Mishnah. It is, of course, also presupposed in the Word6.2 and Word6.1 resources, because these resources accept the definition of the Scriptural *topic* as determined by the figurative meaning. But sometimes the appreciation of metaphorical meaning as privileged by the biblical co-text is more obvious. The following case is perhaps the most explicit in the Mishnah:

[141] mNed 3:11 IV (10)[98]   Jer. 9:25 (E 26)

R. Eleazar ben Azariah says: Repulsive is the absence of circumcision, for by it the wicked are disgraced, as it is said, 'For all these nations are uncircumcised, [but all the House of Israel are uncircumcised of heart.]'[99]

That 'all the house' of Israel are called 'uncircumcised of heart' is accepted at its figurative semantic value, and given an interpretation accordingly: the wicked are thereby being put to shame by the biblical voice. The figurative use of 'uncircumcised' ('of heart') is bound to its concrete meaning (with reference to the 'nations'), but in a metalinguistic manner: 'disgraced' by being so *called*. The concrete meaning makes no contribution to the subject-matter: there is no attempt to explain the wickedness further by applying to it the concrete sense of the absence of circumcision in a specific manner, as is the way of the Word6 resources. Instead, the concrete meaning's importance or value is said to be underscored by the metaphorical use it allows in Jer. 9:26. This is the message: the fact that the word 'absence of circumcision' (*orlah*) can be used as a biblical term of shaming shows how repulsive lack of circumcision really is. This is as near as the Mishnah gets to an analysis of Scripture in *stylistic* terms, although here also the 'lesson' to be drawn is very obvious, and the passage stands at the beginning of a series of midrashic units praising circumcision. Again, as in the case of Word1, one cannot mark all cases in which a biblical metaphor is explicitly or tacitly accepted as such in Mishnaic exegesis, so this resource has no code of its own.

---

[98] ◊•(¶)π¬W6.
[99] The JPS translation offers a footnote on the meaning of this figurative expression: 'i.e. their minds are blocked to God's commandments' (p. 790).

I now turn to biblical expressions whose co-text privileges the concrete meaning, while the Mishnah selects the figurative one. This is the reverse of the resource Word6.1, but it seems to be rarer. In the following dispute, the position of the House of Hillel with regard to the biblical word 'way' offers an illustration:

[142] mBer 1:3 II (3)[100]   Deut. 6:7

The House of Shammai say: In the evening everyone inclines and recites [the *Shema'*] and in the morning they stand up, as it is said, 'And when you lie down and when you get up'. And the House of Hillel say: Everyone recites [it] according to their [own] way (דרכו), as it is said, 'And when you are on the way' (ובלכתך בדרך). If so, why does it say, 'And when you lie down and when you get up'? Rather, at the time when it is people's custom (דרך) to lie down and at the time when it is people's custom to get up.

I will concentrate on the middle part of this dispute, the Hillelite explanation of the expression 'on the way'. This phrase, in particular when taken in its co-textual contrast with the expression 'when you sit in your house',[101] has a concrete meaning: to be on the move from one point in space to another. The Hillelites suspend or weaken the co-textual relationships which favour this concrete meaning,[102] opening up the full semantic range for 'way' (דרך), including the conventionalized figurative meaning 'manner'.[103] This is the meaning selected, which means it can thereafter not be properly connected to 'when you walk' (ובלכתך), because it is not the walking but the reciting whose individual 'manner' is at stake in the Dictum.

However, this interpretation allocates a very specific function to an otherwise inconspicuous member of the biblical sentence. Both Houses agree in taking the expressions 'when you lie down' and 'when you get up' as defining the accepted twice-daily obligation to recite. It is thus perhaps safe to assume that they had no interest in claiming that the two additional expressions, 'when you sit in your house' and 'when you are on the way', created two further obligations, either regularly or occasionally. This leaves these two expressions somewhat pale and lacking in informative punch, in particular if compared with the other two. The Hillelite interpretation solves this problem, at least for 'when you are on the way', by allocating specific relevance to the expression 'on the way' (the Opposition8 resource). In other words, just as with the WORD cases [138] to [140], we find that the elimination of redundancy goes hand in hand with a switch

[100] O8T1W7(way).

[101] This is the JPS translation: 'Recite them when you stay at home and when you are away.'

[102] If the verse were to be taken as meaning, 'Speak of these things all the time and on all occasions', then 'When you are on the way' would have no such concrete meaning. It is the splitting up of the verse into four separate segments (among them 'when you lie down' and 'when you get up'), on which both of the rabbinic Houses agree, which eliminates this option.

[103] The basic meanings listed in Clines, ii. 464–72, are: way, journey, venture, manner, course of life, commandments/actvity of God, hill; our occurrence of *derekh* is taken as spatial (ii. 471).

between figurative and concrete meaning, except that here the hermeneutic movement is from the concrete to the figurative (or abstract).

Word7: Explication of a biblical expression whose biblical co-text privileges a concrete sense in terms of a figurative meaning.

This procedure seems to be what is mainly covered by the rabbinic term *mashal* ('parable') when used as the name of a hermeneutic *middah*.[104] Directly linked to this 'rule' in its transmission in *Mishnat R. Eliezer* is its restriction to three halakhic cases ascribed to R. Ishmael.[105] (As in a number of other *middot*, the rabbinic explication of it is more concerned with limitations and restrictions than with the way it works.) The productivity of Word7 or its variants in post-Mishnaic literature is tremendous, and it is applied wholesale to one biblical text, the Song of Songs (for example, in the Targum).[106]

As in the case of other resource groups, more could be added and finer distinctions could be drawn. However, the resources Word5–Word7 capture the main hermeneutic regularities observable in the Mishnaic material concerning the metaphorical–concrete divide.

---

[104] Number 26 in *Mishnat R. Eliezer* (ed. Enelow, 36), see Stemberger, *Introduction*, 28; Goldberg, 'Das schriftauslegende Gleichnis in der rabbinischen Literatur', 15–18; Böhl, 'Die Metaphorisierung (Metila) in den Targumim zum Pentateuch'; id., 'Der erweiterte Vergleich im Targum'.

[105] Also appearing in the Mekhilta (Neziqin, 6; ed. Lauterbach, iii. 53 f.; see also iii. 102 (Neziqin 13)).

[106] Cf. Heinemann, *Darkhey Ha-Aggadah*, 117 ff.

15

Reflection and Outlook

What exactly has been achieved in the course of this investigation of Mishnaic hermeneutics, and what price is paid for achieving it in this manner? In the following chapter I shall try to give a first answer to these questions. Before doing so, however, I need to reflect briefly on our historical situation as heirs to ancient hermeneutics; and afterwards, I shall point to some avenues of research leading on from this investigation.

ANCIENT AND MODERN HERMENEUTICS

Although I have not spoken about hermeneutics as a general topic, my concern throughout this book was with how reading as reading is done. Insofar as rabbinic reading can be understood and described today at all, on our terms to be sure, it is contemporary with us and provides a current *option* of reading. To see how the rabbis read Scripture is to learn something about what hermeneutics is or can be. I have defined distinct and detailed individual hermeneutic moves, yet they are abstractions delimited by current concepts. I have wrestled with the terminology of modern linguistics, pragmatics, and the philosophy of language to find categories that do justice to the Mishnaic work with Scripture. In doing so, I have perhaps deformed these modern terms, but have also given them historical depth. I have tried to make rabbinic reading visible through these concepts, and thereby allowed it to emerge in the prehistory of those academic disciplines in which the concepts have their home. Hermeneutic practices of antiquity have come to be appreciated as one of the vital links that tie the modern world to its past, in parallel to and in rivalry with the links constituted by Western philosophical discourse. Rabbinic reading is one of the most substantial and sophisticated hermeneutic enterprises known to us. It may well help clarify how notions about language and reading that we take for granted came to mean what they mean to us. The intellectual and conceptual results of the interaction with texts, together with the practice of that interaction itself, are central to the history of the European West, of which modern scholarship and academic discourse are a part. The results of this study of rabbinic hermeneutics in the Mishnah, by reconstructing for our present understanding what reading *was then*, provides a historical background to what reading *is now*.

In making rabbinic reading visible to the modern discourses on language and interpretation, I hope also to make it visible to scholars in other fields who acquire competence in these discourses for their own purposes. Linguistic and hermeneutic terminology has begun to provide a common language for the study of divergent text-centred cultures. The interpretation of Homer by the Greeks, the Muslim commentaries on the Qur'an, or the interpretation of Scripture by the Church Fathers will yield to the *type* of analysis and description realized in this book, although many individual resources will be radically different. Direct, detailed, and meaningful comparisons of hermeneutic traditions may thus become possible, notwithstanding the differences of culture, context, language, and base text. What ensures that like is compared with like is the very fact that all hermeneutic material first undergoes a translation into the terms of our modern discourse. Controlled comparisons also become possible between different stages or documents within any one of these reading traditions. For example, once we have catalogued in explicit modern categories the reading strategies of several rabbinic documents, questions regarding the quality and quantity of hermeneutic techniques can be raised. How is the reading of Scripture say, in *Bereshit Rabba*, the Targums, the Yerushalmi, Rashi, or the Zohar different from that of the Mishnah? There is a precise *sense* in which such questions can now be asked.

MISHNAIC INTERPRETATION THROUGH THE PERSPECTIVE OF HERMENEUTIC RESOURCES

In this book I have introduced, implemented, and illustrated a discipline of description which is meant to enhance comparability, precision, and descriptive rigour in the study of rabbinic hermeneutics. It has been accepted for some time that the rabbis applied their Bible, that they atomized it, that they made it concrete, that they updated it, and so on. This book shows in what sense the Mishnaic rabbis did all these things, and how one goes about satisfying oneself for any individual unit of rabbinic interpretation that these features are indeed present.

The network of hermeneutic resources helps correct any one-sidedness in modern reconstruction. We are not stuck any more with the most obvious hermeneutic aspect of the whole interpretation (see below). The catalogue of resources has the effect of a checklist of hermeneutic options for each unit of interpretation. It provides us with a *procedure* for going beyond first impressions, a test to discover incomplete descriptions. And from the same heuristic procedure emerges the discovery of new resources.

For even where a certain aspect of the interpretation cannot be pinned down with any of the resources as currently defined, the chances are that some come closer than others, pointing us in the right direction (we can form, for example, an opinion on the appropriate resource *family*). This is the manner in which I envisage that future research on rabbinic material outside the Mishnah will expand the current catalogue of resources.[1]

To recapitulate: textually unified interpretations are broken down into functional components, hermeneutic resources. The analysis expects complexity: more than one resource may be required to allow the sense of Dictum and Lemma to converge. Resources are conceived as *abstract* options of handling biblical wording (actually, any wording). Therefore, I had to determine at what level of generality to peg the description of options, that is, how far to take the separation of components within the complex whole. Two pragmatic factors determine the level of generality: the availability of conceptual tools from the modern discourse on language and reading; and the measure in which the *recurrence* of components can be discerned from interpretation to interpretation.

From the latter point of view, the decision to divide textually unified operations into hermeneutic components is particularly important. The tacit assumption that each interpretation is brought about by only one 'technique' of interpretation is unwarranted. Even the notion that each interpretation is accounted for by one *main* component within a complex operation—in principle compatible with the approach taken here—is doubtful. I suspect that what is considered to be the main component is often merely the one that strikes us most forcefully, perhaps the one most at odds with our own reading of Scripture. If we move to a plurality of resources, common features of otherwise totally unconnected interpretations become suddenly visible. And resources recur much more often than complex wholes. A clearer picture might thus emerge of how rabbinic hermeneutics, despite its enormous variety and flexibility, can be a coherent and mutually reinforcing cultural practice. Overlap between disparate interpretations in turn helps firm up the resource definitions.

By claiming that a given unit of interpretation uses a certain resource, it becomes impossible to consider it *in hermeneutic isolation*. The thematic or historical links that modern scholarship has always tended to make between units of interpretation are thus complemented by a third: the hermeneutic link. The description by hermeneutic resource establishes connections which are independent of surface links, such as the name of the rabbi, the identity of the topic, the word chosen as Lemma, and so on. The purely hermeneutic links can therefore be used to contextualize, or indeed test, other similarities or dissimilarities. We can actually *separate out* the evidence of the hermeneutic contents of a rabbinic passage, for example as

---

[1] More about how the current catalogue is meant to accommodate such expansion is found in the introduction to App. I below.

additional type of evidence for broader historical comparisons. Also, resource definitions presuppose a separation of the question 'which hermeneutic operation' from the question 'which literary form or terminology?' Only *after* such a separation can the (vital) evidence provided by literary structures or rabbinic technical terms begin to be evaluated, and make its full contribution to synchronic or diachronic comparisons.

Another methodological decision that has been taken here is the inclusion of phenomena on the borderline of explicit interpretation, and of the thematic embeddedness of interpretation in the wider Mishnaic discourse.[2] I have made a routine part of my description the manner in which a biblical text is drawn into the agenda of its Mishnaic reader, identifying the following main mechanisms: expressive use (π), hermeneutic use of rabbinic paradigms, the resources of the TOPIC family, and the neutralization of biblical co-text. This conceptualizes how 'external' reader concerns can engage hermeneutically with 'internal' biblical structures, that is, how the internal and external are in fact indistinguishable in rabbinic reading. This does not uncouple rabbinic hermeneutics from its historical context; on the contrary. The categories employed here provide mechanisms for linking historical information, including evidence on economic, ideological, or political factors, to hermeneutic rabbinic practice.

PROBLEMS WITH THE APPROACH

The problems linked to the approach taken here are not, in the main, problems that continue from the earlier agenda of scholarly description of rabbinic hermeneutics. Some of the old problems—for example, of whether a rabbinic interpretation is 'genuine' exegesis, or if it preceded the rabbinic conviction now tied to it—are not part of the current study's agenda. The first has no direct role to play in establishing a modern understanding of rabbinic interpretation, for that means a modern understanding of a *rabbinic* standard of genuine interpretation. And the second requires both criteria that are more complex and evidence that is more diverse than scholars have usually suspected.

But there are other problems, mostly linked to the manner of description itself. Infelicities and inaccuracies in the formulation of the individual resources will doubtlessly continue to surface, as they have done during my years of working with them—hopefully, they will be easy to correct. More fundamental is the question of how this descriptive project copes with rabbinic interpretations which appear to make no sense. The project's grounding lies in a pre-theoretical understanding of what does or does not

---

[2] Both of these decisions would have been much more difficult, perhaps impossible, for documents of the genres Midrash or Targum. In the light of the present examination of the Mishnah, however, it may well be feasible to investigate thematic perspectivization in these types of works also.

make sense as an interpretation of a biblical passage. So the first problem is simply the discovery that many Mishnaic interpretations still do not make sense, or at least not quite. In a number of difficult cases a start can be made by identifying *some* of their resources. But there then remains a gap in the hermeneutic profile: the interpretation is not wholly accounted for. The most important decision here is to keep hold of the intuition that there is a gap in the description, otherwise the ground will shift too much under the descriptive project. That there is such a possibility, indeed likelihood, of the ground shifting is both a problem and an advantage of this type of project. Our intuitions can change; they can indeed be educated by a discipline of articulation. But they need to be taken seriously first. Another danger connected to the difficult cases is that a resource definition may be *stretched* to cover some eccentric hermeneutic structure. The reason why this can happen is that the words defining the resources are just that: words. They are flexible in their meaning, and they require a hermeneutic competence (an experience) in *applying* them to the rabbinic material. There is nothing mechanical and nothing eternal about this business of describing rabbinic interpretation, and resource definitions will shift in their application over time. So it needs to be acknowledged that, despite all the apparent precision and objectivity, resource definitions are vulnerable to ambiguity, fuzziness, and uneven application.

There are also resources which look like explanatory cop-outs. Thus, my resource system provides for tacit assumptions entering the rabbinic hermeneutic process (resource Topic0). Such an option is needed, for otherwise one would have to assume that all material factors involved in the interpretation are always spelled out. And such an assumption would simply be implausible for rabbinic literature in general and the Mishnah in particular. A word of clarification is necessary, therefore. If an interpretation makes no sense, Topic0 can be used to bridge the gap only in very limited circumstances; it is not a resource of last resort. But does the resource definition unambiguously tell us, in absolute terms, when not to apply it? Of course not.

There are also ambiguities in the description arising from the fact that the resources stand in for components of complex hermeneutic operations. For cases have been encountered in which the same interpretative result could be achieved by way of two *different* sets of resources. Depending on how one component of the operation is identified, rival sets of resources emerge. This introduces a moment of uncertainty into the descriptive system, in particular where there is no rabbinic terminology.[3] The pragmatic way to deal with this is to include two alternative hermeneutic profiles. Some of these ambiguities may be cleared up in the light of material from outside

---

[3] This uncertainty is, however, not wholly new. Even among the much less numerous rabbinic *middot*, different 'rules' can, in certain circumstances, achieve the same interpretative result. This is implicitly acknowledged in many post-Mishnaic rabbinic discussions (in particular in the Babylonian Gemara).

the Mishnah; and perhaps a sharper focus can be defined later for some of the resources in the present configuration. A related point is that some pairs of resources are insufficiently distinct from each other, or are difficult to separate in practice. Thus, it is not always clear if a biblical sign is focused because it is considered as potentially redundant (Opposition8), or because an emphatic commitment spreads from the centre to the periphery of a biblical sentence (Opposition6).

So, this approach involves the researcher in new difficulties which are neither negligible in quantity nor trivial in quality. But I think that many of them surface because the new procedures make it less easy for us to be satisfied with vague explanations, or the absence of explanations.[4]

OUTLOOK

There are a number of empirical questions which can be followed up on the basis of a comprehensive description of Mishnaic interpretation (and its availability in database form). Among them is a quantitative picture of hermeneutic resources. This needs to go beyond the information on frequency contained in Appendix I below, for what is required is a picture of how many and which resources *occur together regularly*. It is possible that in this respect regular differences between the Mishnah and some other documents of rabbinic literature will emerge. Are midrashic units in such works as Mekhilta or Sifra 'simpler', that is, do they involve on average fewer resources per unit? Also, are their interpretations less perspectivized (for example, by TOPIC resources)?

Another theme worth pursuing are those Mishnaic Dicta which are plausibly linked to Scriptural formulations, or are so linked by post-Mishnaic rabbinic tradition, but of whose hermeneutic intent the surface of the Mishnah gives no hint. Could these be accounted for by the configuration of resources as here established, or are different resources required?

Linked to this question is the following. Why do we have Scriptural support only *sometimes* in the Mishnah? Why is there no attempt to tie Scripture into the Mishnaic discourse at every turn? Perhaps this way of framing the problem is too narrow, though. For biblical wording is just one type of *reason* given for Dicta. The halakhic discourse routinely invokes warrants, exempla, traditions, generalized maxims, rankings of norms, or other reasons. For all of these the same question could be asked: why only sometimes, not always?[5] The Mishnah formulates no independent, universal principles which could be separated from the halakhic discourse as

---

[4] I vividly recall a famous expert on Jewish literature teaching a class on Midrash as visiting professor. After being challenged twice over an explanation of how the midrashic unit under discussion actually worked, he exclaimed: 'Well, it's just—midrash!'

[5] For some aspects of the question, see my 'Delaying the Progress from Case to Case' and 'From Case to Case'.

it moves through the legal cases. The explicit principles we find are all *occasional*, the warrants all limited to a context, the generalizations all tied to a concrete case, the exegetical strategies all encapsulated in their application. Scripture is not declared to be, in principle, a standard of halakhic validity. Nor is the manner in which the Mishnah reads Scripture accounted for in the abstract. So the Mishnah's treatment of the role of Scripture is of a piece with its treatment of warrants in general. The reason for this may have to be sought in the nature of a discourse which avoids spelling out any information whose availability could weaken its links to the social and situational context of its intended use.

The explicitness of rabbinic hermeneutics increases in rabbinic literature outside and after the Mishnah.[6] Very likely, however, the intensity and richness of the hermeneutic activity also increases, thereby perhaps modifying the nature and goal of the rabbinic enterprise. By the Middle Ages large parts of rabbinic literature are devoted exclusively to the explicit interpretation of Scripture. The Mishnah marks one of the main beginnings, not of the rabbinic activity of interpretation, but of its literary representation. Its hermeneutics must eventually be integrated into a historical understanding of rabbinic Judaism's extraordinary hermeneutic creativity as a whole. Until then, the picture presented in this book will remain a fragment.

---

[6] I have drawn attention to the fact in Ch. 4 that explicating an interpretation affects the substance and resources of interpretation.

Appendix I: The Hermeneutic Configuration of the Mishnah: An Overview of Resources

THE CONFIGURATION OF HERMENEUTIC RESOURCES

The list of all resources and formats presented in this Appendix repeats the definition of the resource as given in the body of the book. Each definition is followed by the number of occurrences of the resource in the Mishnah. In the note to each resource the page number is also given on which it is introduced in the body of this book, and the Mishnaic references of its occurrences. If the resource is found more than twenty times, only selected passages are listed. The selection concentrates on the passages that have been translated in this book (i.e. our sequentially numbered sample cases). A full listing of all Mishnaic passages and their resources is contained in Appendix II.

In this Appendix the arrangement of resources according to families is systematic. Many resources form closely related clusters within their family. Often neighbouring resources are defined in parallel or in contrast to each other. This logic of relation is expressed in the numbering (or their systematic 'proximity'), and their systematic arrangement here makes these relationships visible. This Appendix therefore offers three things: a complete picture of all the resources together; an idea of the quantitative relationships; and an additional layer of explanation, namely, the commentary each resource receives from the resources surrounding it. (Table 1.1 gives the systematic arrangement of resource families.)

As a list of just these resources, and not others, this Appendix offers the configuration of hermeneutics which characterizes the use of Scriptural wording in the Mishnah. It is likely that this offers a unique hermeneutic 'fingerprint' for the document Mishnah, in that other rabbinic documents will have additional resources, and some found here may be missing.[1]

THE 'LOGIC' AND THE GAPS OF THE SYSTEM

On the whole, my allocation of numbers to resources is largely one of convention and convenience. Important for the descriptive project is that each resource consists of one definition attached to one and only one name, not what that name 'means'. Yet there are a number of trends that emerged in the labelling of resources. There is a tendency to assign the lower numbers to more fundamental members. And in several resource families there are gaps in the sequential numbering to accommodate additional resources that are likely to be found in other works of rabbinic literature. Where there is no resource number 1 in a family, I suspect that the most fundamental (or simplest) resource of this family type has yet to be found, namely,

---

[1] See on this the final section of Ch. 1, and Ch. 15.

outside the Mishnah. But usually the gaps left in the system are pure guesswork. Such gaps are unused numbers within resource families (sometimes between neighbouring resources), and unused letters of the alphabet between families of resources. Because of a need for abbreviations, each family occupies only one letter of the alphabet. This means that each resource name can be abbreviated to a letter and one (or more) numbers. Thus Word1 can be represented as W1, and this is how it is found in the footnotes labelling each of the Mishnaic passages translated in this study, and in the list of passages in Appendix II. My *Database of Midrashic Units in the Mishnah* also uses these abbreviated resource names.

The gaps in the system will make it possible to construe hermeneutic configurations of resources for other rabbinic works without having to reuse for any new-found resources a 'name' already taken. Where additional resources need to be defined they can be assigned as-yet unused alpha-numerical 'names'; and where a resource first found in the Mishnah does not occur in that other rabbinic work, it will simply appear as a 'gap' in the hermeneutic configuration belonging to that work.

If there should ever be a 'full' inventory of rabbinic resources across all its documents, I would expect it to have some unused numbers in some families, and crowded numberings in some others (for example, double letters as well as double digits), because of the number of resources to be accommodated.

Where a resource is taken to be a sub-type of another resource it is given the same name with an added second digit. In other words, some hierarchical relationships are immediately visible in the resource name. In four resource families the second digit has a different function: it allows the combination of two parameters of description to produce new (two-digit) resources as necessary (EXTENSION, REDUNDANCY, DIFFERENCE, and NORM). Second-digit resources of this type are marked by an asterisk, in the following way: Norm*.1.

Occasionally the numbers represent something like a constant 'meaning' across several resource families. Thus, the numeral zero is used to indicate that the resource is anomalous in some respect; Analogy0 is an analogy, but not used hermeneutically; Topic0 is an assumption that imposes a perspective on a biblical segment, but remains unexpressed; Opposition0 restricts the meaning of the biblical term, but not by using a contrast *term*, and so on. The numeral 8 has a link to phenomena of deixis in the USE and the PERFORMANCE families. There are some more tenuous correspondences between the numerals and their functions;[2] they are merely of mnemonic importance, and I am sure they will not be preserved if and when additional resources come to be defined on the basis of extra-Mishnaic material.

Of the Greek and mathematical signs used for formats, some have tenuous links to their function here: the *omega*-sign (Ω) signals end-position; the *delta* sign (Δ) a difference (in time); the *sigma* sign (Σ) points to a 'sum' of biblical segments found together in one place as a chain; the *pi* sign π marks the adoption of biblical wording for a Mishnaic expression, in parallel to the letter 'p' of the PERFORMANCE resources; 'r' in the sign ® stands for *reprise* (of the Dictum, after the quotation of the Lemma); the logical 'non'-sign ¬ indicates that the application of a hermeneutic resource to a specific Lemma is rejected; the 'section' sign § shows that the biblical term is part

---

[2] Thus Redundancy*.2 involves duplication or repetition; Opposition2 is the multiple occurrence of contrast terms (as opposed to Opposition1, which indicates only one contrast term); Extension1 indicates the presence of one biblical term, Extension2 that of two or more, etc.

of a list given earlier in the Mishnah; and the wavy equal sign (≈) shows that the the same resource occurs in two (or more) neighbouring units of interpretation.

USE OF THIS APPENDIX

Resources only found once in the Mishnah are marked by an asterisk *in front* of the letter. Resources which are not found in the Mishnah with some degree of certainty are placed between square brackets. The total number of occurrences for each resource given after each definition is in many cases approximate. This is indicated by use of '*c.*' in front of the number. In all other cases the numbers are also somewhat preliminary, but give what I believe to be a safe *minimum* number of occurrences. Where a resource is very frequent (Word1, Opposition1, Cotext1, Cotext5, Topic1, Topic2, and Topic3) no specific passages are identified in the footnotes. Examples can easily be found in the list of passages in Appendix II. The same goes for the formal features (π, §, etc.), whose definition and frequency is found at the end of this Appendix.

For any passage identified as involving a given resource, Appendix II gives further information. It offers the *whole* hermeneutic profile for each passage, i.e. shows which other resources are used apart from the resource in question, or which formal features are present. It also indicates if the use of the resource in that passage is doubtful or ambiguous in some manner (although, on the whole, all doubtful cases have been excluded from the consolidated listings and totals in Appendix I). As explained in Chapter 1, the sixth chapter of Avot (containing about thirty-four units of interpretation) is omitted from these listings and the totals.

1. WORD CONSTITUTION AND SEMANTICS

Choices for Word Constitution and Word Meaning (Word)

Word1 Explication of a biblical word-form by choosing a meaning from the full range of polysemous, homonymous, or extended semantic possibilities for that word-form. The word-form is thus taken in independence from its limitations in the biblical co-text, and in turn calls either for an adjustment of the co-textual relationships or for their active suspension. Occurrences: *c*. 69.[3]

Word1.2 Explication of a biblical word-form representing a particle, preposition, conjunction, and the like, by choosing a meaning from the full range of polysemous, homonymous, or extended semantic possibilities for that word-form. The word-form is thus taken in independence from its limitations in the biblical co-text, and in turn calls either for an adjustment of the co-textual relationships or for their active suspension. Occurrences: 19.[4]

---

[3] See p. 365. Occurrences if W1.2 is deducted: 50. Examples: mBer 1:5 I (2) **[13]**, mBer 9:5 II (9) **[114a]**, mPeah 7:7 I (3) **[115]**, mPeah 8:9 I (4) [Ch. 1], mShebi 10:8 I (2) **[132]**, mSot 8:4 ? **[126]**, mQid 4:14 IV (4) **[17]**, mSan 6:2 I (2) **[56]**, mSan 8:1 **[101]**, mSan 10:1 I (2) **[82]**, mMak 2:5 II (2) **[11]**, mMak 2:8 **[12]** = mSheb 10:8 II (2), mMak 3:16 **[133]**, mYad 4:3 III (3) **[41]**.

[4] See p. 370. Occurrences: mBer 1:3 II–III (3) **[142]**, mBer 7:3, mBer 9:5 II (9) **[114a]**, mPeah 7:7 III (3) **[130b]**, mTer 6:6 I–II (2), mTaan 1:2 **[114]**, mSot 5:5 I (2), mSan 10:3 IX–X (10) **[70] [71]**, mSan 10:6 VI (6), mMak 1:6 I (3), mMak 1:9 I (2), mMak 3:10 **[8]**, mEduy 8:7, mAvot 3:9 I (2), mAvot 4:1 I (4), mMen 11:5 **[134]**, mUqtsin 3:12 II (2).

Word2 Tacit selection of a meaning from the full polysemous, homonymous, and extended semantic range of a biblical word-form as part of an adjustment of co-textual relationships within a biblical sentence; that adjustment is called for by the Mishnaic explication of another word-form in the same sentence, or the convergence of sense between the Scriptural segment and its Mishnaic co-text. Occurrences: 6.[5]

Word3 Explication of a biblical word-form in the light of the meaning of a partially similar word-form (belonging to a different lexeme). The word-form is thus taken in independence from its limitations in the biblical co-text, and in turn calls for an adjustment of the co-textual relationships or for their active suspension. Occurrences: 18.[6]

Word5 Explication of a biblical word-form, in independence from the figurative (or figurative-idiomatic) meaning privileged by the biblical co-text, in terms of a concrete meaning without direct relation to the subject-matter as determined through the figurative meaning. Occurrences: 5.[7]

Word6.1 Explication of a biblical word-form in terms of a concrete meaning whose biblical co-text privileges a figurative (or figurative-idiomatic) meaning. The word-form is thus taken in independence from the biblical co-text, but is nevertheless applied to the subject-matter as determined by the biblical co-text (and the figurative meaning); it therefore calls in turn for a partial adjustment of the co-textual relationships or their suspension. Occurrences: 9.[8]

Word6.2 Explication of a biblical word-form whose co-text suggests one figurative meaning as conveying a different figurative meaning, in the following manner: (1) the new figurative meaning applies to the subject-matter as determined by the figurative meaning privileged by the biblical co-text; (2) it is thus integrated into the sentence or wider co-text to some extent; (3) the new figurative meaning can only be derived from the biblical figurative meaning by way of a consideration of the concrete meaning of the word; (4) the concrete meaning cannot be focused unless the co-textual determination of the biblical word as figurative is initially or partly suspended. Occurrences: 17.[9]

Word7 Explication of a biblical expression whose biblical co-text privileges a concrete sense in terms of a figurative meaning. Occurrences: 5.[10]

Word9 Identification of a meaning for a biblical proper name in terms of the meaning of its semantic component(s). Occurrences: 2.[11]

---

[5] See p. 367. Occurrences: mNaz 9:5 I (3), mGit 9:10 II (3), mSan 10:6 V (6), mMak 3:16 **[133]**, mBek 8:1 **[83]**, mUqtsin 3:12 I (2).

[6] See p. 378. Occurrences: mBer 9:5 IV (9), mKilaim 9:8 I (2), mShab 9:2 I (2), mSukkah 4:5, mTaan 1:2 **[114]**, mMeg 4:9, mNaz 9:5 II (3) **[93]**, mSot 5:2, mSot 5:5 I (2) (verse 15), mSot 9:9 II (2) **[42]**, mBM 2:7 I (2), mSan 6:5 I (2), mMak 3:10 **[8]**, mMak 3:15 I (4) **[137]**, mBek 7:5 II (4), mBek 7:5 III (4), mBek 7:5 IV (4), mKer 2:5 I (3).

[7] See p. 387. Occurrences: mMeg 4:9, mSot 1:6, mSot 8:4 **[126]**, mSot 9:9 I (2), mTem 6:3 I (3) **[140]**.

[8] See pp. 384f. Occurrences: mBer 1:3 I (3), mPeah 8:9 IV (4), mShab 9:1 = mAZ 3:6 II (2) **[69]**, mShab 9:2 I (2), mHag 1:1 **[139]**, mAZ 3:3, mAZ 3:6 I (2), mAvot 3:2 I (3) **[36]**, mMen 11:4 [135].

[9] See p. 384. Occurrences: mBer 1:3 II (3) **[142]**, mShab 9:2 I (2), mSot 8:1 VII (7), mSot 9:6 II (4), mGit 9:10 III (3) **[2]**, mBM 3:12 II (2), mSan 10:4, mSan 10:6 III (6), mMak 1:9 I–II (2), mEduy 2:10 II (2), mEduy 8:7 III (3), mAvot 3:2 III (3), mZeb 9:1 I (2) **[138]**, mZeb 9:1 II (2), mZeb 12:2 I (2), mTam 7:4.

[10] See p. 391. Occurrences: mTaan 4:8 III (3) **[51]**, mBM 5:11 II (2), mSan 10:1 I (2) **[82]**, mEduy 8:7, mAvot 3:3 I (2).

[11] See p. 376. Occurrences: [mSot 9:15 I (2)], mTam 7:4, mMid 4:7 **[136]**.

Semantic and Paradigmatic Opposition (Opposition)

Opposition0 Explicating the meaning of a biblical expression by stressing its exclusive effect in a paraphrase using, for example, 'not... unless' (...שׁ עַד), 'only' (בלדם אלא or ...אַיִן), or employing it in a negated phrase. Occurrences: 15.[12]

Opposition1 Explication of the meaning of a biblical expression in the light of its opposition to another expression. The other expression would fit the same biblical syntagma and is a member of a paradigm of Mishnaic relevance. By taking this expression to be excluded, the perspective of the Mishnaic paradigm is imposed on the meaning of the biblical expression. All occurrences: *c.* 109.[13]

Opposition1.3 Explication of a biblical personal pronoun or personal affix in the light of its opposition to another member of the paradigm of grammatical persons. Occurrences: 11.[14]

Opposition1.4 Explication of the number of a biblical expression in the light of its opposition to another grammatical number. Occurrences: 31.[15]

Opposition1.5 Explication of the gender of a biblical expression in the light of its opposition to the other gender in the grammatical paradigm. Occurrences: 3.[16]

Opposition2 Explication of the meaning of a biblical expression in the light of its opposition to several other expressions. The other expressions would fit the same biblical syntagma and are members of a paradigm of Mishnaic relevance. By taking these expressions to be excluded, the perspective of the Mishnaic paradigm is imposed on the meaning of the biblical expression. Occurrences: 15.[17]

Opposition6 Extension of the full commitment attaching to the grammatically central parts of a biblical period to its periphery or to elements which are unstressed, presupposed, incidental, or absent. Occurrences: *c.*20.[18]

Opposition7 Inclusion of the extreme quantitative, spatial, temporal, or numerical limits of a biblical expression through emphasis. Where appropriate, limiting or oppositional members of a subordinate paradigm are named. (Cf. Logic1.) Occurrences: 16.[19]

---

[12] See p. 293. Occurrences: mBik 1:2 I (2) **[34]**, mPes 9:1 II (2), mRH 2:9 I (2), mHag 1:1 **[139]**, mYeb 10:3, mSot 5:5 II (2), mGit 4:5, mBQ 7:1, mSan 11:2 III (3) **[106]**, mSan 11:4 **[84]**, mMak 2:2, mShebu 3:5 I–II (3) **[79]**, mHul 10:1 II (2), mParah 2:3 II (2).

[13] See pp. 288 f. Occurrences if Opposition1.3–5 is deducted: *c.* 66. For a preliminary list, see my 'Stressing Scripture's Words'.

[14] See p. 289. Occurrences: mMS 5:14, mBik 1:2 I–II (2) **[34]**, mBik 1:5, mYoma 8:9 II (3), mRH 2:9 I (2), mTaan 4:2, mSan 10:6 II (6), mSan 11:5, mAZ 3:4 II (2), mHul 2:3.

[15] See p. 291. Examples: mYeb 6:6 II (3) **[55]**, mYeb 6:6 III (3) **[102]**, mSot 6:3 II (4) **[85]**, mSot 9:1 II (2) **[19] [121a]**, mQid 4:14 IV (4) **[17]**, mSan 4:5 I (9) **[105]**, mTem 1:6 II (3) **[103]**, mNeg 2:3 **[104]**, mNeg 12:6 III (3) **[97]**.

[16] See p. 291. Occurrences: mYeb 8:3 I (2), mYeb 8:3 II (2) **[63]**, mAZ 2:5 (Yehudah).

[17] See p. 286. Occurrences: mMS 5:14, mBik 1:2 II (2), mBik 1:5, mYeb 8:2 III (3), [cf. mNed 6:1], mSot 2:4 I–II (2), mSot 4:1 **[108]**, mSot 8:3, mSan 10:5 I (2), mMak 3:13, mZeb 9:5 II (2), mMen 7:4, mArak 9:1, mTem 1:6 I (3), mNeg 14:2.

[18] See p. 311. Occurrences: mBer 9:5 I (9) **[15] [82] [114a]**, mBer 9:5 II–IV (9) **[114a]**, mShebi 10:8 I (2) **[132]**, mBik 1:9 **[117]**, mYeb 12:3 II (2), mYeb 12:6 I–III (5), mGit 9:10 II–III (3) **[2]**, mBM 8:1 I (2) **[37]**, mSan 2:4 II (6), mMak 2:6 I (2), mHor 2:3 **[112]**, mNeg 12:5 I (4) **[107]**, mParah 3:7, mNid 8:3.

[19] See p. 311. Occurrences: mTaan 1:2 **[114]**, mYeb 8:2 II (3), mSot 2:2 **[38]**, mSot 3:2 II (2), mSot 6:3 II (4) **[85]**, mSot 9:1 II (2) **[19] [121a]**, mBQ 4:9 II (3) **[87]** (Yehudah), mSan 10:1 I (2) **[82]**, mMak 1:6 I–II (3), mMak 2:6 I (2), mMak 3:16 **[133]**, mAZ 3:3, mMen 11:7, mHul 12:3 I (5), mArak 8:5.

Opposition8 Allocation of a separate meaning, subject-matter, or referent to a biblical expression or clause on the basis of contrasting the biblical syntagma with an alternative syntagma which is identical except for not containing that expression or that clause. This tacit comparison points to the meaning surplus or meaning differential provided by the apparently redundant expression or clause. Occurrences: 91.[20]

Opposition9 Explication of a biblical syntagma in terms of a syntagmatic position not provided by it (that is, a tacit contrast with a richer or more complex syntagma). The absence of the position is taken to imply the exclusion of a member (or members) of a Mishnaic paradigm which could occupy that position. Occurrences: 11.[21]

Taxonomic Relationships Between Lexemes (Extension)

Extension1 One biblical expression is identified with Mishnaic expressions on a level of generality different from that suggested by the biblical expression's meaning alone. If combined with Extension*.1–3 this amounts to an extension of scope, effectively *generalizing* the biblical term in a certain perspective. Otherwise (in combination with Extension*.4/Extension*.0) this involves a superordination or an application of the biblical term. If the Mishnaic generalization can be linked to other features of the biblical text, one of the other EXTENSION resources defined here will be used as the label instead of Extension1. Occurrences: *c.* 37.[22]

Extension1.0 A biblical expression (as superordinate) is taken to subsume a Mishnaic expression (as hyponym). Occurrences: 15.[23]

Extension2 Two or more biblical expressions which are presented alongside each other in the same biblical sentence and in parallel syntactic position (usually linked by 'or' or 'and') are identified with a Mishnaic list or an expression on a level of generality different from that suggested by the biblical expression's meaning alone. If combined with Extension*.1–3 the biblical plurality of expressions is taken as an *open* list that can be supplemented or completed by (members of) Mishnaic paradigms. Occurrences: 7.[24]

***Extension3** One or more biblical expressions which are presented alongside each other in the same biblical sentence in parallel syntactic position and followed by a general expression (such as 'all') are taken to be extended in scope to (members of) a whole Mishnaic paradigm. One occurrence (mShebu 3:5 III (3) [79]).[25]

***Extension4** Interpretation of a biblical proper name or single referring expression

---

[20] See pp. 297 ff. Examples: mBer 1:3 II–III (3) [142], mPeah 7:7 III (3) [130b], mTaan 1:2 [114], mKet 3:5 II (2)[92] [110a], mSot 4:1 [108], mSot 8:2 I (3) [77], mGit 3:2 [109], mQid 3:4 I–II (2) [110], mZeb 9:1 I (2) [138], mBek 8:1 [83], mArak 3:5 II (2) [58], mArak 9:3 II (2) [16], mTem 1:6 III (3) [73], mNeg 12:5 I (4) [107].

[21] See p. 300. Occurrences: mPeah 7:7 II (3), mRH 2:9 II (2), mSot 9:5 II (3), mBQ 4:9 II (3) [87] (Meir)?, mBM 9:12 II (3) [111], mBM 9:13 II (4) [78] [110b], mSan 2:1 [33] (Yehudah), mHor 1:3, mBek 4:1, mBek 9:1 II (2) [81], mNeg 12:5 I (4) [107].

[22] See pp. 229f. Examples: mSot 8:2 I (3) [77], mBQ 1:1 [25], mBQ 5:5 I (2) [5], mZeb 9:1 I (2) [138], mHul 8:4 I (3) [119]. Occurrences without Extension1.0: *c.* 22.

[23] See pp. 228, 241f. Occurrences: mBer 9:5 III (9), mPeah 8:9 IIb (4) variant, mShab 9:6, mRH 1:9, mYeb 6:6 II (3) [55], mSot 8:2 I (3) [77], mBQ 9:11 [20], mBM 8:1 I (2) [37], mBM 8:1 II (2), mSan 2:4 VI (6), mAZ 3:3, mBek 9:1 II (2) [81], mArak 9:4, mArak 9:8 IV (4), mYad 4:4 II (4).

[24] See pp. 228f. Occurrences: mShab 6:4, mTaan 4:8 III (3) [51], mBQ 5:7 [76], mSan 11:1 II (2), mMak 1:7 II (6), mMak 1:7 IV (6), mMak 1:8 II (3) (Yose).

[25] See pp. 229f.

as standing for a plurality of Mishnaic terms, or for a general concept or class term. One occurrence (mMeg 4:9, if 'Molekh' is understood as a proper name).[26]

Extension5 Determination of the generality of a biblical expression in the light of the occurrence in its co-text of some term of general, inclusive, or exclusive scope, or of an expression of unrestricted scope. The expression whose generality is construed need not be governed syntactically by the second expression. Occurrences: 3.[27]

*Extension5.5 Determination of the generality or taxonomic inclusiveness of a biblical expression in the light of the occurrence in its co-text of a particle of inclusive scope (e.g. או/אף/אם), regardless of whether the latter syntactically governs the former. Once occurrence (mMS 5:10 **[80] [126a]**).[28]

*Extension6 A biblical expression is taken as representing a larger class of items by virtue of being its (most) central or frequently occurring member. One occurrence (mBQ 5:7 **[76]**).[29]

[Extension7] Identification of a biblical expression as representing a larger class of items by virtue of its being a prototypical member.[30]

Extension9 Interpretation of a biblical comparison, simile, or metaphor as implying a substantive and specific similarity or shared class membership between the two subjects; this similarity is thus incompatible with a purely illustrative or stylistic purpose of the biblical construction. Occurrences: 7.[31]

Extension*.0 Mishnaic companion term consists of one hyponym or more.[32]

Extension*.1 Mishnaic companion term consists of two (or more) lexemes of the same level of generality as the biblical lexeme(s).[33]

Extension*.2 Mishnaic companion term consists of a class defined through a complex expression (using e.g. 'all' or 'things which . . .'), or through a superordinate.[34]

Extension.3 Mishnaic companion term consists of the biblical expression used as term for a whole class.[35]

Extension*.4 Mishnaic companion term consists of a proper name or singular referring expression.[36]

Semiotic Options Beneath the Level of the Complete Word (Icon, Grapheme)[37]

[Icon1] Recourse to a transformative Hebrew alphabet (*atbash* or *gematria*).

[Icon2] Recourse to the numerical value of the Hebrew letters (consonants) as transposed back into a new word (*gematria*). (See Icon2.1.)

---

[26] See p. 228, 230.
[27] See p. 230. Occurrences (inclusive of one E5.5): mMS 5:10 **[80] [126a]**, mGit 9:10 II (3), mBM 9:13 IV (4).   [28] See p. 230.
[29] See p. 230.
[30] See p. 231.
[31] See p. 207. Occurrences: mShab 9:1 = mAZ 3:6 II (2) **[69]**, mShab 9:3 III (3) = mYoma 6:8, mShab 9:4 **[129]**, mSan 10:3 IX (10) **[70]**, mSan 10:3 X (10) **[71]**; mAZ 3:6 II (2) = mShab 9:1 **[69]**, mZeb 8:11, mTem 1:1 III (3).
[32] See pp. 228, 241 f.
[33] See p. 228.
[34] See p. 228.
[35] See p. 228.
[36] See p. 228.
[37] All of these except Icon5 are found together on p. 379.

Icon2.1 Recourse to the numerical value of the Hebrew letters (consonants) taken as number. Occurrences: 2.[38]

Icon3 Analysis of a biblical word-form or phrase as acronym (*notarikon*). Occurrences: 2.[39]

*Icon4 Interpretation of the iconic aspects of individual signs in the biblical text (shape of the letter, etc.). One occurrence: mPes 9:2 II (2).[40]

Icon5 Description or prescription of a symbolic representation of the concrete sense of a biblical word-form whose co-text privileges a figurative (or figurative-idiomatic) meaning. (Cf. Word5). Occurrences: 3.[41]

[Icon6] Recourse to a language system other than Hebrew.

Grapheme

A link between the biblical Lemma and the meaning of another word-form is established on the basis of:

Grapheme1 Metathesis of consonants. Occurrences: 3.[42]

Grapheme2 Graphic similarity of consonants (e.g. *dalet* and *resh*). Occurrences: 2.[43]

Grapheme3 Partial overlap of consonants between the word-forms (for example two out of three consonants are the same). Occurrences: 5.[44]

Grapheme4 Similarity or identity of sound (e.g. לא and לו). Occurrences: 3.[45]

Grapheme5 An alternative vocalization of the same consonants, producing a different word-form. Occurrences: 3.[46]

Logical Constants and Conjunctions (Logic)

Logic1 Interpretation of the effect of biblical 'all, every' as including all members of the lexeme governed by it. The totality can be identified as a universal class, or as including even the eccentric members of a paradigm partly selected according to the lexeme governed by 'all', or as uniting the two poles of an opposition whose terms are hyponyms of the lexeme governed by 'all'. Occurrences: 26.[47]

Logic3 Interpretation of the effect of a biblical negation as including all members of the lexeme governed by it. The totality can be identified as a universal class, or as including even the eccentric members of a paradigm partly selected in accordance with the lexeme governed by the negation, or as uniting both poles of an opposition whose terms are hyponyms of the lexeme governed by the negation. Occurrences: 14.[48]

Logic7 Interpretation of the effect of biblical 'and' (*waw*) as making a Mishnaic or

---

[38] See p. 379. Occurrences: mSot 9:11, mUqtsin 3:12 I (2).

[39] See p. 379. Occurrences: mKilaim 9:8 I (2), mSot 9:9 II (2) **[42]**.

[40] See p. 379.

[41] See p. 388. Occurrences: mShab 9:3 III (3) = mYoma 6:8, mPes 10:5 I (2), mYoma 6:8 = mShab 9:3 III (3).

[42] See p. 378. Occurrences: mSukkah 4:5, mMak 3:15 I (4) **[137]**, mBek 7:5 IV (4).

[43] See p. 378. Occurrences: mShab 9:2 I (2), mTaan 1:2 **[114]**.

[44] See p. 378, 5: mBer 9:5 IV (9), mKilaim 9:8 II (2), mMeg 4:9, mSan 6:5 I (2), mBek 7:5 III (4).

[45] See p. 378. Occurrences: mNaz 9:5 II (3) **[93]** (Yose), mSot 5:5 I (2), mBek 7:5 II (4).

[46] See p. 378. Occurrences: mSot 5:2, mBM 2:7 I (2), mKer 2:5 I (3).

[47] See p. 245. Examples: mBer 1:5 I (2) **[13]**, mBer 9:5 I (9) **[15] [82] [114a]**, mBer 9:5 II (2) **[114a]**, mSan 10:1 I (2) **[82]**, mBek 8:1 **[83]**.

[48] See p. 248. Occurrences: mPeah 7:7 II (3), mShab 9:6, mSheq 1:5 **[53]**, mSot 6:3 II (4) **[85]**, mBM 9:13 II (4) **[78] [110b]**, mSan 2:1 **[33]** (Yehudah), mSan 2:4 III (6), mSan 10:6 IV (6), mAZ 3:3, mHor 1:5, mMen 5:2 I (2), mArak 8:6 I (3), mTem 1:2 I (3) **[14]**, mKer 2:5 II (3).

biblical apodosis dependent on simultaneous fulfilment or applicability of all the biblical elements conjoined by it. Occurrences: 8.[49]

2. SYNTAX, TEXT STRUCTURES

Neutralizing or Utilizing the Co-text (Cotext)

Cotext1 Neutralizing the semantic effect of the biblical co-text at the sentence, clause, or phrase boundary, leading to a readjustment or, if necessary, dissolution of grammatical dependencies. Occurrences: *c*. 103.[50]

Cotext2 Explicit or tacit analysis of the meaning of a syntactic collocation in terms of a paratactic, additive, or sequential relationship between its constituents. Occurrences: 6.[51]

Cotext3 Explicit or tacit analysis of the meaning of a biblical word-form, compound, idiom, or fixed collocation, into its semantic components (or in the case of compounds, their word-forms). Occurrences: 7.[52]

Cotext4 Explicit or tacit analysis of the meaning of a biblical word-form or expression according to the semiotic meaning (see GRAPHEME/ICON) attached to its constituent graphemes, individually or in groups. One double occurrence: mKilaim 9:8 I–II (2).[53]

Cotext5 Explanation of the meaning of an expression in the light of the biblical co-text, where the latter is linked by cohesive signals or narrative connectedness beyond the clause. Occurrences: *c*. 102.[54]

Cotext5.2 Explication of the meaning of an expression in the light of a co-text whose limit depends on (or calls for an adjustment in) the scope of a demonstrative pronoun understood as a discourse deixis. Occurrences: 6.[55]

Cotext6 Explication of the meaning of a biblical expression in the light of a contiguous co-text not connected by grammatical links, lexical iteration, or other cohesive signals. Occurrences: 4.[56]

Cotext7 Explication of the meaning of an expression in the light of an extension of the grammatical period to co-text beyond the Masoretic verse boundary. Occurrences: 3.[57]

Cotext9 Explication of the meaning of a biblical expression in the light of its response function in a sequence of reported utterances by different speakers. Occurrences: 9.[58]

[49] See p. 249. Occurrences: mBQ 4:9 II (3) [87], mBQ 9:8, mSan 8:2, mSan 8:4 I (4), mSan 11:1 II (2), mHor 2:3 [112], mZeb 12:1 [86], mZeb 14:1.

[50] See p. 37.

[51] See p. 348. Occurrences: mPes 5:5 [10], mSukkah 4:5, mSot 8:4 [126], mGit 9:10 I (3), mSan 7:7 I (2), mAvot 1:18.

[52] See p. 373. Occurrences: mSot 9:9 II (2) [42], mMak 1:9 I–II (2), mMen 11:4 [135], mBek 7:5 III (4), mBek 7:5 IV (4), mMid 4:7 [136].

[53] See p. 375.

[54] See p. 41 (total is inclusive of Cotext5.2).

[55] See p. 44. Occurrences: mMak 2:5 II (2) [11], mMak 2:8 [12] = mSheb 10:8 II (2), mZeb 9:1 I (2) [138], mZeb 9:1 II (2), mZeb 11:1, mKer 1:2.

[56] See p. 45. Occurrences: mBM 9:12 III (3), mSan 3:7, mSan 4:1 [7], mHul 8:4 II (3) [66].

[57] See p. 46. Occurrences: mSan 10:4 II (2), mMak 3:10 [8], mMen 8:7 (verses 19 f.).

[58] See p. 48. Occurrences: mSot 2:5 I (5) [9] [124], mSot 2:5 III (5), mSot 2:5 IV–V (5), mSan 6:2 I–II (2) [56] [57b], mAZ 2:5 (Yehudah), mBek 1:4 II (2), mNeg 10:2 II (2).

Syntactic Relationships (Syntax)

Syntax2 Identification of a common or partially common referent for two expressions linked paratactically or asyndetically and fulfilling the same syntactic function in Scripture. Occurrences: 5.[59]

Syntax3 A textual direction is chosen for the syntactic dependency of a biblical expression, phrase, or clause which is not supported by the wider co-textual relationships, in the following way. The biblical unit is capable, from a grammatical point of view, of being connected to the preceding or to the subsequent text. Either the rabbinic choice selects the direction not privileged by the co-text, or it selects only one direction when the co-text privileges neither. Occurrences: 7.[60]

Syntax4 Construing a genitive collocation as *genitivus objectivus* when the co-text privileges the *genitivus subjectivus* meaning or vice versa. Occurrences: 3.[61]

Syntax5.1 Construing a biblical syntagma consisting of two paratactic or asyndetic biblical units (clauses or expressions), as indicating a temporal sequence, or as a hypotactic dependency (causal, final, concessive, or conditional). Occurrences: 8.[62]

Syntax5.2 Construing a biblical syntagma consisting of two paratactic clauses for whose relationship the co-text privileges simultaneity or temporal sequence, as indicating cause, consequence, purpose, concession, or condition. Occurrences: 10.[63]

*Syntax6 Construing a biblical period consisting of two clauses in causal, final, concessive, or conditional relationship as indicating an exclusively temporal relationship. One occurrence: mPeah 7:7 III (3) **[130b]**.[64]

Redundancy of Similarity, Repetition, and Synonymy (Redundancy)[65]

Redundancy2 Explication of the occurrence of two synonymous expressions or clauses in similar syntactic function in the same biblical sentence or in each other's co-text as differentiated from each other. Occurrences: 7.[66]

Redundancy3 Explication of the occurrence of two biblical sentences with similar (or identical) propositional meaning as differentiated from each other. Occurrences: 10.[67]

Redundancy4 Explication of the employment of two (or more) biblical expressions from the same lexical field in a similar syntactic function in the same biblical

---

[59] See p. 352. Occurrences: mHal 4:10 and mBik 1:3, mNed 3:11 III (10), mSot 7:5 I (5) **[128]**, mAvot 3:15 III (3), mMiqw 9:2 **[30]**.

[60] See p. 351. Occurrences: mYoma 8:9 I (3) [Ch. 14], mRH 3:2, mNed 3:11 X (10), mSot 7:4 II (2) **[127]**, mMak 3:10 **[8]**, mMen 8:7, mArak 8:6 II (3).

[61] See p. 351. Occurrences: mBM 2:7 I (2), mSan 6:4 III (3), mMak 2:5 II (2) **[11]**.

[62] See p. 354. Occurrences: mHallah 4:10 and mBik 1:3, mSot 5:5 I (2) (verse 27), mSan 6:4 I (3) **[130]**, mMak 2:4 II (2), mMak 3:6, mAvot 4:1 III (4) **[120]**, mHul 5:5, mQin 3:6 II (2).

[63] See p. 355. Occurrences: mPeah 8:9 I (4) [Ch. 1], mPeah 8:9 IV (4), mShab 9:3 II (3) **[3] [57a]** **[130a]** = mShab19:3 **[4]**, mSot 8:6 II (2), mGit 4:5, mSan 2:4 II (6), mSan 2:4 III (6), mShebu 2:5 I (3), mShebu 2:5 II (3), mMen 6:7.

[64] See p. 356.

[65] Resources without page reference are defined on pp. 329–31.

[66] See p. 330. Occurrences: mSot 8:1 II (7), mSot 8:1 V (7) **[121]**, mSan 10:3 III–IV (10) **[50]**, mSan 10:3 VII–VIII (10) **[119]**, mAvot 4:1 III (4) **[120]**.

[67] See p. 330. Occurrences: mPeah 7:7 III (3) **[130b]**, mHag 1:1 **[139]**, mSot 9:6 II–IV **[125]**, mBM 5:11 I (2), mSan 10:6 IV (6), mMak 1:3, mHul 8:4 I (3) **[119]**, mBek 1:2 **[123]**.

sentence or in each other's co-text as differentiated from each other. Occurrences: 14.[68]

Redundancy5 Explication of the employment of two (or more) biblical expressions from distinct lexical fields in a similar syntactic function in the same biblical sentence or in each other's co-text as differentiated from each other. Occurrences: 4.[69]

Redundancy6 Explication of two occurrences of the same biblical expression in the same sentence or co-text in a similar or different syntactic function as differentiated from each other. Occurrences: 17.[70]

Redundancy7 Explication of a biblical collocation employing two different word-forms belonging to the same root (for example, infinitive absolute) as differentiated from each other. Occurrence: 9.[71]

Redundancy8 Explication of two contiguous and asyndetic occurrences of the same biblical expression as differentiated from each other. Occurrences: 5.[72]

Redundancy9 Explication of the significance of a biblical syntagma through the numerically matched pairing of each of its members or subdivisions with one member of a Mishnaic paradigm. Some, but not all, pairings need to be explicable by way of a subsidiary hermeneutic resource producing a one-to-one link, and not all of the links need to involve the same hermeneutic resource. Occurrences: 10.[73]

Redundancy*.1 . . . differentiated from each other in respect of their topic or case schema (Topic2), action, speech act, or referent.

Redundancy*.2 . . . differentiated from each other in terms of a repetition of an action, an iteration, or an accumulation.

Redundancy*.3 . . . differentiated from each other in terms of a semantic extension, or mutual modification.

Redundancy*.4 . . . differentiated from each other in terms of extra emphasis.

Redundancy*.5 . . . differentiated from each other in terms of their separate contribution to a whole of complete or simultaneous parts.

Redundancy*.6 . . . differentiated from each other in terms of a switch of speaker.

Resource examples

Redundancy2.1 Explication of the occurrence of two (or more) synonymous expressions or clauses as differentiated from each other, in the following way: the expressions (clauses) occur in a similar syntactic function in the same biblical sentence or in each other's co-text; and they are differentiated from each other in respect of their topic or case schema, action, speech act, or referent.[74]

---

[68] See p. 330. Occurrences: mMQ 3:9 I (2) **[98]**, mHag 1:5 **[35] [98a]**, mYeb 6:5 I (2), mSot 2:5 I (5) **[9] [124]**, mSot 9:1 I–II (2) **[19] [121a]**, mBQ 9:7 [39], mBQ 9:8, mBM 4:10, mBM 9:13 III (4), mMen 5:6, mMen 8:5, mTem 6:3 I (3) **[140]**, mNeg 2:3 II (2) **[104]**.

[69] See p. 330. Occurrences: mTaan 4:8 III (3) **[51]**, mSan 1:6 III (5), mAvot 5:19 I–II.

[70] See p. 330. Occurrences: mPeah 8:9 I (4) [Ch. 1], mShebi 1:4, mYeb 6:6 III (3) **[102]**, mSot 2:5 III–V (5), mSot 5:1 I (3), mSot 5:1 II–III (3), mSan 1:6 III (5), mMak 2:4 II (2), mShebu 2:5 III (3), mEduy 2:10 I–II (2), mAvot 5:1, mKer 4:3, mNeg 12:6 I (3).

[71] See p. 330. Occurrences: mSot 5:4, mBQ 6:4 II (2), mBM 2:9, mBM 2:10 I (4), mSan 6:4 II (3), mSan 10:5 II (2), mHul 12:3 IV (5) **[122]**, mBek 8:8, mKer 2:5 I (3).

[72] See p. 330. Occurrences: mSot 2:5 I–V (5) **[9] [124]**.

[73] See p. 347. Occurrences: mMS 5:10 **[80] [126a]**, mMS 5:11–13, mShab 9:2 II (2), mPes 5:5 **[10]**, mSot 8:4 **[126]**, mBM 5:11 I (2), mSan 8:4 III (4) **[91] [126b]**, mSan 10:3 I–II, mSan 10:3 VI (10) **[21]**.

[74] See p. 334.

Redundancy3.3 Explication of the occurrence of two biblical sentences with similar (or identical) propositional meaning as differentiated from each other in terms of a semantic extension, or a mutual modification.[75]

Redundancy3.6 Explication of the occurrence of two biblical sentences with similar (or identical) propositional meaning as differentiated from each other in terms of a switch of speaker.[76]

Redundancy4.1 Explication of the occurrence of two (or more) biblical expressions from the same lexical field in a similar syntactic function in the same biblical sentence or in each other's co-text as differentiated from each other in respect of their topic or case schema, action, speech act, or referent.[77]

Redundancy4.2 Explication of the occurrence of two (or more) biblical expressions from the same lexical field in a similar syntactic function in the same biblical sentence or in each other's co-text as differentiated from each other in terms of a repetition of an action, an iteration, or an accumulation.[78]

Redundancy7.2 Explication of a biblical collocation employing two different word-forms belonging to the same root as differentiated from each other in terms of a repetition of an action, an iteration, or an accumulation.[79]

Redundancy8.1 Explication of two contiguous and asyndetic occurrences of the same biblical expression as differentiated from each other in respect of their topic or case schema, action, speech act, or referent.[80]

Inconsistency, Inner-biblical Contrasts and Differences (Difference)

Difference0 A biblical contradiction or discontinuity is noted or tacitly acknowledged but not taken as meaningful. Occurrences: 3.[81]

Difference2 Differentiating two closely related or similar biblical segments by allocating to each a separate subject-matter or referent in the light of a difference in their wording, thereby removing the potential for textual inconsistency. Occurrences: 11.[82]

Difference3 Narrative or propositional compatibility with one biblical segment (segment B) is used as a guiding principle in determining the nature or identity of an event or fact mentioned in another biblical segment (segment A). Occurrences: 3.[83]

Difference4 Narrative or propositional compatibility with one biblical segment (segment B) is used as the guiding principle in narrowing down meaning possibilities in another biblical segment (segment A). The result is a mutual differentiation of topics, referents, or meanings for the two passages. Occurrences: 2.[84]

Difference5 Projection of a narrative or thematic contrast between contiguous or

[75] See p. 338.
[76] See p. 341.
[77] See p. 340.
[78] See p. 336.
[79] See p. 337.
[80] See p. 340.
[81] See p. 273. Occurrences: mSot 3:2 I–II (2), mSot 7:5 V (5).
[82] See p. 267. Occurrences: mPeah 7:7 III (3) **[130b]**, mMS 5:10 **[80] [126a]**, mSot 5:3 I–II (2) **[1] [94a] [94]**, mHul 10:1 III (3), mBek 4:1, mArak 8:6 III (3), mArak 8:7 **[95]**, mQin 3:6 I–II (2).
[83] See p. 265. Occurrences: mYoma 5:5, mEduy 2:9, mMid 3:1.
[84] See page 265. Occurrences: mNaz 9:5 III (3) **[93]**, mSot 5:5 I (2).

close Scriptural segments onto two (or more) contrasting members of a Mishnaic paradigm. Occurrences: 11.[85]

Difference6 Distribution, to two (or more) contrastive members of a Mishnaic paradigm, of co-textual biblical segments set off against each other or distinguished by some linguistic or textual discontinuity. Occurrences: 6.[86]

Difference7 Distribution of two (or more) contrastive members of a Mishnaic paradigm to two discontinuous biblical verses, creating a contrastive relationship between them. By creating this link, the interpretation also increases biblical coherence. Occurrences: 11.[87]

Difference8 Identification of two aspects of one subject treated by two divergent or contradictory wordings in Scripture. These aspects are such that relationships such as harmony, union, cumulation, or combined spatial or temporal presence hold between them. As a result, both wordings can be applied to the same subject without inconsistency. Occurrences: 2.[88]

Difference*.1 Complementary distribution of the members of a binary Mishnaic paradigm to two closely related biblical segments, thereby identifying their difference in meaning.[89]

Position in the Text (Map)

Map1 Interpretation of the relative textual position of signs in Scripture in terms of sequential or spatial figures of speech, taken in their conventional figurative meaning. Occurrences: 5.[90]

3. SUBJECT-MATTER

Imposing the Perspectives of Topical Orientation (Topic)

Topic0 Tacit use of a specific assumption rooted in the Mishnaic discourse for the explication of a Scriptural expression. Occurrences: *c.* 35.[91]

Topic1 Providing a perspective which re-topicalizes, or limits the meaning choices for, a biblical expression or clause. In providing a thematic orientation, or in integrating the biblical expression/clause into a specific place in the Mishnaic discourse, the Mishnah takes over the role of the original biblical co-text. Occurrences: *c.* 110.[92]

Topic2 Determination of the meaning and subject-matter of a biblical expression or clause through its linkage to a Mishnaic apodosis. The apodosis can be one of several rival apodoses, and is part of Mishnaic protasis–apodosis unit (or of a series of such units). The conditional alternatives belonging to this Mishnaic

---

[85] See p. 274. Occurrences: mYoma 3:11 **[40]**, mTaan 2:1, mTaan 4:8 I/II (3) **[95]**, mYeb 8:2 I (3) **[28]**, mKet 3:2, mSan 11:5, mMak 3:6, mMak 3:15 III (4), mAvot 2:13, mAvot 3:2 I (3) **[36]**, mAvot 3:18 I (2).

[86] See pp. 274 f. Occurrences: mYoma 3:1–6, 3:7, 7:1, 7:3 f. (harmonization), mRH 2:9 II (2), mSot 9:5 I (3), mMak 2:4 II (2), mMak 3:15 I (4) **[137]**, mNeg 12:6 III (3) **[97]**.

[87] See p. 275. Occurrences: mMQ 3:9 I–II (2) **[98] [99]**, mQid 4:14 I–II (4), mBM 9:12 II (3) **[111]**, mAvot 5:16, mAvot 5:18 I–II (2), mAvot 5:19 I–II (2), mMen 13:11.

[88] See p. 274. Occurrences: mSheq 6:6 II (2), mYoma 3:4/6 f., 7:1/3 f.

[89] See p. 270.

[90] See p. 357. Occurrences: mKer 6:9 I–IV (4) **[131]**, mYad 4:8 I (2) **[131a] [57]**.

[91] See p. 78. Examples: mPeah 8:9 I (4) [Ch. 1], mSot 9:1 II (2) **[19] [121a]**, mQid 4:14 IV (4) **[17]**, mBQ 9:11 (and see 9:12) **[20]**, mArak 4:4 II (4) **[75]**.

[92] See p. 70.

412 APPENDIX I

apodosis subdivide a larger halakhic theme not so subdivided in the Scriptural co-text; where the biblical text is not part of a conditional structure, this resource also conditionalizes the biblical segment. Occurrences: c. 159.[93]

Topic2.1 Determination of the meaning and subject-matter of a biblical clause or sentence (conditional or not) by linking it to the apodosis of one of a set of Mishnaic protases. This set of protases can be generated from the permutation or stressing of linguistic items in the biblical segment, thereby subdividing the larger halakhic theme not so subdivided in the biblical segment or its co-text. Occurrences: 10.[94]

Topic2.2 Differentiation of elements in the biblical wording of a conditional syntagma into a Mishnaic set of separate protases leading to the same Mishnaic apodosis, the latter being a repetition or rephrasing of the biblical main clause. Two occurrences: mBM 8:1 I–II (2) **[37]**.[95]

Topic3 Explication of a Scriptural expression by way of a Mishnaic companion term whose meaning is specific, standardized, or defined by its recurrent use or interdependence with other terms in the Mishnaic discourse. Occurrences: c. 252.[96]

Topic3.1 Explication of a Scriptural expression by way of an express rabbinic maxim whose validity is treated as unproblematic. Occurrences: c. 57.[97]

Topic4 Explication of two (or more) biblical expressions or clauses by way of functional concepts with a binary (or tripartite, etc.) structure whose meaning is defined by their recurrent use or interdependence with other terms in the Mishnaic discourse. Occurrences: c. 29.[98]

Topic4.1 Explication of two (or more) biblical expressions or clauses by way of a functional proposition which articulates a binary (or tripartite, etc.) structure and whose validity is treated as unproblematic. Occurrences: 7.[99]

Topic5 Determination of the meaning of a biblical expression or clause by embedding it into a Mishnaic account of the same topic whose greater internal diversification is not linked to any differentiation of signs in Scripture. Occurrences: c. 43.[100]

Topic7 Provision of a close rephrasing of a Scriptural expression, clause, or norm. The semantic difference of this rephrasing to Scripture is minimal and not exploited for the allocation of a separate topic or function in the Mishnaic discourse. Thus, the resultant adjustment of links within the biblical co-text is also negligible or imperceptible. Occurrences: c. 33.[101]

[93] See p. 104. Total includes 12 cases of Topic2.1/2.2.
[94] See p. 105. Occurrences: mShab 9:2 II (2), mHag 1:5 **[35] [98a]**, mYeb 3:9 **[100]**, mYeb 9:6, mSot 4:1 **[108]**, mGit 3:2 **[109]**, mBQ 3:9 II (4), mBQ 3:9 IV (4), mBQ 9:8, mBM 3:12 II (2).
[95] See p. 108.
[96] See p. 74. Occurrences if T3.1 is deducted: c. 209.
[97] See p. 77. Examples: mShab 9:1 = mAZ 3:6 II (2), **[69]**, mShab 9:3 II (3) = mShab 19:3 **[3] [57a] [130a]**, mTaan 3:8 **[44]**, mTaan 4:2, mSot 9:1 II (2) **[19] [121a]**, mBQ 5:7 **[76]**, mBM 2:5 **[72]**, mSan 1:4 I–II (2) **[68] [67]**, mSan 8:1 **[101]**, [mAbot 6:3 I (3)] **[52]**, mArak 3:5 II (2) **[58]**, mNeg 12:6 III (3) **[97]**.
[98] See pp. 78f. Examples: mMQ 3:9 II (2) **[99]**, mSan 10:3 VI–VII (10) **[21] [119]**, mAvot 4:1 III (4) **[120]**, mArak 8:7 **[95]**, mNeg 12:6 III (3) **[97]**.
[99] See p. 80. Occurrences: mSot 1:8 I–IV(4) **[22] [49]**, mSot 1:9 I–III (5), mSot 8:1 VI (7).
[100] See p. 108. Examples: mBik 3:2 **[46]** and mBik 3:4 ff., mPes 7:1 I (2) **[24] [37a]**, mTaan 4:8 I/II (3) **[95]**, mSot 2:2 **[38]**, mSot 7:5 I (5) **[128]**, mSot 7:6 = mTam 7:2 **[48] [54a]**, mBB 8:3 **[59]**, mSan 11:4 **[84]**, mMen 11:4 **[135]**, mMen 11:5 **[134]**, mTam 7:2 = mSot 7:6 **[48] [54a]**.
[101] See p. 305. Examples: mSot 2:2 **[38]**, mSot 9:15 III (3) **[43]**, mBM 9:13 I (4) **[113]**, mSan 2:1 **[33]**, mSan 8:4 III (4) **[91] [126b]**, mAvot 3:15 I (3) **[60]**, mMen 10:4 I (2) **[113]**.

Topic8 Explication of a biblical term (or an adaptation of it), when in expressive use (π), by the provision of a legal or otherwise globalized definition. The definition is presented with a view to the term's Mishnaic function and without explicit or discernible recourse to its Scriptural one. Occurrences: *c.* 52.[102]

Topic8.5 Explicit witholding of Mishnaic commitment from what the Mishnah acknowledges to be or explicates as the meaning of a biblical expression or clause. Occurrences: 9.[103]

Topic9 Use of a Scriptural expression or clause as the name of a definite textual entity from Scripture beginning with that expression or clause, or containing it. Occurrences: 12.[104]

4. ANALOGICAL PROCEDURES

Analogy, a fortiori *Argument (Analogy)*

Analogy0 Analogical transfer between two subjects without reliance on Scriptural wording. Occurrences: *c.* 13.[105]

Analogy1 Selection of a situational or substantive similarity (or dissimilarity) between a biblical subject and a non-biblical subject (in particular Topic2) in order to determine the apodosis of a Mishnaic protasis–apodosis unit. Occurrences: 6.[106]

Analogy2 Selection and transfer of a substantive feature between two subjects defined as related on the basis of the textual proximity of their biblical representations, with Scripture also providing a shared or parallel linguistic treatment for them. Occurrences: 15.[107]

*Analogy2.1 Selection and transfer of a substantive feature between two subjects defined as related on the basis of the textual proximity of their biblical representations. One occurrence: mHul 8:4 II (3) **[66]**.[108]

Analogy3 Selection and transfer of a substantive feature between two subjects linked by a biblical expression of a common feature, comparison, or metaphorical similarity. Occurrences: 10.[109]

Analogy3.5 Selection and transfer, on the basis of an equality of relationships, of a substantive feature between two subjects linked by a biblical expression of a common feature, comparison, or metaphorical relationship. Occurrences: 2.[110]

---

[102] See pp. 97 f. and pp. 231 f. Total inclusive of T8.5 cases. Examples: mPeah 4:10 **[31]**, mPes 7:1 I (2) **[24] [37a]**, mBQ 1:1 **[25]**, mBQ 5:5 I (2) **[5]**, mBQ 9:7 **[39]**, mSan 8:1 **[101]**, mBek 7:3 **[29]**.

[103] See p. 313. Occurrences: mShebi 10:3, mTer 3:6 I (2), mPes 9:2 II (2), mKet 4:3 III (3) **[90]**, mSot 9:5 III (3), mBQ 4:9 III (3), mBQ 5:5 II (2), mSan 7:7 I (2) (Lev. 20:2), mArak 5:6.

[104] See p. 99. Occurrences: mBer 1:5 I (2) **[13]**, mBer 2:2, mPes 10:4, mYoma 7:1, mSukkah 3:9, mSot 7:7, mSot 7:8 II–III (3) **[45]**, mMak 3:14, mTam 5:1 **[32]**, mYad 3:5, mYad 4:8 I (2) **[131a] [57]**.

[105] See p. 198. Occurrences detected so far: mErub 4:6, mPes 6:2 II (5), mPes 6:2 III (5), mYT 1:6 I (2), mShebu 3:1, mEduy 6:3 III (4?), mZeb 1:1 **[65]** see mYad 4:2, mZeb 7:6 II (2), mMen 12:5, mArak 4:4 II (4) **[75]**, mTem 1:1 I (3), mTem 2:2, mYad 4:3 I (3).

[106] See p. 209. Occurrences: mRH 2:9 II (2), mMak 2:2, mMen 13:10. Analogy1.5: mAZ 3:5 I (2) **[71]**, mZeb 10:1, mKer 6:9 IV (4).

[107] See p. 203. Occurrences: mShab 6:4, mNed 10:7 II (2), mSot 8:2 II (3), mSan 1:4 I–II (2) **[68] [67]**, mSan 4:1 **[7]**, mMak 1:7 III (6), mMak 1:7 V (6), mMak 1:8 I (3), mShebu 1:3, mHul 2:3, mHul 12:3 III (5), mKer 6:7.   [108] See p. 203.

[109] See p. 207. Total includes Analogy3.5; occurrences: mShab 9:1 = mAZ 3:6 II (2) **[69]**, mShab 9:4 **[129]**, mSan 4:1 **[7]** (one law), mAZ 3:6 I (2), mAZ 3:6 II (2) = mShab 9:1 **[69]**, mZeb 8:11, mTem 1:1 III (3), mTem 1:2 III (3).

[110] See p. 209. Occurrences: mSan 10:3 IX (10) **[70]**, mSan 10:3 X (10) **[71]**.

Analogy4.1 Inference by analogy that the protasis of norm m has the apodosis A, in the following manner: if the protasis n which belongs to the category N, which category is lower on scale X, has apodosis A; then protasis m which belongs to the category M, which category is higher on scale X, logically also has apodosis A (or: logically must have an intensification of the apodosis A). Occurrences: 14.[111]

Analogy4.2 Inference by analogy that norm m possesses predicate A, in the following manner: if norm n which belongs to the category N, which category is lower on scale X, has predicate A; then norm m which belongs to the category M, which category is higher on scale X, logically also has predicate A (or: logically must have more of the quality A). Occurrences: 5.[112]

Analogy5 Inference by analogy that predicate A applies to subject m, in the following manner: if subject n which belongs to the category N, which category is lower on scale X, has predicate A; then subject m which belongs to the category M, which category is higher on scale X, logically also has predicate A (or: logically must have more of the quality A). Occurrences: 3.[113]

Analogy8 Transfer of a (substantive) feature from the more specific to the more general of two Scriptural subjects mentioned in norms or statements which are substantively identical or receive a shared or similar linguistic treatment in Scripture, and are textually contiguous. Occurrences: 8.[114]

Analogy8.1 Transfer of a (substantive) feature from the more specific to the more general of two Scriptural subjects mentioned in norms or statements which are substantively identical and receive a similar linguistic treatment in Scripture. One occurrence: mTem 1:6 III (3) **[73]**.[115]

Analogy*5 Selection and transfer, on the basis of an equality of relationships, ...[116]

Analogy Between Two Occurrences of the Same Lexeme (Keying)

Keying2 Transfer of a feature linked to the co-text of a lexeme at one Scriptural location (location B) to the same lexeme's occurrence in a different co-text at another Scriptural location (location A). Occurrence: 9.[117]

*Keying3 Transfer of a feature linked to the co-text of a lexeme at one Scriptural location (location B) to the same lexeme's occurrence in a different co-text at another Scriptural location (location A) which is in close proximity to location B or exhibiting thematic links with it. Occurrences: 2.[118]

---

[111] See pp. 183f. Occurrences: mTer 5:4 I (2), mPes 6:2 IV (5), mYT 5:2, mYeb 8:3 II (2) **[63]**, mMak 3:15 IV (4) **[61]**, mShebu 3:6, mZeb 7:4, mZeb 7:6 I (2), mMen 8:5, mHul 10:1 II (2), mHul 12:5, mBek 9:1 I (2), mTem 1:1 II (3), mNeg 10:2 I (2), mYad 4:7 **[62]**.

[112] See p. 178. Occurrences: mPes 6:2 I (5), mMak 1:7 VI (6), mBek 1:1 II (2), mArak 8:4, mYad 4:8 I (2) **[131a]** **[57]**.

[113] See pp. 187ff. Occurrences: [mDem 2:2], mYoma 8:9 III (3) **[4]**, mSan 6:5 II (2) **[64]**, [mAvot 6:3 I (3)], mNeg 12:5 IV (4).

[114] See p. 213. Total includes one case of Analogy8.1; occurrences: mBQ 5:5 I (2) **[5]**, mBM 2:5 **[72]**, mMak 1:7 I (6), mMen 7:6, mBek 1:2 **[123]**, mArak 4:4 I (3) **[75]**, mArak 4:4 III (4) **[75]**.

[115] See p. 213.

[116] See p. 209.

[117] See p. 217. Occurrences: mNaz 9:5 I (3), mSot 6:3 IV (4) **[74]**, mSot 7:3, mSot 7:4 I (2), mSot 7:5 I (5) **[128]**, mSan 1:6 V (5), mSan 8:2, mHor 1:4 II (2), mHul 5:5.

[118] See p. 220. Occurrences: mArak 4:4 I (4) **[75]**, mArak 4:4 III (4) **[75]**.

5. NARRATIVE

Biblical Events as Exemplifying a Norm (Norm)

Norm1 Identification of an action reported in Scripture of a human protagonist as conforming to a behavioural norm formulated by the Mishnah. Occurrences: 6.[119]

Norm1.1 Identification of an action reported in Scripture of a human protagonist as the initial and constitutive performance of a Mishnaic ritual or procedure.[120]

Norm2 Identification of human speech reported in Scripture and set in a narrative context as applying a behavioural norm formulated by the Mishnah. Occurrences: 2.[121]

Norm3 Identification of divine speech reported in Scripture and set in a narrative context as example of the application of a behavioural norm formulated by the Mishnah. Occurrences: 6.[122]

Norm3.1 Identification of divine speech reported in Scripture and set in a narrative biblical context as the initial and constitutive creation of a Mishnaic institution or ritual.[123]

[*Norm4] Identification of a divine deed reported in Scripture and set in a narrative context as exemplifying a behavioural norm formulated by the Mishnah. One possible occurrence: mYeb 6:6 II (3) **[55]**.[124]

Norm5 Identification of the speech reported in Scripture of a biblical protagonist as conforming to a norm of verbal behaviour formulated by the Mishnah. Occurrences: 5.[125]

Norm5.2 Identification of the textual format of a passage in Scripture, or of the format of a speech reported in Scripture of a protagonist, as conforming to a Mishnaic norm for the formulation of a legal document or speech act. Occurrences: 2.[126]

Norm8 Identification of an event or speech reported in Scripture in a narrative context as illustration of a general Mishnaic statement articulating a regularity governing nature or the world. Occurrences: *c*. 25.[127]

Norm*.1 Identification . . . .as the initial and constitutive creation/performance of a Mishnaic institution or ritual.[128]

---

[119] See p. 153. Occurrences: mSot 7:6 = mTam 7:2 **[48] [54a]**, mSan 2:2, mSan 2:3 I (2) **[6] [52a]**, mMen 4:3 I (2), mMen 13:10, mTam 7:2 = mSot 7:6 **[48] [54a]**.

[120] See p. 155.

[121] See p. 154. Occurrences: mShab 9:3 I (3), mSheq 1:5 **[53]**.

[122] See p. 154. Occurrences: mYoma 1;1, mBQ 8:7 I (2), mSan 1:6 I–II (5) **[54]**, mSan 6:1, mBek 1:1 II (2).

[123] See p. 154.

[124] See p. 157.

[125] See p. 159. Occurrences (3 if Norm5.2 cases are deducted): mBer 9:5 V–IX (9), mBQ 8:7 II (2), mSan 6:2 I (2) **[56]**.

[126] See p. 160. Occurrences: mQid 3:4 I (2) **[110]**, mYad 4:8 I (2) **[131a] [57]**.

[127] See p. 164, and the overview p. 168. Examples: mShab 9:3 II (3) **[3] [57a] [130a]** = mShab19:3 **[4]**, mTaan 1:2 **[114]**, mSan 4:5 I (9) **[105]**, mSan 6:2 II (2) **[57b]**, mArak 3:5 II (2) **[58]**.

[128] See p. 154.

6. PRAGMATICS

Canonical Traits, Existential Presuppositions (Habit)

Habit4 Explication of one of the canonical semantic traits of a lexeme as possible or definite condition of the application of the biblical norm in which it occurs. Occurrences: 8.[129]

Habit6 Explication of one of the existential presuppositions of a norm as possible or definite condition of its application. Occurrences: *c*. 32.[130]

Habit7 Explication of an expression's semantic encapsulation as possible or definite condition of the application of the biblical norm in which it occurs. Occurrences: 3.[131]

Biblical or Non-Biblical Fixed Wording Used as Utterance About Biblical Events (Use)

Use1 Use of a biblical sentence making no specific reference to a singular event or specific person as utterance about a specific biblical event, chain of events, or person. The sentence (the tenor verse) is thus used to endow biblical happenings or characters with articulated structure, meaning, or evaluation. Occurrences: 4.[132]

*Use2$_\Omega$ Use of a biblical sentence containing no specific reference to a singular event or specific person as utterance about two or more specific biblical events or persons. The sentence (the tenor verse) is thus used to articulate the structure, meaning, or evaluation of these biblical happenings or characters in their relation to each other. One occurrence: mTaan 4:8 III (3) **[51]**.[133]

[Use3] Use of a biblical sentence containing no specific reference to a singular event or specific person as utterance about a specific event, chain of events, or person referred to in a second biblical sentence, also quoted. The unspecific sentence (the tenor verse) is thus used to endow biblical happenings or characters with articulated structure, meaning, or evaluation. At the same time its linguistic relationship to the verse directly referring to these happenings or characters (the event verse) is also highlighted.[134]

[Use4] Use of a biblical sentence containing no specific reference to a singular event or specific person as utterance about two or more biblical events or persons referred to in a second (or third, etc.) biblical sentence, also quoted. The unspecific sentence (the tenor verse) is thus used to articulate the structure, meaning, or evaluation of these biblical happenings or characters in their relation to each other. At the same time its linguistic relationship to the verse(s) directly referring to these happenings or characters (the event verse/s) is also highlighted.[135]

[129] See p. 261. Occurrences: mKet 3:5 II (2) **[92] [110a]**, mBM 2:10 IV (4), mHor 1:4 II (2), mZeb 14:2, mMen 6:7, mHul 11:2 III (3), mArak 7:5, mMakh 1:3 II (2).
[130] See p. 255. Examples: mBer 9:5 II (9) **[114a]**, mPeah 7:7 I (3) **[115]**, mBik 1:4 I (2) **[47]**, mHag 1:1 **[139]**, mKet 4:3 III (3) **[90]**, mSan 10:6 I (6) **[88]**, mHul 8:4 III (3) **[89]**.
[131] See p. 258. Occurrences: mSan 8:4 III (4) **[91] [126b]**, mNeg 2:3 **[104]** (or R4.4), mNeg 12:5 III (4) (Shim'on).
[132] See pp. 128 f. Occurrences: mSan 10:3 IV (10) **[50]**, mSan 10:3 VII–VIII (10) **[119]**, mEduy 8:7 I (3).
[133] See p. 131. There is a second occurrence in *Qinyan Torah*: [mAvot 6:3 I (3)] **[52]**.
[134] See p. 129.
[135] See pp. 132 f.

APPENDIX I 417

*Use5 Use of a rabbinic parable to articulate the underlying structure, meaning, or evaluation of a biblical event or chain of events or the character of a biblical person. One occurrence: mSan 4:5 V (9).[136]

Use6 Use of a rabbinic maxim to articulate the underlying structure, meaning, or evaluation of a biblical event or chain of events or the character of a biblical person. Occurrences: 19.[137]

[Use8] Use of a biblical sentence containing context-sensitive or deictic terms but no specific reference to a singular event or specific person (tenor verse) as utterance placed into the mouth of a biblical protagonist articulating the underlying structure, meaning, or evaluation of a biblical event in which he/she is involved. Page 135, illustration: [mAvot 6:3 I (3)] [52].

Verses Performed. Verses Used as Utterances About Non-Biblical Events (Performance)

Performance2 Use of Scriptural wording as utterance to characterize or judge a singular non-biblical event or person, or unique non-biblical set of circumstances. Occurrences: 13.[138]

Performance3 Use of a Scriptural expression or clause as rabbinic utterance directly expressing (π) the apodosis of a Mishnaic protasis–apodosis unit. Occurrences: *c.* 39.[139]

Performance4 Use of Scriptural wording as utterance necessary in the performance of an obligation prescribed or reported in the Mishnah. Occurrences: 23.[140]

Performance8 Use of context-sensitive or deictic Scriptural wording as rabbinic utterance. Occurrences: 12.[141]

FORMAL FEATURES

π   Use of a biblical word, phrase, or clause, in its original or a modified form, in the expression of a Mishnaic proposition or norm without accompanying restatement or reduplication (*pi* sign). Occurrences: at least 225.[142]

§   Reiteration and explication of a biblical term used expressively (π) in an earlier Mishnaic list (paragraph sign). Occurrences: *c.* 55.[143]

---

[136] See p. 127.

[137] See p. 125 and p. 168. Occurrences: mRH 3:8 I–II (2), mNed 3:11 VII (10), mNed 3:11 IX–X (10), mSot 1:8 I–II (4) [22] [49], mSot 1:8 III–IV (4), mSot 1:9 I–IV(5), mSot 8:1 VI (7), mBB 8:3 [59], mAvot 5:6, mAvot 5:16, mAvot 5:17, mAvot 5:18 I–II (2).

[138] See p. 113. Occurrences: mYoma 3:11 [40], mTaan 3:8 [44], mMQ 3:9 II (2) [99], mNed 9:10, mSot 9:9 I (2), mSot 9:9 II (2) [42], mSot 9:11, mSot 9:12, mSot 9:15 II–III (3) [43], mYad 4:3 II–III (3) [41], mYad 4:4 IV (4).

[139] See p. 106. Examples: mHag 1:5 [35] [98a], mYeb 6:6 III (3) [102], mBM 9:12 II (3) [111], mAvot 3:2 I (3) [36], mHul 4:5, 5:1 [27].

[140] See p. 119. Occurrences: mMS 5:10 [80] [126a], mMS 5:11–13, mMS 5:14, mBik 1:4 I (2) [47], mBik 1:5, mBik 3:2 [46] and mBik 3:4 ff., mPes 10:5 II (2), mYoma 3:8 = 4:2 = 6:1, mSukkah 4:5, mSukkah 5:4 II (2), mTaan 2:1, mYeb 12:3 I–II (2) [116], mYeb 12:6 II (5), mYeb 12:6 IV–V (5), mSot 2:5 I–V (5) [9] [124], mSot 7:8 II (3) [45], mNeg 12:5 I (4) [107].

[141] See p. 116. Occurrences: mMS 5:11–13, mMS 5:14, mBik 1:4 I (2) [47], mBik 1:5, mBik 3:2 [46] and mBik 3:4ff, mPes 10:5 II (2), mYoma 3:8 = 4:2 = 6:1, mTaan 3:8 [44], mYeb 12:3 I (2) [116], mYeb 12:3 II (2), mSot 7:8 II (3) [45], mAvot 5:5.

[142] See p. 85.

[143] See p. 98.

Δ   A situation, Dictum, or practice to which biblical wording applies is marked
as lying in the past or as obsolete, or the application of biblical wording itself
is presented as an act of the past (*delta* sign). Occurrences: *c.* 89.[144]

Σ   Juxtaposition of two or more midrashic units (with the Lemma preceding the
Dictum) or two or more instances of expressive use (π) of biblical wording in
such a way that their sequence corresponds to the sequence of the segments in
their Scriptural co-text (*sigma* sign). Occurrences: *c.* 64.[145]

Ω   Position at the end of a tractate or chapter (final *mishnah*). Occurrences: 48.[146]

◊   Position in the final *mishnah* of a chapter inside a tractate, or in the penultimate
mishnah of a tractate. Occurrences: 54.[147]

¶   Part of a dispute structure. Occurrences: *c.* 238.[148]

•   Ascribed to a named rabbi. Occurrences: *c.* 281.

®   Double representation of the Mishnaic position in a midrashic unit (in addition to a Scriptural quotation). Occurrences: *c.* 59.[149]

≈   Same resource as in a neighbouring unit. Occurrences: more than 71.

¬   Presented so as to be refuted; also indicates that the application of a certain
resource is implicitly rejected by use of an alternative resource for that
Lemma. Occurrences: *c.* 66.[150]

‡   Continuation format of presentation of a paraphrase of the Lemma. Occurrences: *c.* 19.

¡   The Lemma provides the protasis of a Mishnaic protasis–apodosis unit.
Occurrences: at least 10 (mostly linked to π).[151]

---

[144] See p. 123.   [148] See pp. 24, 190 f.
[145] See p. 317.   [149] See p. 326.
[146] See p. 20.   [150] See p. 24, n. 84 and p. 190.
[147] See p. 20.   [151] See p. 111, n. 1.

Appendix II: Index of Mishnaic Units of Interpretation and Their Resources

The index provided below is an extract from my *Database of Midrashic Units in the Mishnah* which, at the time of writing, still has some gaps in the description of individual passages, as well as a number of ambiguities. An updated version will be available on the internet at the time of the publication of this book (http://www.art.man.ac.uk/mes/samely/). The symbols and abbreviations are those used throughout this book and explained in Appendix I, except that all resource names are abbreviated by their first letter (i.e. Topic1 becomes T1, etc.). Where I am unsure which resource to allocate, this is indicated by a question-mark, by use of round brackets, or by use of the words 'or', or 'alternatively'. In some cases the Lemma picked out by the resource is identified in brackets (both Hebrew and English are used). The information here given is exported from two fields of the *Database*: the Mishnaic reference, and the hermeneutic profile. The *Database* offers, in addition to a number of other points of information, a discursive explanation of the allocation of each resource to each passage. An example of a full entry can be found at the end of this Appendix.

Passages containing an interpretation of ordinary language (not biblical wording) are marked by the use of square brackets. The most recent revision of the *Database* is reflected in this list up to mGit 3:2. Entries for mAvot are not included.

mBer 1:3 I (3)	•¶W6.1 x 2 T1
mBer 1:3 II (3) **[142]**	•¶O8T1W7
mBer 1:3 III (3)	•¶D2O8T1W1.2W2
mBer 1:5 I (2) **[13]**	®•¶C1D2≈L1T1T3x2T9W1x2
mBer 1:5 II (2)	•¶≈L1T1T4
mBer 2:2 I (2)	T9
mBer 2:2 II (2)	•¶[M1x2] T3T9
mBer 7:3	•¶C1O1.4T1W1.2 also: P4(Cherubim)
mBer 9:5 I (9) **[15] [82a] [114a]**	ΩL1O6T3
mBer 9:5 II (9) [114a]	Ω®¬H6L1O6W1W1.2
mBer 9:5 III (9)	Ω®E1.0O6W1
mBer 9:5 IV (9)	Ω®G3x2O6W1W3
mBer 9:5 V (9)	ΩA4.1
mBer 9:5 VI (9)	ΩΔN5
mBer 9:5 VII (9)	ΩΔN5
mBer 9:5 VIII (9)	ΩπC1T1W7
mPeah 2:2	¡πC1C5T1 L1?
mPeah 4:10 **[31]**	§πT8
mPeah 5:6 cf. 7:3 II (2)	E1.2(E7?)T2W1
mPeah 7:1	π x 2 •(O1?)
mPeah 7:3 I (2)	§πT8
mPeah 7:3 II (2), cf. 5:6	E1.2(E7?)T2W1
mPeah 7:4	πT8
mPeah 7:7 I (3) **[115]**	®•¶πH6T2W1 (grape-gather)
mPeah 7:7 II (3)	®•¶πL3O9R3.1T2
mPeah 7:7 III (3) **[130b]**	•¶R3.1S6T1W1.2(*ki*)

mPeah 8:9 I (4) [pp. 7 f., 16]
mPeah 8:9 IIb (4)variant
mPeah 8:9 IV (4)
mDem 2:2
mKilaim 9:8 I (2)
mKilaim 9:8 II (2)
mShebi 1:4
mShebi 10:2
mShebi 10:3
mShebi 10:8 I (2) **[132]**
mShebi 10:8 II (2) = mMak 2:8
mTer 3:6
mTer 3:7 I (4)
mTer 3:7 II (4)
mTer 3:7 III (4)
mTer 3:7 IV (4)
mTer 5:4 I (2)
mTer 5:4 II (2)
mTer 6:6 I (2)
mTer 6:6 II (2)
mMS 5:10 **[80] [126a]**
mMS 5:11–12
mMS 5:13–14
mMS 5:15
mHallah 4:10 and mBik 1:3
mBik 1:2 I (2) **[34]**
mBik 1:2 II (2)
mBik 1:3 and mHallah 4:10
mBik 1:4 I (2) **[47]**
mBik 1:5
mBik 1:9 **[117]**
mBik 3:2 **[46]** and mBik 3:4 ff.
mShab 1:1
mShab 6:4
mShab 8:7 I (2)
mShab 8:7 II (2)
mShab 9:1 = mAZ 3:6 II (2) **[69]**
mShab 9:2 I (2) [see 9:1]
mShab 9:2 II (2)
mShab 9:3 I (3)
mShab 9:3 II (3) **[3] [57a] [130a]**
　= mShab19:3 **[130a]**
mShab 9:3 III (3) = mYoma 6:8
mShab 9:4 **[129]**
mShab 9:6
mErub 4:6
mPes 2:2
mPes 3:3
mPes 5:3
mPes 5:5 **[10]**
mPes 6:2 I (5)
mPes 6:2 II (5)
mPes 6:2 III (5)
mPes 6:2 IV (5)
mPes 6:2 V (5)
mPes 7:1 I (2) **[24] [37a]**
mPes 7:1 II (2)
mPes 9:1 I (2)
mPes 9:1 II (2)
mPes 9:2 I (2)

ΩπO1R6.1S5.2T0T2W1(to bless; trust)
ΩC5?E1.0T0T1W1(*darash*)
ΩC1C5S5.2T0W6.1(blinds)
[¶A5T3]
®πC4I3W3
® • (¶)C4G3(I3?)W3T3(Father)
πC1(R3.1)R6.1T1
π_j
• Δ?πP2T8.5
◊≈C1≈O1≈O6≈T2≈W1(*davar*)
◊≈C1≈O1≈O6≈T2≈W1(*davar*)
T2T8.5W1
πC5(K2?)T1T3(¬W9)
πC1?T1T3¬W9
πL1T1T3
πO1T1W1
• ¶A4.1
• ¶¬A4.1? / A4.1?
® • ¶T1W1.2(article)
® • ¶T1W1.2(article)
ΣΔπC1(*gam*)D2E5.5(*gam*)P4R9(from the house)T3
ΣP4R9T2T3T7(mourning) (5:13 ‡)
◊Σ(•)¶H6O1.3?O2?P4P8T3
ΩΔ • T8.5
ΔC5O8S2S5.1?T2(*ma'aseh*)T3
(®)O0O1O1.3T2
O2O1.3T3
ΔC5O8S2S5.1?T2(*ma'aseh*)T3
H6O1.4P4P8T3
H6O1.3O2P4P8T3
®O6T1T3
ΔC5P4P8T3T5
π_j
• ¶A2C5E2.1T1T2T3
◊ • ¶C1T1T2 *zekher*
◊ • ¶C1T1T2 *ra'ayah*
® • A3C1E9T2T3.1W6.1
• A3C1E9G2(*bet*)T0T1W3W6.2
C1O1.4(R9)T2.1T3
C1N2R3.1T1T2T3W1

C5N8S5.2T2T3.1
ΔC1I5E9T1
A3C1E9?T1T2? *zekher*
• C1C5E1.0L3T1T2T3
[A0]
L3O1.3R6.1T2T3
• ¶π¬T2
O1T8(T0)T2
ΔC2C5R9T1T5
• ¶A4.2T3
• ¶¬A4.2
• ¶¬A4.2
• ¶¬A4.2 x 2
• ¶πC5O9R2.1R2.4T1T2
• ¶πT5T8
• ¶O1T5T8
π_j
C5D5O8T2T3
§ • ¶πT8(T8.5)

mPes 9:2 II (2)
mPes 10:4
mPes 10:5 I (2)
mPes 10:5 II (2)
mSheq 1:4
mSheq 1:5 [53]
mSheq 3:2
mSheq 3:3
mSheq 5:1
mSheq 6:3
mSheq 6:6 I (2)
mSheq 6:6 II (2)
mYoma 1:1
mYoma 3:4/6f., 7:1/3f.
mYoma 3:8; cf. 4:2. 6:2
mYoma 3:11 [40]
mYoma 5:1
mYoma 5:5
mYoma 6:8 = mShab 9:3 III (3)
mYoma 7:1
mYoma 8:9 I (3) [p. 350]
mYoma 8:9 II (3)
mYoma 8:9 III (3) [4]
mSuk 2:6, cf. mHag 1:6
mSuk 3:9
mSuk 4:1
mSuk 4:5
mSuk 5:4 I (2)
mSuk 5:4 II (2)
mYT 1:6 I (2)
mYT 1:6 II (2)
mYT 5:2
mRH 1:2
mRH 1:9
mRH 2:9 I (2)
mRH 2:9 II (2)
mRH 3:2
mRH 3:8 I (2)
mRH 3:8 II (2)
mRH 4:6
mTaan 1:1
mTaan 1:2 [114]
mTaan 1:7
mTaan 2:1
mTaan 3:3
mTaan 3:5
mTaan 3:8 [44]
mTaan 4:2
mTaan 4:8 I/II (3) [96]
mTaan 4:8 III (3) [51]
mMeg 1:3
mMeg 3:3
mMeg 3:6
mMeg 4:9
mMeg 4:10
mMQ 3:9 I (2) [98]
mMQ 3:9 II (2) [98]
mHag 1:1 [139]
mHag 1:5 [35] [98a]
mHag 1:6, cf. mSuk 2:5

§•¶π(D0)I4T8.5
T9(U6)
π(biblical I5)
C5D4O1.4P4P8W1
Δ¶E1.0(T2)
ΔC5L3N2T2T3
ΔC1L7T1T3W6.1
[ΔπP4I5]
[(W7)W9]
•¶πΔD5T3≈[W9]
π
ΔC1D2D8T1
•¶C5H6L7N3.1W1
[ΔD8T5]
ΔP4P8
◊ΔC1D5P2
Δ•¶O1.4T5
ΔπD3N3.1
Δ•C1E9I5T1
T9
Ω®•C1C5O1S3T1T3
Ω•C1C5O1O1.3T1
ΩA5E9C1C5T3W1
•¶(P3)T1T2
T9
π
•¶ΔC2G1P4W3
Δ(I5)T3T9
ΔπO1P4
•¶A0
•¶¬A0
A4.1
C5(L1)T1T3W1W2
◊C5C5.2E1.0R6.4T0T1T2W1.2
◊•C5.2D6.1O0O1.3T1
◊•A1C1D6?O9T3
•¶S2T1W1.2
◊≈D5≈N8T1≈T3≈T3.1≈U6≈(W7)
◊C5≈D5≈N8≈T3≈T3.1≈U6≈(W7)
T9
[•¶O1]
•¶C5(G2)N8O7O8T0T1(W3)
◊C1C5G3N8T0T3W3
Δπ(A2)D5 x 2 (P7)P8
¡N8
π¡(list)C5E1.2T1T2
ΔC1P2P8T3.1(mashal)
ΔC5O1O1.3O8T0T1T3.1T5(W1)
ΩΔπD5P8W6.2W7
ΩΔπC5R5.1U2W7
[§πT8T3]
•C2?C5O1.4T1W6.1
◊T0T8?
ΔC5E4.2W1W5
T3 (multiple)
Ω§πC5D7O1.4R4.1
ΩπC5D7P2T4
•¶C1(H6)O0O1R3.1T1W6.1
πC5P3R4.1T2.1
•(P3)T1T2

mHag 1:7 I (3)
mHag 1:7 II (3)
mHag 1:7 III (3)
mYeb 3:9 **[100]**
mYeb 6:5 I (2)
mYeb 6:5 II (2)
mYeb 6:6 I (3)
mYeb 6:6 II (3) **[55]**
mYeb 6:6 III (3) **[102]**
mYeb 8:1–2
mYeb 8:2 I (3) **[28]**
mYeb 8:2 II (3)
mYeb 8:2 III (3)
mYeb 8:3 I (2)
mYeb 8:3 II (2) **[63]**
mYeb 9:6
mYeb 10:3
mYeb 12:3 I (2) **[116]**
mYeb 12:3 II (2)
mYeb 12:6 I (5)
mYeb 12:6 II (5)
mYeb 12:6 III (5)
mYeb 12:6 IV (5)
mYeb 12:6 V (5)
[mKet 1:1] mKet 1:6
mKet 3:2
[mKet 3:5 I (2)]
mKet 3:5 II (2) **[92] [110a]**
mKet 4:3 I (3)
mKet 4:3 II (3)
mKet 4:3 III (3) **[90]**
mKet 5:1
mKet 5:6
[mNed 3:6]
mNed 3:11 I (10)
mNed 3:11 II (10)
mNed 3:11 III (10)
mNed 3:11 IV (10) **[141]**
mNed 3:11 V (10)
mNed 3:11 VI (10)
mNed 3:11 VII (10)
[mNed 3:11 VIII (10)]
mNed 3:11 IX (10)
mNed 3:11 X (10)
[mNed 6:1]
[mNed 7:1]
mNed 7:9
mNed 9:4
mNed 9:10
mNed 10:7 I (2)
mNed 10:7 II (2)
mNed 11:1 and 2
mNed 11:9
mNaz 3:5
mNaz 6:8, mNaz 6:9
mNaz 7:1 I (2)
mNaz 7:1 II (2)
mNaz 7:4
[mNaz 8:1]
mNaz 9:5 I (3)

•¶?π(P3)T1
¬(P3)T1T3
•¶πC5(H6)(P3)T3
®¶πO1T2.1
•¶πC5R4.1?T2T3T8
•¶πC5R4.1?T2T3T8
◊πN3T3
◊•¶N4.1orN3.1(N8)O1.4O9W1
π•¶C5O1.3P3R6.4
¡πT1T2T3
§πR4.1O9?T8
§πO7?T1T3T8
¡πO0O2O9T2T3T8
πO1.5(S2)T1
•¶A4.1O1.5
◊C5T2.1
®•O0O1
•¶C5E1.2O1P4T2.1
•¶C5E1.2O6(P4)T0T2.1T3W7?
∆O8T3
∆P4
ΣH4O6O8T0T1T8W5
Σ•∆(¶)P4W1
Σ•¶P4C1W1
π_i
A2C1C5D5.1T0T3T3.1
[T2(O7)]
π_iO8T2W1
π≈H6O1O6T0T2
π≈H6≈O1T0T2
π¬H6¬O6T3
[•P3?]
•πT8
[O1]
◊C1L1L6T1T2
◊O8(N8?)
◊E1.2S2
◊•(¶)π¬W6
◊•C5T3
[◊•]
◊•N8T1T3.1U6
[◊•T3.1T3]
◊•C1C5N8T3.1U6
◊C1R3.1S1T3T3.1U6W5
[O2]
[•¶E1.0, E7?]
πP3T2
•π
◊∆(N1N5)P2
•¶A4.2
•¶A2
π(¡)(¶)
πL1T1T2
•¶H6O1.4T2
∆πT5
•¶A0T2T3
•¶A0T2T3
A0. •¶A4.1
[•¶H6T2]
Ω•¶C5K2W2

mNaz 9:5 II (3)
mNaz 9:5 III (3) **[93]**
mSot 1:1, mSot 1:2
mSot 1:4
mSot 1:6
mSot 1:7
mSot 1:8 I (4) **[22]**
mSot 1:8 II (4) **[49]**
mSot 1:8 III (4)
mSot 1:8 IV (4)
mSot 1:9 I (5)
mSot 1:9 II (5)
mSot 1:9 III (5)
mSot 1:9 IV (5)
mSot 1:9 V (5)
mSot 2:2 [38]
mSot 2:3
mSot 2:4 I (2)
mSot 2:4 II (2)
mSot 2:5 I (5) **[9] [124]**
mSot 2:5 II (5)
mSot 2:5 III (5)
mSot 2:5 IV (5)
mSot 2:5 V (5)
mSot 3:1
mSot 3:2 I (2)
mSot 3:2 II (2)
mSot 4:1 **[108]**
mSot 4:3 I (2)
mSot 4:3 II (2) **[23]**
mSot 5:1 I (3)
mSot 5:1 II (3)
mSot 5:1 III (3)
mSot 5:2
mSot 5:3 I (2) **[1] [94a]**
mSot 5:3 II (2) **[94]**
mSot 5:4
mSot 5:5 I (2)
mSot 5:5 II (2)
mSot 6:3 I (4)
mSot 6:3 II (4) **[85]**
mSot 6:3 III (4)
mSot 6:3 IV (4) **[74]**
mSot 7:1, mSot 7:2
mSot 7:3
mSot 7:4 I (2)
mSot 7:4 II (2) **[127]**
mSot 7:5 I (5) **[128]**
mSot 7:5 II (5)
mSot 7:5 III (5)
mSot 7:5 IV (5)
mSot 7:5 V (5)
mSot 7:6 = mTam 7:2 **[48] [54a]**
mSot 7:7
mSot 7:8 I (3)
mSot 7:8 II (3) **[45]**
mSot 7:8 III (3)
mSot 8:1 I (7)
mSot 8:1 II (7)
mSot 8:1 III (7) **[99]**

$\Omega \bullet \P$C1G4T3W1W3
$\Omega \bullet \P$C5D4L1L3T0T3
π, §T2
[Δ]
ΔC1L1T5W5
[(I5)S5.1T4.1(U6)]
($\approx$N8)T3.1$\approx$T4.1$\approx$U6
$\approx$C5($\approx$N8)$\approx$T4.1$\approx$U6
$\approx$C5($\approx$N8)$\approx$T4.1$\approx$U6
$\approx$C5(I5)($\approx$N8)$\approx$T4.1$\approx$U6
$\Diamond$C5($\approx$N8)$\approx$T4.1$\approx$U6
$\Diamond$D6O2T3T3.1(T4.1)$\approx$U6
$\Diamond$O0O8$\approx$T3.1$\approx$T4.1$\approx$U6
$\Diamond$C5$\approx$T3.1$\approx$T4.1$\approx$U6
$\Diamond$C1T1W1W2
ΔT3T5T7
Δ(C5.2)(P4)(T9)
ΔO2T3
®ΔO0T3
Σ?$\P$C9$\approx$P4R4.1$\approx$R8.1
Σ?$\P\approx$P4$\approx$R8.1T1
Σ?$\P\approx$C9$\approx$P4$\approx$R6.1R$\approx$8.1T0
Σ?$\P\approx$C9$\approx$P4R4.1$\approx$R6.1$\approx$R8.1T4
Σ? $\bullet$ $\P\approx$C9$\approx$P4$\approx$R6.1$\approx$R8.1T1
πT5
$\Delta\P$C1D0
$\Delta \bullet \P$C1D0O1T7
®O2O8T2.1T3
[$\P$H6O6T0]
$\bullet\pi$
C1R6.1T1
$\bullet \P$(E5.1)(R6.1)T3
$\bullet \P\neg$E5.1R6.1T3
$\bullet$G5O1T2W3
$\bullet \P$C1$\approx$D2T1T3
$\bullet \P\approx$C1$\approx$D2T1T3
$\bullet \P$O8R7.3(R7.1/2)T3
$\bullet \P$C1C5D4G4T0T4W3 and C1C5D4S5.2T4W1.2
$\bullet \P$C1O0(O1)$\neg$T3W1
$\neg$A4.2
L3O1.4O7
$\neg$A4.2
(A2)E1.0K2(O1?)T1
T1T3
$\approx$K2($\approx$T0)$\approx$T3
$\P\approx$K2($\approx$T0)$\approx$T3
$\bullet \P$C5S3T3W1.2
(K2)S2
D3T5T7
D0T5
(T0)
O8T1T3W1
$\Delta\P$C5N1.1(T0)T3T5
T9T5
ΔC1(D3/T0)T1T3T5
π(P4)P2P8T9
ΔT3T9
$\Sigma\pi$T0T3W1.2
$\Sigma\pi$‡(C7)R2.3T3
$\Sigma\pi$‡O1(O2)(O8)

mSot 8:1 IV (7)
mSot 8:1 V (7) **[121]**
mSot 8:1 VI (7)
mSot 8:1 VII (7)
mSot 8:2 I (3) **[77]**
mSot 8:2 II (3)
mSot 8:2 III (3)
mSot 8:3
mSot 8:4 **[126]**
mSot 8:5 I (3)
mSot 8:5 II (3)
mSot 8:5 III (3)
mSot 8:6 I (2)
mSot 8:6 II (2)
mSot 9:1 I (2)
mSot 9:1 II (2) **[19] [121a]**
mSot 9:2 I (2)
mSot 9:2 II (2)
mSot 9:5 I (3)
mSot 9:5 II (3)
mSot 9:5 III (3)
mSot 9:6 I (4)
mSot 9:6 II (4)
mSot 9:6 III (4)
mSot 9:6 IV (4) **[125]**
[mSot 9:9]
mSot 9:9 I (2)
mSot 9:9 II (2) **[42]**
mSot 9:11
mSot 9:12
[mSot 9:15 I (2)]
mSot 9:15 II (3)
mSot 9:15 III (3) **[43]**
mGit 3:2 **[109]**

mGit 4:5
mGit 9:10 I (3)
mGit 9:10 II (3)
mGit 9:10 III (3) **[2]**
mQid 1:7 I (3)
mQid 1:7 III (3)
mQid 1:10
mQid 3:4 I (2)
mQid 3:4 II (2) **[110]**
mQid 4:14 I (4)
mQid 4:14 II (4)
mQid 4:14 III (4)
mQid 4:14 IV (4) **[17]**
mBQ 1:1 **[25]**

mBQ 2:5
mBQ 3:9 I (4)
mBQ 3:9 II (4)
[mBQ 3:9 III (4)]
mBQ 3:9 IV (4)
mBQ 4:3 I (4)
mBQ 4:3 II (4) **[18]** = **[118]**
mBQ 4:3 III (4)
mBQ 4:3 IV (4)
mBQ 4:4 (and see 4:3)

®C5N8T4(U6)
Σπ‡C2R2.1(T0)
ΣπC5(N8)O2O8T3.1U6
ΣπW6.1
ΣπE1.0E1.1(E5?)T3
Σπ(A2)E1.1(E5?)T3
ΣπE1.1(E5?)O8T0(T1)T3
O2(H4)T0T3, O1,T0H4
®C2R9T3W1W5
Σπ•¶C5T7
Σ•¶πC1T0T1T3
Σ•¶π(A2?)C1C5T0T3
Σ‡¬O9T5
C1N8S5.2T3.1
Δ(K2?)R4.3?T3
•¶ΔO1.4O7R4.2T0T1T3.1
ΔC5O1 x 3 O2O8T3
ΔH4H6
ΣΔπD6T3T5
ΣΔπO9T3
ΣΔ¬H6T8.5
ΣΔT5(T7)
Σ‡ΔC2P4R3.1T1T3.1W6.2
ΣΔC5D5P4
ΣΔR3.6T3T3.1
T8.5
◊(•)ΔC5≈P2T1T3W5
πC5C3I3≈P2W1W3
◊ΔπC1I2.1≈P2T0
◊Δ≈P2
[ΩW9]
Ω•πC5P2T3
Ω(•)πC5P2
•¶O8(O1.4)T2.1

•¶πC1?O0S5.2T1T3.1
Ω•¶C2T7?W1¬W6(R9?)
Ω•¶C1E5≈O6W2(*erwah*)
Ω•¶C1O8W1W6.2 or S6/W1.2(*ki*)
πH6T0
πC5?O1H.4
◊C1P3(but not π)T3
•¶πN5.2O6O8T1T3
•¶(¬)N5.2O8T1T3 L5?
Ω•πC1(C5?)≈D7W1?T3T4
ΩπC5≈D7W1T1T3
ΩN8T1T3×3 (U6) or ΩL1T3×3
Ω(•)(O1.4)R4.4T0T1T3(Torah)W1(*torah*)
πC5D6E1.3×3 [E7?]T1T3(crop-destroyer, damage, branches) T8×3
§•¶A4 plus restriction
T2
•πP3T2T2.1
•¶πT2.1
(•)(¬H6)O6T2T2.1
O1T2T3
®O1T2T3
πO1T3
(¬O1?)T2
O1(W3/G5?)L5?

mBQ 4:7
mBQ 4:9 II (3) **[87]**
mBQ 4:9 III (3)
mBQ 5:5 I (2) **[5]**
mBQ 5:5 II (2)
mBQ 5:7 **[76]**
mBQ 6:4 I (2)
mBQ 6:4 II (2)
mBQ 7:1
mBQ 8:1
mBQ 8:7 I (2)
mBQ 8:7 II (2)
mBQ 9:7 **[39]**
mBQ 9:8
mBQ 9:11 (and see 9:12) **[20]**
mBQ 9:12 (and see 9:11)
mBM 2:5 **[72]**
mBM 2:7 I (2)
mBM 2:7 II (2)
mBM 2:9
mBM 2:10 I (4)
mBM 2:10 II (4)
mBM 2:10 III (4)
mBM 2:10 IV (4)
mBM 3:12 I (2)
mBM 3:12 II (2)
mBM 4:4
mBM 4:10
mBM 5:1
mBM 5:11 I (2)
mBM 5:11 II (2)
mBM 8:1 I (2) **[37]**
mBM 8:1 II (2)
mBM 9:12 I (3)
mBM 9:12 II (3) **[111]**
mBM 9:12 III (3)
mBM 9:13 I (4) **[113]**
mBM 9:13 II (4) **[78] [110b]**
mBM 9:13 III (4)
mBM 9:13 IV (4)
mBB 8:2
mBB 8:3 **[59]**
mSan 1:1
mSan 1:4 I (2) **[68]**
mSan 1:4 II (2) **[67]**
mSan 1:6 I–II (5) **[54]**
mSan 1:6 III (5)
mSan 1:6 IV (5)
mSan 1:6 V (5) see next
mSan 1:6 V (5) see preceding
mSan 2:1 **[33]**
mSan 2:2
mSan 2:3 I (2) **[6] [52a]**
mSan 2:3 II (2) **[6] [52a]**
mSan 2:4 I (6)
mSan 2:4 II (6)
mSan 2:4 III (6)
mSan 2:4 IV (6)
mSan 2:4 V (6)
mSan 2:4 VI (6)

•¶πH6
◊•¶πL7O7T2T3; C5O9
◊•¶(H6?)T8.5
πA1C5E1.1E1.2T8
C5L5?T8.5
◊πE2.2E6T3.1
O8T0T3
•¶πR7.3 Eliezer/Aqiva: πT8
O0O1
§®C1?E1.2×2 O8T3 E6?
C1?C5N3T2
(◊?)C5N5T1T3?(merciless)
®πᵢT2T8
L7R4.1T2.1
E1.0T0T2
O8T0T2
πA8[K2?]O8T1
®G5?(inquire)S4W3(inquire)T2
¬O8T2T3W1(return)
≈R7.2
≈R7.2
O8T2
¶ O1? Shim'on:•¶W1?
•(¶?)H4O8
[O1]
•¶(D6)O8W6.2T0T2.1T3
π
◊πR4.1T2T3.1(wronging with words)
¬§ L2.1(T2)
◊πC1C2?R3.1R9W6
◊W7(or W6.2)T2
πE1.0O6T2.2T3
E1.0R7.4?T2.2
πP3T2T8 (*ematay*)
πC5D7(O1)O9P3T3
πC6O1P3T3
◊πC5R6.4?T7
◊C5?L3O9T3
◊(P3)R4.1
◊C5E5.2T3(*okhel nefesh*)
πᵢ
C5T0T5U6
π
≈A2T3.1 × 2
®≈A2C1T3.1
¶®ΔC5N3.1T3 Yehudah: •¶ΔC1N3.1T3
R5.2(judge/deliver)R6.2(congregation)T0T1
C5K2
¬O1
O1(evil)O8T0T3(well)
Yehudah •¶C1C6L3T2T7
•¶C5N1
•¶N1T2
¶C5¬N1T2
Σ π¶T8 (but exegetical background)
•¶πO6≈S5.2
•¶πL3O8≈S5.2
Σ πT5?T8
Σ πT5?T8
Σ E1.0R5.2(R5.5?)R9?L1?T5

mSan 2:5: if D is horse/throne

mSan 3:7
mSan 4:1 **[7]**
mSan 4:5 I (9) **[105]**
mSan 4:5 II (9)
mSan 4:5 III–VII (9)

mSan 4:5 VIII (9)
mSan 4:5 IX (9)
mSan 6:1
mSan 6:2 I (2) **[56]**
mSan 6:2 II (2) **[57b]**
mSan 6:4 I (3) **[130]**
mSan 6:4 II (3)
mSan 6:4 III (3)
mSan 6:5 I (2)
mSan 6:5 II (2) **[64]**
mSan 7:7 I (2)
mSan 7:7 II (2)
mSan 7:11
mSan 8:1 **[101]**
mSan 8:2
mSan 8:4 I (4)
mSan 8:4 II (4)
mSan 8:4 III (4) **[91] [126b]**
mSan 8:4 IV (4)
mSan 9:5
mSan 10:1 I (2) **[82]**
mSan 10:1 II (2)
mSan 10:2 I (2)
mSan 10:2 II (2)
mSan 10:3 I (10)
mSan 10:3 II (10)
mSan 10:3 III (10)
mSan 10:3 IV (10) **[50]**
mSan 10:3 V (10)
mSan 10:3 VI (10) **[21]**
mSan 10:3 VII (10) **[119]**
mSan 10:3 VIII (10)
mSan 10:3 IX (10) **[70a]**
mSan 10:3 X (10) **[70b]**
mSan 10:4
mSan 10:5 I (2)
mSan 10:5 II (2)
mSan 10:6 I (6) **[88]**
mSan 10:6 II (6)
mSan 10:6 III (6)
mSan 10:6 IV (6)
mSan 10:6 V (6)
mSan 10:6 VI (6)
mSan 11:1
mSan 11:2 I (3)
mSan 11:2 II (3)
mSan 11:2 III (3) **[106]**
mSan 11:4 **[84]**
mSan 11:5
mMak 1:1–3
mMak 1:3
mMak 1:6 I (3)

◊?R7.3(R7.4)T1T2W6.1, otherwise ®◊?R7.3(R7.4)T1T2 W6.2
C6T2W6.2?
πA2A3(one law)C1C6E1.2T1T3
◊¶®N8O1.4T1T3
◊¶O1.4T5
◊N8T1 (destroyed), N8T1(peace), N8T1 (*Minim*), N8T1U5(greatness), N8T1 (for my sake)
◊πP3T1T2?
◊π(P3)T1
C1?C5?ΔN3.1T3 E1.2?
C1(*todah*)C5C9N5×2 T3(*widuy*)W1(*todah*)
®C1C9N8O1T0T3×2
(D6)O1O8S5.1T2
‡πR7.4(T3?)T5T7
C1S4T1?T3
• ‡G3E1.2T3W3
(•)A5
πC2O8T8.5(Lev. 20:2)W1(make pass)
π
§πT8?
§π®O1×2 T3T3.1T8(W1 son = child)
C5L7K2×2 T1 *zekher*
®πL7
• ¶πH4?
πD6H4H7R9T1T2T3
®O8T2T3T5
πC1T2
L1O7(forever)T3W1(*olam*)W7(earth)
• ¶πT3
• ¶C5T3W7?(kingdom)
¶O1T3¬W7?
®C1R9T4
C1R9T3T4
≈R2.1T3T4
• ¶πC1≈R2.1T1T3U1
¶πC1O1
R9T3T4
• ¶≈R2.1T1T4 & •¶C1T3≈ U1
• ¶≈R2.1T3×2 T4 & •¶≈U1
≈•¶A3.5C5E9O8(R2.1)T3T3.1W1.2
≈•¶A3.5C5E9T3T3.1W1.2
I: §Σ πW6.2 (drawn away) II: §ΣπC7(from the midst)T3
ΣπO1O2
Σ R7.4T2T4 Σ¬L1O8(in it)T2T4
ΣπH6
O1O1.3T0
Σ •πW6.2(entirely)
Σ π•¶L3R3.4T3 E5?
Σ •¶π‡O8(*od*)W2(build)
Σ ‡C5L5?T0? (W1.2)
I: §π¡T3T8? (own domain) II: •¶E2.2L7O8 (E7?)
§Σπ
Σπ(Isa.)ΔT3
®ΣO0O1T3
• ¶¬L1O0(hear only?)T5
§C5D5.1E1.1O1.3(*anokhi*)T2T4
π[¬H6]
• ¶πP3R3.2
• ¶ΔC5(K2)O7O8T2W1.2(*bet*)

• ¶ΔπO7(conspire)O8(infintive)T2
®(•)O8W1?T2
πA8O8T2T3.1
E2.2T1
•(¶)A2(O8)T1≈T3.1
•E2.2≈T3.1
•¶A2O8T1T3
•A4.2 (A5?)
I: A2T1T3.1 II: E2.2 III (Yose): C5O1T3(civil cases)
•(¶)≈C3T1T3W1.2(bet)≈W6.2(mouth = speaking)
(¶)≈C3O1≈W6.2(mouth = speaking)
π (stylistic variation!)
®A1E1.2O0T2
T7
®D6(six/three)O8R6S5.1T1 H4?
ΔC5T1W5? (way)
•¶C5.2S4T2T3W1
•ΔO6O7(restore)T1
Δ¬C1(anointed with oil)E1.1T2×2T5
exploration of ≈H6 (time of death)
≈H6 several
O8
C5.2T1T2W1
[•¶C5¬R3.2T3] metalinguistic rule T3.1
•¶D5O1S5.1
[R3.2]
®¶C5C7S3W1.2(bet) or G2W3(bet)
O2
P4(reading context)T9
◊•¶®D6G1T1T3W3
◊•¶A4
◊•¶C5D5O8T1T3
◊•A4.1C5T3 several
Ω•C1O7(for the sake of)T3W1(righteousness)W2(make great)
A2×2?T2
•¶≈O1≈S5.2T1T3≈W1(hidden)
•¶≈O1≈S5.2T1T3≈W1(hidden)
•¶R6.2T1T3≈W1(hidden)
A0
•¶O0T3W1(infintive)
•¶¬E2.2(or ¬E3.2)O0(good, bad)T1T3
•¶E3.2(good, bad)E3.2(past, future)T1T3
•¶A4.1
(§πT8)
analogy?
?
πD3N8T3.1(father endows)
¶C5≈R6.1T1T3
•¶C1≈R6.1T3W6.2(Shabbat)
[P3]
[•¶O1]
I ¶≈A4 [C9] II•¶O1≈ ¬A4
•≈¬A4
¶≈¬A4
¬A0T3
•¶U1T1W1(turning)W1.2 (al)(E7?)
•¶T1W6.2 (turning)
•¶T1W7(fathers)
§C5W1T2(T8) (house)

mAZ 2:3
mAZ 2:5
mAZ 3:3
mAZ 3:4 Ia and Ib (2)
mAZ 3:4 II (2)
mAZ 3:5 I (2) **[71]**
mAZ 3:5 II (2)
mAZ 3:6 I (2)
mAZ 3:6 II (2) = mShab 9:1 **[69]**
[mAvot 6:3 I (3)] **[52]**
mHor 1:3
mHor 1:4 I (2)
mHor 1:4 II (2)

mHor 1:5
mHor 2:3 **[112]**
mHor 2:5 I (2)
mHor 2:5 II (2)
mHor 2:7 I
mHor 3:3
mZeb 1:1 **[65]** (mYad 4:2)
mZeb 7:4
mZeb 7:6 I (2)
mZeb 7:6 II (2)
mZeb 8:1
mZeb 8:10 I (3)
mZeb 8:10 II (3)
mZeb 8:10 III (3)
mZeb 8:11
mZeb 8:12
mZeb 9:1 I (2) **[138]**
mZeb 9:1 II (2)
mZeb 9:3 (Zeb 8:1)
mZeb 9:5 I (2)
mZeb 9:5 II (2)
mZeb 10:1
mZeb 11:1 I (3)
mZeb 12:1 **[86]**
mZeb 12:2 I (2)

mZeb 14:1
mZeb 14:2

mMen 4:3 I (2)
mMen 4:3 II (2)
mMen 5:2 I (2)
mMen 5:2 II (2)
mMen 5:6
mMen 6:7
mMen 7:2 I (2)
mMen 7:2 II (2)
mMen 7:4
mMen 7:6
mMen 8:5 I (2)
mMen 8:5 II (2)
mMen 8:7
mMen 9:3
mMen 10:4 I (2) **[113]**
mMen 10:4 II (2)
mMen 10:5 (bSuk 41b)

• πA0?
• ¶πC5C9O1.5 (Yehudah)
¶C1C5E1.0L3(not)O7(any)T2T3W6.1(cling)
Proklos: T2 (bath of Aphrodite) Gamliel: ¬T2
• ¶H4?O1O1.3T1
¶A1.5C1C5O1(upon)T2
• ¶πO8(upon)×2 T2
¶C5(house)≈A3R7.3?(or R7.4)T3(wood, etc.)W6.1
® • ¶C1≈A3E9T1T3
(A5)C5N5T3.1U2U8W1
¬L1≈O1(davar)O9T2(multiple)T3(guf)
L1T2
H4(judge)K2(edah)L1(O8 edah?)T2T3(Bet Din)T3.1(W2 edah)
• ¶®‡≈O1L3T3
πL7×2 O6
πT2
πT2
II (2): π×2 T2
§πC5T0T3T3.1W1(nasi')
• ¶A0
• ¶≈A4.1: several ¬A4.1?
• ¶≈A4.1
• ¶¬A0
π
Eliezer: • ¶πC1P3T2 Yehoshua: • ¶πC1P3T2
• ¶O8(to do)T1T2W1(davar) for both rabbis
• ¶π¬O8(to do)T3.1W1(davar)
• ¶C1A3E9T1T2
• ¶A4
• ¶≈C5.2C5E1.2O1O8R6.1?T2W6.2 (A8?)
• ¶≈C5.2C5E1.2O1O8R6.1?T2W6.2 (A8?)
π
?
O2(flesh)T2
A1.5T2T3.1
®π(washing, eaten)C5C5.2O8(¬O9)O1.4
(E1.2)L7T2
®O1(offered)O8(that he offered)T1T3W6.2(whole offering)
≈®¬A1.5C5L7≈O8(bring it to the door)T2 H4?
≈®H4(offering to the Lord)O8(for)O8(before the tent)
T2×7
• ¶C5N1T3.1
• ¶¬N1
ΔC1L1L3T2
C1E1.2(or E5.2?)L1?T1T3
R4.1T5
®ΔS5.2H4
ΔO1W1(one)T3
L1T1T2T3
®O2T3
®A8O8(herd)(D2)T3T3.1(passover only from flock)
¶A4.1
¶O1O8(for the light)R4T1 (¬A4.1)
¶E10?C1C7(verse 19 f.)S3(verse 31)T2
• ¶ΔO1.4 incomplete
• ¶ΔπT7
• ¶ΔT5
• ¶ΔO7T1S2T5W2?(etsem, ad)

mMen 11:4 **[135]**	•¶ΔC3T5W6.1(face)
mMen 11:5 **[134]**: Num.	•¶ΔC5T5W1.2(*al*)
mMen 11:7	ΔO7T5
mMen 12:5	•¶A0×2
mMen 13:10	®ΔA1N1.1T2T3
mMen 13:11	ΩC5D7O8(pleasing odour)T3.1
mHul 2:3	®A2(O1)O1.3O8?(verse 21b)T2
mHul 4:5: 5:1 [27]	•¶πP3T2
mHul 5:5	πK2S5.1
mHul 7:1 ff.	π
mHul 8:4 I (3) [119]	(E1.2 goat to cattle) ®•¶O1×3R3.1T2.1
mHul 8:4 II (3) [66]	•¶πA2.1C6 (¬O1)
mHul 8:4 III (3) [89]	•πH6
mHul 9:5	C5A2T2T3
mHul 10:1 I (2)	πA4.1
mHul 10:1 II (2)	(®?)πC1D2O0O1¬A4.1
mHul 11:1 I and II (2)	π×2
mHul 11:2 I (3)	π¶≈C1≈T1
mHul 11:2 II (3)	•¶≈C1≈T1
mHul 11:2 III (3)	H4W1(*natan*)T2T3T8
mHul 12:1 **[26]**	π
mHul 12:2	π: T2 permutation?
mHul 12:3 I (5)	O7(sitting or *al*)O8T2W2?(*al*)
mHul 12:3 II (5)	πO8(nest)¬O1.4P3T2
mHul 12:3 III (5)	πA2P3T0T2×2 T3
mHul 12:3 IV (5) **[122]**	πR7.2T2
mHul 12:3 V (5)	O1R7.4?T2
mHul 12:5	ΩA4.2C5
mBek 1:1 I (2)	®O1T2T3
mBek 1:1 II (2)	A4.2N3
mBek 1:2 I (2) **[123]**	®R3.3T2.1
mBek 1:2 II (2) **[123]**	A8
mBek 1:4 I (2)	L1?T2
mBek 1:4 II (2)	C9
mBek 1:7 I (3)	(L7?)≈O8(*im lo'*)≈T5T7
mBek 1:7 II (3)	(L7?)≈O8(*im*)≈T7
mBek 1:7 III (3)	(L7?)≈O8(*im lo'*)≈T7
mBek 2:6	•¶O1.4T2.1
mBek 2:9 I (2)	•¶H6T2
mBek 2:9 II (2)	πO1×2(*rehem, peter*)T2
mBek 4:1	Δ.?πD2O9(R3.1?)T1
mBek 7:2 I (4)	§πT8
mBek 7:2 II (4)	π(P3)T8W1
mBek 7:2 III (4)	•¶πT8W1
mBek 7:2 IV (4)	•¶πT8W1
mBek 7:3 **[29]**	§πT8
mBek 7:5 I (4)	§π(P3)T8
mBek 7:5 II (4)	π§•¶G4≈W3
mBek 7:5 III (4)	§π•¶≈C3/G3≈W3
mBek 7:5 IV (4)	§π•¶≈C3G1≈W3
mBek 8:1 **[83]**	•¶L1O8(in)T3W2(*peter*)
mBek 8:7	πT8
mBek 8:8	O1.4(yours)O8R7.2(R7.4?)T2T3
mBek 9:1 I (2)	¬A4.1
mBek 9:1 II (2) **[81]**	E1.OO9
mArak 3:1	πT3
mArak 3:2	§πT2T3 (pastiche text)
mArak 3:5 I (2)	§πT2
mArak 3:5 II (2) **[58]**	C5(slander of the land)N8O8(ten times)T3.1
mArak 4:4 I (4) **[75]**	§¶A8(A2)K3

mArak 4:4 II (4) [75]	¶A0/A4.2?(¬K3)T0
mArak 4:4 III (4) [75]	A8(A2)K3
mArak 4:4 IV (4)	•¶[K2?]
mArak 5:6	¬O8T7T8.5
mArak 7:5	•¶πH4(his possession)O8T1T2
mArak 8:4	•A4.2
mArak 8:5	C1O7T2T3
mArak 8:6 I (3)	•¶O1(O9?)L3T3(temple treasury)
mArak 8:6 II (3)	•¶C1E1.2S3T2T3
mArak 8:6 III (3)	•¶D2O8T1T3
mArak 8:7 [95]	•¶C1D2.1T4
mArak 9:1	ΔO1.4O2(O8?)T2
mArak 9:2 I (2)	O1T2
mArak 9:2 II (2)	®C1O8T2
mArak 9:3 I (2)	O8(for him)T2
mArak 9:3 II (2) [16]	O8(full)T3
mArak 9:4	E1.0T3: otherwise T7
mArak 9:5	πT8
mArak 9:8 I (4)	(•)O1T2
mArak 9:8 II (4)	®O1×2O8T2
mArak 9:8 IV (4)	E1.0(Levites)T7W1(Levites)
mTem 1:1 I (3)	•¶A0
mTem 1:1 II (3)	•¶¬A4.1
mTem 1:1 III (3)	•¶A3E9T3.1
mTem 1:2 I (3) [14]	L3R4.4?T3(blemished, etc.)
mTem 1:2 II (3)	O8T2T3(blemished, etc.)
mTem 1:2 III (3)	®•¶A3O1.4
mTem 1:5 I (2)	[T8.5?]
mTem 1:5 II (2)	[®¶≈O2]
mTem 1:6 I (3)	π≈O2
mTem 1:6 II (3) [103]	®O1.4T2
mTem 1:6 III (3) [73]	(®)•πA8.1O8T3
mTem 2:2	•¶A0
mTem 6:1 II (2)	πT1
mTem 6:3 I (3) [140]	§πC1R4.1T1T2W5(W1)
mTem 6:3 II (3)	(π)O1O8T1
mTem 6:3 III (3)	O1O8T1T3
mKer 1:2	•¶®C1C5.2O1(does)T0
mKer 2:5 I (3)	§π•¶C5G5(hofdeh)(¬L3)R7.1W3(hofdeh)
mKer 2:5 II (3)	•¶(L3¬R7.1)
mKer 2:5 III (3)	•¶(C5T2)
mKer 4:3	•¶C1O8R6.1T2
mKer 6:7	®A2O1.4/O1.3T2
mKer 6:9 I (4) [131]	Ω•≈M1T1
mKer 6:9 II (4)	Ω(•)≈M1T1
mKer 6:9 III (4)	Ω(•)≈M1T1
mKer 6:9 IV (4)	Ω•¶A1.5≈M1T3
mTam 3:7: see mMid 4:2	Δ?T7 (with future into past)
mTam 5:1 [32]	ΔT9
mTam 7:2 = mSot 7:6 [48] [54a]	¶C5N1.1T3T5
mTam 7:4	ΩΔπW6.2W9(Shabbat)T3
mMid 2:5	ΔπW1(W3?)
mMid 2:6	Δ•¶π(W9?)
mMid 3:1	ΔD3T5
mMid 3:8	ΔT5
mMid 4:1 I (2)	Δ(¬C7)(L7)T5
mMid 4:1 II (2)	Δ(•)(¬C7)
mMid 4:2	see Tam 3:7
mMid 4:4	Δ(H7?)T0?T3(roved)T5(W1yatsia'?)
mMid 4:7 [136]	C1C3(S3?)T1W9

mQin 3:6 I (2)	Ω•D2.1T4W1
mQin 3:6 II (2)	Ω•D2.1S5.1TT34W1
mNeg 2:3 [104]	I: O1.4 (eyes) II: R4.4 or H7
mNeg 6:8	πT8
mNeg 7:4	[P3]
mNeg 9:1	§π×2
mNeg 9:2	π×4 T8
mNeg 9:3	π_i
mNeg 10:1	§π_i(T8)
mNeg 10:2 I (2)	•¶πA4.1
mNeg 10:2 II (2)	•¶C9 (cf. D6)
mNeg 10:10	§πT8×2
mNeg 12:5 I (4) [107]	ΣπO6?O8(like)O9P4T3
mNeg 12:5 II (4)	Σπ•¶L1T2
mNeg 12:5 III (4)	Shim'on: •¶¬L3H7 Meir: •¶¬L3T3.1
mNeg 12:5 IV (4)	• A5×3 T0
mNeg 12:6 I (3)	ΣO8(go out of the house)R6.1(house)T7
mNeg 12:6 II (3)	Σπ
mNeg 12:6 III (3) [97]	Σ®D6O1.4T3.1T4
mNeg 12:7	Σπ
mNeg 14:2	O2
mNeg 14:10	ΔT7 π
mParah 1:2	•¶O8W1
mParah 2:3 I (2)	π_i[O1(*peter rehem*)]T3
mParah 2:3 II (2)	®•¶O0O1O6?H6?T2T3
mParah 3:7	•¶(O0)O1.4O6T2
mParah 8:8	see mMiqw 5:4
mMiqw 5:4 I (3) = mParah 8:8	Meir: •¶T3W1(*miqweh*)
mMiqw 5:4 II (3) = mParah 8;8	Yehudah:•¶ ¬O1.4T3.1
mMiqw 5:4 III (3) (= mPar 8:8)	[•¶T3T8?]
mMiqw 9:2 [30]	§πC1(¬R1.1)S2T3
mNid 1:7	π_i
mNid 8:3	•O1(*dam*)O6(*dam*)T3(stain)T3.1 *ma'aseh*
mMakh 1:3 I (2)	¶§πP3T2
mMakh 1:3 II (2)	•¶πH4T1T3
mZab 2:3	πT3T8
mYad 3:5	T9
mYad 4:1	•¶E1.2
mYad 4:2	see mZeb 1:1 [65]
mYad 4:3 I (3)	•¶A0 x 4
mYad 4:3 II (3)	•¶πC5≈P2
mYad 4:3 III (3) [41]	Δ≈πP2W1
mYad 4:4 I (4)	•¶πE1.4 ×2 (P3?)
mYad 4:4 II (4)	•¶C1C5E1.0(E1.2: all)¬E1.4T0?
mYad 4:4 III (4)	•¶π≈P2?T0T7
mYad 4:4 IV (4)	•¶¬T0¬≈P2
mYad 4:7 [62]	◊Δ•¶A4.1 II:◊Δ•¶ ¬A0 (¬A4.1)
mYad 4:8 I (2) [131a] [57]	ΩΔ•¶A4.2M1N5.2T9
mYad 4:8 II (2)	ΩπC5(D6)
mUqtsin 3:12 I (2)	Ω•I2.1(*yesh*)W2(*yesh*)T3
mUqtsin 3:12 II (2)	Ω•T3.1W1.2(*bet*)

Sample Entry of the *Database of Midrashic Units in the Mishnah*

Code •C1C5E1.0L3T1T2T3

Midrash in the Mishnah

Source   mShab 9:6
Location Deut. 13:18 (E 17)
Rabbi   Yehudah

Text   R. Yehudah [var. ben Batyrah] says: Also he who brings out any at all (כל שהוא) of the things used for idolatry [is liable], for it is said, 'And there shall not cleave to your hand anything of the banned thing [in order that the Lord turns from his fierce anger and show you mercy...]'.

Analysis

C1 the co-text shows the topic to be the punishment of the apostate city, the concrete link to this larger topic (the city is being destroyed, and all movable goods gathered for burning) needs to be suspended before the verse can be applied to the topic of carrying on the Sabbath

C5 so the Mishnaic thematization of idolatry is relevant to the cotext and theme of the verse

E1.0 the biblical term 'banned (thing)', referring to all possessions of the apostate city, is taken to include in its scope the sub-group 'things used for idolatry'

L3 the biblical negation (me'umah min) is understood as absolute or all-inclusive ('all of the things'), i.e. as giving the measurement 'nothing at all'

T1 the theme of Sabbath, and what is forbidden or allowed on it, and what measure of which objects may be carried (which is the point in the discourse at which the midrashic units appears) is used to perspectivize a verse in which it is not thematic

T2 the concrete hypothetical case of a person carrying around even a minute measure of idolatrous objects on a Sabbath is the protasis to which the verse is taken to supply the apodosis (that person breaks the Sabbath)

T3 the term 'brings out' is part of the Mishnaic technical discourse on the Sabbath

☒ Form

Lemma   ולא-ידבק בידך מאומה מן-החרם

List mkd cds   previous marked   next marked

Card 74 of 833   Terms כל שהוא... איסור

© A. Samely 1994–2001

Glossary of Rabbinic, Linguistic, and Other Special Terms

aggadah Rabbinic discourse on biblical narrative and related non-halakhic topics; adjective aggadic.

apodosis See *protasis–apodosis unit*.

Babylonian Talmud Main work of rabbinic literature, consisting of the Mishnah plus a wide-ranging and encyclopaedic discussion, the Gemara; created by several generations of Babylonian rabbis mainly between the third and the seventh centuries CE.

Bavli Short for Talmud Bavli, same as Babylonian Talmud.

case schema Unit in the Mishnah which links a hypothetical situation to a halakhic evaluation or consequence. See *protasis–apodosis unit*.

configuration of resources Complete catalogue of hermeneutic resources which are present in a given work of rabbinic literature.

co-text The immediate (sometimes wider) textual environment of an expression or sentence, in contrast to its non-linguistic situation or historical context.

diachronic Regarding the change which elements of a document or of a system undergo over time. Opposite: *synchronic*.

Dictum Formulation of a rabbinic position which, if linked to a biblical quotation (see *Lemma*), forms a midrashic unit.

event verse Term coined in this study for a verse which contains the report of a singular biblical event or person, about which event or person another, general verse is uttered (the tenor verse). See *Petihah* and *Petirah*.

exegetical midrash(im) Rabbinic work(s) consisting mostly of units of Scriptural interpretation in the sequence of the verses of the Bible (within the boundaries of one biblical book).

existential presupposition That whose existence is assumed, but not thematized, by the use of a certain linguistic expression.

expressive use Term coined in this study for the Mishnaic adoption of biblical wording for directly expressing rabbinic positions, i.e. without providing a second, separate formulation of the biblical message.

Gemara Term for the discourse which, together with the text of the Mishnah, forms the Babylonian or Palestinian Talmud (see *Yerushalmi*). The discourse in both these versions of the Gemara takes the Mishnah as its starting point and theme, but (in particular in the Babylonian Talmud) is not restricted by it.

halakhah Rabbinic discourse on permission and obligation, including civil and criminal law; adjective halakhic.

hermeneutic configuration See *configuration of resources*.

hermeneutic profile Set of resources which together account for the hermeneutic operation of one unit of interpretation. Each resource is represented by its abbreviated name in alphabetical order (footnotes and Appendix II).

homiletic midrash(im) Rabbinic work(s) containing homilies. These homilies consist almost exclusively of units of interpretation arranged in a conventional compositional format presenting a discourse on some theme.

langue Term for the system of a given language, as opposed to *parole*, the individual speech event whose production draws on the system.

Lemma Biblical word or phrase which is the focus of the hermeneutic operation. Its message is reformulated in the rabbinic Dictum, together with which it forms the midrashic unit.

Masorah Rabbinic corpus of (marginal) notes and rules on the exact text, shape, division, pronunciation, and transmission of the Hebrew Bible; adjective: Masoretic.

mention In linguistic philosophy, term for the occurrence of an expression in a (linguistic) environment in which its power to refer is suspended, usually because it is itself referred to as a linguistic entity. Opposition: use.

metalinguistic Speech about linguistic signs (as opposed to extra-linguistic objects).

midrash Traditional name for rabbinic interpretation of Scripture, including rabbinic narrative and preaching; also used for a genre of rabbinic literature (see next entry).

midrash(im) Rabbinic work(s) consisting largely of units of Scriptural interpretation. See *exegetical midrash* and *homiletic midrash*.

midrashic unit Textual unit in rabbinic literature consisting of a quotation from Scripture (Lemma), preceded or succeeded by a rabbinic formulation (Dictum) whose meaning is presented as converging with the quotation.

Mishnah Work containing the early halakhic discourse of rabbinic Judaism (redacted *c.* third century CE), cited according to tractates (see Abbreviations), chapters, and *mishnah* (see next entry).

mishnah (sing.), *mishnayyot* (pl.) Name of a conventional subdivision (approximately of paragraph length) of the chapters of Mishnaic tractates.

operation That combination of hermeneutic resources which allows the convergence of sense of the Dictum and the Lemma in a midrashic unit.

paradigm In linguistics, term for a set of signs which stand in functional opposition to each other in that they exclude each other's employment in the same syntagmatic position.

parashah (sing.), *parashiyyot* (pl.). Rabbinic term for the traditional division of the Pentateuch into weekly portions for public reading.

parole Linguistic term for the individual speech event produced by speakers within the rules and structures provided by the system of their language (cf. *langue*).

Petihah Important compositional form of the rabbinic homily. It provides for the mutual interpretation of two biblical verses (see next entry).

Petirah Main hermeneutic mechanism found in the *Petihah*, providing for the characterization of a biblical event (represented by its biblical report) through a more general verse (see *tenor verse*).

pragmatics Field of linguistics dealing with the contribution of contextual factors, including conversational or social setting, to linguistic meaning.

presupposition See *existential presupposition*.

programmatic exposition Term coined in this study for a hermeneutic attitude which reifies the biblical text and problematizes its meaning in advance of any specific meaning problem encountered for it. Opposite: topical alignment.

protasis–apodosis unit Textual unit in rabbinic literature which links a hypothetical situation (protasis, 'if'-part) to a halakhic evaluation or consequence (apodosis, 'then'-part). Also called *case schema*.

rabbinic Term used in this study to refer to the literature and culture of a postbiblical Jewish group responsible for a literary output between the third century CE (redaction of the Mishnah) and the eighth century in Palestine and Babylonia.

referent, reference The (usually extra-linguistic) entity which a linguistic expression is used to speak about.

resources, hermeneutic resources, resources of interpretation Term coined in this study for techniques of interpretation, defined as hermeneutic components into which whole rabbinic interpretations (operations) can be broken down for descriptive purposes.

segment That part of the biblical text which is quoted or presupposed in a rabbinic interpretation.

Shema' One of the main Jewish prayers, whose text consists of three passages in the Pentateuch, named after the opening word, 'Hear . . .' (Deut. 6:4).

singular (referring) expression Term in philosophy and linguistics for an expression whose referent is a specific individual or a unique item.

synchronic Regarding the elements of a document or a system as simultaneous and functionally related. Opposite: *diachronic*.

syntagma Term in linguistics and literary studies for a complex structure whose elements stand with each other in a simultaneous and functional relationship (used of sentences and of larger textual units). See *paradigm*.

Tannaitic midrash(im) Work(s) of early rabbinic literature of the genre exegetical midrash, largely concerned with the legal parts of the Pentateuch.

Targum Aramaic paraphrases of the Hebrew Bible regularly incorporating or presupposing results of rabbinic hermeneutics.

tenor verse Term coined in this study for a verse of general meaning which is used as utterance about a singular biblical event or person (see *event verse*).

topical alignment Term coined in this study for a hermeneutic attitude which seizes on a biblical wording as valid and relevant thematization of a topic concerning the reader, without reification or distancing of the text of Scripture.

use In linguistic philosophy, term for the employment of a linguistic sign in speaking about something (as opposed to e.g. quoting it). Opposite: *mention*.

Yerushalmi, Palestinian Talmud Work of rabbinic literature, consisting of the Mishnah plus discussion, the Gemara; created by several generations of Palestinian rabbis mainly between the third and the fifth century CE. It is both earlier and less influential than the Babylonian Talmud.

Bibliography

A. TEXTUAL SOURCES FOR QUOTED MISHNAIC PASSAGES

BEER, G., *Faksimile-Ausgabe des Mischnacodex Kaufmann A 50, mit Genehmigung der Ungarischen Akademie der Wissenschaften in Budapest (Veröffentlichungen der Alexander Kohut-Gedächtnisstiftung)* (The Hague, 1930; repr. Jerusalem, 1968).

Die Mischna. Text, Übersetzung und ausführliche Erklärung. Series editors G. Beer and O. Holtzmann (also I. Rabin, S. Krauß), later K. H. Rengstorf and L. Rost (also R. Meyer). The following publications from this (incomplete) project have been used, in tractate sequence (all published 'Gießen: A. Töpelmann', unless otherwise shown):

HOLTZMANN, O., *Berakot (Gebete)* (1912).

BAUER, W., *Pea (Vom Ackerwinkel)* (1914).

CORRENS, D., *Schebiit (Vom Sabbatjahr)* (Berlin: A. Töpelmann, 1960).

BUNTE, W., *Maaserot/Maaser Scheni (Vom Zehnten/Vom zweiten Zehnten)* (Berlin: A. Töpelmann, 1962).

ALBRECHT, K., *Bikkurim (Erstlinge)* (1922).

NOWACK, W., *Schabbat (Sabbat)* (1924).

BEER, G., *Pesachim (Ostern)* (1912).

MEINHOLD, J., *Joma (Der Versöhnungstag)* (1913).

CORRENS, D., *Taanijot. Fastentage* (Berlin and New York: Walter de Gruyter, 1989).

RAPP, E. L, *Mo'ed qatan (Halbfeiertage)* (1931).

RENGSTORF, K. H., *Yebamot (Von der Schwagerehe)* (1929).

BOERTIEN, M., *Nazir (Nasiräer)* (Berlin and New York: Walter de Gruyter, 1971).

BIETENHARD, H., *Sota (Die des Ehebruchs Verdächtige)* (Berlin: A. Töpelmann, 1956).

CORRENS, D., *Gittin (Scheidebriefe)* (Berlin and New York: Walter de Gruyter, 1991).

WINDFUHR, W., *Baba qamma ('Erste Pforte' des Civilrechts)* (1913).

—— *Baba meßia ('Mittlere Pforte' des Civilrechts)* (1923).

—— *Baba batra ('Letzte Pforte' des Civilrechts)* (1925).

KRAUß, S., *Sanhedrin (Hoher Rat) Makkot (Prügelstrafe)* (1933).

MARTI, K., and G. BEER, *Abot (Väter)* (1927).

WINDFUHR, W., *Horajot (Entscheidungen)* (1914).

HOLTZMANN, O., *Tamid (Vom täglichen Gemeindeopfer)* (1928).

KRUPP, M., *'Arakin (Schätzungen)* (Berlin and New York: Walter de Gruyter, 1971).

HOLTZMANN, O., *Middot (Von den Maßen des Tempels)* (1913).

—— *Qinnim (Von den Vogelopfern)* (1931).

LISOWSKY, G., *Jadajim (Hände)* (Berlin: A. Töpelmann, 1956).

BRODY, A., *Der Misnah-Traktat Tamid* (Uppsala: Almquist and Wiksells, 1936).

GOLDBERG, A., *Ohaloth*, see Section B below.

STRACK, H. L., *Pirqey Avot. Die Sprüche der Väter*, 2nd edn. (Berlin: Reuther, 1888).

TAYLOR, C., *Sayings of the Jewish Fathers . . . in Hebrew and English*, 2nd edn. (Cambridge: Cambridge University Press, 1897).

—— *An Appendix to Sayings of the Jewish Fathers, Containing a Catalogue of Manuscripts and Notes on the Text of Aboth* (Cambridge: Cambridge University Press, 1900; repr. Jerusalem: Makor, 1970).

WEIS, P. R., and E. ROBERTSON, *Mishnah Horayoth: Its History and Exposition*, (notes by Weis, translation by Robertson) (Manchester: Manchester University Press, 1952).

Traditional commentaries are cited from the following edition (for Maimonides, see Section B below):

Mishnayyot Tif'eret Israel, 12 vols. (Brooklyn, New York: Zundel Berman, 1993; reprint of the edition Wilna: Romm, 1908 ff.).

B. OTHER LITERATURE

ABRAHAMS, I., *By-Paths in Hebraic Bookland* (Philadelphia: Jewish Publication Society of America, 1920).

—— *Studies in Pharisaism and the Gospels, Second Series* (Cambridge: Cambridge University Press, 1924).

AGASSI, J., 'Analogies Hard and Soft', in Helman (ed.), *Analogical Reasoning* (1988), 401–19.

AICHER, G., *Das Alte Testament in der Mischna* (Freiburg im Breisgau: Herder, 1906).

ALAND, K., and B. ALAND, *Der Text des Neuen Testaments. Einführung in die wissenschaftlichen Ausgaben und in Theorie wie Praxis der modernen Textkritik* (Stuttgart: Deutsche Bibelgesellschaft, 1982).

ALBECK, CH., *Untersuchungen über die Redaktion der Mischna* (Berlin: C. A. Schwetschke, 1923).

—— *Einführung in die Mishna* (Berlin and New York: Walter de Gruyter, 1971).

—— (ed.), *Shishah Sidrey Mishnah*, commentary by Ch. Albeck, vocalization by Ch. Yalon, 6 vols. (Jerusalem and Tel Aviv: Bialik Institute and Dvir, 1959) (*Neziqin*).

ALEXANDER, P. S., 'The Rabbinic Hermeneutical Rules and the Problem of the Definition of Midrash', *Proceedings of the Irish Biblical Association*, 8 (1984), 97–125.

—— 'Midrash', in R. J. Coggins and J. L. Houlden (eds.), *A Dictionary of Biblical Interpretation* (London and Philadelphia: SCM Press and Trinity Press Int., 1990), 452–9.

—— 'Quid Athenis et Hierosolymis? Rabbinic Midrash and Hermeneutics in the Graeco-Roman World', in Davies and White (eds.), *A Tribute to Geza Vermes* (1990), 101–24 .

—— 'Pre-emptive Exegesis: Genesis Rabba's Reading of the Story of Creation' *Journal of Jewish Studies*, 43 (1992), 230–45.

—— 'Jewish Interpretation', in B. M. Metzger and M. D. Coogan (eds.), *The Oxford Companion to the Bible* (New York and Oxford: Oxford University Press, 1993), 305–10.

—— 'Bavli Berakhot 55a–57b: The Talmudic Dreambook in Context', *Journal of Jewish Studies*, 46 (1995), 230–48.

ALEXANDER, P. S., 'How Did the Rabbis Learn Hebrew?', in W. Horbury (ed.), *Hebrew Study from Ezra to Ben-Yehuda* (Edinburgh: T. & T. Clark, 1999), 71–89.

ALEXY, R., *Theorie der juristischen Argumentation. Die Theorie des rationalen Diskurses als Theorie der juristischen Begründung* (Frankfurt: Suhrkamp, 1983); trans. *A Theory of Legal Argumentation* (Oxford: Clarendon Press, 1989).

ALLWOOD, J., L.-G. ANDERSSON, and Ö. DAHL, *Logic in Linguistics* (Cambridge: Cambridge University Press, 1989; first printing 1977).

ALT, A., 'The Origins of Israelite Law', in *Essays on Old Testatment History and Religion*, trans. R. A. Wilson (Oxford: Basil Blackwell, 1966), 79–132 (German original 1934).

ALTER, R., *The Art of Biblical Narrative* (London: Allen and Unwin, 1981).

—— *Putting Together Biblical Narrative: The Albert T. Bilgray Lecture 1988* (Tuscon, Ariz.: University of Arizona and Temple Emanu-El, 1988).

ARISTOTLE, *The Works of Aristotle*, trans. under the editorship of W. D. Ross (Oxford: Oxford University Press, 1928 ff.).

—— *Rhetorik*, trans. F. G. Sieveke (Munich: Wilhelm Fink, 1980).

—— *Posterior Analytics*, trans. J. Barnes, 2nd edn. (Oxford: Clarendon Press, 1993).

—— *Organon 1: Topik. Über die Sophistischen Widerlegungsschlüsse. Griechisch-Deutsch*, ed. and trans. H. G. Zekl (Darmstadt (Hamburg): Wissenschaftliche Buchgesellschaft (Meiner), 1997).

—— *Organon 3/4: Erste Analytik. Zweite Analytik. Griechisch-Deutsch*, ed. and trans. H. G. Zekl (Darmstadt (Hamburg): Wissenschaftliche Buchgesellschaft (Meiner), 1997).

ASHLEY, K. D., 'Arguing by Analogy in Law: A Case-Based Model', in Helman (ed.), *Analogical Reasoning* (1988), 205–24.

ASSMANN, J., *Das kulturelle Gedächtnis. Schrift, Erinnerung und politische Identität in frühen Hochkulturen*, 2nd edn. (Munich: Beck, 1997).

AUERBACH, E., *Mimesis: The Representation of Reality in Western Literature*, trans. W. R. Trask (Princeton, NJ: Princeton University Press, 1953).

AUSTIN, J. L., *How to Do Things with Words: The William James Lectures Delivered at Harvard University in 1955*, 2nd edn. (Oxford and New York: Oxford University Press, 1980).

AZAR, M., 'The Conditional Clause in Mishnaic Hebrew', in Bar-Asher (ed.), *Studies in Mishnaic Hebrew* (1988), 58–68.

BACHER, W., *Die exegetische Terminologie der jüdischen Traditionsliteratur I, Die bibel-exegetische Terminologie der Tannaiten* (Leipzig: Hinrichs'sche Buchhandlung, 1899).

—— *Die Prooemien der alten jüdischen Homilie. Beitrag zur Geschichte der jüdischen Schriftauslegung und Homiletik* (Leipzig: Hinrichs'sche Buchhandlung, 1913; repr. Gregg International, 1970).

—— 'Jewish Hermeneutics', in *The Jewish Encyclopedia*, 12 vols. (New York and London: Funk and Wagnalls, 1901–6), iii. 162–74.

BAR-ASHER, M., 'The Different Traditions of Mishnaic Hebrew', in D. M. Golomb (ed.), *'Working with No Data': Semitic and Egyptian Studies Presented to Thomas O. Lambdin* (Winona Lake, Ind.: Eisenbrauns, 1987), 1–38.

—— 'The Study of Mishnaic Hebrew Grammar Based on Written Sources', in id. (ed.), *Studies in Mishnaic Hebrew* (1988), 9–42.

——(ed.), *Studies in Mishnaic Hebrew (Scripta Hierosolymitana xxxvii)* (Jerusalem: Magnes Press, 1998).

BARTON, J., *Reading the Old Testament: Method in Biblical Study* (London: Darton, Longman, and Todd, 1984).

BAUER, L., *English Word-Formation* (Cambridge: Cambridge University Press, 1983).

DE BEAUGRANDE R.-A., and W. U. DRESSLER, *Introduction to Text Linguistics*, London and New York: Longman, 1981; German original Tübingen: Max Niemeyer, 1972).

BEN-MENAHEM, H., 'Postscript: The Judicial Process and the Nature of Jewish Law', in Hecht *et al.* (eds.), *An Introduction to the History and Sources of Jewish Law* (1996), 421–37.

Bereshit Rabba: see Theodor, J., and Ch. Albeck.

BERGSTRÄSSER, G., *Hebräische Grammatik, 2. Teil: Verbum* (Leipzig 1929; repr. Darmstadt: Wissenschaftliche Buchgesellschaft, 1985, bound with Gesenius–Kautzsch).

BERNSTEIN, M., 'Introductory Formulas for Citation and Re-Citation of Biblical Verses in the Qumran Pesharim. Observations on a Pesher Technique', *Dead Sea Discoveries*, 1 (1994), 30–70.

BHASKAR, R., 'Models', in Bynum, Browne, and Porter (eds.), *Dictionary of the History of Science* (1981), 272–4.

BIALOBLOCKI, S., 'Hermeneutik', *Encyclopaedia Judaica. Das Judentum in Geschichte und Gegenwart* (Berlin: Eschkol Verlag, 1931), vol. 7, cols. 1181–94.

BIRNBAUM, P., *Encyclopedia of Jewish Concepts* (New York: Hebrew Publishing Co., NY, 1993; repr. of 3rd edn., 1975).

BLACK, M., 'Metaphor', in *Models and Metaphors: Studies in Language and Philosophy* (Ithaca, NY: Cornell University Press, 1962), 25–47 (originally published in *Proceedings of the Aristotelian Society*, 55 (1954), 273–94).

BLAU, L., 'Massoretic Studies III. The Verse Division', *Jewish Quarterly Review*, 9 (1897), 122–44.

BLOCH, P., 'Studien zur Aggadah', *Monatsschrift für Geschichte und Wissenschaft des Judenthums*, 34 (1885), 166–84, 210–24, 257–69, 384–404; 35 (1886), 165–87, 389–405.

BLOCH, R., 'Methodological Note for the Study of Rabbinic Literature', in Green (ed.), *Approaches to Ancient Judaism*, vol. 1 (1978), 51–75 (original 1955).

——'Midrash', in Green (ed.), *Approaches to Ancient Judaism*, vol. 1 (1978), 29–50 (original 1957).

BLOOMFIELD, L., *Language* (Chicago and London: University of Chicago Press, 1984; original 1933).

BLUMENBERG, H., *Die Lesbarkeit der Welt*, 3rd edn. (Frankfurt: Suhrkamp, 1996; 1st edn. 1981).

——*Paradigmen zu einer Metaphorologie* (Frankfurt: Suhrkamp, 1998; first published in *Archiv für Begriffsgeschichte*, 1960).

BOCHOROVSKI, E., and P. TROMMER, 'A Semantic-Pragmatic Study of the Sense Relation Called "Opposition"' (Heb.), *Leshonenu*, 57:3 (1993), 215–49.

BOERTIEN, M., 'Einige Bemerkungen zu Bibelzitaten in der Mischna', in Kuyt and van Uchelen (eds.), *History and Form* (1988), 71–81.

BÖHL, F., 'Die Metaphorisierung (Metila) in den Targumim zum Pentateuch', *Frankfurter Judaistische Beiträge*, 15 (1987), 111–49.

BÖHL, F., 'Der erweiterte Vergleich im Targum', *Frankfurter Judaistische Beiträge*, 18 (1990), 23–43.

—— 'Name und Typologie. Zur Form der Namensdeutung der Stammväter im Targum Pseudo-Jonathan', *Frankfurter Judaistische Beiträge*, 21 (1994), 1–6.

—— 'On the Interpretation of Names in the Targums of the Pentateuch and Midrash', *Jewish Studies Quarterly*, 4 (1997), 145–68.

BORGES, J. L., *Labyrinths* (Harmondsworth: Penguin, 1970).

BOYARIN, D., 'Analogy vs. Anomaly in Midrashic Hermeneutic: Tractates Wayyassa and Amaleq in the Mekilta', *Journal of the American Oriental Society*, 106:4 (1986), 659–66.

—— 'Bilingualism and Meaning in Rabbinic Literature: An Example', in Y. L. Arbeitman (ed.), *Fucus: A Semitic/Afrasian Gathering in Remembrance of Albert Ehrman* (Amsterdam and Philadelphia: John Benjamins, 1988), 141–52.

—— *Intertextuality and the Reading of Midrash* (Bloomington and Indianapolis: Indiana University Press, 1990).

BRAUDE, W. G., and I. J. KAPSTEIN (trans.), *Pesikta de-Rab Kahana. R. Kahana's Compilation of Discourses for Sabbaths and Festal Days*, Littman Library of Jewish Civilization (London: Routledge & Kegan Paul, 1975).

BRAVERMAN, N., 'Synonyms in the Mishnah and the Tosefta' (Heb.), *Proceedings of the Eleventh World Congress of Jewish Studies*, Jerusalem: World Union of Jewish Studies (1994), Division E, Vol. 1, 17–24.

BREGMAN, M., 'Seeing with the Sages: Midrash as Visualization in the Legends of the *Aqedah*', in Raphael (ed.), *Agendas for the Study of Midrash in the Twenty-First Century* (1999), 84–100.

BREUER, M., 'Biblical Verses of Undecided Syntactical Adhesion' (Heb.), *Leshonenu*, 58:3 (1994–5), 189–99.

BREWER, D. I., *Techniques and Assumptions in Jewish Exegesis Before 70 CE* (Tübingen: Mohr, 1992).

BRIN, G., 'The Formula "If He Shall Not (Do)" and the Problem of Sanctions in Biblical Law', in D. P. Wright, D. N. Freedman, and A. Hurvitz (eds.), *Pomegranates and Golden Bells: Studies in Biblical, Jewish and Near Eastern Ritual, Law and Literature in Honor of Jacob Milgrom* (Winona Lake, Ind.: Eisenbrauns, 1995), 341–62.

BROOKE, G., *Exegesis at Qumran. 4QFlorilegium in its Jewish Context*, (*Journal for the Study of the Old Testament*, Supplement Series, 29) (Sheffield: JSOT Press, 1985).

BROWN, G., and G. YULE, *Discourse Analysis* (Cambridge: Cambridge University Press, 1983).

BROWNLEE, W. H., 'Biblical Interpretation among the Sectaries of the Dead Sea Scrolls', *The Biblical Archaeologist*, 14 (1951), 54–76.

BÜHLER, K., *Theory of Language: The Representational Function of Language* (Amsterdam: J. Benjamins, 1990); trans. from *Sprachtheorie. Die Darstellungsfunktion der Sprache* (Stuttgart and New York: Gustav Fischer Verlag, 1982; original 1934).

BURCHFIELD, R. W., *The New Fowler's Modern English Usage* (Oxford: Clarendon Press, 1998).

BYNUM, W. F., E. J. BROWNE, and R. PORTER (eds.), *Dictionary of the History of Science* (London and Basingstoke: Macmillan, 1981).

CALDER, N., *Studies in Early Muslim Jurisprudence* (Oxford: Clarendon Press, 1993).

CAMPBELL, J., *The Use of Scripture in the Damascus Document 1–8, 19–20 (Beihefte ZAW*, 228) (Berlin and New York: Walter de Gruyter, 1995).

CARMICHAEL, C. M., *Law and Narrative in the Bible* (Ithaca, New York, and London: Cornell University Press, 1985).

——*Biblical Laws of Talion*, Oxford Centre Papers (Oxford: Oxford Centre for Postgraduate Hebrew Studies, 1986), 21–39.

CASHDAN, E., 'Names and the Interpretation of Names in the Pseudo-Jonathan Targum to the Book of Genesis', in H. J. Zimmels, J. Rabbinowitz, and I. Finestein (eds.), *Essays Presented to the Chief Rabbi Israel Brodie on the Occasion of his Seventieth Birthday*, Jews' College Publications, NS 3 (London: The Soncino Press, 1967), 31–9.

CHAJES, Z. H., *The Student's Guide Through the Talmud*, trans. by J. Shachter, 2nd edn. (New York: Feldheim, 1960).

CHERNICK, M., 'The Formal Development of כלל ופרט וכלל' (Heb.), *Tarbiz*, 52 (1983), 393–410.

CHRISTIE, A., *A Murder is Announced* (London: Fontana, 1953).

CLARK, Y. M., 'Law', in J. H. Hayes (ed.), *Old Testament Form Criticism* (San Antonio: Trinity University Press, 1974), 99–139.

CLINES, D. J. A., *The Theme of the Pentateuch* (Sheffield: *Journal for the Study of the Old Testament*, 1978).

——'Nehemiah 10 as an Example of Early Jewish Biblical Exegesis', *Journal for the Study of the Old Testament*, 21 (1981), 111–17.

——(ed.), *The Dictionary of Classical Hebrew*, vols. i–iv (Sheffield: Sheffield Academic Press, 1993–8) (continuing publication).

——'The Postmodern Adventure in Biblical Studies', in J. Krasovec (ed.), *The Interpretation of the Bible* (1998), 1603–16.

COGGINS, R. J., and J. L. HOULDEN (eds.), *A Dictionary of Biblical Interpretation* (London and Philadelphia: SCM Press and Trinity Press Int., 1990).

COHEN, S. J. D., 'Can Converts to Judaism Say "God of our fathers"?', *Judaism*, 40 (1992) (*Festschrift R. Gordis*), 419–28.

——*The Beginnings of Jewishness. Boundaries: Varieties, Uncertainties* (Berkeley, Los Angeles, and London: University of California Press, 1999).

COSERIU, E., *Textlinguistik. Eine Einführung*, herausgegeben und bearbeitet von J. Albrecht, 2nd edn. (Tübingen: Gunter Narr, 1981).

——*Einführung in die Allgemeine Sprachwissenschaft* (Tübingen: Francke, 1988).

COULTHARD, M., *An Introduction to Discourse Analysis*, 2nd edn. (London and New York: Longman, 1985).

CRUSE, D. A., *Lexical Semantics* (Cambridge: Cambridge University Press, 1986).

CRYSTAL, D., *A Dictionary of Linguistics and Phonetics*, 2nd edn. (Oxford: Blackwell, 1985).

DANBY, H., *The Mishnah*, trans. from the Hebrew with introduction and brief explanatory notes (Oxford: Oxford University Press, 1933).

DANET, B. and B. BOGOCH, 'Orality, Literacy, and Performativity in Anglo-Saxon Wills', in J. Gibbons (ed.), *Language and the Law* (London and New York: Longman, 1994), 100–35.

DAUBE, D., *Studies in Biblical Law* (Cambridge: Cambridge University Press, 1947).

——'Rabbinic Methods of Interpretation and Hellenistic Rhetoric', *Hebrew Union College Annual*, 22 (1949), 239–65.

DAUBE, D., 'Alexandrian Methods of Interpretation and the Rabbis', in *Festschrift Hans Lewald* (Basel: Helbing and Lichtenhahn, 1953), 27–44.

DAVIDSON, D., *Inquiries into Truth and Interpretation* (Oxford: Clarendon Press, 1984).

DAVIES, P. R., and R. WHITE (eds.), *A Tribute to Geza Vermes* (Sheffield: Sheffield Academic Press, 1990).

DAVIES, T. R., 'Criteria for Generalization', in Helman (ed.), *Analogical Reasoning* (1988), 227–50.

DERRIDA, J., *Of Grammatology*, trans. G. Ch. Spivak (Baltimore and London: Johns Hopkins University Press, 1976).

—— *Edmund Husserl's Origin of Geometry: An Introduction*, trans. J. Pl. Leavey (New York and Sussex: Nicolas Hays and Harvester Press, 1978).

—— *Writing and Difference*, trans. A. Bass (London: Routledge & Kegan Paul, 1979).

—— 'Deconstruction and the Possibility of Justice', *Cardozo Law Review*, 11 (1990), nos. 5–6; German trans.: *Gesetzeskraft. Der 'mystische Grund der Autorität'* (Frankfurt: Suhrkamp, 1991).

DODD, C. H., *According to the Scriptures: The Sub-structure of New Testament Theology* (London: Collins-Fontana, 1965; 1st edn. 1952).

DOMMERSHAUSEN, W., and H.-J. FABRY, 'lehem', in G. J. Botterweck, H. Ringgren, and H.-J. Fabry (eds.), *Theological Dictionary of the Old Testament*, trans. D. E. Green, vol. 7 (Grand Rapids, Mich.: W. B. Eerdmans, 1995), 521–9; German original: *Theologisches Wörterbuch zum Alten Testament*, IV/5 (Stuttgart: W. Kohlhammer, 1983), 538–47.

EDGE, D. O., 'Metaphor in Science' in Bynum, Browne, and Porter (eds.), *Dictionary of the History of Science* (1981), 264.

EHRLICH, E. L., *Der Traum im Alten Testament*, Beihefte zur *Zeitschrift für die Alttestamentliche Wissenschaft*, 73 (Berlin: A. Töpelmann, 1953).

ELLIGER, K., *Studien zum Habakuk-Kommentar vom Toten Meer* (Tübingen: Mohr (Siebeck), 1953).

ELLIS, E. E., 'Biblical Interpretation in the New Testament Church', in Mulder and Sysling (eds.), *Mikra* (1988), 691–719.

ELMAN, Y., 'Towards a History of *Ribbuy* in the Babylonian Talmud' (Heb.), in *Proceedings of the Eleventh World Congress of Jewish Studies* (Jerusalem: World Union of Jewish Studies, 1994), Division C, Vol. 1, 87–94.

ELON, M. (ed.), 'Interpretation', *Encyclopaedia Judaica* (Jerusalem: Keter, 1971–2), viii., cols. 1413–29.

—— 'Ma'aseh and Precedent', in id. (ed.), *Principles of Jewish Law* (1975), cols. 112–14.

—— *The Principles of Jewish Law* (Jerusalem: Keter, 1975).

EPSTEIN, J. N., *Introduction to Tannaitic Literature: Mishnah, Tosephta and Halakhic Midrashim* (Heb.) ed. E. Z. Melamed (Jerusalem and Tel Aviv: Magnes Press and Devir, 1957).

—— *Mavo le-Nusah ha-Mishnah* (*Introduction to the Text of the Mishnah*), 2 vols., 2nd edn. (Jerusalem and Tel Aviv: Magnes Press and Dvir, 1964).

Evangelium Vitae: Encyclical Letter Addressed by the Supreme Pontiff Pope John Paul II to All the Bishops . . . on the Value and Inviolability of Human Life (London: Catholic Truth Society, 1995).

EVANS, G., *The Varieties of Reference*, ed. J. McDowell (Oxford and New York:

Clarendon Press and Oxford University Press, 1982).

FAUR, J., *Golden Doves With Silver Dots: Semiotics and Textuality in Rabbinic Tradition* (Bloomington, Ind.: Indiana University Press, 1986).

FINKEL, A., 'The Pesher of Dreams and Scriptures', *Revue de Qumran*, 4 (1962–3), 357–70.

FINKELSTEIN, L. *Mavo le-Massekhtot Avot we-Avot de-Rabbi Natan* (Heb. with English summary) (New York: Jewish Theological Seminary of America, 1950).

—— (ed.), *Sifra on Leviticus*, vol. I: *Text*; vol. V: *Commentary* (New York: The Jewish Theological Seminary of America, 1990).

FINNIS, J., *Natural Law and Natural Rights* (Oxford: Clarendon Press, 1980).

FISHBANE, M., *Biblical Interpretation in Ancient Israel* (Oxford: Clarendon Press, 1985).

—— 'Use, Authority and Interpretation of Mikra at Qumran', in Mulder and Sysling (eds.), *Mikra* (1988), 339–77.

—— *The Garments of Torah: Essays in Biblical Hermeneutics* (Bloomington and Indianapolis: Indiana University Press, 1989).

—— ' "The Holy One Sits and Roars": Mythopoesis and the Midrashic Imagination', *Journal of Jewish Philosophy and Thought*, 1 (1991), 1–21.

—— 'Midrash and the Meaning of Scripture', in J. Krasovec (ed.), *The Interpretation of the Bible* (1988), 549–63.

FITZMYER, J. A., 'The Use of Explicit Old Testament Quotations in Qumran Literature and in the NT', in *Essays on the Semitic Background of the New Testament* (London: Geoffrey Chapman, 1971), 3–58.

FLUCK, H.-R., *Fachsprachen. Einführung und Bibliographie*, 3rd edn. (Tübingen: Francke Verlag/UTB, 1985).

FOWLER, H. W., *A Dictionary of Modern English Usage*, 2nd edn. revised by E. Gowers (Oxford: Oxford University Press, 1983).

FRAADE, S. D., *From Tradition to Commentary: Torah and Its Interpretation in the Midrash Sifre to Deuteronomy* (Albany, NY: State University of New York Press, 1991).

—— ' "Comparative Midrash" Revisited: The Case of the Dead Sea Scrolls and Rabbinic Midrash', in Raphael (ed.), *Agendas for the Study of Midrash in the Twenty-First Century* (1999), 4–16 .

FRAENKEL, Y., 'Bible Verses Quoted in Tales of the Sages', in J. Heinemann and D. Noy (eds.), *Studies in Aggadah and Folk-Literature*, Scripta Hierosolymitana, 22 (Jerusalem: Magnes Press, 1971), 80–99.

—— 'Paronomasia in Aggadic Narratives', in J. Heinemann and S. Werses (eds.), *Studies in Hebrew Narrative Art throughout the Ages*, Scripta Hierosolymitana, 27 (Jerusalem: Magnes Press, 1978), 27–51.

—— *Darkhey Ha-Aggadah weha-Midrash*, 2 vols. (Givatayyim: Massadah/Yad Ha-Talmud, 1991).

FRAWLEY, W., *Linguistic Semantics* (Hillsdale, NJ: Lawrence Erlbaum Associates, 1992).

FREGE, G., *Begriffsschrift, eine der arithmetischen nachgebildete Formelsprache des reinen Denkens* (Halle/Saale: Louis Nebert, 1879; repr. 3rd edn. Darmstadt: Wissenschaftliche Buchgesellschaft, 1977; Georg Olms, Hildesheim, 1964); English trans. in Frege, *Conceptual Notation and Related Articles*, trans. and ed. T. W. Bynum (Oxford: Clarendon Press, 1972), 101–203.

FREGE, G., *The Philosophical Writings of Gottlob Frege*, trans. P. T. Geach and M. Black (Oxford: Blackwell, 1952).

FREUD, S., *Die Traumdeutung* (Frankfurt: Fischer, 1991).

FRIEDMAN, S., 'The Holy Scriptures Defile the Hands—The Transformation of a Biblical Concept in Rabbinic Theology', in M. Fishbane and M. Z. Brettler (eds.), *Minha le-Nahum: Biblical and Other Studies Presented to Nahum M. Sarna in Honour of his 70th Birthday* (Sheffield: Sheffield Academic Press, 1993), 117–32.

GABRION, H., 'L'Interprétation de l'écriture à Qumran', in H. Temporini and W. Haase (eds.), *Aufstieg und Niedergang der Römischen Welt*, II, 19 (1) (1979), 779–848.

GADAMER, H.-G., *Wahrheit und Methode. Grundzüge einer philosophischen Hermeneutik*, 6th edn. (Tübingen: Mohr, 1990) (page references in square brackets refer to the earlier editions); in English: *Truth and Method*, 2nd edn. (London: Sheed and Ward, 1979), with page correlation to the second German edition.

GARVER, N., 'Varieties of Use and Mention', *Philosophy and Phenomenological Research*, 26 (1965–6), 230–8.

GEACH, P. T., *Mental Acts* (London: Routledge & Kegan Paul, 1960).

GEIGER, A., *Urschrift und Uebersetzungen der Bibel in ihrer Abhängigkeit von der innern Entwickelung des Judenthums* (Breslau: Julius Hainauer, 1857).

GEMSER, B., 'The Importance of the Motive Clause in Old Testament Law', *Congress Volume Copenhagen 1953*, Supplements to Vetus Testamentum I, Leiden: Brill, 1953, 50–66.

GENTNER, D., 'The Mechanisms of Analogical Learning', in Vosniadou and Ortony (eds.), *Similarity and Analogical Reasoning* (1989), 199–241.

GERSTENBERGER, E., 'Covenant and Commandment', *Journal of Biblical Literature*, 84 (1965), 38–51.

GESENIUS, W., *Hebräische Grammatik*, ed. E. Kautzsch, 28th edn. (repr. Hildesheim, Zurich, and New York: Olms, 1985; first published Leipzig 1909); English trans. (identical section and paragraph numbering): *Gesenius' Hebrew Grammar*, ed. E. Kautzsch, trans. A. E. Cowley, 2nd edn. (Oxford: Clarendon Press, 1910).

GILAT, Y. D., *Studies in the Development of the Halakhah* (Heb.), ([Ramat Gan:] Bar-Ilan University Press, 1992).

GOLDBERG, A., *The Mishnah Treatise Ohaloth* (Heb.) (Jerusalem: Magnes Press, 1955).

GOLDBERG, ARNOLD, 'Schöpfung und Geschichte. Der Midrasch von den Dingen, die vor der Welt erschaffen wurden', *Judaica*, 24 (1968), 27–44; now in *Mystik und Theologie* (1997), 148–61.

—— 'Kain: Sohn des Menschen oder Sohn der Schlange?', *Judaica*, 25 (1969), 203–21; now in *Mystik und Theologie* (1997), 275–88.

—— 'Form und Funktion des Ma'ase in der Mischna', *Frankfurter Judaistische Beiträge*, 2 (1974), 1–39; now in *Rabbinische Texte* (1999), 22–49.

—— 'Der einmalige Mensch. Der absolute Wert des Lebens und der Würde des Menschen im rabbinischen Judentum (1.–3. Jahrhundert n. Chr.)', *Saeculum*, 26 (1975), 145–56; now in *Mystik und Theologie* (1997), 289–303.

—— 'Die Peroratio (Hatima) als Kompositionsform der rabbinischen Homilie', *Frankfurter Judaistische Beiträge*, 6 (1978), 1–22; now in *Rabbinische Texte* (1999), 395–409.

—— 'Zitat und Citem. Vorschläge für die descriptive Terminologie der Formanalyse rabbinischer Texte', *Frankfurter Judaistische Beiträge*, 6 (1978), 23–6; now in *Rabbinische Texte* (1999), 96–8.

—— 'Petiha und Hariza, zur Korrektur eines Mißverständnisses', in *Journal for the Study of Judaism*, 10 (1979), 213–18; now in *Rabbinische Texte* (1999), 297–302.

—— 'Rede und Offenbarung in der Schriftauslegung Rabbi Aqibas', *Frankfurter Judaistische Beiträge*, 8 (1980), 66–75; now in *Mystik und Theologie* (1997), 337–50.

—— 'Das schriftauslegende Gleichnis im Midrasch', *Frankfurter Judaistische Beiträge*, 9 (1981), 1–90; now in *Rabbinische Texte* (1999), 134–98.

—— 'Die funktionale Form Midrasch', *Frankfurter Judaistische Beiträge*, 10 (1982), 1–45; now in *Rabbinische Texte* (1999), 199–229.

—— 'Der verschriftete Sprechakt als rabbinische Literatur', in J. Assmann and Chr. Hardmeier (eds.), *Schrift und Gedächtnis. Archäologie der literarischen Kommunikation I* (Munich: Wilhelm Fink, 1983), 123–41; now in *Rabbinische Texte* (1999), 1–21.

—— 'Das Martyrium des Rabbi Aqiva. Zur Komposition einer Märtyrerezählung (bBer 61b)', *Frankfurter Judaistsische Beiträge*, 12 (1984), 1–82; now in *Mystik und Theologie* (1997), 351–412.

—— 'Die "Semikha". Eine Kompositionsform der rabbinischen Homilie', *Frankfurter Judaistische Beiträge*, 14 (1986), 1–70; now in *Rabbinische Texte* (1999), 347–94.

—— 'Questem. Vorschläge für die descriptive Terminologie der Formanalyse rabbinischer Texte', *Frankfurter Judaistische Beiträge*, 14 (1986), 99–109; now in *Rabbinische Texte* (1999), 99–106.

—— 'Die Zerstörung von Kontext als Voraussetzung für die Kanonisierung religiöser Texte im rabbinischen Judentum', in A. and J. Assmann (eds.), *Kanon und Zensur. Archäologie der literarischen Kommunikation II* (Munich: Wilhelm Fink, 1987), 201–11; now in *Mystik und Theologie* (1997), 413–25.

—— 'The Rabbinic View of Scripture', in Davies and White (eds.), *A Tribute to Geza Vermes* (1990), 153–66; German original in *Frankfurter Judaistische Beiträge*, 15 (1987), 1–15; now in *Rabbinische Texte* (1999), 230–41.

—— 'Formen und Funktionen von Schriftauslegung in der frührabbinischen Literatur', *Linguistica Biblica Bonn*, 64 (1990), 5–22.

—— *Mystik und Theologie des rabbinischen Judentums. Gesammelte Studien I*, ed. M. Schlüter and P. Schäfer (Tübingen: Mohr Siebeck, 1997).

—— *Rabbinische Texte als Gegenstand der Auslegung. Gesammelte Studien II*, ed. M. Schlüter and P. Schäfer (Tübingen: Mohr Siebeck, 1999).

GOLDIN, J., *The Song at the Sea, Being a Commentary on a Commentary in Two Parts* (New Haven and London: Yale University Press, 1971).

—— 'Reflections on a Mishnah', in his *Studies in Midrash and Related Literature*, ed. B. L. Eichler and J. H. Tigay (Philadelphia, New York, and Jerusalem: Jewish Publication Society, 1988), 141–9; repr. from *Quest*, 2 (1967) (London: New London Synagogue), 44–8.

GOLDSCHMIDT, L., *Der Babylonische Talmud neu übertragen*, 12 vols. (Königstein/Ts: Jüdischer Verlag/Athenäum, 1981; repr. of the 2nd edn., 1967, original Berlin, 1929 ff.).

GOODMAN, M., 'A Note on Josephus, the Pharisees and Ancestral Tradition', *Journal of Jewish Studies*, 50 (1999), 17–20.

GOODRICH, P., *Languages of the Law: From Logics of Memory to Nomadic Masks* (London: Weidenfeld and Nicolson, 1990).

GORDIS, R., 'Quotations as a Literary Usage in Biblical, Oriental and Rabbinic Literature', *Hebrew Union College Annual*, 22 (1949), 157–219.

GRECH, P. S., 'The Regula Fidei as a Hermeneutical Principle in Patristic Exegesis', in J. Krasovec (ed.), *The Interpretation of the Bible* (1998) 589–601.

GREEN, W. S., 'What's in a Name?—The Problematic of Rabbinic "Biography"', in Green (ed.), *Approaches to Ancient Judaism* (1978), i. 77–96.

—— 'Palestinian Holy Men: Charismatic Leadership and Rabbinic Tradition', in H. Temporini and W. Haase (eds.), *Aufstieg und Niedergang der Römischen Welt*, II, 19 (2) (1979), 619–47.

—— 'Writing with Scripture', in Neusner, *Writing with Scripture* (1989) 7–23.

—— (ed.), *Approaches to Ancient Judaism: Theory and Practice*, vol. 1 (Missoula, Mont.: Scholars Press, 1978).

GREGORY, R. L., 'Illusions', in id. (ed.), *The Oxford Companion to the Mind* (Oxford and New York: Oxford University Press, 1987), 337–43.

GRICE, H. P., 'Logic and Conversation', in P. Cole and J. L. Morgan (eds.), *Syntax and Semantics: Speech Acts*, vol. 3 (New York: Academic Press, 1975), 41–58; now in *Studies in the Way of Words* (1989).

—— *Studies in the Way of Words* (Cambridge, Mass.: Harvard University Press, 1989).

GROSSFELD, B., 'The Biblical Hebrew ידה in Ancient and Modern Translations', *Journal for the Aramaic Bible*, 1 (1999), 31–52.

GRÖZINGER, K. E., *Ich bin der Herr, dein Gott. Eine rabbinische Homilie zum Ersten Gebot (PesR 20)*, Frankfurter Judastische Studien, 2 (Frankfurt am Main: Peter Lang, 1976).

—— 'Prediger gottseliger Diesseitszuversicht. Jüdische "Optimisten"', *Frankfurter Judaistischer Beiträge*, 5 (1977), 42–64.

GULLBERG, J., *Mathematics: From the Birth of Numbers* (New York and London: W. W. Norton, 1997).

GÜTTGEMANNS, E., 'Semiotik der Traumerzählung in apokalyptischen Texten am Beispiel von Apokalypse Johannis 1', *Linguistica Biblica*, 59 (1987), 7–54.

GUTTMANN, A., 'Foundations of Rabbinic Judaism', *Hebrew Union College Annual*, 23 (1950), 453–73.

HALIVNI, D. WEISS, *Peshat and Derash: Plain and Applied Meaning in Rabbinic Exegesis* (New York and Oxford: Oxford University Press, 1991).

HALLAQ, W. B., *Law and Legal Theory in Classical and Medieval Islam* (Aldershot and Brookfield, Vt.: Variorum, 1994); article no. II: 'Non-Analogical Arguments in Sunni Juridical *Qiyas*', original in *Arabica*, 36 (1989).

HALLIDAY, M. A. K., and R. HASAN, *Cohesion in English* (London: Longman, 1976).

HANDELMAN, S. A., *The Slayers of Moses: The Emergence of Rabbinic Interpretation in Modern Literary Theory* (Albany: State University of New York Press, 1982).

HART, H. L. A., *The Concept of Law* (Oxford: Clarendon Press, 1961).

HARTMAN, G., and S. BUDICK (eds.), *Midrash and Literature* (New Haven: Yale University Press, 1986).

HASAN-ROKEM, G., *Proverbs in Israeli Folk Narratives: A Structural Semantic Analysis*, FF Communications, no. 232 (Helsinki: Academia Scientiarum Fennica, 1982).

HECHT, N. S., B. S. JACKSON, S. M. PASSAMANECK, D. PIATTELLI, and A. M. RABELLO (eds.), *An Introduction to the History and Sources of Jewish Law* (Oxford: Clarendon Press, 1996).

HEIDEGGER, M.,*Vom Wesen der Wahrheit*, 4th edn. (Frankfurt: Vittorio Klostermann, 1961).

HEINEMANN, I., *Darkhey Ha-Aggadah* (Jerusalem, 1949).

HEINEMANN, J., 'The Proem in the Aggadic Midrashim', *Scripta Hierosolymitana*, 22 (1971), 100–22.

—— 'Early Halakah in the Palestinian Targumim', in B. Jackson (ed.), *Studies in Jewish Legal History: Essays in Honour of David Daube* (London: Jewish Chronicle Publications, 1974), 114–22.

HELMAN, D. H. (ed.), *Analogical Reasoning. Perspectives of Artificial Intelligence, Cognitive Science, and Philosophy* (Dordrecht, Boston, and London: Kluwer Academic Publishers, 1988).

HERFORD, R. T., *The Ethics of the Talmud: Sayings of the Fathers*, text, complete translation, and commentaries by R. T. Herford (New York: Schocken, 1962; original 1925).

HESSE, M., *Models and Analogies in Science* (Notre Dame, Ind.: Notre Dame University Press, 1966).

—— 'Texts Without Types and Lumps Without Laws', *New Literary History*, 17 (1985), 31–48.

—— 'Theories, Family Resemblances and Analogy', in Helman (ed.), *Analogical Reasoning* (1988), 317–340.

HIRSCHFELD, H. S., מדות ודרשת ההלכה. *Halachische Exegese. Ein Beitrag zur Geschichte der Exegese und zur Methodologie des Talmud's* (Berlin: Athenaeum (Verlag M. Simion), 1840).

HOENIG, S. B., 'The Ancient City-Square: The Forerunner of the Synagogue', in H. Temporini and W. Haase (eds.), *Aufstieg und Niedergang der Römischen Welt*, II, 19 (2) (1979), 448–76.

HOLYOAK, K. J., and P. THAGARD, *Mental Leaps: Analogy in Creative Thought* (Cambridge, Mass. and London: MIT Press, 1995).

HONDERICH, T. (ed.), *The Oxford Companion to Philosophy* (Oxford and New York: Oxford University Press, 1995).

ILSON, R. F., 'Lexicography', in Malmkjaer (ed.), *The Linguistics Encyclopedia* (1991), 291–8.

JACKSON, B. S., 'The Fence-Breaker and the *actio de pastu pecoris* in Early Jewish Law', in Jackson (ed.), *Studies in Jewish Legal History* (1974), 123–36.

—— '*Testes Singulares* in Early Jewish Law and the New Testament', in *Essays in Jewish and Comparative Legal History* (Leiden: Brill, 1975), 172–201.

—— 'Maimonides' Definitions of *Tam* and *Mu'ad*', *Jewish Law Annual*, 1 (1978), 168–76.

—— 'Historical Aspects of Legal Drafting in the Light of Modern Theories of Cognitive Development', *International Journal of Law and Psychiatry*, 3 (1980), 349–69.

—— *Semiotics and Legal Theory* (London and New York: Routledge & Kegan Paul, 1985).

—— 'On the Nature of Analogical Argument in Early Jewish Law', in id. (ed.), *The Jewish Law Annual*, 11 (Boston: Institute of Jewish Law/Harwood Academic Publishers, 1994), 137–68.

—— *Making Sense in Jurisprudence* (Liverpool: Deborah Charles Publications, 1996).

—— 'Law, Wisdom and Narrative', in G. Brooke and J.-D. Kaestli (eds.), *Narrativity in the Bible and Related Texts* (Louvain: Peeters, 2000), 31–52.

JACKSON, B. S., *Studies in the Semiotics of Biblical Law* (Sheffield: Sheffield Academic Press, 2000).

—— 'The Original "Oral Law" ', in G. Brooke (ed.), *Jewish Ways of Reading the Bible*, *Journal of Semitic Studies Supplement*, 1 (Oxford: Oxford University Press (2000), 3–19).

—— (ed.), *Studies in Jewish Legal History: Essays in Honour of David Daube* (London: Jewish Chronicle Publications, 1974).

JACOBS, L., *Studies in Talmudic Logic and Methodology* (London: Vallentine Mitchell, 1961).

—— 'Hermeneutics', *Encyclopaedia Judaica* (Jerusalem: Keter, 1971–2), viii., cols. 366–72.

JAKOBSON, R., 'Linguistics and Poetics', in T. A. Sebeok (ed.), *Style in Language* (Cambridge, Mass.: MIT Press, 1960), 350–77; German: 'Linguistik und Poetik', in *Poetik. Ausgewählte Aufsätze 1921–1971* (1979), 84–121.

—— and C. LÉVI-STRAUSS, ' "Le chats" de Charles Baudelaire' (1962); repr. in R. Jakobson, *Selected Writings*, vol. 3 (The Hague: Mouton, 198)1, 447–64.

—— and P. BOGATYREV, 'Die Folklore als eine besondere Form des Schaffens', in R. Jakobson, *Poetik. Ausgewählte Aufsätze 1921–1971*, ed. E. Holenstein and T. Schelbert (Frankfurt: Suhrkamp, 1979), 140–57; first published in *Donum Natalicium Schrijnen* (Nijmwegen, 1929), 900–13.

JAMES, W., *Pragmatism: A New Name for Some Old Ways of Thinking* (London, New York, Bombay, Calcutta: Longmans & Green, 1907).

JASTROW, M., *A Dictionary of the Targumim, the Talmud Babli and Yerushalmi, and the Midrashic Literature*, 2 vols. (Philadelphia, 1903, numerous reprints).

JOHNSON, M., 'Some Constraints on Embodied Analogical Understanding', in Helman (ed.), *Analogical Reasoning* (1988), 25–40.

JOHNSON-LAIRD, P. N., *Mental Models: Towards a Cognitive Science of Language, Inference, and Consciousness* (Cambridge: Cambridge University Press, 1983).

—— 'Analogy and the Exercise of Creativity', in Vosniadou and Ortony (eds.), *Similarity and Analogical Reasoning* (1989), 313–31.

KADUSHIN, M., *Organic Thinking: A Study in Rabbinic Thought* (New York: Jewish Theological Seminary of America, 1938).

—— *The Rabbinic Mind*, 3rd edn. (New York: Bloch, 1972).

KAHLE, P. E., 'The Mishna Text in Babylonia I', *Hebrew Union College Annual*, 10 (1935), 185–222.

—— *The Cairo Geniza*, 2nd edn. (Oxford: Basil Blackwell, 1959).

KANT, I., *Kritik der Urteilskraft*, ed. G. Lehmann (Stuttgart: Phililpp Reclam, 1963), quoted after the pagination of the 1793 2nd edn.; *Critique of Judgement*, trans. J. H. Bernard (New York and London: Hafner and Collier Macmillan, 1951).

—— *Kritik der reinen Vernunft*, ed. W. Weischedel, vol. 1 (Frankfurt: Suhrkamp, 1982).

KASOVSKY, H. Y., *Thesaurus Mishnae: Concordantiae verborum quae in sex Mishnae ordinibus reperiuntur*, 4 vols. (Jerusalem, 1957–61).

KEMPSON, R. M., *Semantic Theory* (Cambridge: Cambridge University Press, 1977).

KERN[-ULMER], B., 'Die Verwendung von Schriftversen in rabbinischen Texten— einige Vorbemerkungen zur Textkonstitution', *Frankfurter Judaistische Beiträge*, 12 (1984), 129–45.

—— 'Paraphrasendeutung im Midrasch. Die Paraphrase des Petihaverses',

Frankfurter Judaistische Beiträge, 9 (1981), 115–61.

KLEIN, M., 'The Translations of Anthropomorphisms and Anthropopathisms in the Targumim', in *Vienna Congress 1980, Supplements to Vetus Testamentum*, 32 (Leiden: Brill, 1981), 162–77.

—— *Anthropomorphisms and Anthropopathisms in the Targumim of the Pentateuch, With Parallel Citations From the Septuagint* (Heb.) (Jerusalem: Makor, 1982).

KLUG, U., *Juristische Logik*, 3rd edn. (Berlin, Heidelberg, and New York: Springer, 1966).

KNEALE, W., and M. KNEALE, *The Development of Logic* (Oxford: Clarendon Press, 1962).

KOCH, H. J., and H. RÜßMANN, *Juristische Begründungslehre* (Munich: Beck, 1982).

KÖNIG, E., *Hebräisches und aramäisches Wörterbuch zum Alten Testament* (Leipzig: Dieterich'sche Verlagsbuchhandlung, 1910).

KRAMPEN, M., 'Ferdinand de Saussure and the Development of Semiology', in M. Krampen, K. Oehler, R. Posner, T. A. Sebeok, and T. von Uexküll (eds.), *Classics of Semiotics* (New York and London: Plenum Press, 1987), 59–88.

KRASOVEC, J. (ed.), *The Interpretation of the Bible: The International Symposium in Slovenia, Journal for the Study of the Old Testament Supplement Series*, 289 (Sheffield: Sheffield Academic Press, 1998), 549–63.

KRIPKE, S. A., *Naming and Necessity* (Cambridge, Mass. and Oxford: Harvard University Press and Blackwell, 1980).

KUYT, A., and N. A. VAN UCHELEN, *History and Form: Dutch Studies in the Mishnah, Publications of the Juda Palache Institute*, IV (Amsterdam: Judah Palache Institute, 1988).

LAKOFF, G., and M. JOHNSON, *Metaphors We Live By* (Chicago and London: University of Chicago Press, 1980).

LAUTERBACH, J. Z., *Mekilta de-Rabbi Ishmael*, 3 vols., translation and edition (Philadelphia: Jewish Publication Society of America, 1933).

—— 'Midrash and Mishnah', in *Rabbinic Essays* (Cincinnati: Hebrew Union College Press, 1951), 163–256.

—— 'Talmud Hermeneutics', *The Jewish Encyclopedia* (New York and London: Funk and Wagnalls, 1901–6), xii. 30–3.

LEECH, G. N., *Semantics: The Study of Meaning*, 2nd edn. (Harmondsworth: Penguin, 1981).

LENHARD, D., *Die Rabbinische Homilie. Ein formanalytischer Index, Frankfurter Judaistische Studien*, Bd 10 (Frankfurt: Gesellschaft zur Förderung Judaistischer Studien, 1998).

LEVINAS, E., *Beyond the Verse: Talmudic Readings and Lectures*, trans. G. D. Mole (London: Athlone Press, 1994).

—— *Collected Philosophical Papers*, trans. A. Lingis (Pittsburgh, Pen.: Duquesne University Press, 1998; Kluwer Academic Publishers, 1987).

LEVINSON, S. C., *Pragmatics* (Cambridge: Cambridge University Press, 1983).

LIEBERMAN, S., *Hellenism in Jewish Palestine: Studies in the Literary Transmission, Beliefs and Manners of Palestine in the I Century BCE–IV Century CE*, 2nd edn. (New York: Jewish Theological Seminary of America, 1962).

LIGHTSTONE, J., *The Rhetoric of the Babylonian Talmud, Its Social Meaning and Context, Studies in Christianity and Judaism*, 6 (Waterloo, Ont.: Canadian Corporation for Studies in Religion/Wilfrid Laurier University Press, 1994).

LIM, T. H., *Holy Scripture in the Qumran Commentaries and Pauline Letters* (Oxford: Clarendon Press, 1997).

LIVER, J., and D. SPERBER, 'Mishmarot and Ma'amadot', *Encyclopaedia Judaica*, 12 vols. (Jerusalem: Keter, 1971–2), xii. cols. 89–93.

LLOYD, G. E. R., *Polarity and Analogy: Two Types of Argumentation in Early Greek Thought* (Cambridge: Cambridge University Press, 1966).

LOEWE, R., 'The "Plain" Meaning of Scripture in Early Jewish Exegesis', *Papers of the Institute of Jewish Studies*, 1 (London: 1964), 140–85.

—— 'Rabbi Joshua ben Haniniah: Ll.D. or D. Litt.?', in B. Jackson (ed.), *Studies in Jewish Legal History* (1974), 137–54.

—— 'Jewish Exegesis', in Coggins and Houlden (eds.), *A Dictionary of Biblical Interpretation* (1900), 346–54.

LONGACRE, R. E., 'Items in Context: Their Bearing on Translation Theory', *Language*, 34 (1958), 482–91.

LOTMANN, J. M., *The Structure of the Artistic Text* (Ann Arbor, Mich.: University of Michigan Press, 1977).

LYONS, J., *Introduction to Theoretical Linguistics* (Cambridge: Cambridge University Press, 1968).

—— *Semantics*, vol. i (Cambridge: Cambridge University Press, 1977).

MAASS, F., 'Von den Ursprüngen der rabbinischen Schriftauslegung', *Zeitschrift für Theologie und Kirche*, 52 (1955), 129–61.

McCARTHY, M. J., 'Lexis and Lexicology', in Malmkjaer (ed.), *The Linguistics Encyclopedia* (1991), 298–305.

MACCOBY, H., Review of J. Neusner's *Uniting the Dual Torah*, in *Journal of Theological Studies*, NS 44 (1993), 315–24.

—— 'Corpse and Leper', *Journal of Jewish Studies*, 49 (1998), 280–5.

MAIER, J., *The Temple Scroll: An Introduction, Translation and Commentary*, *Journal for the Study of the Old Testament Supplement Series*, 34 (Sheffield: JSOT Press, 1985); trans. R. T. White, German original 1978.

—— *Geschichte der jüdischen Religion*, 2nd edn. (Freiburg, Basel, and Vienna: Herder, 1992).

—— 'Early Jewish Biblical Interpretation in the Qumran Literature', in M. Sæbø, in co-operation with C. Brekelmans and M. Haran (eds.), *Hebrew Bible/Old Testament: The History of Its Interpretation, I: From the Beginnings to the Middle Ages (Until 1300)* (Göttingen: Vandenhoeck and Ruprecht, 1996), 108–29.

MAIMONIDES, MOSES, *Mishneh Torah: The Book of Knowledge*, ed. and trans. M. Hyamson (Jerusalem: Boy's Town, 1965).

—— *Commentary on the Mishnah: Mishnah im peyrush Rabbeynu Mosheh ben Maimon*, 3 vols., trans. from the Arabic by Y. Qafih (Jerusalem: Mossad Ha-Rav Kook, 1967).

—— *The Guide of the Perplexed*, 2 vols., trans. S. Pines, introduction by L. Strauss (Chicago: Chicago University Press, 1963) .

MALCOLM, N., *Dreaming* (London, Henley, and Atlantic Highlands, NJ: Routledge & Kegan Paul and Humanities Press, 1977; first published 1959).

MALMKJAER, K. (ed.), *The Linguistics Encyclopedia* (London and New York: Routledge, 1991).

MANN, J., *The Bible as Read and Preached in the Old Synagogue*, 2 vols. (Cincinnati: Hebrew Union College, 1940 and 1966), vol. 2 ed. I. Sonne.

MARGALITH, O., '*Keleb*: Homonym or Metaphor?', *Vetus Testamentum*, 33 (1983), 491–5.

MARMORSTEIN, A., *The Old Rabbinic Doctrine of God*, 2 vols. (London: Jews' College Publications, 1927–37).

MARSHALL, H., 'An Assessment of Recent Developments', in D. A. Carson and H. G. M. Williamson (eds.), *It is Written: Scripture Citing Scripture. Essays in Honour of Barnabas Lindars, SSF* (Cambridge: Cambridge University Press, 1988), 1–21.

MATTHEWS, P., *Morphology*, 2nd edn. (Cambridge: Cambridge University Press, 1991).

METZGER, B., 'The Formulas Introducing Quotations of Scripture in the NT and the Mishnah', *Journal of Biblical Literature*, 70 (1951), 297–307.

MIELZINER, M., *Introduction to the Talmud* (New York: Bloch, 1968; repr. of the 1925 edn., with bibliography by A. Guttmann).

MILGROM, J., 'The Levitic Town: An Exercise in Realistic Planning', *Journal of Jewish Studies*, 33 (Festschrift Yadin) (1982), 185–8.

Mishnat R. Eliezer, ed. H. G. Enelow (New York: Bloch, 1934; repr. Jerusalem: Makor, 1970).

MULDER, M. J., and H. SYSLING (eds.), *Mikra: Text, Translation, Reading and Interpretation of the Hebrew Bible in Ancient Judaism and Early Christianity* (CRINT II/1) (Assen, Maastricht, and Philadelphia: Van Gorcum/Fortress, 1988).

NEUSNER, J. *History of the Mishnaic Law of Purities*, 22 vols. (Leiden: Brill, 1974–7) *part 7, Negaim* (Leiden: Brill, 1974); *part 22, The Mishnaic System of Uncleanness. Its Context and History* (Leiden: Brill, 1977).

—— *History of the Mishnaic Law of Women, part 4: Sotah, Gittin, Qiddushin* (Leiden: Brill, 1980)

—— *Judaism: The Evidence of the Mishnah* (Chicago and London: Chicago University Press, 1981).

—— *From Mishnah to Scripture: The Problem of the Unattributed Saying* (Chico, Cal: Scholars Press, 1984).

—— *The Memorized Torah: The Mnemonic System of the Mishnah* (Chico, Cal: Scholars Press, 1985).

—— *Torah. From Scroll to Symbol in Formative Judaism: The Foundations of Judaism: Method, Teleology, Doctrine. Part 3: Doctrine* (Philadelphia: Fortress Press, 1985).

—— *Writing with Scripture: The Authority and Uses of the Hebrew Bible in the Torah of Formative Judaism* (Minneapolis: Fortress Press, 1989).

—— 'The Mishnah's Generative Mode of Thought: *Listenwissenschaft* and Analogical-Contrastive Reasoning', *Journal of the American Oriental Society*, 110 (1990), 317–21.

—— *Uniting the Dual Torah: Sifra and the Problem of the Mishnah* (Cambridge: Cambridge University Press, 1990).

NIEHOFF, M. R., 'A Dream Which is Not Interpreted is Like a Letter Which is Not Read', *Journal of Jewish Studies*, 43 (1992), 58–84.

—— 'The Return of Myth in Genesis Rabbah on the Akedah', *Journal of Jewish Studies*, 46 (*Festschrift Vermes*) (1995), 69–87.

NOTH, M., 'The "Re-Presentation" of the Old Testament in Proclamation', in C. Westermann (ed.), *Essays on Old Testament Interpretation* (1963), 76–88; the German original appeared first in *Evangelische Theologie*, 12 (1952), 6 ff.

—— *The Laws in the Pentateuch and Other Studies* (London: SCM Press, 1966);

German original, *Gesammelte Studien zum Alten Testament*, 2nd edn. (Munich, 1960).

Noy, D., 'The Aggadic Endings in the Tractates of the Mishnah', *Mahanayyim*, 57 (1961), 44–59.

Ochs, P., 'Rabbinic Text Process Theology', *Journal of Jewish Thought and Philosophy*, 1 (1991), 141–77.

Oppenheim, A. L., 'The Interpretation of Dreams in the Ancient Near East. With a Translation of an Assyrian Dream-Book', *Transactions of the American Philosophical Society*, NS 46/3 (1956), 179–373 .

Partington, A., *The Oxford Dictionary of Quotations*, 4th edn. (Oxford and New York: Oxford University Press, 1992).

Patrick, D., *Old Testament Law* (London: SCM Press, 1986).

Patte, D., *Early Jewish Hermeneutic in Palestine* (Missoula, Mont.: Society of Biblical Literature and Scholars Press, 1975).

Patzig, G., *Tatsachen, Normen, Sätze. Aufsätze und Vorträge* (Stuttgart: Reclam, 1988).

Perelman, Ch., *The New Rhetoric and the Humanities: Essays on Rhetoric and its Applications* (Dordrecht, Boston, and London: D. Reidel, 1979).

Pettit, P. A., 'Shene'emar. The Place of Scripture Citation in the Mishna', Ph.D. dissertation, Claremont Graduate School, 1993.

Pope, R., *The English Studies Book* (London and New York: Routledge, 1998).

Porton, G., 'Defining Midrash', in J. Neusner (ed.) *The Study of Ancient Judaism* (New York: Ktav, 1981), 55–92.

Quine, W. V. O., *Methods of Logic* (London: Routledge & Kegan Paul, 1970).

Raphael, M. L. (ed.), *Agendas for the Study of Midrash in the Twenty-First Century* (Williamsburg, Va.: Department of Religion/College of William and Mary, 1999).

Reichman, R., *Mishna und Sifra* (Tübingen: Mohr Siebeck, 1998).

—— 'Zur Analyse des Applikationsmoments im talmudischen Diskurs', *Frankfurter Judaistische Beiträge*, 26 (1999), 139–47.

Reiss, W., 'Wortsubstitution als Mittel der Deutung. Bemerkungen zur Formel אלא . . . אין', *Frankfurter Judaistische Beiträge*, 6 (1978), 27–69.

Richards, I. A., *The Philosophy of Rhetoric* (London, Oxford, and New York: Oxford University Press, 1936).

Richardson, M. E. J., Review of Clines, *Dictionary of Classical Hebrew*, *Journal of Semitic Studies*, 45 (2000), 147–55.

Roitman, B., 'Sacred Language and Open Text', in Hartman and Budick, *Midrash and Literature* (1986), 159–79.

Rosenblatt, R., *The Interpretation of the Bible in the Mishnah* (Baltimore: Johns Hopkins Press, 1935).

Rothfuchs, W., *Die Erfüllungszitate des Matthäus-Evangeliums, Beiträge zur Wissenschaft vom Alten und Neuen Testament*, 88 (Stuttgart, Berlin, Cologne, Mainz: W. Kohlhammer, 1969).

Ruiter, D. W. P., *Institutional Legal Facts: Legal Powers and Their Effects* (Dordrecht, Boston, and London: Kluwer Academic Publishers, 1993).

Russell, B., 'On Denoting', *Mind*, 14 (1905), 479–93 .

Sacks, H., *Lectures on Conversation*, 2 vols. (Oxford and Cambridge, Mass.: Blackwell, 1995).

Sáenz-Badillos, A., *A History of the Hebrew Language*, trans. J. Elwolde (Cambridge: Cambridge University Press, 1993).

SAID, E. W., *Beginnings: Intention and Method* (New York: Columbia University Press, 1985).

SAMELY, A., 'What Scripture Does Not Say: Interpretation through Contrast in Targum Pseudo-Jonathan', in J. Zmijewski (ed.), *Die alttestamentliche Botschaft als Wegweisung. Festschrift für Heinz Reinelt* (Stuttgart: Katholisches Bibelwerk, 1990), 253–83.

—— 'Between Scripture and Its Rewording: Towards a Classification of Rabbinic Exegesis', *Journal of Jewish Studies*, 42 (1991), 39–67.

—— 'Scripture's Implicature: The Midrashic Assumptions of Relevance and Consistency', *Journal of Semitic Studies*, 37 (1992), 167–205.

—— *The Interpretation of Speech in the Pentateuch Targums: A Study of Method and Presentation in Targumic Exegesis* (Mohr (Siebeck), Tübingen, 1992).

—— *Spinozas Theorie der Religion* (Würzburg: Königshausen und Neumann, 1993).

—— 'Is Targumic Aramaic Rabbinic Hebrew?', *Journal of Jewish Studies*, 45 (1994), 92–100 .

—— 'Justifying Midrash: On an "Intertextual" Interpretation of Rabbinic Interpretation', *Journal of Semitic Studies*, 39 (1994), 19–32.

—— 'Stressing Scripture's Words: Semantic Contrast as a Midrashic Technique in the Mishnah', *Journal of Jewish Studies*, 46 (1995) (*Festschrift Vermes*, eds. P. S. Alexander and M. Goodman), 196–229.

—— 'Scripture's Segments and Topicality in Rabbinic Discourse and the Pentateuch Targum', *Journal for the Aramaic Bible*, 1 (1999), 87–124.

—— 'Delaying the Progress from Case to Case: Redundancy in the Halakhic Discourse of the Mishnah', in G. Brooke (ed.), *Jewish Ways of Reading the Bible, Journal of Semitic Studies Supplement*, 11 (Oxford: Oxford University Press, 2000), 99–132.

—— 'From Case to Case: Notes on the Discourse Logic of the Mishnah', in G. R. Hawting, J. Mojaddedi, and A. Samely (eds.), *Studies in Islamic and Middle Eastern Texts and Traditions in Memory of Norman Calder, Journal of Semitic Studies Supplement*, 12 (Oxford: Oxford University Press, 2000), 233–70.

—— *Database of Midrashic Units in the Mishnah*, available from the following website: http://www.art.man.ac.uk/mes/samely/

SANDERS, E. P., *Paul and Palestinian Judaism: A Comparison of Patterns of Religion* (London and Philadelphia: SCM Press and Trinity Press Int., 1977).

—— *Paul, the Law, and the Jewish People*, (Philadelphia: Fortress Press, 1983).

—— *Judaism: Practice and Belief 63BCE–66CE* (London and Philadelphia: SCM Press and Trinity Press Int., 1992).

DE SAUSSURE, F., *Course in General Linguistics*, ed. Ch. Bally and A. Sechehaye (London: Duckworth, 1983).

SBISÀ, M., and P. FABBRI, 'Models (?) for a Pragmatic Analysis', *Journal of Pragmatics*, 4 (1980), 301–19.

SCHÄFER, P., *Studien zur Geschichte und Theologie des rabbinischen Judentums* (Leiden: Brill, 1978).

SCHECHTER, S., *Aspects of Rabbinic Theology: Major Concepts of the Talmud* (New York: Schocken, 1961; original 1909).

SCHIFFMANN, L., *The Halakhah at Qumran* (Leiden: Brill, 1975).

SCHÜRER, E., *The History of the Jewish People in the Age of Jesus Christ (175 B.C.–A.D. 135)*, vols. I–III, revised and ed. G. Vermes, F. Millar, M. Black, and M. Goodman (Edinburgh: T. & T. Clark, 1973–87).

SCHWARZ, A., 'Die Hauptergebnisse der wissenschaftlich-hermeneutischen For-schung', in *Scripta Universitatis Atque Bibliothecae Hierosoloymitanarum Orientalia et Judaica*, I, sec. IX (Jerusalem 1923), 1–36.

SEARLE, J., *Speech Acts: An Essay in the Philosophy of Language* (Cambridge: Cambridge University Press, 1969).

SEELIGMANN, I. L., 'Voraussetzungen der Midraschexegese', *Congress Volume Copenhagen 1953, Supplements to Vetus Testamentum*, 1 (Leiden: Brill, 1953), 150–81.

SEGAL, P., 'Jewish Law during the Tannaitic Period', in Hecht *et al.* (eds.), *An Introduction to the History and Sources of Jewish Law* (1996), 101–40.

SHARPE, R. A., 'Metaphor', in T. Honderich (ed.), *The Oxford Companion to Philosophy* (1995), 555.

SHINAN, A., *The Aggadah in the Aramaic Targums to the Pentateuch* (Heb.), 2 vols. (Jerusalem: Makor, 1979).

—— ' "Targumic Additions" in Targum Pseudo-Jonathan', *Textus*, 16 (1991), 139–55.

SILBERMAN, L. H., 'Unriddling the Riddle: A Study of the Structure and Language of the Habakkuk Pesher (1QpHab.)', *Revue de Qumran*, 3 (1961–2), 323–64.

SLOMOVIC, E., 'Patterns of Midrashic Impact on the Rabbinic Midrashic Tale', *Journal for the Study of Judaism* (1988), 61–90.

—— 'Towards an Understanding of the Exegesis of the Dead Sea Scrolls', *Revue de Qumran*, 7 (1970), 3–15.

—— 'Toward an Understanding of the Formation of the Historical Titles in the Book of Psalms', *Zeitschrift für Alttestamentliche Wissenschaft*, 91 (1979), 350–80.

SOLOMON, N., review of J. Neusner, *Uniting the Dual Torah*, in *Scottish Journal of Theology*, 48 (1995), 412–14.

SOLOVEITCHIK, J. B., *Halakhic Man*, trans. L. Kaplan (Philadelphia: Jewish Publication Society of America, 1983; Hebrew original, 1944).

SPERBER, D., and D. WILSON, *Relevance: Communication and Cognition* (Oxford: Blackwell, 1986).

STEINSALTZ, A., *Talmud Bavli*, vol. 9: *Massekhet Sukkah*, explained, translated, and vocalized by A. Steinsaltz (Jerusalem: Institute for Talmudic Publications, 1991).

STEMBERGER, G., *Introduction to the Talmud and Midrash*, trans. M. Bockmuehl, 2nd edn. (Edinburgh: T. & T. Clark, 1996).

STERN, D., *Parables in Midrash: Narrative and Exegesis in Rabbinic Literature* (Cambridge, Mass. and London: Harvard University Press, 1991).

STERNBERG, M., *The Poetics of Biblical Narrative: Ideological Literature and the Drama of Reading* (Bloomington and Indianapolis: Indiana University Press, 1985).

STEVENSON, L. F., 'Contextualism', in Honderich (ed.), *The Oxford Companion to Philosophy* (1995), 160.

STRAUSS, L, *Persecution and the Art of Writing* (Glencoe, Ill.: The Free Press, 1952).

—— 'How To Study Spinoza's Theological-Political Tractate', in *Persecution and the Art of Writing* (1952), 142–201.

—— *Spinoza's Critique of Religion*, trans. E. M. Sinclair (New York: Jewish Publication Society, 1965).

—— 'Introduction', in Maimonides, *Guide of the Perplexed* (1963).

STRAWSON, P. F., 'On Referring', *Mind*, 59 (1950), 320–44; repr. in G. H. R. Parkinson (ed.), *The Theory of Meaning* (London: Oxford University Press, 1968), 61–85.

Tanakh: A New Translation of the Holy Scriptures According to the Traditional Hebrew Text (Philadelphia, New York, and Jerusalem: Jewish Publication Society, 1985).

TAYLOR, J. R., *Linguistic Categorization: Prototypes in Linguistic Theory*, 2nd edn. (Oxford: Clarendon Press, 1995).

TEMPORINI, H., and W. HAASE (eds.), *Aufstieg und Niedergang der Römischen Welt, II: Principat*, vol. 19 (1 and 2): *Religion: Judentum* (Berlin and New York: Walter de Gruyter, 1979).

THEODOR, J., and CH. ALBECK (eds.), *Midrash Bereshit Rabba*, 3 vols., 2nd edn. (Jerusalem: Wahrmann, 1965).

TOV, E., 'Harmonisations in Biblical Manuscripts', *Journal for the Study of the Old Testament*, 31 (1985), 3–29.

—— 'Sense Divisions in the Qumran Texts, the Masoretic Text, and Ancient Translations of the Bible', in J. Krasovec (ed.), *The Interpretation of the Bible* (1998), 121–46.

TOWNER, S. W., *The Rabbinic 'Enumeration of Scriptural Examples': A Study of a Rabbinic Pattern of Discourse with Special Reference to Mekhilta D'R. Ishmael* (Leiden: Brill, 1973).

TRUBETZKOY, N. S., *Grundzüge der Phonologie*, 6th edn. (Göttingen: Vandenhoeck and Ruprecht, 1977).

TURNER, M., 'Categories and Analogies', in Helman (ed.), *Analogical Reasoning* (1998), 3–24.

URBACH, E. E., *The Sages: Their Concepts and Beliefs*, trans. I. Abrahams (Cambridge, Mass. and London: Harvard University Press, 1979).

—— *The Halakhah: Its Sources and Development*, trans. R. Posner (Tel-Aviv: Yad la-Talmud, 1996).

VACHEK, J., *The Linguistic School of Prague: An Introduction to its Theory and Practice* (Bloomington and London: Indiana University Press, 1966).

VAN BEKKUM, WOUT JAC., 'Deutung und Bedeutung in der hebräischen Exegese', *Frankfurter Judaistische Beiträge*, 23 (1996), 1–13.

VAN DIJK, T. A., *Text and Context: Explorations in the Semantics and Pragmatics of Discourse* (London and New York: Longmans, 1977).

VAN UCHELEN, N. A., 'The Formula עֹל זֶה נֶאֱמַר in the Mishnah. A Form-Analytical Study', in Kuyt and van Uchelen (eds.), *History and Form* (1988), 83–92.

—— *Chagigah: The Linguistic Encoding of Halakhah* (Amsterdam: Juda Palache Inst., 1994).

VATER, H., *Einführung in die Textlinguistik. Struktur, Thema und Referenz in Texten* (Munich: W. Fink Verlag, 1992).

VERMES, G., 'Bible and Midrash: Early Old Testament Exegesis', in P. Ackroyd and C. Evans (eds.), *The Cambridge History of the Bible*, vol. 1 (Cambridge: Cambridge University Press, 1970), 119–231; repr. in *Post-Biblical Jewish Studies* (1975), 59–91.

—— *Scripture and Tradition* (Leiden: Brill, 1973).

—— *Post-Biblical Jewish Studies* (Leiden: Brill, 1975).

—— *Jesus the Jew*, 2nd edn. (London: SCM Press, 1983).

—— 'Bible Interpretation at Qumran', *Eretz-Israel*, 20 (1989), 184*–91*.

—— 'Biblical Proof-Texts in Qumran Literature', *Journal of Semitic Studies*, 34 (1989), 493–508.

VOSNIADOU, S., 'Analogical Reasoning in Knowledge Acquisition', in Vosniadou and Ortony (eds.), *Similarity and Analogical Reasoning* (1989), 413–37.

VOSNIADOU, S., and A. ORTONY (eds.), *Similarity and Analogical Reasoning* (Cambridge: Cambridge University Press, 1989).

WALKER, D. M., *The Oxford Companion to Law* (Oxford: Clarendon Press, 1980).

WALTON, D. N., *Informal Logic: A Handook for Critical Argumentation* (Cambridge: Cambridge University Press, 1989).

WARFIELD, B. B., *The Inspiration and Authority of the Bible*, ed. S. G. Craig (Philadelphia: Presbyterian and Reformed Publishing Co., 1970; original 1948).

WEINGREEN, J., *From Bible to Mishna: The Continuity of Tradition* (Manchester: Manchester University Press, 1976).

WEISS HALIVNI, D., see Halivni.

WESTBROOK, R., 'Biblical Law', in Hecht *et al.* (eds.), *An Introduction to the History and Sources of Jewish Law* (1996), 1–17.

WESTERMANN, C. (ed.), *Essays on Old Testament Interpretation* (London: SCM Press, 1963); original: *Probleme alttestamentlicher Hermeneutik* (Munich: Chr. Kaiser, 1960).

WHATELY, R., *Elements of Rhetoric*, 5th edn. (London: B. Fellowes, 1836).

WIELAND, W., *Platon und die Formen des Wissens* (Göttingen: Vandenhoeck & Ruprecht, 1982).

WIERZBICKA, A., 'The Semantics of Direct and Indirect Discourse', *Papers in Linguistics* (1974), 267–307.

WIESENBERG, E., 'Observations on Method in Talmudic Studies', *Journal of Semitic Studies*, 11 (1966), 16–36 .

WINCH, P., *The Idea of a Social Science and its Relation to Philosophy* (London and Atlantic Highlands, NJ: Routledge & Kegan Paul, and Humanities Press, 1958).

WITTGENSTEIN, L., *Philosophische Untersuchungen* (Frankfurt: Suhrkamp, 1982); *Philosophical Investigations*, trans. G. E. M. Anscombe, 3rd edn. (Oxford: Blackwell, 1968).

WOLFF, H. W., 'The Hermeneutics of the Old Testament', in C. Westermann (ed.), *Essays on Old Testament Interpretation* (1963), 160–99.

WÜRTHWEIN, E., *The Text of the Old Testament: An Introduction to the Biblia Hebraica*, trans. E. R. Rhodes, 2nd edn. (Grand Rapids, Mich.: William B. Eerdmans, 1995).

ZEITLIN, S., 'Hillel and the Hermeneutic Rules', *Jewish Quarterly Review*, 54 (1963/4), 161–73.

ZLOTKIN, D., *The Iron Pillar Mishnah: Redaction, Form, and Intent* (Jerusalem: Bialik Institute/Ktav, 1988).

ZUIDEMA, W. H., 'Changes in Meaning and Evolution of Meaning: The Evolution of a Ritual', in Kuyt and van Uchelen, *History and Form* (1988), 43–51.

Index of Passages Cited

Index of Authors

Index of Subjects and Names

Note: No attempt has been made to index fundamental terms of analysis, themes to which chapters are devoted, or resource names. The notes of Appendix I identify the page on which a resource is first defined. Manuscript sources mentioned in the footnotes are not included in the index below; 'n.' indicates that the term is found in one or several notes on that page. Words presented on the page in the Greek alphabet are included in the index in transliteration.

Index of Hebrew Terms and Phrases